Sextrology

The Astrology
of Sex and the Sexes

STARSKY + COX

EBURY
PRESS

for laurie litchford

1 3 5 7 9 10 8 6 4 2

First published in the United States in 2004 by HarperCollins Publishers, Inc.

First published in the United Kingdom in 2007 by Ebury Press, an imprint of Ebury Publishing
Random House UK Ltd.
Random House
20 Vauxhall Bridge Road, London SW1V 2SA

Random House Australia (Pty) Limited
20 Alfred Street, Milsons Point, Sydney, New South Wales 2061, Australia

Random House New Zealand Limited
18 Poland Road, Glenfield, Auckland 10, New Zealand

Random House (Pty) Limited
Isle of Houghton Corner Boundary Road & Carse O'Gowrie Houghton, 2198, South Africa

Random House Publishers India Private Limited
301 World Trade Tower, Hotel Intercontinental Grand Complex,
Barakhamba Lane, New Delhi 110 001, India

Random House UK Limited Reg. No. 954009
www.randomhouse.co.uk

Papers used by Ebury Press are natural, recyclable products made from wood grown in sustainable forests.

A CIP catalogue record is available for this book from the British Library.

ISBN: 9780091912949

Printed and bound in Great Britain by William Clowes Ltd, Beccles, Suffolk

acknowledgements

We are grateful to family and friends, associates and even acquaintances who have contributed to the creation of *Sextrology*, sometimes unwittingly, over the past several years. Gratitude goes to Christy Fletcher, Emma Parry, Julian Alexander, Imogen Fortes, Caroline Newbury, Fiona MacIntyre and everyone at Ebury Press.

We extend our deep appreciation to Julie Gilhart, Simon Doonan, Debi Greenberg, Sarah and Colette Lerfel, Linlee Allen, Nadege Mezou, Guillaume Salmon, Alannah Weston, Sarah O'Keefe, Katharina Sand, Marianne Eschbach, Sithara Atasoy, Laurence Antiglio, Vanessa von Bismarck, Maura Egan, Annabel Tollman, Joanne Good, Aatish Tasseer, Matt Tyrnauer, Jessie Brinton, Hannah Sim, Jane Lomas, Brendan Courtney, Tom Ackerman, Pauline Fisher, Robert Duffy and everyone at Marc Jacobs, Guy Trebay, Candy Pratts Price, Sebastian Kaufmann and Mark Wogan.

Our warmest thanks go to Nancy Corbett and Brian Doben, David Rees and Ron Anderson, Justin Bond, Griet Vandekerckhove, John Bartlett, Laurie Pike, Melissa Crowe, Alicia Trani, Michael Slimmer and Corvette and Josh at Mudhoney, Stephen DiCiccio, Stephen Kijak, Craig Chester, Christina Ferrari, Susanne Tide, Jackie and Laurence Llewelyn-Bowen, Andrea Houlton and Dom Smets, Bénédicte and Martin Newland, and especially Pascale Smets and Matthew Pritchett. Lastly, we wish to thank William Leone and Lynne Corbett, without whose imaginings *Sextrology* would never have been conceived.

Introduction

For years, we've contended that men and women of the same astrological sign are actually different signs. Most astrology books lump males and females together, while those that do attempt to treat the sexes separately have never fully explored the distinctions between the so-called sex signs or even so much as ventured to explain why it is they are, as is so often the case, markedly unlike each other. We maintain that astrology must factor in the great divide between the sexes, that the energies that comprise the signs filter through the opposite sexes as through prisms, separate and unique from one another.

We believe that the zodiac has been ignored as a *real* meditative tool for understanding human nature. Even astrologers themselves have had a hand in discrediting its validity, making such a stink about sun-sign astrology, especially horoscopes, being charlatanism while prescribing individual birth-charting. In so doing, the baby went out with the bathwater. Of course, drafting a person's birth chart will outline the potentialities specific to that individual's life. But that shouldn't be used as an argument against a more general sun-sign astrology. Indeed, there is much more to be gained via its exploration than most people realize. Particularly when it comes to sex.

To be fair, we can't completely blame the skeptics. Especially on the subject of sex and astrology, there is nothing cringier than the type of material lining the bookselves on the topic. It's hardly a big epiphany to say, for instance, that Taurus 'gal' likes candlelit bubble baths and pink champagne as a prelude to getting laid. We believe that the subject of sex and astrology is vastly underexplored, and it's our aim in writing this book to show how rich the subject is with potential revelation.

Let's face it, we all like to read about ourselves. Yet, the biggest argument against astrology remains: The whole of the human race can't possibly be divided into twelve (or in this case, twenty-four) categories. Well, guess again: Just because most sun-sign astrology has been so general and gotten such a bad rap doesn't mean it isn't valid. And, for our money, it is most intriguing when investigated via the sexual natures of the signs. In reading *Sextrology,* we believe people will be pleasantly surprised, and in a certain way excited, to discover that men or women of a particular sex-sign share so much more than a string of hackneyed adjectives. They fall under the same personality archetype, the gist of which, as we'll readily explain, you needn't be a Jungian psychologist to comprehend. But let's back up.

The zodiac itself is a dialogue, and often a bit of a battle, between the sexes. And *Sextrology* is an exploration of the astrological signs from the perspective of gender, sexual identity, and sexual behavior. The zodiacal wheel is first and foremost divided along gender lines into six masculine (fire, air) and six feminine (earth, water) signs. This reflects universal balance, existence being one big system of yin and yang. The basic premise of *Sextrology* is that there are twenty-four signs, not just twelve, each sign being divided again into gender polarities.

Men and women of the same sign can actually be very different from one another as they manifest the dynamic of their sign's energy in opposite fashions. Specifically, if a person is aligned with the gender polarity of his or her sign — men in masculine signs, women in feminine signs — he or she *embodies* the elemental-quality of the sign; whereas men in feminine signs and women in masculine signs will *enact* this dynamic. First, when we say elemental-quality, we refer to each sign's particular blend of element (fire, earth, air, water) and quality (cardinal, fixed, mutable) — each sign is a unique amalgam of these two zodiacal components that are key to understanding individual character — which, when paired, one category with the other, four times three, gives us the twelve combinations of the traditional signs.

For example, the masculine sign of Aries is *the* one and only cardinal-fire sign; in simple terms, the cardinal quality suggests initiative and the fire element represents life-spirit. Aries man, aligned with the gender polarity of his sign, thus embodies this dynamic: He is like a spark, or an explosive fireball. Aries woman on the other hand is a rather cool character who is nonetheless the zodiac's little fire-starter, an instigator, inciting others to explosive action while she remains unruffled. To look at Aries man and Aries woman one would say they couldn't be more different in temperament, because, though they are playing with the same astrological recipe as dictated by their sign, they manifest these specific ingredients in an often diametrically opposed manner. This is where personality archetype comes into play.

In the pages that follow, the zodiac will be illustrated as a mandala of human existence and, specifically, human sexuality. Sex, whether referring to gender or 'getting some,' is the primal key to life. We are our sexual natures. And so, in exploring the various personalities of the twenty-four astrological gender-signs, it's not only more fun to focus on the sexuality of these characters, it's essential to do so. To appeal to a primarily occidental readership, archetypes for each sign have been drawn from classical models – the pantheon of various gods and goddesses – as well as their biblical Judeo-Christian equivalents and the echoings of these characterizations throughout ancient and modern literature.

The zodiac itself, having originated in large part in ancient Greece, is steeped in classical symbolism, and individual personality archetypes from that pantheon organically emerge within the rich catalog of imagery surrounding each sign. For instance, taking the example of Aries again, the sign is ruled by the planet Mars, and indeed, we see much of that planet's namesake god of war (Greek: Ares) in the aggressive fireball of masculinity that is the Ram man. When meditating on Aries woman, it naturally follows that she then draws upon the archetype of the war goddess, Athena, who is quite different in character from her often bellicose brother. In fact, mythology tells us that of all the gods, she most loathed him. Likewise, Aries man and woman aren't the most symbiotic couple on the astrological block.

And so it goes: Each of the twenty-four signs of the zodiac is endowed with a certain prototypical energy to such a degree that we see these all too human gods and goddesses come alive in the pantheon of humanity, as it is, characterized by the dictates of astrological placement. And like the rose that blooms in summer, as opposed to the chrysanthemum of winter, life-forms that spring up at certain times of year manifest the character of that time. It is the same with we humans.

Moreover, each of the signs is associated with a seven-year age span, Aries kicking off the zodiac with its correspondence to the period of birth through seven years. When taken metaphorically, we not only see, for instance, Aries man's signature sense of feeling himself 'born' to do whatever he undertakes, but the metaphor extending further to include comparisons on his nature to the very advent of 'big bang' creation on a universal scale. People are that loaded with analogue.

Provided, of course, one accepts the 'noble lie' of astrology to begin with, a plethora of truth is to be gleaned from fully analyzing every zodiacal precept and archetype associated with each of the twenty-four characterizations. Particularly when it comes to sexuality, the myths themselves are a steamy enough soap opera that lend great insight into the erotic nature of every individual in whom the particular proclivities of the associative archetypes are eeri-ly encoded.

Each astrological character's chapter is divided into three sections – *sign + mind,* a psychological profile of the zodiacal personality as dictated by the symbology of the sign: *body + soul,* physical attributes as well as the individual's mode of expression; and *sex + sexuality,* detailing sexual attitudes and behavior. Each chapter finishes with a survey of that individual's relationships with every other sign, male and female, gay and straight. These *coupling* sections are truly just the tip of the iceberg as they entail such a rich complexity of material as to warrant a separate volume unto itself.

It is our hope that *Sextrology* will be read along the same lines, and in the same spirit, as it was written: We set out to compose a pop exploration of astrology and sexuality, intending it to be amusing, if ever so slightly titillating, without taking itself too seriously. As the project got under way, more esoteric dynamics of the subject became simply impossible to ignore; the archetypes especially called out for inclusion in the material (and sometimes during a sound sleep); the creative agendum then became hinged upon facilitating a marriage between the more high-minded musings and the straightforward juicy bits. Indeed it was a process of *letting* the connections be made rather than emphatically making them; in time, everything fell into place. The reader should follow suit by getting into the book for some enlightening entertainment, read his or her particular chapter and those of loved ones, allowing them to turn on a few lightbulbs while tickling the funny bone, if not other portions of the anatomy.

If the book does, however, inspire a deeper fascination by way of its more academic surveying of 'the astrology of sex and the sexes,' then all the better. In that case, one should read *Sextrology* from beginning to end, getting a sense of the zodiac's arc and how each sign, with its inherent symbols and precepts, builds upon the previous, passing a baton of personal philosophy from one character to the next, ad infinitum. Indeed the astrological 'wheel' is a spiraling continuum, rather than a static circle, whereby each of the twenty-four signs has some nuggets of wisdom to offer the rest via his or her individual approach to life, love, and understanding of the libido, without whose precise urgings none of us would be here in the first place.

Aries Man

the one

If an illustration were to accompany the definition of *man* in the dictionary, it would no doubt look more like Aries than any other guy in the zodiac. He is astrology's proto-typical chap – the model-A male – and as such he embodies the strictest utter essence of his sex: Whether eternally boyish or painfully macho, Aries is an exploration of masculinity in its purest form – physically, emotionally, and psychologically. He is most self-assured and unapologetic in attitude and behavior, comfortable in his skin and fearless in his ambitions. He lives life as if he were the only guy on the planet, feeling entitled to take freely from it what he wants, oblivious to obstacles or the admonitions of others. Forthright to a fault, he possesses a conquering spirit, thriving on pursuit in his professional as well as private life. He oozes virility, literally generating an aromatic heat, making no bones about expressing romantic or erotic interest. Beneath his typically clean-cut appearance lies a hormonally raging animal ever ready to take the sexual lead, yet he oft feels obliged to subdue this self-perceived bestial nature, hoping to achieve a higher, spiritual connection with a woman and be her consummate knight in shining armor. In the end, he should come to realize that pure intentions and prurient desire needn't be mutually exclusive. When sexually engaged with a male, the Aries guy manifests an outright need for domination, gleefully bending a man (over) to his will, unequivocally dispelling any and all questions as to who's the boss in bed.

♈

PRINCIPLE

The Masculine Principle. Aries emerges from the watery dissolution of Pisces's primordial womb. Herein lie the principles of form, objectivity, activity, and aggression. The self and its fulfillment are the premier raison d'être. Aries man views the world as ripe for the picking.

Sign + Mind

As the first guy sign of the zodiac, Aries is astrology's primordial male against whose basic, straightforward theme all other men resound in myriad variation. Like Western civilization's premier male prototype – the aptly alphabeticized Adam – the man born under the sign of the Ram isn't created for nuance or deviation; sexually speaking, especially, he exists to get the job done – if not to be fruitful and multiply in the process. For Aries man, existence is a decidedly uncomplicated affair in which his role is startlingly clear. Of all the men in the zodiac the Ram most personifies the masculine stereotype – driven, aggressive, often unemotional or even brutish; and as a result, he finds himself labeled insensitive and self-serving by men and women alike, in every area of life, especially in sexual relationships. This is simply his nature: Like that of any alpha male in the wild kingdom, Aries man's lust for life is inextricably linked with his need to ensure domination. His ruling planet, Mars, represents the Masculine Principle in the zodiac. Often called 'the shield and spear of Mars,' after the planet's namesake Roman god of war (Greek: Ares), the planet signals the active (male) energy in the universe. Mars, whether as planet or war god, symbolizes an outward, objective view of experience that predisposes the Aries to initiative and eagerness if not brashness and a blatant inability to view life from any other aspect but his own. In biblical terms the sign of Aries is associated with big-bang creation befitting this, the only cardinal-fire sign in the zodiac, an assignation denoting an initial spark of life that we see mirrored in each dawning day. Prototypically Aries is the rising son, God's firstborn boy, and as such he embodies an unencumbered spirit of carte blanche. He is, indeed, like Adam freeze-framed before Eve's creation, with no concept of 'other' or, as it so often seems, no sufficient outlet for his relentless erotic urges. The planetary glyph graphically recalls a guy's boner and basket, which sums up the sexual persona of Aries man in a nutshell: He is the eternal human hard-on. He would be: Even on the physical level, Mars rules blood being pumped outward, centrifugally, to the extremities, including the external genitalia, in both sexes, and the dangling male bits, specifically. As Mars' number one son (the planet also co-rules Scorpio), Aries is the pure personification of this primal-male call to arms. He's astrology's valiant little soldier, standing perpetually at attention. Indeed, Aries is an exceedingly imposing figure, devoid of any irony or second-guessing in his signature bold demeanor, cutthroat professionalism, not to mention an unerring yen for booty. His ruling planet's energy is both spontaneous and resolute, making the Ram as impulsive as he is determined in his quest to unleash his libido. However, it won't be just anybody who'll qualify as a suitable object of his ever-pressing desire, save, as we'll see, for a certain caveat.

In strict astrological terms, Mars' glyph is said to signify the emergence of matter (arrow) from the divine (circle), thus representing birth – life matter issuing from the nonmaterial realm or the actual circular womb-source, egg, or seed where spirit first takes form. Aries is a singular human expression of combined body and soul – there's no inherent duality in the Ram guy's nature that would separate one metaphysical aspect from the other. To wax New Agey a moment, he is the model of body-spirit 'oneness.' Unfortunately, as is so often the case, Aries man imposes a psychological split where one ought not to exist – feeling himself so attuned to the raging forces of his body, he may label himself, indeed berate himself for being, too base or animalistic and thus seek to subdue this most striking aspect of his nature. He is a child of the astrological 1st House, after all, one that concerns itself with, among other things, *physicality, selfhood,* and one's *life-force.* And, again, though Aries may be a native of this house, he is also the zodiac's chief fire sign, that element symbolic of spirit. From an astrological perspective, you might say that the Ram man is soul incarnate, one and the same. We see this in his very person, a total presence in full command of his body with no apparent disconnect between his impulsive urges and the physical actions that express them. Unrestrained despite signature attempts to downplay his animal heat, Aries brims with life, the force of which vividly pulses through him.

The red, glowing planet Mars rules the blood – the very substance of fire flowing hot through our veins that literally substantiates our existence from the moment we spring to life in the womb. Fittingly, Aries is associated with birth – the sign rules the first slice of human life, 0–7 years, just as it corresponds to the birth of all creation. Aries man thus vividly embodies that energy of birth – an urgent, bursting-forth dynamic – in all of his life encounters. He feels that he's been 'born' to whatever experience he is inclined to pursue, experiencing his life as if it were a carefully plotted series of predestined circumstances, wherein he is chosen for specific purposes determined, albeit, by his intrinsic goals and strictly personal desires. All fire-sign males – Aries, Leo, Sagittarius – are, to some degree, legends in their own mind; but it is specifically along exact thematic lines of birthright where Aries man is forever self-mythologizing. He inherently feels that he is the one (and only) guy suited to 'do' whatever or, for that matter, whoever strikes his fancy. Just as he might look upon a chosen career as a divine calling, when he is attracted to someone, he loftily believes he's fulfilling his fate by entering into a relationship with

PLANETARY SYMBOL

The arrow (materiality) emerging from the circle (spirit) represents birth as well as divinely inspired action. Often called the spear and shield of Mars, the glyph recalls male genitalia, and the objective, aggressive impetus inherent in the sign of Aries.

SIGN QUADRANT

The zodiacal quadrants correspond to metaphysical planes of existence – physical, emotional, mental, and spiritual. The First Quadrant is that of the self and individual awareness. For Aries man, importance lies in the cultivation and indeed purification of self as a means for achieving oneness with the universe.

that individual. It is a rather egotistical stance, to be sure, but that, too, is an Aries predisposition. His sign's motto, 'I am,' seems to be justification enough for the enormous liberties Aries man naturally takes, as it carries the subtext that only he exists. Indeed, Aries lives life like an eternal infant in the throes of his self-perceptions, all but oblivious to others' concerns.

For Aries, the sign's ram's-head glyph symbolizes ego, and specifically the male ego, sprouting forth, hornlike, as the most definitive gesture of his character. As would befit the profile, even, of an actual ram, horns are a proud declaration of strictly masculine identity; likewise, the Ram man's own horny-ness is in no small way linked to the expression of his healthy ego. Horn size determines a male's ability to assert his dominance – the ram with the biggest equipment usually gets his pick of the ewes – serving as a symbol of masculine supremacy, both as a weapon in his sexual war against other male competitors and as a totem to his own virility, literally, the active power to create life. In mythology, both Ares–Mars and Zeus–Jupiter take the form of a ram, especially when engaged in battle. In the ram's horns, we see that inextricable linking of anger/aggression and lusty sexual expression, both energies that fall under Martian rule.

Aries is the zodiac's personification of the rising-son or rival-god archetype, represented by the savior-warrior deities Ares and Zeus, who are often considered by scholars to be the same god in two aspects – the callow Zeus overthrows his father Cronus-Saturn, who, in turn, had deposed his father, Uranus. These characters, in their youthful upstart phase, all, one and the same, characterize this rival energy, which the flesh and blood Aries man personifies. (The Hindu equivalent is the warrior god Rudra, 'the red one,' befitting the sign's ruddy planetary association, just as Lancelot 'the spear bearer' is the medieval Ares–Mars who can't help but undermine the king, Arthur, despite his initial noble intentions.) Whereas Zeus was born to battle and overthrow the Titans, Ares is thwarted from repeating the patrilineal pattern of uncrowning Zeus and rather comes down to us, in myth, as a whiner who runs to his mother, Hera, the instant he sustains the slightest boo-boo. Such are the two prime aspects of the Aries male persona – conquering hero and/or cruel coward. Still despite Ares's brutish mien, or indeed due to it, he is still so handsome and dashing a deitific stud as to be the first to pluck the über–love goddess Aphrodite fresh from her seashell, just as Lancelot is wedded to the medieval Aphrodite, Columbine, meaning 'dove,' the animal-totem form the Greek goddess takes. It's an age-old archetypal love story – one that likewise ends well for the Aries man: No matter how much women insist they prize emotional sensitivity in a man, most can't resist the straightforward male-animal nature of the Aries, to whom they are drawn on a strictly physical, sexual level. His needs are simple, basic, primal. And for his part, no woman will do but one who is so dripping with femininity as to be a living incarnation of Aphrodite herself. He craves ultrareceptivity, if not outright passivity, in a mate, or a one-night stand for that matter, fleeing from the kind of feminist power that his mother, herself an often overbearing Hera type, typically wields. It is the demure female that he finds exotic and in whose blushing bosom he seeks comfort. As chauvinistic as it sounds, the Ram man looks for a coy lady love, not one who'll compete for a chance to wear the pants. He has a severe allergy to outspoken women, especially those who are wont to swear and swill like sailors.

Sexism, whether it be a negative or a noble objectification of women, has its seeds in Aries's earliest development. Aries guy's mother may be an overwhelming force while his father's influence tends to be negligible, or even hostile. In any case, Aries's dad will be at odds with his mother's invariable spoiling of him. She'll dote on him, label him a godsend, even seem to favor him as her 'little man' over her husband, with whom life may be tense, at least during the formative years of Aries's upbringing – the main thrust of marital discord generally being her disappointment in her spouse's ambition and station in life. She may set up a rivalry between Aries and his father, always holding up the shortcomings of her husband as pitfalls for her son to avoid, lest he similarly fall short, in her estimation, whether in the pursuit of a career or in the development of a moral character. Not wanting to be painted with the same brush of failure, Aries emotionally separates from his dad. His father likewise retreats, just as Uranus shrank from Cronus-Saturn, who, in turn, recoiled from Zeus. Given the synonymous nature of all these characters, one could say that the Aries boy, in a sense, also separates from himself, or at least the 'lesser' parts of his nature, not allowing for even a humble recognition of inherent shortcomings that most of us, to varying degrees, acknowledge. It is important to note that Hera conceived Ares all by her lonesome in retaliation for Zeus' solitarily having brought forth Athena (fittingly the Aries female archetype) from his Aries-ruled head (actually by his first wife, Metis, meaning 'prudence,' who eternally resides in his noggin). Like Hera, Aries's mother may endow her son with the purpose of showing up his father, albeit subconsciously. However, it is a plot that fails – Ares is not Zeus' inheritor; likewise, Aries is, to some degree, forever locked into the Martian role of striving warrior without ever feeling that he can comfortably sit on some metaphorical throne. He is the eternal knight-errant who never stops his life pursuits long enough to enjoy the brand of luxury to which some complacent king is privy. But all is as it should be.

SIGN GLYPH

The Arien emblem is the Ram's head and horns, signifying male dominance, virility, strength, and assertion. It is an expression of male ego inextricably linked to physical virility. Aries's symbol is the Ram, the animal totem of phallic male fertility deities throughout antiquity.

ELEMENT + QUALITY

The fire element signifies life energy. The cardinal quality denotes a call to action and initiative. Together the cardinal-fire combination particular to Aries is best illustrated as a spark, or spontaneous explosion. It points to Aries's creative initiative, forthrightness, and leadership.

POLARITY

Males in masculine (air, fire) signs are aligned with the gender polarity of their sign and thus embody the quality-element combination of the sign. Aries man is an unstoppable fireball. As the zodiac's sparky conquistador, he explodes onto every situation. Life is for the taking, and love and sex must be pursued, never invited.

Via this parental dynamic, Aries boy is conditioned to associate an overage of female affection with the witholding of masculine validation he'll henceforth seek to embrace and, indeed, embody on his own. Meanwhile, he'll draw the better part of his strength from winning female favor, in being a woman's champion à la Lancelot. And yet the zodiac's macho man is ironically fearful of proverbial feminine power when he can't siphon it at his discretion. Instead, it threatens to overwhelm him, whether on a global societal scale or in his own personal life. And for the simple reason that one often fears most what one doesn't understand. In youth, he will eventually flare up at his mother, bidding her to back off, just as he'll avoid flag-waving feminists in adulthood. Especially when it comes to sexual relationships, Aries is programmed with alarms against feminine force, which he, archetypally, suspects might usher in his demise: Guinevere's power over Lancelot was the warrior's undoing – just as Adam's first mate, Lilith, was way too pants-wearing for his taste; he thus saw her demonized and banished to make room for the more seemingly compliant Eve, who, let's face it, was no bed of roses either. The name Lilith still signals female power in popular culture, most notably in its adoption as the name for the 'fair' that constitutes the women's movement in music – concerts where one would be hard-pressed to find assembled a substantial Aries-male population.

Though he owes his original bolstering to his mother, the Ram boy is quick to avoid being seen as the prototypical mama's boy he truly is, and as a result, he begins to vividly eschew what he considers to be 'softer' femmy feelings and behavior, adopting a more impressively impassive demeanor. Enter the Aries swagger, a physical way to signal masculinity. He's a rough-and-tumble kid, the ultimate man's man in adulthood, meanwhile fairly confident his metaphoric horny antlers are impressing the babes. Unfortunately, such displays mightn't stop there: Aries boys can be notoriously scrappy, seeming to always find themselves embroiled in playground conflicts. Fittingly, the planet Mars rules the adrenal system, which regulates the fight-or-flight instinct, which may inspire the Ram male's penchant for butting heads (just as it dictates that female Aries remain forever above the fray). For Aries man, other males more or less fall into a single category: the competition, if not the outright enemy. For the most part, however, he learns to relax his predisposed combative stance, developing a signature strategy for dealing with members of his own sex; in other words, he doesn't. He assumes all men see the world the way he does – from that purely objective Masculine Principle perspective – and he thus believes that other guys need nothing from him. He doesn't bond, he coexists, rarely investing emotionally in his fellow man. Life, in the world of men, is like a pickup game for Aries, who experiences no glitch entering into testosterone-fueled environments, greeting strangers with the same blasé interest as he does his closest male friends. To the straight Aries-male mind, if you turn guys over, they all look the same. He rarely feels impressed, let alone intimidated, by even the most celebrated sports figure or other such societal supermen, and he is perfectly in his element in the butchest milieus whether it be a sports bar, barracks, locker room, or open-trough urinal.

In the Aries world, it's every man for himself. What the zodiac's premier male teaches us, by example, is the power of having a me-first attitude. Aries's take on the survival of the fittest, stemming from his 1st House of self, means not becoming unduly involved with others emotionally, but instead putting energy into liberal, personal pursuits, attacking life, taking from it what he wants. There is no denying that Aries's astrological influences predispose him to an innate sense of grabby entitlement, if not more than his fair share of arrogance. Aries is the only cardinal-fire sign in the zodiac, meaning he literally embodies that sparky initiative spirit. The Ram is a fireball, hurtling himself into experience as well as at any and all objects of his desire; while Aries woman, a cool and detached character, in contrast, nonetheless seems to be forever starting fires of desire for her in the hearts of others. Devoid of subtlety, Aries is his anger and lust personified, metaphorically or literally lunging at whomever ignites his temper or passion. The two greatest weapons in ancient wars were the spear for killing rival male factions and the penis for impregnating women with the conquering race. As the personification of the war god, Aries retains much of this sensibility. But his cardinal-fire nature doesn't end with corporeal campaigns but rather flickers on another metaphysical level as well: Fire, as suggested, symbolizes Aries's self-idealized spirit, and so cardinality, on this score, refers to the Ram's vigilant questing for spiritual fulfillment inherent, even, in his pursuit of a romantic partner, at least to the extent that it is often unclear whether he's following his inbred noble intentions or that perpetual stiffy. The upshot, for this creature of oneness, is that sexuality and spirituality are inextricably linked. But since he can't ever seem to separate them, it may be a painful paradox to endure not only for him but for a would-be mate, who must accept the mantle of responsibility for being Aries's preordained prince or princess bride, as the particular case may be.

Here, we uncover the crux of Aries man's psychosexuality, one that may cause a dangerous schism in his personality: He is forever torn between his anger and lust on one side and his inherent need to be a virtue crusader on the other. When it comes to sex, he fights against his basic instincts and strives to become some transcendent knight-errant who has mastered his predisposed

1

SIGN NUMBER

The number of life: One is the basis for all other numbers. In the cabala it is associated with unity and wholeness in the individual. It is the number of objectivity, viewing life outward from a sole vantage of selfhood.

0–7

SIGN AGE ASSOCIATION

The age of singularity. Birth is violent and bloody and the infant's primal impetus is an animal instinct for survival. Aries man embodies this fight for life all his days. This age is associated with a child's wont to play alone.

The Aries man often suffers from delusions of grandeur, a total disregard of others, and antisocial behavior. He may attach an overimportance, if not divine intervention, to circumstances he encounters. He experiences difficulty with authority and is particularly prone to temper and overaggressive behavior. Aries may express sexism, prejudice, and zenophobia.

beastly nature. Moreover, Aries quests after a sense of spirituality because the strong physicality of his sign leads him to believe he all but completely lacks it. Despite his possible delusions of being divinely directed in life, or even the very reason for them, Aries is insecure about what he perceives as this dearth in himself, and so he often compensates by putting on a soul-man persona, if only a subconscious pose. His 1st House emphasis on physicality confounds him – he is simple, basic, but he confuses that with being base and inaccessible on a 'higher plane.' He doesn't realize that his is no mere physicality. It is rather like the computer hardware on which any introduced software of ideology can be run. As is true for everyone, the ability to 'exist' on more cosmic levels is determined, first and foremost, on the health and integrity of the self as a physical organism. What Aries must understand is that his personal computer came with built-in programs for spiritual understanding, which he might not recognize because they are so perfectly integrated into his singular system. His brand of spirituality isn't one of transcendence, he should come to see, but one grounded in his very being. Aries would do himself a great service by grasping that his spiritual role model isn't an apotheosized figure like Christ, transforming from man to god via a very public self-sacrifice, but rather one of personal transformation like that of the Buddha, an Aries himself, who achieved enlightenment, 'oneness,' by sitting and contemplating his endemic 1st House *selfhood* rather than going on crusades for some external experience of exaltation. Simplicity, Aries can show us, is the most sublime state of all. Yet despite Buddha's example, sitting still, let alone self-scanning, is not the strongest suit of the outwardly objective Aries. Herein lies both his greatest challenge and fondest hope for achievement.

Body + Soul

Aries man, and particularly his sign-ruled head, is always racing. At a party, say, he's generally the guy in an ongoing monologue, directed at a single person, intent on proving some point or theory that (he'll have you know) has been of late occupying his mind. Typically this entails elaborate theses along a specific theme – himself – as he seeks to enlighten others on what defines him, what makes him tick, convinced people are burning to learn what is behind the mind of this most intriguing creature. Just keep nodding (if only in an effort not to nod off). Otherwise, if another person does somehow manage to take the floor, Aries will be lost in solitary physical life and needs – making special requests from a waiter, sneaking peaks at his watch, pager, or text messages, jotting down an idea, adjusting his clothes, and as is most likely, taking glimpses of himself in anything reflective within view. This son of Mars has indeed inherited the war god's dashing looks and notorious ego – besides, he has to keep himself occupied somehow as he's pretending to listen to what you're saying. One is reminded of an old rumor about Marlon Brando that illustrates how he relates to other actors in a scene: He supposedly said something akin to 'bullshit, bullshit, bullshit, my line, bullshit, bullshit, my line.' This attitude is vintage Aries.

A list of famous Aries men – which includes Russell Crowe, Sean Bean, Steve McQueen, Hugh Hefner, Roger Corman, Warren Beatty, Serge Gainsbourg, Ewan McGregor, Charlie Chaplin, Pete Rose, Alec Baldwin, William Holden, James Garner, and Buddha – reveals that Ram men are self-concerned individuals whose all-else-be-damned perspective on life is their greatest asset, but sometimes their most fatal flaw. Suffice it so say, they are not known as the most sensitive of men, particularly when it comes to the opposite sex, lacking any connection to what could be labeled a 'feminine' side. In looks, Aries guys run the gamut from A all the way to B: either eternally boyish figures – David Cassidy, Ewan McGregor, Matthew Broderick, Dudley Moore, Gary Oldman, Michael York, Dana Carvey, Martin Short, Jackie Chan, Robert Downey Jr. – forever clad in jeans, tees, sneakers, and baseball caps, or decidedly manly men – Gregory Peck, James Caan, Spencer Tracy, James Woods, Dirk Bogarde, Timothy Dalton, Jean-Paul Belmondo – who might give the impression they were born with chest hair. Indeed, brimming with testosterone, Aries man may practically have to machete back the pec fur that often threatens to comingle with his beard. One thing all Aries men have in common is the appearance that they've always just had their hair cut – associated with birth, the sign of Aries rules the head, and he always regards this part of his anatomy as the first to show. The Ram man gets sheared, snipped, clipped, or buzzed more than any other guy on the astrological block – usually opting for a close and even cut, squared off in the back above his neck, not tapered. Clean and neat, like a Secret Service agent's. Actually, the whole of his appearance has that same squared-off look – his shoulders are so straight you'd think he left the hanger in his shirt. His clothes generally look as if they've been freshly pressed, with pleats and creases in all the right places; and yet, despite all this apparent crispness, there is something undeniably animal about him. While it's noticeable when he's clothed, naked it's unmistakable: He has a raw, primordial quality, even ever so slightly cavemanesque. Little wonder that, in *A Streetcar Named Desire,* Blanche (Vivien Leigh) comes right out and asks Stanley (Marlon Brando) if he's an Aries – and

ARCHETYPE + MYTH

Aries man draws upon the war god, Greek Ares, Roman Mars. These were originally fertility figures; the phallic spear became an instrument for the hunt and then for martial conquest, aggression in the Aries having equal creative and destructive potential. He embodies the rival or son god archetype. Aries's objective nature is also portrayed by Jason's quest for the Ram's golden fleece. His disregard for the feminine condition (Medea) mirrors Aries's own misogyny. Mars' association with birth is still evident in his namesake month of March, and the vernal equinox, which marks the beginning of Aries.

BIBLE + LITERATURE

The sign of Aries corresponds to creation in Genesis and the male of the sign to Adam, meaning 'bloody clay'. He is, like Aries, without guile and completely objective in his view. Another biblical character is Samson, whose strength is centered in his Arien-ruled hair, a symbol of his virility. The Arthurian Ares is Lancelot, meaning one with a great spear, a questing knight who mates Columba, the dove, Aphrodite's totem. In Don Quixote we see the characterization of the Arien male's infamous crusading becoming delusional. Hesse's Siddhartha (Buddha) portrays the Arien need to strike out on one's own in search of enlightenment. Modern heros like Superman, Zorro, G.I. Joe, and the Lone Ranger are all Arien characters.

though that coarse fictional character turns out to be a Capricorn, Brando himself is so clearly a Ram man. Aries's notoriously bantam physique is undeniably male – even dressed, he appears raw and naked to the imagination, as if his clothes can't quite conceal his protrusive virility. Muscles rippling noticeably beneath his garments, he radiates a stirring aromatic heat. Tough, taut, and eager for vigorous, athletic sex, Aries looks as if he'd be single-minded in his desire to subdue an object of his affection, not to mention get off as many times as possible, pleasuring and exhausting his partner in the process.

His broad neck and chest bulge regardless of whether he sticks to a disciplined workout schedule. Relative to other men, Aries has muscles of the Popeye variety – his forearms are so thick as to nearly outmeasure his biceps if he's not careful. Despite such aboriginal hints, Aries possesses a graceful, bouncy gait and carriage, a low center of gravity that gives him a dug-in quality without the slightest appearance of squattiness. Typically, he has rounded pectoral muscles and rather retiring, unobtrusive nipples, a tough and tightly knit torso with developed lats that fan out, cobralike, accenting a naturally V-shaped frame. A flat upper stomach, typically rippled much to the annoyance of other men, begins to protrude outward well below the navel, which may be so negligible as to be barely visible (like Adam's, questionably existent), tucked into a knot of sinew. Aries's lower tummy, swelled by deep, childlike intakes of air, is supported by open, sturdy hips, which may thrust ever so slightly forward. His pelvic bone, too, is pronounced, thick, coarse pubic hair spreading out generously to either side allowing hardly a glimpse of skin beneath as it trails down along the inside of his thighs, blatantly powerful with thick slabs of muscle atop hairy and sturdy calves. His penis tends to be of average to ample length, though rather thick and stick-straight, the head of which may often end in a markedly sharp point. His balls, though plum-sized, are typically held tight, a signal of tension and aggression in males throughout the wild kingdom, not to mention his body's readiness for release. His ass may be alarmingly muscular and firm even as he ages. Ram guy's feet and hands are always meaningful, often more delicately rendered than the rest of him. Similarly, his face, tightly drawn with high cheekbones and rather flat like a Plains Indian's – a wide canvas stretched and perfectly suited for lines of war paint (a nod to Aries's war-god archetype) – is childlike with features all falling well below its equator, leaving a large and noble forehead to float seemingly far above. Only his dramatically ridged brow bone echoes that recurring primal theme, especially if his strident grooming habits haven't plucked the ever-unpopular unibrow into submission. His nose is small and sharp, eyes quick and expectant, his lip line extensive and perfectly horizontal, though the lips themselves are often thin and pale. This, along with his ruddy complexion, makes a photo-worthy contrast to Aries's constant five-o'clock shadow of razor-sharp barbs (that require careful navigating by sensitive-skinned sexual partners), shades darker than his hair, which, regardless of color, always seems to have a dry, sandy aspect to it. In general, he has a granite jaw that juts out dramatically, perhaps even resulting in a slight underbite. Despite such undeniably manly features, Aries's overall appearance will smack of a certain boyishness suggested especially by an ever-ready way of standing on the balls of his feet, as if he's always about to launch into a sprint. Aries is distinguished among men for boasting a remarkably low percentage of body fat; the whole of his physique seems to fit together perfectly into one streamlined unit. He exhibits a forthright body language in both his erect posture and the way his arms hang open-palmed at his sides. It's an unhindered proclamation of self, which, literally, suggests not the slightest hint of under-handedness in his demeanor. His movements may be somewhat staccato, with little flow, and he holds himself stiffly, like a G.I. Joe. Indeed, Aries's joints and muscles are tight and balled up, and he is continually spraining or pulling muscles during physical or athletic activities.

Aries man always appears as if he's just run off some playing field or another; he's forever flushed throughout his healthy skin. When standing near enough, one senses an actual heat rising from him, a sweet mocha aroma that gets one's hormones flowing, regardless of mental or emotional interest. Mars' fiery influence on his Aries boy is rather more than metaphorical: the planet works centrifugally whereby energy is constantly flowing outward from the Ram male, who is forever shaking his leg or leaning back in his chair, hard-pressed to sit still, having outsized energy to burn off. His skin is typically as dry as his personality – Aries is often challenged in the sense-of-humor department; indeed, others may remark that they've rarely heard the Aries man laugh outright. The truth is, he doesn't take in much that might warrant so hearty a response, being typically preoccupied with what he's thinking or going to say next. He might manage a smile, but he's not one to bust a gut – a nut yes, a gut no. Profusely sweating taking exercise, Aries tends to overheat even when just sitting still, and he can often have overly-strong body odor that needs keeping in check, making him that much more self-conscious and obsessed with hygiene and grooming habits – as if he's attempting to suppress the superman-liness lurking behind his signature Clark Kent-ish appearance. Aries does, in fact, take great pains to look mild-mannered, styling himself in straight-shooting looks, often falling just short of sporting a white hat. Call it righteous-dude wear, tailored to telegraph that he has successfully subdued his savage beastliness. In fact, blatantly male fashions may become a fetish for our

1ST ASTROLOGICAL
HOUSE

self-image
selfhood
identity
personality
constitution
mien/countenance
temperament/disposition
drives
inclinations
individuality
self-expression
how we are seen
way we want to be seen
self-packaging
form/physicality
body language
health and fitness
early years
life approach
worldly outlook
attitude
appearance
new beginnings
enterprise
self-concern
interests
instigation
self-awareness
idiosyncrasies
natural responses
instincts
first impressions
objectivity
aims and goals
adapting to experience
needs and urges
callings

KEYWORDS

self
form
action
body
impulse
initiative
aggression
impact
force
destruction
confidence
ego
masculinity
expectancy
enthusiasm
spontaneity
verve
exposition
vitality
singularity
purpose
penchant
dynamism
vigor
health
cleanliness
aridity
bravado
scholarship
lust
energy
heat
spirit
instinct
vigilance
heroism
morality
grandeur
rivalry
chivalry
militancy
audacity
leadership
candor
destiny

Mars-ruled man. He may wear nothing but athletic gear, or jeans and flannel with workboots, or even sport a sort of leather cowboy look – hopefully, if he's straight, an obliging friend will tell him that these looks went mainstream via the gay community thus explaining the loaded looks he gets from certain guys on the street. Some Aries men are self-styled near-samurais who try to pull off the Eastern martial-arts, no-collar look – typically, a sure signal that this guy is totally absorbed by his grand delusions of being some sort of spiritual warrior. However, all in all, Aries achieves his goal of appearing manly but not brutish. In striking such a balance, he hopes to attract a woman who is as committed to her femininity as he is married to his outré masculine nature.

Sex + Sexuality

Being so fascinated with himself, Aries man is thus acutely aware of, and indeed almost fetishistic about, not only his own masculinity, but the male condition in general. An artist like Matthew Barney could only be an Aries, engrossed as he is in the theme of his own manly body and athleticism, as well as sexual differentiation from females. His masterwork, *The Cremaster Cycle,* is named for the cremaster muscle, which controls the rise and fall of the testicles, its initial usage in the fetal stage being part and parcel of the delineation of the masculine gender. Indeed, just as Aries can't help but be obsessed by what defines him as said male Homo sapiens, he is likewise intrigued by that which stands in sharp contrast to his most human condition. There are two antonyms to *man* that become preoccupations for the Aries: *woman* and *beast.* And his relation to these entities, taken both separately and together, becomes the major theme in the self-exploration that characterizes the whole of Aries man's life. On one hand, all but lacking the proverbial feminine side other male signs are wont to get in touch with to varying degrees, Aries nonetheless strives to relate to females as best he can. On the other hand, he is all too aware of what animal forces rage inside him and thus seeks to divorce himself as he might from what he considers beastly. And these opposite-pulling forces – outwardly seeking to relate to the opposite sex to which he is so naturally attracted while trying to sever the animal nature he senses bucking and rutting inside him – go hand in hand in one heady dynamic: Let's call it Quixotemania.

From early adolescence, Aries will have begun to despise his own bullying, isolating it as his beast within, trying to rise above it. So commences a burgeoning fixation on virtue, his approach to life, and specifically sexual relationships, becoming *quixotic.* Cervantes's windmill-whacking warrior, Don

Quixote – from whom comes this term meaning 'extravagantly chivalrous,' and the inspiration for *The Man of La Mancha*'s aptly titled theme, 'Impossible Dream' – is the quintessential Ram male character, albeit at his most delusional. Herein we see Aries's need to 'die to his animal nature,' as the Buddha did in achieving enlightenment, and his desire to appeal to women, as he will, via a cultivated heroic nature. The valor he develops to appeal to women is often, ironically, chauvinistic at its core, incorporating the notion that females are fragile, which is, we think, a by-product of the man doth protesting too much against his nature – a highlight of urging his inner Gallant to kick his inner Goofus's ass. Childhood fuels this engine as well: His mother had instilled in him the perception that he was better than other boys, a specious notion that contributes to his seeing himself as the best the male species has to offer. Still, his mommy's domineering attitude determines that he'll only be attracted to women who are completely unlike her, meaning demure damsels who are, more often than not, in distress. Confusing his mother's overcontrol with feminine strength, it will be one of Aries's particular challenges in life to learn that women can be powerful without being emasculating. Mothers of Aries boys may also heap misguided romantic love on their sons, a transference of that with which they couldn't reach their detached husbands. As a result, while many men suffer some form of impotence later in life, Aries has trouble retaining erections in boyhood, no doubt due to his potential excess of oedipal stresses. Thus, growing up, Aries man emulates his distant overachiever dad, already beginning to chase needy little-lady types. As well, Aries starts to immerse himself in all things male – enter that masculinity fetish – which can also be a departure point for identifying himself as homosexual, if that is his inclination. He might be the consummate jock or fitness freak whose room is strewn, throughout his lifetime, with athletic gear, vitamins, and men's health magazines; he may be fascinated by all things military and surround himself with war paraphernalia, souvenirs, and actual weaponry; he could be a boxing, car-racing, or smash-up-derby fanatic. Whatever the specifics, Aries becomes obsessed, early on, with male societal roles with nary an interest in their female counterparts. He can't idolize a woman nonsexually – he can barely recognize one from a platonic perspective. A woman can't so much as break from her grooming or utter the odd dirty word without inviting a cold stare.

Aries is the most assertive and ambitious of all males, and the whole of his sexual being depends, first and foremost, upon the physical pursuit of his passions. Like that ram who'll head-butt every rival for a mate right out of the running, the same primal needs are at work in this virile guy: to woo and win as prize a female as possible. Being one of the pickiest men in the zodiac, this

BODY RULERSHIP

Aries rules the head and hair. Men born under the sign are prone to headaches and injuries, sunstroke, inflammation, neuralgia, and accidents stemming from a compulsive nature. Mars, his ruling planet, controls the adrenal system and the centrifugal (outward flowing) vascular system, as well as testosterone, blood, the gonads, and muscles.

is no simple task. He expects a woman to fulfill the idealized requirements of a perfect partner as is foretold in his self-mythologizing imagination. Like Adam, he awaits the miraculous appearance of his Eve, someone heaven-sent (like himself) who is preordained to obey the mandates of his self-professed destiny. She should be the picture of perfection – thin, pretty, if not a tad prim – a trophy who will serve as physical proof of reward for his privileged prowess. And he will demand worship from her in the same way Eve is meant to regard Adam – as a god. For the Aries guy has difficulty perceiving his chosen female as anything more than a part of himself – just as Eve was formed from Adam's rib, he can't but view such bonds from any other angle than his own. Indeed, his partner's attributes will be a direct reflection of his very self. Aries's association with the zodiacal 1st House of *physicality* means the formal packaging and appearance of both himself and other persons will, by astrological decree, be of paramount importance. More readily than most men, Aries will pursue a relationship based solely on appearances – the look can be everything. Empathy for a woman's inner workings, it must be said, is anathema to him. What tops his list of concerns, far more than any thought of a woman's emotional or intellectual content, is the warm form a prospective partner takes – at least initially. To his mind, it would be a cataclysmic crime against God or nature or whatever to settle for any less ideal a partner than is his right to bed and/or betroth – that special someone whom he's been convinced, since boyhood, he'll recognize the very miraculous moment she appears. This best explains why Aries guy tends to fall in love at first sight: He waits all his life for that bell to go off in his head, and so he needn't hesitate or second-guess when it does.

The self-mythologizing that Aries invariably falls prey to begins when he's very young, engulfed as he is by an interest in masculine role-playing, indulging in imaginary superhero games far more than any other males his age. Typically not a team player, he will embrace more one-on-one competitive sports – unless he's the star quarterback or in a similarly singled-out position. Taking a signature interest in martial arts, Aries seeks an outlet for his naturally emerging sexual aggression while cultivating a spiritual calm. Not big on masturbation (for moral reasons, as well as for fear, albeit subconsciously, of 'spiritual' depletion), he would rather overtire himself with athletic pursuits, the modern equivalent of Lancelot's medieval war games, until scoring a desired live partner. And although he may start dating those distressed princesses as early as junior high school, undercutting his erotic needs by playing the noble-prince role to the hilt, bawdy and booby babes will none-theless incite some action in the cremaster zone. He tries to resist, not wishing to appear too Neanderthal; turning his attention even more vigilantly toward the delicate, nearly fragile women who fit the bill of 'noble reward' for all his self-purging and purification – indeed such women are emblematic of what (he wants the world to know) are his ideals in life – he certainly doesn't wish the rest of us to see his animal nature reflected back on him via the sexy slags that *really* rock his hormonal world. Of course, in preserving this immaculate vision of a woman, he vows to keep his pedestaled princess pristine – many Aries guys, in extreme quixotic expression, will even make a chastity pact until marriage. Otherwise his bethrothed may risk toppling in his estimation, even though he'd be the one kicking the podium out from under her. It can border on pathology: Many Aries men are loath to admit they may absolutely lose interest in a woman once having had sex with her. Ironically, women who turn him down turn him on the most, inspiring, indeed preserving, his thrill at the chase. Pulling out all chivalrous stops, he'll persevere until he gets to *yes* or is slapped with a restraining order, whatever comes first.

Meanwhile, his infamous vigil-taking is due to Aries's unusually urgent sex drive, his need to relieve his lance a lot more than any other male sign in the zodiac. And more times than not, his body's insurgent rebellion against his more valiant intentions will carry the day, his pent-up Mars energy driving him in search of sex with no entangling alliances. What to do if you can't drop your fantastical notion of being paired with an eternal virgin? Find no-strings booty. One way or another, Aries objectifies women. If they're not princesses on a pedestal, they are playthings to plow. There must be some reason why Aries has earned a reputation for being rough in bed – for it is rarely a rumor being spread around by his dainty wife or girlfriend. Aries engaging in pure sex, without love, is more than eager to take off the kid gloves and demonstrate, in no uncertain terms, why his is called the sign of the Ram. He's more exceedingly brusque in bed with a female fuck buddy than most fellows simply because he's that much more pent-up. Actually, the more Clark Kentish he is on the street, the more made of steel he'll be in the sack. Luckily, some ladies appreciate healthy sexual aggression, and a bit of nipping and biting back on her part will only act as an everlasting aphrodisiac on our Aries guy. So long as a partner is equally excited by some harmless roughhousing, all will be right with the world. Of course, for our semi- if not grand-delusional Quixote, it will be back to chasing windmills first thing in the morning. Hopefully, Aries will discover, sooner rather than later, that the split he makes in his perception of women – ye olde Madonna/whore complex to be sure – is possible to mend. (The truth is, when Aries man falls in love, he can't help but see that special someone in any other way than through his quixotic lens. It's

Marvin Gaye
Omar Shariff
David Letterman
William Shatner
Leonard Nimoy
Karl Malden
Robbie Coltrane
Buddy Ebsen
Sir Alec Guinness
Sir John Geilgud
Harry Houdini
Marcel Marceau
Roscoe 'Fatty' Arbuckle
Merce Cunningham
John Bartlett
Marc Jacobs
Eric Idle
Al Gore
Thomas Jefferson
John D. Rockefeller
Tennessee Williams
L. Mies Van der Rohe
J. S. Bach
Florenz Ziegfeld
Lawrence Ferlinghetti
Arturo Toscanini
William Wordsworth
Paul Verlaine
Robert Frost
Akira Kurosawa
Ravi Shankar
Raphael
Francesco de Goya
Leonardo DaVinci
Vincent Van Gogh
Juan Gris
Joseph Campbell
Descartes
Buddha
Herb Alpert
Otto von Bismarck
Lon Chaney
Tiny Tim
Charles Baudelaire
Henry James
Rick Schroder
Ram Dass
Colin Powell
Bill Irwin
Ruben Toledo

irreversible; even with a questionable past, she'd instantly be transformed from quean to queen via his idealized vision.) Look at Hugh Hefner, another dyed-in-the-wool Aries, who made it his lifelong pursuit to combine this signature dual objectification of women – bunnies to be both ogled and revered – and in so classy a manner that decades of *Playboy* subscribers have kidded themselves into believing they're really reading the magazine 'for the articles.'

Whether as a wife or a secret wench, no man expects a woman to look as much like an airbrushed centerfold as the zodiac's Don. So aligned with the Masculine Principle is he that overt female functions are too foreign to his framework to be appetizing, let alone intriguing, as they are for many men. He may bristle at the mere mention of menstruation, and any hairy bits on women offend his Barbie-smooth ideal. That muff, especially, should be carefully manicured. He is a sucker for lithe, little, smart, but especially soft-spoken women. Sometimes, even, in an effort to secure a more passive partner, Aries may choose someone who is needy to the point of being disabled by a victimized attitude. She may suffer emotional problems, have been in prior abusive relationships, or be older than he is and verbally lament not having had children. The less self-actualized Aries man may need ever more distressing scenarios in which he can play the rescuer role. Such women, he thinks, will stay typecast as the helpless damsel, forever providing the knight a quest for her salvation while, ironically, ensuring she will stay in a subservient position. This translates into an instant woody for Aries: He's that guy who gets off on submissive women, whether it be a real-life drama or one solely acted out for the purpose of sexual enjoyment. Though one mark of a self-actualized Aries man, vis-à-vis his love life, is his commitment to an equally strong and independent woman, she herself will have to enjoy checking her authority at the bedroom door and let the conquering savior-hero do what he does best in the sack.

There is no getting around the raw fact that Aries man is an athletic lover with a urge for domination. He is all for fast and furious sex, and unlike many men, he'll tire none too easily nor feel a need to pace himself. A native of the 1st House of *self-interest,* he is, above all, in it for his own pleasure; but, as such, he taps into a primal place where the experience is devoid of the bells and whistles that put many people in their head in bed. Aries doesn't subscribe to the kind of societal instructions, like those in men's magazines, on how to please his partner. He is a straightforward animal, in it for his own gain. He doesn't seek to stem the tide of orgasm – he is totally unapologetic, even, if he comes too soon – since that Mars glyph between his legs will either remain at attention or soon return to an erect state, faster than you can say 'Was it good for you?' It's one place, luckily, where the Aries can't tame his savage beast and his higher-plane aspirations go right out the window. Ironically, in indulging his own needs he goes a lot further in satisfying a partner than does many a so-called sensitive man with a how-to manual for a mind. On his infamous second, third, or even fourth go-round, with orgasm no longer imminent, he'll really pour on the energy, bringing a partner to climax again and again amid an infamous monologue of coaxing and baiting. And as cliché as it sounds, he is only further egged on by a series of 'Don't' 's and 'Stop' 's building to crescendo. What a woman might miss is foreplay, something the egoist Ram isn't in the habit of performing. He figures, who needs it? Simple shagging allows for enough variation via positioning, so long as he's firmly in the driver's seat.

First and foremost, the zodiac's questing knight is a missionary man, but in myriad forms – taking a woman from behind, standing, doggie style, or in spoon formation will do the trick, too. Though he wants a woman to commit to a submissive role, it shouldn't be a forced issue. That is, he doesn't go in for such elaborate scenes as call for costuming; he wants the experience to be real, not an enactment of fantasy. The odd restraint spontaneously thrown in the mix might impart a thrill, but planning to employ handcuffs, for instance, rarely appeals to this spontaneous firebrand. He's a passionate but abrupt kisser, just as he's a pro with the quick thrust, not one for long, languid smooches or slow-stroking, sleepy sex. If a woman is after loving affection, Aries may seem too focused on the physical, but plenty of partners would sign on with him for that very reason. And the more appreciation a lover might express on that score, the better. Some well-placed oohs and aahs at the sight of his equipment are enough to satisfy his conceit as (just don't tell him) it's really approval that he's after. Indeed, a lover will notice how he constantly keeps eye contact, forever gauging what effect he's having. Witnessing responses to his efforts only revs the Ram up more – don't forget, it's really all about him – and as his ego swells in response to the obvious impact he's making, so, too, will other parts of him follow suit. Sometimes he'll flirt with inflicting a little pain, the conquering warrior taking characteristic liberties, engaging in behavior that's ever so slightly more slap than tickle. He loves it when you say his name, if not *uncle*. Sometimes, *sir* might even work into the mix. Aries isn't above barking orders, enjoying when a partner hops to, as if playing a very adult game of Simon Says. He'll make some quick moves all his own, switching back and forth between going down on a girl and peppily plowing into her – lickety-split – thinking this is highly innovative (we're not going to tell him otherwise, are you?). Truth be told, it takes a lot to keep up

STR8 TURN-ONS

domination
younger women
lithe bodies
blonds, tans
long legs
small breasts
athletes, dancers
long hair
body scents
shaved, waxed genitals
(active) b + d
(passive) oral
(active) anal
mastery
rough-housing
missionary position
doggy style
cotton, lace panties
teasing, being begged
maids, cheerleaders
marathon sex
tantrism
nudism

with Aries, and a lover might be hard-pressed to pace herself. As it is, she has her work cut out for her, walking a fine line, trying to simultaneously appeal to the alternate sides of his Madonna-whore vision. But it is he who must find resolution with these issues – the good news is that, typically, Aries does eventually marry his contrasting needs and score his own Aphrodite, allowing her to be, like that mythic goddess, as much an eternal virgin as she is an erotic vixen.

Being steeped in so über-masculine a sign, the zodiac's son of Adam very possibly counts the fewest gay males among his sign. Then again, gay Aries is so butch anyway, making most straight men look like sissies in comparison, that it would be difficult to gauge. In fact, being gay only seems to increase the macho identity of an Aries and certainly deepen the sign's penchant for fetishizing all things manly. And just as females seem to be the proverbial 'other' inhabitants of Venus to these straight Mars denizens, women are nearly anathema to gay Aries, who might, in extreme cases, have such a powerful aversion to the fairer sex that it borders on contempt or even revulsion. Whereas many gay male signs appreciate womankind, some to the extent of worship or emulation, the gay Aries guy suffers from an allergy on that score, boasting nary a Barbra or Judy CD in his collection. He basks in masculinity and, he'd be the first to admit it, can't abide the slightest mincing of queens. As he's never the butch top to a submissive bottom, but rather to an aggressive one, his partner must also be a decidedly manly if not straight-acting fellow. Aries likes his men the way he likes his literature – lean and muscular. He's generally attracted to dark, rugged figures, who might appear the strong, silent type, but there will nonetheless be an emotional sensitivity in his mate that appearances belie. Typically attracted to guys his own age or a bit older – he often looks down on younger folks, blanketly labeling them naive and not up to his speed – Aries will defer to his partner on the home front, letting him take the reins of domestic matters such as diet, decorating, and social directing, just so long as, on all counts, minimalism remains the overriding theme. An active lifestyle is crucial to the Ram, who is never content riding the couch – that is, unless someone's lying prone upon it.

Aries wants a playmate, and engaging in sports will be a keynote to his partnerships, just as he will forever plan trips and excursions, not of the hotel-spa variety, but those where he'll get to rough it. He has a particular fondness for the great outdoors and requires a guy sturdy enough to hike by day and then assume the hike position all night long. In truth, just being outside makes our Ram man horny, and he relishes the idea of ravishing a guy up against a tree or on a forest floor. Then again, taking a guy by force, in any setting, tops the Aries's sexual agenda. Especially if there's a bit of a struggle. Wrestling is a big turn-on to the zodiac's warrior, whose fetishism of all things masculine produces a penchant for jockstraps, tube socks, sports kits, workboots, construction gear, and sometimes a hint of leather. He likes a bit of fight in a mate, winning the right to top a guy, which explains his turnoff to submissive, overly acquiescent men. The concept of 'taking it like a man' had to be invented by an Aries, with whom sex always smacks of the autoerotic; thus pinning and otherwise sexually overtaking a manly mate sends the right messages to Aries's mind, that he's even more a stud than the one he's holding facedown in the dirt. Easily bored like his straight counterpart, there often ensues a turnstile dynamic in Aries's sex life, by no means due to his interest in a quantity of men but rather as a result of his radically particular taste. A mate must always keep the Aries guessing, never making himself too available to the Ram, so that the element of quest is always kept alive. Aries, regardless of sexual persuasion, doesn't want what he can have too easily. The Ram indeed does want a long-term relationship, as his lover will also double as his best friend. Still, the Aries is rarely faithful on a purely sexual score. He doesn't have affairs of the heart, however, being forever faithful with his emotions; it's just that he can't help sticking it to some hot booty – quick, safe, easy, no strings attached, and often no names exchanged.

Aries tends to adhere to a near exclusive gay social circle, one that may often have a pointedly activist bent, despite how un-PC he might be in private. In no way living a cozy armchair existence, he can be very out and very loud about it, though, again, his politics don't always embrace the whole of the queer community. Publically, his lover will often be at his side, satisfied to play a second-banana role, which he should be used to given their shared private life. In truth, Aries's libidinous needs must always come first, and he's not inclined to servicing his partner, who soon learns that the culmination of his own pleasure will be a by-product of letting the Aries have *his* way. But even if all is perfect in the bedroom, overly analytical Aries will always find some 'relationship issues' to sort out. Just as he is the most self-congratulatory guy when it comes to actually committing to a relationship – given his me-first approach to life, it does feel like quite a triumph for him to maintain a love bond with another man – he will likewise think nothing of dragging his boyfriend into couples therapy, say, within two or three months of their being together. Guess who'll have all the grievances. Aries demands absolute loyalty from a lover – the more, for lack of a better word, imaginative Ram guys will even play out an elaborate master-servant scenario. But with that weakness for one-night stands, he won't be held to the same hard-and-fast rules, and he

GAY TURN-ONS

topping, forcing
muscle bottoms
military uniforms
skinheads
sports kit, trainers
body builders
outdoor sex
str8 guys
boots, leather
small waists
white briefs, tube socks
nudism
wrestling, pinning
pecs
buzzcuts
grooming
(active) ass play, fisting
(active) b + d
(active) lite s + m
exhibitionism
(passive) body worship
(active) lite torture
   humiliation
clamps, slings

makes no bones about it. What the Aries might not admit to, however, are the rare instances in his life when he's welcomed having the tables turned on him and been bent to another man's will. In such instances, he sees his own masculinity being trumped, as he would only ever submit to a hands-down superman. But such encounters are for the Ram's private journal, or the recesses of his Aries-ruled noggin. Meanwhile, his visions are somewhat more picturesque – alone, or with a lover pal, packs and tents in tow, in quest of adventure and the sense of oneness that comes with silent, solitary communion with life's ever-unfolding landscape.

Couplings

Aries Man / Aries Woman
He's on a quest; she's out of reach. Less ladylike than he sometimes longs for; he's so in-her-face it hurts. Both willful to the core, neither one gives up without a fight. Two fierce libidos means a fair amount of sexual urgency.

Aries Man / Taurus Woman
She's his ultrafeminine ideal; he fulfills the fantasy of stud with an enterprising spirit. As a couple, they're a classic – Taurus boasts of being the woman behind the man. In bed, she's the mistress to his lusty master.

Aries Man / Gemini Woman
She's a fresh pixie to deflower; he's the brute she can't resist. Often purely physical at first, this pairing is eventually founded on friendship. Sexually, she's tireless; he has the staying power to sustain her.

Aries Man / Cancer Woman
She's a Cinderella, inspiring his signature rescue fantasies. He's a self-professed knight in shining armor, all chiseled features and noble intentions. Codependency is a pitfall. But loving support makes them stronger. Sex is a healing experience.

Aries Man / Leo Woman
Her stealth and self-confidence suggest the vigorous sex he craves. Beyond a mutually intense first attraction, Aries and Leo have their traditional ethics in common. It will always feel like an illicit affair – forbidden, exhilarating.

Aries Man / Virgo Woman
She seems pure as the driven snow; he embodies the ambition she finds so attractive. He'll accept her patronage: she may manage his career, if not his life. Often, needs are in conflict. Still, sex is a revelation.

Aries Man / Libra Woman
She's searching for an unfussy affair; he appears the perfect unbeholden partner. From the start, it's a power struggle – both are opinionated, if not combative. In bed, they make the peace – sex is quiet, but may border on kinky.

Aries Man / Scorpio Woman
She seems unattainable; he struggles to win her affection Blasé in the beginning, she eventually assents to his ardor. Often, they have it all: looks, glamour, wealth. Their sex life is enviably active.

Aries Man ∫ Sagittarius Woman

She's a clear conveyor of sexual messages; he readily acts upon them. Aries and Sag share a body consciousness – fitness is often a fetish. Sex is straightforward, spontaneous; no head trips, but never ho-hum.

Aries Man ∫ Capricorn Woman

A rare pair. Her unrelenting faith plus his fighting spirit means life is lived like a crusade. Still, independence is their mutual mantra. Sexually, Cap is less hesitant with him. Indeed, she submits to his will.

Aries Man ∫ Aquarius Woman

She retains a strong selfhood; he's emotionally accessed via their association. Intellectual growth is the outcome. Sex is playful and plentiful. There's more pleasure than she'd imagined in the missionary position.

Aries Man ∫ Pisces Woman

He's found that ultimately demure damsel – few are so willing to be swept off their feet. Subconsciously, she seeks to smother him. Still, they settle into an easy give-and-take. Sex is tender, with oedipal overtones.

Gay

Aries Man ∫ Aries Man

Good grooming and a love of the 'great outdoors' are what these G.I. Joes have in common. Sex will be best in the beginning. Concerns arise around a lack of emotional or spiritual depth. Couples counseling is often in their stars.

Aries Man ∫ Taurus Man

Flab is a four-letter word, so a no-fat lifestyle ensues: neither bites off more than he can comfortably chew. A confident couple – sexually compatible and similarly self-centered. In bed, they keep it simple.

Aries Man ∫ Gemini Man

Their effect on each other is visceral – the beginning of a total transformation. With dominant Aries, Gemini expresses his submissive side. Thriving on drama, life is heightened. Sexually, they're two halves of a whole.

Aries Man ∫ Cancer Man

Cancer is the Ram's Mr. Right. Aries is altered by the Crab's humor and sensitivity. They have a need to succeed; mutual support is their mantra. A dynamic bond, but there's bound to be tension. Sexually, it's a mixed bag.

Aries Man ſ Leo Man

Two über-masculine characters who steer clear of feminine types. An intensely sexual, and deeply spiritual, connection. Together, they see life as a lark, not a labor. Sex is so satisfying, it becomes a preoccupation.

Aries Man ſ Virgo Man

This might begin as a no-strings-attached sex thing. Virgo's aroused by Aries's authoritarian demeanor. But a bond between them yields soulful self-understanding. Sex remains free, 'open' to some extent.

Aries Man ſ Libra Man

Aries and Libra make an impressive package – and they know it: Vanity is their defining feature. Life together is structured, but the Scales struggles to stay on the straight and narrow. Aries likes a little leather on his Libra.

Aries Man ſ Scorpio Man

Their connection is elemental: Sexy, aggressive planet Mars rules both signs. Aries and Scorpio share a profound physical compatibility. Scorpio is often the instigator. Emotionally, their dynamic is complex – anger is ever present.

Aries Man ſ Sagittarius Man

These fire signs share a slew of qualities – palpable masculinity, love of adventure, a bawdy sense of humor. Still, there's discord: Aries is a neat freak; not so Sagittarius. In bed, both men will try anything twice.

Aries Man ſ Capricorn Man

Aries is the arm candy who worships a worldly, well-bred Goat guy. After fascination fades, the focus turns to friendship. From overtly sexual beginnings, this pair may slowly become abstemious.

Aries Man ſ Aquarius Man

Aries might need more affection than Aquarius is inclined to offer. But when it works, individuality and independence await. Somehow, sex stays comfortably casual. Other couples often enter the mix.

Aries Man ſ Pisces Man

Often a purely physical pairing. Pisces man is unusually shallow in his perception of virile Aries as a mere sexual tool. Under such corrupting influence, the Ram's barbaric, conquering erotic spirit emerges.

Aries Woman

the original

For Aries woman, the existential journey lies along the path of least resistance. She is a minimalist of the first order and never crowds her experience with unnecessary obstacles, obligations, drama, or entangling emotional involvements. Single-minded in her artistic or professional pursuits, she adopts a definite plan for their achievement, realizing success by keeping life simple, easily sacrificing extra luxuries. She is the most ascetic female in the zodiac, especially forgoing such feminine trappings as most women would deem essentials. Calling her a 'man's woman' is a gross understatement, as she is far more like-minded and at ease with the opposite sex than with her own. She goes where men go, she does what men do – no double standard, no questions asked. When it comes to sex, Aries is utterly unsanctimonious, requiring no wooing to coax out her carnal desires. She seeks to satisfy her own potent sex drive where, when, and with whom she damn well pleases. Indeed, this unapologetic stance toward sex is a key defining factor in the establishment of her identity. To her, men are, first and foremost, sex objects. She doesn't plan to fall in love – in fact, she often tries her hardest to avoid doing so. Her ideal man is, likewise, a rugged individualist with scant emotional needs and a healthy libido. In same-sex scenarios, however, she invites somewhat more indulgence: Drawn to females with fierce sex drives to equal her own, her bonds are often as intensely possessive and psychologically loaded as they are explosively erotic.

♈

PRINCIPLE

With the first zodiacal precept, from the primordial slime of Pisces's dissolution emerges the solid physical energy of Aries with its directive Masculine Principle of form, objectivity, and action. Selfhood is paramount and the Aries woman is most concerned with its preservation. She is a realist, taking little stock in emotions or spiritual concerns, which, like everything else in life, are simply matters of practicality. Her sign's matter-of-fact motto is 'I am.'

Sign + Mind

Aries is ruled by the fiery planet Mars, which represents the objective or Masculine Principle in astrology. The Aries personality, therefore, is distinguished for being active, directive, and goal-oriented – that which is universally recognized as 'masculine' output power, as opposed to a passive, subjective, receptive input energy, traditionally considered 'feminine.' Being the female native of so über-male a sign means that Aries woman is, in effect, the personification of masculinity in the feminine form. No surprise: As anyone who is intimately associated with her would undoubtedly agree, she is the least 'girly' girl one could hope to meet. Astrology's premier sign is associated with birth, both on the individual scale – Aries rules the ages 0–7 – as well as on a wider human spectrum, the advent of all creation. You might say Aries is astrology's answer to Genesis, or even the big bang theory: Fittingly, Aries is the sole cardinal-fire sign in the zodiac, identified, thus, as an initiatory flame, spark, or flashpoint. Indeed, Aries of both sexes manifest this explosive energy, albeit in different ways, a trait that is often visible as a spirited glint in Aries woman's otherwise steely eyes. She is the least compliant character in the zodiac, one who takes herself most seriously. She is incredibly guarded and doesn't impress easily. Rather she is fully focused on her own objectives and the assertion of her infamous strategies, which she's forever plotting and enacting to her sole satisfaction.

In discerning which archetypes might offer psychological insight into the Aries, the male prototypes are evident enough, both in the first-born biblical Adam and in such classic macho Greek figures as Zeus and Ares (Roman: Mars) – characters who embody the forthright fiery energy of Aries man. Aries woman is no Eve to his Adam, however – that persona is represented by Taurus woman, who, as we'll see, manifests the opposite energies of subjectivity, passivity, and indeed submission. Rather, for Aries woman, the masculinized female, we must discern the archetypal counterparts of Ares–Mars or Adam: Athena, the classical goddess of war and wisdom, and Lilith, Adam's erstwhile first wife.

Like both of these primordial tough cookies, who, respectively, represent the noble vision of female power-wisdom and the flip-side, demonized view of such strength, the Aries woman is an awe-inspiring creature who poses a challenge to the world of men. As the inheritor of such imposing female force, she is not one to be taken lightly. Though it's easy for her male counterpart, aligned with the masculine polarity of his sign, to simply be his unapologetic self in the world, no questions asked – Aries's motto is 'I am' –

the female of the sign is hard-pressed to carve out and sustain her identity in a society that has only in recent history, and, still, just in rarefied Western quarters, begun to allow a woman all the rights and privileges afforded to men. Aries woman cannot simply head-butt her way through life the way the Ram man can; nor would she choose to. It is only by maintaining a healthy distance from circumstances, and people for that matter, that she allows herself the proper vantage point for plotting her successes. Like the biblical Lilith, Aries woman doesn't fit into the patriarchal vision of womanhood – for starters, Lil liked it on top and so wouldn't let Adam assume that power position, and therefore she removed herself, choosing instead to live near the Red Sea (or ocean of *blood,* a substance that falls under Aries's planetary rule). In taking from this archetypal example, Aries woman, too, seeks her cool remove from the domination of men, refusing to fulfill the worldview of woman as a creature of subjugation. She keeps to herself and her own counsel. Though her signature isolationism isn't really due to the fact that she simply 'vants to be alone'; no, she tends to walk alone, eschewing the company of other women, especially, because she perceives herself, and therefore wants to be perceived, as a stand-out: Not in so much to say that she isn't like the others, but rather that there is nobody else quite like her.

No woman is more fiercely or, dare we say, pathologically competitive than Aries. Not surprisingly, every myth featuring Athena seems to be marked by her, clad in signature armour, competing with some god or mortal. Athens is named for her because she bested great Poseidon for the city's patronage. Aries is likewise always showing someone up. And she can be incredibly cut-throat in the process. There's zero irony to Aries woman in her directive approach to life, and she doesn't have a self-deprecating bone in her body (unless it's someone else's). Humor about oneself, which can be so charming in others, is anathema to her. She thus never lets down her guard. And though she will cultivate tact – Athena is the goddess of diplomacy, after all – Aries doesn't afford herself the slightest degree of humility as, for her, that is tantamount to weakness, opening her up to humiliation. Whereas the male war god Ares–Mars is forever on the offensive as is his namesake Aries man, women of the sign are defensive in the extreme. She keeps the safest distance, drawing others' fire, teaching the rest of us, by example, the most valuable lessons in self-fortification, if not edification, the overriding objective of the Aries female, entrenched as she is in self-interest. While the rest of us at some point kick ourselves for wasting valuable time and energy on people-pleasing, Aries will never have need to recriminate herself on such account.

The zodiacal 1st House, ruled by Aries, is one of *worldly outlook* as well as

PLANETARY SYMBOL

The arrow (materiality) emerging from the circle (spirit) suggests physical life stemming from divine origin. This mirrors the full-armored body of Athena – the glyph recalls a shield and spear – emerging from the godhead of Zeus. Formal strength is thus emphasized over emotional or spiritual content.

SIGN QUADRANT

The zodiacal quadrants correspond to metaphysical planes of existence – physical, emotional, mental, and spiritual. The First Quadrant is that of the self and individual awareness. For Aries woman importance lies in the sanctity of her ideas and personal freedom. To keep her identity intact she often seeks reclusion from what she perceives to be a male-dominated world of double standards and restrictions.

SIGN GLYPH

The Ram's head and horns signify the expression of the mind and the emergence of identity. Alternately, it recalls the snake-haired gorgon, vengeful female power, which Athena wears on her breastplate. The female ewe was the animal form of the primordial goddess. The glyph also recalls a human brow and nose, symbolizing wisdom gained via instincts.

ELEMENT + QUALITY

The fire element connotes life and creative power. The cardinal quality signals action and initiative. Together, the cardinal-fire combination particular to Aries is best illustrated as a spark or sudden burst of flame. She is an instigator of the first order, always with an eye on productivity as can arise from blowing the lid off stifled situations.

separateness of being, individuality, selfhood and *self-interest,* just a few of the many attributes that are particularly relevant to the female of the sign. Unlike most human beings, who thrive on connectedness to others, Aries survives in life via staunch independence, if not outright segregation. Under Mars' influence, masculine psychological as well as physiological qualities are most obvious in her makeup, manifesting in this quintessential tomboy long before she starts to morph into womanhood. As far back as she can remember, it is fellow females, not males, who strike her as 'other.' Once she hits sexual maturity, however, Aries no longer hangs as easily with the guys, but is still not chummy with other young women, either. Typically good-looking and confident in the extreme, she appears to be an aloof loner rather than a social outcast. Wholly individual, her presence makes others feel like sheep. She will often be labeled a 'feminist' from early on when, in fact, such political purpose couldn't be further from her mind: Aries has no agenda other than her own. However, she quickly learns that her above-it-all routine works like magic at bringing guys to their knees: While all those 'Eves' are on the sidelines giggling, it is she alone whom boys might be ogling. Without even trying, she seems out of reach, something that only inspires men to pursue her all the more vigorously.

Given her sign's mountain-sheep symbol, Aries is much like the female ewe who holds herself up on some isolated, windswept ledge while rival males duke it out in hopes of winning her affection. Herein one sees the manner in which the sign's cardinal-fire status manifests differently in males and females: The sparky Ram guy, head-butting his way into everything in life, sexual relationships included, embodies his hot pursuits, being a virtual fireball to contend with. In contrast, Aries girl is a notoriously cool customer who ignites others into action. The god Ares rushes boldly into the heat of battle, but Athena is a strategist, the goddess of 'prudent war' or, as also befits her status as patron deity of craftsmanship, the art of war. This is Aries woman in a nutshell: She doesn't merely attack her goals and ambitions, she smokes them out. She makes others want to hand her her successes, because being notoriously unattainable is assumed to be one and the same with being revered and sought-after. It's the same with sex: She lights fires in would-be lovers by being at once self-assuredly blasé – perched upon her ewe's 'bluff' – and disarmingly approachable, more one-of-the-guys than any other gal. She is genius at establishing herself as a lofty goal for those men attempting to capture her heart – typically not a part of her anatomy in the offing. It can be a precarious position to sustain: Holding herself up as one of a kind, an original, she projects an air of superiority that inspires the most ardent of suitors, no wimps or wannabe hotties, all the while breeding contempt in other females whose feminine trappings and societal simpering she can't help but find fatuous. And so, Aries teeters between fostering esteem and desire on one hand and exposing herself to scrutiny and derision on the other.

Aries woman's association with the ages 0–7, the advent of birth for this, the zodiac's Genesis sign, is highly significant. In fact, the glyph of Mars, despite its graphic recollection of male genitalia and signage for men's rooms worldwide, can be read as symbolic of birth, the body (arrow of matter) emerging from the womb (divine circle). And whereas emphasis for the Aries man is on being born, giving rise to lifelong issues along the theme of entitled birthright, for Aries woman it is the feminine aspect of the glyph – the womb-like circle – that speaks to her particular human condition: She experiences life as a creator, and often one who chooses to remain in an isolated private little bubble, birthing her conceptions out into the world. After all, this daughter of Athena is infamously artsy-craftsy in her professional endeavors, typically preferring to work alone, in a removed environment, at her own pace, dispersing her wares with minimal social interaction. It is striking just how many Aries females work with their hands in the fine arts – especially in the design and manufacture of ceramics, textiles, and other such products. Often, too, her trademark handiwork manifests as literature, words of wisdom being Athena's diplomatic domain. Few individuals in the zodiac are as clever as she, and writing – creative, philosophical, journalistic, academic, or psychological – often becomes her perfect outlet. For her, the pen is far mightier than the sword. Whatever the endeavor, one thing is for sure: Aries woman maintains a healthy distance and objectivity toward her vocation, rarely one to be consumed by, or lost in, pursuits. She is a realist of the first order, in no way deluded about her abilities, despite a hardy 1st House-ruled ego. Aries takes a warrior's approach to life and rarely feels daunted – impatient, yes – or discouraged by derision or detractors, who fall under the heading of insignificant others she intends to cleverly defeat.

Athena represents the daughter archetype in myth and literature, as well as astrology. Like Ares, the first Olympian son, she is the premier female off-spring of Zeus and was afforded the same carte-blanche privileges of male gods, never having to marry let alone wear an off-the-shoulder gown. Like her, Aries woman feels singled-out if not spoiled, having her back up in anticipation of any potential impositions; indeed she's like a child first learning the power of the word 'no,' which is her default response to any and all demands made upon her. Indeed, a prime symptom of Aries's correspondence to the 0–7 age group is the Ram female's willful nature – she is an eternal 'terrible' two-year-old: When she wants something in life, she

POLARITY

Females in masculine signs (fire, air) are not aligned with the gender polarity of their sign and thus enact instead of embody the quality-element combination of the sign. Aries woman therefore seeks to 'start fires,' smoking out problems to bring about desired results. As the zodiac's pre-mier strategist, she is able to rile others into a fury or oth-erwise force their hand while she remains cool, calm, and collected.

I

SIGN NUMBER

One being the loneliest number is typically not a problem for the privacy-loving Aries. Independence is of primary concern and a certain oneness with exis-tence is something she is inherently provided to expe-rience. Unlike many others, the Aries woman doesn't feel a burning need to be partnered.

0–7

SIGN AGE ASSOCIATION

The age group of individuality. All her life the Aries personifies a bit of the 'terrible twos,' energy distinguished by a headstrong clinging to selfish need, a reluctance to share, and the ability to launch into a full-fledged tantrum when crossed or challenged.

PSYCHOLOGY

Aries woman can be selfish in the extreme. She typically lacks compassion to some degree, and she is often overly contemptuous of other women. She lacks empathy and her competitive edge can lead to underhanded behavior or cheating. She has great difficulty with romantic commitment and will sometimes quit relationships rather than communicate or compromise. As she's sexually liberated, fidelity is not a particular strength.

simply won't concede to not getting it; and she is not above throwing the most explosive tantrum if she doesn't. To see Aries woman's cardinal-fire feistiness in action, all one need do is stand in the way of her desired objectives, at which point all her Athenian diplomacy will go right out the window – she'll wage an all-out war to secure her purpose or plans. Like a child only just learning to relate to others, interaction is seemingly always something new to the Aries, the whole of her life being a process of learning how to share, cooperate, and indeed play fair. Frankly, she is self-serving, in the extreme adopting the view that, since she requires so little in life, she is therefore entitled to that which she does lay claim – be it property, opportunities, positions of power, or people. Moreover, like a youngster whose discarded toys are picked up by another tot, she often wants things simply because she can't have them. Regardless of the situation, business or pleasure, and despite her signature detached air, at times, in dealing with the Aries, one would swear she could, at any moment, perform the adult equivalent of flipping over the full game board, either because she isn't winning or because she has been caught cheating, something, given her often bratty, grabby nature, she isn't above suspicion of doing.

Except for her trademark tantrums, Aries is otherwise fairly unemotional. She seems to feel only in so far as circumstances concern her, often lacking sympathetic regard for others. She is as steely-eyed as her ruling gray-eyed goddess – and if you don't believe us, just ask her mother, from whom Aries never quite seemed to require tender nurturing or even simple warmth. She doesn't need; she demands, mainly, attention – that, and to be allowed to assert her equally steely will. Just as Athena sprang forth from Zeus' head, so, too, is Aries aligned with her father. She is a female version of him; in keeping with her archetype, her father's brainchild. Usually sired by an independent, self-made man, Aries sees in her father a figure who enjoys perfect authority and undisputed freedom in his family life – and she thinks, 'This is for me.' *Et voilà:* The first seeds of her need for an inalienable identity begin to sprout like the Ram's horns that symbolize her sign. Just as Zeus bequeathed his powerful goat's-fleece breastplate, the 'aegis,' unto Athena, likewise, it is Aries's father's way of life, his attitude, and often his choice of profession that become the protective aegis under which she finds her personal and/or professional identity. Still, Ram girls feel some semblance of compassion, no matter how pale, for their mother. Whereas nurturing can be indulgent and nearly emasculating for Aries boy, the laissez-faire attitude of the Aries girl's mom initiates a framework of self-sufficiency that begins to manifest as early as pretoddler age. Although Aries doesn't necessarily have disdain for her mom, she pities her for having, as she sees it, sublimated her own needs and goals to those of her husband – something that Aries girl is determined never to allow. After all, Athena did have a mother – Metis (goddess of prudence) – whom it was prophesied would bear Zeus a male child to overthrow him, just as Zeus (Jupiter) had overthrown his father, Cronus (Saturn), who had likewise slain his father, Uranus. Happy family. But Zeus swallowed Metis in the form of a fly to keep the prophecy from being realized. And Aries girl, too, feels her father 'swallowed' up her mother via marriage; but she doesn't rebel against her father. He is, after all, her biggest fan: Like Athena, who is Zeus' favorite child, the Aries girl may be the son her father never had, even when he does have boys. Often, Aries comes from a big family with lots of brothers wherein Mother is put-upon, particularly by the males in her life – a private patriarchy of sorts. In light of how she views her parents' relationship, Aries female associates femininity with weakness and identifies strength with the masculine presence of her father. Yet, as we'll see, she's loath to enter a relationship with so strong a guy as would challenge her need for freedom and her all too precariously forming identity.

Body + Soul

Aries woman is an indomitable spirit who seemingly exists to illustrate what a woman is capable of achieving on her own, against societal odds. She is a pioneer, a symbol of strength, self-reliance, and liberation. This fact is especially striking when one considers the list of iconic Aries women of African-American heritage, which includes the likes of such gutsy singers as Bessie Smith, Pearl Bailey, Aretha Franklin, Sarah Vaughan, Billie Holiday, and Diana Ross – breakthrough artists who could only be born under the sign of the Ram. This is a ballsy bunch to be sure, as evidenced by a continuing list of Aries actresses – Gloria Swanson, Bette Davis, Joan Crawford, Sarah Jessica Parker, Julie Christie, Emma Thompson, Simone Signoret, Jessica Lange, Robin Wright Penn, Reese Witherspoon, Natasha McElhone, and Lucy Lawless – none of whom, in life or on film, could convincingly portray some damsel in distress. This is the sign of Camille Paglia, Maya Angelou, Jane Goodall, Eudora Welty, Gloria Steinem, Erica Jong, and Clare Boothe Luce, an unapologetic breed of righteous babes whose beauty stems from a refusal to succumb to society's frilly vision of what femininity should look like. Nowhere but in this female demographic will you see so few brassieres per capita.

If you notice a lanky, natural, decidedly unfussy-looking beauty in the sole company of men, possibly swilling neat drinks and swearing, albeit soft-spokenly,

ARCHETYPE + MYTH

Aries draws on the classic goddesses of the mind. Like Lilith, who predates Eve as Adam's wife, the Greek Metis (Prudence) is Zeus' mate prior to Hera and resides in his head. She is one and the same with her daughter Athena (Wisdom) who springs full grown from his noggin at birth. Aries's prime archetype is Athena, a war goddess, but one of prudence, diplomacy, and strategy. Pallus Athena points to her phallic, spear-toting nature. A patroness of crafts, we also see in her Aries's artisan sensibilities. Like this 'virgin goddess,' Aries woman won't be put upon by males.

BIBLE + LITERATURE

Aries's biblical archetype is Lilith, the original wife of Adam, whose character didn't comply with a male-dominant relationship. Her name recalls the lily or lotus, a symbol of yonic power. Rachel, called 'the holy ewe,' was one of the original matriarchs of Hebraic culture. In modern literature, the Arien prototype is found in handsome heartbreakers like Hemingway's Lady Brett Ashley, the quintessential man's woman, Louisa May Alcott's Jo from the ironically titled *Little Women,* and the ever sapphic Xena, warrior princess.

like a sailor, chances are that woman is a Ram. Being Aries is an attitude: Like some ardent but aloof Hemingway heroine, she freely inhabits decidedly masculine milieus, fraternizing with pals who may easily double as sex partners. To guys, she is refreshingly original, a woman who meets men and accepts them on their own terms – even an avowed bachelor senses he can be his most carefree self, that he needn't alter his behavior in relationship with her. She is one of the boys, and with the wardrobe to match. Though, for the most part, she's one of those women on whom everything looks good, her default duds are jeans and a T-shirt. Not to say she can't throw on a slim and slinky dress and look the model of femininity. Because, much to the vexation of other women, she can pull that off as well; yet with no more panache than when she pulls on her favorite 501s. Her fondness for butch styles makes her all the more fascinating a creature, creating a stark contrast against her naive, lamby looks. Though there is what might be called the 'dark Aries' – a sturdier sort still, with quick, flashing eyes, and an intensely earthy, almost cavewomanesque demeanor – Aries is usually taller, leaner, and lighter-skinned, regardless of race, than other members of her family. Her hair, also fairer, is often fine, dry, and falls straight; she tends to leave it long, uncoiffed or opting for a simple blunt-cut or bobbed style. But it is this woman's face, a feature ruled by the sign of Aries, that is always most striking: A decidedly sculptural bone structure makes her visage wide and planal – not a face so much distinguished by cheekbones as it is by the configuration of her other features – her round eyes with infamously bushy brows, a small, straight nose, and a mouth all in close proximity far below the equator of her face, providing her with a childlike beauty all through her life. Her lips are a contradiction, ample on bottom but slivery on top; sometimes, it even appears as if she has no upper lip at all. Her forehead is high, lending a wise and noble air. Most stunningly, Aries's skin seems stretched over the rather broad plain of her face, as a canvas drawn flat and taut by the vise grip of a tightened frame. This flattened countenance makes her look somewhat like an owl (not surprisingly, Athena's sacred bird). She may have indetectable traces of fine baby hair along her jawline; but typically, having such minute pores, her skin appears flawless and porcelainlike – generally not freckled or beauty-marked. Beneath relatively chipmunky cheeks, Aries's jaw is prominent and may even jut forward a bit (she often experiences a lot of tension in this area and it can become a trouble spot, a place she holds all her stress). Her neck may also have a clenched, slightly strained look to it. But hers is an honest and open face defined by disarmingly cool eyes, often pale, steely gray, or hazel, set in a comely bed of expressive crinkles, which become crow's-feet all too quickly if she's not careful, and a wry regiment of tiny white teeth, gleaming in a decidedly gummy smile.

Aries's back and shoulders are strong and straight, her head held high, exhibiting perfect posture that pitches slightly forward, her arms thin and sinewy. She is generally not big-breasted; and in the off case she is, her boobs will be firm as if they were made of muscle – in either case, she'll boast developed pectorals underneath them. She has dramatic-looking areolae, and nipples that stick out hard and long when she is aroused, nearly as painful as pleasurable when in such a state. Typically more delicate on top and bigger-boned on bottom, Aries nonetheless doesn't have much curve to her shape, which can be rather short-waisted; her hips are often practically nonexistent, and she's long-legged, with powerful though streamlined thighs, which bodes well for athleticism – in one form or another, a definite featured aspect of her lifestyle. Her joints tend to be loose, which, while making her look flexible, can also lend a dangly, puppety effect to her appearance. This quality is accented by a prominent, forward-projected pelvic bone juxtaposed against thin, elongated thigh muscles, creating a U-turn space at the crotch – this is the second place, after her face, that catches one's eye. Although she is not a hairy female overall – barely needing to shave her legs or armpits – she does have a rather dense bush, which may spread wide across her pronounced pelvis, hanging down like a beard at that infamous crossroads between her legs. There is never any lack of moisture here as Mars' centrifugal energy provides all the happy outpourings she needs. And just like those nipples, her clit easily becomes enlarged, due perhaps to Mars' rulership of the more sticky-outy sexual apparatus in both sexes, i.e., the penis and the clitoris. So it's little wonder that her mythical archetype's full title is Pallus Athena – as *pallus* or *phallus* attached to this female deity's name suggests she's the pantheon's original goddess chick with a dick. In fact, Aries's pleasure button can protrude so indignantly, you'd think it was trying to make up for a mythical, missing schlong.

The Aries female walks with a springy gait, moving somewhat ganglingly, though never ungracefully. It's just a sexy bit of boyish energy that bounds right through her waify, sometimes wispy, feminine form. She can be fairly brusque, cliquey, or even outright confrontational upon a first meeting, eyeing those she doesn't know rather skeptically, and not at all subtly. She is highly territorial, her usual domain being with the men. So if you're at a party, say, and the crowd divides, as it's wont to do, along gender lines, Aries is typically not helping out in the kitchen; instead she hovers near the grill, straddles the bar, jockeys for the pool table, samples cigars and cognac, or otherwise hangs with the guys. She often latches onto a man, not her boyfriend, hubby, or even necessarily a first date she came with, rather instituting the buddy system for

1ST ASTROLOGICAL
HOUSE

self-image
selfhood
identity
personality
constitution
mien/countenance
temperament/disposition
drives
inclinations
individuality
self-expression
how we are seen
way we want to be seen
self-packaging
form/physicality
body language
health and fitness
early years
life approach
worldly outlook
attitude
appearance
new beginnings
enterprise
self-concern
interests
instigation
self-awareness
idiosyncrasies
natural responses
instincts
first impressions
objectivity
aims and goals
adapting to experience
needs and urges
callings

KEY WORDS

identity
separation
mind
prudence
animus
distinction
independence
nonconformity
diplomacy
strategy
feminism
detachment
détente
austerity
intent
single-mindedness
controversy
feminism
fitness
libido
exhibition
energy
execution
premeditation
presence
alacrity
competition
simplicity
liberation
contempt
calculation
craftsmanship
mettle
discretion
circumspection
constitution
attitude
anticipation
idiosyncrasy
incisiveness
tact
artfulness
severity
solemnity
skill

the evening with an old guy-friend or even a new male acquaintance (much to the chagrin of whomever he might be paired with). Like her speech, which is succinct but even-toned and devoid of emotional pitches, she emits a monotone laugh, keeping her jaw clenched against it and her body still and straight. One senses a great vitality in this woman: She radiates health and seems capable of meeting tough physical challenges. If she were a tree, she'd be a cross between a willow and an oak – towering, light, and feathery, still undeniably hale and hearty. She is, one might say, ruggedly feminine more than ambiguously androgynous – a handsome beauty, both admirable and sexually appealing to men and women alike.

Sex + Sexuality

Like attracting like, strong, virile guys are Aries's physical ideal, providing her with the promise of the rough-and-tumble sex she craves. Still, as she isn't looking to repeat her mother's mistakes, they should also be the silent type – no amount of prudence in entering a relationship with an overbearing man can substitute for the wisdom of knowing not to go there in the first place. Indeed, of anybody in the zodiac, male or female, nobody is more blasé toward the notion of permanent relationships than Aries woman. But as a native of the 1st House of *physicality,* she cannot forgo sex – it must be an almost daily mainstay of her routine. Like some stereotypical male, Aries is looking to 'score,' with the loophole line that she's not looking for anything more 'serious' forever on her lips. After all, being the catch of the century requires remaining available, or at least seeming so. Although Aries eventually procures a longtime companion, she isn't ever one to jump into marriage – the Ram always keeps her options open. Besides, this willful woman has her own itch to scratch. Unabashedly alert to the physical attributes of men, she is the zodiac's comparative sexual shopper. Fittingly, therefore, she tends to hook up with older, faster guys when she's young, unable to bear the idea of being someone's high school sweetheart. Conversely, as she matures, she prefers younger guys, confidently on the make for sizable studs who might provide some serious exercise in the sack, but still, like her, aren't looking to be tied down. As a rule, Aries has little difficulty realizing this straightforward sexual agenda.

When single life loses its sparkle – for many a Ram gal it never will – Aries will still steer clear of commanding personalities, scoping out guys who'll provide her with nurturing while remaining just enough of a pushover so that she can always assert herself. And given the amount of uncommunicative, reticent males in the gene pool, Aries might slip into relationships fairly easily. Still, she keeps a potential mate in the foyer of her affections for a long time before allowing him into her inner sanctum – meanwhile, of course, there's always a door to the bedroom off said foyer. She doesn't, like many women, have a mile-long checklist of requisite qualities in a man. For Aries, it's a trade-off; given that she demands such absolute autonomy in relationships, she can't be that picky. One dynamic she sometimes falls into, albeit subconsciously, is to have a relationship that actually proves true all her dubious notions about the tyranny of men over women. Throwing her hands up in defeat, as if to say there's just no use fighting this age-old battle of the sexes, she will retreat even further into a solitary life with no-strings sexcapades.

Entering a relationship always smacks of striking a bargain for Aries, the terms of which are that she'll stomach an excess of foibles and/or deficiencies in return for absolute free rein. Often, she'll latch onto a guy who doesn't appear nearly 'good enough' for her, particularly to the queue of men who desire her brand of disaffected affection, that laid-back palsy-walsy bond she seems to promise. The man she chooses may even be disabled, if not physically, then emotionally or psychologically. This can be her 'out' – as if to say, 'I put up with your shortcomings, you should be grateful I'm even here.' Interestingly, while Aries men often look for absolute perfection in a potential mate, akin to the illicit mythic affair between Ares and the primo-pussy deity Aphrodite (who was wedded to the lame, cuckolded Hephaestus), Athena, as antithesis to Ares, was widely worshiped in temples she shared with that same gimpy god; some scholars claim they were sexual consorts as well. In similar fashion, Aries woman may set up house with a 'lame' character whose shortcomings she unconsciously uses as leverage against her guilt at being unable to fully commit. It's a realistic 'working' relationship she's after anyway – being a relative disbeliever in spiritual bonds – one that suits her independent streak while satisfying any basic need for companionship. To be fair, there is a sort of Aries splinter group, those Rams who feel a strong urge to cohabitate or wed as a means, ironically, of garnering literal support for their otherwise 'independent' lifestyle. Still, even when head over heels in love, the typical Aries is loath to marry and become legally beholden.

Cohabitation with a humble everyman who'll make no undue demands actually furthers Aries's lifelong quest for increased freedom. Just as Hephaestus' hammer blow freed Athena from the head of Zeus, a menschlike dude with no domineering agenda will keep the home forge fired up while Aries emerges as a diva in this man's world. Typically, her ideal partner will be

BODY RULERSHIP

Aries rules the head, which, in the case of Aries woman, points to the need for an independent mind as well as a strategic outlook on life distinguished by prudence and self-protection. Mars rules masculine traits in both sexes, the adrenal system, signaling flight rather than fight in females of the sign. The planet also controls outward-flowing functions in the body such as genital lubrication and the shedding of eggs during menstruation.

a handyman like Hephaestus, since having some callused-pawed beefcake on the home front keeps her sexually sated as well. (She doesn't want to *have* to stray.) Aries appreciates hard features as much as hard work – no pretty-boy aesthetes or intellectual dreamers for this sexy straight shooter. She wants physical meat from her mate, not fashion advice or existential musings. Aries female naturally assumes superiority over her significant other, especially intellectually, so she really doesn't want much evidence to the contrary. Feeling herself more man than most men, she desires a guy with whom, in contrast, she can be her most feminine self, particularly when she knows, upon rolling out of bed, that she's the one who gets to pull back on the pants. Sometimes, though, her judgment may truly miss its mark and in her physically focused pursuit of increasingly testosterone-engorged guys, she may snag herself a baddie who'll use his manly body more aggressively than she may have bargained for. Such pitfalls in female character seem lifted straight from the pages of a Hemingway novel – as in *The Sun Also Rises*' Brett Ashley and her penchant for macho, bloodthirsty matadors. Meanwhile, the disabled Hephaestean Jake Barneses of the world continue to chase her to the ends of the Earth. But to Aries's mind, someone is always in hot pursuit of her. For, she has the oft specious notion that nary a guy she meets isn't after her. So high is the opinion she has of herself. And even well into advancing years, she'll still feel a need to deflect imaginary advances of younger men, the irony being that her infamous resistence only piques interest where it might've otherwise not existed.

The atmosphere is always thus loaded, the question of carnal interest forever hanging in the air. Suffice it to say that Aries woman doesn't possess a subtle sexuality. Yet, despite her unapologetic directness, she is enormously misunderstood, often perceived as a tease and a user by men who impose a double standard, disallowing a woman to be as love-'em-and-leave-'em as they accept other men to be. Women may simply label her 'easy' – a projection, typically, of their own sexual repression. After all, most people aren't hip to the astrological influences of objective Mars on the Aries woman: It *forces* her libido into action. She has neither the time nor the inclination to send out invitations, hormonal or otherwise; such focus on others goes against her nature and feels like an imposition on her no-nonsense character, not to mention a phony waste of time. It's that sort of deference to a man that she labels her mother's – and indeed most women's – ultimate demise. Putting out is one thing, being put out is quite another.

Sexually, Aries acts on impulse and responds to whatever she experiences as physical attraction. Only when a man makes her Mars-ruled juices actually flow will she give him the time of day. To squelch such impulses seems, to her, a crime against nature. Contrary to the popular belief of women who may've seen their men swiped right out from under them by Aries, she isn't conniving or even calculated – she simply follows the signals her body sends, feeling justified in doing so. There's nothing romantic or emotional in her actions – she's not generally passionate enough even to be predatory. Few Aries want to work that hard. On the other hand, she may throw a major hissy fit if a guy doesn't take her bait – as pissed off as Athena when Paris judges Aphrodite more beautiful than her – whereby all diplomacy goes right out the window and it's all-out (Trojan) war. Scorn is the one sentiment she will not easily abide from a man.

To be sure, Aries can be a real hypocrite when it comes to sexual relationships: It is fine for her to have a roving eye, acting on her 'honest' impulses; but just let her catch a steady beau screwing around and all ideological diatribing on equality in relationships is discarded. Rejection is anathema to Aries; she is the one accustomed to rifling through the male meat-rack, spitting out the chewed-up bits at will. Of course, such a one-sided view of relationships is a throwback to her upbringing: Her father may have gotten away with sex-on-the-side shenanigans, but there's no way her mother would have entertained such thoughts for herself. And the Aries female expects that same double standard to apply to her relationships. She must have, at the very least, what her father enjoyed – usually, she hankers for more. Topping her father is a stock subconscious force – as mentioned, she may enter into the same career as her dad, only to surpass him. Unconsciously, she seeks to emasculate her father for, what she considers, the foul manner in which he treated her mother. Part and parcel of that subliminal castration – where did Athena get that auxiliary Pallas anyway? – is Aries's tendency to cuckold the men in her own life. It takes balls, certainly, to do so. Which may not be taking the metaphor far enough – Aries female, of all women, has the worst case of penis envy imaginable. Sometimes, it's not such a bad thing: The strong, silent type with whom she often permanently partners might be happy that she's the britches-wearing relationship front person and may prefer her being the motivating force in the bedroom as he can take the backseat while letting her drive the action.

When it comes to sex, Aries craves instant gratification. If single, she'll usually have a booty-call number logged into her speed dial; and in a relationship, she's gotta have it more often than any other woman on the astrological wheel. Not one for nuance, Aries generally opts for skipping the preliminaries and getting to the main event. Foreplay schmoreplay: Intercourse

Hope Davis
Simone Signoret
Aretha Franklin
Mariah Carey
Bessie Smith
Loretta Lynn
Pearl Bailey
Celine Dion
Sarah Vaughan
Maya Angelou
Chaka Khan
Louise Lasser
Ruth Page
Paloma Picasso
Olivia Hussey
Armanda Plummer
Ali McGraw
Lena Olin
Victoria Beckham
Annabella Sciorra
Claire Boothe Luce
Mary Pickford
Marguerite Duras
Ann Miller
Betty Ford
Jane Mansfield
Flannery O'Connor
Barbara Kingsolver
Eudora Welty
Rhea Perlman
Janis Ian
St. Theresa of Avila
Mother Hale
Isak Dinesen
Lucrezia Borgia
Rosie O'Donnell
Lucy Lawless
Sandra Day O'Connor
Reba McEntire
Selena
Marsha Mason
Fanny Ardant
Claudia Cardinale
Ethel Kennedy
Liz Phair
Keri Russell
Dianne Wiest
Astrud Gilberto
Samantha Fox
Isabel Toledo

The mythical symbol for Athena whose namesake asteroid or 'planetette' Phallas also bears the similarly yonic symbol of a diamond atop a cross.

is something she can never get enough of. Indeed, she has so urgent a need for that specific, straightforward form of sexual contact that she finds what most people consider pleasurable preambling far more frustrating than fulfilling. She's totally fine with the fact that her Mars-fueled nature places heavy focus on the physical *act* of love, not to mention directing emphasis on the actual protrusive apparatus, whether it be her hunger for a guy's stiffy or a preoccupation with her own clitoris. She is a woman in pursuit of her own orgasm. And she'll think nothing, for instance, of waking up a lover by shagging him. For Aries's last-of-the-red-hot ruling planets, Mars, allots her more than her fair share of lustful energy, effecting some of the most vigorous sexploits conceivable. Still, Aries is not a sensualist by any stretch of the imagination – such titillation can actually be a turnoff. Her breasts and nipples are often either not especially sensitive, tending to be an uneroticized portion of her anatomy, or they are sometimes *too* sensitive an area that she'd just as soon skim over. No, when push comes to shove, which she inevitably hopes it will, the whole of Aries's sexuality is acutely focused on her yoni, which yearns to be engaged in the one, or two, functions for which it was specifically designed. The mythical symbol for Pallas Athena, incidentally, is basically an inverted beaver on a stick. This goes a long way to explain why it is that Aries is so picky about a lover's physical attributes: Not one to find excitement in suggestive, let alone mental or imaginary levels of sexual contact, she needs to have some meat in her potato – on that score, she is very much conscious of size. Regardless of how much affection she might hold for a man, the unveiling of his equipment must elicit at least some tiny gasp or she'll be disinclined to let a relationship progress any further. However, her emphasis on the corporal shouldn't make her seem superficial. On the contrary, another lesson Aries woman teaches us is that, with this basic level of physical connection fulfilled, relationships may proceed on a wholly natural, unspoken, and decidedly serene level. No emotional or cerebral compensation will be necessary on the part of either party. Aries leaves it to the rest of the zodiacal signs to line the pockets of sex therapists and marriage counselors.

Typically not a day goes by without Aries female getting off, one way or another. She is a notorious masturbator, something she'd readily admit – if she's sleeping alone, especially, she often can't even doze off without a few pointed flicks. She plays with herself during sex as well, not wanting to waste time having the guy do it – no matter how adept he is, he won't get her there as assuredly as she can. Besides, she doesn't want him distracted from the simple role he's there to perform, and that is quite frankly to ram her, expertly and thoroughly. Of course, she enjoys being eaten; but again, it will only ever be a means to an end, with no undue loitering allowed. Sucking a guy is pretty low on her priority list, as the act somewhat offends Aries's no-service sensibilities. She may experiment with anal sex, although it seems to her, quite literally, beside the point. Intercourse is the thing. Still, she'll never fall into a rut with it: She is an aficionado of positions and a connoisseur of techniques, highly skilled in her role as the wildest ride on the planet. Never one to just lie there, nothing but the design of her anatomy suggests she is passive in the carnal situation.

As a nod to her Lilith archetype, she mainly likes it on top — it's that particular penchant that gave rise to this primordial female's marital squabbles with the fragile-ego'd Adam. Aries will simultaneously squeeze, pump, and hump her man with such ardor that he must possess reserves of natural staying power if he's not to disappoint this most insistent female. Just as she can drink most guys under the table, she can easily outscrew them as well, and if that means pulling an all-nighter, then so much the better — sex with her always seems somewhat competitive. Though of any woman, Aries might like it a little rough, she won't take any more than she herself dishes out. She is aroused by seeing a man squirm and may engage in erotic acts aimed at having her way with decidedly submissive types — although, being more male-homophobic than most women, such a fellow might raise her wily eyebrows. Besides, as a basically unpsychological character, one not easily given to fetishes, this proclivity rarely progresses to the whips-and-chains stage. (Though if presented with a pair of handcuffs, Aries would undoubtedly find some use for them.)

Anyway, it's far more exciting still to be in a sexy struggle for domination with a self-professed he-man whose status as such will be called into question by the muscle power with which Aries is wont to push back. Female sexuality, she'll have you know, is not all perfume, plucking and powder puffs — it's a raw, primal and often beastly affair. Indeed, she is animalistically activated, and in no small way, by a man's scent, and, she hopes, vice versa. Often, the riper the body odor the better for Aries and her ideal man, who might also appreciate her more cavewomanesque forgoing of razors as well as deodorant, particularly, of the feminine variety. At some point, too, Aries's penis envy will be played out in one way or another. If her partner is so inclined, she may turn the tables, giving him a good 'go' with the help of a latex instrument or two.

For Aries, all sexual activity should have at least a small dose of shock value to it, especially where there is an opportunity for a bit of exhibitionism on her part. She gets off on being watched — lights on, shades up — and she has a

STR8 TURN-ONS

younger men
swarthy looks
rugged builds
body hair, stubble, beards
large penises, foreskin
f-f-m threesomes
sex on-the-side
mutual masturbation
laborers, lumberjacks
big hands, meaty forearms
girl on top
face sitting
(active) b + d, humiliation
cuckolding, groveling
(passive) analingus
standing sex, on the floor
one-night stands
male rape fantasies
strangers, casual sex
male strippers, escorts
role-reversal
male locker rooms
sweat, body odor

GAY TURN-ONS

younger women
blonds
femmes
straight, married women
(active) seduction
(passive) worship
(active) penetration
performing striptease
threesomes, foursomes
one-night stands
first encounters
face sitting
struggle, rough-housing
fingering
mouth music
(active) teasing, lite torture
strangers
f-f-m threesomes
double dildos
biting, nippling
rubbing, humping, scissoring
mind games
(active) lite s + m

weakness for sex in public, which is really all about her hope that she and her lover will be noticed (whereas for many people it's getting away with *not* being seen that holds a secret thrill). The Ram wants to cause a stir by being caught out as highly sexed. She may discuss in detail a previous night's romp as dispassionately as describing a trip to the dentist. She has a tendency to brag about her sexual conquests, confident that such disclosure will only inspire awe and admiration in others. Her sense of discretion often slips, as she feels no conflict in mixing business with pleasure, even daring to engage in a quickie behind her office door, only to emerge with her partner to suspiciously raised eyebrows. Often even when in a steady relationship Aries will crave extra-curricular activities – indeed, no other woman is bound to stray from her primary commitment as much as the Ram. She may say nothing, thinking it nobody's affair but her own, or she might have been so up-front about her liberated spirit from the get-go that she has established her bond as 'open.' She may even want her partner present while she gets it on with another guy – to have him watch her with, perhaps, a younger stud or even someone she's picked out of a gourmet catalog of paid escorts. However, this type of behavior is a rarity, if only because Aries's partner's affection is too profound to comfortably allow it. In fact, her long-standing heterosexual relationships can be relatively one-sided, with the man becoming the nurturing, maternal presence. For it must be said that the typical Aries is relatively lacking in maternal instincts, which helps to explain why she often seeks a man who will mother her, that is, when they're not in the bedroom. She will rarely make time for simple shows of affection, something that threatens to become her foremost relationship pitfall – it also sheds light on why so many Aries live solitary, albeit satisfying lives late into adulthood. It's just too much work to dredge up warm and fuzzy feelings one doesn't possess.

In many ways, Aries female is very much like a stereotypical man whom women are wont to harangue for not having more sensitivity. Again, the Ram gal is much more aligned with stereotypically male perspective in life, one which, ironically, makes women appear to her to be the so-called opposite sex. This may explain why Aries is easily one of the more bisexual females on the astrological block. Compared with most women, she'd think nothing of forming a threesome with her male partner and another woman, particularly if that woman is distinctly unlike her – superpassive, soft, and seemingly vulnerable. She gets quite a kick out of watching a femmey femme wriggle helplessly beneath her, relishing the role of alpha female to be reckoned with. There is a hint of the sadistic in the way she relates to a woman in a bisexual setting, as she imposes a forcefulness, particularly with someone who is new to girl-on-girl experiences.

She really gets in a woman's face, pressing her for oral pleasure, strapping on the de rigueur dildo. Even the straightest Aries, if there truly is such an animal, would be curious to feel the rush of screwing another woman to orgasm, and to hear a few pleas for more (or less). Though practically all Aries females will find themselves in bed with another woman at some point, when the Ram identifies as gay, she does so unequivocally. Just as straight Aries typically hangs with an all-male cast of friends, gay Aries will seek out the company of other women exclusively, for all intents and purposes turning her back on the male world completely. Privately she may have been undergoing a gradual shift to gay identification, but it would seem to those who know her as if she switched teams overnight: Up to that total turning point, she could have been quite sexually active with any number of men (whose jaws will invariably hit the ground). It's not that the Aries remains closeted longer than other gay women, it's just that having had bisexual feelings for so long, typically acting on them all the while, such open experimentation actually stems the tide of an utterly sweeping sexual epiphany. Indeed, it's not so much a matter of discovering an abrupt desire for women, as much as it is developing an incremental but ultimately violent revulsion for men.

Unlike straight Aries, who, in sleeping with a woman, seeks to express a near-bratty dominance over another female, the gay Aries is looking for the exact opposite experience – she is generally drawn to even more domineering women with whom she can play at being a bit of a sex object herself. Gay Aries can get very girly, indulging in the sort of feminine trappings that would send straight Ram girls running for the hills. And yet, because she so obliterates herself from the gaze of men, the Aries lesbian feels free to explore, indeed fetishize, the female experience without its signaling a surrender to male tyranny. With a woman, gay Aries will do what straight Aries wouldn't dream of: dress up in lacy lingerie and provocative underwear, perform stripteases for her lover – the whole Playboy-bunny routine. On the outside it will be the same jeans-and-T-shirt shell as usual, but underneath may be lurking entire pages of the Victoria's Secret catalog. Gay Aries essentially shares her alpha-female status with a lover, whom she'll let play the part of decision-maker and parental adviser while she commits to her own starring role as a worshiped and indulged ingenue, no matter her actual age. Aries does tend to connect with, even slightly, older lovers, at once butcher and certainly more mothering than herself. Her lover may even be an amalgam of her own parents' energies, someone who confers and consults with Aries's father in offering her professional advice, just as she'll powwow with Aries's mother on how to best negotiate the Ram's moodiness. For the lover of an Aries woman, attention will always be on caretaking, that and staving off her trademark terrible tantrums – whether she's straight, gay, or, as is most often the case, somewhere in between.

As a rule, gay Aries wants to be done for in the bedroom, the rather one-sided recipient of sexual activity, requiring her lover to be happiest in the position of service to her, orally or otherwise. The only thing Aries may miss about heterosexual contact is the very real penetration it afforded – still, she can't quite stomach the idea of what's attached to a genuine penis. In a steady lesbian relationship, it will be her lover who'll need to do the requisite strapping-on or endeavoring to stimulate the Aries with similarly probing toys or techniques. Much to her partner's delight Aries will give audible testimony to the incomparable pleasure this provides, especially satisfying the erotic desires of a more dominant companion. If her lover is decidedly butch, Aries will only play the femme even more, forever trying to fulfill the extent of whatever fantasies her partner might possess. Aries, for her part, thrives on an erotically charged relationship, and she'll do anything to keep an aura of electricity in the air. In truth, to the Aries, life is just what happens between sexual experiences.

Swimming in the all-girl pool as gay Aries tends to do, increasingly limiting her contacts with men in every sector of her life – even in her career, gay Aries will continually gravitate toward or nurture an all-female environment – she will typically befriend other photo-ready females, mainly femmes, with whom to mix and mingle. When single, she'll gal-pal around, fairly exclusively, with other lookers like herself, turning more female heads in her search for sexual partners or a permanent relationship. When already seriously involved with someone, she maintains a bevy of chic girlfriends, often those like her who have more behind-the-scenes mates, with whom she can continue to check out the ever-changing lesbian social scene. Like straight Aries, all her friendships will border on flirtation, and she may even dare to have the occasional dalliance. But because she yearns for the unadulterated worship of a blatantly unaffected mate, someone for whom her good looks and glamour are an aphrodisiac (not a source of competition as with a similarly inclined lipstick lez), she mostly saves her loving for that emotional rock waiting for her at home. If anything, she'd prefer to make a party of it, sharing a sexual conquest with her lover, bringing home a pretty present for a mate to play with. In such a scenario, she and the third will engage in sensual play designed, in the Aries mind, to provide a visual treat for her partner, who might then get the pleasure of having her way with the visiting newbie. Still, other than for another woman being sexed up from either end via their mutual consent, nothing or no one should ever come between Aries and her lover. If what they have together alone isn't enough, the Ram will be out of there like a shot. She's happy to respect her partner's limits; if that means no third parties, so be it. After all, Aries doesn't effortlessly invest her heart. When she finds a lover to commit to, she will do anything and everything to protect and preserve that bond.

Couplings

Straight

Aries Woman / Aries Man

He's on a quest; she's out of reach. Less ladylike than he sometimes longs for; he's so in-her-face it hurts. Both willful to the core, neither one gives up without a fight. Two fierce libidos means a fair amount of sexual urgency.

Aries Woman / Taurus Man

She sees vast carnal possibilities. He's slow to read her blatant signals; Aries's unfussy demeanor is what finally fastens his affection. Sex is a psychological affair – roles are reversed, master/servant fantasies explored.

Aries Woman / Gemini Man

They'll take a party approach to life. He's a rousing, robust sexual ride; she seems built for speed. A sordid one-night stand could fuse them as best friends. They're a liberated pair – threesomes are standard.

Aries Woman / Cancer Man

The attraction is subtle – less physically felt, rather more subconscious. Their pairing is antidotal – an emotional cure for past pain. He provides the support she's sought. Sex exorcises ex-lovers.

Aries Woman / Leo Man

Love at first sight: He sees an easy coexistence; she finds her alpha-male match. A hot affair that quickly becomes committed. A threat to domestic bliss: her dalliances. In bed, there are no bells and whistles; ecstasy is automatic.

Aries Woman / Virgo Man

They're a mystery to each other. Best-case scenario: This match means positive psychological change. When challenged, it disallows personal growth. With her, he's free to explore kinkier proclivities.

Aries Woman / Libra Man

Allies from the outset, sharing a need for sexual freedom and intellectual expression. As a couple, believing themselves an exclusive elite, they have cachet as others buy into the perception. In bed, she's the aggressor.

Aries Woman / Scorpio Man

They might not embody each other's ideal, but their similarly defiant natures intrigue. A subversive pair with a complicated sexual dynamic – both hot *and* heavy in the extreme. Erotic addictions are explored in tandem.

Aries Woman / Sagittarius Man

Bucking authority, they live way outside the rules. He's unhurried and askew; she's unbeholden and autonomous. This is a supercouple that easily finds professional success. Sexually, they're exceptionally open-minded.

Aries Woman / Capricorn Man

If looking for complication, she'll connect with complex Cap man. A messy match – dramatic, chaotic, unclear. Extreme fantasies are comfortably expressed: Gender-bending, swapping, or S&M may be status quo.

Aries Woman / Aquarius Man

He has a sobering effect; her remote nature mirrors his own. Each inhabits a separate sphere – the overall effect is either meditative or mismatched. Sexually, they're unrestrained: Limits might be lacking.

Aries Woman / Pisces Man

With this ultrareceptive man, she softens, stimulating maternal instincts. He's expected to clean up his emotional act or take his exit. Sex is no simple affair: She wants it long and hard; he's comfortable cuddling.

Gay

Aries Woman / Aries Woman

Two uncomplicated characters who need no validation. They agree that androgyny is a supreme state of being. There's a goodly dose of narcissism wrapped in their desire. Mutual masturbation might be how it begins.

Aries Woman / Taurus Woman

A social pair, they want to see and be seen. Aries has that glow of good health; Taurus is fetching but unfussy. The Bull offers Aries the protection she herself usually seeks. Sex is earthy and orgiastic.

Aries Woman / Gemini Woman

A boarding-school scenario: Aries initiates Gemini, who is invariably infatuated with the Ram, allowing herself to try acts she's only ever read about. In every aspect, Aries is the leader. In bed, there are no inhibitions.

Aries Woman / Cancer Woman

There's a promise of hedonism here: Danger and excitement are the attraction. Together, they thrive on social spontaneity and serendipity. Sex, especially with a buzz, is mind-blowing. There's a thrill in threesomes.

Aries Woman ∫ Leo Woman

A warm, romantic, optimistic pair. Leo assumes the role of mentor. In the extreme, she'll exploit her power over Aries, seeking ever more worship and obedience. But most often, it's a keeper.

Aries Woman ∫ Virgo Woman

They're a joy to behold: Aries finds her ravishing, reverential consort. Artistic leanings are lovingly pursued, creative passions sparked. Often, they're joined at the hip. In bed, it's Aries who's pussy-whipped.

Aries Woman ∫ Libra Woman

In the glint of each other's eye, there's a challenge: Who's the more evolved sexual animal? Antagonistic from the start, they process tension as pent-up erotic aggression. Sex is each woman's wildest.

Aries Woman ∫ Scorpio Woman

Scorpio holds herself up as a prize – the role Aries ordinarily assumes. Tables turned, the Ram is floored with feelings for the sultry Scorpion sexpot. This all-consuming tie might not last, but it's lusty.

Aries Woman ∫ Sagittarius Woman

Competitiveness creates a healthy sexual tension. Aries is the more overt character; Sag keeps her emotions uncharacteristically cached. Superficiality is a pitfall. Still, it's a homey, cozy twosome.

Aries Woman ∫ Capricorn Woman

Their learning curve is steep, but knowledge gained is power: Self-improvement takes precedence; individual pursuits are promoted. The infatuation lasts. Sex is rapturous – it's all about worship.

Aries Woman ∫ Aquarius Woman

At first, they hide their hook-up from others. But taboo is what keeps them tempted. Even when committed, this coupling remains one of the most erotic and exotic lesbian combinations. Raunchiness is de rigueur.

Aries Woman ∫ Pisces Woman

With utterly unlike agendas, Aries and Pisces feel free to protect and promote each other's pursuits. Together, life is richer. In bed, Pisces is the consummate femme fatale to the ardent, adoring Aries.

Taurus Man

the idol

Dude the obscure: Taurus male is purposefully vague. Achieving his life's ambitions, he operates best by keeping his intentions guarded and others guessing. He is not a man of action but of reaction, a brilliant strategist who, in both professional and personal dealings, forces people's hands before playing his closely held cards accordingly. Seemingly guileless, he disarms those around him by having no apparent agenda to assert — a strong defense is his best offense. Letting experiences unfold rather than forcing things to happen, Taurus remains veritably stress-free in even his loftiest maneuverings, exhibiting what comes to be known as his signature grace and elegance. Hanging back in situations, he is master of all he surveys, and like a wide-eyed kid in a candy store, he maintains an appetite for pleasure and no real barometer for abstinence. Romantically, as in business, Taurus embodies a come-hither attitude that wins him the title of the zodiac's preeminent male love-object. He wants to be wanted, and in the worst way, his seeming insouciance inspiring would-be mates to make all the requisite moves. He is thus attracted to dominant women who'll treat him like a trophy while indulging his notorious little-boy habits, for better or worse. With such a powerhouse female, he's willing and able to take a backseat, often going along for a lifelong ride. In a man-to-man bond, Taurus takes a more direct tack, clearly signaling affection, sexual interest, and relationship needs. Still, he will retain enough emotional and psychological distance as to make a lover work at continually keeping him happy.

Sign + Mind

PRINCIPLE

The Feminine Principle. The second zodiacal precept of Taurus is the counterpoint to Aries's Masculine Principle. Here objectivity is replaced by subjectivity, and content takes precedence over form. Planet Venus desires and demands quality in all things. In keeping with his sign's motto, 'I have,' Taurus man views existence as does a collector, filling his life with delightful possessions, people included.

Taurus is one of two signs ruled by Venus – the other is Libra – the celestial sphere signifying the Feminine Principle in the zodiac. Taurus may be seen as the opposite of Aries, which precedes it on the astrological wheel, that sign being ruled by Mars and the Masculine Principle. Taurus's governing Venus is named for the Roman goddess of love (Greek: Aphrodite), giving rise to such centripetal energies as passivity, receptivity, subjectivity, integration, and any number of other quiescent-themed concepts. So here at the beginning of the zodiac, the basic point-counterpoint battle of the sexes is laid out before us: outward male action and aggression, as befits Mars' war-god namesake, versus alluring feminine invitation, symbolized by Venus. The twist, however, is that in the case of Taurus man the Feminine Principle is embodied in the male. Not to say this automatically makes him feminine, but rather that even the straightest Bull guy won't be a hard-and-fast he-man. Venus' come-hither energy combines with Taurus's fixed-earth quality to make him that much more inert, if not seemingly submissive, than other men. He is the flip side of forthright Aries, from the get-go nearly unknowable – indeed any relationship with Taurus feels like pulling teeth. In making social plans, he has a compliant, obsequious manner, thusly putting the onus on others to run the show – and take the fall if plans should fail. Probably nowhere is Taurus's inability to be assertive, or just plain forthright, more apparent than in his conversation: You get the feeling he's trying to tell you something, but it's not always clear exactly . . . what? He's cryptic, to say the least, so lost in his subjective perceptions that he often cannot objectify his thoughts and impressions into words. He hems. He haws. He stumbles. Unable to grasp the obvious in life, he is all subtlety and nuance. Yet this very 'inability' defines the Taurean brand of expression and artistic vision: He is an unusual, twisted thinker – the 2nd House of the zodiac, which falls under Taurean rule, is one of *uniqueness,* branding him astrology's original avant-gardist, someone who achieves exaltation by going, if just ever so slightly, against the grain of what is considered the norm.

It is the Bull's birthright to remain obscure, thus constantly arousing others' curiosity in him. He knows the power of provoking interest, and he employs it like a tractor beam, drawing desirable people and situations to him. By disclosing less and less of himself, keeping his intentions hidden, he purposely forces people to jump to conclusions, which he'll then tweak to his best advantage. As the zodiac's subjective male, this boy Venus sees particular beauty in becoming what others want him to be – it gets him further, with far less effort, than fighting for what he wants. To him the Aries of the world are just so much bluster and spinning of wheels, their pointed directness an obstacle to taking in the big picture. Taurus believes that strict agendas limit possibilities and serendipitous opportunities, which might then exceed such expectations. In truth, Taurus makes far fewer decisive moves during his lifetime than any other man in the zodiac: He waits. He weighs. He watches. Then, like his symbol Bull, an essentially still and meditative creature that must be incited to attack, Taurus man charges full force at his goals, but only once they're securely within his grasp. Needless to say, he's no risk-taker. And though he often appears to have achieved his successes in one fell swoop, that's not the full story: Much planning goes into Taurus's trademark acquiescence – putting on a poker face is a slick ploy he'll hone over a lifetime. Meanwhile, in his perpetual state of bluff, he appears the very image of easeful elegance.

But here's the rub: What may be perceived as Taurus's passivity is actually a powerful, active force. Whereas Aries's motto is 'I am' (. . . a force to be reckoned with), Taurus's mantra is 'I have' (. . . you in the palm of my hand). The Bull employs Venus' demure strength as a means of acquiring all things he fancies, people included, as if they were *possessions*, things to have and to hold, another key attribute of the 2nd Astrological House. He never quite escapes this dynamic, in fact, whether collecting art, plotting a series of corporate takeovers, or shopping for a lover. Experience for the Taurean guy is all one big come-to-papa, with little sweat needing to be mopped from his brow. But his lurid allure is no less puissant than the action it inspires – that action being worship, in one form or another, something that cannot be had by force. Rather, Taurus coaxes worship from others, presenting himself as a blank surface upon which they may graffiti their own projected agendas: He incites, then relies upon the vandalistic urges of others to write his proverbial ticket. Passivity is pretty powerful stuff – the only caveat is that Taurus often gets locked into the roles others cast him in. But that's the backlash of asking for idolization. Fittingly, in ancient times, the bull (and bovine images in general) were ubiquitous emblems of worship, particularly as male fertility figures. Thus it is no accident that our expectant Bull is a living archetype of this desire for idolatry.

Coming second in the zodiac, Taurus is the fixed (center) sign of the zodiac's First Quadrant, that which is associated with the self and the metaphysical level of the body. While Aries, via Mars, is concerned with physical action, Taurus, in contrast, is steeped in physical sensation, the unseen aspect of corporeal experience that is instead receptive and reactive to stimuli.

PLANETARY SYMBOL

The glyph of Venus – circle of spirit above the cross of matter – represents content over form. Called the mirror of Aphrodite, it points to a certain physical vanity, recalling the myth of Narcissus, which reflects that Taurus even looks on himself subjectively, watching with an often obsessive concern for how others see him.

SIGN QUADRANT

The zodiacal quadrants correspond to metaphysical planes of existence – physical, emotional, mental, and spiritual. The First Quadrant is that of the self and individual awareness. For Taurus, physical sensation takes precedence over action.

No surprise there: Taurus is completely caught up in his five senses, enraptured by Venusian beauty in all its forms. This is the most basic symptom of Taurus's distinction as the sole fixed-earth sign in the zodiac: He is focused on terrestrial pleasures. The premier pastoral male of the zodiac, Taurus is a naturally docile but hedonistic character, like Ferdinand the Bull eternally rolling around in life's bed of roses. The glyph of Venus is often said to be representative of a flower, that tiny expression of earthly delight that captivates with its pleasing appearance and perfume. Like Taurus, the flower is completely passive and nondirective whilst inspiring people to simply reach out and pluck it. Aroma is its means of ensuring sexual propagation of the species – similar to the signals our little Bully sends out. As such, Taurus also draws much of his archetypal nature from the springtime male flower gods, figures such as Adonis, Hyacinthus, and Narcissus, in whom we see reflected Taurus man's subjective vision of self (not to mention his infamous vanity). In light, too, of the sign's affinity with the ages 7–14, when one is in the proverbial 'flower of youth,' these adolescent gods portray malehood on the brink of sexual maturation, still oblivious to its temptations. All his life, Taurus retains this same sense of untarnished innocence, if not blissful ignorance – at the very least, this is what those who seek to seduce him are led to believe.

Likewise, in biblical terms, Taurus represents the archetypal pastoral landscape of earthly delight, Edenic paradise – the garden is the symbol of Taurus's fixed-earth status. Herein, as Joseph Campbell suggested in *The Power of Myth,* one lives in a mythic 'dreamtime,' a sort of blissful oblivion that exists outside of the temporal where one is unaware of the world of opposites, oblivious to the concept of duality. For, like Adam with Eve, before the fall, Taurus is ignorant that 'other' is separate from himself. As mirrored in this story of Adam, Taurus experiences a partner's agenda as being one and the same as his own. As well, he is notoriously oblivious to traditional gender roles. In the floral paradise where Taurus 'lives' (ancient agricultural cultures were matriarchal in structure), man is the proverbial second sex, subordinate to female will. But, as that age-old story suggests, there's a price to pay.

Mythology is also lousy with stories about bulls and the women who love them. One such tale is that of Europa (a descendant of the nymph Io, from whose 'prequel' myth Taurus woman takes her archetypal character). Zeus, attracted to the nubile Europa, disguises himself as a snow-white bull, offering the girl a ride on his back. Straightaway, he gallops off across the sea with her, establishing Europa as queen of Crete. Their union yields a son, Minos, who with his queen, Pasiphaë, rules the island, its palace walls crowned in golden bull's horns, its people worshiping the animal, holding it sacred. But there's trouble: Envious of his brother Zeus' legacy, Poseidon sends the king a white bull, too, demanding it be sacrificed to him. But Pasiphaë is so taken by the virile creature that she has a life-size wooden cow built with a conveniently retractable back door she hops into, bending over. And bingo: She inevitably gives birth to the horrible half-man, half-bull monster Minotaur, who is kept imprisoned in a labyrinth and fed the live bodies of nubile maidens and youths. This myth lives on in the hearts and minds of all Taurus men: For when the Bull gives himself openly as an expression of his own desire, as Zeus approached Europa, the result is ennobling. But when he presents himself for worship, a door is left open to corruption, literally breeding perversion in place of purest desire. Taurus does himself a great disservice by not taking a forthright stance in his professional life, too. Simply accepting offers because they're flattering or prestigious will usually leave him wanting. Likewise, not being the aggressor in love but available to a woman's advances might only make him wonder what 'better' female he might incite to fall at his feet. Easy come easy go. The trap becomes wanting ever more to be wanted: Desire only begets more desire. Like the Minotaur, Taurus man must find a way out of the psychological maze constructed by his need for worship. Sure, Taurus should embrace being his laid-back self, like Ferdinand, forever stopping to scratch and sniff the roses. But, in so doing, no doubt also like dear Ferdi, the Bull boy could fertilize his own garden of dreams instead of forever fecundating someone else's.

The 2nd House is also associated with *value(s), self-worth, comfort, contentment,* and a host of other esteemed attributes one might seek to garner. Indeed, Taurus is the zodiac's gatherer and collector, in contrast to Aries's hunter-warrior, who looks on life as a process of cultivation. Invariably, he has amassed a pack of friends, of whom he is the appointed leader. While in the workplace, he makes himself the darling of higher-ups. His efforts are often painstaking in this department, as he schmoozes and strokes those in power, playing the part of the complicitous, ingenuous greenhorn, just one of the guys, a team player and affable bullshitter, often with a respectable handicap in golf – his favorite sports are leisurely ones – while, with women in senior positions, he's a walking-talking innuendo. As befits his Edenic archetype, Taurus cultivates familiar ground instead of seeking to conquer new territory, fixing himself into situations and tending to them as would a gardener. Jerzy Kosinski's famous character Chauncey Gardner may be seen as the quintessential Taurean male figure in modern literature, one who recognizes the power of just *Being There*. On the surface, Taurus's fixed-earth status depicts his notorious fixation on material goods. But there's a deeper meaning: He affixes price tags to people based on

ELEMENT + QUALITY

The earth element connotes materiality and substance. The fixed quality signifies focus, concentration and a certain magnetism. Together the fixed-earth combination particular to Taurus is best illustrated by a garden, symbolizing earthly beauty and delights, sacred space, careful cultivation, property, and a sense of the proprietary.

POLARITY

Males in feminine (earth, water) signs are not aligned with the gender polarity of the sign and thus enact, instead of embody, the quality-element combination of the sign. Taurus man seeks to possess material goods and people as furnishings in his life that reflect meaning and value back onto him.

2

SIGN NUMBER

The number of relatedness: Two represents the combining of male with female into one entity. It signals the primordial androgyne, Adam and Eve fused into a single being prior to the need for the fig-leaf fashion statement.

7–14

SIGN AGE ASSOCIATION

The age of innocence and first flowering of youth. This period is associated with prepubescence and, thus, a time of shy awkwardness and androgynous male beauty wherein the hormonal ragings, soon to ensue, are all but latent.

their substantial value to him. He is forever subtly attempting to possess the interest of others, whether having business associates in his back pocket or in hoarding a harem of women worshipers for no other purpose than to bolster his self-worth. For the Bull often has a line of female admirers as long as his arm if not another outsized part of his anatomy. It's part and parcel of his particular obsession: Some people take vitamins every day, Taurus routinely inspires people to fall in love with him. He does little to keep his ever-growing flock of worshipers on a leash, save for dangling himself before them. Then again, Taurus gives the impression of having a lot to dangle. For him, there is an all-important 2nd House *comfort* in knowing that, at a moment's notice, he might simply snap his fingers and there would appear a stampede of women at the ready to do whatever it takes to make Taurus their man. In truth, he's terrified of rejection – this is the root cause of his compulsion to procure that harem in the first place and why it is he won't 'make the moves.' Similarly, in his professional life, he feels safer insinuating himself into the hearts and minds of his associates, allowing for such advancement as that might bring. Rarely will he come right out and profess his ambitions for fear of hearing the dreaded word *no*.

Taurus's trademark relinquishment of the reins finds its seeds in his early childhood. Bulls of both sexes are generally raised in mother-dominated households where the father, though present, may be passive. As it turns out, Dad often has a more compliant chickie on the side; his psychological absence is thus a symptom of his attentions being diverted elsewhere. In an effort to compensate for his dad's inadequacy, Taurus becomes a consort of sorts to his mother. In return, Taurus's mother showers him with affection, but in transferring feelings meant for her husband, she also puts the screws to her boy. She begins making most of his decisions, disallowing his opinions, stifling his shows of spontaneity, and ultimately squelching his emerging sexual self. Meanwhile, based on his parents' model, Taurus sees relationships as synonymous with instability and he seeks instead to channel energy into endeavors that might add grounding (fixed-earth) to his existence: Money and the things it can buy – tangibles – become paramount. Likewise, he keeps friends and love interests on a shelf, expecting them to be available when he deems fit. Such people are his to play with when he pleases, and he expects them, as belongings, to comply. He, on the other hand, remains unbeholden. Meanwhile, having been subordinate to his mother's overbearing nature, he can't help but become wrapped around the finger of similarly ball-busting women. In the myth, Adonis' mom was called Myrrha – another name for Aphrodite–Venus herself – reinforcing the fact that, like his flower-god archetype, metaphorically speaking, Taurus wants to marry his mother.

Body + Soul

As his Bull symbol would suggest, Taurus often appears the strong, silent type. Having difficulty articulating his thoughts, Taurus decides early on that the less said, the better. However, he risks seeming obtuse, straightaway giving the specious impression that he's little more than beefcake. His body language doesn't help counter that image: Like some curved sculpture of a young god, Taurus's very presence is suggestive. Languid and physically at ease, he's at once alluring and allusive. With sidelong glances, sly, through weighted eyes, he exudes a seductiveness that nonetheless seems unintentional. His slow, meditative movements imply a willowy, weighted-down quality – indeed, Taureans are legendary for a certain largesse – which speaks to hours of slow, satisfying, sleepy sex. He isn't the zodiac's male love object for nothing: Despite any awesomeness in his size, his inherent sensuality is seen as totally nonthreatening to women. Taurus personifies masculine perfection on the physical plane, but, most importantly, via the Feminine Principle, the epitome of manhood from the female point of view. Rarely an overtly erotic entity like the imposing Mars-fueled Aries, Taurus is an eroticized one glimpsed through Venus' Vaseline-gauzed lens. In myth, Tauros was an island of matriarchal rule where men were enslaved and used for procreation and ritual sacrifice. Indeed, more than any other man, Taurus fits the bill of a scantily clad extra in some 1950s B movie, entitled something like *They Came from Venus,* about a female-dominated planet where males are the second sex, expected to speak only when spoken to, foreshadowing many a romantic Taurean relationship.

Blessed with Venus' soft, refining energy, her 2nd House sons tend to be real 'beauts,' as the planet rules the manifestation of feminine traits in the body. Still, Taurus is more than just a pretty face. His quiet expression is not symptomatic of himbo emptiness, but rather part and parcel of a naturally understated elegance. A list of famous Taurean males – which includes the likes of Duke Ellington, Burt Bacharach, Fred Astaire, Bing Crosby, James Mason, Charles Mingus, Richard Avedon, Andre Gregory, William Inge, Henry Fonda, Gary Cooper, Jimmy Stewart, Michael Palin, David Byrne, Richard E. Grant, Peter Townshend, Steve Winwood, and Bryan Eno – reveals a decidedly tasteful lot, though sometimes with a definite twist. Taurus is typically leaner, if not taller, than other males in his family; and even when he is small of stature, perfect proportions help Taurus project a tall appearance. He possesses a supple, sinewy physicality that sets him strikingly apart from bulkier adolescent boys. As well, his transition through puberty is slow and subtle. Much to the

PSYCHOLOGY

A Minotaur in the making, Taurus can suffer from over-possessiveness just as he might express gluttony in food, drink and other substances. He can be obscure and withholding in his emotions, experiencing difficulty with self-expression. He is obstinately fixed in his ways and may be secretive if not closeted in his obsessions, sexual or otherwise. He is often fetishistic when it comes to feminine trappings and may indulge in transvestism.

ARCHETYPE + MYTH

Taurus man personifies classic flower gods – Hyacinth, Narcissus, Adonis – representing nature as male, a second sex, subject to the advances of a dominant female, or even a male deity. Bulls were an ancient symbol of desire, Zeus taking taurine form in his infamous rape of Europa. The Minotaur symbolizes desire (for food, drink, sex) run amok, the labyrinth that traps him being a psychological maze of his perversion. Theseus is the Taurean hero who still relies on feminine direction – he finds his way out of the trap by following a thread woven by his lover Ariadne, 'fertile mother.'

annoyance of other young men, Taurus is often that kid who sails through his teens pretty much unscathed – no zits, no unibrow, no excessive hairiness. His complexion tends to be somewhat smoother and creamier than that of his male siblings, with hardly a detectable pore. He produces precisely placed facial hair, often heavy on his lip and chin. He has a nonchalant style distinguished by casual but costly clothes – typically, clean, crisp, and 100 percent natural – as he practically lives in jeans, blazers, sweaters, loafers, moccasins, and the like. Despite his often impeccable grooming, there's something of a just-rolled-out-of-bed look about Taurus, mostly due to his hair, which, regardless of its consistency, tends to appear unruly and may suffer from errant, aptly named cowlicks. In many cases, his hair thins early in life, and he goes bald before reaching middle age. Still, balding only seems to add to Taurus's masculine appeal.

One way to spot a Taurus guy is by the manner in which he seems to speak to you sideways, a physical manifestation that mirrors his obscure mode of discourse. Truth be told, Taurus may seem perpetually off on some weird tangent, his responses somehow not matching or following what has previously been said. His subjective comments may even stop conversation dead in its tracks, with a proverbial *Henh?* hanging in the air. In short, if a goofily good-looking man with a body like a young David starts chatting you up (but you have little to no idea what the hell he's saying), chances are he's a Bull. Like his totem animal, Taurus's eyes are set wide apart so that it appears he can only see out of one side of his face at a time. His skull and forehead are distinctively narrow, often so much so it's as if he's just been squished by elevator doors. He has a high hairline and a bony face, deeply hollowed at the cheekbones. His brow is fairly delicate, with fine, light hair, his eyes big and heavily lidded and luxuriously lashed, his nose, long, thin, and prominent, if not ever so slightly flattened and flared at the tip. And just as his eyes appear lazy, so, too, is his jaw somewhat slack; and his mouth is often cherry red, his lips full, moist, and blatantly sensual. His infamous Taurean neck – the body part ruled by his sign – tends to live up to its reputation as being ultrastrong and sturdy, never squatty, square, or stocky, as is often asserted by popular astrology. Rather, it is long and sinewy, like that of a dancer. Indeed, along with male Pisceans, the Bull man is, fittingly, considered one of the zodiac's foremost hoofers. His shoulders are broad but finely boned, though he is by no means unmuscular here, his sinew draped like damask around his skeletal structure. Taurus is like an art-class life drawing come alive: There's a delicacy to this creature that his sheer bulk belies – the feminine and masculine Venus-Bull energies working in perfect harmony. Taurus's body movement is languid, but never lumbering in the least; in fact, there's a poetic ease to his gait and a deliberate, nearly choreographed grace in his slightest gesture, from crossing a leg to sipping his drink. Indeed, Taurus man may be most indulgent with his appetites for food, drink, sex, or anything that provides a buzz to his all-important senses – other symptoms of his insatiable Minotaurian cravings for earthly delights. Fortunately, his particular brand of natural refinement diffuses any impression of gluttony. In fact, Taurus man can make raiding the fridge look more like practicing tai chi.

As befits Taurus's correspondence to the ages 7–14, this man possesses a physical beauty that is unmistakably boyish. More smooth than hairy, any body fuzz he does have is typically arranged in tightly contained areas. Wispy strands often sprout out around his nipples, which though they sit atop firmly masculine pecs, are nonetheless slightly protruding, budding like those of a eleven-year-old girl. Don't worry – this looks a lot better than it sounds. Taurus's back is as strong as a bull's – good thing, because his front middle is surprisingly soft, suggesting an emotional sensitivity. He's often long-waisted with strong, wide hips, his lower abdomen pronounced and traced with a hairy 'highway to heaven' leading down to his pubic area. Down below, this boy is big, boasting one of the healthier-sized cock 'n' bulls ever to be unzipped in the zodiac. Taurus man's package tends toward the loose and low-slung sort, a symptom in male animals of low stress, while his ass is typically firm and high below an arched lower spine. He's often bowlegged, his limbs seeming to move independently from the rest of his body. And he has proportionately large, sexy hands and feet. Still, despite the grace that Venus bestows on her beauty boy, Taurus at times exhibits a clumsiness – the bull-in-a-china-shop syndrome – which has to do with a general deficiency in his depth perception. Taurus man is often actually myopic, and especially when tipsy or otherwise overly relaxed, he may fail to properly negotiate his environment – just as his voice will boom beyond the polite limits of his surroundings, eliciting the occasional *sshhh* from his mate. To boot, when Taurus is angry, elated, or generally excited, his voice can become strangely high and squeaky, like a prepubescent child's. But again, it must all be chalked up to his natural, boyish exuberance, rather than the slightest social crassness requiring more serious admonitions. Though his antics may invite some quizzical stares from strangers, such behavior only endears Taurus all the more to his ever-widening circle of admirers.

∫ex + ∫exuality

Through his upbringing, Taurus was conditioned to believe that female affection is achieved by letting a woman take control. And much to his delight,

BIBLE + LITERATURE

The fixed-earth sign of Taurus corresponds to the Garden of Eden. Taurus man draws upon the passive characterization of the Edenic Adam who is *subject* to female influence, power, and temptation. As in the story of the golden calf, taurine figures were ancient fertility idols. The blood of bulls was also a fructifying agent. In the pansy-picking Ferdinand the Bull, the taurine idol is combined with fecund male flower gods. Chauncey Gardner in Jerzy Kosinski's *Being There* illustrates the suggestibility of the Edenic male archetype.

somewhere during his sexual development, he learns that idleness leads to his increasing, well, idolness. Perhaps as early as junior high, Taurus boy is given reinforcement for this nonchalant behavior: He's the unassuming lad being gawked at, and giggled over, by a gaggle of girls – all the while, pretending not to notice. Yet, by the time he reaches college, he has typically met with so many erotic experiences, through little effort of his own, that he figures, 'My sex life's not broken, why fix it?' For Taurus, passivity becomes a most powerful pussy magnet. To the opposite sex, he appears the ultimate malleable male: that guy who'll let a girl get her hooks in and mold him. Unfortunately, what accompanies his compliant attitude is apathy to commitment. In his early days, when venturing out in search of sex, Taurus is often found in a pack of other young men, most often those who are his physical inferiors – not too hard to imagine considering the Taurean's pleasing looks and physique. He especially eschews the company of other overly good-looking guys as might outshine him, forever fearful of competition and possible defeat. To his mind there can only be one true Bull per pen: In a sense, Taurus sees his guy friends as steers, eunuchs of sorts, meant to amuse and calm him until such time as he is singled out by some determined female matador. And – *toro, toro* – it never takes too long.

Taurus's first sexual encounter will typically be with a much older woman. With her, he'll play a sort of soft-core gigolo role, perhaps throwing his youth in her face, indulging in immature antics. In short, he might carry on like a seven-to-fourteen-year-old with an all-too-lenient mommy. With such a partner, he feels a built-in freedom whereby he won't be expected to take the relationship too seriously. Nor will he have to exert much energy in the bedroom, letting the more seasoned woman take on the obligation of driving the sexual action. He wants proof of a woman's desire, and characters who give off a whiff of desperation often provide it more vividly than those who don't. What the woman won't realize, however, is that the Taurean is getting off on this dynamic of him letting her 'have her way.' Of course, in entering a relationship with an older woman, Taurus man seeks to relive his childhood, but this time with a more overindulgent mother figure, as opposed to a strictly overbearing one. And chances are he'll get away with proverbial murder in the company of one so obviously thrilled to be with a young, vital stud. He may in fact treat her like crap, pushing the limits of her willingness to forgive his rowdier antics, if even subtly abusing the sexual power he wields. Nothing thrills Taurus more than a woman who professes she'll do, or take, anything to keep him as her own. Even if his initial sexual experiences are not with an older lady, that younger female, too, will take on a similarly doting, demanding (albeit drooling) demeanor. And by this point in his development, Taurus's outsized self-confidence trumpets his conviction that any female would find herself lucky to be linked with him. Like his virile Bull mascot, he is thus often accused of jumping anything that makes a move on him, even if meanwhile pining for the affections of a less 'available' female. As that story goes, however, the more gourmet brand of girls out there generally demand a good deal of wooing if not outright chasing down – but our passive Bull is simply not a predatory animal.

Taurus man approaches sex in a way that would be regarded as feminine throughout nature's kingdom: He signals readiness, but to clinch the deal, he expects the opposite sex to do the prerequisite pouncing. Nine times out of ten, Taurus is seemingly seduced into sex; eight of those nine times, the supposed seduction is puppeteered by the Taurean master himself. It's automatic for him – not so much a matter of cunning – he simply finds it less work, and for this 'dreamtime' inhabitant, the whole of life should be one big easy. He's not about to waste precious time and energy making a play for a woman when he might very well find himself shot down in the end. And so, he provides himself the luxury of rarely (read: never) being dumped or otherwise failing in relationships. As one might imagine, someone who doesn't (let himself) experience failure has no pesky compounded failure feelings with which to contend. This is the key to Taurus's brand of unselfconscious confidence and natural esprit de corps. Still, the question remains, what kind of women does the Taurus attract if he's not actively pursuing those he might otherwise objectively fancy?

Certain women will regard Taurus, for all his hanging back, as the proverbial strong, silent type. Still others might be suckered into believing he's shy. He often appeals as a 'cute but clueless' character over whom women shrug their shoulders, roll their eyes, and pout out something akin to 'What would he do without me?' And that's exactly the reaction Taurus hopes to inspire – after all, he not only avoids taking an active role getting into a relationship, he also counts on retaining that hands-off involvement once it's up and running. Still, some women will blatantly get off on the pure idea of seducing him. Meanwhile, the single Taurus often has several women, simultaneously, in each category. In all given scenarios, one thing is certain: The zodiac's male love-object lives in the reflective heat of others' desires for him. The Taurean sheikh is nothing, after all, without his worshipful wives and concubines. More than any other guy, he has the ability, and indeed the luxury, to inspire a female cult following, a symptom of his magnetic fixed-sign standing, which goes hand in hand with his archetypal status as the fertility idol incarnate. In fact, many a

KEY WORDS

temptation
bliss
delight
determination
methodology
acumen
routine
withholding
obstinacy
equanimity
passivity
fertility
appetite
taste
incitement
longing
possession
entreatment
capability
beauty
idolatry
jealousy
tenure
subjectivity
reflex
composure
magnetism
influence
allure
custody
union
relatedness
trust
affection
difficulty
strength
stability
endurance
steadfastness
practicality
caution
repression
intensity
sensuality
fulfillment

domineering female looks at Taurus and simply sees a hot stud engineered for producing pleasure if not providing some quality sperm. Bull guy's marriages – and there are typically more than one – often begin with a bun already in the oven. As the Minotaur myth suggests, an obsessive desire for idolization is no cinch to satisfy, requiring ever more human sacrifices to his lust for worship. Even when in a relationship, Taurus is hard-pressed to pass on any seductress who might throw herself at him. In playing the field, Taurus rarely lets his lust for even his most coveted acquisitions show – he is a coolheaded collector of such priceless pieces, in this case, of ass. Obvious investment, emotional or otherwise, would run contrary to the signature detachment for which he is worshiped. There is, however, a possible paradoxical pitfall here: that he, the zodiac's premier fancier, is nonetheless always placing himself up for auction, available to the most fervent aspirant for his affection and sexual favor.

Rarely a risk-taker, Taurus requires a 'sure thing,' someone who'll demonstrate, beyond a shadow of a doubt, that she is indeed pitching for him harder than any other bidders on the block. The other shoe falling, however, is that the most ardent woman for his affections *will* prevail, and often despite how much or little sentiment Taurus may actually feel for her. He submits to the woman who shares his most torrid passion – himself – blind to other considerations. This often makes those close to the Bull wonder at his judgment in choosing partners, leading to the age-old 'Is he really going out with her?' line of questioning. Yet, to be fair, what most of us fail to realize is that Taurus prizes tenacity in a person – such a trait signifies caretaking stability and grounded focus, which, for this fixed-earth sign, is of prime importance. Moreover, Taurus may *sense* assets in a partner that aren't readily apparent to others' naked eyes. To his credit, he generally values personality and intelligence above looks. He's often insecure about his own brainpower, such that obviously superior smarts in a partner easily eclipse an emphasis on beauty or any blatant lack thereof. The sign's association with the 2nd House, that of *content* rather than form, astrologically programs him to see beneath the surface – in fact, this is one of his best qualities. At his core, Taurus is looking for security and guidance – he doesn't endeavor to steer the love boat but rather luxuriate in all that's being afforded him on board. This slice of beefcake is totally submissive, and moreover, he likes it that way. When alone with a woman, he's incredibly cuddly and cooing, needing constant coddling and physical signs of reassurance. Sexually, too, he's not at all what he appears.

Taurus has little inkling that he often appeals to women on a strictly sexual basis. Likewise, he's usually in the dark as to what is expected of him in bed. And so he goes on strutting his stuff, unaware he's a big tease, sending out a nearly palpable magnetism that is in no small way attributed to his own pent-up sexual energy begging for release. Laying so much responsibility for hookups in a lady's lap, Taurus can sometimes spend a lot of time in the sexual bull pen – like the Minotaur, trapped in his own complex of desire without any easy escape. This sexual confinement manifests physically as well, as the Bull arguably suffers from blue balls more severely than most. Typically, Taurus is disinterested in masturbation – a predisposition not based on moral principle, as is often the case for the vigilant, ascetic Aries, but stemming from the Taurean inability to objectify his thoughts and even conjure up the appropriate images without his signature obscure and random notions pressing their way into his mind's eye. Moreover, what gets him off most is seeing a partner getting off on *him*. Even in this most intimate of circumstances, he isn't able to view experience directly, but rather needs to glimpse it through another's eyes. This may explain why Taurus can be indiscriminate as to whom he jumps into bed with. Women who might not seem 'up to snuff' at face value are indeed those whom Taurus may find the most adamantly appreciative in the sack. Being mismatched with an expectant beauty, the Bull will instead often exploit any truth there is to the argument that girls who, let's just say, couldn't capture the cover of *Vogue* simply work harder in the sack. And in this guy whose namesake zodiacal animal has to be provoked into action by overt gesturing, we glean new meaning from the concept of 'screwing anything that moves.' As the male love-object he will, in fact, only ever become a fraction as excited as his lover, who might really have to chew the scenery to elicit even the most meager response. Indeed, left to his own devices, Taurus is pretty placid in bed. In some instances, a partner will have a hard time telling whether he's even enjoying himself, so imperceptible are his reactions; he may just lie there letting himself be done. This is often a symptom, however, of becoming lost in sensual stimulation, as the less he moves about, the more he may be open to mounting excitement. For if there's one guy who can breathe into such feelings of arousal, letting them wash over him and build to extra-ordinary levels as would drive most men to thrashing about, it's the Taurus. At the point where most guys would be climaxing, the Taurean is just beginning his slow rise to the heights of 2nd House *sensation*. Meanwhile, like Chauncey Gardner, he 'likes to watch' a woman using him as a boy blowup doll, relishing seeing lust for him burning in a take-charge partner's eyes. For other people, eyes might be the mirror to the soul, but for the zodiac's Narcissus, they are mirrors reflecting back on himself. And if his lover is looking for a slow and easy session, all will be right with the world – but here's where those who've misjudged him as a sexual dynamo get off, or don't, as the case may be.

Bernard Malamud
Vladimir Nabokov
Georges Braque
James Beard
Orson Welles
Donovan
Chris Franz
Stevie Wonder
Bono
Busta Rhymes
Harvey Keitel
Dennis Hopper
John Corbett
Jet Li
Anthony Quinn
Jack Klugman
Tony Danza
Lee Majors
Jean Gabin
Robert Montgomery
Edward R. Murrow
L. Frank Baum
Iggy Pop
Justin Bond
John Cameron Mitchell
John Ebersol
Harry S. Truman
Malcolm X
Honore de Balzac
Louis Farrakhan
Sigmund Freud
Glen Campbell
Eugene Delacroix
Ulysses S. Grant
Andre Agassi
The Rock
Jerry Seinfeld
George Carlin
Socrates
George Lucas
Willie Nelson
Joey Ramone
Bill Paxton
Immanuel Kant
Pete Seeger
Robespierre
Stewart Granger
Eric Satie
Niccolo Machiavelli

BODY RULERSHIP

Taurus rules the throat and neck, respectively symbolic of expression and a supportive strength. There is a tendency toward ear and throat infections, obesity, and other glandular issues. Planet Venus rules feminine attributes in the body, estrogen, and the centripetal flow of blood back to the heart.

Sensing his infamous aura of sexual power, a woman may only naturally assume she's in for a right pounding, something, however, Taurus is not generally disposed to deliver. Indeed, the burning desire that the Bull inspires in a woman, and even the gasp of anticipation at the generally generous size of his apparatus, creates far more buildup than any payoff can equal. Taurus male's legendary sexual magnificence exists, it would seem, mainly in the imagination of those who've yet to bed him. Not to say Taurus guy is a lousy lay – *au contraire* – it's just that sex with him can be like seeing a movie you've heard too many raves about – it can't but fall short of blockbuster expectations. Much of what he's after has already been satisfied by the time sex itself occurs anyway – that being, the ego boost he gets from a woman wanting him so badly she practically lassos him into bed. Besides, the blissfully ignorant Bull might himself buy so far into the preproduction hype promoting his abilities that even he doesn't realize if and when he's failed to deliver 'at the box.' Rarely the premature ejaculator that Aries can be, Taurus has the opposite problem, if any – he loses his erection easier than most males on the wheel. It's not a matter of impotence, per se, but simply a testament to how high a stimulation threshold is necessary to make all his systems go. Still, our subjective, insouciant fellow feels the beefiness of his wiener, or lack thereof, is a barometer for how titillatingly talented his lover is, and not a matter of blame or shame on his part. Meanwhile, he barely entertains such lines of thinking, happy to linger in the wings between sexual acts, bodies entwined, lost in that infamous dreamtime, simply enjoying the kind of intimate exchange many women are often complaining men don't engage in enough.

It is key to remember that Taurus man is steeped in the feminine experience. He seeks tenderness, and he longs for patient understanding in the bedroom. He feels, perhaps subconsciously, that he suffers from a sort of sexism: that he's not allowed to want what many women desire from sex – a loving, sensitive experience – but rather that he's expected to perform like some professional stud. (In truth, doing just that is often a pure sexual fantasy for Taurus, something he may act upon of his own accord in a stealthier mood, but it's not a role he wants to play out in a light-of-day steady relationship, and certainly not when he feels under obligation to do so.) In any case, Taurus rarely embodies the big bang; and if he is able to find his way past the leering lady lechers to a woman who'll let him be his typically tranquil ol' Ferdinand self, and indeed love him for it, all is as it should be. In truth, Taurus is a slow, meditative lover who, when allowed to be his lolling best, is uncommonly capable of sustaining marathon sex sessions. The zodiac's male darling, he will let himself be actively adored for hours, just as he'll roll around letting slip certain bits of him – fingers, tongue, phallus – into any place warm and welcoming. As befits his idol status, he loves to taunt and tease his lover, increasing her literal devotion, if not her outright desperation, for his body; offering her only subtle and brief stimulation as will drive her into action, seeing her beg and indeed grab for what she wants from him. Astrology's eternal nubile boy, one might suspect from his complete lack of sexual cunning that he hasn't had much experience; but of course this is the Bull's de rigueur ruse, the mental maze he subconsciously draws a partner into while he waits and watches her very human self-sacrifice, seeing what demure decorum she typically embodies being forfeited for the flesh-hungry abandon of a quean. Though sweeping, Taurus's game-playing begins and ends here, as, again, he in no way consciously messes with a woman's mind. The eternal adolescent, he has no rational agenda, but is the eternal Adonis asking to be deflowered. Even his orgasm comes upon him as if by surprise, like one – what's this? – experiencing it for the first time. Fittingly, the color associated with Taurus is *green*.

Taurus doesn't possess much in the way of a psychological relationship to sex. He is a sensualist not an eroticist, and he doesn't go in for elaborate scenes or fantasies. Group sex, especially, is too impersonal and thus a major turnoff to him; unless, of course, it's an intimate ménage à trois with two women going at it to please him sensually. Full-on lesbian scenes, a boon for many men, are especially tantalizing to the Taurean male: Being so nearly fetishistic about all things feminine, the mere idea of two similarly inclined, succulent girls expressing mutual delight in his presence provides almost more tingle than he can take. Besides which, he actually feels so at home and at ease with women – particularly in such a scenario where he's not saddled with sole responsibility for providing sexual ecstasy – that he is able to relax and share in their pleasure, fine with not being the main focus. But his fetish doesn't always stop there: For one, he may have a big-girl fantasy, more likely to be turned on by 'fat chicks' than any other male sign, reveling in being overwhelmed by a woman of de Kooning proportions. Moreover, it must be said that Taurean males are the preeminent cross-dressers of the zodiac. Without elaborating on the mythological implications of donning 'goddess raiment,' squeezing into a pair of panties awakens a desired sexual thrill in the Taurean, which just so happens to have unmistakable archetypal implications. And it's something that he's totally unashamed of – just ask any Taurus male, he'll tell you, particularly as it has little or nothing to do with sexual preference or identity. Taurus loves women – even the straightest Bull could get stuck on the Oxygen network while flipping through channels. But his being so naturally empathetic to females does have distinct disadvantages for Taurus's partner. He may all too

STR8 TURN-ONS

older, dominant females
dark features
Asian women
round, solid bodies
short hair
epic foreplay
slow, sleepy sex
gymnasts, dancers
(passive) body worship
exhibitionism, teasing
(passive) seduction
humiliation
married women
cuckolding other men
gigolo role-play
(passive) anal play
(passive) b + d
hairy bushes
cuddling, caressing
wearing panties
stockings, garters
food, drink, substances
bisexuality

easily fall into extracurricular sexual relationships – not out of maliciousness, or wile, but almost out of sheer laziness with relationship 'rules.' Typically, if he does play around with another woman, she'll be a neighbor or work colleague – someone right in the Bull's face – who is, often, also in an existing relationship. Even single Taureans are known to hook up with a lady who's 'taken' – as if he expects to slip right in without expending the effort of building something new. In fact, many women who settle down with a Taurus do so fresh from another long-term relationship, one in which she was still ensnared when she met the Bull guy. As the zodiac's premier collector of admirers, one could say Taurus has a special interest in 'ready-mades.' Still, the best part of waking up with a Taurus male in your bed is that, being female-centric, he naturally understands what a woman wants. Given time and patience, he'll eventually get around to doing everything one could ever hope to have done. Taurus man is a clitoral connoisseur whose tongue tends to be as lovingly long as a certain other sizable part of his anatomy. His oral fixation on the mons veneris is proof that this boy is Venus's original lover: Indeed, Taurus elevates eating-out to a rite of worship. Of course, he'll expect reciprocation; but the length of time it can take him to climax, not to mention the often mighty length and girth of his member itself, can make returning the favor a tiresome prospect.

Sometimes, it's a man's job. And if any male sign would sign up to receive a bit of no-strings service from another guy, it would be our easygoing Taurean, who is as suggestible as the age group associated with his sign, regardless of how he sexually identifies himself. Given Taurus's swirl of masculine and feminine energies, most Bull boys tend to be rather bisexual by nature instead of polarized, one way or another, gay or straight. Few straight Taureans haven't had it off with a guy at some point in their life, just as many a gay Bull could see himself falling for a woman at one time or another, making strong emotional connections with the opposite sex. There are exceptions, and they are striking ones: Certain Taurus gay boys are so palpably effeminate they seem to be male only in the strictest biological sense. Just as cross-dressing is commonplace among straight Taureans, gender-bending is also common among gay men of the sign, as well as cases of sexual reassignment. Venus working her magic on the physical earth plane can have some very real and tangible effects. When simply identifying as gay, not as a woman – and it's important to note here that many straight Taureans do identify as women and end up lesbian transsexuals; this can be true of any sign, but Taurus more so than others – the Bull guy will tend somehow to be less at the mercy of a need for worship as a love object than is his heterosexual counterpart. Perhaps because overt sexuality is already such a striking keynote to gay life, and the gay Bull is generally pretty well sated by the ardor he's wont to inspire, he thus wears a need for deeper affection instead of blanket attention more openly on his sleeve. Straight Taurus may field a steady stream of pitches for his sexual favor, but gay Taurus contends with even more approaches. What the gay Bull feels is lacking in his life is finer focus on such Taurean concerns as emotional attachment, and the stability that long-term relationships can bring. Gay life, by its nature, tends to involve more sex for sex's sake, something that makes this male native of the 2nd House seek the solace of *creature comforts* all the more.

The gay Taurean male, having been bombarded with so many requests for his sexual favor, is eventually forced into a stricter discernment, concentrating his attention on the less superficial attributes of a potential lover. He generally wants a mate with whom he can share a sensually fulfilling lifestyle – one that would include a quality home, filled with beautiful furnishings, regular luxury vacationing, preferably with the same comfy circle of friends. He is definitely not one for the bar scene, and the bulk of his friendships may actually be with straight women. Yet, unlike other gay men who also bond better with female friends, Taurus doesn't play a wifey role in his own relationship. In fact, he tends to take on a more stereotypically husbandlike or fatherly position in partnerships, perhaps living out some image of the perfect male parental figure that was lacking in his own upbringing. He's a real nurturer and enjoys imparting advice to an often younger, less experienced lover. Sometimes this parental dynamic takes a different twist, with Taurus falling in love with the boyfriend or husband of a close female friend – or with the couple itself. In such a case, he may be projecting his own arrested need for happy parents onto the beloved pair.

To Taurus man, a hint of bisexuality is always intriguing. Even the most strictly gay-identified Taurean male may find himself in bed with a woman at some juncture. Because he lives on such a sensual level, where the graphic physicality of sex doesn't always fully enter his mind anyway, an emotional attachment to a member of the opposite sex could lead him down that particular garden path. Meanwhile, his sexual behavior with men is generally straightforward and psychologically uncomplicated. Gay Taurus man likes to be in charge, but not so as to ever dominate; rather, he enjoys physically demonstrating to his lover the pleasure that can be derived via being topped by a passionate, yet tender lover. Especially if his partner's previous experience has taught him that top guys are really only truly interested in submissive men, the Taurean lover wishes to dispel such a stigma and even offer a sense of sexual healing. As befits his astrological makeup, Taurus can be seen as a passive top, often preferring to be sat on, doing his partner from below. What Taurus

GAY TURN-ONS

youth
pretty boys
dark hair
clean-cut looks
smooth bodies
stomachs
necks, ears
wining and dining
(passive) body worship
mutual oral
deep massage
friction, rubbing
tongue baths
(passive) analingus
(passive) lite b + d
straight, married men
business suits
boxer shorts
cross dressing
stripping
homemade porn
cigars
body art, piercings
nibbling, biting

man does generally demand is a fair amount of body worship. He especially enjoys having someone seemingly grovel at his feet – or balls or ass. To him, such fawning signals an intense experience of intimacy. Role-playing is a bore for the Bull; and adding a third male party into the mix is usually out of the question, for the gay Taurean male is especially jealous and possessive. If one truly wants to unleash the beast within the Bull boy, all he'd have to do is have a dalliance – *once*. Because brewing behind Taurus's still, meditative demeanor is a temper that, though rarely revealed, is so ferocious as to floor and gore someone with one go. So fierce is Taurus's need for a secure sense of belonging that anything that might seem a threat is instinctively stamped out. To the Taurus male, straight or gay, a lover is his most valued possession. Such that, if his partner plays the tramp, he or she is bound to get trampled.

Couplings

Taurus Man ∫ Aries Woman

She sees vast carnal possibilities. He's slow to read her blatant signals; Aries's unfussy demeanor is what finally fastens his affection. Sex is a psychological affair – roles are reversed, master/servant fantasies explored.

Taurus Man ∫ Taurus Woman

This bond is intense in the beginning, but often somewhat static later. Still, it's a simpatico astrological coupling. Sex is comforting, emotionally validating: They could stay in bed for days.

Taurus Man ∫ Gemini Woman

She's been searching for someone so sensitive *and* strong; he's found a sexy, spitfire sort. Their friendship is foremost, so sex is rarely the focus. Indeed, in bed, they sometimes seem reluctant. Still, there's hope.

Taurus Man ∫ Cancer Woman

She sees a safe, steady guy – someone she can trust. Her volatility stimulates Taurus's caretaking instincts. It's a ten-hankie twosome – much ado about nothing; they cry till they laugh. In bed, she's a skillful sexual teacher.

Taurus Man ∫ Leo Woman

Fixation: A relationship between two stubborn types – she's doggedly ambitious, he's complacently immovable – is difficult to sustain, but there's a reward for trying: Emotional tensions create exceptional sexual heat.

Taurus Man ∫ Virgo Woman

Marriage material: He's easily swayed by the adoration she showers. She accepts his tender tutelage. There are obstacles, but they're often overcome. Either way, it's a smoldering sex thing from the start.

Taurus Man ∫ Libra Woman

She storms into his life, introducing new sensual experiences. They luxuriate in all manner of excess. This bond may never push on past superficial – they're in different 'places' – but the erotic connection is serious.

Taurus Man ∫ Scorpio Woman

He's the submissive sort she hopes to reshape. Any alliance between these astro-opposites is nothing short of obsessive. Sexual addiction – to each other – is to be expected: Passion borders on savagery.

Taurus Man / Sagittarius Woman

Sharing much in common – especially a need for attention – they clash when it comes to the essentials: She's happiest out in the world; he prefers the pleasures of home. Still, sexually, it's sumptuous.

Taurus Man / Capricorn Woman

Each finds a counterpart capable of true love. Still, though these earth signs are emotionally aligned – feathers rarely ruffle – she, thinking he'll stray, imposes restrictions. In bed, clearer communication is called for.

Taurus Man / Aquarius Woman

She sets out to nest with someone 'normal.' Ironically, he's exploring the dark side of his psyche. Enormous, uprooting changes occur. Aquarius is accustomed to more passion; for him, she's the exotic exception.

Taurus Man / Pisces Woman

She's the über-feminine female of his fantasies. His instant devotion is all the proof she needs: He's 'the one.' Harmony is in the stars. Their sexual desire is pressing – each pleases and pampers the other.

Gay

Taurus Man / Aries Man

Flab is a four-letter word, so a no-fat lifestyle ensues: Neither bites off more than he can comfortably chew. A confident couple – sexually compatible and similarly self-centered. In bed, they keep it simple.

Taurus Man / Taurus Man

An uncommon gay combination – two narcissists seek an adoring mate. Both men want the center of attention. Togetherness is tense, tempers regularly flare. At its best, in bed, this is a mutual admiration society.

Taurus Man / Gemini Man

Gemini's interest is primarily sexual; Taurus feels a profound emotional pull. When it works, life feels free and easy. Sexually, they click: Gemini plays slave to the big lug Taurean master; roles are also reversed.

Taurus Man / Cancer Man

A conservative and quiet couple – homebodies who enjoy a rich quality of life. There's nothing to prove: Taurus is his most placid self; Cancer takes the lead. Hidden dalliances may mean hearts get broken.

Taurus Man / Leo Man

Life with Leo seems to promise luxury, the good life. The Lion, a lookist, leaps at the beautiful Taurean Adonis. Loyalty to each other is their leitmotif. Friends and family abound. Sex is ceremonial, sometimes self-conscious.

Taurus Man / Virgo Man

Erudition is the attraction. Communication is extraordinary. Each gives the other endless attention, without resentment. In the extreme, giving so much means enough is never enough. In bed, they're gracious, good-natured.

Taurus Man / Libra Man

Taurus is Libra's homoerotic ideal. Beyond the physical, they share an appreciation of the finer things. Socializing is an art form. Food and drink are copiously consumed. They'll dote on each other. Sex is an intense exploration.

Taurus Man / Scorpio Man

Evasive, indirect characters whose sexual relationship often remains secretive. Contempt and power struggles are built into the bond. A classic male skirmish, like Archie and Reggie. Scorpio's sadism may be their undoing.

Taurus Man / Sagittarius Man

A force of nature. Together, they feel capable of ruling the world. Still, there's trouble – Sag takes the upper hand, Taurus tags along too willingly. A purely sexual scenario is perhaps preferable.

Taurus Man / Capricorn Man

A fondness for each other might go unspoken; sexual involvement, too, might stay under wraps. Friendship is guaranteed – Taurus–Cap combos are great roomies. In bed, the Goat's well-honed handiwork unearths the Bull's desire.

Taurus Man / Aquarius Man

A bond that's bound to have ballast. Each feels he's found the perfect partner. Dynamic Aquarius introduces his Bull boy to new and exhilarating situations, sexual and otherwise. They raise each other's professional profile.

Taurus Man / Pisces Man

Pisces seems that 'missing link' in Taurus's life. It's a symbiotic bond. Being with the Bull is like a dream come true. Life is productive, professional goals are met – and more. In bed, selfish motives are put aside.

Taurus Woman

the ideal

Taurus woman is the zodiac's barefoot contessa, a sort of tribal princess who embodies the combined spirit of regal immunity and pastoral naïveté. In every aspect, she is a 'living doll' – an infinitely fun-loving character who approaches life with an unspoilt, childlike vision and in so doing, she freely spreads joy. Taurus feels it her purpose to create a little bit of heaven here on earth, on one level procuring, and indulging in, as much epicurean delight as she might; while, on another, living as if it were a sacred right to do so. Professionally, she tends to pursue careers that perpetuate her carefree sensibility, providing her a sense of play while offering amusement to others. Though she is a materialist of the first order, she espouses simple luxuries, viewing wealth as a natural birthright, often dedicating herself to the needy, and particularly to children. Her guileless glee and secure sense of self make others feel as if they're in the presence of a favorite baby-sitter. In truth, no other woman enjoys being a girl more than this eternal nymphet, the whole of whose existence is an exploration of the feminine experience – from trial to exaltation. Her greatest goal in life is to be worthy of having lived it. As such, Taurus seeks to surround herself with 'quality' people: In a man she demands the full package – looks, personality, sense of humor, roguish charm, sexual ability, a boyish spirit, and a bankroll that could choke a bull – expecting to be cherished unerringly and in the extreme. Her same-sex bonds are an all-out celebration of womanhood, an often earthy-crunchy affair marked by mutual nurturing and a shared journey of self-discovery.

Sign + Mind

Venus rules Taurus, as well as Libra; but in this most vivid of earth signs, the planet's powers are fully focused on the material plane. Representative of the Feminine Principle in astrology, planet Venus signifies the concepts of subjectivity, and thus responsiveness, unity, integration, and harmony along with a slew of attributes borrowed from its namesake goddess – beauty, grace, charm, love, and desire. In Libra, an ideological (air) sign, these qualities are crucial in their consideration as abstract values, but in Taurus they are to be taken far more literally, explored tangibly, in their application. Indeed, the Taurus woman cares little for theory – she deals in substance, that which she can see, feel, smell, and taste. And as the female embodiment of her planet's patroness, thus aligned with the feminine position she so firmly holds, Taurus woman seeks to manifest these Venusian qualities as visibly, or indeed palpably, as possible. The looks of things, and people for that matter, are far more important to her than they are to any other sign – the planet's glyph is often referred to as the 'mirror of Aphrodite' – in so far, at least, as the power and value they might contain. First impressions are crucial to Taurus, her natural disposition making her susceptible to a certain vanity of the 'mirror, mirror' variety. And yet, Taurus's concern with looks can be deceiving – they possess far deeper meaning to her than one might readily imagine. Even Taurus mightn't realize that in her notorious love of clothes, cosmetics, and designer doodads for herself and her home, she is channeling a spiritual energy specific to her sign. She isn't the zodiac's preeminent material girl for nothing: Taurus is the terrestrial goddess incarnate, and as such she adorns herself in vestments with such signature ritualistic fervor (ever wait for a Taurean to get ready for a date?) as would recall the goddesses' own temple priestesses – from those of the libidinous Venus to the attendees of virginal Vesta – who, as history has it, employed the sacrament of costume to become the goddess in preparation for sacred sexual rites with the sacred kings or god-priests.

Think of all those over-the-top Taurean entertainers just screaming in their resplendence, often via Bob Mackie designs – Cher, Barbra Streisand, Carol Burnett, Joanna Lumley, Pia Zadora, Rita Coolidge, Janet Jackson, Grace Jones, Shirley MacLaine, Bea Arthur, and Ann-Margret. It might as well be a marquee of drag performers. And such a summation would be apt: Transvestism in men has its roots in shaman-priests also putting on the goddess's holy vestments as a means of being granted her power. Taurus woman, already fully femininely endowed by nature, might thus be labeled the zodiac's *vestite* – a term, like *vestment,* which stems from Vesta herself. The point of all this *garb*-age comes down to one thing: expression. Just as the sign rules the voice, symbolically interpreted as that which gives rise to personal idiom, the sign of Taurus woman is all wrapped up in a need to embrace and celebrate herself as a woman in so vivid a manner. Indeed, one wonders how the cosmetics industry might suffer if it weren't for the lady Bull, forever softening herself with lotions, perfuming and polishing herself to ideal female perfection. The 2nd House of the zodiac is one of *expression,* and whereas the Aries woman who precedes her on the astrological wheel seeks to enjoy all that men in this world do, forgoing feminine trappings as fatuous, Taurus finds power in the powder puff, seeing her second-sex status as providing an advantage in life: Doors are continually held open as she sashays her way toward whatever goal she seeks to achieve.

As the only fixed-earth sign in the zodiac, Taurus is predisposed to, well, fix herself up materially, just as she is inclined toward having all the 'right stuff.' Her sign's motto is 'I have,' and rarely is she ever one of the 'have-nots' – a condition she'd like to see universally eradicated in fact. Even more essentially, Taurus spends a lifetime developing an ever-expanding list of attributes that might fall under the heading of her motto. First, she is exceedingly concerned, if not obsessed, with her very person, as female physical traits are ruled by Venus. And so it goes that the Bull woman is hyperaware of what she takes into her body – and, yes, on every level – being most precious about food, drink, and other substances that she allows to pass down her Taurean-ruled throat. Likewise, as Venus's glyph vividly recalls a hymen-crossed vagina leading to a uterus, purity and discernment are also underscored in the sexual arena. Overall, Taurus treats her body like a temple, taking special care with her physical charms. She shows us, by example, the beauty of viewing oneself as a sacred place – that we must treasure and never trash our bodies. On a more metaphorical level, Taurus believes that in cultivating herself, she makes her little patch of the world a far better place for others as well.

Content, value, and *power* are prime attributes of the zodiacal 2nd House associated with Taurus. This goes a long way toward explaining why she is forever taking up hobbies – endeavors that speak to what one is 'made of' – adding to her coffer of valuable assets. She may have the best of intentions, but with hands in so many pots, Taurus might be considered something of a dabbler. She is often as conscious of her personal belief system – those more metaphoric *values* – as she is about the price tags on cashmere shawls or her preferred shabby-chic decor. What Taurus has and holds true is powerfully endowed, loaded, and *sacred* to her. And lest one forget it, she is sure to offer

PLANETARY SYMBOL

The glyph of Venus – circle of spirit above the cross of matter – represents the unseen spiritual, and indeed sensual, content over physical form. Called the mirror of Aphrodite, it points to a certain vanity and subjective view of self. The symbol's cross recalls a hymen, suggesting the virgin aspect of Earth. The glyph's outstretched 'arms' are an invitation to union.

SIGN QUADRANT

The zodiacal quadrants correspond to metaphysical planes of existence – physical, emotional, mental, and spiritual. The First Quadrant is that of the self and individual awareness. Whereas Aries is focused on outward action, Taurus is steeped in incoming sensations and focused on a quality of life and personal attributes. Taurus woman seeks to cultivate her many charms in a lifelong pursuit of an increasing sense of value and self-esteem. Her motto, 'I have,' might easily be followed by the phrase 'the best womankind can offer.'

SIGN GLYPH

The Taurean emblem, the head and horns of the bull, signifies the inherent power of response. It is the same as the symbol of the Egyptian goddess Isis, who, like Eve and Io, is a deified embodiment of feminine nature.

reminders: Taurus enjoys performing her temple rituals in front of people, demonstrating how well she takes care of herself and her loved ones. Similarly, she'll have you know how superior the stuff is you're sitting on, staring at, or stuffing into your face when within her hallowed halls. But it's all part of her charm: For nobody could ever say Taurus is jaded toward even the little things. She naturally understands that life is a gift; and so it's difficult to begrudge her anything. In any case, as far as the concept of value goes, the 2nd House doesn't distinguish between material wealth and self-worth, and neither does the Taurus woman, for better or for worse.

The sign of Taurus is associated with the biblical experience of Eden, that most fixed portion of earth, just as the female of the sign personifies the archetype of Eve – the essential female prototype, the top-of-the-line female. The proverbial Garden, paradise, is thus literally heaven *on* earth. And it is in this state of grace, before the fall, that Taureans of both sexes 'live,' metaphorically speaking. Just as Taurus male is represented as the Edenic Adam, the Greek Adonis – their names (*Adonai* meaning 'lord') are one and the same – and other agrarian 'flower gods,' so, too, does the Taurus female draw further archetypal energy from the mythic maiden-earth goddesses, the nymphs, who embody the spirits of *fixed,* sacred terrestrial spaces – specifically gardens, groves, and the temple-shrines erected therein. In ancient literature and religions, the garden is always symbolic of the female – it is the fertile place where seeds are planted. With all this primordial feminine power piled up inside her, who can really blame Taurus for being a bundle of self-concern. It is merely her particular archetypal cross to bear. Like a garden, it takes work to tend to Taurus – luckily she makes much of the effort herself. Still, anyone with whom she intimately associates will feel obliged to pick up a big hoe and share in the work of tilling the soil of Taurus's experience.

Nymphs, those adolescent earth goddesses, are a perfect match to Taurus's association with the age group 7–14. On the basic level, this is a time in a girl's life when she looks forward to womanhood, forever playing dress-up on that theme – the fun and excitement of Venus-ruled fashion and beauty is something of which Taurus never tires, no matter her age. But the significance of this age group doesn't end there: This is also a time of life marked by a girl's developing awareness of her own burgeoning sexuality, and the responsibility that goes along with it – overriding themes in the Taurus's life. Bring on the nymphs: These frolicking, pubescent vegetation goddesses, forever being chased by licentious gods, live on in the hearts and minds of our naturally naive Taurean.

The myth most apt in laying out the basic themes of the Bull girl's struggles with self-worth, and her subsequent relationships with men, is that of the beautiful nymph goddess Io, who had a hard time saying no to the supreme god, Zeus–Jupiter, disguised as a black cloud, such foreshadowing being lost on her. His queen-goddess wife, Hera, in a fit of jealous rage, nearly catches the two in the act but for Zeus transforming Io into a pretty, snow-white heifer. Hera's intuition not to be outwitted, she knows the score and asks if she might have the cow as a pet. Zeus has no choice lest he give away his ploy, and Io is kept captive. In the end, she's helped to escape and Hera lets loose a stinging gadfly that chases her out of Europe across her namesake Ionian Sea into Asia, where she's changed back to her old self and worshiped as an über-goddess in her own right, the Egyptian Isis. Voila, Taurus woman in a nutshell: Attracted to high-powered he-men, those she feels most likely to provide all those requisite *goods,* she risks being overpowered by them and looking like a silly cow, especially in the eyes of other, older and wiser women. But only in going through the experience of being stung in the ass enough times will she finally smarten up and recognize herself as self-sufficient, just like that ballsy broad who ran Io out of town. Taurus, in all her glorious über-feminine subjectivity, cannot help but attract male attention to herself, whether it be positive or negative. Both Eve and Io – the same character, really, being the antediluvian mother of mankind viewed from separate traditions – invite their respective snakes in the grass. And such is one of the many pitfalls that await Taurus, for whom the only way *out* of such destructive patterns is *through.*

Bulls, in nature, don't see so well. And Taureans of both sexes share this myopic vision; symbolically, the female of the sign, especially, lacks discernment. She is so focused on herself, even as a means of attracting desired situations and people, that she doesn't often properly filter out what or who gets in despite her astrological focus on treating herself like a temple – indeed, these dynamics go hand in hand, an underdeveloped discernment giving rise to conscious quality-control. It's this way: Whereas Taurus man is a collector of admirers, affixing little price tags of worth on everyone he meets, Taurus woman seeks to make herself into a priceless treasure in hopes of luring that one special, worthy someone. It's a conceited conceit, to be certain – and Taurus's relationships are often a mutual-admiration society *à deux.* The good news is, this dressing for romantic success usually does work in attracting a perfect catch – with one, well, catch: She necessarily attracts those undesirables as well. She's not so great at spotting snakiness, particularly in her youth; Taurus must learn that looks can be deceiving and it may be a rude awakening to realize that not everybody wraps himself in the true raiment of his soul the way she does. Taurus feels herself a paragon of girlhood, so she *fixes* up to

ELEMENT + QUALITY

The earth element connotes substance, materiality, and content. The fixed quality signifies a need for stability, comfort, focus, and cultivation. Together, the fixed-earth combination particular to Taurus is best illustrated as a garden, like Eden, or the flora therein. Any grove, glade, or temple could be considered a sacred Taurean space.

POLARITY

Females in feminine (earth, water) signs are aligned with the gender polarity of their sign and thus embody the quality-element combination of the sign. Taurus woman envisions herself as her best possession, a substantial focus as befits the fixed-earth status of her sign.

substantiate that belief, becoming a walking-talking picture of the feminine ideal, at least the way she sees it or, often, rather, the way she imagines men might want her to appear. In all her blatant subjectivity, Taurus can't help but see herself through other people's eyes, particularly male peepers. Assuming that this is standard behavior, she goes for guys based on their looks as well, believing in the old what-you-see-is-what-you-get adage. To boot, because the 2nd House makes no distinction between *financial value* and *human value,* Taurus often assumes that money equals merit, making her one of the most likely women to be taken in by a chubby wallet. She is hard-pressed to learn that, when it comes to matters of the heart, or simply shopping the proverbial meat market for dates, there is often precious little truth in advertising.

Of course, much of Taurus's view of relationships stems from patterns played out by her parents during her childhood. Her mother may be an overbearing figure, a quintessential Hera character, that goddess's province being women, marriage, and motherhood (the goddess also bestows *wealth* and *power,* two 2nd House concerns). Her father will tend to be on the passive side. And whereas Taurus boy attempts to play a companionable role with his mother, Taurus girl sides with her father, subconsciously blaming her mom for unmanning him with her ballsy nature. Meanwhile, also subconsciously, Taurus begins to associate males in general with passivity, sowing the seeds of her signature managerial streak with men. Trapped in this parental struggle, of course, Taurus's early life mirrors Io's – she comes between Mother Hera and Father Zeus, pitting primordial female power against a rather shaky male domination. The Bull girl feels that much of the tension in the household could easily have been avoided if only her mother hadn't been so controlling a figure – that if she'd embraced a softer spirit of acquiescence, more like the namesake of her planetary ruler, Venus-Aphrodite, the Bull's father mightn't have been so beaten down and psychologically castrated. Taurus tries her hardest not to be like her mother, who, even when beautiful, is decidedly steely and severe. This is often the impetus for Taurus to first begin outfitting herself in frilly pastels, whipping herself up into a feminine confection, someone sweeter and more supple than Mommy for Daddy to come home to. At this point, she's unaware that such a penchant for painstakingly prettifying herself will become just as shrewd a ploy as any perpetrated by the matriarchal shrew she's trying to eschew. Unsurprisingly, competition ignites between Taurus and her mother as the Bull increasingly becomes the love of her father's life. With each application of lipstick and cascading tress of hair, Taurus further rubs her mother's nose out of joint, albeit unconsciously. Often, the cosmetic effects become so exaggerated and artificial – enter the 'vestite' – that even the fourteen-year-old face Taurus wakes up with isn't the one her peers will ever see. Talk about *The Mirror Has Two Faces* – it's enough to make you break a nail. And while we're on the subject of Aphrodite's freaky little looking glass, here's two words for you: *Snow White*. This famous fairy tale is merely the Io story in disguise. Hera is the beautiful queen of mean, Io, the 'snow-white' heifer, is . . . well, you get the idea.

Although, like Snow, Taurus girl threatens to outshine her mama, it isn't typically a full-blown conflict, but rather an underlying contest. Mainly it is her mother who feels the burn while the Bull girl may remain unsuspecting for the most part. Indeed, like Ms. White, Taurus lives in that idyllic, Edenic state associated with her sign, moving in mythic dreamtime, as if attended by a flurry of cartoon bluebirds and small woodland animals scurrying at her feet, where animated flowers metaphorically spring up with every step. She is *that* blissfully ignorant. Life is lived like Eve's in that garden with no dualistic distinction between good and bad, let alone evil. As such, she often doesn't recognize when things aren't *right* for others, certainly unaware if she herself is doing them *wrong*. Of course it is only that much more infuriating for those at odds with Taurus to realize she has no ill intent. Snow or Io, after all, weren't out to incur the wrath of anybody, especially not their powerhouse mother figures. Still, there will be women throughout her life – you can call it a pattern – who won't buy Taurus's innocent routine, certain it's all an act. It begins with her mother, who wonders if Taurus's guilelessness is a guise, unable to fathom that someone could be so self-centered as not to even notice her effect on others. Bliss. Many other women will be convinced she's conniving. The aptly titled film *All About Eve* explores this very dynamic with Taurean Anne Baxter batting her eyes in the title role. Really a retelling of the Io–Hera myth, Eve is an upstart who idolizes a grande dame of the theater, ingratiating herself to her while slowly taking over her life and position. It is eternally debatable just how much of a viper she is – or does she seem evil to women because they recognize themselves in her? Perhaps the character is detestable through her saccharine sweetness because she has the often enviable quality of stopping at nothing to get what she wants – tunnel vision is often exactly what 'it' takes, while worry about stepping on some other babe's Blahniks only diverts one's gaze from the bull's-eye.

Whatever the case, being born to this sign means it's all about Taurus. The underlying psychological upshot is that the Bull girl overcompensates because she feels lacking – that, as the eternal nubile nymph, she isn't quite the woman others are, like Io faced with a world of Heras. So it becomes her most pressing issue, over which Taurus doth protest too much: to try to be *more*. Her 'I have'

2

SIGN NUMBER

A feminine number of unity and sympathy. In the cabala, this number signifies the blending of male and female. Ancient teachings saw Eve as half of the primordial androgyne with Adam, united in one soul-body before being torn apart by the consciousness of duality.

7–14

SIGN AGE
ASSOCIATION

The age of nubility: The sign
of Taurus is associated with
this period when a female
blossoms from a child into a
young woman. This transformation is metaphorically
applicable to the Taurean all
her life, as her life lessons
focus on what it means to
fulfill her role as a woman of
substance.

motto becomes an obsession, and those 2nd House attributes of *wealth, worth,* and *power* are raised to pressing needs. Thus the dolling up, thus the overage of hobbies and would-be accomplishments, attempting to fill in the holes with *stuff* if not rounding out her person with makeup and voluminous hair. She wants to be a big girl, but is plagued with feelings of unworthiness and underreadiness. As a result, many Taurean female performers, for instance, suffer from stage fright; and, by the same token, it's why they become such extreme divas: overcompensation.

Little wonder that, even in her youth, the castle walls often aren't big enough for astrology's Snow White and her mother, who tend to bicker constantly during the Bull's adolescence. Her mother may worry that Taurus is attracting a wee bit too much attention, not only of the doting-father variety, but of the more snaky-male sort. And Taurus, being a girly girl, is already making googly eyes back at the boys she excites. As girls mature faster than boys, soon our rapidly developing Snow will have a string of boyfriends whom she'll dwarf – but we'll get to the symbolic significance of those industrious diminutive fellows as the Taurean saga unfolds. Suffice it to say, however, that Taurus loses ye olde snowiness earlier than many other princesses in the kingdom, and her domineering matriarch will be none too happy about it. As the original myth suggests, mums and daughts are really mirror images of each other, and much of her mother's angst is actually geared toward seeing Taurus not repeat the mistakes of her own youth. (There is, however, more method to the Bull's madness, if not boy-craziness, than meets even her mother's eye.) As the Taurus matures, she and her mother will gradually reconcile their differences. Eventually, they end up as generational reflections of one another, cut from the same mold, two peas in a pod.

Body + Soul

Without the dubious benefit of big hair and bold makeup, Taurus is probably the most naturally beautiful female on the astrological block (when she can resist the urge to do herself up in drag). She embodies the form and spirit of her nymph archetypes so completely that, all her life, there will be something fresh and girly about her. A list of famous Taurean Barbie dolls – including the wingy-haired likes of Bianca Jagger, Penelope Cruz, Anouk Aimee, Debra Winger, Glenda Jackson, Cate Blanchett, Audrey Hepburn, Katharine Hepburn, Uma Thurman, Natasha Richardson, Michelle Pfeiffer, Candice Bergen, Renée Zellwegger, Valerie Bertinelli, Shirley Temple, Leslie Gore, Ann-

Margret, Kirsten Dunst, and Sandra Dee, many of whom came to notice during their tender Taurean-ruled years – reveals that the beauties born under this sign are earthy blatantly female characters. Indeed, the grounded Bull is rarely an ethereal creature. Rather, she has a vivid presence, and a visceral one: The appeal of her particular charm hits a man below the belt. No amount of structured clothing can hide her physical sensuality – so pastoral a creature, she fairly aches to be barefoot and naked. She may seem stiff in tailored clothes, like some nubile beauty freshly plucked from the countryside, then plopped into an urbane setting. This goes a long way to explain why Taurus wears soft, flowy, or drapey fabrics and styles – otherwise, this natural woman feels hemmed in. She can sometimes be swathed in so elaborate a complex of tunics, peasant blouses and skirts, shawls, capes, scarves, and such that she is like a precious treat, packaged in delicate multilayers of wrapping.

One sure way to spot Taurus in a crowded setting is to activate all five senses: One might listen for the jangling of myriad silver bracelets and bangles, or the clinking of a beaded shawl, or follow the scent of the strongest, sweetest perfume in the room, or listen for a loud cascade of girlish laughter. Other-wise, scan for the woman with the middle-parted, tousled hair, dressed in muted, dusty pastels that recall any number of flavors of Turkish delight. Then check out those eyes: Like Taurus male, her peepers tend to be set far apart, seemingly on the sides of her head. These big, beautiful, aptly named cow eyes boast exceedingly long, luxurious lashes that blink in slow motion as if she were capturing you with a low-speed camera shutter. She is the incontestable queen of deliberate glances, scrutinizing a man without so much as turning in his direction. Her face is generally narrow, photographed far better, and far more often (knowing this), in profile. There is something childlike if not 'premature' to her looks, an echo of her basic psychological condition of feeling unaccomplished or incomplete. Another striking feature of the Taurean visage is her ultrasoft and creamy complexion. Whatever her race, Taurus tends to be fairer-skinned than other females in her family and often exhibits a light sprinkling of freckles about the nose, which is long, thin, and ever-so-slightly upturned. She may suffer from incongruous tiny skin eruptions – not acne per se – perhaps due in part to her über-feminine biology. Venus's influence floods Taurus with estrogen, sometimes turning her dewy complexion downright oily. Her lips are full and sensuously curved, such that even a hint of gloss makes them appear 'irresistible.' Taurus typically chooses to leave her hair long and free-flowing, styling it in wavy Rapunzel ringlets or curls, notoriously trimmed or fringed or feathered to frame her brow and marked jawline. Her chin is determined and, as a rule, held high, a nod to her bullish resolve, if not

PSYCHOLOGY

Vanity is rampant among Taurean women. She tends to overpersonalize experience, failing in objectivity. She can be too concerned with appearances and thus have difficulty with aging. Taurus may struggle with low self-esteem. She may also put too much emphasis on material concerns, being greedy for and miserly with money. Eating disorders may also plague her.

ARCHETYPE + MYTH

Taurus woman is the living representative of the Virgin Earth and the nubile nature goddesses (nymphs) who personify the natural energy of ancient groves, glades, and gardens where temptation arises. Nymphs are forever being chased and deflowered, just as Eve was courted by the serpent. The thematic dilemma for the Taurean archetype lies in a polarized vision of womanhood – relation to men versus responsibility to self and femalekind.

outright obstinacy. And her Taurean-ruled neck is long and swanlike, though never so delicate as to appear the least bit fragile. For it is here that she most clearly exhibits an earth-sign sturdiness. As well, her physique is healthy and strong, even when diet-thin. In contrast, her shoulders are graceful, and her arms delicate, ending in soft, small, childlike hands. Like her lustrous hair, Taurus's nails have a naturally buffed quality, as if she's always just stepped out from the manicurist (which is usually the case, anyway). And as befits Taurus's correspondence to the ages 7–14, her breasts are often firm and high, regardless of their actual size, which tends toward small to medium and rather cone-shaped, like a nubile's budding protrusions. It must be said, too, that they often point, like her eyes, in sidelong directions. There's usually no skimping in the ass and hips department, both of which appear all the rounder in contrast to her signature long, willowy waist. Many Taureans are natural dancers, their sometimes overly strong legs longer in proportion to their torso. However, Taurus's biggest complaint about her body will be thick calves and ankles.

As her sign rules the throat, bull girls typically boast a rich and velvety vocality. And unlike Aries, the natural belter of the zodiac, Taurus's voice is like a well-worn woodwind, effortlessly emitting rounded, sonorous tones. She gives good phone – whether talking business or engaging in a bit of tele-eroticism; and there's simply no getting around her soundings-off in the bedroom – something akin to the sweet lowing of a cow. Her pillowy lips hint at the similarly puffed lower-placed pair she possesses, just as her satiny throatings suggest yet another silky instrument where many of the Bull's other talents naturally lie. Indeed, even on a purely physical level, this girl's Taurean power of response is strikingly evident both in the way her pussy swells with excitement and how incredibly juicy it becomes at even the mere suggestion of sex. Her bush tends to be soft and fine; yet, despite it's natural spareness, the Taurean female typically trims it farther back into a whispered hint of a V. Her mound makes a rather vivid protrusion, as if in some silent tribute to her planetary namesake deity, for whom the mons veneris is named. However, for all the prominent aspects associated with her privates, she often has a tricky trigger that takes a keen finger or tongue to find. The inner thighs and tummy are erogenous zones for the Taurean female, as is the perineum. Her nipples, too, are special pleasure points, never overly, uncomfortably sensitive. Indeed, more Taurus women pierce their nips, probably, than any other female in the zodiac, enjoying a teensy twinge of pain twirled into the erotic delight her breasts are wont to deliver.

Taurus is the female body cultist of the zodiac and, as such, is more likely than most to venture a tattoo or two to go along with the odd piercings which, besides offering herself pleasure, are often meant to deliver a possible added element of ecstasy to a lover: Ask many a Taurus to say 'ah' and a tongue stud is often revealed. Still, sex aside, Taurus female simply enjoys such elements of adornment; and she chooses less drastic variations as well, including toe rings, anklets, her noisy multiple spangles, and a plethora of earrings. Overall, there is a twinge of the tribal to any style Taurus espouses. Unbeknownst to her, in most cases, Taurus is enacting the ritualistic process endemic to the earthly nymph and temple-priestess archetypes attached to her sign. Whether she opts for a more natch neo-flower-child bohemian look or something ultraurban or rocker-glam, she seems to signal that she belongs to some metaphorically consanguine society of like-minded individuals – she often does actually associate with a horde of metro-hippies, or a band of bohemian cronies. Regardless, any pack she travels with will always manifest some combination of total earthiness and utter extravagance – the term *hippy chic* had to be originally coined after a Taurus. And just as she manages to appear natural and naked even when made-up and decked out, Taurus can also make a veritable rag right off the rack look as if it were riding the back of royalty. Still, she will always insist on appearing comfortably sexy; and what particular style she chooses will depend, to some degree, on which sociological pool she's fishing in, especially for a life mate. (Leather means 'rock star.' Tiny suits say 'investment banker.' Little – though rarely black – dresses scream 'society mogul.') But one mustn't misconstrue the Taurus as antifeminist, *au contraire* – she isn't so much a stereotypical female as she is a prototypical one. Her practical earthiness, as well as her 2nd House associations with *value* and *substance,* instill in her a need to advertise the self-product she's proffering, becoming something of a billboard that isn't easy for a would-be partner to miss. Of course, she can sometimes miss the mark, and in trying to make herself appear the consummate treasure or treat, she might come off looking more like a tart. (Sorry, Taurus, but you know it's true.) Just don't say it to her face. Although Taurus has a broad, unselfconscious brand of humor – the sign boasts scads of comediennes – she possesses scant ability to laugh at herself. From an astrological point of view, she can't: She embodies subjectivity – a feeling that all eyes are on her – and being so grounded an earth sign disables her even further from looking at herself objectively. Taurus feels it is her duty to be beautiful, and it is certainly one obligation she truly takes to heart.

BIBLE + LITERATURE

The sign of Taurus is likened to Edenic bliss. The biblical prototype of the Taurean female is Eve, who represents the female condition. Eva is the virgin Earth, the nubile aspect of Mary, whose salutation Ave anagrammatically reverses the original sin of eating the apple. Snow White is taught a lesson by her mother, who gave her the poison apple, just as Hera (to whom apples are sacred) taught the snow-white heifer Io a thing or two. Joseph L. Mankiewicz's screenplay for *All About Eve,* from Mary Orr's short story 'The Wisdom of Eve,' explores a presumed innocent taking the place of her powerful female role model.

2ND ASTROLOGICAL HOUSE

values
matter
time
obtainment
financial dealings
possessions
investments
earning capacity
gain through effort
latent talents
inner resources
desire for fulfillment
expression
self-worth
personal freedom
material debt
personal protection
money earned
money spent
personal stock
self-reflection
uniqueness
endowment
contribution
ingenuity
comfort
rest and relaxation
priorities
inner strength
supporters/mentors
what we stand for in life
what guides our actions
happiness
tastes
resources for existence
power of attraction
spending capacity
how obligations are fulfilled
responsibility
husbandry
symbiotic union

Sex + Sexuality

From the time she's very young, Taurus longs for a traditional, old-fashioned relationship in which men and women play customary fairy-tale roles. And though, as she progresses to maturity, she'll learn to amend this pat stance, she is naturally cynical about heterosexual bonds, believing they can only function well in this cookie-cutter fashion. For any misery her parents suffered, she blames her mother and pities her father, just as her archetypal Io may have felt sorry for Zeus for having such a ball-busting mate. However, what Taurus, like Io, mightn't realize is that her own mother, in being so characteristically hard on her, might be trying to head off at the pass Taurus's mistakes with men. The myth itself isn't so much about Hera's catching Zeus as it is about the goddess – who was, incidentally, referred to as 'the cow-eyed' – saving Io, indeed the maiden aspect of herself, from the lecherous power of a self-styled omnipotent man; for, in so doing, she makes Io her pet and pupil, whipping her ass into having more respect for her own womankind. Taurus's mother has a similarly uphill battle. As the most feminine of the zodiac's females, the Bull is designed to be receptive, even submissive, in relationships and, indeed, as regards actual sex with men. But along with her label as the sign of sexual response goes a heap of responsibility: In being too open and available, the ideal dolly, she might give women a bad name.

In proving herself the opposite of her domineering mom, the Bull girl hooks up with typically older, popular guys early on, those with whom she feels valued in the public eye of her peers. In some instances, Taurus's love story might end there, as she, more than any other female sign, often marries her childhood or high school sweetheart. Still, despite the noble intentions she might inspire in a boy, it is generally not her brain most guys will be after. Plucked, perfumed, and prettified to perfection, the Taurean treat looks good enough to eat. What piques a boy's interest, too, is her combination of obvious femininity and 2nd House *power:* Even when a slip of a girl, a veritable Audrey Hepburn type, she will still look sturdy, her weighty neck and legs preventing her from ever appearing too demure or delicate a flower. Besides which, she has a forceful and spunky attitude; she's no withering wallflower to be sure – indeed, she may already exhibit her mother's domineering spirit despite attempts to subdue it. Boys see what amounts to her bull energy and decide she's not so unbreakable that they couldn't take her for a right tumble in the hay. In truth, young Taurus's sex drive is as strong as any adolescent boy's, and she's designed for some fairly heavy sexcapades. But what the pretty young

Bull mightn't realize, in her zeal to play house, is that she could be confusing love with an urge for sex. Usually, one advises girls the other way around – not to confuse sex with a need for love; but for the Taurus, the opposite tends to be true. She is astrologically engineered, first and foremost, for physical union as befits her status as the Venus-ruled earth nymph. Feeling the ultrafeminine force of her sign ever since she can remember, she's long perfected playing dress-up – acting the ideal woman – and now, with the onset of hormones coursing through her body, she immediately feels herself ready to play house. She mistakes her surfacing sexual urges for a call to matrimony, or a reasonable facsimile thereof. Why do so many Taureans marry their childhood sweet-hearts? Often because they're barely out of high school when they do so. But the success rate of long-lasting marital bliss is dodgy. The moral of the Io myth, cautioning against being one more notch in some power-monger's bedpost, isn't designed to teach the Cowgirl not to give away the farm; rather it's meant to instill the belief that women have the power, and it's she who can thus whittle a tally on her own bedpost. Deeper study of the myths reveals that Io was no virgin. She was a nymph who did what nymphs do, having many lovers. Zeus was just one in a string. Her crime wasn't in taking Zeus as a prize, but that he already belonged in Hera's box of Cracker Jack. Our vision of nymphs bolting from pursuing gods and heroes isn't about protecting their maidenhood but rather not wanting to be subdued by male tyranny. They were already getting it off with every satyr roaming the woods. Hera mightn't so much have been protecting the sanctity of her own marriage as helping Io to escape the tyranny of a similar bond. But, Taurus thinks to herself, I don't want to *top* a man the way mom did, not being one to wear the pants as, say, the Aries women of the world, as the female embodiment of the Masculine Principle, are wont to do. What Taurus, aligned with the Feminine Principle, will eventually realize is that she can run the show while still remaining on her back. But, like Io, she generally learns the hard way.

Being materially minded, Taurus is anxious to get on with adult life and start ticking off items on her infamous acquisition list. This is another reason for Ms. 'I have' to start playing house sooner than later, as she feels that she and a young mate should get while the getting's good. To boot, in a rush to get out from her mother's thumb, she may leap before looking into a live-in relationship and end up with a 'lesser' man than she bargained for, if not one in a long line of trolls – enter the symbolism of Snow White's dwarfs. Sure, these mini-men might be money-oriented, whistling off to work to mine the world for 2nd House *riches,* but look what she's got to deal with: all those seven vices men are apt to let surface once a woman agrees to play house, if not clean

KEY WORDS

content
vanity
arousal
attraction
belonging
inertia
subjectivity
beauty
symbiosis
nature
innocence
endurance
persistence
ownership
restraint
domestication
materialism
acquisition
patience
acceptance
security
sensuality
sweetness
composure
grace
aquiescence
growth
luxury
sustenance
modesty
tradition
capability
cultivation
response
craving
receptivity
accomplishment
artlessness
impeccability
candor
taste
cultivation
value
aplomb
ingenuousness

up after them. If she's not coping with a hypochondriac, she could be suffering some know-it-all, a dope, an agoraphobic, a manic, a depressive, or a rage addict. Best thing that witch ever did was slip Snow the apple – for she finally woke up and saw all she wanted was a prince, minus the complicated, deadly boring sins. (Hera, of course, possessed magical apple orchards and often showed up in the guise of an old crone to teach some bimbo or another a lesson.) If only this reaction were so automatic for all Taureans. In her early years, she too often focuses strictly on would-be sheikh-shopping – no other woman needs to be shown the money the way she does – which invites men whose preoccupation with materialism might preclude a wholesome morality, not to mention simple human kindness. At the same time she wants a man who'll play Ken to her ever-loving Barbie. Indeed, she thrives in relationships with men just her own age, those with whom she can grow old rocking by the fire. Even when a famous citizen of the world, the Bull girl usually attaches herself to a handsome hottie, if not a compliant himbo, with whom she can walk through life as she once surfed the halls of high school with a main squeeze, hands lodged into each other's back pocket. In the end, relationships, sex, and all things couple-y should be a decidedly simple affair, no more complicated than it was back in the day when she locked lips at her locker. Her particular challenge, when it comes to love, then, is striking a balance between her need for that eternal boyfriend, an equally sweet and synergistic Adam to her Eve, and her desire for wealth and the power she believes that money buys. In truth, she is not just Snow White in that saga but – mirror, mirror – she's potentially that vain and greedy old witch as well. If she's lucky, as most Taurean women are, blessed by fortune-bringing Venus, called the 'lower benefic' in the zodiac, astrology's Gidget will live happily ever after with her Moondoogie, *je m'appelle* Barbie *avec* her Ken, and still manage, in extending all analogies, to pay for their Malibu dream house in cash.

Meanwhile the problem is often not being able to separate Venus-propelled love from 2nd House *possessions* should they not be combined into a tall, dark, and handsome package. The color associated with Taurus being *green,* our little Cowgirl typical puts 'lettuce' first on her notorious shopping list for ingredients in a mate. Again, just as she can't separate material value from the moral or even spiritual brand, her motivation for 2nd House *comfort* sees her assuming that a man who shares her want of financial security will also be inclined, as she is, to be emotionally warm and fuzzy. (Sound of loud game-show buzzer.) It's not easy scoring a bigwig who also indulges in back rubs and backyard barbecues. Still, if anyone's going to find him, Taurus woman will. And once faced with someone she's labeled a suitable candidate, she'll leave nothing to chance. After all, Taurus is playing for keeps, and like her male counterpart, she doesn't like to spin her wheels or waste energy on faulty attempts at love. Inevitably, she blunders on the first few tries, falling for guys who only feign to share her passions – again, that faulty depth perception – making the Bull a real sucker for the old cape trick: Olé! Then again, in targeting a potential partner, her notorious dolling-up might strike certain men as startlingly superficial – unable to see through to the 'real face' underneath, such a mensch might label her a bit of a bullshitter. Still, more times than not, Taurus woman's attention to detailing sees her falling under the heading of a man's ideal.

Love is generally a win-win situation for Taurus. If she's lucky enough to score a well-heeled mate who's also not a heel, all is right with the world. If she goes for the bucks and bags a baddy, she'll sooner bolt than keep unhappiness bottled up. If she happens to fall for a down-on-his-luck dreamboat, she'll learn in a flash that, when push comes to shove, love will win out over money – it might not be the method of her mind, but it certainly is the modus of her heart – and though she'll be a nervous wreck about it, she'd never kick Ken out for making peanuts, or, for that matter, eating crackers in bed. Enter the fairy-tale bit that Taurus longs for throughout her life story: Our Bully, herself, is quite the little money magnet once she stops trying to grab from the universe and lets abundance flow in. The girl can't help it: practically every time she turns around the universe goes *ch-king* – it's her astrological birthright. So, before she knows it, that blessed Venus energy coursing through the 2nd House starts working its financial wizardry. As if Taurus woman didn't have enough self-confidence. Though her planetary ruler makes her nearly obsessive about romantic union, it is most often her solo talents, something toward which she is uncharacteristically humble, that pay off the biggest. Those hobbies and interests she procured in her youth in hopes of making herself more valuable a human being are ironically where Taurus places the least monetary expectation but often see her becoming, as is befitting, the biggest cash cow on the astrological block. Let this be a lesson to all Tauruses with natural talent – cultivate your gifts and mighty forces, even financial ones, will conspire to help you.

Meanwhile, bully for the boyfriend. In truth, more Taurus-female relationships entail business partnership with a mate, exactly how the sign's love and money aspects are meant to go together. Often, Ken manages or produces Barbie's talents or otherwise shares in a mutual enterprise where she finally sees herself, as the zodiac's treasure, being cherished and tended to. Less often it's the other way around, with Taurus as the anchor, the proverbial

Elaine May
Jamie-Lynn Sigler
Betty Page
Ella Fitzgerald
Anita Loos
Sandy Dennis
Ann B. Davis
Alice B. Toklas
Bea Arthur
Carol Burnett
Grace Jones
Phyllida Law
Celeste Holm
Eve Arden
Sheena Easton
Shirley Temple Black
Lesley Gore
Kelly Clarkson
Valerie Bertinelli
Joyce DeWitt
Eva Peron
Golda Meier
Coretta Scott King
Queen Elizabeth II
Catherine de Medici
Mary Robinson
Madeleine Albright
Anne Baxter
Margot Fonteyn
Carolyn Roehm
Hedda Hopper
Alice Faye
Judith Jamison
Martha Graham
Daphne Du Maurier
Charlotte Brontë
Mary Wollstonecraft
Katherine Anne Porter
Kate Smith
Alice Liddell
Harper Lee
Blossom Dearie
Catherine the Great
Ida Rolf
Odette Sanson
Pia Zadora
Tammy Wynette
Nancy Walker
Florence Nightingale
Nora Ephron

BODY RULERSHIP

Taurus rules both the throat, symbolic of expression, and the neck, connoting a certain poise and grace in bearing. There is a tendency toward ear and throat infections, obesity, and other glandular issues. Venus rules feminine attributes in the body, estrogen, and the centripetal flow of blood back to the heart.

woman behind the man. Either way, Taurus will take a 'family business' approach to whichever of their individual endeavors looks to be the most bankable at any given time, pooling resources to optimize chances for success and ensure as bullish a household economy as can be. She prefers all facets of their partnership to remain private and self-sustaining. There should never be a need for outside influences. This, of course, extends to the bedroom, where, if the Taurus can't fulfill even the tallest erotic order, indeed no woman can.

Of all the possible milieus in which to mingle, Taurus woman is most in her element in bed – unabashedly lusty and instinctual, her sexuality is unencumbered by psychological bells and whistles. Like her Taurus brother, her brain doesn't function as a sexual organ; her interaction with a lover remaining purely sensual. She is enlivened by a man's desire to be pleased, ready and eager to entertain his every request and make a few of her own. This girl lives up to her assignation as the zodiac's earthy nymph, like those mythic nubiles, seemingly designed for the taking, not to mention possessing if just a tiny dose of their namesake mania. As the sign of sexual response, Taurus is an exceedingly reactive recipient in the bedroom – though generally not in any other room in the house as she likes sex in a sanctified boudoir setting – getting off on playing a traditional female role, particularly in her choice of sexual positions. She is decidedly a real bottom girl, of all the female signs, the most strictly passive. Hungrily, and most audibly, she invites a man into whichever nook and cranny achingly begs for penetration. In her exaggerated penchant to please a man orally, one might suspect she has an extra G-spot lodged somewhere in that Taurean-ruled throat. She is a temple harlot come to life, programmed to receive a man as some sacred prince or sacrificial priest, her very being a glorious gateway to divine ecstasy where there is no division between the sublime and sinful aspects of getting it on. She is that archetypal Eve, remember, who has no concept of a dualistic division between sexual rights and wrongs.

Taurus takes the exploration of her femininity to near fetishistic heights, organically falling into role-play as striptease artist, geisha, or even expert call girl, without any forethought or shade of irony. To her mind, she's simply expressing herself, tapping into natural sexual proclivities. This is perhaps the most enviable aspect of the Taurean sexual persona: She easily accesses her primal erotic self, guilelessly giving herself over to a man's more dominant urges. Sex isn't something to engage in lightly or to participate in slightly – for Taurus it requires complete surrender, which in turn culminates in a kind of transcendent ecstatic state. This is rarely had by assuming control or taking an assertive position in the sack à la Aries woman. Taurus is the literal flip side of that sign that precedes hers and thus requires to be thoroughly worked over by a man. She doesn't want to be ransacked, however, in any way, shape, or form. Rather she craves a slow, sensual, systematic detailing of her entire being, the bulk of her sexual excitement stemming from utter acquiescence to a man's exploration and domination of her, executed sweetly but deeply. The Bull girl really appreciates a bit of beefcake, particularly if it extends to her eternal boyfriend's bits and pieces. For her it's both the meat *and* the motion. And if anything could dispel her wide-eyed, unquestioning view of a mate – and fast – it's a failure to sufficiently deliver such goods.

The simple truth is that Taurus will rarely commit to a guy for the long run unless he's stellar in the sack. Money, looks, sense of humor – all such other bulleted points on her checklist go right out the window if her man lacks in the lovemaking department. If Taurus does enter a relationship with, say, that aforementioned childhood sweetheart, she may have nothing to compare her guy to, gaining an ever sneaking suspicion that she's missing out on something. Taurus may want to explore her options, curious as to what might be dangling in the trousers of each potential Mr. Big she meets. Taurus is not promiscuous; she'd find that word offensive and sexist as it is rarely applied to men. Though she looks, she's not inclined to touch, at least not indiscriminately. If she does marry young, for instance, or if she is not being sexually satisfied to the extent she senses she could be, she may act upon a select situation, not actively looking but open to the possibility that a certain someone might come along who triggers her hormonal instincts in such a way as to dispel all doubts. She doesn't institute a blanket 'open marriage' situation per se, but she will honestly express her need to expand her horizons if and when she feels that doing so is part and parcel of her own development, sexual or otherwise. Taurus isn't one to sneak behind a partner's back. And making so bold a move is rarely a result of her nymph archetype running rampant in her psyche, rather it's an integral part of cultivating a deeper understanding of herself as a woman. Sex, in and of itself, holds little fascination for the Taurus – it is, however, often a vital component of her all-important journey of feminine self-discovery, a means of giving voice to her individual expression, singing the song of herself. Her own sexuality is a source of liberation for the pastoral Taurus, who, when coming upon societal conflict with her own personal instincts and desires, will always follow what she maintains to be a *natural* inclination. If, though in a relationship, she has a hankering for a hunk who's not her boyfriend or husband, that must be right *because* she feels it. It's another instance where Taurus might raise the ire of other women, for whether the man Taurus fancies is taken or not will typically be of little consequence – she thinks about what is right for her, not what is wrong to her

STR8 TURN-ONS

tall men
size
swimmers' builds
smooth torsos
clean-shaven looks
hairy legs
executives
silk, satin lingerie, sheets
blue eyes, big noses
(active) oral
sixty-nine
submission
lite b + d
erotica, softcore porn
muscular hands, feet
flattery, (passive) seduction
nibbling, licking
pillow talk
gifts, surprises
(passive) anal sex
money, success
call girl role-play
m-m-f fantasies
seduction, stripping

fellow women, falling into that All About Taurus pattern at its least circumspect. The earthy nymph operates via her very human sexual responses, and just so long as she accepts the Hera-imparted responsibility of her actions, she will trust that her personal path is the right one, regardless of the consequences. It could be a deal-breaker for her cuckolded Ken, who might have avoided such developments, perhaps, if he were more anatomically correct; but Taurus is never one to regret. All experience is valuable to her.

Of course, meeting her sexual match in a mate would make Taurus's life far less messy – maybe if Adam had been more attentive, Eve wouldn't have been open to the seduction of the snake. Though never commanding, Taurus is nonetheless the most demanding of dames in the bedroom. Her fantasy life is especially steeped in thoughts of submission and might even border on acts many other women would label demeaning. As a bachelorette, she may outright serial-date for the very purpose of sampling the smorgasbord of men, reviewing their potential, practically meeting them at the door with a clipboard. Variety might spice up life for a while, but it isn't something that sustains her. The hands-down lookist of the zodiac, she is a sucker for fresh-faced family scions and frat boys, thrilled as much by the element of male society as she is by the individual fellow. Indeed, her fantasy life might include being 'taken' by two flush(ed) studs at once – she certainly can be more girl than one guy can handle. But even when this remains a glint in her infamous cow eyes, she will get off on flirting with a group of male friends, playfully pitting them against each other, enjoying the sensual delight if not the palpable whiff of hormones that her pointed coquetry might stir up. In signature style, of course, she does so candidly, her camaraderie being up-front and honest with nary the cock-tease about it. In fact, she is often a sort of female mascot to men, if not the spotlit diva with her male dancers in the background. The image of Shirley MacLaine comes to mind as the only lady to infiltrate the infamous all-male Rat Pack. As this sort of female presence, neither slaughter girl being passed around, nor just one of the guys, the Taurus is capable of meeting men on her own über-feminine terms. She seeks their same privileges, especially that of sexual freedom, but she does so from the unmistakable perspective of oh so enjoying being a girl.

In same-sex relationships, as well, Taurus rarely casts herself in a butch role. Our nymphet is typically not bisexual, but more definitively polarized, straight or gay. Though in adolescence the straight Bull might experiment with another girl, usually one who has a crush on her, rather than vice versa, interaction is really about relieving the Taurus's pent-up sexual energy. And so she might simply lie back and let it happen, grateful for release that isn't self-induced. (She isn't big on masturbation in any case.) Likewise, in adulthood, she may passively play-act at lesbian sex for the purpose of pleasing her man should he request such a showing. However, if and when Taurus comes out full stop, there's absolutely no going back. For her, sexuality is a tremendous source of strength and personal power, and she'll seek a like-minded lover who'll live as resolutely as she does – Taurus will often play a key role in championing gay causes, acting up on her sisters' behalf. Still, she doesn't so much march as stroll when taking issues to the streets, and she's not a big believer in banners and labels that set the gay community apart from society at large. Not consumed by the near stereotypical trappings of womanhood in which straight Taurus is so boldly steeped, the gay Taurus is nonetheless intently focused upon sharing and commemorating, with her lover, the finer, more solemn virtues of femaledom. She revels in the kind of sexual tenderness that can only be shared with another woman, just as she enjoys picking out the perfect piqué sheets between which to do just that.

The typical gay Taurus is a lipstick lesbian, only without the lipstick. She tends to be eternally girly, but often over time simultaneously sinks deeper into a naturalist state, quite unlike her notoriously adorned, cosmetically inclined straight counterpart. Instead of transforming her outward appearance in an attempt to telegraph availability, she explores other 2nd House attributes such as *comfort* and *stability* in both the presentation of her person and of her environment. Gay Taurus is quite the homebody, preferring to cultivate her domestic arts and craftiness rather than to spend money socializing in restaurants, bars, or clubs. Typically, Taurus will espouse her nymph archetype all the more in lesbian relationships, drawn to older, wiser women who will mother her, albeit in a rather tough-loving way, furthering Taurus's education on the boon of female empowerment. Taurus is often drawn to more beautifully butch lovers than herself, and even her briefest romance will start with the same brand of seduction she might have experienced in her youth via the ardent attentions of an already decidedly gay girlfriend.

Taurus is the girl with the *Personal Best* fantasy: She enjoys being mastered in the bedroom, particularly by an athletic, Amazonian lover. She prizes physical attributes most highly in a potential partner and makes no bones about not even looking at another woman unless she's sufficiently stunning. A smug superiority exists in many a gay Taurean relationship – a belief that, in bonding, she and her lover have become an unsurpassably perfect pair. Like straight Taurus, the gay Bull is designed to be the recipient of a sexual offensive, but she diverges from her heterosexual counterpart when it comes to that trademark need to please. For gay Taurus the pleasure is typically all hers, and she

GAY TURN-ONS

older women
submission
athletes, butches
drag kings
dark features
being pursued
big breasts
body hair
massages, caressing
deep kissing
luxuries
cliché mood music, candles
piercings
creams, lotions
musky scents
mutual oral
(passive) penetration
licking, teasing
student-teacher role-play
whipped cream
(passive) foot play, worship
feathers, ticklers
monogamy

is often somewhat remiss in the reciprocation department. She'll dally with her lover, rather than outright diving on in. Enjoying the loving, tender process of kissing and touching, she'll nibble, lick, and unconsciously tease her lover while demanding to be eaten-out with unrivaled gusto. The trick is finding a lover who relishes taking on the sole role of aggressor, willing to sufficiently address Taurus's designation as the zodiac's prime receptor. Regardless of sexual identity, Taurus woman craves penetration and will urge her spitfire lover to oblige. She thrills at displays of female power, and the mere mention of an aggressive top woman is often enough to make her toes curl. Fingering and dildo play, especially, are standards in her sexual mix, providing Taurus her de rigueur multiple orgasms. She prefers ardent chowdowns to the artful, finessed licks and nibbles that characterize her own signature style. Sixty-nine is a particularly intense turn-on; and yet, for all her passivity, she's not much for bottoming out in that configuration. Sitting on her face is often completely out of the question. Still, despite such specific sexual tastes, she's one female who'd be content to simply cuddle in a lover's arms as an erotic end-game unto itself.

Even when with a dynamic, independent or outright butch lover, Taurus requires a femmey pajama-party element in her relationship. She loves late-night prettifying pedicure sessions, flipping through magazines for clothes or home-furnishing inspiration, sipping wine while making a meal together. She adores shopping and lunching with other ladies and throwing dinner parties for a close circle of friends. She will bond with a coterie of like-minded women – typically well-bred bohemians with beefy bankrolls – who also espouse an adherence to long-term bonds. To be sure, gay Taurus woman is a die-hard monogamist whose idea of eternal bliss is growing old with that one special someone.

Couplings

Taurus Woman / Aries Man
She's his ultrafeminine ideal; he fulfills the fantasy of stud with an enterprising spirit. As a couple, they're a classic – Taurus boasts of being the woman behind the man. In bed, she's the mistress to his lusty master.

Taurus Woman / Taurus Man
This bond is intense in the beginning, but often somewhat static later. Still, it's a simpatico astrological coupling. Sex is comforting, emotionally validating: They could stay in bed for days.

Taurus Woman / Gemini Man
Two extravagant individuals drawn to the promise of glamour the other offers. Life is a whirlwind; their every move is contingent on the current trend. In bed, he likes a quick fix; she favors more drawn-out sessions.

Taurus Woman / Cancer Man
She's his fantasy in the flesh – all soft skin wrapped in a fuzzy pastel sweater. She knows his placid nature is a pose, and that extraordinary experiences await. In bed, it's titillation and tenderness in equal measure.

Taurus Woman / Leo Man
He longs for a natural woman – subtle, accessible Taureans appeal. She basks in Leo's glow, energized by his powerful presence. She stimulates his self-actualization. Tactile expression is her strength.

Taurus Woman / Virgo Man
She has what it takes – beauty, virtue. After those dangerous types, he seems a safe choice. Their bond is about personal growth, newfound optimism. Sex involves experiment – swapping might be an option.

Taurus Woman / Libra Man
They take time to warm up, but then it's hot. Each invests much energy in the other's emotional health. In artistic pursuits, this partnership is peerless. Sexually, imaginations are stimulated: Role-playing is one ritual.

Taurus Woman / Scorpio Man
Illicitness is inherent; they turn on to the taboo of togetherness. In the long run, their love may be a barren landscape in which little grows. But an extraordinary sexual connection keeps them from taking a hike.

Taurus Woman ∫ Sagittarius Man

Fixation at first sight. Sag's colossal self-confidence transforms this twosome. In her, he's found a 'savior.' Financially, they don't see eye to eye. She's one lover who'll satisfy his outsized libido.

Taurus Woman ∫ Capricorn Man

He often keeps his women undercover – not so now: She's a classy piece of arm-candy. She exists to create a stable environment in which he might thrive. Life together is *haute* everything: Only the best will do.

Taurus Woman ∫ Aquarius Man

Lurking tension requires exploration. She must clear her mind of prior expectations. For him, it's time to get real. Another caveat: they might be careful not to constantly contradict each other. Saving grace: Sex is stellar.

Taurus Woman ∫ Pisces Man

Allies: An emotional attachment develops instantly. He's ready to commit. If she accedes, life will be peaceful and productive. In bed, the focus is on entertainment – both require plenty of playful attention.

Gay

Taurus Woman ∫ Aries Woman

A social pair, they want to see and be seen. Aries has that glow of good health; Taurus is fetching but unfussy. The Bull offers Aries the protection she herself usually seeks. Sex is earthy and orgiastic.

Taurus Woman ∫ Taurus Woman

Like painters whose every brushstroke is carefully applied, the Taurus twosome pays ultimate attention to all aspects of living. Appreciation for each other means added value individually. Lavish foreplay is foremost.

Taurus Woman ∫ Gemini Woman

With provocative Gemini, the Bull girl taps into her own toughness. They agree on the essentials; joint professional ventures are a natural partnership path. Sex is endlessly enjoyable, at turns rough-and-tumble and tender.

Taurus Woman ∫ Cancer Woman

They get off on being 'girls' together – it's all dress-up and makeup. They may lead a lewd lifestyle, one that includes sex with strangers and swapping. If intimacy is lacking, this pair may opt to be pals and not partners.

Taurus Woman ∫ Leo Woman

The Taurus-Leo liaison is about learning to give way – letting go, allowing deepest feelings to surface. Often, they flirt with the rougher edges of existence. Sex is raunchy from day one. Love with a buzz appeals.

Taurus Woman ∫ Virgo Woman

Two cultivated sexual personae culminate into one powerful, potent whole. In the extreme, erotic appetites are unappeasable. More often, they're slaves to the ecstasy they experience together. Still, each is renewed via their association.

Taurus Woman ∫ Libra Woman

This starts as a crush. Taurus explores femininity; Libra experiments with androgyny, allowing latent longings to surface. In bed, Libra takes charge, lavishing her lover with all manner of sexual attention.

Taurus Woman ∫ Scorpio Woman

Taurus sends a shock wave through Scorpio, who, in turn, takes the role of guru to the suggestible Bull. A sexual relationship may develop ever so slowly. Months could pass before so much as a kiss is risked.

Taurus Woman ∫ Sagittarius Woman

They're a testimonial to the good life. Though Taurus is easily sated by simple luxuries, Sag can't help but yearn for more, more, more. Even if they end up just friends, an erotic connection endures.

Taurus Woman ∫ Capricorn Woman

Taurus pushes all Cap's buttons: How does one dare such outlandish relaxedness? To Taurus, Cap is a wise woman to be worshiped. Together, they live a principled, luxurious lifestyle. In bed, Cap takes command.

Taurus Woman ∫ Aquarius Woman

In Taurus, Aquarius has an eager audience, someone who'll listen lovingly to her high-minded monologues and learn. Sex is best when conceptual – it's all about exaggerated role-play and complex mind games.

Taurus Woman ∫ Pisces Woman

Initially, they clash. But it's intriguing. They have career goals in common; each works to reinforce the other's reputation. Often, emotional balance is elusive. Sex is untamed – a workout, if you will.

Gemini Man

the goodfellow

Gemini man is an operator. He can't sit still, constantly striving to set the wheels of his myriad plans and projects in motion. He is the zodiac's premier urbane figure, the proverbial man on the pavement with his ear perpetually to the ground and his finger on the pulse of cultural trends, especially those rooted in localized experience. The quintessential insider, Gemini infiltrates whatever milieu, private or professional that strikes his fancy – forming close alliances, ringleading, and invariably living by his own set of rules. He has the soul of a street poet, if not a rabble-rouser, with a knack for voicing the needs of the common man. Indeed, he may be something of a rogue, in conflict with, and even fighting against, 'establishment' views. He gravitates toward media-driven vocations, those steeped in the commercial exchange of ideas, which brings him into contact with an ever-revolving cast of characters. In rare moments of downtime, he still craves stimulation, reveling in close ties with family and friends, as well as being drawn to private clubs, lodges, and cliquey associations. Partygoing is a particularly Geminian penchant. Something of a playboy, he nonetheless seeks to settle down with a real hometown type of girl – his perfect counterpart – with whom he hopes to share a lifestyle, in any number of variations, along an American-dream-like theme. In same-sex relationships, he's irascibly fun-loving, forever negotiating a need to explore the 'scene' aspect of gay life against the building of an unbreakable, near brotherly bond.

PRINCIPLE

The Principle of Consciousness. Whereas Aries is objective and Taurus subjective, the sign of Gemini can step to one side and mentally view experience from both angles at once. He takes in impressions and information, at the same time delivering his own messages and agenda. Interaction is what it's all about for Gemini man, a master of commerce, communication, and all such exchange. Fittingly his sign's motto is 'I think.'

Sign + Mind

Gemini is ruled by the planet Mercury, whose smallest of orbits around the Sun is echoed in the Twins guy's inclination toward the inside track of life, always close at hand to a hotbed of activity. The planet, namesake of the Roman 'messenger' god Mercury (Greek: Hermes), represents 'pure intelligence' in the universe, the astrological Principle of Consciousness, and the astrological 3rd House attributes of *commerce, community,* and *communication,* to which it gives rise. Where Aries is associated with masculine-objective (outward) energy, and Taurus with subjective-feminine (inward) energy, Gemini is something of a two-way street, wherein both dynamics are simultaneously in play – one of many aspects of the sign's duality. Just as Hermes was a neutered or bisexual god – combining with Aphrodite to form the proverbial Hermaphroditus – Mercury's government over Gemini is fitting as, though traditionally considered a masculine sign, its quality is mutable – every third sign of the twelve-sign zodiac is – in a sense, dualistic or neutralistic, synthesizing the two that precede it. Such that, Gemini takes in as much as his infomaniacal mind will allow, while putting all his own notions in motion, being objective and subjective at the same time. And this combination of masculine and feminine energy often adds up to his being AC/DC in his sexuality, too. It is thus fitting that his patron Mercury was called god of the crossroads – a sort of streetwise deity, metaphorically downtown with the lowdown. In this sprightly, somewhat sneaky god we see the Gemini character, often all too glaringly, perpetually involved in handshaking, wheely deal-making, and the like, communing at the most fundamental, intimate level of human *interaction.*

Combining the respective objective and subjective dynamics of the two previous signs, Gemini is the first individual in the zodiac to step out of a narrow, personalized view of existence, to thus focus on what's 'happening' outside himself and negotiate a field of experience. Indeed, he directs the flow of information (pure intelligence) every which way. As Mercury's glyph suggests, with hands outstretched and antennae attuned, the Twins guy is all about plugging into his *immediate surroundings,* just one in a seemingly endless string of attributes that fall into the Geminian 3rd Astrological House. The notion of *immediacy* is crucial to Gemini, both in terms of time and space. The quick and dirty: He wants what he wants, here and now – lack of patience and long-range planning are typically his biggest pitfalls. Still, he is the first bright–lights–big–city thinker to come down the astrological pike, and as such, he embodies a scrappy, street-survivalist stance. He is notoriously clever, able to anticipate people's needs and moves, smoothly steering situations to his best advantage. It is no accident that Mercury is the god of merchants and of thieves; as well, it was his responsibility to conduct each departing soul to Hades. Suffice it to say that the Twins guy tends to have his own underworld connections. He would: The 3rd House rules *guilds, gangs, fraternities,* and other such *localized organizations,* in addition to *immediate family* and *close intimates.* On one level, Gemini places strong emphasis on the role of actual kith and kin in his life. But it also determines that he nurture a 'family of friends' — a small network, or band of brothers, on whom he can rely for both affection and support.

His 3rd House concern with *the immediate* not only manifests as his urge for instant gratification — constant stimulation, information, having to be at the hub of excitement — it also surfaces as an overwhelming need to experience life in the 'hood. This small-orbit lifestyle demands being surrounded by a steady troupe of cronies — if not a regular roster of homies whose ranks rarely change — not to mention a steady pool of easily accessible female playmates. Herein we see one startling aspect of his sign's correspondence to the ages 14–21: All his life, Gemini smacks of teen spirit, evidenced especially by his somewhat anxious attitude toward romance and sexuality. Like some school-yard Romeo, he's continually perfecting his spiel, his well-rehearsed sales pitch — engaging in elaborate though ingenious courtship rituals and constantly gauging his prowess against his inner circle of *boon companions* (literally, 'goodfellows'), such relationships also falling under 3rd House rulership. Gemini guy lives in a world contingent upon male pecking orders; and typically he's at the top of the heap — indeed, he tends to only associate with guys whom he can boss around. When it comes to the opposite sex, life is like some eternal high-school dance, a central, essential field of activity defined by the negotiating of friendly business and an outsized preoccupation with sexual hooking-up. Indeed, in the Geminian existence, manly worth is, in no small way, determined by the caliber of arm candy one manages to cart around. Just as Taurus guy can be a real boudoir gigolo, the proverbial midnight cowboy, Gemini is a presentable daytime escort, a paparazzi-ready playboy. He is easily impressed, generally overexcited, and often embarrassed by his sexual exploits, one moment bragging to his buddies, the next, sheepishly avoiding the subject. It is the process of courtship that thrills him most — playing the field, that mutable range of immediate experience — just as he revels at being a mercurial character in business. Whatever his career, Gemini tends to act the upstart, exhibiting a certain juvenile disregard for existing rules, riding roughshod over superiors, either gaining a reputation as a creative free spirit or a renegade to

PLANETARY SYMBOL

The glyph of Mercury recalls the winged-capped god himself as well as the caduceus, the wand he carries that represents the dualistic nature of life, two serpents wound round a single staff. The 'antennae' of the symbol signify the emergence of the human mind from the integration of divine (circle) and earthly (cross) forces.

SIGN QUADRANT

The zodiacal quadrants correspond to metaphysical planes of existence – physical, mental, emotional, and spiritual. The First Quadrant is that of the self and personal experience. For Gemini man, importance lies in his need to commune and communicate with small circles of friends and associates. The interchange of information and commercial dealings are paramount.

SIGN GLYPH

The Gemini emblem portrays the understanding of duality – pairs of opposites as the dynamic of all experience. The twins represent the divine (soul) and mortal (body) parts of the self, which must be negotiated via human consciousness (mind).

be rousted. He simply can't do a job by rote, feeling compelled to shake it up and fly by the seat of his pants, surviving by his wits and living on nerve. This may be a direct result of Mercury's rule over the body's central nervous system. Inhabiting such a small sphere, Gemini necessarily becomes expert at honing his tricks and questionable tactics so as not to interfere with his reputation; at least that is his hope. Mercury is also the patron of jugglers, jokers, and magicians, and Gemini is guided by that god's tricky shtick.

Just as in biblical analogy Aries guy personifies Adamic big-bang creation, and Taurus, Edenic earthly delight, Gemini corresponds to that precise moment in the Bible's Book of Genesis when, biting into the apple, the notion of duality is born. On the most essential level, Gemini is aware of himself and his metaphoric nakedness, his visibility in the world, just as he is prone to focus on all the naughty-and-nice bits about everybody else. The sign of Gemini personifies the knowledge of good and evil; and indeed, every pair of ideological opposites that exists under the sun. He is pure, unadulterated consciousness tuned in and turned up to full throttle. Talk about living at the crossroads: The whole of the Gemini male experience is a process of synthesizing what appears to be a world of inherent disparity. Thus, he seems to be firing from double barrels, expressing contrasting and conflicting sentiments. He can be, at hairpin turns, the friendliest and fiercest character on the astrological block: Smiling one second, sneering the next, Gemini man swings between emotional extremes so quickly that he seems to be one big mixed message. As the only mutable-air sign in astrology, he is changeable on the intellectual and social planes – as a male aligned with the masculine gender-polarity of his sign, he not only embodies black-and-white duality, but every shade of gray in between. In light of Gemini's Twins symbol, the sign itself can be viewed as representative of the world as a system based on the pairings of opposites – the guy of the sign is *both* sides of every coin, simultaneously, while the Gemini gal is *either* one way or another depending on which way the wind takes her. He, thus, possesses a 'multiple' personality, while she has a 'split' one; and, as such, he might strive to establish more boundaries in life, while she typically works for resolve and synthesis.

Gemini is a tough nut to crack: Like a hormonally raging teen, he's a bundle of raw energy. Being so vividly mercurial, he may be the most difficult sign to understand, and though his exuberance makes him easy to love, he's oft considered the hardest to trust. In a relationship with Gemini, the rules change constantly, as freely as the breeze blows – one second balmy, the next kicking up a storm. Employing the biblical analogy that sees the knowledge of duality (good and evil) as synonymous with being cast out of the proverbial garden with all its blissful ignorance, Gemini is employing every fiber of himself, scrambling to survive in the world any which way he can. To him, existence is chaos, a free-for-all, with no rules except one: every man for himself. That is the crux of the story of Cain and Abel (each of whom is curiously purported to have had a twin sister), thematically based, as it is, on their fending for themselves in the wilderness. As well, not living in Edenic grace like Taurus, who forgoes much in the way of Geminian self-awareness for blissful ignorance, Gemini nonetheless sees himself as an underdog. And even when born with a silver spoon in his mouth, Gemini might be overshadowed by circumstances or other siblings – whatever the case, he feels that he must therefore *make* good in life. And he usually does so, first and foremost, by creating a bit of a buzz about himself, as any self-respecting native of this mutable-air sign should, relying on bravado where pure bravery doesn't exist, employing a bit of Mercury's merry-trickster affectation and artifice, in short, putting on a very good show.

In literature, the character of Robin Hood is Geminian from the get-go: First, the legendary figure is the mythic Robin Goodfellow or Puck (Irish: Pooka), who is a male sprite, fairy, a versatile creature of the air, indeed, the medieval incarnation of Mercury–Hermes himself, sharing, as Oberon's gofer, in that god's role of messenger. As Robin of Sherwood, he is guardian (god) of thieves, tricksters, rogues, minstrels, wastrels, and all such disadvantaged underlings that make up his merry band of boon companions. What is the aptly named Hood's occupation? He is the original antihero, a good-guy gangster using the wrong means to the right end – stealing from the establishment to give ye olde folks in 'da hood' the goods. Fonzie, of 1970s TV land, is the pop-culture equivalent, a righteous hoodlum, locked so long into his teen years that his middle-aged ass got a bit too big for his Levi's jeans. The Fonz, remember, could never admit he was 'wrrr . . . wrrr . . . not right.' Ever disagree with a Gemini guy? It's the same story. He cannot be told he's mistaken, ever. And there's a deep-seated reason why: Gemini's personal belief system is the only solid element in his ever-changing world despite, as Geminian Paul Weller put it, his 'ever-changing moods.' Like Fonzie, he is not to be challenged – he's the boss, the top of the pecking order – and to question any of his tenets is tantamount to conspiring to dismantle his whole modus operandi. Gemini man exists on the power of his own positive thinking, fondly subscribing to his own spin and hype. Undo one of his carefully crafted credos and you threaten to unravel all he's built up to house and protect him from what he perceives as the cruel chaos of the world. Seeing the inherent duality in everything can be a bit maddening – if Gemini didn't adopt hard-and-fast prejudices, proverbial bottom lines, and emphatically reinforced rationalizations, he might second-guess every little thing he said and did.

ELEMENT + QUALITY

The air element signifies mental and social experience; the mutable quality, a call for versatility and change. Together, the mutable-air combination particular to Gemini is best illustrated as ether, static electricity, information, and pure consiousness.

POLARITY

Males in masculine signs
(fire, air) are aligned with the
gender polarity of their sign
and thus embody the
quality-element combination
of the sign. Gemini man is
like Adam having just bitten
that apple, a bastion of conscious perceptions and
buzzy ideas. He is a walking-
talking news bulletin, a
human Rolodex with myriad
connections, opinions, and
advice on all subjects.

Basically, it all comes down to an outsized fear of death. Yes, death. What this apple-eater carries with him in light of the dichotomous 'biggie' of them all is a consciousness of the opposite pairing of mortality and that slippery little bugger immortality. That is the price to be paid for consciousness, a theme emblazoned into the sign of Gemini as represented by the mythical Twins, Castor and Pollux — the celestial Dioscuri (sons of Zeus). Long story short: Their mother, the goddess Leda, had a mortal husband, Tyndareus, the king of Sparta, but she did it with Zeus while he was in the form of a swan. The lady lays two eggs, one with two mortal children, Castor and Clytemnestra, and another containing two immortals: Helen, of Troy fame, and Pollux. The boys are eternally entwined, together pointing to the duality of mortal and immortal being. When Castor falls at the battle of Troy — thanks a lot, Helen — Pollux strikes a bargain to share his immortality with his brother, living half the year in Olympus, and half (dead) in Hades. Gemini man would jump at the chance to swing this ultimate deal.

From the winged Mercury, to the air sprite Robin Goodfellow, to the egg-hatched twins that make up the symbol of this sign, the sign of Gemini is lousy with bird imagery. Our fine feathered friends are symbolic of the soul taking flight from the body — whether in death or in the achievement of immortality, which may or may not occur with death, or even in the simple expression of the soul's inspiration. Since Gemini can't bank on the first two, he sets his sights on the third option, trying to make his mark on the world as a means of being remembered, thus living forever in the hearts and minds of mankind. Why do you think this guy is constantly going full-stop? He's dancing as fast as he can in hope of effecting some semblance of eternal life, all the while whistling in the graveyard. Fittingly, Robin Hood isn't the only character winging around the Geminian male psyche in green tights: Peter Pan, and the complex that bears his name, lives on in the personality of this eternal fourteen-to-twenty-one-year-old, hell-bent, as he is, on not growing old. Like Hood, he's a daring gangster-ringleader, forever attempting to escape the proverbial Hook! But time has a way of creeping up on a person, leaving only one escape: Neverland (no time). And it is that very realization that sends Gemini in search of solace amongst the familiar 3rd House faces of his upbringing. So long as he keeps to the herd, he subconsciously hopes to avoid being picked off by predator death.

Gemini's goosey frame of mind finds its roots in his earliest childhood. The Twins guy tends to grow up in surroundings that appear stable but are usually anything but — his parents may remain married despite inhabiting completely different spheres, trotting out in a show of solidarity only for appearance's sake. So parental relations are and aren't 'a way' — the basic home atmosphere is thus dual from the get-go. Such an environment is static, in both senses of the word: It is stagnant and also fraught with nervous tension, an undercurrent of buzzy stress that sees the Gemini growing up with perpetual butterflies in his stomach. With parents often psychically too preoccupied with their own ongoing drama to be a supportive, loving presence — his father is typically off somewhere in his own Neverland, while mother is a strong but agitated figure who plays the disciplinarian with a rather iron fist — the Twins boy finds solace in the company of siblings and a slew of other males his age. Mother may make the mistake of complaining about her husband to her Geminian son, even sending him on spying missions to report back on Dad's doings. Gemini is the quintessential Mercurial go-between, his mother's scout but often his father's accomplice as well — delivering apologetic missives on one or the other's behalf. As a result, Gemini boy may learn to distrust other males in general, save for those in *his* gang, which *he* rules, often with that same iron fist he witnessed at home. He strives to please his mom, wanting most to win a 'good boy' pat on the head. With his father, Gemini eventually strikes the casual bargain of vague interaction, or formalized indifference. Life, he learns, doesn't give handouts. Still, ask any Gemini if he had a happy childhood — he'll answer in the affirmative. He doesn't know he's overcompensating, playing the big shot, the playboy, the operator, the ringleader, as a means of healing the hurt he feels inside for being all but ignored by those whose attention he sought most.

Body + Soul

Working the room with an edgy enthusiasm — shaking hands, kissing cheeks, polishing connections, generally running the show — is Gemini's usual role in a social setting. Just as he is famous for organizing outings with friends and colleagues, he is continually calling meetings in the workplace, perpetually aghast when associates don't work at his quicksilver pace. Professionally, too, he'll have his pack, a coterie of insiders whom he handpicks, hot shots who will follow his self-styled example and function in the same freewheeling way. Gemini's notorious street-smart mien can manifest in a number of ways. Typically, he plays the ultraslick and flashy urbanite. Sometimes he espouses a gritty inner-city chic; or when an artist or musician, he'll fully embrace the spirit of the street, adopting the look of the workingman with whom he so intrinsically identifies. A list of famous Gemini men, one that includes such

3

SIGN NUMBER

The number of circumstance. Events happen in threes, and all experience has a beginning, middle, and end. Gemini signifies the presence of a third-party perspective of knowing the difference between dual forces. Three is the number of life's cyclical nature, most clearly illustrated by the couple giving birth to a child.

14–21

The teen age: Geminis are eternal bachelors with a rat-pack mentality, based on birdlike pecking orders, and likewise steeped in courtship ritual. Often prankish if not punkish, the Gemini is generally a leader of a merry band of men. There is always something of the mischievous juvenile delinquent about him.

spritish, pointy-eared chaps as Errol Flynn, Johnny Depp, Mark Wahlberg, Michael J. Fox, Noah Wyle, Ian McKellen, Mike Myers, Gene Wilder, Jackie Mason, Donald 'Art of the Deal' Trump, Paul Weller, Boy George, Prince (or whatever), Paul McCartney, Lenny Kravitz, Bob Dylan, Noel Gallagher, Morrissey, and Allen Ginsberg, reveals eternally boyish characters shot through with nervous energy, intent on expressing it. Despite Gemini's size – even when tall, he's typically slight – it's his signature electric presence that one immediately senses.

Gemini definitely has style – he walks the walk (a snappy, bouncy gait that is at once youthful and confident) and talks the talk (a clear and deliberate form of speech, as if he's overpronouncing each and every syllable). Given his astrological placement as the mental (air) sign of the First Astrological Quadrant of Self, he is highly *self*-conscious and thus employs wardrobe and grooming habits to telegraph the image he wants most to project: that he's an in-the-loop character. Exceedingly fashion-conscious, if not painfully trendy, he opts for exclusively cosmopolitan looks that specifically suggest a *downtown* sensibility. His fashion taste, like his musical preferences, usually has its origins in inner-city experience: modish looks that have a hint of the street about them. More than anything, as the zodiac's mutable-air embodiment of ether, Gemini wants to look hip and 'happening,' providing visible evidence of his 3rd House association with of-the-moment awareness. His style will never be too prim or formal, even when the occasion strictly calls for it, as he wants to communicate that he is, in some way, a humble neighborhood figure who is never divorced from what might be called common experience or ethos. He is suspicious of bourgeois sensibilities and the people who espouse them, and he makes it a point in his physical expression to set himself apart from that sociological sector. So when other guys are in suits, he might be in some Fonzie variant of Levi's-and-leather, but you can bet that, piece for piece, his garments carry a heftier price tag than those of the stuffed shirts and suits surrounding him. And since, for him, time is of the essence, he'll typically sport a snazzy watch. His haircut is trendy, of-the-moment, and he opts for short, whimsically laddish coifs. And, perhaps due to Gemini's rule of the hands, this guy probably has a burning penchant for rings, forever flashing metallic reflections from his infamously gesticulating mitts. Also in Fonzie fashion, many Gemini males ride a motorbike or scooter, which guarantees this mercurial character will avoid traffic more readily than the rest of us.

As it is, he's naturally flashy. The Twins guy's face lights up like a beacon, shiny-skinned and full of color; the whites of his darting eyes sparkle, as do his typically pearly teeth, which beam from a nearly perpetual, impish grin. His movements are quick and choppy, fittingly like those of a bird, and his facial expressions flip in an instant from delight to disdain to downright indignance in reaction to whatever bit of information one's feeding him in the moment. His eyes, marked by a swath of crinkles from these constant responsive gymnastics, are typically dark and beady, and he tends to squint or blink them incessantly, like lenses set on a high shutter speed. His face is often quite round, sometimes appearing flat, like a plate, his cheekbones being more broad than high, and his hairline fairly low and childlike. His nose is almost always proportionate with his features, and he has a dramatic line to his lips, which, when parted, often reveal a set of squarish, gapped teeth that are dead center of his smile, as if he's been cleaved in two – a physical nod to his astrological duality, separate halves ever working toward cohesion. He is generally small-boned, shorter, slighter, and more aerodynamic than other males in his family; and yet, he holds himself in a puffed-up stance, often determined to improve his musculature, like some weedy teen forever attempting to put on mass. As befits his Mercurial nature, the Twins guy has a hard time sitting still. He dashes about a room adjusting lighting and temperature, changing music, offering snacks and refreshments, and jumping from one topic to another. 'What's that?' you'll hear him say if he has ducked out of the room momentarily, never wanting to miss a single shred of conversation, or the opportunity to offer a quip or a dig. He is the king of sarcasm and revels in setting others up for jabs and heckles – lightning quick with a one-liner – ironically giving himself away by smiling wildly or laughing before the butt of his joke even realizes he's taking the piss. Indeed, Gemini always looks as if he's up to something, even when he isn't. Holding his expression in a forced look of innocence, he'll smirk outright, only adding to his already puckish mien – large, pointed ears, arched brows, a small, sharp chin, and those trademark shifty, mischievous eyes. Like a teenager, he's up on the latest lingo and physical expressions gleaned from favorite TV characters or other media influences.

As befits his air-sprite status, Gemini is notoriously light on his feet and he shines in athletic pursuits that require quick thinking and wiry moves. Just as in his professional life, Gemini is fantastic at faking out an opponent in team sports like football, hockey, or rugby, wherein he is distinguished as a player who hits low and often employs the surprise tactics of a mosquito. Gemini is arguably the most energetic male in the zodiac, restive where Aries man is directive. His body, with its proportionately low degree of body fat, is built for speed. And he's blessed with a rather teenaged-appearing physique – a sinewy neck, squared but delicate shoulders with overpronounced blades, a lean and lithe torso bookended by strong, elongated lats, and a small stomach that may

PSYCHOLOGY

Gemini man can be an excitement addict. His thrill for deals and risk may give rise to lying, cheating, or other underhanded behavior. He is Machiavellian, maintaining that the end always justifies the means. Dual in character, he overrationalizes. He can be sexually immature, an eternal playboy with an often compulsive need for variety. He can suffer nervous complaints and inferiority complexes, overcome through the power of positive thinking.

ARCHETYPE + MYTH

Gemini personifies the mythical spirit beings of the air, primarily the winged Mercury. As the patron of merchants as well as thieves, Gemini draws upon that god's urbanity. Castor and Pollux, the Dioscuri or star gods who form the constellation of Gemini, are air creatures, too, hatched from eggs laid by Leda (who was laid by Zeus in swan form). Pollux is divine, Castor mortal. Wanting to stay together for eternity, they spend half the year in Olympus and half in Hades. Their story mirrors the Geminian condition, steeped as it is in sibling bonds, a mixture of heavenly and hellish experience, and marked by a burning desire to cheat death.

nonetheless be soft and exhibit tiny rolls of flesh when he sits or bends. He tends to boast powerful thighs and sturdy calves, his legs rippling as he darts about, endowing him with a low center of gravity, which appears offset by what seems a slightly oversized head on slight shoulders. This may be a physical manifestation of his sign's inherent mind-body disconnect, something that he tries so hard to meld. Generally, Gemini is not the most heartily endowed of males; rather, he tends toward painfully average in the penile department. It's the same story testicle-wise: not too big, not too small, just the right size to make the majority of Goldilockses out there feel right at home. In fact, just as it often becomes the Twins guy's goal to appeal as the perfect middle-of-the-road mix of strength and sensitivity, so, too, does his physicality present the perfect blend of opposites. Even the potential averageness of his package seems engineered to attract women who might be put off by either extreme. Indeed, this perfect physical proportionality allows the Gemini guy a great deal of bodily confidence. He can slip on a Speedo like nobody's business, never worrying that he's under- or overfilling it – either scenario being fodder for poolside sneers and snickers. The one area where physical size might be an issue are his hands and feet, which can sometimes be so disproportionately small as to make one wonder how he keeps from toppling over. As the consummate air sign, it's as if he doesn't require the grounding others do. But, on second look, you'll notice that what he might lack in bulk he makes up for in polish, always having, for instance, perfectly clipped, if not buffed, nails. Gemini is no dirty birdy: Typically obsessed with cleanliness, which he considers next to *good*liness, the Twins guy is spiffed to a sparkle, his face scrubbed, his hair coiffed and lacquered into place, his body spritzed (if not oversplashed) with cologne, his breath regularly reminted. Of any male, too, he's most likely to shave or wax his body hair, feeling most comfortable with a smooth teenagelike torso. In this way, Gemini signals to the population of would-be lovers that he's as far from some great unwashed character as a woman could hope for. He makes it clear there's nothing to be squeamish over – that she'll find him literally palatable should things progress to such a point.

Sex + Sexuality

In a nod to his 3rd House's rule of *awareness,* as well as his patron Mercury's omnipresent nature, Gemini's main concern is to be the most 'going on' of guys, sexually or otherwise. With his keen antennae, this two-way radio of a man is always picking up a woman's signals, then instantly telegraphing the desired feedback, releasing information tailored to meet with her approval. On a larger scale, he's sending more sweeping messages as well, signaling sexual interest by flirting and posing, making a visible show, if not an outright spectacle, of his affections. He works to perfect his suitor's delivery, honing his words and gestures, reveling in the happenstance surrounding the securing of a mate or even an evening's date. Indeed, he creates an exciting environment, that mutable field, around the advent of what he hopes will be literal *intercourse,* as opposed to objectively professing interest like Aries or subjectively inviting it like Taurus. The Geminian character, who sees life as an eternal crossroads, focuses on the proper setting wherein he and a woman might literally intersect. He is a master of mood, employing lighting, music, and other such atmospheric accoutrements to provide fertile ground for romance to blossom. Of any sign, Gemini is the consummate lad with the swinging bachelor pad, replete with the coolest furnishings, a killer home-entertainment center, bar, and a bed, which often has some novelty aspect to it. Put it this way: If any guy were to have a vintage waterbed or a rotating circular bed or one housed in a giant Lucite martini glass, it would be our groovy Twins guy. He'll light candles, lubricate a would-be lover with liquor, even present her with a couple of thoughtful gifties, so long as it will help to clinch the deal. Everything *about* him says he's the slickest bachelor, the perfect date, if not the ultimate mate. Funny and fitting, too, that Geminis are the zodiac's birds, sons of the Twins laid by Leda, who was herself laid by swan Zeus. For we see him behaving similarly to a male bird of paradise, hell-bent on dazzling a female with elaborate displays: Chatting and gesturing, puffing himself up, he suggests an ability to provide an exciting and colorful life. Gemini communicates his prowess and passion in the same multimedia fashion – through sound and sense, spoken word, music, special effects – as in any bird's ritual courtship presentations. Like his winged friends, the Gemini fellow believes that the male who puts on the best show wins. He wants to be thought of as fun. And he's certainly not above fabrication to that much further feather a potential love nest: As if he didn't have enough to do, Mercury is not only the god of jesters and clowns but also of liars and cheats – a deific blend of nice and naughty qualities as befits a ruler of this dual sign. And like this god who slips so easily between Olympus and the underworld, Gemini inhabits at least two worlds at once. He is a living testament to the coexistence of life's disparate planes of existence. In brass tacks: No matter how squeaky choirboy a *neighborhood* character he appears, he often has more experience with life's shadier dealings than most males. It's part of his appeal to have an edge, an ever-so-slight aura of danger about him – just enough to impress the chicks. The Gemini believes

BIBLE + LITERATURE

Gemini is associated with consciousness and the duality arising from the biblical Fall. Life for the Gemini is lived outside Eden, in the 'wilderness' where a street-survivalist stance is required. The story of Cain and Abel, both of whom had twin sisters, details the origin of dual-natured humanity. Shakespeare's Puck is the medieval Mercury, messenger to the Fairy King. Called Robin Goodfellow, he is the precursor of Robin Hood, who did bad things for good reasons. Peter Pan is likewise a rogue hero with a dual nature, determined to keep the shadow side of himself all sewn up and to never grow up.

that 'thoughts have wings,' and he is a master of letting his personal notions fly, thereby creating a buzz about himself.

With a typically open-door dating policy effected quite early in life, he's forever toting a different type around on his Geminian-ruled arm, no doubt scratching après-sex notations next to her name in some form or another of a little black book. So cunning is he that, with a word or mischievous glint, this little devil, as his Mercury glyph suggests, can send shivers racing up and down a girl's spine. Like magic, he'll parlay the slightest possibility of erotic interaction into an ecstatic reality – even when a girl might originally be dead set against it. Such is the power of the Geminian sleight of hand: By creating an atmosphere of excitement, many a rocking female will go out with the zodiac's artful dodger on the sheer impulse that an evening out with him promises to be fun. He seems happy and shiny, not at all a wolf or snake in the grass to guard against. But astrology's firstborn son of Mercury inherits his patron's hocus-pocus to such an extent that the little scamp inevitably scams his way into a woman's drawers, if not her heart, when she least expects it. He possesses such verve, and quite a bit of nerve, making his move with incredible speed. Caught unawares, a woman feels no harm in giving over to kissing this lovable rogue with whom the mere idea of sex seems more like light confection than it does serious invasion. This is what Gemini hopes. Especially if he has lured her back to his lair, that tender trap where he can fully play his hand. Combined facility and elfin quickness will see him slipping a woman out of her dress in no time – indeed, there isn't a guy in the zodiac who can go from zero to sixty-nine faster than he.

Variety is certainly the spice of Gemini's life. Indeed, the mutable quality of his sign sees him adapting, dating women from seemingly every walk of life. To this Mercury-ruled guy, with his tiny orbit, it is indeed a small world after all. Another reason why so many men of this sign make haste to the bright lights and big city as soon as they can – there, he is guaranteed a plethora of pusillanimous pulchritude that he can thus overpower. Indeed, when playing the dating game, Gemini often goes for pushovers who are at once more likely to guarantee him a good time while guarding against his falling in love. He is that eternal teen, remember, who forever credits a date on the basis of her being easy and thus, nonthreatening to his bachelor status. He wants to have fun and not work too hard when playing the field; and the airier the head a girl has, the more amusement he'll have messing with it, not to mention coaxing it to perform its namesake act. Let's just say that the zodiac's sneaky operator is always looking for an opening. Once our little Mercury has sexually gone 'around the world' enough times – or at least bedded his way through as many ethnic neighborhoods as his local city will allow – our 3rd House lad, being thus tied to his *familiar surroundings,* will ultimately seek to permanently bond with a lass of his own social species.

When Gemini mates, it is typically like some chatty magpie, for life and with a bird of his same feather. It is eerie, actually, just how vividly this dynamic will play out as the Twins guy is distinguished in the zodiac for settling down with his, well, *twin,* a female carbon copy of himself – the Bonnie to his Clyde if not the Jeckle to his Heckle (remember those witty cartoon magpie tricksters?) – a clever partner in crime who would make his merry gangster-prankster patron Mercury proud. For all the airheads he's screwed with, Gemini's main squeeze must be intelligent; he is truly respectful of a woman's mind, at least one who wouldn't fall for his usual tricks. The 3rd House also rules *side-by-side* and *sibling* relationships, so the Twins guy doesn't meld into a ball of oneness with his mate as does Taurus, who precedes him on the wheel; rather he remains pointedly separate from the righteous sister of his choosing, seeing himself and his loving clone as dividing and conquering in the world together, covering more bases in their shared struggle for survival. Both Gemini and Sagittarius men, who share a zodiacal axis, being so-called 'opposite' signs (actually they are sort of octaves of each other, concerned with similar astrological experience on different scales), have a similar cloning aspect to their relationships, Gemini looking for an already existing twin while Sag fuses with a partner into a sort of third entity, typically assimilating a mate, transforming her into a likeness of himself. Gemini indeed looks for a girl with a similar upbringing to his own or one from the same geographical location or social stratum. He prizes personal class over the culturally assigned highfalutin variety – the kind money can't buy – seeking the sort of streetwise nobility that comes from living by one's wits, cherishing that kind of hearty spiritedness in a woman, a folksy sophistication that might have characterized a heroine in a twentieth-century Depression-era, wartime Hollywood film.

When the Goodfellow falls in love, he expresses his emotions by adopting a big-brother bearing, breeding that all-important familiarity between him and a would-be mate, becoming an immediate fixture and shoulder to lean on. He makes a woman feel as if she's known him all her life. And before you can say two-car garage, she might find herself being heaved over the threshold. He really pours it on, adjusting his signature affects away from presenting that swinging-single persona to painting a picture of sure-bet relationship material and family man. As such, he schmoozes her brood just as he will whisk her back to his own family homestead – the Gemini courtship ritual, as it is geared toward matrimony, entails a goodly amount of Sunday dinners. In his quest for

KEY WORDS

community
multiplicity
ubiquity
commerce
urbanity
ingenuity
whimsy
courtship
stimulation
contradiction
exploitation
savvy
fellowship
mentality
display
readiness
amusement
commotion
transaction
versatility
polish
pettiness
geniality
spontaneity
connection
transmission
artfulness
trickery
information
legerdemain
adaptability
versatility
change
eloquence
camaraderie
expression
alacrity
bravado
thought
curiosity
cunning
poetry
activity
experience
speed

a mate, there is an unspoken desire to achieve a solidarity of vision that, he's loath to admit, Gemini's parents never shared. However he does seek the personal space and freedom they did enjoy. Ah, wilderness: In the dog-eat-dog world where our antediluvian Twins guy 'lives,' he is hell-bent on establishing a secure nest to weather the gathering storm that is his view of existence – indeed, the mutable-air sign of Gemini is akin to the staticky, unpredictable atmosphere of ungodly human roguery that necessitated the biblical flood represented by the succeeding cardinal-water sign of Cancer – and he and his lifemate must man their separate battle stations, all hands on deck, battening down the hatches. To Gemini, the odds are always at least halfway stacked against him. For his part he still focuses on appearing the compromised local boy who nonetheless *makes* good. He promises to be nose-to-the-grindstone, a real worker bee, projecting this image to the world, happily embracing his humblest beginnings while building a 'better' life for himself, an attitude that will define his MO even when promoted to CEO. Although, being too much the buzzy drone often sees him typecast into that role and thus overlooked for professional advancement. Yet, even when Gemini comes from buckets of money, silver spoon stuffed down his gullet, he often dresses in ratty clothes as a youth to dispel any stigma, and it later becomes an obsession to machete his own path through life's jungle and thus emerge a self-made man.

Nothing is more important to Gemini than garnering respect for his of-the-people persona, especially from his partner, who should applaud his Robin Hoodiness. To his mind, she must be a bastion of moral goody-goodiness, just what one expects from a little sister. His own Maid Marian must support his swashbuckling worldly endeavors, appreciating his attempts to make the world a better place, particularly for her, though not always by employing the most aboveboard means. Like Mr. Hood or his cartoon equivalent Underdog, whose own Marian is sweet Polly Purebread, Gemini man has a you-and-me-against-the-world attitude in relationships. He is an insular character from the get-go, but his partnerships reinforce this dynamic all the more. Surviving by his wits in the wilds of the world often necessitates our own underdog employing the more swindling aspects of his hoodier self. Gemini is Machiavellian to the core, and making good often means playing by the rules of the streets. Thus he endows his mate with all the homespun goodly qualities he feels he's fighting the good fight for. Not the quixotic knight that Aries is, questing after high ideals while keeping women on a pedestal as an emblem of lofty virtue, the Geminian rogue isn't so blind in his romantic ambitions. Rather he sees his wife or lover as a flesh-and-blood helpmate whom he simply wants to portion off from the harsher realities of life he feels are his duty as a man to wade through. The world is a dualistic place to his mind, remember, so while he deals daily in the den of thieves, he hopes his partner will stake out their caravan of dreams, preferably via the use of picket fencing or the modern equivalent as might suit his modish bungalow or sleek, terraced apartment. Such is the level of Gemini's taste and aspirations, superchic yet modest and unassuming.

Gemini is generally not chauvinistic; actually, he tends to consider women a whole lot smarter than men. Still, he believes the fairer sex should be protected from the world, which, as he sees it, is rife with evils; and the more he runs interference and deals with the dirty work of existence, the more payoff he hopes to garner and bring back to feather and indeed decorate the nest. Goodies are important to the zodiac's Goodfellow, and just as he decks himself out in spanking new fashions, so, too, does he like to see his wife dressed to the nines – he sometimes buys them matching outfits – and kits out his home as best he can. Again, he isn't into opulence, rather he has a modish, trendy aesthetic that he might gain pleasure in achieving through a bit of DIY. No matter his age, Gemini prides himself on being part of a hip, happening couple. He may actually insist upon picking out his wife's clothes, ensuring that she will be costumed in a manner that suits him, such that the necessarily staged production that is their relationship will appear seamlessly designed. Though he encourages his mate to work – two incomes are always welcome in the Twins's household – he will nonetheless be adamant about having children (he'll pick their clothes out, too, to match) and, most importantly, he'll want to have them young, which always makes for prettier photo greeting cards. Being seen as the callow, sexy, procreative couple is fairly crucial to the Gemini, who can't help but contemplate and therefore manipulate the public relations image he and his perpetually put out.

Being the zodiac's original excitement addict, the Twins man needs to make a splash in tandem with his partner. He prethinks how they'll look together, say, arriving at a party, appreciating, without pushing the issue, if all eyes are on them. It's not a question of vanity, but a matter of kick, that all-important Geminian electricity coursing through his sign-ruled nervous system. He and his partner of choice will be sociable in the extreme, attending parties, frequenting cafés, clubs, and restaurants known for being a 'scene.' As a couple, he and his mate, for lack of a better word, *date* other couples, 'going steady' in foursomes with the Gemini typically playing ringleader, guiding his merry band through mini-bacchanals, going slightly out of bounds in partying, just enough so that emotions run high – laughs becoming more riotous, run-ins more dramatic, and flirtations more frequent and acceptable.

Joe Namath
Ian Fleming
Bob Hope
Maurice Sendak
Richard Thomas
Morgan Freeman
John C. Reilly
Alfred Molina
Jacques Cousteau
Jerry Stiller
Allen Ginsberg
Henry Kissinger
John F. Kennedy
Jean-Paul Sartre
Ian McEwan
Ian McKellan
Denholm Elliot
Vincent Price
Jim Broadbent
Laurence Olivier
Barry Manilow
Martin Landau
Clint Eastwood
Bjorn Borg
Jim Thorpe
Johnny Weissmuller
John Wayne
S. I. Newhouse
Bill Moyers
Igor Stravinsky
Frank Lloyd Wright
Ellsworth Kelly
Jean Tinguely
Herman Wouk
William Styron
M. Scott Peck
Norman Vincent Peale
Alexander Pope
Thomas Hardy
R. W. Emerson
Walt Whitman
W. B. Yeats
Paul Gauguin
Dashiell Hammet
Al Jolson
Frank Oz
Tommy Chong
Liam Neeson
Danny Elfman
Christo

BODY RULERSHIP

Gemini rules the central nervous system, the lungs and respiratory system, arms and hands, chest, shoulders and shoulder blades – the wings. Mercury rules the brain, sensory organs, reflexes, and the thyroid, which controls metabolism. The planet also governs physical changes and the growth and development of intelligence.

He might squeeze the other lady's leg under the table, reinforcing the fact that, even though he's married, it doesn't mean Peter Pan is six feet under. He chats up the waitress, the coat-check girl, the busboy, whoever strikes his fancy at any given time. His mate will be the one to roll her eyes, full aware that her winky man is eternally steeped in that teenage sort of courtship ritual. She may or may not be so forgiving of his more infamous dalliances.

The Twins guy often can't help but seek the thrill that potential sexual triumphs provide. Flirting affords an escape valve, but only to a point. As such, many a Gemini will forgo channeling his obsession with immortality into procreation and instead attempt to remain forever young, playing the dating game until he seems, well, dated. Think Austin Powers (not to mention his twin, Dr. Evil). As is more typical, the ubiquitous son of Mercury will seek to cover all the bases, bringing up babies while still cruising the babes. Sometimes the siblinglike aspect in his relationship manifests all too literally, and he'll view his sister-wife as a sainted figure, seeking to preserve the good in his mate – the maid in Marian, the pure in Purebread – to the extent that the relationship will be all but sexless. In such a case, he may use his partner's beneficence as a bargaining chip, playing the part of the lovable schlub who doesn't deserve so good a woman; being, like poor Castor, 'only human' in his failings, which might easily include slipping the salami to some other girl. This is, after all, the danger of life lived in the concrete jungle – sometimes one succumbs to its vices – but, he convinces himself, putting himself out there is how he can provide for his family. Our multiplicitous Twins man can *rationalize* anything, his usual disclaimer being something along the lines of 'I love her, but I got needs.' Indeed, he may feel he's doing his mate a favor, not subjecting her to his more lewd longings. Though this is an extreme case, most Goodfellows make a definite split between what they would do in bed with their sister-woman and what they'd get up to with some *goomah*.

When it comes to sex, Gemini consciously considers what it takes to be good in bed. He isn't going on pure animal instinct like Aries, or satisfied with pure sensation as is Taurus. Instead, the Twins guy uses his head. And nobody is better with his hands. As befits his planet's rule of communication, Gemini is not just a cunning linguist, his oral skill extends to the bedroom as well. If speed is the aim, no guy can get a girl off quicker, so long as we're speaking strictly of clitoral stimulation as a vehicle to orgasm. For it takes a sexually seasoned Gemini to sustain his signature fast and furious pace when it comes to plain old fucking around. But knowledge is power, and the Twins will actually make it his mission to overcome any carnal shortcomings. As it is, this original power-house of positive thinking is famous for looking in the mirror and giving himself verbal pep talks of the rah-rah variety (not only when gearing up for sex but also in other instances, such as when warming up for an interview or business presentation). In all arenas, what he lacks in true confidence he'll make up for in bravado, which translates into putting on the air of a powerful, badass stud, employing that much more talk than action – telling a woman how he plans to ransack her while working his foreplay magic, using those sign-ruled hands during intercourse to bolster the excitement and quicken a woman's pace to match his signature own. He'll twiddle, squeeze, bite, pinch, lick, and blow while poking, providing a woman with the feel of a full-body climax, no pale substitute, in the end, for a straight-on plowing. In some cases he may seek to overcome a sense of sexual inferiority through dominant role-play, a soupçon of which is all it takes to impart a major thrill to the Twins, whose trademark fantasy involves subjecting women to compromising, but rarely all-out-humiliating, positions. Think *The Story of O* via Disney.

For the Gemini male, sex must always, first and foremost, be fun. Like a terrier, he'll root out every corner of a female's fantasy life, urging her to admit, and submit to, her kinkiest longings. He thrives on experimentation and detests routine. Indeed, variety of experience, if not partners, is Gemini's most pressing penchant. At even the slightest show of interest from a female, he has a hard time keeping it in his pants despite long-term commitment. It's the breach in his dual nature he finds most difficult to broach. In extreme cases, sexual compulsion provides death-defying thrills, and with each *petite mort* he feels all the more alive. His penny-bright appearance often belies an if-just-slightly-sleazier sex life, the curse of his sign's inherent burning curiosity that drives him to experience all that human sexual behavior has to offer. At least once; as he's rarely one to get locked into anything too depraved. He has a weakness for high-class hookers who don't mind going around looking like they've just stepped out of the pages of *Penthouse*. Just as that magazine is distinguished from *Playboy*, with its solo layouts, by portraying couples going at it, so, too, does Gemini have a wee voyeuristic streak. Moreover, he is specifically turned on by the idea of tag-teaming a female with another fellow, just so long as he needn't play second banana. Puns aside, he'd like to be both director and featured actor. It's an in-your-face manifestation of his Castor-Pollux complex to be sure, that myth at once treating the Geminian themes of siblings and boon companions while flirting ever so slightly with homo-eroticism. In such a fantasy there is as much a thrill imparted by overwhelming the woman with two sets of everything as there is being partnered with another guy in the process. In a sense, Gemini, in directing the action, will vicariously participate through the other man just as he takes part himself, in a

STR8 TURN-ONS

small women
home girls
red heads
hour glass figures
white panties
snake eyes
long legs
m-f-f threesomes
girl-on-girl porn
little boy role-play
high-class hookers
lite b + d
(active) oral
(active) humiliation
spanking
mind games
high heels
peep shows, striptease
g-strings, lingerie
manicured muffs
swinging, swapping
facials
lipstick, nail polish
tag-teaming

sense being the two of them. That certainly works as an antidote against feeling like not enough man in bed.

Ironically, Geminis have few insecurities surrounding their sexual identification. Usually aware of 'natural' homosexual feelings early in life, and perhaps part and parcel of being born under the neutral (bisexual or neutered) rule of the planet Mercury, he's willing to accept any duality within himself as just one more personal paradox. In fact, there's a strong bisexual streak in all straight Gemini men, if only a purely mental predisposition. When the Gemini does self-identify as gay, however, he generally chooses a partner as much on the basis of attraction as he does for cerebral stimulation. He is partnership-oriented in the extreme and seeks out a potential lover whom he feels will be capable of committing to a long-term relationship. Still, he'll require that all-important freedom, including those occasional peccadilloes. He's attracted to intellectuals, which raises one of the most misunderstood inferences regarding Gemini as a whole: Those born under the Twins are typically credited with being brainy in their own right when, in fact, it is a *need* to be stimulated mentally that characterizes the sign. But for the gay Gemini male, this inherent want is tantamount, as he often lives vicariously through his lover in this regard, content to know that mental faculties are being well represented within the relationship, without having to fatigue his own mind – he prefers to focus on fluffier creative and entertaining endeavors. The same dynamic applies to his ambition: Gay Gemini man wants a total mover-shaker, but doesn't necessarily feel obliged to be highly motivated himself. As long as achievement is also being covered by a lover in the relationship, he can look upon it as a done deal in his own life, indeed sharing in the accomplishment. This relegated way of thinking, whereby the Gemini includes the capabilities and interests of his partners under a larger, umbrella-shaped sphere of his own experience, is symptomatic of his own, often rampant, narcissism.

The gay Twins man seeks his soul mate in the literal, Platonic sense of a lover embodying his other half: someone without whom he cannot achieve wholeness in his life. There's a sense of Gemini and his lover having been hatched from the same egg: He goes for a guy his own age, and of approximately his same size and stature. And like his straight counterpart, he acts according to his astrological association with the 3rd House, gravitating toward men who come from a similar background or home environment. Nostalgic to the core, the past is a gay Gemini obsession – he needs to feel as if he 'comes from the same place' as a lover. Indeed, his ideal bonds are brotherly. This may explain why Geminis are notoriously relaxed about infidelity. More than most signs, he'll overlook a partner's sexual indiscretions, hoping, often against hope, that he'll be afforded that same slack should the right opportunity ever present itself. Generally he's not looking for side action anyway. Ironically, Gemini's liberal stance on sexual shenanigans outside his committed relationship really stems from the fact that he makes such deep bonds: If the Twins guy deigns to be tied down in the first place, it's because he feels so connected to his partner – to him something as *lite* and superficial as sex couldn't begin to shake the foundation of his profoundly loving feelings. For gay Gemini a quick fling is rarely something to sweat.

Gemini man thrives on fun and excitement, and being able to share a stirring social life with his lover is a crucial requirement for their success. Making a scene – being seen – and attending sophisticated gatherings with other gay male couples are his favorite forms of entertainment. His approach to life is playful, and he tends to assume the part of Peter Pan even more than his straight Twins counterpart. Gemini is painfully attracted to men who are equally youthful in countenance, as he relishes the envious glances and flirtatious come-ons that are flung in their shared direction. If his lover is up for it, nothing is more exciting than the prospect of a third male party to play with. And he especially enjoys indulging his more overt bottom fantasies, particularly if that feature is sorely lacking in his relationship. Often, because Gemini seeks out such a strong emotional bond, he may have sacrificed his purely sexual needs to achieve it, hooking up with a heartfelt lover who isn't as sexually experimental or adventurous as himself. Still, many a gay Gemini man enjoys a well-integrated sex life with an unwaveringly loving partner. Regardless of their erotic repertoire, affection will be a keynote – constant cooing, kissing, touching, as well as exhaustive foreplay routines, are must-haves for the gay Gemini.

But when the Twins does get itchy for sleazier scenarios, it usually centers on his penchant for pleasing: His primary fantasy is generally to become wholly subservient to a sexual badass – leather, boots, the whole kit and caboodle. This sexual dynamic is often the polar opposite of the emotional dynamic that manifests with a committed partner: If there's one thing Gemini guy cannot deal with in his waking life, it's authority. He simply won't be told what to do, or when to do it. Even when his partner is the real breadwinner, which is often, Gemini will revolt at any command that he perform even a single chore. His time is his own. Period. And he indulges himself in it, frequenting the gym if for no other reason than to enjoy the regular, daytime social scene it provides. Curious, too, that the amount of time Gemini spends 'working out' doesn't seem to translate to much ameliorative change in his body shape. At least his mouth would have gotten some exercise from gabbing

GAY TURN-ONS

bottoming
sugar daddies
hairy chests, legs
rough trade, bears
bikers, truckers
(passive) b + d
(passive) lite s + m
briefs, jockstraps
circle jerks
forced submission
clubs, private sex parties
goatees
nipple clamps, piercings
dirty talk/phone/cyber
gang-bang fantasies
group sex
(passive) rimming
swallowing
(passive) tea-bagging
slaving
leather, rubber, latex
lite scat
gay outings, cruises

away with his gym buddies or chatting up his personal trainer – whose real function is to pump up the Gemini's ego as much, if not more, than his muscles. Of course, other oral activities might also often present themselves in the sauna or steam room. In any case, it does seem that gay Gemini is 'between jobs' much of the time. However, even when in the throes of a thriving career he will retain a lot of freedom and incorporate leisure elements into his workweek. Life, Gemini teaches us, should never feel like a grind. And when in a relationship with a real mogul and raising eyebrows and ire from others who label him a bit of a freeloader, both he and his lover know there's more there than meets the eye: that having a Gemini in your life is like being automatically programmed every day with the latest news, gossip, information, trends – being plugged into the Mercury-ruled ether – which makes a person hip to what's happening. In this way, he is often a constant source of inspiration for anyone lucky enough to be his lover, giving his mate much in the way to move and shake about.

Couplings

Gemini Man / Aries Woman

They'll take a party approach to life. He's a rousing, robust sexual ride; she seems built for speed. A sordid one-night stand could fuse them as best friends. They're a liberated pair – threesomes are standard.

Gemini Man / Taurus Woman

Two extravagant individuals drawn to the promise of glamour the other offers. Life is a whirlwind; their every move is contingent on the current trend. In bed, he likes a quick fix; she favors more drawn-out sessions.

Gemini Man / Gemini Woman

Slick, innovative Geminis come together fast and furiously. At first, it's a blast – a social, sexual, creative whirlwind – but making a deeper commitment is challenging: He's restless; her disquiet increases.

Gemini Man / Cancer Woman

He's a man of action, a guy with great prospects. She's that someone who'll see him through struggles. Their rapport seems caustic – constant quipping calls for patience. In bed together, they constantly try new tricks.

Gemini Man / Leo Woman

They have so much in common: commitment to family, appetite for achievement, a love of lavish spending. Happily, they allow each other plenty of personal space. Sexual independence is often admissible as well.

Gemini Man / Virgo Woman

First impressions are deceiving: He seems perfect; she calls to mind mighty maternal figures from his past. But they're two fickle souls troubling to find a through-line; still, they enjoy plot twists along the way. Exotic sex is their asset.

Gemini Man / Libra Woman

There's a natural flow – an easy rhythm into which they fall, often forever. If one attempts to take the upper hand, their groove turns into a grind. Creative freedom is crucial. Sexual drama is alien to such cool characters – it's all about ease.

Gemini Man / Scorpio Woman

Living proof that chemical attraction exists: There's a tug too powerful to resist – pheromones are flying. Other aspects are less harmonious – ideologically, there's opposition. In the long run, their lust won't wane.

Gemini Man / Sagittarius Woman

She lives large; he invites such expansiveness, living vicariously. She believes his strengths offset her weaknesses. Sex is touchy-feely, with lots of flirtatious foreplay. She encourages his lewder tricks and touches.

Gemini Man / Capricorn Woman

Cap is a conquest for Gemini. For the Goat, he's a guilty pleasure in her otherwise serious existence. Still, they share an interest in all things au courant – fashion, news, culture. In bed, she takes control – he's not complaining.

Gemini Man / Aquarius Woman

Their only concern: pleasing each other. He's her ideal fling; she relishes the role of minx and mentor. Free-spiritedness creates a combined social and political consciousness. Sex is robust and randy.

Gemini Man / Pisces Woman

They share a classy, cosmopolitan sensibility, a worldliness that allows them to live large, beyond the status quo. A divide-and-conquer approach to career means they often make it big. In bed, she's a queen.

Gay

Gemini Man / Aries Man

Their effect on each other is visceral – the beginning of a total transformation. With dominant Aries, Gemini expresses his submissive side. Thriving on drama, life is heightened. Sexually, they're two halves of a whole.

Gemini Man / Taurus Man

Gemini's interest is primarily sexual; Taurus feels a profound emotional pull. When it works, life feels free and easy. Sexually, they click: Gemini plays slave to the big lug Taurean master; roles are also reversed.

Gemini Man / Gemini Man

The double-Twins bond smacks of boyhood romance – like the love between two naive campmates. They're all about style and trend. This duo is distinguished by youthful ebullience that outsiders find appealing.

Gemini Man / Cancer Man

Cancer has rare insight into the Geminian character; he's not put off by a slick veneer. Together, they find an emotional center. Over time, mutual caretaking becomes their raison d'être. Sex is dramatic, passionate.

Gemini Man ∫ Leo Man

These guys see great possibilities in getting together. Often, a bit of exploitation takes place. Leo is smitten with the tricky Twins guy, who seems to have no shortcomings. In bed, Gemini hankers for saucier sessions.

Gemini Man ∫ Virgo man

They're buzzed in each other's company – in a literal sense, partying is a preferred pastime. Both are prone to rage, so tempers will flare; sometimes, fights feel dangerous. Frequent time-outs are taken. In bed, they're boisterous.

Gemini Man ∫ Libra Man

These boys should agree to disagree. But a strong attraction exists: It's like going to bed with a best friend. Lively arguments lead to heated reconciliation sex. For both, fooling around should be fun, frisky.

Gemini Man ∫ Scorpio Man

Scorpio is subversive; Gemini is the happy, shiny creature who exists on the inside track of life. Often, this is simply a sex thing – the Twins entertains prostitution fantasies and stern Scorpio longs to enslave.

Gemini Man ∫ Sagittarius Man

Volatility is their shibboleth. Gemini's temperamental nature knows no bounds; the Archer is a fiercely fickle fellow. One or the other may be unwilling to commit. Still, at least for a few nights, this pairing is unparalleled.

Gemini Man ∫ Capricorn Man

Financial gain may inspire this twosome's togetherness. Little wonder tensions arise if resources dwindle. Taunting each other is a way to play – they call it quipping. Sex is 'dirty,' the kinkier the better.

Gemini Man ∫ Aquarius Man

Gemini's fantasy of being devoured by a big, bad man – Aquarius is the sometimes scary, 'supreme' sign of the zodiac. This is a dynamic and exhilarating ride for two intellectually inclined guys.

Gemini Man ∫ Pisces Man

Gemini is the 'little brother' to the Pisces mentor. The odd Fish guy will abuse such influence, reducing a green Gemini to mere minion. Sex is masterful, both an erotic work of art and a chance for Pisces to dominate.

Gemini Woman

the gift

Gemini woman rides a fine line between innate vulnerability and an aggressive need to assert her own agenda, both professionally and in her personal life. She is acutely aware of her feminine wiles, using them to her best advantage, often playing coy or precocious in order to disarm people and gain necessary ground. Indeed, no other female creates more of a stir; whether in expressing her signature outsized spirit in awesome displays of talent, or upsetting the proverbial apple cart in the trademark coups she's wont to launch, or both. Gemini is not a casual or even overly considerate character, easily claiming the title of nerviest creature in the zodiac – she's capable of achieving the greatest triumphs as well as causing the gravest trouble. She puts everything, and then some, into scoring any goal, embodying a take-no-prisoners attitude in each endeavor. Gemini is iconic, if not cyclonic: She leaves every circumstance, and indeed each individual, she encounters irrevocably altered in the wake of her presence. When it comes to relationships, she throws herself into situations out of an alternating need to indulge desire and impose dominance, letting herself be swept away by curiosity. At times, she will full-tilt flirt with disaster. Eventually, Gemini touches down and settles into an understanding bond in which she may safely swing between her two distinct personalities – helpless baby doll and ruthless boss. With other women, she is all the more imperious, drawn to doting lovers who will unquestioningly do her bidding, in public as well as in private.

★★★

The Principle of Awareness. Gemini is acutely cognizant of mental mechanics. Her motto is 'I think,' and she is a master at mind games, for the sake of her own amusement as well as putting the wheels of her success in motion. She consciously alternates between the two previous forces of (Arien) aggression and (Taurean) passivity, avenger and victim, to outwit others.

Sign + Mind

The sign of Gemini is ruled by the planet Mercury, which, like the messenger god of the crossroads (Greek: Hermes) for whom it's named, represents the zodiacal Principle of Consciousness and the 3rd House attributes of *commerce, communion* and *communication*. Ancient traditions likened him to the *logos,* or word of God, and thus he came to represent the 'pure intelligence' of the universe. It is fitting that Gemini is the first air (mental) sign of the zodiac, one for whom the cognitive faculty is key. One look at Gemini female and it's clear: She is a woman with much in the way of machinations going on in her mind. As her planet's glyph suggests, with its tiny feelers and antennae, Gemini is forever looking to 'put a bug' in someone's ear. Whereas Gemini man is caught up in his own need for buzz and stimulation, Gemini woman seeks to incite such excitement in others, if not send them into a complete frenzy. The Twins symbol is representative of the strict division between two distinct expressions of her personality, both of which emerge in the Gemini woman at different times in her life, if not within any given day. You might say Gemini guys are simultaneously *both* sides of their duality (and every point in between), while the Twins woman is *either* one extreme of herself or the other. On first introduction, she makes a clear-cut impression – but fittingly that's only half the story. When next one meets her, she may have made a complete switcheroo – being not just slightly altered, but completely opposite in demeanor. Gemini pours on her separate personalities as something of a defense mechanism. She can sit at a dinner party and, quite literally, turn a separate face to the guests seated to her right from that to those at her left. She's tough as leather or frilly as lace, depending on the way she perceives those around her and how they may be of use. If playing the guileless, giggly waif works to her best advantage, so be it – but if being the wickedest witch in the Western world is called for, she can pull that attitude out of her pointed hat faster than you can say 'my little pretty.' And though it will typically take a lifetime, Gemini works toward integrating these alternate sides of her rather borderline personality, often for the sake of her own mental health. For Gemini woman risks depersonalization, a condition characterized by a 'distortion in how one's self, and body feel,' as a result of splitting off into her signature separate characters, a predisposition that often surfaces full force during her early adolescence. But fear not: She will make it her existential mission to 'get herself together,' fostering increased integrity, in every sense of the word.

In biblical terms, the sign of Gemini is associated with dualism: Reality as perceived upon biting into the apple swiped from the tree of knowledge of good and evil. The zodiac's first (cardinal-fire) sign of Aries is likened to that of the big-bang Adamic creation, while the second (fixed-earth) Taurus is associated with garden-variety Edenic delight, which provided the perfect backdrop for temptation. Gemini, it follows, is all about munching on experience – *awareness* being another of the many traits associated with the Gemini 3rd Astrological House. Indeed, Twins of both sexes are like Adam and Eve made newly conscious of themselves and their *immediate surroundings,* yet another 3rd House concern. Gemini woman could be considered the embodiment of the two-faced Eve – a self-empowered-female-cum-troublemaking-temptress, or personal-fall-victim-cum-progenitor-of-humanity. To be sure, she is no walk in the park. Gemini is rarely the innocent she pretends to be. Even as a young girl, she's often attracted to older, slick, if not shady types on whom she develops killer crushes, seemingly seeking sweet corruption. Sometimes, like Eve, she's bitten off more than she can comfortably chew. Meanwhile, she turns around and tosses the apple at innocent guys whom she, in turn, might seduce into action. It's the same in business: She is often the consummate agent, holding 'prized' clients in the palm of her hand for others to fight over. Sometimes, she is that creative property herself, pitting people against one another for her talented participation. She can be both catalyst and monkey wrench, a dream come true or someone's worse nightmare. Whatever the case, she approaches life with an unapologetic 'deal with me' demeanor.

Gemini is the only zodiacal sign with the quality-element combination of mutable-air, air and fire signs being masculine from the zodiacal perspective. As a female in a masculine sign, therefore not aligned with the gender polarity of her sign, Gemini woman doesn't embody the mutable-air status, rather she projects it onto others, keeping them guessing if not initiating a flurry of disinformation in the process. As well, mutable-air signifies a versatile, changeable, or indeed random mentality, just as it denotes the Mercurial ether or ethos, a world of pure information, intelligence, and creed. Gemini guy is himself a walking-talking bit of this buzzy atmosphere, engaged in a constant exchange of ideas and dollars, wheeling and dealing his way through life, negotiating experience with the street-smart, swashbuckling piracy of Robin Hood or Peter Pan. The same cannot be said for Gemini woman: The world in which she lives is filled with people who must constantly negotiate *her.* Gemini is as unpredictable as a pixie – after all, she is the astrological daughter of winged Mercury, god of trickery and magic. Gemini woman's particular talent is to perplex, making people peg her as one thing only to shape-shift into another. If Gemini man is Peter Pan, she is the zodiac's Tinker Bell, that

PLANETARY SYMBOL

The glyph of Mercury recalls the fairies of medieval lore, whether kindly angels or pesky insects. These air sprites alter reality, whisper ideas in one's ear, and cause mischief, all of which the Gemini is generally guilty as charged. The 'antennae' signify the emergence of the human mind from the divine sphere: She can alternately soar to great heights or be the proverbial moth to a flame.

The zodiacal quadrants correspond to metaphysical planes of existence – physical, mental, emotional, and spiritual. The First Quadrant is that of the self and personal experience. For Gemini woman, importance lies in her ability to effect change in her intimate surroundings, whether by administering to the immediate concerns of a family life or career, or by promoting a certain *air* about herself that establishes an irresistible aura of attraction to her talents or ideas.

little brownie with the twinkly but maddening personality who is all sweetness and light when in love, but woe to any foe who might stand in her way – particularly those wholesome Wendys of the world for whom her heartthrob might throw her over. Like Tink's, Gemini's attempts at cruelty might come off as merely comical. Besides which, with her being so subtle a mischief maker, one is often hard-pressed to pin Gemini down as an out-and-out culprit of chaos. One must simply cope with whatever confusion she creates. This is, after all, what this mind-alterer is after.

Just as all humanity has dealt with the metaphoric fallout of Eve's actions, so, too, does every person with whom Gemini comes in contact have to alter (mutability) their own thoughts (air) to accommodate her. In Greek mythology, the goddess Eris (Discord), having not been invited to some divine soiree, gets even with the party planners by chucking an apple (what else?) into the proceedings, having scribbled upon it 'For the fairest goddess among you,' or some such provocative statement. Long story short: Athena, Hera, and Aphrodite all think the apple is for them. So they find this cute shepherd boy from Troy, called Paris, to decide; the goddesses bribe him with gifts: Athena offers wisdom, Hera promises wealth and power, and Aphrodite puts forth the most beautiful woman in the world, Helen (henceforth of Troy), whom Paris picks, instigating all-out war (Eris' ultimate goal to be sure). In terms of archetype, Gemini woman is Eris, just as she is the Eve of expulsion. To boot, she's all three of those über-goddesses as well. (As a mutable sign, Gemini seeks to negotiate and indeed integrate all the female energies that come before her in the two previous signs, personified by Athena, Hera, and Aphrodite, to be exact.) But it doesn't stop there: Gemini is most poignantly the living prototype of the victimy Helen herself; but no less so is she the personification of her vengeful twin sister, Clytemnestra.

As a mutable sign Gemini combines the energies of the two signs that precede it on the wheel (every third sign of the zodiac is mutable and does this, rounding out each of the astrological quadrants). In this case, Gemini combines the aggressive, objective, masculine force of Aries with the come-hither, subjective, feminine energy of Taurus. Aries is ruled by planet Mars, named for the war god, and Taurus by Venus, the goddess of love. Gemini combines these dualistic forces of love and war, poignantly personified in the character of Helen, for whom the love of various suitors presaged the Trojan War. Helen means 'torch,' something that every Greek hero carried for her, the metaphoric flame to which every Gemini woman, like a tiny moth, is drawn. Helen certainly flirted with danger and ultimate disaster as every Greek suitor for her hand in marriage swore an oath to protect her, no matter who was granted this sexy little gift as a wife. The sign of Gemini is associated with the age group 14–21, a time of courtship, which manifests in the Twins guy as elaborate ritual wooing displays akin to those of birds of paradise. Okay, time to tie all this into a neat little Geminian package: Not only is Gemini's archetypal Helen a mutable collage of the Aries and Taurus female prototypes, the ultimate gift bestowed to Paris, not to mention a little baggage needing to be negotiated and fought over, she is also part bird (flight being a symbol of immortality as Zeus fathered her in the form of a swan) and she is a twin, with a rather conniving female counterpart in her sister Clytemnestra, whose name just so happens to mean 'divine courtship.'

The mythical twins who make up the sign of Gemini are the brothers Castor and Pollux, not so much twins as they are quadruplets: Zeus wanted to sleep with the goddess Leda, who was married to a mortal king, and so he took on that swan guise. Nine months later Leda lays two eggs – in one are her mortal children, Castor and Clytemnestra, in the other are her divine kids, Pollux and Helen. That Castor is never mentioned in the same breath without Pollux, while hardly anyone associates Helen of Troy with Queen Clytemnestra of Greek tragedy fame, is terrifically telling when it comes to the respective natures of Gemini man and Gemini woman. The myth of Castor and Pollux is a story of struggle between mortality and immortality, and of the need to strike a bargain so that these inseparable brothers might remain together – all of which is mirrored in the Twins guy's psyche. When it comes to these twin girls, it is their division from one another, and indeed their diametrically opposed natures, that speak to the Gemini woman's condition: Helen is the consummate passive, the face that launched a thousand ships, while Clytemnestra is depicted as a violent plotter and killer of her husband, Agamemnon, whose own brother, Menelaus, is Helen's groom whom she dumped when ditching out of Greece with that pretty boy Paris. Taken together you have the Geminian female personality, the perfect amalgam of passive and aggressive: In the girl Twins of the zodiac, represented by Helen and Clytemnestra, we see yet another example of the combined mutable forces of subjective and objective realities.

The sign of Gemini, associated with that age group 14–21, is characterized by this stage in a girl's life when she is on a hormonal seesaw between the alternating duality of childhood and emerging adulthood. Meta-phorically speaking, the Twins girl is in a perpetual state (read: rage) of adolescence, well into her old age. (Hello, Joan Collins. See you soon, Sadie Frost.) She is an angst-ridden lady locked into a state of freshly awakening awareness, as if every circumstance is one of new, and therefore momentous,

SIGN GLYPH

The Geminian emblem stands for the duality of all experience and the ability to negotiate conflicting forces from an outside perspective. Whereas Gemini man is *both* sides of his dual nature simultaneously, Gemini woman is typically *either* sweet as pie *or* tough as leather, at any given time.

ELEMENT + QUALITY

The air element signifies mental and social experience; the mutable quality, a call for versatility and change. Together, the mutable-air combination particular to Gemini is best illustrated as the atmosphere surrounding each and every circumstance. Gemini woman seeks to effect situations, to create a certain buzz if not a commotion in promotion of her needs and desires.

import. She is acutely aware of experience, and yet she will never readily admit to being 'experienced' per se, particularly as concerns sex. The most apropos literary representation of the Twins brand of womanhood is embodied in the character Lolita, Vladimir Nabokov's provocative teen. Herein, we have a character smack-dab in the age group associated with the sign, hovering at the crux of maturity, the proverbial human crossroads of development from child into adulthood. Lolita is blatantly sexual, but she's still young enough to feign naïveté. That is Gemini woman, forever toying with that Mercurial crossroads, walking a perpetual fine line between vulnerability and perpetration. As such, she forces others to determine what the crux of her being is – in other words, to suss out the 'decisive factor' in her personality. Which isn't easy: Like Helen *and* Clytemnestra, the Gemini represents both triumph and trouble, and any association with her is steeped in such irony. Taking up with her is akin to kidnapping a killer: One must always negotiate Gemini's nearly diabolical diametrics. Consider such famous females of the sign as Judy Garland, Marilyn Monroe, Isadora Duncan, Josephine Baker, Sadie Frost, Kathleen Turner, La Toya Jackson, Angelina Jolie, Anne Heche, Stevie Nicks, Joan Collins, Wallis Simpson, Michelle Phillips, just to name a few of the Twins women known for being as potentially disturbing (to themselves if not to others) as they are creatively gifted. In business, Gemini is a bulldozer in barrettes. In love, she *is* Lolita, a cutesy diminutive form of the name Delores, meaning 'sorrow' – a seeming innocent who'll rip your soul to shreds as soon as look at you – a provocative pixie licking the proverbial lollipop all the while making a man wonder if she's staring at his crotch. She tears people, particularly men, in two: The dualistic character who lusts after Lolita is fittingly named Humbert Humbert. Unwittingly doing her bidding, he is part lecher, part lackey. Gemini woman possesses that same power of manipulation, a talent she began to hone at just around the same age as Lolita (that is, when readers first meet that wanton waif). Indeed, the adolescent Twins girl may become the living Nabokov nightmare for her parents, whose unfortunate reactions to their daughter set in motion the wheels of Gemini's personality polarization in the first place.

Like Gemini boy, the Twins girl grows up in a family where the father is the absolute ruler, albeit a practically nonparticipatory one. In fact, Gemini isn't much parented at all. Her mother is often caught up in her own life, involved in some business or study, if not struggling with emotional issues. There is little in the way of family ritual, and Gemini girl is left, in part, to her own devices. Rather than its fostering independence, the Twins girl feels overlooked. As a masculine sign, Gemini is naturally aligned to the ideologies and sentiments of her father, though she clashes with him, too. Often MIA, he is a covert character indulging in secret activity – many a Gemini's father is hiding an addiction or sexuality issue. With her mother, a sisterly relationship is engendered whereby a close emotional bond involves a good deal of bickering. In the spirit of role reversal, Gemini feels parental, if not sometimes a bit pitying toward her mother. On top of all this, the 3rd House rule of *brothers and sisters* becomes a keynote in Gemini girl's life, if not a thorn in her side. She never blames her parents for a lack of love. Instead, she points the finger at siblings, whom she cites as having caused her life to be less than idyllic. Gemini is one of those rare birds who could easily shove her fellow fledglings out of the nest. She wants every bit of her parents' attention, and when she doesn't get it, she lashes out – the quintessentially difficult teenager, Gemini might be in a nasty funk that lasts for years, as bitchy to other students as she is unbearable to other kids in her family. But all this bile is typically a mask to hide deep hurt.

Though Gemini embraces her father's sneaky modus operandi, her emerging lifestyle outside the family usually involves activities that her father would find unacceptable, especially when it comes to relationships with boys. Gemini's sexuality develops early, and she is drawn to older bad-boy rogue or hoodlum types. Indeed, in a nod to Gemini's air-sprite archetype, she can be, like Mercury orbiting closest to the sun, attracted to fiery situations, that moth to a flame. Thus she all too often gets burned. Her sign's association with visceral awareness manifests as an unquenchable curiosity, such that she is typically intrigued by people from the proverbial other side of the tracks. She may enter sexual relationships with characters her father would find unsavory – Dad is often blatantly biased, if not outright bigoted, a projection of his own repression. In this way, too, Gemini emerges as two people: the eternally dutiful daughter, and the naughty, sexually knowing ingenue. Unfortunately, her own needs often get overlooked in an effort to satisfy the expectations that she imagines are being projected onto her. As Gemini matures, she becomes something of a caretaker to her mother, specifically in the sense of doing her mother's *thinking,* affectionately bossing her around much in the way she witnessed her dictatorial father doing in the past. Emotionally, and indeed sexually, Gemini tends to shut down or, on the other side of the spectrum, act out in ways that could only be considered a cry for attention. In many cases, being 'trouble' is her way of getting back at the world for feeling robbed of tenderness. Appearing and acting provocative, the Geminian Lolita invites sexual attention, subconsciously hoping to fill the emotional void left from a lack of fatherly affection.

POLARITY

Females in masculine (fire, air) signs are not aligned with the gender polarity of their sign and thus enact instead of embody the quality-element combination of their sign. Whereas Gemini male is the mercurial mutable-air changeling caught up in his rapid-fire ideas and impressions, wheeling and dealing his way through life, the Gemini female instead plants ideas. An unseen spin-meister, she hatches plans that typically promote *herself* as a commodity.

3

SIGN NUMBER

The number of existence – past, present, and future – and the dimensionality of reality – length, width, and depth. Three also signifies the advent of the child off-spring, corresponding to Gemini's association with siblings. It is thus the number of procreativity and the renewal of life. Triangles and circles are both based on this numeral.

Body + Soul

A list of famous Gemini women includes such gorgeous gamines as the aforementioned Monroe, Collins, Garland, Baker, Hurley, et al., as well as the less controversial likes of such cheeky urchins as Kylie Minogue, Helena Bonham Carter, Natalie Portman, Courteney Cox, Isabella Rossellini, Jeanne Tripplehorn, Rosalind Russell, Paulette Goddard, Laurie Anderson, Annette Bening, Grace Mirabella, Gena Rowlands, Adrienne Barbeau, and Brooke Shields (who emerged as the advertising world's answer to Lolita). In fact, Gemini women are often the face that launches a thousand products – something about the Twins' particular brand of spritish beauty excites the general public. Gemini's representation, via Mercury, of the astrological principle of *commerce* herein becomes clear: She is bought and sold as a commercial product more often than any other woman. Think Helen of Troy, Marilyn Monroe, Judy Garland – divinely gifted commodities men haggle over and capitalize upon. Though an air sign, she is anything but ethereal; rather she seems to be an accessible pixie, fresh and wholesome but with a signature twinkle in her eye that suggests she can get up to a bit of mischief. She is the original ragamuffin. As a child she is the quintessential tomboy, looking every inch a guttersnipe as befits her planetary namesake Mercury's rule of the streets. As a teen, in the actual ages associated with her sign, she is provocative – sexually pointed toward males in a sea of shrinking innocents and giggling prudes, she is often seen as a fast, sexualized schoolgirl, all pigtails and cigarettes, busting her blouse buttons and aware of the power lurking beneath her pleated skirt. To other females she is edgy and challenging, just as soon kicking another girl's ass as trading clothes and gossip with her. The premier air sign, her mind develops earlier than others' making her the consummate ringleader. However, the innuendo she's wont to employ invariably goes over her peers' heads, urging bored, frustrated rollings of eyes and the seeking out of an older, 'quicker' crowd. All of these qualities are still in evidence in the adult Gemini, whose boyish body language and no-fuss, low-maintenance appearance only makes her beauty, and indeed her sexuality, all the more candid.

Gemini is a tough little bird, a typically pint-size woman who packs an enormous punch. Like a sparrow on the attack, the Twins female's sweet, unassuming appearance belies her capacity for sudden bursts of bellicosity. And like some teensy tweety, this babe can't sit still for a second – she fidgets and fusses, jumping in and out of her chair, dashing about, doing a handful of tasks simultaneously while making sure she doesn't miss one snippet of conversation

– that Mercury-ruled nervous system is forever on overload until she totally crashes, spent. Many a Gemini suffers from exhaustion nearly half of the time. That's why learning to conserve and pace herself is the most essential way to ameliorate her physical well-being. It's as if her body has a hard time keeping up with her rapid-fire mind, which leaps from one subject to the next – you hear it in her voice, which is breathy and often catches, a symptom of not respirating deeply, not speaking from her diaphragm – urging her in this direction, then in that. Talk about a short attention span: This girl is hard-pressed to focus on what is being said to her as every word out of anybody else's mouth immediately reminds her of the 40 million things she forgot to tell you or someone else, or meant to do, or needs to do, or plans to do, or – ahhhhhhhh! One word of counsel for Gemini woman: meditate. Of all the characters on the zodiacal wheel, the wound-tight Twins girl would most benefit from such a practice, one that is designed to still and soothe the mind, in turn helping her to sustain energy that is otherwise only issued in spurts. Of course, Gemini woman isn't always aware of the metaphysical origins of her innate nervousness; in fact, she tends to be the least self-analytical character in the astrological pantheon (and ironically, the one individual who could benefit most from a healthy dose of introspection). Gemini doesn't realize that she's two different people, mainly because she is only fully *one* at any given time – which can be most confusing for those with whom she comes into contact. As if suddenly thrust into a *Patty Duke Show* rerun, one may meet a clever and captivating conversationalist, only to be confronted with what seems like a brash and boisterous bubblehead in a future exchange. She'd be the perfect chameleon, if only she could consistently control when and how her changeling personalities came and went. For Gemini seems unable to stop her moods from swinging, experiencing spates of manic enthusiasm for life that are nonetheless followed by the deep, dark indigo blues.

Still, despite her vacillating psychological state, all eyes in the room tend to be on the Gemini woman. She's quite simply captivating, an irresistible mix of childlike beauty and expressive exuberance. She can be 'on' in a social milieu, matching her face which is typically beaming, her eyes bearing a lit-from-within sparkle. Her face is often round as a penny, her hair short and arranged like a frame around it – even when she keeps her 'do' long, she may opt for bangs as a fringe to set it off. She usually has apple cheeks, made all the more pronounced by eyes that are deep set and slanted, even squinty, and a delicate, if not a too weak, chin. Gemini's nose rescues her from too cutesy a countenance, being straight and pronounced, if not slightly beaky. As well, her ears can be a bit oversized and rather pointy and elfin. Her lips are usually luscious and look glossed without the

14–21
SIGN AGE ASSOCIATION

The age group of female sexual awakening. This is when most girls lose their virginity and discover the power of their own erotic nature. It is an age of curiosity, exploration, and incentive – a conscious desire to attract sexual partners. All her life, the Gemini personifies this inquisitive and experimental age.

PSYCHOLOGY

Dual-natured, Gemini is often passive-aggressive and may suffer from borderline personality disorders or even manic depression. Her craving for attention may see her using sex or troublemaking to gain notice. Prone to nervous exhaustion, Gemini may find stimulants to be her drug of choice.

slightest cosmetic application, her teeth pearly and perfectly straight. Gemini's neck is typically both short and delicate in the extreme – it may even give her trouble and necessitate strengthening through pointed exercise. Her shoulders and cervical spine are similarly fragile despite a tendency to hold herself in a tough and sturdy manner. Posture is often an issue for Gemini and, regardless of the fact she's generally petite, she may carry herself like someone quite tall, sloping her shoulders and dropping her sternum as if trying to appear smaller than she is – which she isn't. This crouched comportment is more a symptom of the emotional unrest that causes an actual caving in around her chest cavity. Her body may best be described as dumplinglike; though she's often slim due to a speedy metabolism, she is, still, naturally round and bouncy. Breasty as a rule, she has a tiny waist and voluptuous hips, ass, and thighs. Gemini's bottom half is worlds more sturdy then her daintily structured torso, and she may often complain of having chubby thighs and too bubbly a butt. Still, her calves and ankles are as finely boned as a finch's, and her feet and hands are quite small and childlike, a trait she shares with her Gemini brothers. Overall, the way she holds herself gives one the impression that she's really robust, if not a bit strapping, when in actual fact she's a physically tender creature. Her extrasensitive nipples are a source of great pleasure, evidenced by the way she often toys with them lavishly during sex. Her nether regions may not only be supertight, but rather shallow as well, which will make a guy who's not especially endowed feel somewhat more of a sexual giant than usual. Her skin is quite soft and supple – one pointed poke and she comes out in a bruise. And despite her spritelike semblance, she can be ever so slightly klutzy, forever bumping into the corners of kitchen cabinets in her signature haste, or walking headlong into a door she left open, having dashed off to do something else entirely. Even when draped in couture, there's still a hint of the awkward schoolgirl about her. For all her heaven-sent beauty, there persists in Gemini a raw and pleasantly unrefined quality – and she's far too much the gamine to ever completely pull off looking stately or glamorous; even Marilyn Monroe could never be considered truly elegant or sophisticated for all her golden-age screen idolization. Rather, an oomphy precociousness was her very appeal. Indeed, Gemini girl is a precarious sexual persona, an eternal Lolita forever teetering between erotic curiosity and total carnal abandon.

Sex + Sexuality

Whether drawing upon the Eve of expulsion, Helen, or Eris, Gemini woman is metaphorically endowed with a controversial character. Just as Helen's name translates to 'torch,' so does it carry the synonymous meanings of firebrand, hellion, agitator, ringleader, marplot, or provocateur, all of which are applicable to astrology's little Tinker Bell. But Gemini isn't conscious of this archetypal weight, at least not wholly so. As the zodiac's daughter of Mercury, she is perpetually lodged at his crossroads domain. Controversy, literally 'alternating directions,' is her birthright. The expression 'the girl can't help it' had to have been coined after a Twins. And when it comes to love, especially, our Gemini is bound to be star-crossed. Indeed, she is most definitely challenged in affairs of the heart; still, at the same time her experience of love is something many of us can only dream of.

Gemini girl storms the sexual arena, chewing on that apple, her mind newly awake to the myriad stimuli that electrify her sign-ruled nervous system. And just as eating the fruit of the tree of knowledge gave rise to understanding the world as a system of pairs of opposites (which is what sent the first couple frantically groping for fig leaves), Gemini is perpetually eager to play 'you show me yours and I'll show you mine,' her infamous curiosity driving her at the core. Not only that: It seems that part and parcel of munching forbidden fruit is an attraction to a fellow who's extremely opposite to herself, causing controversy, first and foremost, on the home front and especially in the eyes of her father. She may be drawn to someone considered too old, too fast, too married; she may form a killer crush on an outright hoodlum; a boy across a racial fence; one from that 'wrong' side of the tracks, or the 'right' side as it is often Gemini who is the societal underdog. She is the daughter of Mercury after all, the urban god of rabble-rousers, who was the primo deity of Roman plebeians, the working class, at whom the ruling-class patricians looked down their noses. Gemini, often regardless of how silver a spoon she is fed from, tends to espouse an urban homegirl sensibility, the proverbial 'hood being under Mercury's rule. In medieval times, the god was the patron of 3rd House *guilds* and *merchants,* the latter term being derived from his name. Helen was indeed a most precious commodity, her marriage, like that of all women historically up to the modern age, a point of trade.

Likewise, in the biblical line, the Fall, brought about by Eve's actions, necessitates living by one's wits, which, extending the analogy, were purchased at a heavy price: The expelled, antediluvian Eve and her progeny had to survive by the sweat of their brow, amid family feuding – Cain and Abel are each purported to have had twin sisters, such suspicions of incest being unavoidable. And before you can say Angelina Jolie, we see the emergence in Genesis of the wheely-dealy side of human nature, rife as it is with Mercurial deceit, trickery, and thievery, key ingredients in the gathering storm of post-Fall human

ARCHETYPE + MYTH

Gemini personifies the demigoddess, half-divine, half-mortal, like winged sprites or fairies. The Gemini, Castor and Pollux, have twin sisters, Helen and Clytemnestra, meaning 'divine courtship.' Eris, goddess of discord (Gemini in troublemaker mode), causes an uproar by tossing an apple into a party to which she wasn't invited. On it is written, 'For the fairest among you.' Athena, Hera, and Aphrodite all pounce. During the judgment of Paris, the divas bribe him with wisdom, power, and the love of the most beautiful woman in the world (Helen). Gemini, at various times, pretends to offer any combination of these endowments herself.

BIBLE + LITERATURE

The Geminian archetype in literature draws upon the sign's association with the biblical Fall and the proffering of forbidden fruit. Gemini woman is a master manipulator, as provocative as Eve holding out that apple. Shakespeare's Juliet personifies love at the Geminian crossroads. Nabokov's Lolita is the tempting apple of her lecherous stepfather's eye; she sends mixed messages to Humbert Humbert, his name signaling the same duality that Gemini incites in men – paternal love and unadulterated lust. Peter Pan's Tinker Bell is the two-faced air sprite who is loving toward him and vengeful toward everybody else, particularly the Wendys of the world.

decadence culminating in the purging flood, represented by the succeeding sign of Cancer, fittingly the cardinal-water sign of the zodiac. Meanwhile, the metaphorical experience of these streety 3rd House attributes are packaged into our pretty little Geminian bird, making her the tough-and-tender gamine she is. In short, her love life is all very *West Side Story,* characterized, as it was, by a sort of social divide. The element of air signifies the mental experience as well as the social one. Such that, just as the Twins girl is subject to a division in her rational relation to the often harsh realities of the world, she also tends to have to cope with one form or another of a cultural crossroads.

Just when you thought the mention of *West Side Story* was a throwaway reference, there's more: When it comes to the advent of love, Shakespeare's *Romeo and Juliet,* the basis for the aforementioned musical, is an exploration of the Geminian experience, from soup to nuts. The play treats the mutable-air world of social disorder, played out in an urban landscape. Every Mercury-ruled 3rd House theme under the sun is folded into the mix – a *family* feud between two *merchant* houses is the backdrop for Romeo and Juliet (nigh on completing her fourteenth year of life), who hastily rush into star-crossed love. The play itself is already a retelling of the Helen myth, or rather an untelling of it, as Shakespeare has Juliet betrothed to Paris, making him now into the Menelaus whom the beloved girl throws over in favor of the forbidden fruit of Romeo. Romeo describes Juliet, too, in Helenesque terms, saying she 'teaches the torches to burn bright.' They first profess their love to one another in the Capulets' apple orchard, only to end up in their shared tomb, like Adam and Eve expelled from the garden and ultimately robbed of their immortality. What Shakespeare calls their 'death-marked love' isn't lost on the Gemini girl, for whom, as in all great romances, an element of the unrequited is de rigueur. First, like Juliet, Gemini is living proof of love at first sight, all else fuzzing out of focus when she spots a boy who takes her sign-ruled breath away – the existence of this phenomenon is still debated by dubious philosophers; for sure, not one of whom are Gemini women. The 3rd House rule of *immediate* experience isn't just relegated to that of the *familiar,* indeed *familial* surroundings, but to Mercury's rule of the *instantaneous.*

Although Gemini is a mental air sign, it is not a rational one. The sign corresponds to the reptilian brain, which is the primitive bit in humans, similar to that in modern reptiles and their flying cousins, birds. Fittingly, many Geminian concerns are housed in this part of the organ: It rules those antediluvian survival instincts like hoarding and mating as well as ritualistic behavior, including courtship. It also controls automatic responses like breathing as well as the opposite instincts for fight and flight, fear and lust, love and hate, the last two comprising the thin-lined main theme of Shakespeare's play. Indeed, the name Juliet, a feminine diminutive of Julius, comes from the Greek *oulos* meaning 'downy,' another aviary reference chalked up to the Twins bird. Love at first sight is thus an automatic response that seems to control Gemini girl more than any other sign; but, by the same token, its exclusive usage is something out of which she must evolve, learning to employ her conscious thought more, well, mindfully. Like Juliet, and all her archetypal figures, Gemini acts hastily, without thought to consequence. Though she tends not to look both ways at the intersection of love, which might see her getting clobbered, many would give their frontal lobes for such a full-on experience of love overwhelming. For Gemini, it is unavoidable that she hurtle head over heels into the abyss of *l'amour*. And doing so, for ill or nil, only serves to toughen this bird up as time goes on.

Just as the 14–21 age group associated with the sign portrays a shift from dependent to independent thought in the individual, so, too, does Juliet shift in the play from an ancillary, conditional character to a freethinking unconditional one. She moves from using her reptilian, ritualistic brain associated with inherited automatic responses (which, by rights, should signal repulsion to a Montague) to employing her own noggin, as if for the first time, like Eve independent of God's conditional world where He does the thinking for you. In the urban jungle, however, one must develop one's sustainable plots for survival. Such a process will come to characterize the whole of the eternal 14–21-year-old's life, whereby, you might say, her inner Clytemnestra, the human, rational, indeed calculating (if not ironically cold-blooded) part of herself systematically replaces the instinctually vulnerable and thus potentially troublemaking Helenesque side. In the meantime, Gemini tends to lose her head every time love comes to town, or so it seems to those intimately associated with her. Her motto, 'I think,' thus becomes a quantitative question of how much or how little. Poor star-crossed Gemini: Unlike her male counterpart, who indulges in the 3rd House attributes of *friends* and *immediate family,* not seeming to get enough of this level of companionship, the Twins girl can't seem to escape it becoming a trap.

As with Juliet, Eve, or Helen, expectations are heaped on the Gemini girl that she adhere to a vision of her future, typically designed and held by her parents, who nonetheless fail, in her estimation anyway, to fully meet her immediate needs. She may, in fact, unconsciously seek out such Romeos as she knows will raise the ire of her loved ones. Whatever the case may be, when it comes to love, her decision-making, or lack thereof, tends to upset the familial

3RD ASTROLOGICAL
HOUSE

thought
friendship
comprehension
maturation of the mind
neighborhood
errands
merchants
brothers and sisters
communication
transportation
short trips
adaptability
relating
taken-for-granted talents
consciousness
objective mind
primary schooling
local milieu
relatives
acquaintances
informal discussions
mental circuitry
mental connections
periodicals and newspapers
phone calls and letters
conversation
gossip
information
gestures/signals
television/radio
logic and reasoning
intelligence
give and take
buying and selling
business and marketing
thought structure
assimilation of information
dealmaking
brainstorms
mental state
mechanical dexterity
resource management
public relations
learning

KEY WORDS

whimsy
curiosity
intimacy
activity
occupation
instigation
skepticism
intercourse
separation
discovery
beguilement
mirth
intrigue
ingenuity
volatility
provocation
scrutiny
imagination
commodity
comportment
manipulation
discord
agitation
precocity
broadcasting
division
contradiction
complexity
flirtation
faculty
finesse
execution
nerve
interference
realization
gratification
motion
management
friendship
effect
friction
antithesis

applecart. Even when the choice of fellow is fine by them and Gemini brings home the school valedictorian, the reaction to the relationship might be the same as it would have been if she had brought home a forty-five-year-old, tattooed, nipple-pierced, ex-con cult leader named Daddy, and for one simple reason: The Twins girl's personality tends to shift so abruptly from what is her usual autocratic, if not tyrannical character on the home front – where she's incidentally always been that calculated Clytemnestra – to a suddenly simpering invertebrate that it would seem to anybody who knows Ms. Bossy that the relationship is turning her into an unequivocal bimbo. It's only natural to blame the guy as the newly introduced stimulus. Whatever the case, the notoriously scrappy and clever schoolgirl seems to go out the window with the advent of love, and those close to her can't help but worry that the Gemini's sense of self (at least as they always knew it) is in jeopardy. To be fair, she might have doormat written all over her and even fellows with noble intentions are hard-pressed not to turn into opportunistic snakes in the grass. And the pattern repeats. Of course, the knee-jerk reaction is to try to stop, indeed forbid, the Twins girl from further ingratiating herself via relationships. But we all know what that does psychologically. As in the *Fantastiks,* yet another Romeo-and-Juliet-based musical, the fathers of the would-be lovers prevent their growing children from seeing one another, twisting the familiar theme, in a plot to ensure they'll marry in defiance. Likewise, the surest way to see a Gemini engage in any behavior is to tell her she's disallowed, barred. The defiant goddess of discord rises in her and social disorder ensues.

Revolting against rules is what Gemini, with that apple in her, is all about. The truth is, love interest from a male, specifically in Gemini's early development, is tantamount to the attention she has felt lacking all her life, generally as a result of parental focus being placed on one or more either shining or troubled siblings. If Eris teaches us anything, it's that feeling slighted is the root of all discordant social action. Unfortunately, the adopted airheaded personality Gemini presents to a beau often sees her getting carried away, and her haste to be loved, please, and be pleased might result in her being left holding the bag. Circumspection in sex, especially, isn't the Gemini's strongest suit. Overtones of succumbing to the snake in the garden being obvious, Gemini's own personal paradise is all too often lost by the dashboard light – signature fallout ensues – and the result of heedless sexual action tends to plague Gemini in any number of forms. She risks sending a would-be Romeo the wrong message: that screwing around so easily isn't something she does just with him. There is the *rumor mill* to think about and her local *reputation,* both aspects of the 3rd House. There are the de rigueur I-told-you-so's by nosy *friends, family,* even *neighbors.* Poor Gemini, she can't seem to do anything without its affecting those in her immediate vicinity, a power, however, she can and typically will come to harnass as her own special astrological weapon for conquering the world. For better or worse, there is no such thing as an isolated instance in her experience. For all her lack of forethought, she torments herself in hindsight. Her motto, 'I think,' now carries the subtitle 'too much' as she neurotically examines every possible consequence to her actions. Guilt, especially, becomes the downside of her Mercury-ruled guile. Suddenly that apple gets stuck in her throat.

Love at first sight, for the zodiac's Juliet, invariably morphs into the unrequited variety, amid a cyclone of variables. Since she's typically so young, falling hard for an equally callow fellow, there isn't much chance outside of sixteenth-century Verona that she'd be considered old enough to marry. There's that familial disapproval. Perhaps ensuing gossip surrounding her 'fast' Mercurial nature. Her mind becomes a whirl of every possible opinion others might have of her. Sometimes, as is human nature, rejection by an inamorato sends her reeling into a need for validation. Ironically taking on what (she thinks!) are others' projections, she might fall into a sort of sexual perdition, looking for love in all the wrong places. More gossip. More neurotic thoughts. Of any female, she is most easily targeted by often older snakes who see in her an opportunity to assert a sexual agenda. More wanting to please; seeking validation, Gemini flirts with disaster. Drugs might ease the pain, silence her thoughts. She's sending signals of vulnerability. It can become a feeding frenzy, Helen's forsworn suitors breaking their oath to protect her. There is a parallel pattern: When the Gemini is creatively gifted, she often has such divine talents, that they, like her capability for love, are immortalizing. The zodiac's precious cargo, thus, is likewise haggled over and exploited by the world of men as a near analogy of the dynamic her love life can take. More gossip. More derision. Guilt. Self-loathing. Nervous anxiety. The gathering storm. The ensuing cyclone: And like Dorothy Gale (her surname a symbol itself of mutable air) she gathers up her all (*Toto,* in translation) and longs to get away, to fly away, like that happy little bluebird. But before you can say *Eve: Portrait of a Teenage Runaway,* such an exodus of biblical or made-for-TV proportions, we realize, is strictly a metaphorical one. Gemini girl never gets to Oz. Her world is the black-and-white experience of good-versus-bad duality expressed by familial Kansas; as we'll see, Leo woman, drawing on the Huntress archetype, embodies the Technicolor chase along some golden path or another, while for the Twins it will rightly remain a dream.

Expulsion will take the form of self-imposed exile while Gemini comes

BODY RULERSHIP

Gemini rules the central nervous system, the lungs and respiratory system, arms and hands, chest, shoulders and shoulder blades – the wings. Mercury rules the brain, sensory organs, reflexes, and the thyroid, which controls metabolism. The planet also governs physical changes and the growth and development of intelligence.

FAMOUS GEMINI WOMEN

Precocious Pixies and Dualistic Divas

Michelle Phillips
Elizabeth Hurley
Kylie Minogue
Brooke Shields
Angelina Jolie
Heidi Klum
Helen Hunt
Ally Sheedy
Jewel Staite
Juliette Lewis
Anne Heche
Lauryn Hill
Natalie Portman
Leelee Sobieski
Alanis Morisette
Mary-Kate Olsen
Ashley Olsen
Yasmine Bleeth
Adrienne Barbeau
Venus Williams
Kristin Scott Thomas
Annette Bening
Joan Collins
Judy Garland
Marilyn Monroe
Judy Holliday
Gena Rowlands
Colleen Dewhurst
Billie Whitelaw
Emmanuelle Seigner
Josephine Baker
Isabella Rosselini
Helena Bonham Carter
Julianna Margulies
Courtney Cox
Susan Strasberg
Jane Russell
Jeannette MacDonald
Carol Kane
Paulette Goddard
Paula Abdul
Stevie Nicks
Laurie Anderson
Judith Malina
Molly Sims

to grips with some brand of personal fall into the pits, a normal disposition of her astrological inheritance – fearing that her all, again *Toto,* will be swallowed up by that ugly Gulch. If still living at home – she can be in her thirties before leaving the roost – Gemini may end up behind a closed door at the end of the hallway, leaking sad songs that speak to her pain and isolation. The storm has overwhelmed her mind. And though she may stay for years in a cocoon of segregation, rolling her eyes and sneering her lip at loved ones, she will eventually change identities, Juliet to Lolita, Helen to Clytemnestra, underdog to butterfly, still delicate but, unlike the rest of us mere mortals, able to let fly her myriad fascinations. Solitary confinement, if only of the metaphorical kind, brings Gemini to her senses, literally connecting her winged Mercurial head to the raw, heretofore flailing nerve upon which she lives. Not to suggest that she'll emerge from the pits with some new spiritually awakened personality, not at all. She'll be the same two people she's always been. Only now, she will channel them at will, not unconsciously causing a stir, but resolutely doing so. So now if some snakey Humbert Humbert comes along, she turns the tables, letting him think he's getting his way while she works her own agenda. Lolita, remember, had a secret Romeo stashed away the whole while she sucked that lollipop and used her lecherous father figure as a vehicle to establishing her own life, where she was boss of the bungalow, a helpmate to a young husband who seemingly appeared out of nowhere. Gemini thus turns to the world of men who were once beyond her ken and asks the musical question 'Who's zoomin' who?' She harnesses the power of her vulnerability, bringing opportunistic wheeler-dealers out of the woodwork, those who, thinking they have a pushover on their hands, unwittingly do her bidding. She releases that schoolgirl sexuality right smack-dab in the middle of her most professional of dealings. Indeed there isn't a sector of life in which Gemini doesn't disarm the so-called ruling patriarchy, grabbing the good old boy network by the balls and twisting their dual Humbert[2] designs, to be her patron-cum-partner, to her best advantage. She comes to realize that she's able to work mutable-air magic, making others think what she wants them to think with nothing more than a wink and a prayer. This is her gift: to make people feel her only game plan is to please. And, thereby, Gemini is sought after; her very association feels like a favor that's been selflessly granted. And, here's the kicker, who can say no to someone who asks for so little?

With all the stops she pulls out, portraying the ingenue to gain ground in virtually every endeavor, she will have put an end to such game-playing in her personal life. She is far too naturally susceptible to emotional pain and suffering to expose herself to even the slightest possibility of hurt. Bruising oh so easily in situations through which others might sail unscathed, she steers clear of any man with whom the possibility of a romantic bond might give rise to a roller-coaster ride, which, quite frankly, her nerves cannot abide. Practicality becomes her primary focus in the securing of a relationship. Crossing the street if some slick male character comes her way, she'll start to shadow guys who pose no imaginable threat. Boyish fellows with whom she establishes a pals-y friendship are the safe bets she seeks, slowly transitioning the relationship into one that includes romance. Before the guy even knows his new best friend has bigger plans for him, she might already be perusing china patterns. What Gemini wants most is to be stimulated mentally, to find a mate with whom she has shared interests if not parallel professional designs where, pooling resources, two heads can be more powerful than one. Just as Gemini guy looks for an almost exact female counterpart who'll perpetuate a lifestyle similar to his own upbringing, Gemini girl seeks to trade in her set of familial circumstances for a whole new one. Typically, this informs her choice of mate more than she might admit even to herself. She wants to wave good-bye to anything she deems dysfunctional in her past, and as she will invariably become part of her mate's family – in many respects like a sibling – she is picky as to the kind of brood she chooses to marry into. What she especially prizes is a family with strong parental influence, in contrast to what she might consider the stifling force of her own, one where both emotional and even financial support could be forthcoming. She is not symbiotic with a mate; rather, she sees marriage especially as two people rolling up their sleeves and digging into the day-to-day duties at hand, in a very businesslike partnership. Whether or not she and a mate work together, she will take on the role of the eyes and ears of the relationship, information central. You want to get to him? You'll have to go through her. In this way, she determines that her mate will have no distraction from his (read: her) plan and thus have no excuses for not increasing productivity and their own financial payoff. Even when going off to their separate places of employment, she will typically act as his public relations representative, a mouthpiece geared at casting a wider net so he needn't waste time on such outreach. It's automatic for her anyway – she is a spinmaster, facilitating her loved one's endeavors. When she has children, it will be the same with them, much to the skulking chagrin of offspring, who'll label her overbearing to say the least. Often, she will choose a mate with questionable social skills who won't fight, but wholeheartedly welcome her being the front man. She cannot and will not be in a lasting relationship where the man is under some lord-and-master delusion. She is astrologically predetermined to feel like a potential bird in a gilded cage who nonetheless yearns to fly free.

Melanie Brown
Sadie Frost
Wallace Simpson
Hedda Hopper
Rosalind Russell
Jessica Tandy
Sally Kellerman
Kathleen Turner
Jeanne Crain
Wynonna Judd
Leslie Uggams
Phylicia Rashad
Joan Rivers
Sandra Bernhard
Lindsay Wagner
Pam Grier
Peggy Lee
Nancy Sinatra
Patti LaBelle
Rosemary Clooney
Roseanne Cash
Gladys Knight
Melissa Etheridge
Lea Thompson
Sharon Gless
Olympia Dukakis
Katherine Graham
Grace Mirabella
Joyce Carol Oates
Marguerite Yourcenar
Jamaica Kincaid
Colleen McCullough
Pauline Kael
Elizabeth Bowen
Mary Cassatt
Agnes Varda
Martha Clarke
Isadora Duncan
Dorothea Lange
Harriet Beecher Stowe
Steffi Graf
Anne Frank
Anna Kournikova
Ruth Westheimer
Suzi Quatro
Colleen Dewhurst
Meredith MacRae
LaToya Jackson
Robin Tunney
Nikki Cox

This, more than anything, will inform her choice of partner. Ironically, though she'll keep her guy on a rather short leash, she typically has clauses written into her contract that see her jetting off with friends, or on solo business, where she can practice her more glamorous persona of the eternal coquette.

When it comes to sex, it is Gemini's habit to feign naïveté. Even in her practical, long-term relationships, the bedroom is one place she can't help but put on a bit of a show. While still in that dating pool, there's something intriguing, to many a man, about a woman who appears wet behind the ears, especially when one senses she's similarly conditioned in a certain other key spot. More importantly, this so-called sexual illiteracy disarms any guy who (even if kidding himself) believes that such neophytism means she has no great experience with which to compare him. In this way, Gemini instinctually lets a man off the hook of having to perform spectacularly, something she finds (from experience) to be a hurdle to the kind of low-stakes roll in the hay she enjoys anyway. Most importantly it takes any burden off her – she can't be pressured to engage in any acts that are too elaborate or invasive, and so she'll claim exemption on the grounds of her supposed novice status. She doesn't like to go too deep into a sexual experience, literally or figuratively, much preferring to keep activities light and superficial. Moreover, she likes the focus of behavior to be geared toward her pleasure. To her credit, this ruse tends to work like a charm, inspiring a guy's gentlemanly nature, insuring he proceeds gingerly, easing her into more advanced play. What she withholds in actual participation she makes up for with a show of enthusiasm. Part and parcel of being that ingenue is embodying a certain eager curiosity, a teach-me-teach-me attitude that motivates a man to take a protective if not a professorial attitude toward her sexual education. In a sense, all men become Nabokov's nutty professor, Lolita's sexual mentor, Humbert Humbert, a name that perfectly represents the duplicity Gemini woman projects onto a man, as either the laudable educator or downright lech. It is indeed amazing what she can accomplish with a simple vacant (all the while knowing) look, leaving it up to a man to handle her with care. She may be blatantly vulnerable, but she pretty much goes willingly, rarely needing to put up a fuss since it's already planted in her partner's mind that he's conveying precious cargo when he takes Gemini on an erotic trip. She plays the protégé, literally the 'protected,' seeking to be taken under her man's wing.

In Eve's archetypal perspective of fallen angel, Helen's going along so willingly with her kidnapping, or Lolita's losing her lolly with a pop, we see that it's in Gemini's erotic nature to portray the good girl going bad. Role-playing is endemic to her sex life as, in a way, she's never *not* engaging in it. So long as one indulges the noble lie that she is undertaking certain activities only because they are being sprung on her, as if for the first time, Gemini can be a fairly adventurous sexual partner. She will alight upon many acts and positions during a single interlude, so long as she's never made to explore any one too profoundly. Her skin is sensitive and may react wildly to even the slightest touch. The innate vulnerability associated with the sign is poignantly expressed during sex, where it seems to take so very little to please the nervy bundle that is our beautiful Gemini. Just as she is a master of psychological manipulation, she, in turn, likes to be physically teased, the element of surprise being highly arousing to her. She may even enjoy being tied down occasionally, with a steady partner, that is, who'll take her to the edge, with light touches and licks, of how much tactile torment she can take. For the Gemini, whose mind is always racing ahead, there is much excitement to be derived from expectation. While in such a helpless Helenesque state, she'll thrill at being baited by a man, say, rubbing his dog around her kitty, dipping in and out, or, if she feels emotionally secure, even screwing her while she remains restrained. Despite the particular delight she feels in being bridled, she may banish such behavior entirely if those old feelings of insecurity are released as a result. A lover must always remain alert and flexible to her ever-changing moods.

When it comes to intercourse, the Twins actually prefers to be on top, where she can control the pace and positioning. Having a guy plow her often feels too much like a violation, and she has no patience for a man, even her long-term lover, just wanting to get off. There is always a sense of the Gemini self-pleasuring in bed, as if her partner is a mere tool for her own masturbatory masterwork. She won't, however, tolerate being similarly engaged. Gemini will always retain an aspect of wanting to lose herself in sex. Playing capture can be cute, but it's total rapture she's really after, being transfixed by the sexual act without necessarily having to credit the man who's on hand to help her achieve this aim. He's there to provide the ride. And Gemini can be downright bossy in the bedroom, often forgetting that her lover's role isn't only to do her bidding. Consequently, she often enters into relationships with sexually imma-ture men, or even somewhat namby-pamby ones – opting for an opposite type to the overbearing men she may have felt abused by at some point in her past. Besides, as a mutable mix of masculine and female energies, as befits Mercury's androgynous neutered glyph suggests, Gemini feels a commonality with a guy who possesses a strong, sensitive feminine side. In some cases, she may even thrive on sexually overpowering a decidedly fey male. Whereas most women find male homosexuality a hands-down turnoff, the Gemini may be both psychologically intrigued and erotically titillated. In fact, she'd sooner engage

STR8 TURN-ONS

younger, boyish men
married men
seduction, playing ingénue
basketball players
Africans, Latins
one-night stands
exhibitionism
mutual masturbation
standing sex
speedy thrusting
quickies
teachers, professors
masturbation during sex
doctor/nurse role-play
phone/cyber sex
treasure trails, goatees
(active) oral sex
(passive) lite b + d
bi men, bi porn
vibrators, dildos
tickling, pinching, teasing
(passive) nipple play
swapping, girl-on-girl

in a threesome with two men as opposed to the more commonplace girl-guy-girl ménage, knowing she won't be the overwhelming focus. She might get off on watching what transpires sexually between guys, if for no other reason than to satisfy her infamous curiosity, seeing what she knows most women will never see. Watching such a tryst, she is rather unshockable as, like her Libran air-sign cousin, she can be something of an honorary gay man herself.

Gemini is probably the most versatile sexual creature in the zodiac. Life lived at the proverbial crossroads sees her going where the wind takes her more than any other woman on the astrological block. She approaches sex like a schoolgirl armed with a little four-way, folded-paper 'cootie catcher,' randomly exploring all directions, often opening a new 'door' onto unexpected and unexplored sexual territory. No female is more naturally bisexual, and Gemini often acts on same-sex curiosity early in life. Anything that smacks of forbidden fruit, remember, begs Gemini to be sometimes literally munched, the ruby variety included. For all this sexual 'blowin' in the wind' (Bob Dylan is a Gemini, of course) she tends to eschew hard-and-fast labels, deeming herself a 'people person.' Having said that, when the Gemini does identify as gay (even if on a temporary basis — not an unlikely scenario either), she tends to be most in-your-face about it. If and when she is made to feel she *shouldn't* be doing something due to societal pooh-poohing (let's face it, it's not a perfect world and biases do exist), the Twins girl will go that much further to cause controversy, the proverbial apple lodged deep in her gullet. Meaning, if, say, Gemini attends a stodgy family gathering, she won't discreetly bring her girl-friend but will sooner arrive in matching outfits, each wearing one of a set of earrings, and make quite a little show of her bond, affectation taking priority over pure affection. Call it the Eris in her. Or the Anne Heche. Either way it begs the question: Is Gemini sometimes in gay relationships simply for the effect? At least, it's a question that might occur to her lover, perhaps after Gemini has up and flown the coop. Making a display is Gemini's astrological legacy, just as it is for her so-called opposite sign of Sagittarius — not really opposites at all but rather 'octaves' of one another. Whereas for Sag, the Lady Godiva of the zodiac, all is pomp and circumstance, for Gemini life is rather like a staged coup or demonstration, launched from a rather underdog perspective.

Perhaps as a symptom of that 14–21 age group associated with her sign, the Gemini bird is acutely aware of pecking orders and so-called popularity. When actually that age herself, she is rather more advanced then her peers and tends to seek out the company of those just that much older than herself. She is drawn to a more mature in-crowd, emulating if not outright imprinting on glamorous girls, that is, as she sees them. Being so naturally bisexual a character, she will rarely experience all-out lesbian crushes; rather her feelings, even of lust, will be wrapped up in worship, friendship, envy, and 3rd House *sibling adoration* all in equal measure. As her ruler Mercury is the closest orbiting planet to the Sun, our little Geminian moth is drawn to sunny golden girls whom she hopes will dote on her with that same sense of sisterly affection. She basks in such reflected light, adopted as the *kid,* that eternal gamine to those she considers estimable goddesses. By association, those her own age see her as an exalted figure. Again, our Gemini is, in a sense, two people. Gay Gemini incorporates this sort of dynamic into her adult experience. For the interminable teenager, the world is one big high school; and the Gemini is just as proficient at infiltrating the *beau monde* as she is getting in good with the senior cheerleaders when she herself is merely a freshman. Developing an appetite for glamour and gossip early in life, while the Taurus teen might selfishly be scanning *Vogue* and *Harper's Bazaar* for beauty tips, Gemini is perusing *Vanity Fair* and other glitterati rags for the latest dish-and-dirt. Once venturing out on her own, the zodiac's original urbanite will typically gravitate toward the big city, attracted by professions that perpetuate this buzzy lifestyle. Fashion and entertainment are big draws to the Geminian, who prefers to 'work it,' in these industries, even if just behind the scenes. She is the perfect fashion, hair, or makeup stylist; she's a human Rolodex who makes a great artist, model, or photographer agent or booker; the consummate manager or public relations consultant – jobs where she might find herself gilded by association with the rich and famous. Even when Gemini is herself a celeb, she will generally be self-effacing in the face of more glamorous notables in contrast to whom she'll remain her gaga gamine self.

That proverbial people person, gay Gemini is rarely exclusively lesbian in her associations, having a slew of straight friends and especially gay male friends with whom she'll cavort. She will, however, be a card-carrying member of the gay-girl mafia, an exclusive set of stylish women who love women, aiding and abetting her sisters in their personal and professional lives as she is likewise given such assists. Gemini is the preeminent networker and is often 'the person to know' in whatever industry one might be attempting to maneuver. She is a lookist and will typically only associate with a highly presentable crowd, that viewpoint carrying over to her love relationships as well. Though she doesn't have a specific type, of anyone, gay Gemini is something of a modelizer, bound to bag as many waify would-be mannequins as she might. She may also be a bit of a starfucker, thinking nothing of dating someone purely because she's famous. Popularity is forever impressive to Gemini, as she tends to venture her own success on ye olde adage 'It's not what

GAY TURN-ONS

younger women
models, glamazons
blonds, redheads
athletes, gymnasts
femmes, straight/bi women
toys, gadgets
domination
double dildos
fingering, licking, biting
threesomes, foursomes
g-strings, lace, leather
erotica
mastery
cross-dressing
carpet-sweeping, scissoring
phone/cyber sex
mindgames
(active) penetration
strap ons
role-play, masks, costumes
anonymous sex
(active) worship
paying, prostitute fantasies
private parties, sex clubs

you know, it's *who* you know.' This carries over into her world of wooing just as it is a mantra in her professional life. Though there is a strong splinter group of ultrabutch Geminis who are so fetishistic about masculinity they practically live as men, exhibiting no irony in palling around with straight guys, even falling into such stereotypically macho behavior as would make the casual armchair feminist cringe, the majority of gay Twins girls are enticingly androgynous in look and demeanor. A sexy sprite, manicured and pedicured beneath her catcher's mitt and cleats, Gemini is a tenderhearted toughie who wants to be romanced by a lover but also likes to call the shots. She and her invariably gorgeous girlfriend will generally be attached at the ultrahip, attending what the Twins girl deems to be important social events, often never far from the snap of paparazzi. She likes the ritual of dressing for a date (almost more than the date itself), sharing the mirror, swapping jewelry and accessories with her mate, who is also, well, her *mate*. Something about Gemini's relationships smacks strongly of continental, urban-dwelling teenagers, pinkies locked, strolling down life's boulevard — *side-by-side bonds,* and *boon companions,* being attributes of her astrological house. And, in a certain sense, Gemini's lover is like the sister she never had — even when she does have them, the association is characterized by rivalry more than it is camaraderie. She can be Twinsy in the extreme, opting for those matching outfits (thankfully irony is employed here) and two-for-one, typically pixie haircuts. Already sentimental by nature, the Twins girl can be a real mushpot in the expression of her affection, often buying her lover little gifties and celebrating the moments of their life. She is the queen of quick getaways, generally opting for a sunny retreat and a convertible rental car. Indeed, many Geminians seek subtropical metropolises for their infamous relocations, which, as luck would have it, are often the setting for, among other attractions, year-round photo shoots and a model-infested nightlife.

Just as this mutable-air character demands a lot of social stimulation, she also requires a home atmosphere replete with special effects, particularly when it comes to creating the right sexual ambience. She will meticulously clean her space and then strew it with candles, which, along with her myriad mementos, framed pictures, beauty products, and other personal effects, will define the relief landscape of her boudoir. Invariably, there is a dimmer switch — it's all about mood and buildup. Indeed, sex for the gay Geminian often amounts to what others might consider extended, if not epic, foreplay, involving her sign-ruled hands, breath, and nerve endings. Her idea of rapture is spending hours arousing one another with the ubiquitous employment of fingertips, inhaling the pleasure and thus allowing the sensation to spread over the entirety of her gooseflesh. It's all about surface tactile exploration for this bird, that and a shallow employment of tongue, as to deliver little zaps and tingles. Of any gay girl in the zodiac, Gemini can most easily forgo the phallic sculpture others stash in their nightstand. She will do the strapping on, however, if it is important to her partner, typically taking a pass at being passive. Clitoral orgasms are the ones she comes to trust, and she's more than satisfied with no-fuss, no-muss contact. Impatient and impetuous as she is, she doesn't like to, shall we say, beat around the bush, locking onto her lover's trigger and not letting go until she's fired off a number of shots. It's how she likes it in return, too, and, indeed, no woman gets off quicker or has so instantaneous a refractory recovery as she, the enviable possessor of multiple-O capability. When she goes, she's gone – losing herself in the chaos of sensation, the Twins girl falls into a near pit, if not fit, of passion. Indeed she often descends into semiconsciousness, which may require the metaphorical equivalent of a popcorn trail to find her way back to the reality at hand. While many people become increasingly jaded by same-samey sexual experience, feeling a need to raise the stakes to attain altered ecstatic states, Gemini is almost overwhelmed by the simplest, straightforward erotic involvement and, indeed, comes to rely on a regular sexual routine. An insular character, she rarely has a mind to engage in expansive scenarios such as group sex. She enjoys flirtation more than anyone, however, and will often ride a fine line, even with members of her close circle of girlfriends – it can all be so incestuous. Gemini's lover is better off granting her the casual indiscretion, as it rarely amounts to anything more serious. Her natural coquetry is, in itself, an aphrodisiac to the Gemini, who might steal a kiss just for the thrill of being spied by her lover, hoping it might spice things up later in the sanctity of their own sack. Harmless mind games come to define the behavior of the Gemini. She can hold you hostage mentally or free your mind to endless possibilities. She is the flea in society's ear, forever bending others to her perceptions, making us think the thoughts she silently suggests.

Couplings

Gemini Woman ∫ Aries Man
She's a fresh pixie to deflower; he's the brute she can't resist. Often purely physical at first, this pairing is eventually founded on friendship. Sexually, she's tireless; he has the staying power to sustain her.

Gemini Woman ∫ Taurus Man
She's been searching for someone so sensitive *and* strong; he's found a sexy, spitfire sort. Their friendship is foremost, so sex is rarely the focus. Indeed, in bed, they sometimes seem reluctant. Still, there's hope.

Gemini Woman ∫ Gemini Man
Slick, innovative Geminis come together fast and furiously. At first, it's a blast – a social, sexual, creative whirlwind – but making a deeper commitment is challenging: He's restless; her disquiet increases.

Gemini Woman ∫ Cancer Man
Typically passive, he pursues her anyway – Gemini's impish appeal makes him behave surprisingly, even shockingly. The Crab appears the ultimate catch – charismatic, clever. In bed, it's a mixed bag – a mess if she's moody.

Gemini Woman ∫ Leo Man
He's the object of her doting attention. With time, Leo evolves into the dream guy Gemini imagined. They'll often take a walk down the aisle. Laughter is their saving grace. With her, he's forever in his sexual prime.

Gemini Woman ∫ Virgo Man
A challenging psychosexual dynamic. He's a Svengali to the plucky, 'youthful' Gemini; but surprise, she's more self-sufficient than he imagined. In bed, Virgo gets a reeducation – less repression, more expression.

Gemini Woman ∫ Libra Man
Where she goes, he'll follow: Libra is positively passive when compared with the enterprising Gemini. They have something to prove – success is the consequence. Sex is comfortably secondary in their nonstop lifestyle.

Gemini Woman ∫ Scorpio Man
He's bewitched – she's the one who'll alter his perception from dark to light. As time passes, she hopes he'll remain so reliant. Their commitment appears unbreakable. In bed, lavish fantasies are revealed.

Gemini Woman / Sagittarius Man
She's addicted to bold, beguiling Sag man. They're in absolute accord – their bodies, too, snap into place like puzzle pieces. Sex, like all other aspects of their shared life, is wild with rounds of overt experimentation.

Gemini Woman / Capricorn Man
From the start, they seem set on different speeds – he's slow; she's swift. At best, they help each other adjust to a more moderate pace. Sexually, she feels snubbed; but he's dreaming up ways to draw out her desire.

Gemini Woman / Aquarius Man
Instant attachment. Codependence could be a pitfall. Emotionally bound, sexually rapt. At best, they embody the power of positive thinking. Otherwise, unreality dissolves into disillusionment. Sexual appetites are unwieldy.

Gemini Woman / Pisces Man
Pisces appeals as a consort. He may hang on her every word. Together, worldly ambitions are given fullest focus; other aspects are often left in disrepair. Sexually, she gets a surprise: Mild Pisces makes many demands.

Gay

Gemini Woman / Aries Woman
A boarding-school scenario: Aries initiates Gemini, who is invariably infatuated with the Ram, allowing herself to try acts she's only ever read about. In every aspect, Aries is the leader. In bed, there are no inhibitions.

Gemini Woman / Taurus Woman
With provocative Gemini, the Bull girl taps into her own toughness. They agree on the essentials; joint professional ventures are a natural partnership path. Sex is endlessly enjoyable, at turns rough-and-tumble and tender.

Gemini Woman / Gemini Woman
When they meet, two Twins are often looking for a pal more than a partner. They'll enjoy a liberal liaison founded on solid friendship. Both bore easily, so dreaming up new ways to excite is essential.

Gemini Woman / Cancer Woman
Mother issues abound, but a certain amount of healing takes place. Gemini lightens and learns to love more, without fear. The Crab has an emotional leg up on her enchanting Geminian ingenue. Sex stays spontaneous.

Gemini Woman ∫ Leo Woman
They invite controversy – indulging differences, these two are often playfully at odds in public. Egocentric sorts, domestic bliss may elude them. If love languishes, friendship blossoms. Sexually, each is the other's 'best.'

Gemini Woman ∫ Virgo Woman
Both are prone to moods and whimsy. This combo is challenged from the start. Gemini must learn to compromise, almost constantly. Virgo morphs into a more mature self. Sexually, too, the energy is tempestuous.

Gemini Woman ∫ Libra Woman
An aesthetically inclined couple with a common vision: to be expressive in all aspects of life. *Et voilà:* They easily engage in a liberating, invigorating liaison. A no-fuss affair in which both partners thrive – sexually and otherwise.

Gemini Woman ∫ Scorpio Woman
Two become one: From the start, they're happiest alone. Scorpio transforms jumpy Gemini into a serene sort. The pressure to be everything to each other may overwhelm. Sexually, outsiders are off-limits.

Gemini Woman ∫ Sagittarius Woman
A winning twosome. Gemini rides strapping Sag's coattails. Their partnership means more professional power. But business and pleasure blend beautifully. In bed, it's a question of who's the boss.

Gemini Woman ∫ Capricorn Woman
It's a learning experience. With a glib 'Get over it,' Gemini stills the Goat's soulful, strained searching. But it's Gemini who's subdued in bed: Her lover demands the command position.

Gemini Woman ∫ Aquarius Woman
They'll say it was predestined. This connection is empathetic in the extreme. As a couple, they're insular; neither feels beholden to those on the outside, even friends. In bed, one is only more generous than the other.

Gemini Woman ∫ Pisces Woman
From inauspicious beginnings, Gemini and Pisces build a solid bond. First, they'll weed through a litany of harsh preconceived notions. Often a haphazard, compulsive relationship. Sex is too often an afterthought.

Cancer Man

the player

Cancer man is the zodiac's Prince Charming, a self-professed perfect gentleman – clean-cut, polite, coolly composed, and thus seemingly tailor-made to the specifications of a traditionally minded woman. He appears caring and sensitive, nice and funny, the very picture of respect, moral soundness, and earnest ambition. The consummate marrying kind who feels an inbred need to nest, nurture (and be nurtured), Cancer's prime motivation is to be recognized as *that* proverbial good provider. Notoriously artistic, he gravitates toward careers in which his sensorial spirit might flourish. Still, he expects to be handsomely remunerated for his endeavors – art and commerce are inextricably linked in the Cancerian male mind. Even when working within a corporate structure, he generally performs in special, solo capacities, channeling his signature creative imagination. He is, in any case, a hopeless romantic, forever lost in daydreams that feature him in heroic roles, a veritable Walter Mitty with not just one secret fantasy life but typically a slew of them. To women, he portrays himself as a stable, safe bet who'll lavish a mate with attention and seek to satisfy her every whim. He prides himself on being the model boyfriend, husband, or lover, and no guy is more a family man than he. For Cancer, sex is an act of worship, whereby he gives himself utterly to a woman, investing his every emotion. In same-sex bonds, he retains his straight-arrow public air, playing the part of a prized but companionable lover who won't be defined by his sexual orientation. In private, however, no male is more compliant and eager to be immersed in the depths of erotic experience.

iV

PRINCIPLE

The Mother Principle. Via its ruler Moon, Cancer represents a model of the world environment as having a tangible feminine *source*, Mother Nature, from whence all life stems. Cancer man subscribes to this principle in the organic way he lives his life, rarely imposing his will, but functioning by 'going with the flow' of his inherent instincts and emotions. His motto is 'I feel,' and he is disposed to ride the tide of life experience. Cancer seeks assimilation into this feminine nature rather than to assert any mastery over it.

Sign + Mind

From an astrological perspective, it is no accident that the most consistently popular leading men in Hollywood are Cancerians. The cosmic 4th House, governed by the sign, rules the *general public* at large, and in particular the female portion of the population. One might say that Cancer man embodies the vision of male virtue from that collective female point of view. He's the consummate romantic hero – sugarcoatedly masculine, without a hint of misogyny – one seemingly manufactured to appeal to the estrogen crowd. Not surprisingly, Cancer is ruled by the Moon, symbolic of the Mother Principle in astrology; and as the fourth sign, Cancer initiates the Second Quadrant of the zodiac, that which is concerned with the human environment and emotional experience. Thus, taking all this together, the sign of Cancer represents the ideal perception of the universe, or *yoni*-verse if you will, as female – a tangible source (Mother Nature) from which all life springs – as opposed to a male paradigm for existence, which emphasizes an intangible sky-god Father Principle of creation, associated with the Sun and the fifth zodiacal sign of Leo. The one man born under the Mother Principle, Cancer personifies the male role in what he perceives to be a matriarchal world – as a consort to any number of queens – recognizing the 'female' as authority in the cosmos. As anyone intimately associated with a Cancer man would readily admit, it is to womankind the Crab feels he must answer. He doesn't enter into relationships with a woman as some swashbuckling rogue who spirits away his princess-bride or hauls her off caveman style. Rather, the Cancerian man is wedded *to* a woman – he is her eternal bridegroom, doing right *by* her – deferring to the female in his relationships as the one who wears the pants – at least up to a point.

The sign of Cancer corresponds to the ages 21–28, a time when a young man has come of age and is on the brink of maturity, being at once wet behind the ears and all potential for the future. At this 'marrying age,' wild oats have been sown, and one is embarking on a path toward desired goals and ambitions. Metaphorically speaking, Cancer male embodies the notoriously unjaded qualities of this age all the years of his life: He is forever the wunderkind in the workplace and, in his private life, that proverbial charming prince looking for his perfect match, groomed to be wed and to live happily ever after with some godmother-fueled Cinderella. There is something forever fresh and pure about him. Sex, in particular, is not something about which he will ever be cavalier – casual contact is typically an anathema to the straight Crab. He tends not to squander his precious swimmers – this spermatic euphemism is especially apt for astrology's premier water sign. Of all the guys in the zodiac, he's the one who will voluntarily save himself for marriage, just as he'll play the savior role within his relationships. Cancer man is the romantic hero, the Perceval whose reputation for purity proceeds him, just as he is the sacred and sacrificial consort of queens – the Osiris, the Heracles (Hercules), whose name means 'beloved of Hera,' fittingly the Greek mother goddess who weds him for all his trials, in her virgin form, Hebe. In mythology, Heracles is tasked to perform his twelve labors (one for each of the zodiacal signs), which included slaying the giant Crab in the heavens – Cancer's namesake constellation. Likewise, the medieval Perceval must fulfill obligations to his instructress, Blanchefleur, who reveals to him the mystic meanings of chivalry. These are parables for Cancer's psychic and emotional needs: He feels obliged to appear the perfect male protégé, specifically to women through whose interest in him he may be ennobled. Even as a boy, before hitting the pivotal age of twenty-one, Cancer will try to appear at least that grown-up. Characteristically career-minded and motivated, he seeks to register on the romantic Richter scale as a potentially 'primo' provider. Thus, he'll put overwhelming effort into securing such external trappings as might befit the earnest go-getter role he's bent on playing – the perfect watch, classy car, tasteful wardrobe – such accoutrements as would hint at his ability to caretake himself and thus generate affluence for a partner. He's not all trendy flash like Gemini; rather he goes for traditional quality labels. Indeed, subtlety is, ironically, Cancer's hardest-hitting weapon in his battle for love. And the persona he cultivates, almost insidiously, is aimed at looking most agreeable to what he perceives as the mass feminine sensibility. Indeed, no man grasps the workings of the female mind, and its reasonings, better. As his ruler Moon is the feminine 'planet' that governs intuitive power, and female intuition in particular, Crab man has the unique ability to empathize with women and view life from their perspective. He literally *feels* what it is a woman seeks in a man, and he becomes a living testament to that ideal.

Unlike Taurus, which is associated with the Feminine Principle, Cancer doesn't simply personify the male as a fertility idol; instead, under the Mother Principle, Cancer man is about being the perfect moral and emotional consort, the chivalric ideal. The rather testicular glyph of the sign must, of course, be read less literally: It is symbolic of the *seeds* of experience – past conditioning – which define one's future promise. Fittingly, the sign of Cancer is associated with the 4th Astrological House, that which concerns both *the home one comes from* and *the home one creates* – the metaphoric 'marrying age' of twenty-one is

PLANETARY SYMBOL

The Moon signifies rhythm in the zodiac; it is in a sympathetic relationship with Earth, in orbit around the planet while still remaining in the Sun's gravitational pull. Moods, like tides, are regularly controlled by the Moon, and the Cancer man especially can't escape such effects. The half-circle of the planet's glyph symbolizes this constant process and the potential for fullness that personifies the callow Cancerian prince who forever pretends to kingly greatness, but feels incomplete without a nurturing emotional relationship.

The zodiacal quadrants correspond to the metaphysical planes of existence – physical, emotional, mental, and spiritual. The Second Quadrant is that of emotional and indeed moral environment. For Cancer man, importance is on his sign-ruled gut instincts and an approach to life circumstances from that essential feeling level.

a particular hingepin. These two interrelated *environments* become Cancer man's prime preoccupations, if only unconsciously. Little wonder: The 4th House also rules the *unconscious mind,* in particular, its childhood *conditioning,* and thus *character development,* which directly points to the Crab's nearly compulsive focus on his personal evolution. Herein, too, we see a blatant nod to his innate ability to become so ubiquitously appealing as a matinee idol – he is most able to project himself onto the collective consciousness as a thoroughly likable fellow, a middle-of-the-road regular Joe. Still, as his ruler Moon's glyph suggests, the orb depicted as not fully waxed, Cancer is a man very much in the process of becoming whole. And though he may pretend to be a power player, his potential is more inherent, latent even, than it is realized.

Cancer is the zodiac's only cardinal-water sign, distinguished first and foremost as emotional initiative – water symbolizing feelings and intuition, or divine feminine inspiration – as compared with the physical-energetic action associated with Aries, the previous cardinal (masculine-fire) sign on the wheel. Indeed, Cancer man is thoroughly involved with action on the unseen, sensitive 'feeling' plane. In an instant, he touches a woman's soft spot, inspiring the affection worthy of so exemplary a romantic hero, grooming himself to appear the part of perfect young gentleman – unfortunately, he often looks like he just walked off the set of a Lifetime original movie – cloaking himself in his signature soap-opera air of dashing good-guy promise. He's the eternal female champion, clean as a whistle and seemingly pure of heart. His presence is like that of one freshly bathed in the sanctifying waters of divine inspiration, achieved through chastely holding vigil until the perfect woman comes sauntering along. With his infamous lost-boy expression, Cancer leads one to believe he's indeed still wet behind the ears. But don't buy it: Even the peerless Perceval's very name gives away his true intent as it literally means 'to pierce the valley,' specifically, the one found lying between some available lady's legs. But, like that of Cancer man, Perceval's hidden agenda goes mainly undetected, being all unassuming stealth, lurking in the watery (emotional) world until . . . *gotcha*. He isn't, however, only actively emotionally (cardinal-water) disarming dames in hopes of worming his way into said valley, he's also hoping to inspire mother love for him in a woman's heart. Of course, not all women are willing to oblige, but in this way, he's able to weed out those who don't seem capable of such combined sexy–mama sentiment. As oedipal as that sounds, this cloying need for such a dual dynamic is endemic to the Cancerian male sexuality. Actually, it is emotional life-or-death to the Crab guy that he find a female who can provide that double-barreled expression of affection.

Just as Cancer woman, as the embodiment of her cardinal-water nature, is personally transformed by embracing her own flow of emotion, the Cancer man is, figuratively speaking, reformed or made whole by the flood of feeling he invokes in his lover; and not one of pure romantic love or lust, but such sentiment combined with a sense of mothering protection and, often, a dash of pity. The (s)mothering lover that Cancer boy seeks will be credited with making the male Moon child into a man, helping him realize his potential, something this eternal bridegroom is unable to achieve all by his lonesome. The environment that Cancer man's wife or lover provides must be like a womb in which he can fully develop and be reborn. And by extracting a flood of emotional feeling from her, he is purified, renewed, and most of all, enriched. In this way, a woman becomes the *source* of his new life, just as the advent of the Nile flood, a symbol of renewal that is the ultimate characterization of water-cardinality, signals the coming of the resurrected god, the Osiris-Horus, who is both lover and child to the mother goddess Isis. Similarly, in the Greek flood myth, the goddess-creatress Themis instructs Deucalion, the Greek Noah, and his mate Pyrrha, on how to repeople the planet, the ultimate take on the 4th House attribute of *home that one creates*. In the biblical line, Cancer corresponds to the Flood, which wipes out all the evils of post-Fall Genesis, symbolized by the preceding sign of Gemini in the zodiac. Cancer marks a new beginning, and men of the sign are branded with that same need. He is also Jonah, transformed via his experience in the Cancerian-ruled belly-womb of the whale; as well as the baby Moses sent down the proverbial river, more cardinal-water, from one mother to another. And it is under the watchful eye of some righteous mama that the emotionally orphaned Crab will be happiest. As the Moon represents the Mother Principle, it is astro-logical to assume that any paucity of self-realization in the Cancer male is in part due to the role, or lack thereof, that his actual mother played in his early development. Again, whereas Cancer woman is a 'wet' wellspring of emotion, our generally cool and collected Crab guy looks to a woman in his life for such outpourings of sentiment, which he'll suck up like a sponge.

One could argue that Cancer man seeks the care of a protective female because it mirrors his cosmic vision of the universe – as a womby mother-earth source of awe and protection. And so he will strive to structure his personal life accordingly, living within a female system, welcoming the scrutiny and instruction of women. With men, on the other hand, he is extremely guarded. Since the time he played childhood boys-against-the-girls games, he has secretly sided with the pigtailed population. Terrified of masculine scorn, he learns early on to mask his thoughts and disguise his emotions in a vague attempt to go along with the guys. After all, it's not a popular locker-room

SIGN GLYPH

The Cancer emblem is a crab. The glyph recalls two individuals floating along in the same vessel, like a couple surviving a flood, as the Crab, both a sea and a land dweller, inevitably would. The symbol may also be read as a man's testes, a source of human life and procreation, a Cancerian pre-occupation in a – pardon the pun – nutshell.

ELEMENT + QUALITY

The water element connotes feeling and instinct. The cardinal quality signifies a call to action and initiative. Together the cardinal-water combination particular to Cancer is best illustrated as a source, spring, river, or tide, and it is on this current of emotion that the Cancer rides, particularly in the sentiments he elicits in romantic bonds.

POLARITY

Males in female (earth, water) signs are not aligned with the gender polarity of the sign and thus enact instead of embody the quality-element combination of the sign. Cancer man, therefore, isn't a wellspring of emotion, but rather he seeks to elicit emotional responses from others. Particularly in love relationships, Cancer wants to be carried away by a partner's deepest feelings.

boast for a guy to admit he likes sappy songs and chick flicks. So he adopts a stoical veneer – like his sign's symbol Crab, he forms a shell. During the course of his sexual development, Cancer is intensely apprehensive of being ridiculed for his inherently sensitive side. As a result, this potentially most feeling male sign in the zodiac often ends up becoming the most shut down. Gay or straight, the male Moonchild is suckered by bogus macho stereotypes that dictate that men must be poker-faced in situations that call for emotional expression. Hemingway was a Cancer, after all – so butch it hurt, so sensitive he opted out. Though the Moonman is a born romantic, he may be well into his twenties before breaking through his adopted nonchalant exterior, letting this softer side show. Meanwhile, he'll keep his Celine Dion and Norah Jones CDs as cached as his emotions. Only when Cancer male 'secures' a steady relationship will he feel comfortable revealing his more delicate sensibilities. More than being reborn in his romantic relationships, he is rather allowed to rediscover his true self, complete with a full range of feelings – from moony-eyed in love, to deeply melancholic when dejected. It's little wonder Cancer makes such a convincing actor, as, in one way or another, he's been pretending all his life. Like Pinocchio, the Jonah myth Disney-fied, he wants so much to be a 'real boy' and yet he's stuck in performance mode, dragged through imitative motions of what he perceives to be acceptable male behavior. Not embracing his true self, especially his deep and varied sexual imagination and desires, he risks having more than a growing nose give his true feelings away, despite attempts to retain that cool and detached demeanor. Like actual crabs who can live both on land and in water, the Cancer guy inhabits two worlds at once, presenting himself as a concrete, down-to-earth type while possessing a murky and mysterious sensuality. Ruled by the Moon, he can't escape the tidal ebbs and flows of natural callings surging through him; and his infamous moodiness is due mainly to the internal effort of suppressing his wilder sexual imaginings, all for the sake of appearances. Sooner or later, however, Cancer man must 'come clean' and admit his deeper, darker urgings, both to himself and existing or prospective sexual partners, without fear of being pegged any less savory a character. For he must eventually learn that there must be a limit to caring what others – and particularly women – think of him. He does himself a great disservice by assuming a picture-perfect posture since, being only human, the Crab is bound to fall short of impeccability sooner or later.

In truth, many Cancer males are brought up in households with a paradoxical image of mothering: His own mother may loom quite large on an emotional level, but be incredibly passive and needy in all actuality. In fact, it might be in her passivity or, even, outright attitude of victimization that she takes the entire household emotional hostage. Even in a family dominated by females, as Cancer boy's typically is, he will take on a mothering role to his siblings, and especially to dear ol' mom herself, while maintaining a more brotherly relationship with his father, whom he'll tend to view as lovable but weak. Still, as if that weren't enough of a dearth in parenting, his father might be missing from the scene altogether, or be so detached as to make little impact upon his son's emotional environment. Lacking in emotional fulfillment, Cancer looks to recuperate from this sense of loss through a romantic bond. He aims to attract a powerful alpha female – one, as nature would have it, who is singled out to breed (mothering in the strictest sense) – as he hopes such a woman might provide a nourishing, motivational *environment* in which he can cultivate, indeed incubate, a feeling of psychological wholeness. This is a distinction that astrology often fails to make: In no way is Cancer looking for coddling or saccharine mommying to make his life easier; rather he seeks a home environment that'll challenge him into accessing latent greatness, and with a woman who'll put him through his paces. Contrary to popular belief, the level of attention Cancer seeks goes far beyond baby talk or being served his favorite meals.

Body + Soul

Cancer man tends to look more like a Mr. Nice Guy than any other male in the zodiac. Cancer's 4th House rule of the *general public,* and of females in particular, is perhaps responsible for the preponderance of successful Crab movie actors: Tom Cruise, Tom Hanks, Tobey McGuire, Josh Harnett, John Cusack, Harrison Ford, Robin Williams, Topher Grace, and Kevin Bacon – all exude big red, white, and blue box-office appeal – America itself is a Cancer. The Crab's appearance tends to be pleasing but placid, and not exactly seething with sexuality. Rather he is the kind of guy a girl would feel readily comfortable bringing home to mother. Even when blessed with extraordinary good looks, he doesn't generate much heat; rather, he is as cool and pale in spirit as the moon. He may even be downright innocuous as a result of wanting to blend in and be that 'real boy.' To pick a Cancerian out of a crowd, one should scan for the man who seems most intent on avoiding detection, that invisible shell going everywhere he does. Even the most drop-dead gorgeous Moon child may escape notice by downplaying his features – hiding behind an overgrown haircut, glasses, wearing inconspicuous styles of clothing. With friends, he huddles in close circles, typically addressing only those within

---

4

SIGN NUMBER

The number of structure, completion, and protection – the square is the most solid of objects. There are four elements, four compass directions, four seasons, and four archangels.

21–28

SIGN AGE ASSOCIATION

The age of the bridegroom. Cancer is the marrying kind who cleans up real nice to take home to mother. He personifies the quality of this age all his life, embodying the spirit of promise and potential, characteristically committed to relationships as if forever saying 'I do.'

PSYCHOLOGY

Cancer feels overly responsible. He may live in a fantasy world, more of a dreamer than a doer. As a pretender, he can fall prey to pretention. A role player, he can be overly sycophantic. In relationships, he can be needy. He often suffers from disassociative feelings, a sense he is a phony or a fraud not in touch with his truest goals, feelings, or desires. He can be reclusive if not agoraphobic.

earshot. He may even face the wall, his back to any larger audience, conducting one-on-one conversations standing sideways instead of chatting face-to-face. When caught in an eye-to-eye conversation, he wears a smiling, vacant expression, pretending to hang on every word being said. And though he nods and laughs appreciatively, asking a string of leading questions, it is often fairly evident that he never quite listens to the answers being given.

Even the Crab's physicality can be painfully vague: Generally neither too tall nor too short, Cancer will usually hover in height somewhere around the five-nine or five-ten mark. He's fairly well proportioned, neither overtly muscular or broad-shouldered, nor wimpily underbuilt. The most derisive term used to describe him might be *weedy*. Usually lighter-skinned than other men in his family, he can have a somewhat washed-out expression regardless of his ethnic background. And when he's a white guy, his hair will often be a sort of mousy brown meets dirty blond, making it difficult to put one's finger on a particular hue. The texture of his hair tends toward fine and wispy, and he'll have a rather high hairline, especially at the points straight above his temples. Probably the most distinct feature to his countenance is the form of his face, which is fittingly rather moon-shaped, oval, or even oblong. Though he may be slightly hunched over, his head and neck jutting out somewhat storklike (made all the more noticeable by a typically gawky Adam's apple), Cancer is rather sturdily built. Not one to ever be burdened by excess body fat, he'll nonetheless tend toward some softness around the chest and middle. Indeed, it seems no matter how much weight he bench-presses, Cancer man's pecs always have something of a feminine look to them, protruding as they do just about the nipples – a highly sensitive area on this guy, and a possible source of great pleasure, if he'd ever get over feeling it's too girly for a guy to enjoy such secretly lurking sensations (the Cancer man caveat in a nutshell).

His figure, in fact, may be ever so slightly reminiscent of a woman's: His trunk curves in, most high-waistedly, then rounds back out as it leads down to his hips. And whereas most men wish they were as naturally blessed with lateral muscles as Cancer is, this only seems to accentuate his, dare we say, hourglass physique. He's usually less hairy than other guys in his family, though what fuzzy patches he does possess tend to be more straight than curly and rather scattered and insignificant. His stomach, especially, will be accentuated by hair. Cancer man's lower abdomen is protrusive, perhaps due to the sign's rulership of this area, and his pelvis is broad, which, what with his rounded sides and requisite hint of love handles, makes him look somewhat hippy, even when he's ultraslim. With strong shoulders and ample, naturally toned arms, as well as a fairly flat butt, he is saved from ever looking pear-shaped. His legs are as well defined and sturdy as they are graceful, lending him the air of a dancer. Like his body, his penis size hovers somewhere around average. Still, the Crab guy does tend to be rather thick in this area; and his balls, though not often of the low-hangers variety, do err on the large side. He will have a rather profuse shock of hair about the pubis, which, given the spare quality of the hair on his head, can appear rather incongruous. More than most men, the Cancerian may have an oddly shaped member – one that bends to the side, curves downward, or has a bulbous mushroom head – and if left uncircumcised, his foreskin can be overlong or too tightly fixed.

Cancer has a distinct manner of moving and gesticulating. A nod to his Pinocchio nature, he has a puppety, staccato means of physical expression, often tilting, nodding, or throwing his head back in conversation, just as he will bend and straighten his wrists, or even his ankles, unconsciously, in quirky little flipping motions as if he were floating in water. There is always something decidedly goofy about the Cancer guy, the precise quality that one finds most endearing about him. That, plus his creative ingenuity, which translates to a quick, razor-sharp wit. Still, it's clear that, if he wasn't styled so conservatively, he might appear quite a bit more offbeat than most guys. His countenance is akin to that of a collegian trying to pass for slightly older with a fake ID – as if he's always attempting to keep a straight face – and even when he is being dead serious, it's hard to take him as such. Literally wide-eyed, his lenses are usually paler than those of other family members – hazel, for instance, when everyone else's are brown, or a blanched blue when others' are piercingly bright. His lids look opalescent, pale pink beneath a light brow, his eye sockets shallow and somewhat Asian in character, even when he isn't. As a rule, he has a beaky nose, and a somewhat pinched upper lip that lends him a lisping quality, if not literally translating into a slight speech impediment. His expression is made all the more idiosyncratic by a generally irregular or downright crooked set of teeth. His head is generally round and pumpkin-y.

But just as Cancer man spiffs himself up to signal that he's 'going places' to a would-be alpha chick, there's something undeniably lost about his expression – like an orphan, all buttoned up and spit-shined in his eagerness to appear a perfect candidate for adoption. In this way, Cancer man tugs at a woman's heartstrings, getting a girl *right here,* appearing at once needy for love and determined for success, a one-two punch many a woman finds irresistible in her search for a man to have and to mold. Even his haircut looks administered to him, as if in an effort to spruce up his foundling impression – Cancer guy, like Aries, tends to focus his grooming efforts on having freshly cut hair. Overall, Cancer's appearance and expression is one of utter sweetness.

ARCHETYPE + MYTH

Cancer personifies the consort god, who often wed his mother. Deucalion is the Greek Noah who was guided by Themis, an oracular mother goddess whose name means 'waters.' The yearly flooding of the Nile was said to presage the coming of Osiris, whose bride-mother Isis swallowed him (as Jonah was gulped down by the whale), giving birth to him anew. Heracles is put through the ringer by mother Hera, via a series of labors including the slaying of the zodiacal Crab, a symbol of the end of one aeon, and the beginning of another. Heracles means 'beloved of Hera,' and he marries her in her virgin form, Hebe.

BIBLE + LITERATURE

As the cardinal-water sign Cancer is associated with Noah, the Flood, and the renewal of the human moral condition. He also draws from the baby-Moses arche-type as well, being sent down the river, from one mother to another. Jonah's stint in the Cancer-ruled belly of the whale is a tale of personal transformation. Pinocchio goes through the same journey on his voyage to becoming a real boy. The medieval Perceval is trans-formed by the fairy queen Blanchefleur into a pure and valiant being, thus becoming the prototype for Cin-derella's Prince Charming. Walter Mitty, who forever imagines himself a romantic hero and savior of mankind, is a modern Cancerian char-acter. The ithyphallic figures of Perceval and Osiris live on in wounded characters like Hemingway's Jake Barnes in *The Sun Also Rises* and Buck Henry's Benjamin in his screenplay, *The Graduate*.

No matter how hard a shell he tries to maintain, he can't help but appear terminally sensitive. His hands, especially, give him away: Though his fingers are often finely tapered to near points – a nod, perhaps to his crabbish clawing – the Moon man probably possesses the most beautiful paws of any guy in the zodiac. They seem to say all there is to say about him: strong but gentle, artistic, graceful, and capable. But it is his fresh-faced innocence that causes potential sexual partners to lower their guard, never expecting so unassuming a guy to be as engineered or determined as he is to go in for the kill.

ʃex + ʃexuality

The significance of Cancer's being both metaphoric lover and son to a female is that she is an all-encompassing figure of constancy in his life, in whom and from whom all life energy, his own included, flows. He, as consort, is there to protect and respect the awesome power that she, a living, breathing expression of the Feminine Principle, undeniably represents. The ancient matriarchal dynamic whereby the female takes a spouse merely to further her familial line is the one in which our Crab seeks to exist. In his search for a strong woman, he will consider it a bonus to enter into a family distinguished by this brand of matrilineal power. Not only is he being 'adopted' by a mate, but often by her entire clan as well which, much to his delight, is typically lousy with ballsy ladies. There is an added perk to mating with a woman with an omnipresent familial influence. Just as he wishes to appear the ideal husband, he also wants to be sure that his wife or lover will be sufficiently occupied emotionally so that she won't hijack his time and energy with any cloying needs of her own – with a distracting brood of her blood relations, he'll be that much more off the hook. Lest we forget: He's the one with needs, so his mate really shouldn't have any. In return for sacrificing himself to his partner's and ultimately his family's provision, he will expect to have his other day-to-day affairs catered to – never having to cook a meal or wash a dish or plan an evening or probably even pay a bill. He wants a life where he can just show up and nonetheless do what he's told. Like Moses in that basket, he's happy to just kick back and go with the flow his determined mate is manifesting, not having to expend energy on setting any agendas. They will be set for him. Like a crab, Cancer man moves with the current (read: present moment), and in so doing he may thus preserve his strength for personal, professional pursuits in which nobody, not even his iconic partner, can share.

Cancer man is a notoriously clever, inspired type, who generally seeks the greatest financial reward to be reaped for his talents. To him, the term 'starving artist' is oxymoronic. Action via impressionability is yet another symptom of his being the zodiac's sole cardinal-water male, symbolically combining the respective qualities of initiative and creative sensitivity. He has an amazing knack for tapping into the emotional climate of a culture, sympathetically speaking to, if not stirring up, common shared feelings. He executes this best via art forms that allow him to express the sentiments others experience, often doing so through witty social commentary or other outlets where humor or pathos may be employed as a curative means, purging people of more fearful or pessimistic passions. He is irony personified. Like a walking-talking *New Yorker* cartoon, he can sum up a situation from a sidelong angle – always sidling up to a punchline, never hitting one over the head with it. It's the Crab way: to make a sneak attack (but really grab you). Meanwhile, he feels that accomplishment in such lifelong pursuits is predicated on his being able to live life, as much as possible, from that strictly right-brain perspective, while his female partner becomes a substitute for his left side. If he is out in the world turning a buck, he won't want to deal with the nuts and bolts of quotidian living. In some rare instances, if his partner is the primary breadwinner, he might become the literal husband (original meaning: housebound), tending to the domestic environment and undertaking the leading role in rearing the children. It is typically impossible for Cancer, and thus his partner, to mix it up and do a bit of both. His mate is an essential part of himself, the yin that usually allows him to yang out and pursue his singular, sweeping dreams.

To focus fully on his typically artistic ambitions, Cancer often sacrifices responsibility for himself on all other levels. Ironically, he must give himself over completely to a significant other in order to succeed in his solo endeavors – with a constant rush of inspiration flooding Cancer's consciousness, there is simply no space for other, more practical concerns. Indeed, there is an element of his entering into a master class when he starts a serious relationship. His woman becomes the mentor shaping his character, providing the appropriate all-important healthy and motivating *environment* in which he can grow and achieve his goals; so long, that is, as he puts himself, completely, into her capable hands. In Cancer's relationships it would seem that his lover is the boss on so many levels that he is nothing more than her willing slave, something that often raises the ire of his male friends. Of course, an inversion is inherent in all master-servant relationships, and this is certainly the crux of the Cancer man's love bonds: Like the curiously named crabs, those pesky parasitic lice, the Cancerian male also figuratively feeds on his female host. Typically, the woman remains unaware of this – at least the itchy critters let you know you've got

4TH ASTROLOGICAL
HOUSE

self-protection
conclusions
parents
conditioning
blood ties
home/residence
family foundation
pedigree
psychological base
private life and matters
houses and real estate
parent of greater sway
mother influence
theoretical self
basis of character
self-recovery
accumulated factors
domestic setting
domestic environment
operational base
collecting
household items
land and property
the drama of life
intellectual training
nurturing
unconscious mind
emotional life
subconscious fears
instinctive response
habits set in childhood
beginning and end of cycles
patriotism
childhood memories
sentimentality/nostalgia
maturity
the past
public opinion
the (female) population

KEY WORDS

potential
pacifism
irony
control
commiseration
trust
calculation
regret
convention
sensibility
guardianship
impression
self-protection
mood
emotion
ceremony
evasion
nourishment
purification
shrewdness
sympathy
melancholy
opportunity
dissatisfaction
procreation
matriarchy
patriotism
sensitivity
shelter
concern
sentimentality
attachment
pretension
suppression
immunity
romance
husbandry
concealment
conversation
self-confidence
intuition
commitment
memory
nostalgia
subtlety
tone

them. But Cancer man is sneakier still. Just like the ocean crab that obliquely approaches its prey, undetected, before bearing down with those viselike claws, the Cancer man sneaks up on a woman, insinuating himself and his (un)conscious intentions. So cool and detached is his demeanor that, when she suddenly finds herself captivated, she's already unable to imagine life without him. It's the same with his libidinous needs: One wouldn't expect such acute lust, literally experienced as an insistent surging in his loins, from this seemingly reserved boy-next-door. Sustaining his placid veneer, cloaking his panting need to pounce, he thus bides his time, feigning to want nothing more than a platonic interaction. Pretending to be nonchalant, he not only disarms a would-be lover, but also plants the seeds of desire for him in her psyche. It's a strategy that works: He draws her in, then gradually lowers the boom. Like that crustacean you accidentally happen upon, our tenacious Crab won't let go once he gets his pincers in.

Still, when it comes to sex, females are never mere physical objects to be plowed for pleasure; they are venerated *sources* of life from whence he, sometimes all too gratefully, receives his inspiration and to whom he must offer himself as a desirable partner-in-reproduction. In fact, it's all but impossible for the Cancer guy to approach sex without entertaining the basic, procreative function of the act. Thus, he tries to appear the very embodiment of gourmet seed: Like a crème de la crème sperm-bank donor, Cancer man wants his 'profile' of personal qualities to appear most intriguing to a woman. So, consciously or not, he grooms himself for female scrutiny, offering all the requisite attributes he intuits one might seek, all the while seeming to assert no overtly masculine agenda of his own. In a nutshell, he plays Prince Charming, careful not to come across too kingly and, thus, tamper with the archetypal matriarch he seeks as a mate.

Most of all, Cancer man makes a woman feel secure. After all, he is the living embodiment of the archetypal sacrificial hero, presenting himself as someone who'll remain eternally by her side, if not be at her beck and call. Thus, he acts the antithesis of some wild man or flaky freak. Rather, he becomes a rapt audience to a woman, who will, in turn, find herself talking up a storm, typically revealing far more about herself than she otherwise would. Without consciously knowing why, a woman instinctively invests herself emotionally in Cancer man. But if she were to look more carefully, she might notice that he's only really half-listening, *playing* at being intent, simply because he knows that's what a woman wants. Cancer man sends a message: He's sensitive, different from other guys. But unfortunately, it might become painfully clear over time that he's actually contemplating what car he's going to buy next, or how the waitress might look in a tight fuzzy sweater, or how he might look driving the waitress away from the drudgery of her life, rescuing her and her sweater, in his new car. Still, he's a skilled actor on the stage of life, and he usually gets away with it, especially with the self-absorbed women he often attracts. With just a soupçon of effort, Cancer is most often able to make a woman feel she is endlessly interesting, which works like a charm in paving the way for the relationship to progress – quickly – to the next level. He will have achieved in short order what most men struggle to effect: not only the speedy putting out of pussy, but the impression that it was primarily the woman's idea to offer it up, practically on a silver platter. So it might then come as a bit of a surprise that the sexual experience is really so much about *him*.

Cancer isn't pushy in bed; rather, he's notoriously cloying, asserting an intensely emotional agenda. Sex with him is, in a word, loaded. He may seem so damned grateful, and audibly so, that a woman starts to wonder whether he might not have engineered the whole shebang after all. Sex with the typical Cancer man is often even accompanied by a running apology: 'Oh, that feels good – sorry about this – I really like that – sorry, sorry, sorry.' Seems he has a hard time understanding that it's not necessarily being *done* to her, that she might, too, be enjoying herself. Politeness has its place, but someone might need to tell the all too courteous Crab guy that you can't play sex like a game of Mother, May I? But taking the reins is simply not his forte – one instance where being programmed for deference can be somewhat a detriment. Eventually, Cancer may have to trade in his grateful-little-boy routine for the more flattering role of big daddy – a self-vision that always (pre)occupies his imaginary life anyway.

To *realize* these 'real man' reveries is no easy task for the zodiac's Pinocchio. He is plagued by insecurity such that, even if he achieves the unapologetic sexism of a Hemingway, he will still defer to women (as the aptly named 'Papa' did). Even this pompous pugilist of a Cancerian immortalized his own malehood as wounded, castrated like Perceval and Osiris. His thinly veiled auto-biographical figure, Jake Barnes in *The Sun Also Rises,* embodies these ithyphallic gods in the characterization of a Lost Generation's sacrificial male, emasculated via his affection for the iconic Lady Brett Ashley. (Cancer has an easier time with the Lady Bretts of the world, who would necessarily seek to be on top.) Like Hercules, it is Cancer's birthright to be taken to task, and he must perform the sacrificial purpose of following the female's decree – even in bed, the dubious expectation is he's there to satisfy a woman's lust, not his manly own. Herein the eternal twenty-one-year-old Cancer is cast in the recurring role he was born to play: The Graduate. Graduation, literally 'developing

BODY RULERSHIP

Cancer rules the stomach and there is a tendency toward digestive and gastric afflictions. It also rules the alimentary system, the female reproductive system, the breasts, womb, and ovaries. The Moon rules the lymphatic system, bodily fluids, the pancreas, and the sympathetic nervous system, controlling the reflexes and responses to emotional stimuli.

gradually,' is the planetary energy associated with his ruler as the waxing Moon glyph suggests. Having an eternal mother-lover, metaphorically akin to Mrs. Robinson, to go home to provides him the perfect sexual and emotional environment for the development of his character. The onus is on him to do nothing, except carry out matriarchal mandates – Mrs. Robinson is just Hera with a skunk stripe. And as it is for the story's hero, Benjamin, Cancer's reward for being put through hell by this domineering mommy dearest is that he eventually gets to *graduate* and marry her 'daughter,' or younger aspect, as Heracles married Hebe, Hera in her virgin form. Such is the allegorical sexual journey every Cancer man must take, gradually letting his lady love transform him into a wholly complete man who will eventually become, if not her lord and master, than at least self-possessed enough not to be emasculated by her. In some cases, Cancer misses the transition, forever becoming blindly bonded with a castrating woman. Sometimes he will purposefully have 'learned' on a mommy mentor with the intention of building enough confidence to double back and pick up that sweater girl. Other times, when he does make the psychological and emotional shift, the relationship doesn't survive Cancer's metamorphosis, the ballsy mate refusing to allow the Cancer to develop his own set of *cojones*. In that case, the eternal bridegroom is either left fondling his bachelor's degree, washed back onto the shore of single life, or, now, consciously in the market for a more equal partner – someone with whom to navigate life's ebbs and flows, like Pyrrha to his Deucalion, two peas, floating along in a pod.

Meanwhile, whatever the arrangement his relationship takes, the Crab will always be sexually aroused by the assertion of female power. Cancer is typically a much better lover, anyway, when he isn't tasked as the prime mover. Pressure to perform makes him nervous, and he risks either losing his erection or shooting the moon too soon. However, in a more passive role – the proverbial male ingenue – it's quite a different story: In this instance, he may be the most sexually tireless man on the astrological block, capable of not only recurring orgasms but multiple ones as well. And with the strain off to be some sexual he-man, he is able to fully embrace his sensitivity as sexual excitement often sees him tapping into some fairly sappy emotional outpourings. Of any man, he is the premier softie, loving to kiss, hug, spoon, and moon. He needs that showering of cuddly mother love as much as, if not more than, getting his rocks off. On that score, nothing imparts more of a pure erotic thrill than letting an energetic top woman have her way with him, boobs bouncing, as she barks imperatives and instructions.

In fact, very little in Cancer man's vision of worthwhile sex doesn't include breasts in one way or another. He is the zodiac's preeminent tittiefucker, and most of his sexual fantasies involve big-bosomed babes in the proverbial pole position. The Crab guy relishes being (s)mothered by a female, and his masturbatory visions feature ladies who loom large and in-charge. But that's just the beginning: Whereas many men choose to remain in the dark about more intimate female functions, the Cancerian embraces all of a woman's more scatological workings. He is anything but squeamish when faced with a partner's outpourings, a proclivity that may easily extend to the peepee department, urine falling under Cancerian rule. As well, he's way up for anal sex; though if his mate flashes a red flag, he's fine with forgoing it. Of course, he loves being blown – what man doesn't? – but for him the act imparts a particularly soothing and secure, pacifying sensation. He can be fairly kinky in his makeup, especially where his love for a dominant woman drives him to the extreme: savoring the role of a submissive or even an outright slave to a die-hard dominatrix.

For the most part, however, the Crab rarely acts on his more intricate fantasies. He will certainly be reluctant to broach the subject on the home front, where he neither wishes to risk shaking the emotional foundation of his permanent relationship nor tamper with the pristine carnal bond that is procreatively driven at its core. It makes sense that his mythic savior-consort archetype owes his raison d'être to his ability to properly impregnate his goddess mentor. It's the same for Cancer: He seems designed to propogate, parent, provide, and protect. And compared with most, or dare we say, *all* men, he can't seem to divorce the natural function of sex from the simple pleasure of it. Sex is, on some unconscious level, duty first and desire second. Perhaps for that very reason many a Cancerian marries early, having had few prior sexual partners – a fact that only further fuels both his fantasies and his frustration. Though he considers sex sanctified, this homebody isn't above extracurricular activity. Ironically, the more secure he feels with that strong, roost-ruling woman, the more likely he is to fulfill his secret yearnings elsewhere. Sooner or later, it seems, he needs to live out his fantasy fuck with that fuzzy sweater. It's not inconceivable that Cancer man will find a girl – even pay for one – to perform a sort of sexualized schoolgirl routine for his pleasure. Or, at the opposite end of the spectrum, this may be where he indulges his submission desires, seeking to be disciplined as any dirty-minded schoolboy deserves to be. Either way, his fantasies always surround the balance of power between himself and a woman. And all too often, these are imaginings he'd never dream of attempting with his mother-lover. He is the zodiac's purified male, remember, and he simply can't bring his 'dirtier' Mittyish daydreams to light. It's not just a matter of fearing rebuke on the

Ingmar Bergman
Charles Herman-Wurmfeld
Jean Anouilh
George Orwell
Nathaniel Hawthorne
Franz Kafka
J. J. Rousseau
Hermann Hesse
Jacques Derrida
Saul Bellow
Ken Russell
Tom Stoppard
Clifford Odets
Neil Simon
Jean Cocteau
E. B. White
Henry David Thoreau
Pablo Neruda
Nelson Mandela
David Brinkley
Gerald Ford
John Glenn
John D. Rockefeller
Richard Branson
Oscar Hammerstein
Ray Davies
Vince Guaraldi
Arlo Guthrie
Woody Guthrie
Cat Stevens
Gustav Mahler
David Hockney
Marcel Proust
Andrew Wyeth
J. M. Whistler
Camille Pissarro
Modigliani
Edgar Degas
Edward Hopper
Rembrandt van Rijn
Julius Caesar
Giorgio Armani
Richard Simmons
Arthur Ashe
Matthew Pritchett
Jeff Beck
Mick Fleetwood
Sidney Lumet
Peter Lorre
Antoine de Saint-Exupéry
Yazid

home front – rather, he himself needs to live an unsullied reality. He typically won't be happy knowing he and his lady wife *actually* get up to those acts that pollute his private imagination. That's not whom he wants to be. So it isn't a matter of convincing Cancer to build a bridge, connecting his more 'perverted' visions with his somewhat puritanical, albeit fetishistically passive, carnal behavior. That will rarely, if ever, happen. What the Cancer must come to grips with, instead, is that he will always have more savage notions – whether or not he acts upon them is a different story – that have nothing whatsoever to do with his actual love life and domestic existence.

In any case, Cancer will typically immerse himself in that household reality, focusing on his primal need to be the pristine husband, the unadulterated consort, regularly coddling, cooing, and conceiving with his woman. Just as he is almost pathologically intrigued by those de rigueur female bodily functions – if any man would think nothing of having sex with his woman when, for instance, she's not quite finished with her period, it is our crusty Crustacean – his Greek Deucalion archetype was married to Pyrrha, whose name means 'life blood,' so you do the math. Likewise, he is all over his mate when she's pregnant, whereas this often drives a wedge into other couples' sex lives. For our ithyphallic hero, however, the swelling of a woman's belly, like the waxing of his ruler Moon, awakens a deep desire. Indeed, his mate might have to kick Cancer off in the middle of the night more than usual – as it is, the Crab has the distinct sexual habit of sneaking *in* when his woman least expects it, his favorite windows of opportunity being those fluid states – just falling asleep or upon waking. One would be hard-pressed to find a longtime partner of the Cancer man who hasn't actually awoken to his slowly shagging her, the actual experience being subtly woven into her dreamscape. That's how talented he is at insinuating himself in this very literal sense. And such fetishizing of his little mama won't end there: Once she's given birth, his woman's milk might also become a fixation, to the point where the baby could have some fairly stiff competition. In a sense, Cancer's more fantastical sexual contemplations will naturally be subjugated by his equally ardent eroticizing of his relationship with the mother of his children. And since Cancer tends to have a lot of kids, there are typically plenty of years that go by where Cancer is lost in the near ecstatic throes of parenthood, aroused by all the permutations his partner will undergo. Their bedroom will often be a damp heap of bodies, baby things, and bedding, a veritable love nest where the nice and the naughty comingle comfortably.

If and when Cancer is to venture forth from his mushy domestic nexus in a quest to fulfill unrealized carnal desires, it tends to occur at or about midlife, when most Crab men have reared their families – remember, he generally gets an early start. Sometimes it will manifest in a rather hands-off manner, with furtive visits to peep shows or even video booths. Indeed, he may try to satisfy his wanton appetites with a minimum of human contact, his idea of cheating entailing no more than paying for a lap dance. Of course, he'll choose the inevitable 'performer' in the pigtails and baby-doll dress. Like his so-called opposite sign of Capricorn, not really opposites at all, the Crab has a very questionable attraction to nubiles. At least in the Player's case, he will doubtless have the moral wherewithal to keep his peccadillo just that – a petty sin – decidedly preferring to see a consenting adult female acting the *wittle* girl part than ever entertaining the unthinkable alternative. He may have quite elaborate scenarios running in that creative mind, often involving white cotton panties and a lollipop or some unreasonable facsimile. Fantasies of this sort, acted upon or not, generally see him fully clothed. Indeed he may pay a Lolita-alike to do little more than fish for candy in his pocket. There may be a bit of spanky, spanky. On the total other side of the spectrum, Cancer may play out elaborate humiliation fantasies where some big-haired, riding-crop-toting mama grinds her stiletto into some part of him, as it is, splayed spread-eagle at her feet. No other man in the zodiac likes to be called a lowly worm the way our often tweedy boy-next-door does. In extreme cases he may want to be stripped, bound, gagged, and taunted by some fierce mistress, all the while wimpering his way to ecstasy if not, in rarer instances still, trying not to wet his diaper. You heard us. We might as well deal with the tinkle factor right here and now: No man is more prone to take the odd golden shower than he, whether it be provided by someone in schoolgirl costume or full leather regalia. It's probably the most graphic interpretation of his sign's cardinal-water status. There is, in fact, very little a woman can do to turn the Cancer off – every possible working of her being is up for grabs to be fetishized by the Crab. He doesn't objectify women along the more usual lines – as a manicured, lingerie-clad centerfold – but as a source of natural awe. He is at once fascinated with the female form, as *other,* and yet he deeply identifies with women emotionally, even spiritually, regardless of his own sexual preferences.

Unlike many gay men, the homosexual Cancer may find himself physically excited by women as well; and he may even reach for bi porn over the purely gay variety. Still, he'll mainly watch the guys doing the women – nothing imparts a bigger thrill than a hetero he-man in action – wishing he was the player cast in the enviable part of the inevitable third wheel who 'just happens' upon his straight roommate screwing his girlfriend and (to the strains of a bad synthesizer sound track) is casually asked to join in. Any lingering

STR8 TURN-ONS

strong women
Nordic, Germanic types
tall women
big breasts, implants
kissing, licking, sucking
(active) oral
(passive/active) discipline
titty-fucking
waitresses/flight attendants
(active) anal sex
submission fantasies
strippers, porn stars
pregnancy, lactation
schoolgirls
shaved, waxed genitals
(passive) bondage
leather, biker chicks
(passive) golden showers
cuddling, spooning
home porn
hotel rooms
crops, whips
nymphomaniacs
dominatrixes

doubts that Cancer man loves women will be otherwise dispelled by his CD collection of female vocalists. And because he's astrologically geared to be the quintessential male consort to females, it's rarely ever completely out of the question for him to entertain a love relationship, if not a sexual one, with a woman. In his lifetime, at least one of his close friendships with a woman may cross the line, dipping briefly into sexual territory. He prefers the company of young women who share his need to land Mr. Right (read: rich). And nobody has a stronger sixth sense for sussing out where the most successful guppies gather; so, he'll put on his crispest clothes (Cancerian males, regardless of orientation, are ironing freaks) and subtly schmooze with such a crowd, knowing his signature insouciance will see him chatted up within minutes. Gay Cancer dates a lot, but rarely second-dates. That is, until he finds his perfect man — the exact big-daddy antithesis of his father — worldly, connected, cultured, and hopefully, brimming with cash. He requires all that riches signal: comfort, security, and the means by which he'll be able to concentrate solely on his creative or intellectual pursuits, without having to concern himself with a temp job. While straight Cancer will make up for his orphaned feelings in the nurturing rearing of his children, gay Cancer often calls for a do-over of his childhood: Lamenting having missed out on the princely origins that he feels befit him, he'll seek to secure a relationship with a blatantly well-heeled fellow. Wanting to be the eternal son-lover to his mate, he may even hunt for a husband in venues that attract a mature clientele, rarely wasting his time clubbing with guys his own age. Unlike his straight counterpart, the gay Cancer won't as readily concern himself with earning a hefty income, but will instead play the more wifely role of domestic engineer, allowing himself plenty of free time to focus on those burning dreams. He wants what he never had: a childlike existence, in a stimulating, urbane, and sophisticated setting, in which current events are discussed over breakfast, holidays are planned, and real-estate investments are debated — all as an antidote to what he typically considers the numbing, status quo atmosphere of his own upbringing. He'll usually insist on having his own room, separate from the one he shares with a lover, a place where he can spread out and surround himself with images and fixtures that reflect his true self — especially since he was probably cramped into a corner at home, having to constantly share with siblings.

This is perhaps how that age of twenty-one manifests in the gay Cancerian psyche: His home smacks of someone having just moved into his own apartment, just short of hanging a wooden initial on the wall like that spunky Mary Richards on the *Mary Tyler Moore Show*. And the 'Mary' comparisons don't end there. Though gay Cancer guy is what's commonly deemed 'str8-looking, str8-acting,' one only needs to scratch the surface of his personality to awaken the divalike Mother Principle within. Male Cancer, despite his sexual orientation, has what might be called a female soul. He's protective and nurturing and can be rather persnickety and even school-marmish in demeanor. In some cases, he maintains the careful, protective spirit of a prudish dowager. There's no getting around it: Of all the gay men in the zodiac, Cancer can be the biggest sissy. So, as if being son and lover to a mate isn't enough, he will also play the role of wife and mother. He is decidedly attracted to str8-ultramasculine guys, often making love bonds with men who have heretofore been heterosexual and, often, married. Cancer sees himself as a trophy boy – the better-looking, more pleasingly put together, or generally youthfully spirited one of the two. And this dynamic will spill over into the bedroom as well, where the Cancer needn't 'work' so hard – his lover should be the more passionate and ardent one, as Cancer kicks back and simply goes along for the ride. He loves being the object of a partner's doting adoration, but soon, he'll want more than fatherly sugar from his daddy.

The wounded warrior, the castrated fertility figure, the milksop in pinstripes, the Crab is the embodiment of irony. His straitlaced looks are often deceiving as, of all gay males in the zodiac, Cancer has the most prurient desires, secretly longing to be the bottom feeder on the sexual food chain, as befits his more crusty crustacean status. Hands down, the gay Moon child is the biggest cock pig in the zodiac, wanting to be of blatant service to as rough and rugged a man as he might find. Of course, the tanned and tweedy man he typically mates with mightn't realize his Cancer's dirty little secret, nor will the Crab always reveal it. He is, on all accounts, programmed for receptivity, passive to the point of no return. But often for fear of rocking the foundation of his desired cushy domestic situation, Cancer might look elsewhere to fulfill his longings. In truth, it would shock most anyone who knew him in the light of day to discover what this man gets up to in the dark, if not in back rooms of gay bars. As unsqueamish as straight Cancer is, the gay Crab can be that much more into scat. He generally draws the line at pain, however, in any way, shape, or form. And despite the danker depths of his sexual desire, gay Cancer is still a sucker for tender romance, seemingly so utterly content to indulge in the scented-candles, champagne, and Calgon-bubble-bath scene. Like Gemini, he can be fetishistic about foreplay, but with a decided twist: Rather than such stimulation being designed to make the inevitable climax more dramatic, Cancer enjoys the frustration it affords, isolating it for his own ironic pleasure. As it is, he isn't in those back rooms for his own objective release but rather is deriving excitement from servicing others who'll let loose on, if not in, him.

GAY TURN-ONS

daddies, bears
hairy bodies
nipple play
piercing, clamps
bottoming
swallowing
rimming
showers, bathing
bi porn
(passive) b + d
humiliation, torture, slaving
gags, blindfolds, collars
cross-dressing
kink, raunch, lite scat
frottage
glory holes, tea rooms
truckers, bikers, skinheads
whips, chains, slings
rubber, latex
watersports
(passive) lite s + m
felching
rape fantasies

(Indeed, when it comes to which sexual page this boy is on, he is very decidedly a *recto* rather than a *verso*.) Reciprocation is often adamantly not what he's after. He might prefer to get off, or *not* as the case may be, simply by being kissed for hours, elevating that act to an end in itself. Cancer man is probably the only individual to whom dry-humping appeals as a cause célèbre. Frottage, or the aptly collegiate-termed 'Princeton rub,' is likewise a favorite sexual proclivity – especially when it results in him bearing the climactic brunt. Like straight Cancer, the gay Crab enjoys being sprayed, one way or another. And yet, through all this sexual *mishegoss,* he is the most romantic of gay men – his more dank desires and sappier visions are rarely mutually exclusive, both stemming from the watery realm of his sodden astrological rule. His motto 'I feel' points to sex, like everything, having to play on the full range of his emotions, from humiliation to euphoria, that are often bundled into one paradoxical package.

Couplings

Cancer Man / Aries Woman

The attraction is subtle – less physically felt, rather more subconscious. Their pairing is antidotal – an emotional cure for past pain. He provides the support she's sought. Sex exorcises ex-lovers.

Cancer Man / Taurus Woman

She's his fantasy in the flesh – all soft skin wrapped in a fuzzy pastel sweater. She knows his placid nature is a pose, and that extraordinary experiences await. In bed, it's titillation and tenderness in equal measure.

Cancer Man / Gemini Woman

Typically passive, he pursues her anyway – Gemini's impish appeal makes him behave surprisingly, even shockingly. The Crab appears the ultimate catch – charismatic, clever. In bed, it's a mixed bag – a mess if she's moody.

Cancer Man / Cancer Woman

Two Moon-ruled souls share a rare and rarefied emotional and sexual connection. They seem to live on their love alone. At home, everything looks a wreck; but chaos is comforting. Bed is a safety zone where anything goes.

Cancer Man / Leo Woman

He's clever and commanding; she confidently holds court. They're meticulous about career matters. Self-concerns are joyfully sacrificed for the common good. Sexually, Leo tries tenderness; Cancer takes it up a notch.

Cancer Man / Virgo Woman

They become fast friends. Together, they manage stresses. Life has a flow. She's happy to stay at home; Cancer softens into professional success. As they crave each other completely, too much sex is never enough.

Cancer Man / Libra Woman

He's that rare 'regular' guy; she seems, at first, too perfunctory a personage. Relating requires tolerance. At best, they're harmonious and hilarious. Sex eases tensions: Cancer's passive so Libra has the power.

Cancer Man / Scorpio Woman

Cancer requires mothering; Scorpio's a cunning caretaker. Together, they cultivate a snug coexistence. Prosperity and progeny are anticipated. In bed, it's all-out eroticism. But mum's the word.

Cancer Man / Sagittarius Woman

She's unpredictable, something he's unequipped to handle. Sexually, she falls into a category: fantasy fling. They share a soulful ideology. She uses sex to fasten his affections. In bed, he'll feel like James Bond.

Cancer Man / Capricorn Woman

He's the Eagle Scout of her dreams; she's that perfect, postmodern beauty. These astro-opposites are often ideal counterparts, easily finding a comfortable, conducive middle way. Sex is a slow process of chipping away at constraints.

Cancer Man / Aquarius Woman

She's his wake-up call. He's less an epiphany, more of a reality check – a sign it's time to get serious. They're an ideological society of two, living an inspired life. Sex is transformative – a step up for him, an enhancement for her.

Cancer Man / Pisces Woman

Two sensitive souls with acutely creative spirits. With him, she delves into a vocation, inching closer to goals. He breaks through lingering emotional limitations. Bed is their messy center of activity.

Gay

Cancer Man / Aries Man

Cancer is the Ram's Mr. Right. Aries is altered by the Crab's humor and sensitivity. They have a need to succeed; mutual support is their mantra. A dynamic bond, but there's bound to be tension. Sexually, it's a mixed bag.

Cancer Man / Taurus Man

A conservative and quiet couple – homebodies who enjoy a rich quality of life. There's nothing to prove: Taurus is his most placid self; Cancer takes the lead. Hidden dalliances may mean hearts get broken.

Cancer Man / Gemini Man

Cancer has rare insight into the Geminian character; he's not put off by a slick veneer. Together, they find an emotional center. Over time, mutual caretaking becomes their raison d'être. Sex is dramatic, passionate.

Cancer Man / Cancer Man

A clinging, clawing bond. A similarly wry sense of humor sustains them through inevitable relationship travails – highs and lows are endemic to the Crab chap. Sex is conventional, but there's no criticism.

Cancer Man ∫ Leo Man

Leo is suspicious of Cancer's sneaky ways. Over time, often on the sly, these charismatic characters become companions, enchanted by each other. They're a popular pair. In bed, it's a loving, affirming affair.

Cancer Man ∫ Virgo Man

Workaholics who tend to social climb. In tandem, sharp wit and sarcasm surface – it's a contest of who can be more clever. Professionally, this partnership is pure gold. In bed, they handle each other with care.

Cancer Man ∫ Libra Man

Cancer is Milquetoast to left-of-center Libra. But the Scales guy is famous for making exceptions, especially if sex is in the offing. Cancer acclimates to a spot of scandal in his otherwise spotless existence.

Cancer Man ∫ Scorpio Man

They're masked and cool in public, but not so behind closed doors. Their object: to live and love ecstatically, in a sustained state of rapture. A completely compatible couple who merge mentally as much as they do sexually.

Cancer Man ∫ Sagittarius Man

Cancer is a tough nut to crack – he's especially guarded with straight-shooting Sag. Soon it's clear their quality-of-life concerns correspond. The Archer's extensive sexual past shouldn't prohibit partnership: Cancer's hiding quite a history himself.

Cancer Man ∫ Capricorn Man

These astro-opposites face many challenges. There's trouble lurking behind the straight surfaces they present. In the end, Cap is labeled 'the villain.' But from the first, sex is so fine as to become a fetish.

Cancer Man ∫ Aquarius Man

Cancer directs Aquarius down a more traditional life path – to the Moon man, success is measured by the money one makes. Resentments resound if creativity is sacrificed to status. Sexually, tables turn: Aquarius is the authority.

Cancer Man ∫ Pisces Man

Together, they probe remote corners of experience – spiritual exploration is a possibility. Soul-searching enhances their chances of relationship success. They both crave romance and often find it with each other.

Cancer Woman

the pearl

Unplugged: Cancer woman is the most emotive character in the zodiac. A wellspring of raw feelings, she wears her heart on her sleeve, needing to express her emotions even when others might consider it unwise to do so. More than any other female, she is consumed by her sentiments, brutally unabashed in both her affections and her aversions. She comes on strong, unhinging set rules and systems, as well as the nerves of the more reserved or regimented people in her midst. Cancer is a master at washing away outmoded restrictions, 'cleaning house' and otherwise causing a welcome upheaval on both social and professional fronts. Free-form in her approach to life, she goes on gut instincts, and her actions may seem uncontrolled or irrational. Eternal commotion in the unfathomable ocean of her emotions might see Cancer manically swinging from proverbial party girl to sorrowful soul, especially in her tender years, during which she's fairly aching for loving care. In truth, she often feels at sea, challenged to establish firm emotional footing, secure a healthy lifestyle, and land the right kind of mate. In early relationships she expects to be saved by men and thus risks attracting tyrannical types who take advantage of her natural urge for dependence. Ultimately, she will realize that the best man for her is a stalwart type, a 'rock' who'll go with the flow of her invariably eddied existence. With other women, she tends to play mother hen, doting on her lover while dictating constant demands. She is politically and socially motivated in her sexual orientation and charged with an often cloying need for romantic demonstration, affectionate stroking, and validation.

ſign + Mind

Cancer is ruled by the Moon, representative of the Mother Principle in the zodiac, which presides over flows of fluids in the body as well as all that water symbolically represents – emotions, mood, and intuition, among other attributes. For this reason, Cancer woman seems to be all feeling. Being born under the Mother Principle manifests in a number of ways: First, it means that Cancer tends to view females over males as authority figures, for better or for worse. It also instills in the girl Moonchild an inherent sense of existence itself as being feminine in nature: That Mother Earth is the sovereign, tangible source of life as opposed to the masculine paradigm, whereby power is perceived as emanating from a distant, intangible sky-god. As heady as it may sound, this is typically the way of the world for the Cancer female, who grows up in a female-dominated household where her mother is the unequivocal master, and her father is a rather vague, if amiable, figure. Whereas a masculine (patriarchal) model of existence emphasizes stoical *form* the feminine version, meanwhile, features expressive *content,* and Cancer female can be seen as the personification of loaded sentiments, which are themselves as seemingly unguided as the ocean, and thus overwhelming to the more restrained, ordered creatures among us. But chaotic looks can be deceiving.

Though the Moon is associated with elusive moods and instincts, it nonetheless represents the principle and power of *rhythm* in the universe, literally discernible in its control over our planet's waters via the clockwork regularity of the tides, just as it regulates women's menstrual cycles – *mens* means 'moon.' Thus, the lunar-ruled Cancer female most poignantly embodies this dynamic. That silvery, slivery orb, in all its routine, monthly (moon-thly) waxing-and-waning permutations, offers itself as the preeminent example of order within our immediate cosmos, the solar system, just as this pearly sphere has come to denote chaos – the dreaded nocturnal world, rife with unpredictable, howling fears and perils giving rise to the confusion of the mind, from mild moonstruckedness to outright lunacy (*luna:* Latin for 'moon'). Herein lies the particular paradox associated with Cancer woman: a seeming ball of chaos who is actually a broadcast of natural order, albeit on an unseen, internal level. The whole of her life will be a process of embracing herself as a natural rhythmic expression of rhyme and reason; that is, not subjugated to, or indeed victimized by, external pandemonium. To be sure, she has a tough cosmic road to hoe – the sense of turmoil Cancer experiences is real to her despite any potential ability to perceive it as mere illusion. Understandably, in youth her first instinct is to fight her feelings – squelch, subdue, and simply not accept her outsized emotional state. But, in refusing to embrace internal unpredictability, pain is only compounded. Once she does make that psychological shift, embracing her ebbs and flows, Cancer is not only liberated from daunting emotional demons, but she is also able to express them freely within the confines of daily life and interpersonal experience – family, home, relationships – mainstays of living that are ironically most challenging for the Cancer female. The reason here, even Cancer woman would tell you, is she has a hard time finding her all-important rhythm in such situations; and it's little wonder. She feels inherently disenfranchised from her most elemental beginnings – in particular, she typically feels cut off from strong male influences, simultaneously (and utterly) plunged into a female-dominated environment. Born under the sign of the Mother Principle, Cancerians generally exhibit a lack of the Father Principle as well.

In metaphorical terms, Mother represents nurture, especially of the emotional sort, while Father characterizes protection, control, and discipline. And so, just as Cancer female embodies complete connection with her mother *source,* she lacks any stoical mechanism as might act to guard her against her emotional onslaught. On this score, she often feels dangerously exposed, which may explain why many a Cancer female soon becomes hardened (a nod to her Crab sign's protective shell). A number of Cancer girls dramatically withdraw from interpersonal dealings, while others 'act out' obnoxiously – most swing dramatically between these two scenarios. At the negative end of the sentimental spectrum lurks Cancer female's strongest one: fear. Indeed, the whole of her life's evolution will consist of finding the proper sensible distance from that scary sensation without denying it as her most elemental, psychological jumping-off point: Healthy fear – as opposed to the more irrational sort, a kind of neurosis or anxiety about living – is like an internal red flag that shoots up, signaling one to 'watch out.' Cancer possesses this immense inner-guidance system as her birthright, and with proper perspective, she may use it as an uncannily precise way to negotiate life's inherent dangers. As Joseph Campbell once pointed out, fear is the first experience of the human being while in the womb – a body part ruled by the sign of Cancer – which makes perfect sense: It is due to fear that an individual seeks *comfort* and *security,* which, along with *home, heritage*, and *emotional conditioning,* are attributes of the astrological 4th House falling under Cancer's rule.

The glyph of Cancer recalls the nurturing aspect of the female (mother) condition, seen as symbolizing either breasts or ovaries, the former offering nourishment, and the latter being the female seeds of life, which upon

♈ iv

PRINCIPLE

The Mother Principle. Via its Moon ruler, Cancer represents a model of the world environment as a tangible feminine entity, a *source* from whence all life stems. Cancer woman embodies this nurturing principle, engineered much like Mother Earth herself, predisposed to give and sustain life as well as being given to what might be perceived as chaotic rumblings and revolts. Her motto is 'I feel' and she does so in spades.

The Moon signifies rhythm in the universe as it controls the cadence of ebbings and flowings with its every wax and wane. The Cancer woman especially feels this hold on her being, which may give rise to chaotic feelings. In time she will settle into the rhythm and learn to pride herself on being so organic a component of the natural world.

fertilization will be nurtured within the womb. Astrologically, the breasts along with the stomach (womb) also fall under Cancerian rulership, offering clues to the Moon woman's metaphysical condition: As scholars have revealed, ancient matriarchal mystery cults, like that of Eleusis, celebrated the fact that females are born *as* mothers – girl babies already contain their eggs at birth, in contrast to boys, who slowly develop sperm – metaphorically speaking, thus, girls are born pregnant. In this way, heredity (*where you come from*) and heritage (*what's then passed on*) are simultaneously represented in the female condition. It would seem, then, that the nature of humankind is inherently matriarchal, something that the sign of Cancer symbolically reminds us of. It is from this bio-mythic ancestry that Cancer female ultimately draws her strength, transcending the perceivable chaos of her existence, ceasing to see herself as only needing said nurturing, instead feeling capable of offering it, both to herself and to others. Indeed, Cancer woman's whole life is a process of developing from expectancy to self-deliverance. Meanwhile, she may meet a sizable hurdle in heaping her need for (lacking fatherly) love upon a potential mate – otherwise known as the infamous Cancer-female static cling: that cloying and oft most annoying need for reassurance that points to her totem Crab's viselike claw.

As astrology's fourth sign, Cancer is the first sign of the zodiac's Second Quadrant, that which is primarily concerned with one's emotional environment, linking perfectly to the sign's rulership of the 4th Astrological House of *feelings,* as well as *the home one comes from* and *the home one establishes.* Fittingly, too, Cancer is associated with the age group 21–28, a time of maturity when a female moves from maidenhood into marriage and motherhood – again pointing to the sign's association with the womb. The key to Cancer's happiness is to embrace the matriarchal power she wields in the world. In linking astrological signs with biblical evolution, Aries represents big-bang creationism, Taurus expresses Edenic delight, Gemini symbolizes 'the fall,' and so Cancer is the flood. As the only cardinal (initiatory) water (emotion) sign in the zodiac, she personifies that rush of water, that matriarchal source, spring, or swelling river. In this way, the sign represents the re-creation of the world, this time along feminine rather than masculine lines. Judeo-Christian flood myths all but ignore the female figure, save for the sign of the dove, a symbol of the goddess in matriarchal religions, later adopted as an emanation of Christ. However, in the Greek flood myth, Themis, notably a creatress and goddess of order, is credited with helping Deucalion and Pyrrha, the Hellenic Noah and his wife, repeople the earth by throwing stones, 'the bones of Mother Earth,' over their shoulders, whereupon they turned into human beings. Point being: Zeus, like Yahweh, gave up on the world he created – thus the father god abandons the world of men – leaving a mother goddess to purify it with water, thereby starting all over again; this might be seen as the ultimate interpretation of the 4th House concepts of *old home* versus *new home*. Where the father abandons, the mother sympathizes and kisses the universal boo-boos of the world to make them all better. In the biblical line, the antediluvian (Gemini 'Twins') world of duality – the knowledge of good versus evil and the awareness of all other pairs of opposites characterizing the fall from grace and leading to wheely-dealy human corruption, bargaining, and haggling, even down to the machinations of Geminian-ruled *courtship* – gives way to Cancerian *mating* and literal *repairing* of circumstance as represented by all those two-by-twos being taken upon the ark, itself a word that means 'promise,' a most Cancerian concept. Not only is the flood itself a symbol of the sign's cardinal-water status, but so, too, is the activity going on inside the ark, wherein fluids are flowing every which way – the passengers weren't playing pinochle, after all. The flood washes away, purifies, and repairs the world. The animals inside are a promise of new life in this floating metaphorical womb upon the sea. This is Cancer woman in a nutshell: her symbol Moon's glyph waxing full like the swelling pregnant belly or the creation of a perfect pearl. She is a walking-talking harbinger of hope that must necessarily smile through her tears just as the sun shines unseen behind the clouds of torrential rain or in the dark of night.

The particularly Cancerian quality-element combination of cardinality and water signifies a need for action via emotion, or *feeling* action, as opposed to the previous cardinal sign of Aries's, *bodily* action. What this means specifically for the Crab girl is that her power lies in actively purging her emotions. Cancer's Moon rulership endows her with intuition, making her a receptor of impressions, while the cardinal quality emphasizes her role as one of astrology's action figures. From that perspective, she's wired to do both simultaneously – to take information in and then to act – really respond – in kind. Themis, whose virgin aspect, Artemis (Ar-Themis), is oft credited with being goddess of the Moon, seeks to re-create the world in response to her feelings of remorse at its being destroyed by Zeus. As such, Cancer female embodies that Mother Goddess archetype. And as the flood myth associated with Cancer suggests, it's quite literally a clean break that Cancer female needs in her own life – ending her vision of the male-created world, in which she feels downcast, re-creating a new world for herself. She has a built-in purification system: Like that flood cleaning up the world, Cancer's emotions are meant to wash away negative influences from her life environment – the home she comes from – and allow for a new, pure future – the home she creates. The home life the Crab girl is often born into is one in 'ruins' racked with emotional unrest and most often

SIGN QUADRANT

The zodiacal quadrants correspond to the metaphysical planes of existence – physical, emotional, mental, and spiritual. The Second Quadrant is that of emotional and indeed moral environment. For Cancer woman, importance lies in trusting feelings, developing instincts, purging herself of pain, and the transformation of emotional need into a source of power.

The Cancer emblem is a Crab. The glyph recalls two individuals floating along in the same vessel, like a couple surviving a flood, as the Crab, both a sea and land dweller, inevitably would. The symbol may also be read as a woman's breasts or ovaries, both ruled by the sign of Cancer and suggestive of her lively, literally life-giving, qualities.

ransacked by divorce. Often, Cancer girl is the offspring of a first marriage, faced with stepsiblings, or that of a second one, representing the issue of a reconstituted family. Perhaps the most important manifestation of Cancer's cardinal-water status is the activation of her emotions into wishes. To wish is to act, emotionally. But the trick for the Cancer female is to act on her emotions in a manner that ultimately leads to the purification of her own condition. Like her symbol Crab, that hard-shelled inhabitant of water, she is designed to endure torrents of emotions. Or, to extend the raw-bar analogy even further, it is the actual chaos of the watery (emotional) environment, the literal daily grind of sea and sand, that, within the soft underbelly of the oyster, forms into the perfect-symbol of purity and perfection, as well as wisdom: the pearl. Cancer female can only achieve this perfected state by letting the turmoil of emotions wash over her completely, embracing rather than fighting them, allowing even negative conditions to crystallize her character – not being selfish but rather shellfish in her motivations. As a female in a feminine sign, Cancer woman personifies her quality-element combination. She *is* that rush of emotion, whether a waterworks of self-pity or a font of feminine wisdom; whereas Cancer guy, a rather unemotional character, instead *plays* on the emotions of others by taking on a hero-savior role in relationships. But that is not Cancer woman's job in life. Contrary to popular astrological belief, the Crab female is not the nurturer of the zodiac – this bulletin should come as a great relief to her as she is continually typecast in a role she has trouble playing – she is of little help in trying to 'fix' things for others, particularly men, as a substitute for facing her own self-improvement process.

The archetypal blueprint for the Crab female condition is revealed in the story of Cinderella. It's a tale steeped in Cancerian and 4th Astrological House imagery: In a household dominated by women, where the absence of a father has caused victimization for our poor, pitiful Cindy, we witness a shift from the house in which she's brought up to the home, or castle, that she creates. And just how does she make it? Not through any physical action, but by wishing, all the while embracing the degradation and the ensuing sadness associated with her less than ideal environment, literally raking the ashes of her failed existence – she doesn't act out or tell her stepmom or stepsisters where they can go; rather, she accepts her condition. She *feels* her pain and fear, which in turn fuels her dearest wishes – cardinal actions on the nonphysical, Moon-ruled, intuitive plane. Without negative circumstances, there's nothing to transcend. Cinderella doesn't merely overcome her upbringing, she scores real big – landing a prince and a palace and all that happily ever after stuff – while never compromising her own moral character, getting even with all life's bitches without so much as uttering one moan. Complaining is a waste of emotional energy that's meant to be channeled into one and only one emotional action: having hope. Hope floats in the flood of mourning.

Taking her cue from Cinderella (literally, girl of ash, thus, one in ruins), directing energy into hopeful action, puts Cancer in touch with a fairy God Mother who materializes (*mater* meaning 'mother') after Cindy's had a good cry (mourning loss, purging negative feelings) while still having hope, that ark or promise that carries her to a secure, emotional dry land. There's more Cancerian imagery: All the action happens at night; Cinderella is whisked off in a pumpkin, a vegetable ruled by Cancer as it grows at night, you might say, by the light of the moon, drawn by nocturnal mice; the glass slipper as an image of the 'crystal cave' or entrance to Delphi, the world womb; and the appearance of the fairy godmother, the medieval Themis, symbolizes Cinderella's own wise-womanliness, those magical powers of intuition that eventually transform her into a princess, literally achieving serene 'highness' in moral character. Armed with all she's wished for, Cinderella doesn't wait around for her prince to trot up; she goes and gets him, adorned in the raiment of her ennobled (princesslike) nature. Likewise Cancer isn't going to be 'saved' by playing the victim – this is Cinderella, not Snow White – but must instead pull herself up by the emotional bootstraps and take action, letting the world, particularly that of men, see her very best resolute self. Her higher character comes from going through, not around, the negative aspects of her condition. And this is a Cancer female's most valuable lesson: Life is all about process; and escape is not an option. And nowhere is that concept better drawn than in the glyph of her ruling Moon, not full, but rather a first-quarter one – the First Quadrant of the zodiac is already behind her, but there's much more growth ahead. This first-quarter stage is referred to as the Virgin Moon, just as the full Moon is coined the Wise Moon. And, as we said, it often takes a good many years for the Cancer female to recognize herself as a pearl of wisdom. Still, as any pagan will tell you, it is during the waxing of the Moon that one is meant to cast one's spells of wish craft, the growing manifestation of the Moon taking up the cause on the unseen, mystic level that is characterized by this witchy, nocturnal sign. All Cancer women are witches without quite realizing it, though those around them will at times attest to this fact for reasons of their own. Cancer woman is engineered to naturally 'vibe in' to situations and project her immediate emotional reactions and intentions into the ether, trusting to these feelings, which are more acutely real to her than they are to any other sign in the zodiac, actually experiencing the growth of her intendments within her emotional being, until they are made manifest, almost miraculously. She

ELEMENT + QUALITY

The water element connotes feeling and instinct. The cardinal quality is a call to action and initiative. Together, the cardinal-water combination particular to Cancer is best illustrated as a life-giving source, spring, or river, a symbol of Cancer's emotional expression and nurturing urge. Lifeblood, Moon-ruled menses, and mother's milk are also signified.

feels things are going to happen, and by trusting to these inklings, they do. Indeed, Cancer woman teaches the rest of us by example the power to create by trusting to our instincts. The cardinal quality, as the dual meaning of the term denotes, signifies the initial and spontaneous, as well as the leading and directive, energies in the zodiac. In short, Cancer *goes* with her *gut*.

Meanwhile, she endures more than her fair share of situational chaos. Cancer girls generally grow up in female-dominated households with a mother who, perhaps subconsciously, places herself as a wedge between the Cancer girl and her father. In some cases, she is under her mother's thumb, 'enslaved' by constant chores or restrictive curfews. Cancer's mother may also be something of a doormat to men – setting no example of feminine strength – compensating by becoming dominant, if not downright shrewish, toward other women, daughters included. This sends the Crab girl a mixed message about what it means to be female, something she has plenty of time to bitch about – albeit under her breath – while performing the myriad obligations that her mother sets out. Early on, Cancer girl begins to bottle up her emotions for fear of some punishment, emotional or otherwise. She often feels downtrodden. And even if her mother is as sweet as pie, she'll still spoon-feed Cancer girl a laundry list of tasks, under the guise that such responsibility is simply a female's lot in life. Most damaging of all, Cancer's mother doesn't often put much stock in the opinions of her own sex, but instead defers to the supposed omniscience of the man or men in her life. This may put the Crab girl at the compound disadvantage of having neither emotional access to father nor the kind of mothering that teaches, by example, female power.

As her symbol quarter Moon suggests, Cancer might possess a sliver of wise understanding about the kind of woman she'll need to become to achieve happiness. And so, usually as soon as she is legally able to do so, Cancer girl moves out of the home – initiating her first of many *endings*, another 4th House notion, a series of which will define the Cancerian experience for years to come, seeking escape from mother while looking to fill the void of lacking male influence in her life. More than most women, Cancer female is inclined to shack up at a tender age, not only seeking emotional rescue after feeling so undervalued, but also wanting to catch a whiff of some testosterone for a change. And though some Cancer girls do begin an early Cinderella-style introspective journey toward fulfillment, most Crabs grab at the first ray of hope they see floating by. This is the big cosmic joke of Moon-ruled Cancer's Mother Principle: In an effort to escape and transcend her own mother issues, Cancer may be so grateful to the first prince who comes along that she gives her full (quarter) self to him, unquestioningly, making a god of him much in the manner her mother made of men. But being a Cancer female means that, eventually, your god must be a goddess – revering femininity in herself, as well as other women, against whom she often unwittingly puts herself at odds.

Body + Soul

In her emotional quest, which leads straight to men, Cancer woman projects an aura of caring little for her own sex. In fact, in the single active objective of becoming the be-all-end-all little woman to a guy, she might have such utter disregard for other woman her own age that she seems to them a nemesis, a term whose meaning, in this context, should not be understated: The Egyptian counterpart of our archetypal Greek creatress Themis is the goddess Isis, a figure associated both with the Moon – she wears a Moon diadem like Themis' virgin incarnation – and with the advent of the flood. Nemisis (Nem-Isis or Nepthys) is Isis' 'dark sister' or shadow self, which is how Cancer woman represents herself to all her 'sisters,' other women to whom she only shows her dark side while, like the Moon, turning her other, shinier face to men. Like those infamous stepsisters in *Cinderella,* Cancer can come across as conniving, vainglorious, phony, and manipulative, not to mention totally unsimpatico to fellow females. It isn't just Cinderella who represents Cancer female in this story; rather, all the female characters are potential aspects of the Moonchild's personality – such as her own (step) mother, needing to achieve womanly wisdom (godmother) and, in the process, alternating between the perfect princess (to men) and a wicked pain in the ass to women.

Being the demure darling to men, no matter how disingenuous, is a popular tack for Cancer to take. She makes a man feel like the big, strong protector. At times, she'll trade in her sweetheart pin for a lampshade crown, presenting herself as the proverbial party girl who promises a good time. Yet, such a display is usually the mark of a Cancer in a lot of pain and denial – often, literally dancing as fast as she can in an effort to escape the chaotic emotions being put into her self-evolutionary path. What Cancer senses, mainly (the sign's motto is 'I feel'), is acute loneliness, something she'll remedy the best way she knows how: Whether by being the dutifully doting damsel in distress, or ensuring a ball will be had by all, she acts in a way to bring about the desired result: Notice. A glance at a list of famous Cancer women, which includes the likes of Meryl Streep, Princess Diana, Frances McDormand, Linda Ronstadt, Carly Simon, Pamela Anderson, Christine McVie, Isabelle Adjani, Edie Falco, Courtney Love, and Liv Tyler, reveals that this is a sign with tremendous emotive power. Indeed,

4

SIGN NUMBER

The elemental number, it is the substance of the universe – fire, earth, air, and water. The sign of Cancer, the first water sign, completes the primary square of the zodiac. It thus comprises the substance of life and solidity. Also called the number of man, it refers to humans as four-limbed creatures.

21–28

Cancer often looks like one who is just about to cry – it is her default expression, all pouty mouth and welling eyes – and indeed she can do so at the drop of a hat. She is an emotional wellspring and is sometimes just plain messy. Actresses of this sign seem to draw strength from their raw emotional natures. Whether it's the eternal victim Janet Leigh, or the put-upon drama queen Meryl Streep, or the embodiment of emotional chaos Courtney Love (never mind the Delphic implications of her band's name, Hole), emotion is Cancer woman's power. The more Cancer feels, or indeed aches, the more formidably alive she becomes. And if the Moon girl is anything, she is vivid, a disposition that tends to rub other women the wrong way. True, the Crab certainly takes up more than her fair share of space, emotional or otherwise, becoming a Nemesis in the most literal sense: She cancels other females out by absorbing most, if not all, the available male attention – think Cinderella entering that ball. Indeed, no female inspires more jealousy than Cancer woman, a vivacious and, often consciously, scene-stealing character.

There's no denying that Cancer woman pushes the limits of emotional abandon – a result, no doubt, of feeling abandoned – often becoming hooked on a desire to shock, a propensity that becomes far more addictive than even partying does. In fact, despite her raw openness of emotion, drugs or alcohol are not typically her demise. Which isn't to say they won't help fuel her desire to be the life of the party, the centripetal force that draws others, particularly men, to her. More often than not, you'll hear Cancer well before you see her. She's the one laughing a bit too loud, her voice carrying over all others. Then again, she could just as easily be the girl moping in the corner whispering only to her boyfriend. In either scenario, she still draws attention to herself. Many a Cancer gravitates between these extremes, as if her mood depended on the course of the Moon. She'll dump that party-girl persona as necessary, playing instead the proverbial lass one takes *home* to *mother,* both excruciatingly important Cancerian concerns. She looks the part: Despite her country of origin, Cancer is generally as wholesome and all-American as apple pie. Added to which, she styles herself in colorful, curvaceously cut, rather middle-of-the-road fashions that portray a sort of feminine stereotype. Even when presented satirically – as in the case of Courtney Love's baby-doll getups gone bad – Cancer wants to look as much the girl-next-door as possible. Makes sense: Cancer's association with the ages 21–28 manifests in the girl Moonchild as a sort of wifey taste, whereby she appears eternally marriageable and, more than any woman, ready to settle into any suburb in the offing. Still, the neighbors might be surprised to discover she has a penchant for key parties. Indeed, calling Cancer a flirt doesn't even begin to describe her overt gestures toward the opposite sex, if she feels inclined to deliver them. When sexually inspired, Cancer throws herself at the object of her lust, leaving no question as to her interest. Unlike her male counterpart, the female Crab is no creature of subtlety.

There is even something exaggerated in her looks. Her complexion is bright, her physicality bubbly and boundless, her eyes beaming and her smile naturally pasted on like that of some beauty-pageant contestant. Indeed, of all the women in the zodiac, nobody can flash a set of pearly whites the way a Crab can, as she is generally gifted with a beautiful, albeit exaggerated, mouth and oversized teeth. And with a fresh, creamy, often lightly freckled complexion, Cancer is a contradiction in terms – a congenial hometown girl who'd just as soon grab a guy's package as stand there smiling at him. Perhaps because the years 21–28 are associated with mating, Cancer seems born to make a love connection. Whether or not she's in a relationship, the Crab requires, even demands, regular sex. Still, because of her generally conservative, sometimes corporate style of dress, there is rarely anything truly 'sleazy' about her. Even the 'slagier' likes of Courtney Love and Pamela Anderson have been known to scrub up nicely. Some Cancers take their watery Mother Earth status quite seriously, albeit subconsciously, espousing a sort of crunchy-granola, often witchy-medieval style, opting for such items as leotards, tunics, peasant dresses, and shawls meant to deemphasize the bosom, if she's thus endowed. It seems Cancer women are polarized along the breast-size spectrum, having either sizable 'jugs' or the barely there mosquito-bite variety – either way she tends to suffer from a serious case of boob envy. If she is chesty, this will tend to be her most overtly feminine feature, the rest of her remaining relatively slim-hipped, short-waisted, and long-legged. She looks great in jeans; only she'll opt for a woman's cut rather than just pulling on a pair of 501s. Often, Cancer has the lean build of a runner, with rather light bones that are nonetheless large. Her frame appears most slight when viewed from the side; whereas, looking at her face-on, she appears more broad-shouldered, her arms dangling a bit far out from her sides. Even if willow thin, Cancer still has a gentle curve about her figure, a swanlike stature, marked by a longish neck, upright carriage, and arched back. She often has the bearing of a Degas dancer. Generally graced with a flat tummy, a definite source of pride, she may even put off pregnancy to retain it, obsessing on snapping her shape back after giving birth. Her ass is usually round, though not overly ample. And more than any other zodiacal sign, Cancer takes pride in the appearance of her pussy, prettifying it with a whisper-thin coif as to somehow make it more lovable a treat – a little present *sans* the bow – to that prince who sweeps her off her feet.

Cancer tends to be very much the blond, if not literally, then in

PSYCHOLOGY

Cancer can be over-emotional, self-pitying, and overanxious to please. She typically has mother issues, suffers psychological abuse, and may act out in rebellious or promiscuous ways. She has difficulty establishing boundaries with friends and romantic partners in particu-lar, and she is given to melancholy and fits of hyste-ria. A certain 'lunacy,' named after her ruling Moon (Luna), can plague the female Crab.

ARCHETYPE + MYTH

Cancer personifies the mother goddess. Themis, meaning 'waters,' saves the Greek Noah, Deucalion, and his wife, Pyrrha ('life blood'), from the wrathful flood waged by Zeus and teaches them to repopulate the world. In both Themis and Pyrrha we see the natural function of the female as the proliferator of life. The moon goddess Selene had a shepherd she fancied put into an eternally youthful sleep – while he snoozed, she 'had her way,' giving birth only to daughters. Rivers and springs were personified as female deities. In India the Ganges was synonymous with the mother goddess, endowed with powers of purification.

personality. Actually, she will be lighter-haired, just as she is lighter-skinned, regardless of ethnic background, than other females in her family. And if such lightness doesn't happen naturally, there's something about the sign that sends its native girls straight for the bottle (of bleach, that is). Maybe it's a symptom of being that mythic Cinderella who must appear literally fairer than the rest. She wears her hair loose and long, and if it's not naturally straight, she'll lend it a hand. Not generally big on makeup, Cancer instead opts for a natural-beauty look. Except when it comes to her lips and eyes, which she paints and mascaras, sometimes in the extreme, so as to better be able to smile and bat her lashes at the potential stags she seeks to snag.

Sex + Sexuality

Starved for male affection, Cancer really clings to the first eligible boy who takes romantic notice of her – she's the girl with a serious steady relationship while still in high school. Nevertheless, she has her standards: In fact, she will already have edged her way into a shiny-happy social scene in which the pool of guys are rather traditionally minded, athletic, all-American male versions of herself. Even at sixteen, she's already thinking marriage. To her mind, stranger things than living happily ever after with your childhood sweetheart have been known to happen – in truth, however, they rarely occur for Cancer. Coming off the chaos of her upbringing, mired in the mayhem her mother created, the Crab is drawn to stoical males from stable, if not rigid, backgrounds. She assumes that the void left by a lack of father love is best filled with a perfect stereotypical cutout of a male; and so she often gravitates toward unemotional, insensitive, or even unattainable types, believing such qualities are linked to conventional masculinity. Indeed, all the hackneyed gender images are covered: A guy must be tall, sporty, authoritative, and stoical. Thus, she is drawn to males from cultural backgrounds that emphasize male domination if not a hint of the Fatherland – Aryan (and often Aries, the zodiac's own militant macho man) as well as Anglo and Scandinavian types whose rearing is disciplined, impassive, and stiff-upper-lipped.

As is often the case for the Cancerian Cinderella, she tends to come from a broken home, or from the proverbial wrong side of the tracks. Hence, this put-upon maid seeks to social climb – not necessarily to great heights, but just high enough to rise above what she, at least, perceives as the drudgery of her lowly station, arriving at that comfortable middle class. Likewise, if the Cancer is born into a life of privilege, she tends to ditch the silver spoon in favor of a more democratic existence – the affluent Cancer girl goes the extra mile to appear all grassrootsy, typically styling herself in hippy-dippy fashions. Like Cinderella, Cancer simply wants her due – some human dignity – it's not as if she longs to be a bonbon eater like her (step)mother may have been. One imagines that Cindy would have been most kind to her servants in the castle, forgoing any caste systems already in place, becoming the proverbial 'people's princess' like that real-life, iconic Cancerian royal who tragically fell victim to the inordinate chaos of her existence. Princess Diana's Cancerian nature was, in fact, all too vividly drawn in the collective conscious, her on-the-verge-of-tears expressions indelibly etched in media memory. Her emotional life was, arguably, in conflict with the inherent stoicism of such a romantic bond as she made. Not able to fit into the stiff-upper-lip ideal of such an existence, her feelings overflowed the ages-old confines of the royal arrangements, and she indeed re-created the image of the monarchy, re*pairi*ng the us-and-them quality, as did Cinderella, inherent to aristocratic societies. Feeling like the low woman on the totem pole, young Cancer does a bit of pulling herself up by the bootstraps, not letting her background stand in the way of mixing and mingling with the beautiful courtiers in her school courtyard. To be sure, she wants a strapping prince, a scion of suburbia who literally stands head and shoulders above the rest. But she's not like the self-assured Taurus, who is blissfully unself-conscious of her own desires, simply attracting attention with her self-obsessed feminine wiles. No: Cancer is a floodgate of churning yearnings. She is utterly needful of expressing her loving emotion to a man. She doesn't simply aim to please, like the Bull she is desperate to do so, pulling out all stops to shower affection on the male who gut-wrenchingly inspires her love. Cancer doesn't have casual crushes. She swoons, cries, and pines for love and the want of its being returned.

Poor, poor, pitiful Cancer: So dire are her sentiments that she expresses them blatantly, shooting the moon in making her exaggerated feelings known. She's like Marianne in Jane Austen's *Sense and Sensibility,* all the former and none of the latter, and thus ripe to be picked as doormat of the year. In a nod to her water-cardinality, Cancer rushes like a river into things without much circumspection. Sex may be the most startling means for Cancer's self-expression, a vehicle for declaring a deep-seated need for the unconditional love she's after. Ironically, such profound sexuality may prevent her from attaining affection, as 'giving it away' can become something of a negative pattern. Of course, to the untrained eye of a teenage boy, it simply seems 'she's gotta have it.' For more than any other girl, sex for the Cancer is too easily confused with love. She pours her heart out to boys who are willing to

BIBLE + LITERATURE

Cancer is associated with the Flood. As in the Greek myth, gnostic biblical teachings credited the Mother Goddess with saving humanity – the dove was originally her totem. Jonah's whale is actually the Babylonian Derceto (the goddess mother of Queen Semiramis), who rebirthed him in her womb. Cinderella sees her (antediluvian) life in ashes, weeps, and wishes for a new one – her godmother hooks her up. She is all of the former, as the character Marianne, and none of the latter in Jane Austen's *Sense and Sensibility*. In Eugène Ionesco's play *The Chairs,* the character Semiramis is wife and mother to her mate, and they are together trapped in a circular, womb-like structure in the middle of the sea. In popular culture, tv's Eddy Monsoon, both watery names, from *Absolutely Fabulous* fame is a Cancer in character, the show, a twist on the Cinderella story, depicting a household of women, from the perspective of a less-than-nurturing mother.

**4TH ASTROLOGICAL
HOUSE**

self-protection
conclusions
parents
conditioning
blood ties
home/residence
family foundation
pedigree
psychological base
private life and matters
houses and real estate
parent of greater sway
mother influence
theoretical self
basis of character
self-recovery
accumulated factors
domestic setting
domestic environment
operational base
collecting
household items
land and property
the drama of life
intellectual training
nurturing
unconscious mind
emotional life
subconscious fears
instinctive response
habits set in childhood
beginning and end of cycles
patriotism
childhood memories
sentimentality/nostalgia
maturity
the past
public opinion
the (female) population

entertain her need for affection in return for a little nooky. And it's a deal Cancer girl is willing to strike: This maid whose sign is archetypally steeped in mating needs contact far more than she needs the protection of her so-called virtue. Sex, she believes, is a means to emotional repair.

It is Cancer's gut instinct to look for a savior in a mate. But she isn't the damsel in distress she perceives herself to be; rather, our moony Cinderella must take responsibility for her own survival. The hero she requires is more the sacrificial sort. In Egyptian mythology, Osiris was the savior-god wedded to Isis, who swallowed him up and then gave birth to him as her son, Horus — talk about your Mother Principle at work. Indeed, Osiris was known as 'he who impregnates his mother,' more apt for Cancer man, but the point is well taken here: Cancer woman doesn't require a man who'll come to her emotional rescue, but one who'll sacrifice himself to the watery rush of her emotions, willing to be swallowed into her delightful vortex. Osiris, as the story goes, was yearly torn to pieces and reassembled by Isis, all but for his 'lost' penis, which she then replaced with a fake one made out of clay. (Right, cheers, thanks a lot.)

The metaphorical significance is that, being the consort of the zodiac's own Isis does require a bit of ritual castration: The male can't impose any patriarchal dominance, but rather must take a second-sex role in the relationship, subject to Cancer's authoritative whim. Cinderella isn't swept off her feet; she wows the prince, who then spends his life metaphorically groveling at hers — the significance of his kneeling at her piggies, putting on that glass slipper, a symbol of the uterine entrance, the 'crystal cave,' where male initiates entered the world womb at Delphi. Trouble is, these aren't the guys Cancer generally goes for early in life. Instead, she often confuses a man's steady outright inability to love, a horrid stoicism, with the loving anchor she truly needs. She is perpetually being drawn to such loveless creeps, domineering guys whose tyranny she misreads as loving attention. Such a character will not make a suitable consort to the Cancerian princess. She needs a true equal partner, a prince among men, not some tyrannical king who'll expect her to do his bidding. In the matriarchal mind, kings are to be sacrificed. Such an autocrat won't be able to take the brunt of her increasingly surfacing emotions. Ironically, it is those overbearing men onto whom she'll eventually unleash the overage of her pain and anger, castrating these callous cads in any case. Going against the flow of Cancerian emotion, these dictatorial dudes drown, while the more charming, compliant fellows will be carried along on the current of her outpouring love. Meanwhile, even the imperious boyfriend she couples with will forgive any volatility he may suffer at her hands; that is, while she's using them, as well as other parts of her anatomy, to pleasure him. He will, for a while, delude himself into thinking that his putting up with emotional tantrums only leads to Cancer's making up in bed for the commotion she causes.

In truth, Cancer woman does have a voracious sexual appetite that is no cinch to satisfy. Even when she's on the giving end, which is her usual, and indeed her favored, place to be – blowing her mate or doing all the major maneuvering, even in a submissive position – her lover should realize that he's being engulfed for her pleasure, not his. It's probably what made those bootleg Pamela Anderson videos so enthralling – Cancer woman is a most willing recipient of anything being dished out. Indeed, it may seem as if no job is too big for the Crab girl. For when it comes to sex, she doesn't take her 'I feel' motto lightly. Cancer wants to experience erotic sensation as acutely as possible, requiring a deep rogering for a reasonable duration, though she'll expect it to be done with enthusiasm and gusto. She isn't into rough poundings. Rather the rhythm should be long and deep. Similarly, going down on a guy is never the chore it can be for many women; in fact, one would think the Cancer girl had an unhingeable jaw, as she really hunkers down on her hunk, moaning all the while in ecstatic delight. And praise be to Isis, she really does swallow her lover whole. After all, the Moon rules both saliva and vaginal lubrication, facilitators of her desired profound penetration.

But there's another meaning to this cardinal-water sign being 'wet,' i.e., overly sentimental, doting, and mothering toward men. Probably nothing leads to the Cancerian's being walked all over by guys more than the sickeningly gooey manner in which she relates to a man. She might be a total bitch to other women and dismissive of men who don't make her stomach flip, but toward a guy she has feelings for, the young Crab especially will act the wide-eyed, baby-talking, overly adoring, and indulgent worshiper. It is one exaggerated symptom of the Mother Principle channeling through her – a predilection that could easily make onlookers loose their lunch. She'll fawn and fondle her partner, always having to touch or kiss or cling in some coy manner. Indeed, it is often a put-on as it runs counter to what her true nature would dictate; such desperate shows, she thinks, will strengthen her bond. In time, all that constant doting will begin to take its toll – what was originally meant as a means for puffing up her man will only become a glaring symptom to him of a ridiculous dependence. In time, it will even strike her man as phony, as, increasingly, in private, she will express her inevitable anger at playing the submissive in public, using her partner as a veritable piñata for venting these bottled-up feelings (not to mention the full line of baggage filled with her childhood scars).

Even hitting the sheets, which has always been the salve and the glue that

KEY WORDS

magic
rhythm
feeling
instinct
affection
becoming
demonstration
tenderness
introspection
concern
withdrawal
creation
purification
wisdom
fluidity
sorrow
sarcasm
morality
retreat
hope
chaos
instinct
strength
modesty
fortification
sensitivity
womanhood
promiscuity
rapaciousness
sentimentality
safety
depression
reaction
deliverance
lunacy
regularity
motherhood
sexuality
rebellion
promise
melodrama
intuition

keeps her and a lover together, doesn't quite do the trick anymore. Cancer woman is predisposed to sexual addiction as she might use 'the act' to anesthetize her feelings, often causing her to seek out more elaborate and edgier erotic scenarios to achieve that click of oblivion she seeks. Along the way, urging a lover to go 'faster, deeper, harder' may eventually see him heading for the door in search of a less psychological sexual relationship. Indeed, nobody uses sex to fill the emotional void as much as she. Cancer vies with Virgo for the proverbial title of woman who loves too much, and yet *giving* is the true nature of the zodiac's very own *source*. As with most experiences chez Madame Crab, her sex life and especially the nitty-gritty activities therein, might seem a maelstrom to the more staid observer, but any suspected chaos isn't generally the problem, but rather part of the *solution* (double entendre intended, as even etymology makes this link between the liquid and the 'answer'). It's all math to the Cancer, anyway, as she metaphorically solves her problems two-by-two, throwing herself into a very literal mating game, without the slightest guilt at doing so, and not exclusively for the quick, dirty reason that it feels good; the fact is, no other act is more natural to the Cancer in that it provides a profound release and a channel for her *dammed* emotions. Remember, she is the very embodiment of gut feelings, so what might be considered emotionally overwhelming to the rest of us is generally absorbed by Cancer, unfazed. A creature of the deep, the Crab is uniquely equipped, of all women, to safely negotiate sexual waters that most might alternately consider profound or abyssmal, complete with a cymbal-crashing nod to being a crustaceous bottom feeder. But never fear: the *ark* of the lifelong covenant Cancer makes with herself is salvation. And survival, as she knows it, depends first and foremost on dependence, which most often takes the literal form of sexual union, so graphically illustrated by the flood-myth, replete, as it is, with its mass copulation 'at sea.'

Accusations that Cancer looks to lovers and lovemaking for emotional rescue are typically true, but what most people don't realize is that she doesn't do so in vain. Meanwhile, the Crab is equipped to weather the flood of any ensuing consequence, forever able to sally away, leaving behind (never amassing more) emotional Samsonite. Whereas the precocious Gemini female tends to flirt with overwhelming sexual experience and often *falls* in the face of invoked disaster, Cancer, the personification of *deluvian* experience is, hence, born into damage, often both real and metaphoric, spending her book of days drifting toward repair. All is entropy for Gemini, while despair is a default starting line for astrology's Cinderella. Life, in Cancer's estimation, has always been a broken proposition, the home she's brought up in smacking of that quality, in one way or another. Just as the concept of water breaking describes both shattered levees and the liberated rush of embryonic fluid, any past dilapidation ushers in a deluge of emotional relief, release, and rebirth. Cancer pours her guts out *via* experience. Sex, specifically, will be no placid affair, indeed it can be torrid, torrential. However, the moral of any flood myth is that life goes on, and such is the psychological modus Cancer holds firmly in her mind. She is forever parlaying all the baggage from the 4th House storage of *the home one comes from* into furnishing *the home one establishes.* And every day brings new hope and promise despite her signature moping and whining. She may wallow in the deepest of sentimental and indeed sexual mires, often ending up labeled a mess as a result, but every melancholy state will be a means of mourning and attaining *deliverance* from enduring sadness. Cancer doesn't skirt over 'issues;' rather, she employs her sign's motto and *feels* their full import – she embraces her feelings, finds closure and moves on. To be fair, it must be a drag having to constantly do this – she doesn't want to be a wet blanket – still, it's the Cancer who isn't 'dealing,' the one pretending life is a party, wearing that lampshade crown, who should cause the real concern. For most Crab women, life is about securing emotional dry land. And sex plays a huge part in Cancer's feeling her way toward such providence.

In the process, Cancer provides herself, and indeed a partner, an abundance of erotic experience to choose from. Ironically, she is at once the most experimental *and* the pickiest of female signs – that is, there's nothing she won't try once, thrice, or more times in this process of defining, for all time, what suits her sexual self. Kudos to the fellow who finds himself in the throes of Cancer rummaging the depths of carnal knowledge – he might easily assume he's hit the motherload. Which, of course, he has. She approaches every act as a new beginning, and even if with a mate for a million years, she'd still seek to stir something fresh into the sexual mix. Any one of the eyebrow-raising activities mentioned in this book might find their way onto Cancer woman's sexual menu at one point or another. The barometer for what this tempestuous character enjoys is that infamous connection to her feelings, something she never loses, even in the midst of a so-called sexual debauch. She could be drenched by some cardinal flow or another and still smile up at her partner with an expression of purest affection. She is no victim, even when consenting to activities of the most submissive kind, those many might well consider sexually degrading. If such proclivities pass the checkpoint of her gut instincts, so be it – they will be waved on through, inspiring little cause for Cancerian unrest. She not only leans, but learns on her lovers. With every sexual interlude, the Crab gleans a little bit more about herself, growing via these experiences into a solid

Della Reese
Kristi Yamaguchi
Michelle Kwan
Deborah Harry
Cyndi Lauper
Martha Reeves
Nicolette Larson
Cheryl Ladd
Jessica Simpson
Shelley Duvall
Kelly McGillis
Katherine Helmond
Frances McDormand
Suzanne Vega
June Lockhart
Harriet Nelson
Nancy Reagan
Lindsay Wagner
Susan Hayward
Michelle Lee
Shirley Knight
Marianne Williamson
Gilda Radner
Phyllis Diller
Phyllis George
Phoebe Snow
Twyla Tharp
Anne-Sophie Mutter
Faye Wattleton
Frida Kahlo
Iris Murdoch
Helen Keller
Elizabeth Kubler Ross
Mary Baker Eddy
Mother Cabrini
Rose Kennedy
Diane Feinstein
Sally Priesand
Louise Erdrich
Oriana Fallaci
Pearl Buck
Ann Landers
Abigail Van Buren
Mildred 'Babe' Zaharias
Missy Elliot
Michelle Branch
Gloria Stuart
Bess Myerson
Vikki Carr
Eleanor Parker
Louise Fletcher
Phyllis George
June Carter

BODY RULERSHIP

Cancer rules the stomach and there is a tendency toward digestive and gastric afflictions. The Moon rules the lymphatic system, bodily fluids, the pancreas, and the sympathetic nervous system, controlling the reflexes and responses to emotional stimuli.

pearl of womanly wisdom in the form of which she can offer her hand some day, when that prince *will* inevitably come. She isn't just sexually messing around, but readying herself, building that *ark,* both as a promise and a throughline for her inter-dependent future with a mate. Although this mechanism might be years in development vis a vis her lovelife (having more than her fair share of fun in the process), Cancer will exhibit this same sort of MO in less touchingly personal sectors, namely career and her social existence.

Anticipation, as braless Crab lady Carly Simon once crooned, is Cancer's watchword. Defined as 'confident expectation' we herein see her Cinderella-like modus of not merely wishing for but manifesting her dreams. Generally entering the job force early in life, often working her way through school, she finds a financial rock to stand on as well as an atmosphere of order in the workplace that provides grounding against any upheaval at home. A cardinal sign of the first order, Cancer is rarely content to be low lady on the totem pole and, from her first day on the job, she will begin anticipating her own advancement. Other women, especially, sense she's forever cooking up some scheme for success. Indeed, in so doing, she makes quantum leaps on the careerfront. But anticipation too often turns to *precipitation;* that is, hasty, indiscreet or even reckless moves geared toward her own promotion. Of course, that term has its watery connotations as well, while all of Cancer's secret plans mirror the pattern of a slow pregnancy followed by a sudden delivery. The Crab seemingly rushes into the status of boss, or often becomes her own, under the turned-up and out-of-joint noses of stymied colleagues. To them, she simply doesn't play fair: She may use associates as stepping stones, blurring the lines between professional and personal involvments, specifically with men who'll make up the bulk of her supporters. (Indeed, Cancer may often be killing two birds with one stone, advancing her carnal wisdom while furthering her own career aims with the same individual.) Mutual back-washing is de rigueur, as Cancer, in signature style, pulls out all stops to get what she wants. In the face of the flood, there are always casualties. And when it comes to her own fulfillment, Cancer takes an all-others-be-damned attitude, particularly sandbagging fellow women. She may have few female friends as it is, and she certainly won't make many in the workplace, perpetuating that wicked stepsister disconnect with her own sex. What girlfriends she does have will be unapologetic types like herself with whom she may get up to 'no good,' forming little covens of like-minded, sexually liberated ladies with whom to compare mathematical notes on length, width, and volume of men cum notches on their bedposts or to commiserate over the many complaints of the female condition. She can juggle more than one guy at a time, still clinging fast to her ideal of marriage; continuing to pursue those clean-cut Clark Kents whom she'll put through their sexual paces while keeping them in the dark about her murkier exploits. She may even keep a stud or two on a string whom she'll use purely as sex tools, 'liking 'em dumb' because it's easier to do so. Otherwise, she might rock in the opposite direction, hooking up with a hardcore swinger who's looking for a woman willing to explore the depths of sexual experience. Often, that would be her.

Cancer woman unconsciously embodies the sexual freedom of matriarchal societies, those pagan females persecuted as witches by the patriarchal church for all their bawdy, medieval bra-burning. For Cancer, there is no shame in indulging in even the raunchiest scenarios so long as they don't conflict with her gut. Only a Cancer female can describe, in mixed company, a night spent with a lover and a double-sided dildo without a sniff of guilt or irony. Indeed, Cancer is conducting what even modern-day wiccan would call a wee bit of sex magic each and every time she hits the sheets. She is so completely involved in the act and, naturally attuning herself to the experience, never letting it consume her, she harnesses the transformative power of the proceedings, forever conjuring from it what she needs as emotional sustenance. There's power in that: Often literally riding the waves of such experience, she releases angst and feels optimistically refreshed in her future outlook – getting her ya-ya's out, for all sisterhood (despite her many detractors) as well as herself. What's more, leaving no stone of her sexual self unturned – here's where the magic comes in – she eventually conjures up the exact kind of guy for whom she'd pack in her past experience and settle down, just as Pyrrha and Deucalian tossed those rocks over their shoulders, re-peopling the planet, two-by-two. *Feeling* out every dark corner of her sexuality, and calculating her likes and dislikes, Cancer woman develops a very distinct sense of self on this score. Her 4th House ruled *intentions* are ever clear. And as any witch will tell you, intention brings about desired results and, sure enough, that desired Prince will trot on up, grateful, and not at all judgmental of Cancer, despite she herself being so infamously hot to trot. The Cinderella myth, in fact, is all about sex magic. That consummate worker of *wish*craft leaving her glass slipper, a symbol of the uterine entrance, in the hands of Mr. Charming himself. And finally we hit the mother lode of Cancerian paradox: like Cindy, Cancer only loses her footing when confronted with this man of her dreams, the one she's been dredging up her whole life. Inevitably, he is a fellow who'll fall somewhere between the extremes of past sexual 'pacifiers' – any *dummy* she's meanwhile sucked upon – and the sexual 'provocateurs' who have enjoyed, if not sought to outright exploit, her erotic unabashedness. Her perfect prince

STR8 TURN-ONS

tall men
Nordic types, blonds
businessmen, collegiates
jocks, body builders
smooth torsos
nudism
lite s + m
slaving
double dildos, strapping on
father figures
couples, swinging
anal sex
(passive) b + d
sex clubs, hedonism
swapping
polyamory
swallowing
intense nipple play
downers, Qualudes
firemen, cops, deliverymen
water sports
submission fantasies
prostitute fantasies
dungeons, whips, chains

won't himself be a sexual player, neither will he be condemning toward those who may've been one. No, the reason she loses her footing is because, in the midst and mire of Cancer's tumultuous life, she doesn't fully factor into her equation encountering that other four-letter word, love. When *it* hits, the challenging bit of Cancerian life is called into question, namely, the day-to-day living with a male-partner, not just doing the deed and being done. For once (and ever after), Cancer finds herself emotionally out of her depth, and she'll spend the rest of her lifetime happily struggling to honor that paragon of sentiments. In the bat of an eye, she will leave her wild ways behind. Her critics, of course, will suspiciously balk and indeed damn her happiness in light of what sexcapades she might have previously gotten up to. Meanwhile she will be as blessedly blissful as can be, looking behind her without a single regret and certainly without any unrequited erotic longing. As with everything that outgrows its usefulness, Cancer will make jetsam of her past so-called wicked ways. Despite the fact she will have kissed an overage of frogs, indeed due to it, she faces the prospect of a partnership with nary a backward glance; and achieving certain deliverance from life on her own, she'll eagerly take on the role of happy homemaker in the light of day — even when she's more nine-to-five than her fine fellow — while nailing the part of the happy hooker, much to her mate's delight, in the not-so-still of the night.

In the female Moonchild, these two seemingly opposite dynamics are not mutually exclusive. Cancer can easily leave the kids with the sitter and then accompany her man to some classy strip joint or swingers club. She thrills at knowing she's in the minority of women who are comfortable and secure in such a setting. And she might even be the first to start stuffing bills into some dancer's G-string. As well, the prospect of a threesome with her guy and another girl is rarely out of the question. She'd even participate in a foursome, provided the same-sex shenanigans were limited to her and the other woman, and the men either watched or joined in, though never engaged in sex between themselves. Cancer woman is fairly contemptuous of men who do with men, while she herself can be the consummate bisexual. From an astrological perspective, you might say that an erotic equation that didn't include a dose of the female is anathema to this über-feminine Moon mama. Her breast envy/obsession certainly becomes a driving force in her sexual interest in girls. Cancer is aware that she's typically more sexually advanced than other females, and she thrives on the idea of seducing a straitlaced, more 'proper' type than herself in bed. Unlike Aries female, who might feel a need to dominate other women — teaching them a lesson — Cancer wants to open a woman up, demonstrating her knowledge of how to pleasure another girl — she is, after all, an aficionado of her own erogenous zones. And, as the sixty-nine symbol of the Cancer sign suggests, the Crab will put her notoriously expert oral skills to use, diving into a woman's muff as only this inhabitant of the deep can do.

When the Cancer woman does self-identify as gay, she will do so completely and never look back. Typically, the lesbian Crab is quite a different animal from her straight counterpart. It would seem that taking men out of the equation has a drastic effect on her, as if skipping all that Cinderella posturing for a prince also removes the obstacles to her wise-woman ways. Or, at least she'd like to think so. In any case, real or put on, the gay Cancer woman does embrace a rather self-righteously feminine view of the world, and with a decidedly parental bent: More likely than not, she will take on the role of both nurturer and the one to rule the roost. Again, unlike her straight counterpart, she is faced with no male impediment to linking her inherent femininity with an innate sense of leadership. On this score, heterosexual Cancer could learn a lot from her lesbian sister. And as Cancer females of either inclination are uniquely capable of committing to a career as well as creating a cozy home environment, the gay Crab girl will be especially adept at melding these two dynamics into one integral lifestyle, usually finding or creating moneymaking ventures whereby she can set her own free-flowing hours. It's this sort of going by her own rhythm, being an emblem of self-sufficiency, by which she primarily attracts other women to her — she appears a beacon of female strength and womanhood. She can be alluring to women who respect and wish to emulate her, as well as opportunistic sugar babies looking for a big mama. Either way, the Cancer woman will be an inspiration to her lover, giving constant reassurance and wise advice as to how the disorder of life might best be negotiated. Cancer is gently pushy with a partner, investing more than most women in her mate's well-being. She is an emotional mentor, not a logistical one, never barking orders but nonetheless cautioning and careful, rather like a second-grade teacher as opposed to some hard-nosed *professoressa*. Though age needn't be a determining factor in Cancer's choice of a partner, she's most attracted to wholesome girls-next-door in whom she seeks to instill her own intensely feminine wiles. There is a sense of her offering a lover a taste of empowerment via their sexual activity. Foreplay, especially, may be a fulfilling, extended affair, rife with lingering, lauding, touching, and kissing. Lovemaking for the gay Cancer female is a momentous occasion, though she rarely holds out any longer than her voracious heterosexual counterpart. Regardless of frequency, sex is something to be engaged in über-consciously, if not ceremoniously. Worship is a keynote to the gay Cancer's sex life, and she expects to receive such venerational affection, just as she revels in offering it.

GAY TURN-ONS

submissive women
big breasts
dark hair
cunnilingus
(active) b + d
mastery, domination
tattoos, piercings
straight couples
flavored lubrication
sixty-nine
belly/nipple rings
(active) heavy s + m
water sports
toe-to-clit stimulation
shaving, grooming
rimming
(active) heavy nipple play
edible underwear
public sex
groups, swapping
pimping, enslaving
stripping
teasing, torture
rubber, leather, latex

She loves to have her breasts fondled, sucked, nibbled, and squeezed, giving and receiving massages, cuddling and mutually stroking for hours on end. Reciprocation in the bedroom is a must to the Cancer female, no matter how much the mommy-giver she may be in other aspects of the relationship.

It's one long, extended vagina monologue as the Crab invariably seeks to explore every deep-seated aspect of she and her partner's shared feminine experience via their relationship. Emphasis will often be on gender issues and self-help with Cancer seeking to inspire them both toward self-realization. Often, gay Cancer is a new-agey character, the kind of *womyn* who all but turns her back on the world of men. Her trail will loop through a decidedly 'conscious' professional environment, the whole-foods store, several body work venues and back to her 4th Astrological House *domestic environment* which might very well be an assault of cooking smells, naturally scented candles, and kitty litter. It can be quite an *au naturel* affair with nary a razor in sight as Cancer makes a statement via her own person against societal images of, and constraints put upon, females. The literal outpourings of femininity will be something to savor as she immerses herself, mostly orally, in the juicy role of sexual guru to her girlfriend, often employing all she has absorbed from the many volumes on the joys of lesbianism lining her trademark towering bookshelves. Sex, she feels, is something to be practiced as a spiritual discipline; and she endows each and every erotic experience with that sort of significance. The Crab's world is her own private *yoniverse* where she takes on the role of wise-woman, full-out, for a cozy coven of friends. If she's a more urbane sort, the scale of her social life will still be heavily tipped away from the Y chromosome crowd. And still, her digs will have an elegant crunchy feel, the whiff of hair product mingling into the melange of usual homey odors, a lady-shaver stored neatly in her powder room.

Whatever the particular social mileu she espouses, gay Cancer tends to be that much more a social climber than her hetero sister. She generally embraces the lesbian cause, politically, and tends to use the platform of her sexual preference as a means of wielding power, not only within the gay community, but in society at large. Whereas Gemini might be part of the gay-girl mafia, Cancer marches her agenda into power breakfasts and board meetings; with a hairdo spritzed solidly into place, she's a telegenic spokeswoman with any number of axes to grind. While straight Cancer might employ her sexuality as a viable means of getting to the top of her profession, the gay Cancer, with that particular ingredient removed, will instead ball-bust the big boys all the more in insuring she gets the gold if she's the right individual for the job. Not that she doesn't mix business with 'getting busy'; indeed, the gay Cancer boss will surround herself with gorgeous gay hirees whom she'll groom in her image. Many a Cancerian match is made in the workplace. And whether she's composting her dinner scraps in some ritzy bohemian enclave, or chopping the competition to pieces in the multicorporation conference room, gay Cancer generally maintains a high opinion of herself and her accomplishments. Regardless of particulars, she will always fancy herself and her lover the power-couple-to-beat, making key social appearances together at functions of social, cultural, or political import. And this dual dynamism is a distinction she works toward upholding in the bedroom as well. *Lite* is never something one might label the Cancerian sex life. The Crab, it seems, need never come up for air as she strives to profoundly pleasure her partner, the concept of a quickie being anathema to her. She expects the same in return and won't long tolerate any, shall we say, beating around the bush. Her lover must dive headlong into the deep-end, the vivid appreciation on Cancer's part at doing so nearly warranting a snorkel set. Sex is a private affair for the Crab who, though willing to throw the kitchen sink into bed with her and a mate, tends to draw the line on introducing a third party. Far more so than her straight counterpart, gay Cancer is ultimately concerned with establishing a stable homelife. To her, monogamy is of utmost importance and sanctity on that score is a most effective aphrodisiac. Woe it is to a partner with even a potentially roving eye as the Crab employs her signature vice-like grip in sexual bonds, becoming more and more emotionally attached, not less, as time goes on. She intends to live happily ever after, with all the trimmings and trappings, and she deserves a lover who is woman enough to ride the tide of this lifelong dream.

Couplings

Cancer Woman / Aries Man
She's a Cinderella, inspiring his signature rescue fantasies. He's a self-professed knight in shining armor, all chiseled features and noble intentions. Codependency is a pitfall. But loving support makes them stronger. Sex is a healing experience.

Cancer Woman / Taurus Man
She sees a safe, steady guy – someone she can trust. Her volatility stimulates Taurus's caretaking instincts. It's a ten-hankie twosome – much ado about nothing, they cry till they laugh. In bed, she's a skillful sexual teacher.

Cancer Woman / Gemini Man
He's a man of action, a guy with great prospects. She's that someone who'll see him through struggles. Their rapport seems caustic – constant quipping calls for patience. In bed together, they constantly try new tricks.

Cancer Woman / Cancer Man
Two moon-ruled souls share a rare and rarefied emotional and sexual connection. They seem to live on their love alone. At home, everything looks a wreck; but chaos is comforting. Bed is a safety zone where anything goes.

Cancer Woman / Leo Man
Cancer's father issues might finally get fixed; Leo's warm nature is awakened. It's soul asylum: a safe place to purge emotions. He's compelled to control, under the guise of being 'helpful.' In bed, she teaches him a thing or two.

Cancer Woman / Virgo Man
He's in rescuer mode, sweeping Cancer off her sore feet. But her sexual history might be epic, causing him concern. With candor, such troubles are surmountable. In bed with no-holds-barred Cancer, Virgo really lets go.

Cancer Woman / Libra Man
Openness is this pair's ongoing theme: Sexuality is a liberal subject for Libra, giving Cancer license to color outside the lines. Their erotic repertoire will always be original – bisexual scenarios are stimulating.

Cancer Woman / Scorpio Man
Her effect on him seems instantaneous – she's that princess he'll perch on a throne. Cancer is unafraid of his spooky disposition. This is rarely a casual coupling. Sex is vigorous and athletic; still sensitive and intimate.

Cancer Woman ∫ Sagittarius Man

He's undaunted by her turbulent temperament. Exhausted from taking life so seriously, she finds relief in his lively approach. A notoriously wild couple, they might live hard and fast. In bed, immense appetites are indulged.

Cancer Woman ∫ Capricorn Man

A first, mind-blowing sexual encounter paves the way for a commiserative bond – whether as carnal cohorts or something more committed. Erotic activity borders on extreme – strange, rough, sex could be standard.

Cancer Woman ∫ Aquarius Man

He dotes, taking responsibility for her feelings. In a constant process of catharsis, this couple is exhausted and exhilarated. Sexually, they're often at odds: She needs intimacy; he's happiest somewhat detached.

Cancer Woman ∫ Pisces Man

They push each other's buttons, though with the best of intentions. An absorbing bond: He especially uncovers old burdens, healing in the process. Cancer opens up, too. Sex is an escape from stresses.

Cancer Woman ∫ Aries Woman

There's a promise of hedonism here: Danger and excitement are the attraction. Together, they thrive on social spontaneity and serendipity. Sex, especially with a buzz, is mind-blowing. There's a thrill in threesomes.

Cancer Woman ∫ Taurus Woman

They get off on being 'girls' together – it's all dress-up and makeup. They may lead a lewd lifestyle, one that includes sex with strangers and swapping. If intimacy is lacking, this pair may opt to be pals and not partners.

Cancer Woman ∫ Gemini Woman

Mother issues abound, but a certain amount of healing takes place. Gemini lightens and learns to love more, without fear. The Crab has an emotional leg up on her enchanting Geminian ingenue. Sex stays spontaneous.

Cancer Woman ∫ Cancer Woman

Moon mamas are moody together. A liaison, regardless of its length, that boosts self-esteem. In the extreme, this pair puts on airs. Crafts and homemaking are emphasized. Sex is secondary to cozy cuddling.

Gay

Cancer Woman / Leo Woman
Emotionally fulfilling after an initial period of 'testing.' If they survive struggles, it's often a loving, long-term coupling. But to others, they're exclusionary. In bed, Cancer submits to the Lioness's supremacy.

Cancer Woman / Virgo Woman
Cancer seems lost at sea. But Virgo doesn't give in to the Moon woman's mood swings and changes of heart. Earthy-crunchy sensibilities are exacerbated. The scent of patchouli may well waft from the bedsheets.

Cancer Woman / Libra Woman
Cancer seems the ultimate catch, but she, too, falls, infatuated with vivacious Libra. This relationship is romantic – gifts are constantly bestowed. At home, they're surrounded by beauty. In bed, atmosphere is utmost.

Cancer Woman / Scorpio Woman
Hooking up means hitting partnership payload. Both carry baggage, but togetherness treats old wounds. Conflict may surround domestic duties. Sex seems always to involve the element of surprise.

Cancer Woman / Sagittarius Woman
They embody different aspects of womanhood – here, opposites attract as much as they annoy. Physical contrasts are exploited for erotic potential. Still, on an emotional level, this couple struggles.

Cancer Woman / Capricorn Woman
They're searching for salvation – a soul mate. With Cancer, the Seagoat learns to heed her sign's watery half: That tendency to emotionally fishtail. It's all about forgiveness. In bed, patience is required.

Cancer Woman / Aquarius Woman
Big issues abound when these supernatural sisters sign on. They're so in sync, it's scary. Still, they go through phases of fierce fighting. Chaos can be exhausting. Sex is like their social life – wild, fast, frenzied.

Cancer Woman / Pisces Woman
They experience their first meeting as a 'religious' experience. Little wonder: Vivid déjà vu accompanies an intense, undeniable physical attraction. A long-term bond will be life-altering. Sex is heightened.

Leo Man

the natural

Leo man is the zodiac's *quint*essential golden boy, a gleaming figure with great charisma and an innate sense of ease and entitlement. He lives life like a king, the world being his playground, assertively satisfying his desires, which are, nonetheless, noble by nature. With nary a duplicitous bone in his body, he prizes honesty and purity above all other virtues. Leo grabs what he wants out of life, with pure conviction, his unshakable self-esteem inspiring awe and worship in others who seek to bask in his reflected light. Exuding such confidence in his masculinity, indeed recognizing no equal among men, he assuredly assumes leadership roles, socially as well as sexually. He can be so notorious a cutup, the proverbial class clown, that even his wholesome good looks may be overshadowed by an 'all-personality' label. Women regard him with a shy, schoolgirl wonder. Like some sexualized Tom Sawyer, he is not only preposterously, almost comically, self-serving, but also a man in possession of a mammoth heart of gold. Leo doesn't fall in love easily, but when he does, it will be regarded as something sacred and ennobling, driven by strong emotion rather than any simple expression of lust. There will rarely be anything sordid or kinky about Leo's sex life, and his heterosexual relationships always smack of an old-fashioned sweetheart sensibility. In love relationships with men, he is even more vehemently moralistic, longing to share an abundance of affection, while feeling left cold by the more overtly sexual aspects of gay life.

V

The Father Principle. The fifth zodiacal precept represented by the Sun and Leo is centered on the concepts of authority, absolutism, power, and supremacy, as well as a sense of wholeness, if not totalitarianism. The Father Principle represents the belief that divinity does not stem from a natural, tangible (feminine) *source*, but from an unknowable, abstract, but all-powerful (masculine) *force*. Leo, thus, rules. His sign's motto is 'I will.'

Sign + Mind

Leo man is ruled by the Sun – which he can't help but believe rises and sets by him. In the zodiac, this life-giving sphere symbolizes a number of astrological precepts, chief among them the Father Principle, and thus, authoritative energy in the universe – in diametrical opposition to the preceding sign of the zodiac, Cancer, which is ruled by the Moon, representing the Mother Principle and nurturing energy. In simple terms, this means Leo man can be a real know-it-all, an obvious symptom of a more deeply embedded psychology that disallows him to view the world from any other perspective than one of unquestioned command. He isn't so much a scene-stealer but someone who pins that label on others, considering the default mandate, in conversation or otherwise, to be his own. To his mind, what others think or say is so much bluster and pretense, while he is forever in control of the sovereign truth and, one might say, the divine right to express it. He steers clear of anyone with an obvious agenda, preferring deferential company who will hang on his every word. His slow diatribes often entail the retelling of his quotidian experience as to make it into some exalted, indeed legendary saga. Left unchecked, one might wish this guy came with an 'off' switch. Still, it is often preferable to simply let Leo stay in filibuster mode. For, when silent and withholding, one can safely assume he's stifling some hurt or outrage. Like the proverbial lion with a thorn in his paw, injury makes him dangerous. He'll usually either sulk, seeking to make those around him miserable, or eventually succumb to one of his infamous temper tantrums – one scenario being worse than the other. In his general good humor, though, Leo can't help but hold court, shining benevolence and approval on family and friends, who notoriously gather, if not run circles, around him. Fortunately, Leo is generally a brilliant raconteur, despite the fact his monologues might rival *Beowulf* in length. As his animal symbol suggests, he is the zodiac's undisputed king of the jungle and therefore recognizes no glitch or irony in taking center stage in all proceedings. Indeed, he is astrology's noble savage, the sign of Leo corresponding to the point in both human evolution and mythos marked by the rule of kings, God's representatives here on earth.

In making the transition from Cancer to Leo on the astrological wheel, there is a philosophical shift from the Mother prototype of existence (a *material* source of life, the planet) to that of the Father model (an abstract *author* of life, a sky god). This segue also mirrors a passage from matriarchal rule to patriarchal imposition, consort-princes (personified by Cancer men) to divine kings, stationary agrarian societies to conquering nomadic ones like that of the Hebrews. In biblical context, the sign of Leo corresponds to the Book of Kings, and our powerhouse Leo to the figures of Solomon and especially David. Arthur (*author*) is the medieval David, the boy wonder in whose image Mark Twain's Tom Sawyer was created – Tom's triumph over Injun Joe mirrors David's felling of Goliath. The Lion man, as the incarnation of these archetypes, is likewise a divinely ordained inheritor of patriarchal power, his word being law. But it is an ancient law-of-the-jungle, survival-of-the-fittest, might-as-right framework into which the Leo man is metaphorically born. Only when we arrive at the next masculine-polarized sign of Libra do we see the principle of democracy represented via that sign's motto 'We are.' Leo's motto is the seemingly straightforward 'I will,' desire and determination being cojoined in that creed. Leo's view of the world and indeed of his own masculinity stems from this position of *authority,* linked as that word is with *authenticity,* such that he perceives himself as a natural-born leader in a world of pretenders, phonies, and parvenus.

The 5th Astrological House is, among other things, that of *cocreation with God* as well as *fun and games;* thus, recreation, in both senses of the word are Leoan concerns. More than any other individual, Leo man maintains that his way of thinking and doing is the 'right' way, his view of existence being a distinctly absolute one. This may explain why the Leo boy is such an infamous wiseacre in school; indeed, he has little respect for any authority other than his own, with the exception of that of his father, whom he tends to worship. As a masculine sign, Leo is aligned with a traditionally male-objective perspective, convinced that more subjective, intuitive views (those typically associated with the feminine mind) are decidedly inferior. Ruled by the Sun, symbolic of the harsh reality of day (as opposed to the Moon, which deals with the mystical world of impressions), Leo is very much the realist, suspect of anything that smacks of overfeeling or a woo-woo sensibility. As the fixed sign of the zodiac's Second Quadrant of Emotions, Leo is a concentrated hotbed of what might be considered manly, indeed, kingly feelings – courage, pride, valor, nobility, dignity, respect, and *amour propre* – in contrast to his astrological neighbor Cancer's 'female' feelings of sensitivity, sympathy, and susceptibility. That female-polarity water sign is about gut instincts and responses, fitting its rule of the stomach, while Leo rules the heart and back, symbolizing passion and resolve respectively, which, again, combine into the sign's signature *will.* Though the 5th House is that of *creativity* and the *fine arts,* the Leo is forever on guard for artifice. His creativity is natural, whether focused on the strictly reproductive responsibility inherent in any divine kingship or in terms of his

PLANETARY SYMBOL

The symbol of the Sun – the point depicts the individual comfortably ensconced within the divine sphere – signals the integration of the self with the whole of creation. Called the Shield of Helios, Leo, like the central Sun in the zodiac, is similarly fixed at the hub of the wheel of human interaction – like a king surrounded by his court, or Arthur encircled by the knights of his Round Table.

own role as an *artist,* itself a word that shares the same etymological root as *Arthur* and *Artemis,* male and female Leo archetypes respectively. Indeed, Leo will eschew most others' creative attempts as arsty-fartsy, false or fluff, assuming a particular disdain for anything with even a slight whiff of the culturally highbrow. Similarly, he despises formal settings and attire, not so much wanting as *needing* to feel relaxed and comfortable at all times. He isn't interested in pleasing or impressing anybody, and one either takes him as he is or he's happy not to be taken at all. This rule applies to his professional as well as his private life. He is equal parts noble and savage: Just as Leo generally thinks himself better than other people – something he may readily admit without even a hint of irony – he considers the conspicuous finery of those who've achieved certain wealth and power in the world as symptomatic of a superficial soul, masking a weak and generally unmanly character. To him, the early birds on the work front are nothing but pets and brownnosers; and the spit-shined Percevals of the planet, with their sappy notions of courtship, are doormats waiting for women to walk all over them. He pretends to be no romantic hero transformed by love. Like everything, he will have it on his own terms.

Leo truly is a Tom Sawyer at heart, the original picaresque figure – defined, as that word is, as your *everyday* roguish hero – bucking oppressive authority, recognizing none but his own, while exerting his formidable power over others. The 5th *fun and games* House is also one of *sport* and *amusement,* which predisposes the Leo to a natural athleticism, though he's typically not infused with much in the way of team spirit, unless he is the undisputed captain. Collectivism in any form only works for this fellow if he is the one orchestrating the action – think Arthur assembling his knights or Tom duping his mates into believing that work, whitewashing that picket fence, is fun and creative. Thus, the sport and amusement associated with the sign are typically at others' expense. He is not the merry prankster that the Mercury-ruled Gemini is; rather, if he is a jokester at all, he is an extremely practical one who, like the Sun, is inclined to have others run circles around him, sometimes for mere amusement. Indeed, Leo seems to turn other people into jesters. And even as far as his friendships go, there is an element of his having associated with those whom he has cast in some role or another geared toward his own entertainment. Leo is the only fixed-fire sign of the zodiac, thus distinguished as a concentrated, magnetic focus of life energy or spirit – falling into the Second Quadrant of Emotions, he thus hones his passions into purposes, his recreative spirit shifting, as he matures, from one of pure laddish enjoyment to that of laudable self-invention: His noble intentions become fervent fixations. Like Shakespeare's born king Prince Hal, the young Leo will live a life of knavery, to some extent, often experiencing an outright obsession with gaming and gambling – horse racing is a particular fascination – full knowing he must ultimately 'imitate the Sun' and take up the reins of a responsible, well, reign.

Leo is archetypally associated with Helios, the Greek Sun god – his Sun symbol is deemed the shield of Helios – the dutiful but notoriously put-upon charioteer who daily races his steeds around Earth with the same kind of devotion many a Leo man exhibits in both his professional and private life, if not his daily trek to the track. The Helios archetype has meaningful manifestation in the Leoan male psyche: Like that ancient Sun god whose very divinity is linked to the function he performs, the Lion man often finds it impossible to shirk his responsibility as the zodiac's ultimate father figure – never failing to be perceived as a leader, at home or in his career. Despite any deliberate attempts to lose himself in the throes of his myriad leisure activities, he is typically one upon whom others unceasingly depend. It is, after all, the image he has fostered since youth and is thus one aspect of self he can't easily escape. Part and parcel of the Sun's principles of absolutism, wholesomeness, and completion is the 5th House ideal of *integration of self*. On one hand, this 5th House-given quality makes Leo man uncannily comfortable in his skin, a seemingly at-ease and natural character. But on the flip side, he is unable to successfully separate himself from his vital societal roles and the mantle of his obligations. Fittingly, the age group associated with Leo is 28–35 years, a time of life when a man leaves the ladder-climbing of his young life behind and really 'comes into his own,' a metaphoric state of fully ripened self-realization, which Leo male embodies all throughout his life. Like some ancient sun king, he has, by virtue of his zodiacal placement, inherited a position of majestic power; and yet he's hard-pressed to fulfill the role of God's little representative here on earth. All fire signs share this heady sense of divinity within themselves, as the element of fire also represents spiritual force. So whereas the cardinal Aries male is, like some errant knight, forever *questing* to prove himself spiritually worthy, the fixed Leo man is born with his sense of worthiness intact and burning bright like a furnace. And just as this makes him a secure, entitled, and highly egotistical individual, it also signals that much more for him to potentially rebel against, like Helios refusing to drive his chariot or the perpetually truant Tom Sawyer venturing out in search of fun and adventure instead of tending to his chores. Being the center of attention is Leo's zodiacal birthright, but sometimes the center cannot hold.

As these examples suggest, the Lion king's neglect of his obligations may have disastrous effects, not so much for himself, but for those who rely heavily on him and, indeed, love him. Capability and culpability, then, go hand in hand

SIGN GLYPH

The Leo emblem depicts the Lion's mane, a representation of masculine power, virility, and vitality. It symbolizes the might-is-right rule of the natural world, where survival inevitably belongs to the fittest. If humanity still inhabited the jungle, chances are the Leo men would be the natural overlords.

ELEMENT + QUALITY

The fire element symbolizes life energy, spirit, or the divine force. The fixed quality denotes magnetism, sustainment, and concentration. The fixed-fire combination particular to Leo is likened to a star (the Sun), the heart (seat of love and life force), and the hearth (center of the home).

for the Lion, to whom, like King Arthur being divinely empowered to pull the proverbial sword from the stone, even the most daunting challenges come more easily, naturally, than most. First, the Leo man tends to be physically powerful from an early age, and that might is mirrored in his intellectual capability, clever wit, creative talent, and moral fortitude. In fact, no other male in the zodiac can boast this kind of across-the-board strength. Yet, despite his prowess, or indeed due to it, Leo feels pangs of guilt and more disappointment than most in failing to achieve predetermined goals. Perhaps this is a throwback to having been the pride and joy of his family, especially singled out by his mother, who pinned her greatest hopes solely on him. From his being set apart from other family members, a psychological rift may ensue, wherein the Leo experiences an intense sense of blame for outshining his siblings in particular; and so it seems his signature prowess becomes a sword that cuts both ways. He may even begin to downplay his accomplishments, behavior that is ironic, since at the same time he delights in his mother's preferential treatment, slowly beginning to perceive himself as a rising family star. However, no matter how hard he tries, the Leo can't get that same sort of feedback from his father, whom he both respects and relates to intellectually, but who is, nonetheless, not as overt in his regard. He may even be chastised by his dad for 'trying too hard'; and so, he stops trying, often after just one painful incident of patriarchal reprimand. Fittingly, in the myth of Helios, we see a similar attempt to find connectedness with a father via some blatant display designed to impress others. The Sun god's son, Phaëthon, is reproached by his peers, who refuse to believe the magnificent Sun is his father. Confronted by Phaëthon, Helios pledges to grant any wish as proof of his paternity. Unfortunately, Phaëthon asks to drive the Sun god's chariot, which ends with his Icarus-like demise. Archetypically, both characters in this story may be read as symbolic of the Leo male: We see his need to be like his father – the real family star, albeit a detached one, just as later, in adulthood, Leo can't help but project a similarly removed demeanor with his own children, particularly his sons. The parental dynamic of his own youth gives birth to the Leo man's psychological paradox: He believes that he is a superior being destined for success, instilled via his mother's extravagant favor; but, on the other hand, he sees no payoff in trying to achieve such an exalted status, as demonstrated by his father's censure and withholding of approval. Since it was his father's opinion that most mattered in his youth, and because he wishes to avoid his infamous feelings of guilt when failing to fulfill high goals, Leo man adopts a no-effort attitude toward life, only finding success when it comes easily and naturally. He learns, sometimes Pavlovian style, that *striving* is a punishable offense, forming a lifelong psychology that fits like a glove.

As a nod to his ruler Sun's Principle of Completion, the Lion presents himself as one who is in no way lacking for anything he does not already intrinsically possess. He is, quite literally, full of himself. In this way, Leo goes through life feeling wholly confident – an especially easy stance to affect if one never takes the slightest risk, emotional or otherwise, save for those he ventures in gaming. Indeed, in his every interaction with others, he'll make little or no effort to establish a personal connection, only securing friendships that, like everything else, develop naturally with zero strain. This works both ways: As his father's son, Leo is incredibly wary and disdainful of people who 'try too hard,' for as the guy who 'has it all,' he possesses no empathy for those who wear their insecurities, not to mention their hearts, on their sleeve. To Leo, shyness, nervousness, and indeed earnestness are all signs of weakness – even people who fail to exhibit definite physical strength, a visible wholesomeness, may be labeled *less* by him.

Upon meeting Leo man, one might immediately sense that waggish Tom Sawyer aspect of his personality. He may, at turns, be flippant, curt, coarse, or blatantly prankish – fibbing, making up wildly vivid tales about his personal life or profession in the face of a stranger's sincere interest, which he, of course, finds fatuous – as if to say one isn't truly worthy of his time and effort to be open and honest as, in most instances, he expects never to see them again. This dismissive air recalls a disinterested king who cares not one iota to know the 'little people': The hinge of the Leo male's behavior, after all, forever teeters on one regal theme or another. As the embodiment of authority, Leo is faced with the same brand of decision-making as all kings: whether to be a good one or a bad one. Though, for this fittest of survivors, might *is* right, as evidenced by his signature allergy to, indeed contempt for, personal weakness in others. Leo man must, as did the mythic King Arthur, make a psychological shift, adopting a might *for* right philosophy, if he wants to avoid spending his life as some tired sort of tyrant. A glance at the list of famous Leo men – including one, if not two Caesars, Napoleon, Mussolini, Bolívar, Selassie, and Castro – reveals that Lion males are notoriously above reproach and can be dictatorial in the extreme. The sign boasts professional autocrats like film directors Huston, Hitchcock, DeMille, and Kubrick as well as self-professed fathers of industry or leaders of whole movements within their professions. Leo is the sign of Henry Ford, Carl Jung, George Bernard Shaw, Aldous Huxley, and Jerry Garcia. Norman Lear, the pathos king of sitcoms, created the quintessential tyrant in Archie Bunker, the human Garfield, portrayed by Leo Carroll O'Connor, whose character's 'throne' is enshrined in the Smithsonian. This is Leo man in caricature. Yet, despite any real shows of despotism, the Cat man's

POLARITY

Males in masculine (air, fire) signs are aligned with the gender polarity of their sign and thus embody the quality-element combination of the sign. Leo man is a fixed star, the natural center of attention around whom others invariably gravitate. And yet, one can never get too close lest one finds oneself getting burned.

superior sense of self and will of steel are employed most often as natural instruments of benevolence.

Whereas Gemini man blurs the line between opposites, including good versus bad, the Leo man prides himself, wholly, on his good *will*. Of course good to him isn't always right for others; something that this man, with his absolutist terms and visions, has most difficulty understanding. Conviction is a quality of the heart, really, rather than the mind. As is the courage to back it up. The zodiac's Lion rarely falls into the old refrain 'If I only had the nerve'; nonetheless, like Oz's Lion, a bullying personality signals a deep-seated cowardice toward living. For better or for worse, Leo is near pathological in his *will* to wave some sort of righteous sword like Arthur's Excalibur – from the Latin *ex* meaning a 'drawing out,' *calibur* deriving as a 'mold' or 'cast,' thus the sword in the stone. Etymology sees the first figurative usage of *caliber,* fittingly, as referring to 'merit' or 'importance,' Leo watchwords that become determinant yearnings of the Lion's heart. A good guy who strikes attitudes, Leo's white hat is a jewel-encrusted crown of Siegfried and Roy proportion. It is in his most righteous expression, thus, that we glimpse Leo's nativity to the 5th House of *drama*. Here he goes whole hog chewing the scenery. There is no irony in, say, T. E. Lawrence, of Arabia fame, setting himself up as some banner of a being, ruling people by virtue of his passionate devotion to their cause, being the one to rally around and fuel it. He would be king. Both he and Peter O'Toole who portrayed him on film are Leos of the first order. Men of this sign are – it's a cliché, but must be said – the center of attention. The kicker is that, even in the most intimate of relationships, he is challenged to relate to others from any perspective other than that suggested by his planetary glyph, a decided point within the sphere, graphically suggesting the bestowal of attention *outward* from within his private bubble. He doesn't invite or indeed allow inspection into his own endeavors; however, he naturally assumes a position of overseer to others. Someone has to do it. Via his Father Principle he is *patronizing* in the right, more often than the wrong, way, not only empowering his *peeps* but just plain old making them feel good about themselves. There's something about having a Leo man around that makes one feel all is righteous with the world. He is a testament to wholism; indeed, he defines it. His confidence is complete and it inspires others to stop second-guessing themselves. Think of 'Pops' Louis Armstrong, with his eternal croakings of 'yes.' Leo man exudes the same positive fatherly strength and protection – that shield of Helios. He is Midas turning others to gold, although sometimes with that king's overly objectifying touch, bidding pawns to move around while he kicks back kinglike with a most deserved economy of motion. He is the human embodiment of the supreme god personified as the Sun by the ancients, not the rising one of Aries but the majestically fixed, high-noon, seasoned, and *august* Sun, a nod to Leo's birth month unavoidably endemic. What person doesn't want to be in the presence of such greatness, if not grandeur. Imagine having an affirmative strong arm like Satchmo in your life – a totally benign male presence who would nonetheless kick the punks of the world's asses for so much as looking at you sideways. To his loved ones, Leo is such an emotional bodyguard.

The fixed status of Leo signifies the consolidation and protection of feelings and the *will,* the determination, of these emotions into a strong defense against the world of fear and barbarism, at least as he sees it. Leo man is a fortress, a Camelot, armed to the teeth with pride. He often literally acts the part of an ancient sun-king wrought in the postdiluvian age of miracles. Recounting the tales of his encounters with signature dramatic flair, he's a walking myth and legend, like all fire signs to some degree – while Aries strives to be *first* and Sagittarius seeks to explore *most,* Leo personifies the *best* – flouncing around like a monarch nobly held on ransom, trapped in an egalitarian-anarchical society, still keeping a heroic golden-age sensibility beating in his mystic heart. Think of Leos Robert Plant's or David Crosby's fantastical, not to mention Arthurian-themed, lyrics; or the utterly defensive 'Teflon' presidency of Bill Clinton, the inheritor of the American Camelot ideal; or the ennobling work of Alex Haley's exploration of his roots; or the mythologizing documentary style of Ken Burns. Here is a sign who sees himself as the sole inheritor of man's most noble, indeed, divinely sovereign qualities. He teaches the rest of us, by example, to approach life from that perspective, not as a mere human, but as a cocreator with God, thus ordained to do right by the world. To be fair, it's a most valid, and indeed attractive, viewpoint to hold.

Body + Soul

When consciously brandishing his metaphorical sword of righteousness, Leo's brand of confidence isn't viewed as priggish arrogance but rather a fiery magnetism that no other man can equal – in its best light, his no-effort approach to life is perceived not as smug or lazy, but rather as self-assured, devoid of any overeagerness or artifice. Whereas many men resort to fanciful displays – male posturing or slick shticks – especially in their quests for sexual relationships, Leo is sure he's appealing enough without such fandango. To him, less is always

28–35
SIGN AGE ASSOCIATION

The age group associated with the sign of Leo signifies the advent of full male maturity, still free from the second-guessing of middle age. The Leo 'king' is in full realization of his person, particularly as regards his inalienable manhood.

PSYCHOLOGY

The Leo man is given to temper tantrums and other tyrannical behavior and suffers, in some degree, from a superiority (god) complex. Surpressed emotional issues, typically feelings of abandonment by the father, can lead to the repression of creativity, laziness, and underachievement. Gambling can become a psychological obsession, one way the Leo can experience the excitement of risk without the responsibility of failure.

more, and like his symbol Lion, whose mane is proof of masculinity, the Leo man prides himself on a naturally rugged manly manner and style, requiring little more than soap and a disposable razor for personal grooming. Consider the list of famous Leo actors – Robert Mitchum, Kevin Spacey, Robert Redford, Robert De Niro, Phillip Seymour Hoffman, Sean Penn, Edward Norton, and Woody Harrelson – all decidedly unshowy jeans-and-blazer types whose acting styles are forever being touted as honest and naturalistic. As well, each of these men is private in the extreme, exposing another common misconception about the Leo male: that he longs for the spotlight on a global scale. As the personification of a masculine-fixed-fire status, by the time he's an adult Leo already considers himself a star, regardless of his profession, and as such, he doesn't need proof in the form of universal attention on any kind of grand scale. Rather, he knows that plenty of people will be drawn to him; he'll simply select those he deems worthy to enter his personal, private sphere – just as Arthur fills the seats at his Round Table with only the best and brightest, while Shakespeare's Henry must eschew such losers as Falstaff and company. In this exclusive circumstance he is, like the Sun, designed to inspire growth, whether fostering others' creative development, like Robert Redford with his aptly named Sundance Institute; or in the fatherly focus upon his favorite children; or even in his notoriously 'Who's your daddy?' approach toward women.

Leo man projects a sense of health and vitality. Unlike his predecessor, Cancer, who strives to appear the golden boy, somehow always missing the mark, Leo man can't help but exude a florid radiance, no matter how discreet or brooding he may wish to look. He's like a Thomas Eakins subject come to life, a sanguine potentate of the natural environment. It's as if he can't quite escape his sunny planetary rulership; and try as he may to slink into a corner or get lost in a crowd, he unwittingly attracts attention, indeed adoration, from an ever-widening circle of both male and female admirers. Simply put, Leo man has a palpable presence, a super-natural bearing that suggests complete comfort with self – a physical ease that's easy to envy: literally *wholesome,* every part of his well-proportioned body seeming equally strong and perfectly connected, his typically ropelike muscles creating one continual flow from his majestic head down to his wide, steady feet. His ruling planet Sun's glyph, remember, symbolizes the Principle of Completion in the zodiac. He is, first and foremost, a self-contained individual, one in full possession of his faculties, able to fire on all metaphysical levels, from the physical on up to the spiritual. Indeed, Leo man appears, on the surface, to have no disabilities or dysfunctional behaviors. Nothing in his body language suggests weakness or disease – he'll seldom be seen leaning, shuffling, or shifting his weight from one leg to another; rather, he stands square, his entire self held solidly in space. Rarely will there be even the slightest hint of tension, anxiety, or overeagerness in his expression. Like all fixed signs (Taurus, Leo, Scorpio, Aquarius) there is something 'come-hither' about the Lion, which, for him, manifests as an entirely laid-back physicality and a candid, nearly expectant look on his face. Many may mistake this open quality as the mark of an outgoing personality; while in truth, the male Lion is anything but extroverted. Not to suggest he's shy either, it's just that most people don't hold anything but the vaguest interest for him.

Ironically, one might say he's *blatantly* nonchalant; and it's this double whammy of glowing presence and arm's-length insouciance that combines to form the infamous Leo charisma: Like the Sun, he radiates such heat – actual vitality, power, and authority – that others are simply prevented from getting too close. Which, of course, suits Leo man just fine. When it comes to male friendships, Leo is notorious for having few to none, and save for the one queen (or boy prince) this maniacally monogamous man is forever *expecting* to meet, he makes no room in his life for close relationships. Indeed, he is delighted to go through his daily routine solo, casually happening upon people – a slew of acquaintances – thus avoiding the bother of having to invest himself emotionally. To 99 percent of the population, he will remain an untouchable, unattainable entity. Indeed, a lot of people get burned by the Leo, whose decidedly sunny looks belie his ferociously smug personality, and it often comes as a shock to be snubbed or scorned by someone so seemingly shining and affable – like approaching what appears to be a sweet tabby cat only to find you've just tried to pet Garfield.

As befits his 'golden boy' status, Leo man's general coloring is auric and ruddy. Like Cancer, he will be fairer than other members of his family – though not pale and watery like the Moon man, but rather flushed and often blotchy, with blond or red hair – even when of Latin, Mediterranean, or African descent. As a nod to his symbol lion's mane, Leo guy sports thickly tousled locks, coarse or strawlike in texture, often atop a splendidly low hairline. His face can best be described as weathered; and even from a young age, his kisser is crinkled with what one naively assumes are welcoming laugh lines about the cheeks, temples, and even his bushy brow. His dry skin is terribly sensitive, sunburning or freckling readily; and ironically, he must be careful to protect himself against moles and small skin cancers caused by the harmful rays of his ruler Sun. The best way to spot a Leo is by the sheer size and perfect symmetry of his head and facial features – big-headedness is not a purely metaphorical attribute of the Leo man. In getting close enough to see the details of his expression, one might wonder what exactly seemed so warm

ARCHETYPE + MYTH

Leo male falls under the archetype of the Sun (father god), such as the Greek Helios, whose chief myth concerns paternal love and responsibility: The character-istically distant god is called upon by his son to be allowed to drive his chariot, ending in a fatal fall for the boy. Scholars have equated Helios with Elias, the father for whom Jesus calls out when on the cross. In Egyptian mythology, Ra is the sun god, from whom every royal pharaoh is descended – fittingly, he took the form of the Great Cat. The zodiac's own cool cat is as unbe-holden, and yet expectant of praise, as these supreme deities.

BIBLE + LITERATURE

The male sign of Leo is associated with the Bible's Books of Kings, particularly Solomon and David, the boy king. This theme is echoed in the stories of Arthur, the boy king whose name means divine authorship and authority by virtue of his possession of the sword Excalibur. Leo embodies the Arthurian motto as E. B. White laid out in *The Once and Future King* – might for right. Mark Twain's Tom Sawyer is Arthur redux, his name implying that same blade-toting birthright, literally 'one who saws.' Like Arthur attracting knights to the Round Table, or Tom recruiting lads to do his chores, the Leo man is likewise a magnetic figure to whom others naturally defer.

and welcoming; for there is a decided edge to his mien. What looked, at first, like laughing eyes may indeed narrow and fix one cautioningly in their gaze: One soon realizes, too, that it's no easy task to get this guy to crack so much as a smile. Leo keeps his typically ample lips tightly pursed into a pucker, a place where he tends to store hidden tension. Fittingly, he is reluctant to express pleasure with even the most meager of grins – such shows of favor, he feels, are not easily won. Thus, his winningest smiles are reserved for momentously pleasing occasions. Even when he does grant the occasional sly, dogged grin, he is not so much smiling *at* people as he is smiling *on* them. Indeed, in a quest for Leo's approval, we may all, at one time or another find ourselves reduced to the court jesters he casts us as, jumping through hoops to elicit even the most reluctant smirk.

Leo is a naturally fit fellow. Not surprisingly, he may be something of a fat-phobe, projecting a kind of body fascism onto others, particularly his sexual partners. Blessed as he is with an undisputedly masculine physique, Leo is confident enough neither to accentuate nor deemphasize his shape with any special style of clothing. An aversion to anything artificial means cotton and wool are the mainstays of his wardrobe. Classic 'preppy' brands like Brooks Brothers, Polo, and Lacoste are a bastion of Leoan style; indeed, oxford shirts seem made-to-measure on his enviably V-shaped torso, though he'll forgo ironing for a clean but crumpled look. Born with pectoral muscles most men spend their lifetime in a gym trying to develop, his chest may be especially well-defined. Rarely does Leo fight the battle of the bulge, generally boasting a flat middle that is, nonetheless, nearly impossible to chisel into a neat six-pack; there is a meatiness to this big-boned man that forms into a hard mass, though any heft to his tummy is typically more thick skin than fat. Leo man is as powerfully built in the legs as he is in the torso – another clue to picking him out of a lineup: He'll never be the gym rat with a pumped-up top and weedy legs. On the contrary, everything flows in perfect proportion through the male Leo body, right down to his often oversized hands and feet, an anamolous feature that gives him an ever more solid and grounded countenance. His 'package' is similarly designed, as Leo is rarely one to be seriously lacking in that department – not overly hung, perhaps, but considerably thick. His *cojónes,* too, may share the outsized quality of his other extremities; after all, *creative power* is an aspect of Leo's native 5th House, and the source of that virility, symbolically or otherwise, seems to reside in his relaxed low-hangers. Naturally, too, Leo sports some goodly body hair, symetrically situated and often blondish in hue, rarely, if ever, will he be hirsute in the extreme. In the pubic area, his hair will be sparse, wiry rather than dense, often trailing into his buttocks and inner thigh region. However, those sensitive areas of his anatomy are rarely glimpsed. Let's just say, Leo is seldom one to sport a Speedo. And even on an infernal August day, he is wont to be conservatively but casually outfitted in full-length trousers and button-down shirt. For, of all the men in the zodiac, Leo is easily the most modest, not to mention the least promiscuous and the absolute pickiest-choosiest.

Sex + Sexuality

When it comes to sex, nobody can hold out on 'getting some' like the Leo. He is literally vigilant in his determination to 'do without' until someone worthy enough comes along; as the zodiac's sacred Sun king, he cannot consort with just anyone. Sex for him is sacrosanct, an empty experience if his all-important heart isn't in it. In this Second Quadrant of Emotion, Leo's rule over the heart extends to the sacred, mystical significance of this organ and the power in its purity; he operates from this chakra point, if you will, which is the very embodiment of his sign's fixed-fire status. Just as flowing Mars-ruled blood is the emblem of Aries's cardinal-fire, the heart is the central existential force of the body, beating with tribal rhythm, responsible for the sustainment, the *fixed*ness, of life. Leo is one and the same with this organ, metaphorically; and he literally follows the inclinations of his own, bent on being true to its desires and keeping them pure by never settling for second best to what passions burn in his breast, trusting his heart over the noise and distraction of his mind. He shows us that *amour propre* must come before the loving of any other, that is, if it's to be significant. Until an estimable queen appears on the scene — whether it be female *or* male (we'll get to that) — remaining sexually unattached suits the Leo just fine. Still, his search for a meritorious mate is an active one, and if he's not lucky enough to marry his childhood sweetheart, the Becky to his Tom Sawyer — more Leos marry their prom dates than any other man in the zodiac — he'll uniformly work his way through a string of ladies, holding an ongoing contest for his permanent affections, putting each woman he links up with through a trial by fire, gauging her emotional capacities, especially those 5th House sentiments of *courage* and *devotion*. It is not someone easily put off by his signature imperiousness that he seeks; rather, Leo hopes to appeal to a woman who'll buy into his presumption of superiority, sharing in it and, thus, imbuing herself with that same dominance and authority. Meanwhile, it should be obvious to any potential mate that Leo surrounds himself with a sphere of friends and associates who genuflect to

5TH ASTROLOGICAL
HOUSE

love given
self-expression
amour propre
creative talent
imagination
procreation
offspring
passions
emotional perspective
speculation/gambling
spending habits
ancestry
genealogy
hobbies
games/sports
originality
social life
drama/dance
artistic outlets
publishing
joie de vivre
power plays
dynamism
image projection
popularity
stardom
politics
pleasure
fame/renown
life force
competition
romance
love affairs
love-making
legacy
teaching
trysts
fêtes
fine arts
playing with children
fun/amusement

popularity
morality
wholeness
insouciance
nobility
might
cordiality
playfulness
solitude
autocracy
comfort
self-esteem
athleticism
victory
appeal
charisma
rectitude
vehemence
asperity
resplendence
domination
magnificence
honor
virility
majesty
facility
judgment
piety
control
intolerance
eminence
lightheartedness
vitality
enthusiasm
royalty
prowess
stardom
flourish
remove
pride
ritual
sanctity
tyranny

him; and on some subconscious level, he hopes this will be a selling point to an equally power-hungry female. One definite aspect of Leo's fixed-fire status is that he lives in the spotlight, no matter how localized it may be; and consciously or not, he hopes that 'place in the Sun' will lure potential lovers. Never one to be on the make, he revels in watching women throw themselves at him. In truth, it's the only way he makes a love connection. He approaches dating as entertaining; that is, *considering* various female consorts for his affections; and as a native of the astrological 5th House of *sports and games,* he's happiest when the competition for him really heats up. Witnessing this race is a spectator sport; and Leo is resplendent in the role of first prize. Leo man wants a woman who is at once strong and feeling, automonous yet fiercely loyal, a haughty diva in public but a vulnerable little girl in private — not so that he might overpower her, but rather please, protect, and, as a baggy-lipped Leo Brit once crooned, come to her 'emotional rescue.' Often unbeknownst to him, Leo is drawn to women who lack father love in their life — ladies with a necessarily toughened exterior hiding an ultratender, aching heart. Such markedly paradoxical requirements make for a tall order in a mate, since most females' emotional states fall into either one category or the other (at least to his mind) — so needy as to be cloying, *or* so strong as to be blatantly ball-busting. This male Goldilocks has a tough time finding that woman who is 'just right.'

Despite his noble intention of attracting a quintessential queen, Leo's habit of putting prospective mates through the mill can make him a royal pain in the ass: He will purposefully run hot and cold, testing a woman's emotional stamina. For instance, he may expect her to be Janey-on-the-spot, while he slacks off himself. Or he may toy with her affections, even when he's decidedly disinterested and has no intention of investing emotionally himself. It's in just such a case that Leo's sadistic streak can really surface, as he gets a sick thrill out of stringing girls along, especially those whom he'll label bimbettes, sometimes going so far as to let a woman know that she's not the only one vying for him. Call it a game of cat and mouse. In this way, he'll kick back and watch various females jockey for his affections as if taking in his favorite pastime. Leo in a more malicious mode will invite flirtation, or even mere interest, expressly for the opportunity to rebuff it, getting off on telegraphing his ennui via dull stares and a barely audible *mm-hhmm.* (Ever seen De Niro on a talk show? It's as if he's granting the host, and the world, a huge favor just by showing up.) Little does he realize how bratty the whole display seems. Ironically, because Leo man is ultimately searching for his regal counterpart, he'll only ever sour on women who continue to make themselves too obviously available. Certainly, such overt behavior may be amusing at first, but it soon elicits a giant lion yawn. It is the woman powerful in her own right who captures his discriminating heart. Unlike Taurus, the preceding fixed (come-hither) male sign of the zodiac, Leo won't simply succumb to the pushiest female on the prowl – Taurus willingly responds to aggressive women. Instead, Leo seeks a forcefully feminine partner, one who will, at some point in their courtship, demand to be wooed in such a way as would befit a queen; an ultimatum, in word or deed, on her part, is proof of her moral pedigree. Simply put, Leo man looks for a woman who deserves him; and who better than one demanding to be deserved by him? Thus, he thinks: I have finally found my *rightful* mate. For, we must remember, the Lion sees life in absolute terms – a symptom of being born under the Sun – such that situations and, indeed, people are either good or bad, winners or losers. A woman is either right or wrong for him: There is no gray area. Relationships are all-or-nothing to the Leo man, who spends much of his early life holding back, both emotionally and sexually, until he finds a love worthy of pouring his whole self into. Never would he settle for anything even approximating a compromise situation, as so many people do – Leo can't be that cavalier with his affections – and still, by the same token, once he finds a relationship he deems deserving of his involvement, he has a hard time letting go should the association somehow go awry.

In stark contrast to Cancer man's desire for mothering, Leo man feels the need to be a father figure to women. He isn't looking to *be* adored, but rather to find himself a lover worthy *to* adore. And remaining Mr. Unavailable *is* his MO for finding such a suitable mate: In keeping his signature distance – for him, thus, acting natural – he will have systematically weeded out anyone who requires more static cling in a relationship. Likewise, if a woman is too comfortable with his arm's-length routine, he hypocritically finds her laissez-faire attitude suspect. Believe it or not, what he really wanted all along was to be called on the carpet and delivered an ultimatum – that he can be a tyrant with other women, but he must treat her like gold, or she's gone. Bingo: That's the romantic pay dirt Leo has been waiting to hit all his adult life – to find a female with courage enough to demand he become her paladin, both champion and protector, considering herself worthy of royal treatment. Offering such a mandate is tantamount to passing his infamous test – that trial by fire – and insures she'll never again suffer the slings and arrows of his emotional withholding. Moreover, this display of haughty female imperiousness works like an aphrodisiac on our heretofore sexually truant Tom Sawyer.

What Leo looks for in a woman, physically, is the same as what he seeks in a mate, philosophically: He wants an earthy woman of substance, a regal peasant to play counterpart to his picaresque hero, a *noblesse primitive* along the

BODY RULERSHIP

Leo rules the heart, the controlling mechanism of the entire organism, the upper back, and spine, and there is a tendency to cardiac and spinal afflictions. Likewise the Sun rules the circulatory system and the thymus, which is credited with stimulating growth. These functions mirror the Leo man's ability to integrate others into a wholistic unit or working system.

same archetypal line as Guinevere, unto his Arthur, Cleopatra to his Caesar. He is like the male lion who, if lucky enough to mate at all, will only do so with the one alpha female of the pride, a distinction determined by physical strength as well as symmetrical perfection, that sense of literal wholesomeness that signals health and beauty in (and out) of the animal kingdom. Still, Leo man isn't drawn to golden, fair-haired beauties like himself; rather, he is typically enticed by dark, sloe-eyed women who exude a sultry sensuality encased within a sturdy, full-figured frame. Waifish females, he imagines, would be unequipped to satisfy his emotional and sexual demands. Though he is by nature an avowed fat-phobe, he still holds the curvy, hourglass gal in the highest esteem. We're talking about the Sun personified here; thus, it is appropriate that this man's most compatible love is a fertile earth mother, one upon whom he can shower his (procreative) power, which in actuality might mean eventually bearing his children. To his mind, all things being equal, a man as mighty as he *demands* a comparably fierce female. Surely, he'll never feel that any woman could be 'too much' for him; and so he gravitates toward vivacious ladies who seem to be full of good health and vigor, perhaps by way of athletic capability. He's never quite able to escape his infamous attraction to those primitive-peasantry races, wildly pure and sturdy *stock* on whom he can try out his rather *patronizing* lord-and-master act, if not literally *father* a slew of children (*offspring* are an important aspect of the 5th Astrological House). For, despite his chosen woman's sense of her own 'highness,' her Leo partner must be ever so slightly elevated in rank – a queen in her own right, nonetheless only conquerable by so worthy a king as Leo imagines himself. Within this analogy, too, we see Leo has a soft spot for exotic, va-voomy women, particularly those of Middle Eastern, Latin, Mediterranean, Indian, or African origin. To some extent, Leo man is of the school of thought that 'the darker the berry, the sweeter the juice.' It's interesting to note, too, that the lion is a native of Africa, a land distinguished by intact primitive customs and a tribal system of chieftain-kings.

Life with our noble savage has its brutal moments. Like the male lion prowling the veldt, he is essentially a loner, the unavoidable solo occupation of any self-professed monarch. There is little symbiosis with Leo in love relationships. He's generally on his own path, even in the course of the day, like Helios, unwavering in the marks he's determined to hit. He is unwilling to deviate. Life is ritual, indeed sacrament. He doesn't function on fleeting feelings or whims – the fixed-fire of his sign signifies sustained emotion, heartfelt interests that, like his personal bonds, are few. But they burn intensely, like an eternal flame. And he must keep those fires going, deepening them, increasingly, into passions. Leo's 5th House is that of *drama,* particularly of the ritual sort, theater and religion being synonymous in the ancient soul of the Lion. To him, all is a passion play, wherein the characterizations of his daily routine are imbued with symbolic import. The ritual that is Leo's quotidian existence reinforces his role as a solemn presence here on earth, just as the ceremony surrounding a sacred priest-king is meant to reinforce the unseen power of divine sovereignty. In other words, you can't spring any plans on the Leo; and woe it is to even his loving spouse if she questions how he chooses to spend his time or even his mandate on which restaurant to, and this is the word for it, *frequent.* The glorious outcome of this view on life is that committed relationships, particularly those solidified by the sacrament of marriage, are more sacred to him than to any other man. He is not only the most monogamous of males; he also believes that looking at foreign goods is almost as bad as fondling them. The more vernacular F-word is outright sinful to consider, even to the Leoan agnostic. Leo prides himself on loyalty, and when in an unhappy marriage, he may grin and bear it rather than admit defeat. Still he won't stray. He's not one to seek sex. But he will let love find him. If his heart begins to pound for another female, he'll pick up and pad his way into the sunset. And when he goes, he's gone – as deeply as he loved, the loss of it will be that much more profound. It's a thin line to cross, as this Cat can be hateful to say the least. If, however, he is the one left in the lurch, he has the hardest time recovering from lost love of any guy out there. He will be so shocked and crippled at being cast aside that the sulking could last for years. It's a case of the bigger they are, the harder they fall. And as Leo is so careful to let only the most loving, loyal subjects into his 'circle of trust,' he never entertains the possibility of his devotees defecting. In the case of a lover, especially, the sexual bond is the most profound of ritual experiences that cements the union on a moral, emotional, and spiritual plane. The Leo doesn't see such covenants as easily broken.

Sex for Leo man should be as natural an occurrence as any coupling in the wild kingdom. However, ironically, when the time comes to consummate a relationship, it is, to his mind anyway, quite the ceremonious affair. One imagines him hearing a drumroll, if not a proclamatory fanfare, when he finally unzips his fly; and he's on the lookout for an appreciative glint to that effect in his partner's eye. The actual act of sex is a big deal for Leo, and it's a turnoff if his lover doesn't share this heightened, somewhat dramatic perspective. On some level, he hopes she'll admit that a sexual experience of this magnitude has yet to occur in her lifetime. Indeed, if Leo gets even the slightest whiff that she is 'too seasoned' in the sack, he'll do a hasty retreat, though not before hitting her up with a heavy moral head-trip. Arthur, after

Blake Edwards
Norman Lear
Gus Van Sant
Alfred Hitchcock
Nicolas Roeg
William Powell
Ring Lardner Jr.
Neil Armstrong
John Huston
George Hamilton
George Bernard Shaw
Gene Rodenberry
Ray Bradbury
Robert Mitchum
Garrison Keillor
T. E. Lawrence
Peter O'Toole
Yves Saint Laurent
Andy Warhol
Larry Rivers
Willie Shoemaker
Mike Douglas
Malcolm Forbes
Samuel Goldwyn
Henry Ford
Alex Haley
Bert Lahr
David Crosby
Jerry Garcia
Carroll O'Connor
Roman Polanski
Napoleon
William Bennett
Benito Mussolini
Fidel Castro
Claus Von Bulow
Claudius I
Thomas Eakins
Carl Jung
Herman Melville
V. S. Naipaul
Percy Shelley
Alfred, Lord Tennyson
Marcel Duchamp
Jean Dubuffet
Cecil B. DeMille
Michael Kors
John Landis
Sam Elliot
Russell Baker
Charles Bukowski
Ogden Nash

all, fully expects his Guinevere to be pure. In truth, few other men are as sexist as the Leo on this score. Unlike his flip-side astrological neighbor, Cancer male, who feels subjected to the collective scrutiny of female-kind, therefore bearing them no moral judgment, the Leo male considers himself the final word on, well, *everything* – but especially on issues of ethics, which fall under his sign's jurisdiction. Leo possesses a striking inability to view moral questions with the slightest smidgen of subjectivity, let alone irony. Sex, though a natural outpouring of passion for the Lion, must never smack of anything even a tad sleazy; and he'd find it highly suspect if his partner did not wholeheartedly agree.

Fittingly, then, Leo's favorite flavor, hands down, is vanilla. He prides himself, in fact, on having few to no so-called perversions, looking to appeal on that very premise to women as a righteous Cat. It is the lion's share of his attraction, drawing women on the basis of embodying noble intentions, just as he invites a certain corruption from those who'd get off on seeing his signature rectitude slip. Most often, it is the woman who must take the driver's seat upon entering, shall we say, sophisticated sexual territory. If anything, he may have an inclination toward dominance role-play, with his partner in the submissive position; when this sadistic streak exists, it is a flagrant exaggeration of Leo's inborn superiority complex – he believes himself justified in ruling, with a firm hand, even the one he most loves and cherishes. However, in most cases, Leo man simply doesn't have a kinky bone in his body. For his more imaginative mates, this (lack of) preference may leave them, if not wanting, than wondering what erotic variations they're missing out on as they continue to mix it up with only him. As a male sign in the Second Quadrant of Emotions Leo is not as fixated on the physical aspect of sex as are men in the First Quadrant, nor is he so sexually stimulated on a mental level as are those in the Third Quadrant. His erotic interest is strictly determined by the emotional connection made in his Leo-ruled heart. Still, there's a lot to be said for indulging oneself on this plane: The Lion is nothing if not intensely passionate. When he reveals his emotions to the 'right' woman, he'll do so utterly; thankfully, this manifests as marathon lovemaking sessions distinguished by playful hours spent kissing, spooning, holding, and heatedly rolling around. However, no matter how rough-and-tumble a romp becomes, sex must always be taken slowly, if not outright lazily. As a nod to his association with the 5th House of *love affairs,* every sexual encounter for the Leo should feel like the first time, or at least a special occasion (contrary to the standard interpretation that Leo has lots of love affairs – even during his serial-dating days, he rarely goes further than a girl's front door). This may even remain true when the Leo and his partner have been married for decades. For him, the bedroom is a sacred space, and regular sex with a steady mate is as revered in his mind as would be, for the rest of us, a sweet but fleeting tryst from our past. Still, his sexual tastes are often perceived as bland, which may leave his lover craving a little spice in their ardently wholesome routine. For all his noble intentions, Arthur did see his Guinevere go for the French (read: oral) guy who she apparently hoped would lance her, *a lot*. Indeed, despite Leo's legendary-self-stylings, he isn't one to 'go down' in history. Not to say he isn't willing to accept such favors himself – it is, after all, good to be the king.

With a substantial dose of patience, any lover of a Leo man will be allowed to slowly shake things up, especially if she does so under the guise of *playing* the hoochie-koochie courtesan whose role it is to pleasure her benevolent ruler. In this way she might release the beast, inciting him out of his usual kick-back mode, which, to be fair, does have its moments: For all his lolling about in the bedroom, Leo is actually one of the more tireless men in the zodiac, comfortably spending whole days crumpling the sheets, alternating between sex and sleep. He expects *it* often – with one full day of sex on the weekend, if lifestyle allows – and boasts the ability to maintain a hard-on long after most men would have withered. Indeed, once a woman gives over to *his* natural rhythm, she may be surprised how multiorgasmic slow-moving sex can be. Leo elevates simple acts, like kissing, to a heightened state of ecstasy; with him, the most wholesome and natural expressions of sexual desire should be more than enough to satisfy anyone, even those who usually need more bells and whistles in the bedroom. It is this precise realization that the Leo hopes to inspire in his lover, bringing about a sense of sexual healing by showering pure affection and devotion. Of course, certain maneuvers will make the Lion roar more audibly than usual: Playing with his testicles, especially by running ones fingernails across them, albeit lightly, during intercourse is a surefire way to have him, well, by the balls. Other key erogenous zones are his chest area, in general, and his back; gently clawing along his *entire* posterior during sex sends electric shivers through his body, as does lightly scratching his scalp and neck. As would befit our ritualistic Sun king, he never tires of the same sexual program, for it is this son of Helios' unique ability to experience what others might label routine as perennially fresh, like each new day. For the most part, he elicits that same craving for the familiar in his lovers, who find themselves rapt by his sunny and wholesome approach to sex, basking in the spotlight of the devotion Leo showers, apparently to the exclusion of the rest of the world.

The spicier aspects of Leo's sex life tend to run along specific lines: The Father Principle with its inherent need for authority takes on a decided twist with erotic interests falling under the general heading of light B&D (that's

STR8 TURN-ONS

dark skin
long, raven hair
sloe eyes
ethnicity
innocence
vanilla
massage
touching, fondling, groping
passionate kissing
hugging, spooning, cuddling
natural beauty
missionary position
scratching, biting
fresh scents
sex outdoors
(active) lite b + d
(passive) worship
(passive) oral
dancing, striptease
schoolgirls, cheerleaders
begging, groveling
ball play
(passive) analingus

'bondage and dominance' to you larger lot of Leos who wouldn't otherwise have a clue). Desires might be so subtle as to require a partner to spend some quality time on her knees in service to her king, while he nearly ignores her efforts to please him. She may have to deliver a dramatic discourse on his awesome prowess and manly magnificence, sometimes in an effort to fully erect the monument to which this monologue is dedicated. More elaborate fantasies might include some version of the cliché French maid's uniform, or no uniform at all, his partner being at his beck and call, cleaning, cooking, and performing other domestic duties as a prelude to his barking out other commands. The Leo may fancy retaining his complete control, remaining fully clothed and comfortably seated while a woman is made to graphically expose and pleasure herself for his amusement. Tying a lover up with the mutually consensual proposition of 'using' her at will could work its way into the mix of Leo's carnal vision, as might role-play centered on a woman being an out-and-out sex slave. Though not one for accessorizing with leather leashes or collars, Leo will rather get off on a woman pretending to be some captured wild woman whom he must tame with a somewhat iron fist. If you ever wondered who those adult-magazine layouts depicting women as cavewomen were geared toward, it is the zodiac's king of the jungle. Spanking a female into submission is probably the prime Leo variation on a straightforward sexual theme of masculine domination. He doesn't much go for the slappy-slappy of a woman made up as some submissive schoolgirl, however, the way Cancer man will. Rather, Leo likes a bit of a fight, whether it be from some captured Queen of Sheba or that saucy French maid. Strong women who will play along at being subdued only fuel the ego of this Cat, who might then expect a bit of struggle to work its way into the signature follow-up to this sexual play of straightforward copulation. If the scratches on his back are that much more pronounced as a result, all the better. Dominating a fierce pussy is much more an accomplishment to his mind, and a wee bit of a wincing reminder cached beneath his all-cotton shirt puts a contented Cheshire grin on his face that his friends and colleagues can only begin to guess at.

Sex is definitely something Leo doesn't discuss outside the privacy of his home, where, even there, it's something that is preferably avoided in conversation. He is not what one would call an open character, preferring to remain sheltered in the bubble of his standoffish aura. As such, he is the least likely of individuals to participate in any adult sexual group dynamic. He is a one-on-one kind of guy, and even the de rigueur male fantasy of bedding two women has little appeal to the morally uptight Leo. When it comes to his own feelings of homosexuality, even in his adolescence the Leo is disallowed any sort of self-loathing that might plague other young males. For one thing, gay Leo is typically still a decidedly butch, athletic fellow who feels just as at home in the locker room or on the line of scrimmage as his straight buddies. In fact, being as self-possessed as he is, the Lion is arguably less prone to sneak peeks in the shower than his hetero mates. As he matures, gay Leo, though no more a 'joiner' than his straight counterpart, typically seeks out a more global and ardent fan base, unlike his hetero brother, who prefers a low-key, localized kingdom in which to rule. Gay Leo is far and away more out and proud than most of his homosexual friends; pride itself is a more prominent virtue (or vice) for the gay Leo man than it will ever be for the straight one. Still, you won't see him strutting in any parades as one of the people, though he might consider the role of grand marshal; typically, he's an armchair activist who feels he's furthering the gay cause by example rather than by demonstration. Gay Leo man may even fancy himself a poster boy for normal, wholesomely natural, and indeed enobling homosexuality. In truth, he really is one of the more straight-appearing and -acting men on the wheel, as if naturally dispelling the notion that gay men are any different from straight ones. Sometimes this gay king may have to flex his muscles a bit more to ward off any doubts as to his worthiness to wield power – which explains why gay Leos do so on a grander, more public scale. Meanwhile, it's not surprising that gay Leo man is psychologically somewhat more complex(ed) than his straight counterpart, who prides himself on leading as simple and unanalytical a life as is humanly possible.

Looking 'straight' also serves another purpose: It attracts female friends, who make up the greater part of his adoring fan base. Leo notoriously drops hints as to his 'past' exploits with the ladies, conscious of keeping a number of female hearts on a string. For, regardless of sexual orientation, Leo man needs to know that he appeals to a pride of women; and whereas straight Leo will eventually zero in on one mate, the gay Leo, never taking that next sexual step, is left in a perpetual state of being surrounded by devoted females from whom he withholds emotional involvement – and, of course, sex itself. Most of his male friends are straight, and they, too, are subject to his dominion, being typically weedier and wimpier pussy-whipped fellows in whose presence the Leo will feel a natural superiority, *might* being *right,* and all that rot. Even here Leo directs his attention onto the females in his midst, forever putting his male friends' dates through the same sort of trials by fire to which straight Leo subjects prospective mates, as if asserting a heterosexual agenda, vicariously, through his straight vassals. Meanwhile, conversely, one is forbidden to express an opinion about Leo's choice of lover, though it will always be tempting for his circle of friends to do so.

GAY TURN-ONS

younger men
Asians
submissives, twinks
lifeguards, Speedos
farmboys, rentboys, guidos
denim, t-shirts
cowboy boots
smooth bodies
swimmers' builds
mind control
(passive) oral
(active) tea-bagging
buttockry, frottage
bearcubs
transsexuals
muscular backs, lats
sports kit, jockstraps
wrestling
locker rooms
exhibitionism, adulation
hygiene
(active) nipple play
father role-play
animal noises
monogamy

In most cases, Leo man selects a lover who seems 'out of character' to those who know him best, or so it would appear: For all his button-down goldenness, Leo tends to seek out streety, even tricky types whose character might be, if not suspect, than at least wholly out of sync with his own. Still, more often than not, the guy that captures Leo's heart only *looks* like a one-night stand – something that appeals to the Lion's association with that 5th House of *love affairs*. While straight Leo wants a ready-made queen, at once on par with himself, gay Leo seems to enjoy slumming it in search of some 'lost' male orphan whom he can adopt and have benefit from his natural fatherly energy. Not to say that Leo only goes for younger guys; in fact, he also has a penchant for men *just* his own age. This points to a pathology particular to his sign: No matter how dysfunctional the Leo's upbringing may have been, he'll tend to view it as almost perfect in hindsight; often, to reinforce this perspective, he'll connect with a guy from a similar background – same town, school, socioeconomic sphere – though one that is decidedly less sunny, the shadow side of his own. Take Tom Sawyer: In a heterosexual sphere, his perfect partner is the equally ecumenical Becky Thatcher; but his primary same-sex relationship is with Huck Finn, a déclassé outcast from the other side of the tracks who, it naturally follows, simply needs the right sort of patronage in order to transcend such dodgy circumstances. This is precisely what Leo man longs to do in gay relationships: to shower affection in such a way as to have a healing and stabilizing effect. On the one hand, Leo's natural sense of superiority is thus assured. Yet this is where we see the same problems arise for the gay Leo as arise for his straight counterpart: Ennobling passion may take precedence over straightforward carnal desires in the Lion's desire to heal the cruder side of his lover's personality. Even Mark Twain may have had insight into the nature of the Sawyer-esque Leo's proclivity for a lover along the Huck Finn archetype, as the character's name itself serves as an anagram of sorts designed to inform the Leo that he should go ahead, already, and just *Fuck Him* (the double *n* thus becoming an *m* in the transposition). For, in truth, a dearth of sexual experimentation might derail a gay relationship even faster than a straight one; and the saltier sorts Leo consorts with are not typically those who tend to be churchgoing in their sexual appetites, living on Leo's higher love alone.

Anyone who knows a Leo man will readily admit he has something of a God complex. To be fair, a great number of men, gay and straight, relish the direction of such an authoritative figure; and so, at least initially, Leo man appeals to a lover who seeks such patronage. While Leo's attention may be in 'noble' pursuits such as exercise and nutritional regimes, styling and grooming, networking for career purposes, building equity, buying real estate, and otherwise seeking to be the most successful good-looking, masculine gay couple of all time, his lover might simply have his eye on the perks, wanting to leave the more ambitious pursuits to his Leo king, enjoying, instead, a decidedly cushy existence of ultimate queendom. But bonbon eaters beware: The lover of a Leo man must, at the very least, *pretend* to have some ambition. Only an uncharacteristically codependent Lion will refrain from kicking his stud-muffin sidekick out on his ass if he thinks it is being used to warm the couch all day – or worse, bouncing around in bed with somebody other than him. Which brings us to a point that can not be emphasized enough: Leo is a most jealous man with, hands down, the hottest temper of any man in the zodiac, and he takes 'cheating' as a crime against nature, God, and along such lines, himself.

When it comes to nuts-and-bolts sexual behavior, then, threesomes seem distinctly out of the question. The only way Leo would entertain the thought of anyone but his lover in the bedroom is if that third party wanted nothing more than to watch. Indeed, Leo man is foremost an exhibitionist and to a specific end: He believes his lovemaking is so authentic and quintessentially passionate that he wishes (secretly or otherwise) to share it with the world. Have you apartment dwellers ever wondered which gay couple is the one without window shades? Safely assume one of them is a Leo. He makes love in a nearly soap-operatic fashion, his 'favorite things' being somewhat soft-core in sensibility: Deep kissing and body contact typically top the list, along with massage and mutual masturbation. Though he will use his mouth sensually over his lover's body, he's not particularly oral per se. He will 'let' his lover blow him, to be sure, but he's uncomfortable in the service position. Ironically, when it comes to any anal penetration, he will sooner adopt the passive pose, as if to say he's the one being *done* and not doing *for*. This can be surprising to Leo's lover, who naturally assumes his fatherly friend would drag his daddy act into the bedroom. Still, even on the receiving end, Leo is rarely one to engage in any outright fuck fests. Anal penetration should never feel like anything more than a surge of passion, the same fleeting expression as deep kissing; all should remain as wholesome and innocent as possible, with emphasis heavily placed on love as opposed to sex. On a subconscious level, too, Leo is attempting to force an epiphany in his lover: to show him that the sharing of emotion *is* the ecstatic aspect of sex. Though most agree that all sex acts are better when passion is present, to the Leo man, regardless of sexual preference, even the most basic bedroom behavior is empty, if not dirty, without it.

Couplings

Leo Man ∫ Aries Woman

Love at first sight: He sees an easy coexistence; she's finds her alpha-male match. A hot affair that quickly becomes committed. A threat to domestic bliss: her dalliances. In bed, there are no bells and whistles; ecstasy is automatic.

Leo Man ∫ Taurus Woman

He longs for a natural woman – subtle, accessible Taureans appeal. She basks in Leo's glow, energized by his powerful presence. She stimulates his self-actualization. Tactile expression is her strength.

Leo Man ∫ Gemini Woman

He's the object of her doting attention. With time, Leo evolves into the dream guy Gemini imagined. They'll often take a walk down the aisle. Laughter is their saving grace. With her, he's forever in his sexual prime.

Leo Man ∫ Cancer Woman

Cancer's father issues might finally get fixed; his warm nature is awakened. It's soul asylum: a safe place to purge emotions. He's compelled to control, under the guise of being 'helpful.' In bed, she teaches him a thing or two.

Leo Man ∫ Leo Woman

It's a battle of the wills. A shared need to shine incites glaring problems. At best, they merge into one supernova; otherwise, they might fall into an emotional black hole. Regardless, they're a lusty couple.

Leo Man ∫ Virgo Woman

Leo's floored by Virgo's exceptional femininity. She recognizes a talent worth championing: He might become her mission. They'll enjoy an even-keel existence. In bed, she's the seductive schoolmarm; he's her dominant pupil.

Leo Man ∫ Libra Woman

They connect as intellectual equals, each inspiring the other to think more progressively. A fast-paced, industrious duo. In the bedroom, they're bonded: Sex is fun-loving, relaxed – no head trips, no taboos.

Leo Man ∫ Scorpio Woman

Life is a banquet – a feast at which they devour separate areas of experience. Together, they're 'takers.' This couple craves notoriety. Offspring are inevitable. Sexual hunger for each other seems insatiable.

Leo Man ſ ſagittariuſ Woman
Vigor and drive are what they share in common. Two colossal egos, in tandem, produce one of astrology's quintessential power couples. In bed, he's robust and ever ready; Sag matches such heartiness.

Leo Man ſ Capricorn Woman
Often a snobbish 'power' sign pair. They share traditional values, an old-fashioned work ethic. Still, as they're emotionally dissimilar, disappointment develops – she's capricious; he expects compliance. Sexually, it's cozy, but careful.

Leo Man ſ Aquariuſ Woman
Together, they're big and bold, gifted, but unpredictable. Leo adopts a contemplative countenance. Her unusual, extraordinary qualities emerge. Sex is passionate, energized by envy, as well as esteem.

Leo Man ſ Pisceſ Woman
She's their spiritual barometer; he keeps the romance rolling. Emotionally, she underwrites his quest for professional power. Their bond affords a dose of detachment from others. In bed, Pisces is his estimable goddess.

Leo Man ſ Arieſ Man
Two über-masculine characters who steer clear of feminine types. An intensely sexual, and deeply spiritual, connection. Together, they see life as a lark, not a labor. Sex is so satisfying, it becomes a preoccupation.

Leo Man ſ Tauruſ Man
Life with Leo seems to promise luxury, the good life. The Lion, a lookist, leaps at the beautiful Taurean Adonis. Loyalty to each other is their leitmotiv. Friends and family abound. Sex is ceremonial, sometimes self-conscious.

Leo Man ſ Gemini Man
These guys see great possibilities in getting together. Often, a bit of exploitation takes place. Leo is smitten with the tricky Twins guy, who seems to have no shortcomings. In bed, Gemini hankers for saucier sessions.

Leo Man ſ Cancer Man
Leo is suspicious of Cancer's sneaky ways. Over time, often on the sly, these charismatic characters become companions, enchanted by each other. They're a popular pair. In bed, it's a loving, affirming affair.

Gay

Leo Man / Leo Man

A challenging match. For two kings, it's a constant question of who's the boss – someone wins, someone loses. Egos may abate; cooperation and humility are the lessons. Sexually, it just feels 'right.'

Leo Man / Virgo Man

Virgo seems harmless and charming – captivating, but no threat to the Lion's alpha status. The Virgin is happy to be Leo's coveted companion. They transcend differences over time. Still, their sex life needs spicing.

Leo Man / Libra Man

Ideological differences are a hindrance here. Leo's dogmatic; Libra's liberal. Still, a little lively debate stimulates. Sexually, it's simpler: Libra takes the lead, persistently inciting Leo's deeper desires.

Leo Man / Scorpio Man

This pair is polarized: Leo seems too sunny to Scorpio, who lingers even longer in emotional darkness, as if to annoy the Lion. In bed, they do battle. But Leo is enlivened by the scrappy Scorpion force.

Leo Man / Sagittarius Man

Together, two high-rolling he-men live even larger – Sag is especially audacious. Fortune seems to surround them. Sexually, too, they've hit the jackpot: It's all a game; extreme behavior gets much play.

Leo Man / Capricorn Man

Leo feels out of the loop: He's a neophyte compared to the cultured Goat guy. But the Lion learns to accept the guidance of such a socially adept sophisticate. In bed, Cap hopes to expose his 'hick' to a soupçon of sin.

Leo Man / Aquarius Man

They exist to support each other. Before long, Leo reevaluates his lifestyle, reconfiguring priorities. Aquarius creates their new order – his rules take precedence. Passionate love frees Leo of any self-doubt.

Leo Man / Pisces Man

A head-trippy gay-guy duo. Egos clash and verbal sparring is expected. Holding out emotionally becomes a game that no one wins. In bed, peace is restored – this is where these boys shine.

Leo Woman

the knockout

Leo woman is the prime mover of the zodiac. No other individual possesses her power and determination for achieving goals, sexual or otherwise. Burning with desire, she attacks life, letting nothing stand in the way of her hunt for fulfillment. Incapable of distancing herself from her passions, she embodies the romantic and erotic urges that drive her forward in pursuit of satisfying a constant craving for love and lovemaking. In a sense, Leo woman *is* sex, her every action fueled by a natural lust for life – and she looks the part: A fiercely energetic woman with vivid coloring and flashing eyes, she hungers for experience, never doing anything by halves. Without the slightest timidity, she makes her needs and feelings known, boldly proclaiming sexual interest in a would-be mate, subsequently proving to be a boisterous wildcat in the bedroom. She is attracted to men who possess passions that equal her own, but, like her, won't be completely consumed by them. She presents a challenge to the male of the species, requiring a guy to be so stable and commanding as to make her seem feral and feminine in contrast – no easy feat for the one woman who can't help but beat most men at their own game of dominance, whether in a professional or personal circumstance. In same-sex bonds, Leo is provocative, seeking to draw out a woman's concealed desires and uncover her wild side, only to then later subdue her, both within the bedroom and without. Leo is always the leading lady in gay relationships, playing the role of protector to the hilt.

V

The Father Principle. Via the Sun's rulership, the sign embraces a patriarchal view of the world, as a place of male mastery, authority, and domination. But Leo woman doesn't represent compliance to this rule. Rather, drawing on her mythic archetypes, she embodies the spirit of a matriarchal power in exile – Artemis on her hunt – and its revered relegation by the patriarchy to the home, like Hestia at her hearth. Leo is a determinant force to be reckoned with – her sign's motto is 'I will.'

Sign + Mind

Leo woman's ruler Sun represents the authoritative Father Principle in astrology. For the male of the sign this precept translates into a big-daddy sense of innate ease and entitlement, while in the Leo female it signals a rebellion against patriarchal subjugation, a call to flee and get out from under the thumb of the more universally accepted male-dominant social paradigm. As the one female born into the puissant sign of patriarchal rule, Leo is anything but passive or compliant in the face of such ersatz authority. Rather, she possesses the spirit of a Cleopatra faced with a Caesar – a mighty matriarch confronted with male-dominant society, equipped with the power to fight in her flight against it. The animal lion itself, an emblem of male majesty, is inherently a matriarchal species: Females take on the 'lion's share' of hunting and tending to the family pride, while the male remains a rather lone figurehead. Fittingly, the oldest matriarchal goddesses, Artemis (Roman: Diana) and Hestia (Roman: Vesta), are Leo woman's prime archetypes. As goddess of the hunt and goddess of the hearth, respectively, they represent the same double-duty energy – provider *and* protector – that both the real lioness and the astrological one personify. Both deities are self-possessed 'virgin' goddesses who refuse to marry and be subjugated by the world of men. Virgin status attached to these goddesses doesn't signify chastity but rather the refusal to submit to the male. Indeed, such female deities as these who remained 'intact' in their godhead were viewed as too powerful to make into the wives of the male gods of the conquering patriarchy. Like Athena, the prime archetype of Leo's sister-fire sign Aries, Artemis is a beloved of Zeus and the inheritor of his divinity, just as an ancient queen such as Cleopatra (meaning 'father-love') was seen as descending from the gods. Indeed, the cult of Diana in Rome was the largest and last surviving rival of Christianity. The only other deity to achieve more attention was Hestia-Vesta, to whom more sacrifices were offered than to any other god. As goddess of the home, she was the hub, just as she sat tending the eternal Olympian fire, letting the other twelve gods get up to their hubbub. She was still like the Sun around which all else revolves – her sacred round table depicting the zodiac becoming medieval Arthur's Round Table. Artemis, as her name suggests, is also linked with the legendary king. It is apt that these most popular of goddesses archetypally represent the Leo, who in a nod to her sign's Absolute Principle tends to be, shall we say, rather full of herself. Taking Artemis and Hestia together, the She-Lion can bring home the bacon and fry it up in the pan. Such is the mythological stuff of which Leo woman is made.

She is the incarnation of both the fiercely wild goddess of the hunt and of the gentle domestic goddess of the hearth, aspects paradoxically rolled together into a cohesive whole that *is* the lady lion. Indeed, her life is one continual, exhilarating chase for those goals she hungers to achieve. Still, she keeps the home fires burning and generally becomes the one person in her brood upon whom the responsibility for maintaining familial solidarity falls. No individual in the zodiac, male or female, is as fierce a control freak or as fervent in the pursuit of passions.

Metaphorically speaking, the hunt represents freedom in expressing creative or procreative urges – though a virgin deity, Artemis is also the creatress mother goddess of all wild things, ancient proof that the virginity associated with her was never interpreted literally. As Carl Jung theorized, the hunt is symbolic of the sex act itself; it would thus extend to more figurative acts of creation. Such interpretations are perfectly fitting considering Leo's association with the 5th Astrological House, which rules, among other things, the *creative life force,* as both *artistic expression* and *lovemaking* with the subsequent bearing of children – as if to say that the offspring of one's mind (ideas) and of one's body (children) come from the same impetus inside the self. Leo woman is the human materialization of this impulse: Like her ruler, Sun, she is the most vital entity on the astrological wheel, far more determined to demonstrate her abundant energy than is her Leo male counterpart, who embodies the Sun's unreachable-star aspect – rather she portrays its active, omnipresent nature. She is an irrevocable force, an overriding distinction that surfaces early in the Leo girl's development. Like Artemis, the Leo female usually knows precisely what she wants out of life, practically from infancy. She makes sure of one thing: She *will* be utterly free to express herself however, whenever, and to whatever degree she sees fit. 'I will,' after all, is the sign of Leo's motto. As the zodiac's huntress, she has a certain through-line to her life, marked by definitive goals determined by her notoriously untamed passions. It must be said that the pursuits of the Leo female are not cerebral. Instead, they are fueled by a heartfelt need for exposition, befitting a sign that not only rules the physical heart, but is also a native of the zodiacal Second Quadrant – comprising the 4th, 5th, and 6th Astrological Houses and the signs that rule them. Cancer, Leo, and Virgo all represent life as lived on the metaphysical emotional level. Cancer represents gut instincts and the outpouring of feeling; Virgo, the weighing of the conscience. And right in the middle of the quadrant is the fixed Leo focused on, as Kate Bush once put it, the 'constellation of the heart,' the patterning of passion into a purpose to hotly pursue. Incidentally, one of that particular Leo's record covers sees her as Artemis-Diana flanked by

PLANETARY SYMBOL

The astrological symbol of the Sun signifies the individual needing to be at the center of the collective consciousness. The circle suggests divinity, making Leo woman a diva who loves the spotlight.

The zodical quadrants correspond to the metaphysical planes of existence – physical, emotional, mental, and spiritual. The Second Quadrant is that of emotional environment, wherein one's feelings about the world are of prime concern. The fixed Leo is a concentrated and conservative generator of heartfelt passion. For her, importance lies in carefully tending to and honing her creative expression into the hottest ticket in town.

her 'hounds of love,' astutely linking *l'amour* with the hunt. On another cover, she's outfitted as Arthur, brandishing a sword. Yet another depicts ruby slippers, which, in a foreshadowed metaphorical click of the heels, will bring all this extended analogy home.

First, let's say that even as a child, Leo is never one to drift or feel at a loss – her huntress's path is ever clear. Leo's family life will have been suited to her autonomous, driven nature as, more often than not, she grows up a latchkey kid with both parents noticeably absent from her day-to-day environment. Left to her own devices, Leo girl becomes a bastion of self-reliance, honing her (Artemisal) survivalist skills in the practice of creating a stable (Hestian) home environment – for herself. Like Dorothy in *The Wizard of Oz,* she lacks consistent parental guidance, but rarely suffers as a result. Rather, feeling exempt from such supervision, she is free from an early age to set out on a fantastical journey on a golden road through life – her very own quest for the great and powerful qualities of Oz. Whereas 'wet' Cancer is forever wishful, Leo is fiercely determined to be wonderful, if not wonder-filled. Often, there are dramatic reasons for the conspicuous absence of a parent, usually her mother – divorce or death – while more generally, it is the result of having a notoriously weak, if not entirely ineffectual, mother figure. Most often, Leo's father is strict and strong-willed, though a sporadic presence at home. In the extreme he is a tough disciplinarian, dogmatic politically, religiously, or both, against whose dictatorial nature the little Lion girl privately begins to rebel. She doesn't advertise her feelings with the kinds of coup d'états Gemini girl might launch, rather she strategizes, the eternal queen on the chessboard, all stealth and surprise offensives, like the animal lion itself. She pretends to comply with parental mandates but nonchalantly dismisses and disobeys them, secretly following her own path, rarely of the garden variety. Ironically, she rules herself with as firm a hand as her father's. Indeed, despite the times having suffered his severe temperament, Leo woman will forever credit her father for having instilled in her the sign-ruled backbone necessary to stand up for her convictions.

As befits her sunny rulership, she lives each day as if it were sacred, a ritual drama calling for exactitude and economy in the way she spends her time. Fulfilling her chores, tending those infamous home fires, Leo takes special care to focus her free time and inexhaustible energy on her most burning passions – typically those that entail stepping into some sort of spotlight. She never wallows or complains as will Cancer. She gets on with it and easily gains the respect of teachers and other grown-ups for being so self-reliant. Like an ambitious adult jockeying for a corporate promotion, she knows how to play the game, win friends, and influence people. She lies low, like the predatory lioness, biding her time until it's appropriate to spring into action – in contrast to Leo man, who can't help shooting his mouth off in the face of authority. Still, when Leo woman does make a power play, watch out. Her take-no-prisoners approach to realizing ambitions – going in for the kill – knocks any and all competition out of the running. If the zodiac's Lioness shares one essential trait with her wild namesake, it is the realization that survival depends upon cooperation with others, particularly other females whom she can amass into a 'pride' of sorts – women who will uphold her alpha pussy position in the pack, doing her bidding, if not outright serving as her pawns, and later as her well-instructed vassals. As the undisputed queen on life's chessboard, she needs underlings to run interference and to provide the requisite strength in numbers it takes to achieve the positions of authority she seeks. As well, such subordinates assist her greatly in capturing whatever king she is currently hoping to topple. In return, she heaps her particular brand of parental guidance and support upon these friends. But this loyalty, for which she is famous, works both ways: It at once wins her trust and coveted leadership roles, but also guarantees that she'll be eternally expected to take responsibility, emotional and otherwise, for those same fierce supporters.

Opportunism can be a keynote in the Leo female's life. As the one fixed-fire (read: concentrated spirit) female in the zodiac, she excels at pursuits that require sustained action and creativity. Though Leo isn't always adept at coming up with creative ideas, nobody can run further with what is already 'out there' than she. If Leo sees a chance to intercept a creative plan or concept that isn't presently being done justice (even if by its originator), she may 'develop' it into something more fully realized – a scheme to which she can hitch her *own* star. Still, as suspect as that may sound, it is the Leo's birthright, as one born under the sign of wholeness and completion, to envision how a half-baked concept could be sufficiently fleshed out and then accomplished. In all fairness, too, the Lion queen isn't always conscious of this tendency to usurp other people's territory – regardless, she may easily gain a reputation for being cannibalistic. Still, Leo teaches us, by example, that it is indeed natural to base our outlets for expression, creative or otherwise, on the inroads that pre-decessors have made. With her keen sense of knowing where and when to grab the baton and start boogying, few others give chase to such ambitious desires as does this fast-track daughter of Artemis. The Absolute Principle of Leo's ruler Sun determines that she must give ambitions her 'all,' leaving no stone unturned in the pursuit of her passionate interests. The calendrical time of Leo's birth is characterized by the height of the growing season, and indeed,

SIGN GLYPH

For Leo woman, the glyph is best understood as the lion's tail, a barometer of feline emotion that acts as a rudder, giving balance to the cat on its infamous hunts and high-speed chases. The circle represents divine mind linking the strong emotion she feels and her determi-nate will into a single focus.

ELEMENT + QUALITY

The fire element symbolizes life energy, spirit, or the divine force. The fixed quality denotes magnetism, sustainment, and concentration. The fixed-fire combination particular to Leo is likened to a star, the fame and fortune that women of the sign are forever chasing.

the Lioness sees life as filled with opportunities ripe for the picking. Not so much embodying the 'divine right' sense of entitlement Leo man feels – he's content to be king of his own castle – the Lioness's own fulfillment requires far grander successes, often on a global scale. And because she shoots so high, she may achieve a sort of superstardom even when only halfway toward the fulfillment of her ultimate goals.

More than any other astrological character, male or female, the Leo woman dreams of wordly renown. Like the Sun, which shines to the farthest corners of the globe, she seeks to have her influence felt ubiquitously. A list of famous Leos, which includes the likes of Annie Oakley, Mata Hari, Amelia Earhart, Dorothy Parker, Coco Chanel, Lucille Ball, Julia Child, Martha Stewart, Madonna, Jennifer Lopez, and J. K. Rowling, reveals fierce, in-your-face females who went so far in the exposition of their individual talents as to become, in fitting Hestian fashion, household names. Many of these women have had whole industries built around them, blessed as they are with the unique ability to elevate their chosen genre to the level of pop mania. Who else but a Leo woman could bring French cuisine to the masses? Or make a multimedia conglomerate out of telling people how to make strawberry pincushions? Even Madonna or J. Lo. might have to admit they're not *great* singers . . . or dancers . . . or actresses, but they certainly know how to amass a following. Sheer *will* is what makes these ladies tick, and the Leo is living proof of its omnipotent force. However, regardless of how much notoriety or glory she achieves, the Leo woman will still hunger for more, seemingly unable to grasp that fame may be too fleeting for even her, the fleet-footed Huntress. In fact, this reality rings true for the celeb and nonceleb Leo alike: The Lioness's particular psychological hurdle to overcome in life is learning to know when enough *is* enough, how to gracefully 'go out' on top – megalomania is too often her undoing. Leo's outsized creativity is matched only by her *willing*ness for attention. Fame cannot unnerve her, rather it is the nourishment on which she feeds.

Even as she chases her star to the ends of the earth, Leo woman has a unique ability to retain a centered sense of home and heart(h). Like Dorothy following her 'golden' brick road, all she need ever do is remember that home is where her sign-ruled heart is. Likewise, just as her creativity is inextricably linked to her sexual expression, the Leo girl, even at a tender age, will step out with her fair share of (often decidedly older) men, preferably those with the full metaphysical package – brains, heart, and spirit – and have not one shred of difficulty holding her own. From youth, she's attracted to fast crowds and edgy back-street Casanovas who, like her, seek to transcend the climate of their upbringing, one she'll inevitably label, like her own, a two-bit existence.

Body + Soul

Leo woman, infused with so much physical and emotional energy, always seems, despite her actual size or stature, somewhat larger than life. No matter how conscious an effort she might make at appearing demure, the sheer power of her being belies any such stabs at subtlety. She is haughty, cunning like a cat, somewhat savage in her movements, athletic, often exhibiting a defined musculature. Her brand of beauty is distinctly fiery, made all the more vivid by overt personal style choices, as she often kits herself out in boldly revealing clothes, brightening her hair to a golden red or flaxen blond. If she's not careful, Leo may miss the golden-girl mark completely, coming across instead as brassy, a quality that too often matches her *broad* outgoing personality. Indeed, there is rarely anything fragile in her physicality. She is, after all, the huntress of the zodiac and, as such, exudes a ferocity that befits her Lioness totem. It is this very rough-and-tumble mien that makes Leo the most tangibly sexy woman on the astrological wheel. Her presence poses a challenge to a would-be lover, as if to say, *Are you up to this?* Even when pint-size, she can't help but give a man pause. A potential mate need only be introduced to a Leo woman to sense the depth of her passionate nature; and despite her obvious physical appeal, it is this underlying fire that is most daunting: He realizes, right from the start, that to survive a relationship with Leo woman requires a lion's share of energy, sacrifice, and above all, emotional stamina. As the queen of the jungle, she packs a one-two punch of raw earthiness and regal imperiousness, designed to communicate that she feels comfortable, and absolutely empowered, at the top of any human heap. Particularly in her numerous platonic relationships with other women, she is forever reinforcing her alpha status – like Artemis with her troupe of nymphs or even her hunting dogs, the Leo, too, has her bunch of 'bitches' – fiercely taking the lead in every social situation. Unlike the male Leo, who guards his autonomy at all emotional costs, the Lioness eagerly invites a circle of admirers who'll unfailingly honor her inherent self-styled VIP status. She may even keep company with a bevy of queenie males – Leo is the zodiac's preeminent fag hag – although, in such a scenario, she'll invest her affections even less. For, in truth, Leo woman is not generally loving; rather she saves her fervent devotion for just one or two lucky, and hopefully hardy, individuals. More than most fully matured females, Leo remains devoted to one long-standing best friend from childhood, someone whose life should revolve around her, though rarely vice versa. However, such close confidants aside, she is a flashy female who

POLARITY

Females in masculine (fire, air) signs are not aligned with the gender polarity of their sign and thus enact instead of embody the quality-element combination of their sign. Whereas Leo male *is* the fixed-fiery star, a legend in his own mind no matter his station or occupation, the Leo woman instead goes on a hunt for stardom. She can fixate on people with an ardent passion for life with whom she hopes to find a glorious place in the sun.

5

SIGN NUMBER

The number of health and protection; the pentacle expressed such power. Called the emblem of Morgain or Guinevere, it was drawn on battle shields. The cabalistic meaning of the number is that of expansion, creativity, and sexuality.

rarely leaves the house without a doting entourage deferring to her command, surely making her one of the easier females to spot in a crowd.

Leo lady doesn't so much enter a room as *storm* it. Her vivacious body language is as eye-catching as her colorfully coordinated appearance. Even her voice stands out, a gravely honeyed growl that regularly crescendos into explosions of full-bodied laughter. Like her male counterpart, she is naturally fit, blessed with a low percentage of fat and a muscled physique. The odd Leo woman is known to suddenly balloon up, but this is generally the physical manifestation of a 'blocked' emotional life; and often she'll deflate as quickly as she expanded. But even in such an uncharacteristically swelled state, Leo isn't one to hide her robust appearance, for whatever she has, she *flaunts*: The Lioness always appears built to last, a countenance that can't help but hint at strength and endurance in the bedroom, too. Though generally beautiful, there may be a hardness to the Leo's face that saves her from ever being considered *pretty*. As one might expect of the premier Sun-kissed kitten, she is typically (literally) thick-skinned and may look 'weathered.' Her skin is often pale, freckled, or uneven in tone – tanning herself into a tawny hue, though easy to do, usually has a detrimental drying effect – and she may have fine traces of barely detectable hairs about her jawline and above her solidly set lips. Extraordinarily, she does look much like her animal namesake: Her brow is furrowed above flashing, inescapable eyes; her somewhat flattened nose flares intermittently; her mouth seems designed to devour and, ironically, masks a cunning, if not jagged, smile. Framing Leo's signature heart-shaped face is her infamous mane, a great head of hair that often causes her some stress in styling. As it is surprisingly straight, sparse, and dry, she goes to great lengths to make her mop look more voluminous, often wildly overhandling it. With her typically low hairline, and the addition of artificial curls and endless products, she will truly appear very much the tousled lioness.

Leo's jaw, like the rest of her, is strong and well-defined, her neck sinewy, her shoulders athletically square, as is her upper torso, which boasts very little curve, even at the waist. As a nod to her bare-breasted Artemis archetype, Leo's tits are legendary: Perfectly formed and almost always symmetrical, these high and mighty masterpieces are certainly worthy of exhibition; and though her back and chest may be broad, those lovely orbs are neither too big nor too small, just perfectly ample. And don't think she doesn't know it. In fact, nothing in the Leo's body language suggests she's insecure – about *anything*. She moves deliberately, with a natural grace that is slinky like a cat's rather than, say, delicate as a swan's. Overall, she is sinewy, and her Leo-ruled back muscles, in particular, tend to ripple when she moves. Her tummy can be a weak spot – most Leo women overcompensate here, working hard to develop abs of steel – while her ass is generally on the high side and rounded, without the slightest wobble. In some cases, Leo woman's behind will be bodacious – a marvel of nature, plump if not slightly overgrown, envied by friends and endlessly focused upon by a mate. Though her hipbones may protrude somewhat, Leo's pubic region is, ironically, the most demure part of her body: Encased in a fine, soft peach-fuzz, the Lioness's pussy doesn't appear the fierce *vagina dentata* one might expect to uncover. With lips tightly drawn in, the crevice itself is short and subtly situated, her clit decidedly retiring. Still, Leo's kitty is highly sensitive and naturally strong in its ability to grip and squeeze, whereby she's easily able to achieve vaginal orgasm, with little need for supplemental stimulation. Her legs tend to be lean and mighty, the calf and thigh muscles visibly ripped like those of an adolescent boy – physical evidence of Leo's masculine rule, as well as the swift, athletic energy of her huntress prototype. Boyish, too, are her feet and hands, which can be rough and dry, a condition that no amount of cream or other cures seem to counteract.

Even when dolled up in Versace or Dolce & Gabbana (quintessential Leoan designer garb: exotically sexy *and* tastefully flamboyant), there is still a decidedly unfussy and low-maintenance quality to the Lioness's appearance. She can't help but exude a naturally raw sexuality, despite fashionable trappings, careful grooming, or the constant cosmetic makeovers she gives herself. Even Lucille Ball, with all her war paint, red hair, and Hollywood wardrobe, was never able to pull off the part of glamour queen. She was much more in her element, say, catfighting in a grape vat. Madonna, too, with her myriad disguises (and attempts to seem aloof), simply never looks sublime, ethereal, or even truly untouchable. Indeed, no amount of artifice masks Leo woman's authenticity: What you see is what you get. And she's generally willing to let you see more than most. In the dead of winter, for instance, she'll go strapless, intrigued as she is by *chica*-chic styles inspired by tropical climes, regions where, like her, the Sun is *always* shining. (Who will ever forget J. Lo and her barely there Versace number – you know the one that helped to make her name as common as Kleenex?) Leo woman is literally hot – her body temperature tends to hover just above normal – and in her search for a lover, she seeks someone who projects a similar heat. The naked truth is, Leo woman's personality cannot help but be revealed, and it often sees her reviled to boot. Most Lionesses don't *do* phony. When she tries, she never quite pulls it off – something to which anyone who has suffered Madonna's ersatz Brit accent will attest – for the simple reason that she tends to *over* do it, as in everything she endeavors. Certainly, she finds success by being a bit of a copy-Cat, running with others' only half-baked ideas. She *completes*

28–35
SIGN AGE ASSOCIATION

The age of parenthood. Even Artemis, a supposed virgin, was depicted with multiple breasts to represent her as the provider and protector of wild things. Like the female lion, who does the hunting while her mate hangs around roaring, Leo feels it a necessary part to bring home the bacon *and* fry it up in the pan.

PSYCHOLOGY

Leo has father issues; she generally finds the male-parental influence weak or arbitrary. She may project this view on men and could be at once predatory and emasculating. She can be imperious and dictatorial, particularly toward other women. She may be ritualis-tic in the extreme. Leo woman has difficulty admit-ting fault and is given to rage. She can be preoccu-pied with perfection – an overachiever and workaholic. For all her passions, she struggles with showing sim-ple affection, falling into cold and calculating attitudes and behavior.

what others stumble upon or pioneer, doing *up* all she takes on. That includes her attendance at a social function: She will have you know she's in the house, no half measures. Leo is truly a whole person, meaning she embodies, 100 percent, whatever she is undertaking at any given moment. She's on that hunt, remember, a ritual drama of self-sacrifice to which she gives over utterly. In astrology's 5th House *drama* department, she is its undisputed queen. A native of the Second Quadrant of Emotion, she plays life by heart, relating to experience spontaneously and viscerally, often in the extreme. She is showy, swashbuckling, and shrewd, if not shrewish, in her dealings. She breaks into conversation. Every reaction surfaces in her as if in Technicolor, flashing in her eyes, flushing in her cheeks, flaring up in her speech. Of all the women in the zodiac she is the most saucy and brazen. She can be a loud and pushy *prima donna,* though rarely demure enough to fully pull off that title. In time, she should evolve a sense of calm in the candid expression of her passions and opinions. A poorly aspected Leo personality will be characterized by brutal curtness and bullying directed primarily at those she maniacally curses for being 'better' than herself, unwitting objects of her signature insane jealousy. Whatever the case, Leo will have you know that she never caters to anyone but herself; *au contraire,* she expects others to do any and all grunt work, while she remains a calm, cool central command. As evidenced by her usual posse of female devotees, others exist to entertain her. From her perspective, everyone else is infinitely more dull than she, the dramatic dame. Only people with visible passion akin to her own will catch her notice; those lacking this particular trait, in her estimation, deserve to play the part of handmaiden or fool for her emotional edification.

ſex + ſexuality

Leo woman is drawn to men with ardent natures, those who appear to wear their heart on their sleeve and will commune with the Leo on this particular level where she lives. This simple fact goes a long way to explain why it is Leo women are so notorious for falling head over clicking ruby heels in love with Latin, Mediterranean, Caribbean, and other mother-loving emotionally fueled cultures prone to fervent displays. Leo is a native of the month of August – her world is meant to feel, metaphorically, tropical. And when it comes to men, she can be as corny as Dorothy's Kansas in that same month. Faced with a fellow she fancies, the typically fierce Leo turns into something of a goofball. (It's charming, really.) Not adept at disguising her feelings, she practically 'goes into heat' around such fervent, darkly dashing types – big, blond Nordic dudes leave her cold – while she often 'lightens up' her own look so as to seem like the Sun itself to these hotties she hungers for. Guys of such swarthiness have more than a purely physical appeal: They embody passion to the Leo woman's mind; and men so seemingly ruled by their hearts are those the Lioness seeks to capture. She tends to make her feelings known in a blatantly obvious sometimes even screwball manner, so there's no guesswork required of the man Leo fancies. Unlike men of the sign, Leo woman rarely stands on ceremony when it comes to bestowing her affections. She's far more viscerally passionate than ideologically romantic, practically purring in the direction of a lust object, drawing him in, and then . . . she pounces. Leo woman is a focused predator – she zeroes in on only one man at any time, marking him, like a cat, as her exclusive territory. In total contrast to her male counterpart, she's not come-hither. Rather, like her huntress–lioness archetype, she does the pursuing. Which means, for the man she craves, there's nowhere to run and nowhere to hide. Like that queen on a chessboard, she has all the requisite moves – free rein to knock a man right out. Like several of those aforementioned über-celebs who try to tackle too many modes of entertainment media at once, every Lioness must be careful not to emotionally overextend herself, and most especially in making her intense affections known. As in chess, this zodiacal queen ought to exercise circumspect economy in carrying out her bold plan to conquer a man; otherwise, she'll leave herself open to savage attacks of emotional hurt. As well, her overly audacious nature does put a portion of the male population *off*. The Leo is often *on*. Her dramatic personality is a *loaded,* and often *loud* proposition to take on in partnership, the very expressions that qualify her social character. Indeed, it can be a raucous court she holds. She attacks experience. The opposite of demure, the force with which she shows her feelings is matched only by her own devastation should they not be returned. The Leo lady learns this about herself early in life, and so she becomes ever more strategic in her all-or-nothing approach to securing that *one* relationship. Her standard game plan is simple: She concedes, like any she-cat complying to a mate, appearing soft, unassuming, and submissive to the man she's targeted. (At first, this docile behavior comes as a shock to her devoted posse, subjected as they are to her persistently fierce demands.) Purring and cooing, she disarms a would-be Romeo by rendering unnecessary his seductive lover-boy strategies, working her way into position until the time comes to clasp him in her claws. A master of flirtation, once she's convinced of a man's interest, she'll play cat and mouse, toying and teasing a guy unabashedly. As she expects to be entertained by those whose attention she demands, so, too, does she provide entertainment to a man she desires, playing the clown or fool for a fellow's enjoyment – though never just plain old dumb.

ARCHETYPE + MYTH

Leo woman is associated with the so-called virgin provider and protector goddesses, Artemis (Diana) the Huntress, and Hestia (Vesta), goddess of home and hearth. Taken together, they signify the dual nature of Leo – wildly expressive and yet domestic to the core. Artemis, called Art (Morgain) by the Celts, was the mother, sister, and wife of Arthur. Meanwhile, scholars credit Hestia with the construction of Arthur's round table, which like the goddess's hearth is an interpretation of the sign's Sun glyph. Artemis was called the Mother of Cats, like the Egyptian Bast, who carried the same title.

BIBLE + LITERATURE

Both Bathsheba, King David's wife, and her son Solomon's mate, the Queen of Sheba – arguably the same character – are Leoan figures. Like sought-after Leo woman, the huntress Artemis-Diana had such a huge cult following that she was folded into biblical lore as Mary's mother, Anna. St. Genevieve ('generator') is synonymous with the Arthurian Guinevere, the medieval Artemis. Shakespeare's Cleopatra ('Father's glory') and his aptly named Kit in *The Taming of the Shrew* are fiercely Leonine characters. *Oz*'s Dorothy also embodies the goddess of the chase's ambition and mirrors the Leo's ability to rally her mind (Scarecrow), her heart (Tin Man), and her undaunted spirit (Lion) to achieve the object of her ironic hunt, Hestia's province: home – there's no place like it.

A look at a list of famous Leo actresses illustrates their skill in this particular area: Lisa Kudrow, Loni Anderson, Rosanna Arquette, Barbara Eden, Victoria Jackson, Gracie Allen, Debra Messing, Melanie Griffith, Lucille Ball, and even Madonna (during certain incarnations) have all made a mark playing 'flaky' while nonetheless holding men in the palms of their hands. (Note, too, their shared penchant for those swarthy-male sexpots – Lucy and Desi, Arlene Dahl and Fernando Lamas, Madonna and her ex, Carlos, Melanie and Antonio, Lisa Kudrow and some French guy.) Indeed, it is a particularly Leoan talent to infiltrate a man's heart and disarm him by acting 'kooky,' both amusing and humoring him till she gets her claws in. Being funny is meant to disguise, for a time, just how fierce she is. Thinking, perhaps, that her naturally tough, ambitious self may frighten a prospective mate, Leo instinctively acts comically feeble-witted, like the school brainiac who swears she'll fail tests, only to ever score A-pluses. It all comes down to the thrill of the chase, the huntress herself deigning to be pursued though unwilling to entertain any would-be hound dogs. However, to be fair, if she's on the prowl at all, it is because deep passion is present. Love is not an emotion she experiences every day, so she pulls out all stops to guarantee she's left nothing to chance in winning her objective. If concealing her fangs requires a wee song and dance, so be it. If nothing else, she'll send her hot-blooded Valentino a clear message: At the very least, he'll get to pet the pretty pussy.

Though she's not quick to fall in love, especially not on first sight like the Geminian Juliet, Leo is certainly no saint in between times. She is an outrageous flirt with a killer's appetite for sex, yes; but sex, to the Leo, is a vividly demonstrative means of making an – if just a brief – emotional attachment. The Lioness is passionate for her prey, eye on the prize, fixed on her need to express her outsized, bubbled-up emotional aggression. The 'wet' cardinal-water Cancer is always on some jag, letting her gut feelings flow. But Leo guards her emotions in her mystic heart of hearths, cooking them into a heated froth. Through sex, exercise, and ambition she ultimately expresses them. A woman isn't labeled a wildcat for *not* letting her fierce feelings show. Likewise, Leo can handle a fairly active life of sex and dating without getting hurt as much as most, the guys she chews up and spits out included. Though getting some is high on Leo's agenda, she's always holding in her heart that most fiery fixture, hoping that this guy is *the one*. She is a true romantic, predicated on the belief that men with visible passion will love her more fully than what she perceives to be, often via her father's example, society's de rigueur stoical male. And so she rumbas her ruffles into run-ins with unreserved, illustrative loverboys, barnyard Romeos to whom she may feign to play Juliet, a character that couldn't be further from her true self. Gemini, a flesh-and-blood Juliet if ever there was one, sees the world, dually, in black-and-white terms, experiencing love in the same all-or-nothing way, which adds up to a lot of unrequited feelings. She's like Dorothy pre-bump-on-the-head knockout, subject to the authoritative mandates of right and wrong heaped upon her. Our Leo lady, however, is that same character who fell from a star (the Sun), a Madonna-esque ray of light crashing into the world of the 'little people' in full Technicolor delight, quite dramatically, if not violently, making her presence known. This is not the kind of girl to deliver a believable balcony scene, some bird in a gilded cage – she's far too take charge for that. Her gold is the trail she blazes, and our Leoan Dorothy never surrenders: Just as she typically lived outside the box of parental rule as a girl, she colors beyond the lines in her adult life, rarely restraining herself in her expression, the many-breasted Artemis having an overage of metaphorical mouths to feed. Take it any way you like, but the point is, she hungers. And she makes nary a distinction between the longing in her heart and the heat in her loins, impassioned pangs being one huge umbrella under which she operates. She's no cool femme fatale detachedly luring men to her – this is the sign of Mae West or Mata Hari in the Queen of Sheba's gold-link underwear doing a hootchy-kootchy number. Such is the attention Leo seeks to draw. She is one and the same with her libidinous intentions, embodying the mutual lust she senses passing between her and a man, but nonetheless lies in wait, compelled to feign an unassuming mien as to inspire a man's ardent advances, which she'll return without hesitation. You might say, the Lioness full well puts the *bush* in *ambush,* attacking her loving assailant like Artemis letting loose her hounds (of love), tearing Actaeon to shreds for pursuing and spying on her. Likewise, the lover of a Leo is hard-pressed to survive a relationship with her intact.

Indeed it is the promise of sex, not sex itself, that Leo uses to get a man. To give her hot-blooded beau the impression he's running the show, she'll let him carry on as his usual lothorio self. However, it is she who is stalking *him,* lying in wait as he approaches, performing the role of a woman who'll make no real relationship demands, hoping to not scare him off. In truth, no female mate in the zodiac is more commanding than the Leo. What she wants most in life is to love, and it's something she's wildly capable of doing. Leo rules the 5th House of *love you give* (as opposed to the Cancerian 4th House of *love you receive*), making her ability to express this grand emotion at once sweeping and profound. The rub, however, is that she looks to be loved as much in return. Fittingly she falls for those obvious types because they seem most up to the task – but it's no easy feat, and most men fall short of her often unrealistic

KEY WORDS

power
will
drive
ferocity
perseverance
attention
drama
principle
flagrance
hunger
voracity
impatience
commonality
expression
praise
success
passion
ambition
determination
authority
dominion
pride
fixedness
completion
bravery
prestige
acquisition
intensity
exuberance
renown
magnanimity
humor
idealism
stamina
creativity
profit
fealty
vitality
sovereignty
exaggeration
covetousness
defiance
autonomy

expectations. It might take a lifetime for the Leo to realize that it must be enough that she, herself, feels such lust for life – possessing both an unparalleled zeal for living as well as a passionate commitment to people and pursuits – without expecting a man to wholly match that ability.

In truth, nobody is more devoted than Leo woman. Under the Sun's Absolute Principle, her participation on all metaphysical levels is total. Her fixed-fire status assures that she'll attach her full, feverish energy to whatever *creative* or *loving* pursuit has her attention. Such that, to be loved by a Leo woman is akin to being offered a challenge, one that demands a man express his feelings to the fullest capacity. It must be said that Leo woman may put her mate through the emotional ringer, constantly demanding ever more proof of his heartfelt interest. That is, until she learns a particularly piquant Leoan lesson in life: *to back off.* Far too often, she's simply been barking up the wrong tree, especially when it comes to those romantic philanderers (read: *dawgs*) she had fully expected to make heel. In playing the balmy bimbo, it seems she ended up with her dreaded macho equivalent: the *him*bo. Eventually, Leo woman discovers that she's better off easing up, both in her hunt to bag a passionate man and in her constant pursuit of validation once she's secured herself into a relationship. Unfortunately, she usually learns the hard way that love chased in earnest often remains the most elusive. That which is literally central to her, the loving Leo-ruled heart, is, after all, a lonely hunter.

Artemis is the huntress precisely *because* she's turned her back on love and men. When similarly inclined, Leo woman devotes her feverish attention to other pursuits, namely professional success with its promise of acceptance and respect. Like Actaeon, turned into a deer by the goddess and devoured, as it were, by his *own* hounds, the stag who gets to see ambitious Leo naked will have to overwhelm her. Only in so doing does he prove himself worthy. In short, Leo wants a man who can keep up with her, some healthy competition. She enjoys besting, and being bested, even in bed. She thrives on high-powered men, those who generate growth in the world – makers, shakers, movers, and manufacturers – self-made men and kings of industry, chieftans worthy of her company. The Actaeon myth, after all, recounts the ritual drama of the hunt whereby the stag king is sacrificed to Artemis, called Art in Celtic tradition, her male consort son being Artio or Arthur. Leo man might be the king. But Leo woman is one to whom a king is subject. And it will take an impassioned potentate to stand up to the ever-loving ripping to shreds that Leo woman is wont to provide, whether it be in the amorous display of her affections or for the slightest impropriety to her person. It takes a special kind of man to be with Leo, one who gives way to her fiercest dramas, remaining unruffled, but who will nonetheless refuse to be pussy-whipped by her. It's a combination that doesn't necessarily come around all that often, and Leo learns that for her, of all women, Mr. Rights are few and far between. She may even adopt an antimale stance. Enter self-love, and we're not just talking vibrators here. The whole of the huntress's journey through life is hinged on *amour propre*. And not only that — Leo will fuel her love of self with the admiration of others, sometimes on a grand scale, the lady of the Leo Sun being the zodiac's quintessential superstar. Via the 5th House, she has so much love to give, another interpretation of the many-breasted Artemis expressing for the masses. Here, too, we glimpse Leo's more humble zodiacal archetype, Hestia, whose myth holds many clues in uncovering the straight Leo's psychosexual state of being.

As goddess of the hearth (fixed-fire), the mythic *heart* of every home, sitting in the center of heaven tending her 'eternal flame,' Hestia is the symbol of solitude, self-sufficiency, and inner peace. Disinterested in the ho-hum love-and-war soap opera of other gods, she literally *tends* to herself. As a living archetype, Leo woman augments her own happiness by following suit. Indeed, Hestia's exclamation of self-love must, at some point, be adopted as the Lioness's anthem. Unlike Artemis, Hestia isn't antimale, but rather vehemently *pro-self,* a quality that all Leos inherently possess. And in the necessary process of converting all the energy she uses chasing down affection into a mighty force of self-love — shifting from Artemis the hungry huntress to Hestia the 'tender' protectress — Leo woman begins to stoke the fire of her powerful 5th House creativity all the more. In regaining her 'center' this way, she will begin to summon heretofore intangible love and attention — and those *horned* stags and mambo kings she craves will come, shaking their maracas, out of the woodwork. In the end, Leo tends to find the love she's looking for when she least expects it — whilst fixedly focused on her personal ambitions. In this Hestian 'self-contained' mode, like the dot in the protective sphere of her symbol Sun, she poses a completely different challenge to a man, demanding whether he can break her self-protective barrier and love her as much as she loves *herself*. Meanwhile, until such a man successfully picks up the challenge and 'enters in,' an emotionally evolved Leo is living proof that if you love yourself, the whole world loves you back. This, it seems, is the main reason for many a Leo's dramatic popularity: Their self-love works like captivating bait — all fixed signs are magnetic — attracting affection to them on a global scale. Interesting that the so-bad-it's-good film *Dr. T & the Women* — a Leo legend if ever there was one — depicts a pride of females and just one male, whose mate suffers from a 'Hestia complex,' a syndrome resulting from being overly loved.

BODY RULERSHIP

Leo rules the heart, the controlling mechanism of the entire organism, the upper back, and spine. There is a tendency to cardiac and spinal afflictions. Likewise, the Sun rules the circulatory system and the thymus, which is credited with stimulating growth. The heart works in unison with all other organs, and the circulatory system extends to the entire body. This mirrors the Leo woman's need to have control over all aspects of, and everybody in, her life.

It's what Leo woman invites and often has to struggle with, as it brings great emotional responsibility, that which any monarch would have toward her people, if she plans to remain popular. Of course, the zodiac's queen of hearts is also capable of chewing, if not chopping, off the heads of those with whom she closely associates, just as she is the mother lion to her myriad cubs. In any case, she can inspire a sort of loving dependence upon her that poses its own set of challenges.

The difficulty in preying on people's affections is that she risks ensnaring the weak and otherwise impaired. Especially when it comes to potential mates, it can be a real problem: What she perceives as passion in a guy may indeed have been an oversensitivity or, if one reads the Actaeon myth from another angle, a self-destructive streak. If she does, however, protect herself, as Kate Bush put it, in a 'circle of fire,' really a sphere of self-love, only a strong-willed male counterpart can enter into her affections, not intimidated but charmed by her dramatic, diva-esque defenses. It is this echelon of devotion that she has ardently been after her whole life: That a man dared to woo her while in her Hestian 'selfish' state may be proof enough of his passion, minus all those hot-blooded bells and whistles with which other men have attempted to win her. Still, it's an enormous leap of faith for a control freak like Leo to let love find her while she simply hangs back in waiting. But if she's been burned enough times trying to engineer relationships, she may one day find herself willing to let a man take the reins in driving a love bond forward. As the pursued, too, she'll take a *real* passive role, rather than a make-believe one – no more pretending to be some unsuspecting sex kitten. In such a case, where she isn't the covert aggressor, Leo no longer feels so 'put upon,' continually pressured (both in bed and out) to invigorate the passions of her man. Administering to her own ambitions, she has automatically eliminated high-maintenance men from pursuing her – male weaklings who would feel slighted, actually intimidated, by her fierce self-focus. Self-consumed, she can't help but attract a man secure enough in his masculinity to not feel threatened. He is just the emotional tough guy, a *richy* or not, she craves, someone who'll stand up to the rigorous rough-and-tumble lifestyle and sex life she enjoys without fear of crushing his ego, never mind his very bones, to dust.

In the 5th House *spirit of competition,* Leo likes to battle her lover for dominance in the bedroom. Like Annie Oakley, or her fictional incarnation, at any rate, for whom every interaction was a contest at which she secretly hoped to be bested, Leo woman, to varying degrees of subconsciousness, seeks to be physically restrained or subdued in some way or another. Unlike the preceding fire sign of Aries, Leo has no special affinity for the dominant girl-on-top position. Rather, she prefers a carnal contest: some heated writhing, if not all-out wrestling, flipping, and switching, in the course of lovemaking, all the while feverishly kissing, licking, groping, and clawing her lover. Ironically, whereas Leo man is mainly vanilla in his sexual tastes, there seems to be nothing the naughty little Lioness won't try once or twice. In truth, Leo tends to be one of the later sexual bloomers, but that in no way thwarts her heated development. She is an enthusiastic lover, and a fast learner. What she might lack in finesse, she makes up for in gusto. However, she needs to realize that it's best not to think and behave in those terms – such know-how, special skills, and fancy tricks tend to come off as rehearsed when employed by the Leo, who is designed to engage in sex, like everything, from the heart, and not with the mind. For women of the Second Quadrant, carnal knowledge of a man is a visceral experience. If anything, she should lose her head. Still it won't totally keep her from trying out some new move in the sack. She may want to one-up her lover, revealing a new erotic stunt, in the spirit of contest. Indeed, for Leo, sex should feel like play. The 5th House is that of *fun and games* after all. And Leo is one to go in for the extreme sort. She is astrology's original wild thing, securely under the protection of her goddess Artemis, who has a certain knack for making grown guys grovel. This is not to suggest Leo seeks a submissive male. On the contrary, she expects her man to successfully, indeed willingly, put her through her sexual paces – the more vigorous and athletic her lover the better. This explains her penchant for youthful studs in between times stalking a lifelong mate. She appreciates the wide-eyed appreciation and exuberance newbies have to offer, and she actually takes pride in adopting the role of teacher in her favorite subject, sexual education, looking for that impassioned spark in a student's eyes. Leo woman can, in fact, be fairly nymphomaniacal in her notorious robbings of the cradle. She shares the same attitude toward sex as these fellows: Junior cats don't demand any more attention than she's willing to give in the moment, satisfying her sexual hunger, while keeping her eyes open for a serious partnership. In simpler terms, they tend to be as indefatigable as she is in bed. Leo woman is all about that life-force furnace, the most striking interpretation of her fixed-fire status, and just as she learns economy in dispensing energy, so, too, does she harness her power, saving it for the ritual attention she gives her few, burning passions. Perhaps the most difficult bit of entering a full-time relationship is saying good-bye to the smorgasbord of fresh goodies the infamously famished Huntress is wont to devour. It also determines her need to find an expert lover in a mate, not one to bargain on that score. In truth, this is why she doesn't hesitate in jumping into bed with a man early in the relationship, if not on the second date. Before

Arlene Dahl
Rosanna Arquette
Maureen O'Hara
Kim Cattrall
Barbara Eden
Kate Bush
Katherine Hamnett
Clara Bow
Lucille Ball
Vivian Vance
Valerie Harper
Connie Chung
Anna Paquin
Helen Mirren
Ethel Barrymore
Esther Williams
Eydie Gorme
Vera Miles
Whitney Houston
Monica Lewinsky
Myrna Loy
Jane Wyatt
Norma Shearer
Geraldine Chaplin
Edna Ferber
Annie Proulx
Dorothy Parker
Coco Chanel
Amelia Earhart
Zelda Fitzgerald
Louella Parsons
Madame Helena Blavatsky
Annie Oakley
Gracie Allen
Beatrix Potter
Edith Hamilton
Julia Child
Jacqueline Onassis
Elizabeth Dole
Rosalyn Carter
Lillian Carter
Iris Love
Bernadine Healy
Princess Anne
Shelly Winters
Rose Marie
Rhonda Fleming
Maureen McCormick
Delta Burke
Emily Bronte
Peggy Fleming

she invests, she needs to check out the merchandise. Glorious is the Leo woman who has an immediate inkling that love is in store only to discover the object of her burgeoning affection is sufficiently equipped. But woe is it to her if ye olde weenie isn't up to snuff. In truth, she'll turn on her heel, never allowing herself to think what might have been. For when she does get involved with a man who doesn't fully satisfy her in the bedroom, she will begin to develop a roving eye. Further down to the nitty-gritty, unlike some women, to Leo size *does* matter, especially when it comes to girth. She encourages a great deal of friction, more than most women can withstand before soreness overcomes them. Marathon sex is always on the menu chez Leo, indefatigable in the extreme, who would just as soon skip dinner if there's the chance of an erotic bout going into overtime. She hungers for passionate lovemaking as evidenced by her prolific squealing, moaning, and growling in bed. She's not so much verbal as she is just plain noisy. Making love is a primal act for Leo, and her guttural responses – let's just say, she's a screamer – are a clear sign that she's indulging profoundly animal urges. Indeed, she approaches sex from a purely instinctual place, vividly in touch with her feelings and candidly expressing excitement. Leo has little interest in games or fantasy role-play and is decidedly turned off by guys who seem too in their head in bed. For her, nothing can replace just plain going at it, full force, with no need for titillating detours, which, to her mind, only break the natural rhythm of two bestial bodies doing the *deed* they were designed to do. This is not to say she has a just-get-me-there attitude. Rather, she feels both parties should enter the erotic arena with the goal of getting off not as fast, but as *furiously* as possible. For Leo, the best sex imaginable is an equal give-and-take: At once passionately attacking a man's body in the pursuit of her own orgasm, she willingly propels the pleasurable offensive her partner is aggressively launching. Then it's all about getting into a sustainable, though fervid, rhythm. She's rarely content to remain long in a slow, vibey mode, unless she's simply catching her breath, after popping, before gearing up for yet another climax.

For the Leo woman, great sex must have many peaks and valleys. Not one to ever bother with the quickies so many other signs enjoy, she won't get out of bed until she's sufficiently satisfied, which often means having had more than just the one, or even two, orgasms – hers are so explosively complete – and she'll take the interval 'recovery time' to play with her lover, urging him to stay inside, squeezing him as to keep hope alive for another round, or perhaps trying to beat her own record for getting him *back* up should he go down. Speaking of going down, this is an area about which she's generally unenthused, though certainly not outright squeamish. She performs fellatio with savage, if not toothy, abandon, making a man fear for his parts. But her haste might just be a by-product of hurrying the 'job' along. Despite the obvious pleasure oral sex conveys, she sees having her kitty licked as merely a fleeting precursor to penetration. While Leo woman easily reaches climax via clitoral stimulation, she considers the sensation rather too acute to completely satisfy, not to mention being a pale substitute for the full-body orgasms she luxuriates in when aroused vaginally. This is yet one more reason why those tender types don't stand a chance with Leo woman. She requires a real he-man in the sack, a guy who is less about technique and more about just powerfully plugging away. Emotional sensitivity isn't even a quality she admires in her women friends, whom she often ribs or outright bullies for it just to assure they remember who's boss. She certainly isn't much impressed by sensitivity in a man, eschewing such a mate who feels the need to be in touch with his feminine side. She's rarely in touch with her own. Born under a masculine sign, Leo woman is intrinsically ungirly, despite the cha-cha sexpot persona she might adopt. However, she still needs to feel as feminine as possible, regardless of any tomboyish astrological predispositions. She requires a fiercely masculine lover precisely so she can be her ferocious, aggressive sexual self and still manage to come off like a delicate flower in comparison. (In the extreme, a need to telegraph how femininely sexy she is might find her looking like a bad Charo drag queen.) Leo is so often the leader in all other aspects of her life that her relationship with a man might eventually be the one place where she'd actually prefer to be somewhat demure, saving her ferocity for private, often professional, pursuits; so long as she finally finds a guy who'll steer them both in a healthy direction.

Not so with the Leo lesbian. The Lioness, who even when straight-identified can be rather bisexual by nature, has intense relationships with women overall. She is especially provocative in female company, always pushing buttons – pointing out weaknesses, challenging opinions, questioning motives, and especially poking fun – behavior that is intended to test other women's mettle and elicit emotions. Leo is compelled to 'turn up the heat' on other females, whose placid natures she blames on society's crushing domination of her gender. Like Hestia stoking her flame, she welcomes even an angry flare-up with a smile that says, 'I knew you had some fire in you.' Such shows of passion are, to the Leo lesbian mind, proof that the patriarchy hasn't claimed every woman in the world as its own.

In fact, gay Leo's relationships often start with the Lioness teasing a woman, gauging whether she has the requisite impassioned responses she'll later hope to encounter in the bedroom. But constant *digs* often have another purpose: To

STR8 TURN-ONS

swarthy looks
dark hair, darting eyes
body hair, stubble
Mediterraneans, Latins
rough trade
defined pecs, biceps
legal teens
flirtation, seduction
penis girth
staying power
struggle, play-fighting
wrestling
being filmed
outdoor, beach sex
m-f-f threesomes
'primitive' role-play
(active) teasing, tickling
torture
ball play
handcuffs/whips
exhibitionism, masturbation
male models
male strip clubs
sixty-nine
(passive) anal sex
girl-on-top, doggie style

unearth any lingering lesbians-in-waiting. The gay Leo woman doesn't simply step out of the closet, she's *fired* out of it, and she has a penchant for pulling others out, too. She often just plain has the hots for 'straight-acting' women, eliciting a thrill from being the first to initiate someone into same-sexuality. Like Artemis, she insists that other women take a walk, if not an all-out sprint, on the wild side of life. Even better, she enjoys luring a prospective partner away from a man – the ultimate power trip for this gay-power sign. Unlike straight Leo, the gay Lioness is A-Ok with her masculine side – the whole drag *king* concept was no doubt initiated by a Leo, who can be fetishistic about male attire – and she intends to play the traditional husband role with a partner, in keeping with her generally butch persona. But bolo ties aside, Leo readily appoints herself the authority in a relationship, reveling in showing a less experienced lover the lesbian ropes. Often an adamant gay activist, she'll recruit her mate into a cult of female cronies. Like a lioness on the Serengeti who does all the hunting for, and nurturing of, the pride, Leo views the male of the species as, well, specious – a lazy figurehead who doesn't quite deserve his kingly title.

Relationship-oriented in the extreme, gay Leo woman wants a pretty, waifish wife to call her own. In some cases, Leo will seek out a plain Jane whom she identifies as having 'potential.' As a native of the 5th Astrological House of *cocreation with God,* the Lioness lesbian naturally views her partner as a project. Unlike her straight counterpart, the gay Leo will typically forgo any temptations to serial-date when looking for her perfect partner. Sex without love is particularly empty for the lesbian Lioness since what she longs for rarely occurs during a one-night stand. Sex, for her, means an absolute sharing of emotion, and quite frankly, if she's not feeling the love, she'll have nothing to give. However, when gay Leo does find someone to love, she falls hard, and the subsequent outpouring of emotion can indeed overwhelm any woman who doesn't completely share her feelings. One would be hard-pressed to find an individual more able to become entirely immersed in a relationship. She is profoundly loyal and demands the same in return. The energies of Hestia (self-protector) and Artemis (protector of wild things) combine to pack a defensive punch in the Leo lesbian, who guards her private life with a lover as fiercely as a lion would her cubs. Being born under the sign of *parental authority,* she projects this quality onto her partnerships, in the extreme, barring her lover from relationships with exes-turned-friends or even standing friendships as well – much like a male lion, ironically, who, upon encountering a female with cubs, may kill them off to start anew, with no competitors for his mate's affection. As would be expected, this domineering attitude makes its way into the bedroom.

Though she's the undisputed president of the he-woman man-haters' club, Leo nonetheless emulates the traditional male sexual behavior for which she has so much disdain. Reveling in her dominant role, she demands that a lover play the femme in bed, wearing frilly lingerie, performing seductive stripteases, and otherwise indulging in stereotypically female trappings. Leo loves to kick back, letting her lover do the oral servicing, urging her on with verbal taunts before flipping her over to deliver an even more vigorous tongue-lashing, licking her in places one wouldn't have imagined lingually reachable. Working her lover over with toys, too, puts a glint in the Lioness's eyes, as does strapping on a dildo and driving her woman to orgasm after orgasm. In the spirit of variety, the Leo may periodically thrill her lover with a fresh phallus, newly purchased from a sex shop. Happily, she'll bestow more decidedly elegant gifts as well: The hopelessly romantic Leo is forever surprising a partner with tokens of her affection, or spontaneously whisking her off for a candlelit dinner or surprise weekend away. So long as they can be alone, all is right with the world. Leo wants a captive audience, and her mate might even need to be dramatic in the display of her devotion. The Lioness may even do the whole dominatrix act to her slave-lover.

That is until the Lioness lesbian decides she wants to raise a family. Leo's association with the 5th Astrological House of *procreation* and *children* means that gay Leos of both sexes are generally determined to bear offspring, to insure the continuation of their heritage. Sperm is sometimes all the Leo thinks men are good for. While adoption is always an option, Leo woman in a same-sex relationship may prefer to produce her own kids with a mate. She would also insist that her child(ren) not be born out of wedlock as such. The lesbian Lioness doesn't take her progeny lightly and is ultimately concerned with establishing dynastic roots, heredity being a near preoccupation. (Those genealogy Web sites had to have been invented by a Leo.) As such, more Leo lesbians take a trip down the aisle than any other gay girl, in whatever form of commitment ceremony they fancy. She often wants to signal, via dramatic ritual, that she has left her wild life behind, choosing to revel instead in the comfort and safety of a committed relationship. At least for a time. Despite every good intention, the Leo can fall in and out of love without warning. She is rarely promiscuous, rather she'll serial-marry, remaining eternally hopeful she'll ultimately meet her match.

Although Leo likes to wear the pants in the relationship, she's nonetheless drawn to status and power. In other words, if the girl she's landed is a latent lesbian who just so happens to be a CEO somewhere, so much the better – such perks only make life potentially more creative and dramatic. She revels in

GAY TURN-ONS

submissive/naïve females
femmes
married, straight women
blond hair, blue eyes
perky breasts
tight bottoms
shaved muffs
long legs
extended foreplay
top positioning
cross-dressing
strapping on
(active) forced penetration
flattery/fawning
(active) heavy b + d
(active) lite s + m
mastering
dressing in drag
colorful, kinky lingerie
animal sounds
spanking
showing off
sitting on face
monogamy, marriage

flaunting herself, and her sexual identity, meeting every straight woman's gaze with an open-faced question mark, and every man on his own terms. Like other gay fire-females she is comfortable in an all-male milieu, just as scrappy, stoic, and matter-of-fact toward men, if not more so, than they are to each other. She'll breezily commune, discussing sports or stocks, while her invariably girly girlfriend clutches it up with the girls. Leo woman is a class act, and she gives her partner the royal treatment, with an eye on the envy she's amassing from lookers-on. Pride is of prime importance to this egoistical lady, and how she provides for her loved ones is a big barometer for her own self-importance. It's simply a symptom of the 5th House of *the love you give,* something the Leo queen of hearts does in spades. One is as much under scrutiny as under her protection, passionately, at once guarded and appreciated. She doesn't have laissez-faire relationships; she fiercely bonds and extravagantly luxuriates in the lush environment of a fertile, thriving, infinitely hot and heavy relationship.

Couplings

Leo Woman / Aries Man
Her stealth and self-confidence suggest the vigorous sex he craves. Beyond a mutually intense first attraction, Aries and Leo have their traditional ethics in common. It will always feel like an illicit affair – forbidden, exhilarating.

Leo Woman / Taurus Man
Fixation: A relationship between two stubborn types – she's doggedly ambitious, he's emotionally inflexible – is difficult to sustain, but there's a reward for trying: Emotional tensions create exceptional sexual heat.

Leo Woman / Gemini Man
They have so much in common: commitment to family, appetite for achievement, a love of lavish spending. Happily, they allow each other plenty of personal space. Sexual independence is often admissible as well.

Leo Woman / Cancer Man
He's clever and commanding; she confidently holds court. They're meticulous about career matters. Self-concerns are joyfully sacrificed for the common good. Sexually, Leo tries tenderness; Cancer takes it up a notch.

Leo Woman / Leo Man
It's a battle of the wills. A shared need to shine incites glaring problems. At best, they merge into one supernova; otherwise, they might fall into an emotional black hole. Regardless, they're a lusty couple.

Leo Woman / Virgo Man
When Leo lands in Virgo's life, there's a shift: She's someone he won't seek to change. Heady on adoration, she relaxes into the role of queen consort to this gentleman. In bed, Virgo is eager to take Leo's orders.

Leo Woman / Libra Man
Flattery gets them everywhere: Validation is the basis of their jovial bond. He learns to compromise; her energy is infectious. In bed, Leo wears the pants, but Libra's content to play passive.

Leo Woman / Scorpio Man
A stressy couple, exceptionally intent upon success. She's out to prove her worth, no matter the cost; he'll cash in on her credibility. Tempers often flare. His fantasies can be hard-core, but she may well entertain them.

Leo Woman ∫ Sagittarius Man

Their courtship is formal, enveloped in etiquette, played by the rules. She's a nurturing presence; he's that stud she's been searching for. 'Waiting' is a way to build excitement – their first encounter is explosive.

Leo Woman ∫ Capricorn Man

Two precocious characters whose individual independence dwindles once they're a duo. He is especially possessive. In bed, it's 'dirty,' perhaps more daring than either would venture with another. *Worship* is the key word.

Leo Woman ∫ Aquarius Man

An indelible impression is made. Their bond develops via emulation – she might mimic him. Furthering ambitions is a prime motivation. He's inventive and erotic; she needs straightforward sexual expression.

Leo Woman ∫ Pisces Man

He's a mystery she's keen to uncover. Resolute, she pursues with a frightening intensity. Together, natural aptitudes turn a profit – everything is accomplished her way. Lovemaking moves at Leo's fast pace.

Gay

Leo Woman ∫ Aries Woman

A warm, romantic, optimistic pair. Leo assumes the role of mentor. In the extreme, she'll exploit her power over Aries, seeking ever more worship and obedience. But most often, it's a keeper.

Leo Woman ∫ Taurus Woman

The Taurus-Leo liaison is about learning to give way – letting go, allowing deepest feelings to surface. Often, they flirt with the rougher edges of existence. Sex is raunchy from day one. Love with a buzz appeals.

Leo Woman ∫ Gemini Woman

They invite controversy – indulging differences, these two are often playfully at odds in public. Egocentric sorts, domestic bliss may elude them. If love languishes, friendship blossoms. Sexually, each is the other's 'best.'

Leo Woman ∫ Cancer Woman

Emotionally fulfilling after an initial period of 'testing.' If they survive struggles, it's often a loving, long-term coupling. But to others, they're exclusionary. In bed, Cancer submits to the Lioness's supremacy.

Leo Woman / Leo Woman

Huge egos are hoisted even higher. Often an elite, irksome twosome. This is rarely a casual affair. At best, they find phenomenal success. In bed, it's all about tough love: Sex is rough, perhaps a tad punishing.

Leo Woman / Virgo Woman

A stimulating association. Life is lively. Often, a shared spiritual practice develops. Virgo finds power in passivity – especially in bed where she's the object of Leo's lust. Jealousy is a possible pitfall.

Leo Woman / Libra Woman

Libra plays hard to get, often abstaining until Leo absolutely insists. Socially, they're a superficial pair. With the focus on personal pursuits, they mightn't develop much depth. Sexually, stimulation comes from confrontation.

Leo Woman / Scorpio Woman

A shift: Leo's agenda is unalterable, so Scorpio's forced to face herself. Often, she'll simply lose interest. Sex is their way to recover from distress. In the light of day, it's far more difficult to doctor.

Leo Woman / Sagittarius Woman

A classic combination: Friendship is foremost, but sexually they don't suffer. Arguments erupt over extravagant spending. Life is glamorous. Lovemaking smacks of luxe: Pampering each other is a passion.

Leo Woman / Capricorn Woman

They make a formidable pair – stylish, ambitious, ostentatious. Making mischief is their social modus. Still, with mature Cap, Leo gleans life lessons. As for sex, it's purity in public and prurience in private.

Leo Woman / Aquarius Woman

More reciprocity makes this relationship a success. So Aquarius should dodge some of Leo's demands. Best case: They're a droll duo – lively, larger-than-life. Sex is luscious when Leo lets herself be led.

Leo Woman / Pisces Woman

Romantic and unrestrained, this relationship is at turns exhausting and enlivening. Pisces is attached; but the Lion needs her space. Professionally, they're perfectly suited. Sexually, Pisces has her lover by the short hairs.

Virgo Man

the vehicle

Virgo man is a complicated, often confounding character. To him, the world is an imperfect place fraught with potential pitfalls and disappointments. He is especially predisposed to a defeatist view of relationships, which can't help but fall short of his signature pristine expectations. Masking profound sensitivity and a wealth of emotional wounds behind a superior cynicism, Virgo man projects an impenetrability that alternately puts people off or piques their curiosity – especially those who sense the soft core of vulnerability masked behind his cool marble facade. He is a master of disguises, putting on different faces for different people, careful to keep his friendships separate and, thus, others' illusions of him alive. He fears upset – conflicts are to be avoided at all costs – so he keeps his distance in relationships, typically entering into bonds where clear-cut control can be maintained. With women, he takes on the role of mentor, playing Pygmalion in an attempt to mold his partner into an ever more distinct vision of his ideal. Despite a typically rugged, ponderous appearance, he is a gentle giant, the optimal caretaker in the bedroom – demonstrating such carnal knowledge and dexterity as to suggest a startling empathy for a woman's sexual needs. In relationships with men, it's a different story: Drawn to stable, often older men from whom he may expect some degree of patronage, young Virgo desires to be prized and protected by a lover, but otherwise left to his own devices. Inevitably, he will strike out on his own, seeking to nurture an intellectual bond with a similarly self-possessed mate.

Vi

PRINCIPLE

The Principle of Compromise. Virgo must find a middle ground between the Mother Earth and Sky Father views of existence that Cancer and Leo respectively represent. He must *negotiate* a will to master his environment with a *yielding* compassion for it. Virgo's motto, 'I serve,' expresses his desire to make a mark without leaving a mess.

PLANETARY SYMBOL

Just as Mercury signals mercurial effects on mental and social (air) dealings for Gemini, here in Virgo the planet portrays sustantial (earth) change akin to the alchemical transmutation of lead into gold, and all that symbolically suggests. Mercury's glyph, called the caduceus, is an emblem of the medical profession. Some claim that Vulcan, an as yet undiscovered orb, is Virgo's ruler. (The start of Virgo, 23rd August, marks the namesake Roman god's festival of Vulcanalia.) Others credit Chiron, a broken chip of a planet orbiting between Jupiter and Saturn.

Sign + Mind

Mercury is credited with the planetary government of Virgo. However, many modern astrologists dispute this rulership, theorizing that the sign's sovereign sphere, already dubbed Vulcan, has yet to be discovered. Others cite Chiron, a tiny planetette thought to be the ruins of a once mighty orb, as Virgo's patron planet. Some even claim that other bodies in the asteroid belt, Juno in particular, reign over the sign; or that Earth itself is Virgo's ruler. Whether or not any of these theories are 'true,' the fact that this sign's rulership cannot be pinpointed bears the most meaning for, and insight into, the Virgoan persona – a slippery nature fitting its generally designated Mercurial rule. This aura of uncertainty and disenfranchisement that surrounds the sign's planetary rulership is analogous to the Virgo male's psychology. He feels cut off, if not cast out, from a solid placement in the world. As anyone who intimately knows a Virgo man will readily admit, he often goes MIA from his dealings with others – as hard to reach physically as he is emotionally. The mythical characters who lend their names to Virgo's phantom planets – Vulcan (Greek: Hephaestus) and Chiron, one a smithy and one a healer – are similar in that they removed themselves from the glitzy, vainglorious aspects of Olympian existence, making themselves instead of service to both gods and men, tinkering and doctoring up the world to make it a better place for mankind to live. Hephaestus is a deity who became lame as a result of being trapped in the middle of a dispute between Hera (Roman: Juno) and Zeus, the bickering big mama and big daddy of the pantheon. This story of being caught in the middle of a divine squabble makes sense in terms of Virgo's placement on the zodiacal wheel: As the third sign in the Second Quadrant of Environment, just following Cancer and Leo, whose ruling Moon and Sun, respectively, represent the contrasting Mother and Father Principles in astrology, Virgo is likewise caught in the balance.

As a mutable sign, Virgo is a synthesis of these opposing precepts and thus epitomizes the astrological Principle of Dissonance and ultimate Resolution, using mediation, give-and-take, and compromise in his quest for *healing* and *productivity,* the two main attributes of his zodiacal 6th House. On the cosmic level, this makes Virgo uniquely capable of incorporating the matriarchal Earth-cult view of the world (mother-source) with that of the patriarchal Sky-cult vision (father-creator) into a single modus operandi. In real terms, Virgo man is particularly adept at imposing his intellectual ideas onto the natural environment while being mindful not to abuse it. Hephaestus-Vulcan, in his volcanic workshop, forged tools and weaponry, via the masculine element of fire from the feminine earth. And despite being compromised by personal injury, or indeed due to it, Hephaestus takes the lemon fate has dealt him and makes lemonade. This is precisely what Virgo man is cosmically urged to do in life, for he, too, is often faced with some (perhaps subconscious) sense of emotional disability. In addition to being a metalworker, Hephaestus, from whose name the literary figure of Dr. Faustus may be derived, is also an alchemist; so, too, is Chiron, whose curative miracle work falls into the same category of 'hermetic magic.' Mercury (Greek: Hermes), Virgo's traditional ruling planet and the namesake patron god of alchemists, has as its symbol the caduceus, which remains to this day the emblem for the medical profession.

Though Virgo's cosmic connections are as sketchy in nature as he is, a solid framework emerges from the seemingly disparate celestial clues astrology gives us. The fleet planet Mercury, in its rule of the buzzy air sign of Gemini, presides over communication, commerce, and speedy interchange on the social and mental (air) planes. Here, in the earth sign of Virgo, Mercury works those same dynamics, but on the material (earth) plane, suggesting slow transmutation as opposed to immediate transmission. For the volatile Gemini male, life revolves around a zippy interchange of thoughts and ideas; whereas for the more deliberate Virgo, life is a long, steady course toward substantial, permanent transformation – like a gradual alchemical permutation or a healing process, which both require time and patience. As a mutable earth sign, many Virgo men actually wind up working in professions that involve the alteration of substances, in some form or another – as ceramicists, engineers, product designers, builders, architects, inventors, scientists, medical researchers, doctors. Fittingly, *work, health,* and *service* are other chief attributes of the 6th Astrological House of Virgo, whose sign's motto is 'I serve.' Existence for the Virgo man is meant to be a servile, humbling experience. Still, it may take him a lifetime to fully perceive humility as a virtue. For, if and when the planet Chiron exploded, it left an enormous chip on Virgo man's shoulder.

In making the transition from Leo to Virgo, the male archetypal personality shifts from that of the quintessential Sun king, the embodiment of divine right, with an unconscionable ego to prove it, to that of the Everyman, hard-pressed to answer to his own very human conscience. (The zodiac is an evolutionary spiral that mirrors history – as kingly power abates, people power intensifies.) Indeed, it is on this John Doe level where Virgo man lives. Whereas things come easy for the Leo, who inexorably leads a life o'Riley, the Virgo man has a tougher road to hoe. Typically, without such 'God-given' masculine endowments as athletic prowess or a winning way with the ladies,

SIGN QUADRANT

The zodiacal quadrants correspond to the metaphysical planes of existence – physical, emotional, mental, and spiritual. The Second Quadrant is that of emotional environment, wherein a person's feelings about the world are of prime concern. Virgo deals with the conscience and its battle for moral rectitude. Matters of the conscience are visceral, corresponding to Virgo's rulership of the intestinal workings, not to mention his oft bilious disposition.

SIGN GLYPH

The symbol of Virgo is that of *M* for 'material,' literally that of the Mother Earth (Mater). The crossed arm of the glyph suggests virgin purity but also a need for introspection, self-analysis, and soul-searching. The sign of the Virgin means utter discrimination and, in Virgo man's case, his notorious skepticism and a need to hide himself away from the societal mainstream.

ELEMENT + QUALITY

The earth element connotes materiality and substance; the mutable quality, versatility and change. Together the mutable-earth combination particular to Virgo is best described as pliable clay or rock ore that can be transformed in a fiery furnace – just like the magma bubbling at the earth's core.

POLARITY

Males in female (earth, water) signs are not aligned with the gender polarity of the sign and thus enact instead of embody the quality-element combination. Virgo man is hard-pressed to make something substantial out of his life. Sometimes, he does so by literally working with his hands or in the health or service industries.

Virgo is vulnerable to a litany of doubts, insecurities, and fears from an early age. He not only feels socially cast off, but because Virgo is often born at a time when his parents are embroiled in struggle or strife, he also senses a lack of familial love. Though smart in school, often musically and artistically gifted, Virgo fights an uphill battle in the trenches of human relationships. He is the zodiac's misanthrope, a Charlie Brown, the cartoon Everyman who often finds himself positioned low on the totem pole. He may be mocked or otherwise made fun of, which causes him to project a wounded and dejected personality. However, these early experiences often fail to breed the true humility upon which Virgo man will, later, thrive. Two particularly distinct personalities may emerge from the knotty Virgoan psyche: On the one hand, not privy to automatic personal status, like the Leo, Virgo may spend a lifetime bitterly seeking revenge by amassing enormous wealth and/or power. This particular pathology is the primary theme of both Marlowe's and Goethe's Dr. Faustus, who uses his alchemical knowledge to gain such ephemeral sway – humility is all that can save him from an abysmal fall. (As anyone who knows him well will tell you, there are times, indeed whole aeons, when Virgo plays Mr. Bigshot, 'overcompensating' with exaggerations about his wealth and status, showing off by spending way too much on clothes, gadgets, trips, food, drink, and gifties – mind you, all for himself.) On the other hand, the maimed god of menschhood, Hephaestus, forging tools in his volcanic workshop, is a symbol of Virgoan masculinity at its best – a modest, unassuming character who uses divine inspiration for the common good, not for personal vengeance. Harry Potter, J. K. Rowling's orphaned prodigy, is an apt Virgo male archetype: Thrown into a loveless environment, Potter, whose name seems a nod to 'muggle'-friendly potter gods such as Hephaestus and Prometheus, never gives into the self-loathing one might expect of a boy so ill-treated. Then, magic happens: Harry alchemically transforms from reject to righteous instrument of power despite any touch of evil lurking in his lightning scar, Zeus's signature mark, wounding him like Hephaestus. Meanwhile, Harry's shadow opposite, the character Draco Malfoy – a Little Lord Fauntleroy from hell – is a model for that former Virgoan inclination: a draconian coward who hungrily clings to material wealth and increasingly sadistic critical power as a means for overcoming insecurities, acquiring what will only ever be a fleeting sense of superiority – in short, someone headed for a long, Faustian fall.

From his youth, Virgo walks an emotional and, indeed, a moral tightrope. He is visited equally by vice and virtue, just as he must resolve fear with faith, self-denial with self-acceptance, plain old right with wrong. Avoiding conflict, he sidesteps tense situations, holding his tongue when feeling compromised –

like a volcano, he bottles up his emotions until they cannot help but blow or sink him into a dark depression. By virtue of his sixth-sign placement as the hinge of the zodiac, Virgo's sees his whole life as a turning point, one long, continual crisis. Still, he must be careful of building up too much real or meta-phoric bile in his system – the result of feeling forever star-crossed – and learn to let the healing begin. Many a wounded Virgo will become a social or arts critic, jobs in which he can earn big bucks by being his naturally bilious self. Fittingly, the sign of Virgo rules the liver, an organ that secretes bile, regulates metabolic function, and helps filter poisons, thus purifying the body – apt, too, as it is Prometheus' liver that is daily devoured by Zeus' eagle as punishment for his signature service to mankind. Virgo's symbol (a capital M that curls back on itself), the Greek word for virgin, is an obvious emblem of purity pointing, in no small part, to the Virgoan male's psychosexual need to remain unsullied, pristine, perfect. Being born under the sign of the Virgin can be a real head trip: He can't help but project his need for perfection, not only onto himself, but onto the world, and indeed onto other people. Nothing – and nobody – it seems, is ever good enough. Often, he'll get stuck bellowing, rather than making even the slightest attempt to alter his world for the better, unaware that it is his birthright to be a vehicle for change. Fear of failure, fear of success, and above all, fear of mediocrity may cause Virgo to get stuck as a sideline critic, which, nonetheless, has its perks: People view him as an expert of superior, discriminating taste, unaware that he mightn't endeavor to accom-plish any feat himself for fear of putting his head on the kind of chopping block to which he subjects others. Like most critics, he can't take even a fraction of what he's capable of dishing out.

Fear and self-loathing, as well as his obsession with perfection, have strong roots in Virgo's childhood. Like Hephaestus, he is often disabled by his upbringing, having been made to feel somehow flawed. Virgo is famous for his phobias and hypochondria, which are often caused by overprotective parents, in the same way that anal retentiveness (a particularly Virgoan affliction) is often the result of trauma caused by a squeamish parent during toilet training. As such, Virgo man adopts a feeble self-image, seeking out similarly dis-advantaged friends and love interests with whom to sulkily associate – he is infamous for being sullen if not Gothic in his temperament. Unconsciously echoing his phantom planet Chiron, Virgo, too, feels lacking. There's no easy way of convincing him that, from an astrological perspective, this is exactly how he should feel. Though he fills the void with pride, an arguable virtue in the sign of Leo, here, in Virgo, it's a definite vice. Like the glyph of the sign suggests in curling back onto itself, the path to Virgo's happiness lies along a

6

SIGN NUMBER

Virgo's number is often called the devil's number, especially in triplicate. Yet it is also considered the num-ber of God's creation, which took six days. As such, it is associated with work and productivity. The cube is six-sided and, when opened, forms a cross.

35–42

SIGN AGE ASSOCIATION

Middle age. Life is a crisis. This is a time when a man's so-called glory days are gone. Virgo never feels like a golden boy; rather, he is dis-enfranchised. He is the everyman, a true mensch, hard-pressed to make his mark. Humility becomes the benchmark of his success.

PSYCHOLOGY

Virgo may suffer from many irrational fears, such as dis-ease phobia. He can be dis-trustful and critical of others. Feelings of disappointment may fuel pathological lying, especially surrounding his origins. Innate self-loathing may lead to psychosomatic illnesses and/or an obses-sion with his physical being. Virgo tends to tamper with his looks, falling prey to eat-ing disorders or even a com-pulsion for plastic surgery.

artistic ones. Virgo man is often a creative genius who finds great satisfaction not only in working with his hands, literally demonstrating his mutable-earth status as an artisan – sculptor, metalworker, carpenter, potter – but also as an arranger-composer, filmmaker or film editor, novelist or choreographer, molding *compositional* masterpieces. But even if he trades a perfectly pressed suit for an actual smith's apron, he'll never completely quit rolling his eyes. As a list of famous Virgo men reveals, one that includes the likes of Peter Sellers, Elvis Costello, Paul Rubens (Pee-Wee Herman), Robert Blake, Stephen King, Hugh Grant, Richard Gere, Peter Falk, Michael Jackson, Leonard Cohen, and Leonard Bernstein, they are a shrewd, sardonic, somewhat cagey lot who can't help but come across as slightly skewed (if not suspect) despite their widely recognized genius.

If you happen to spot a serious fellow who looks as if he's been sucking on a lemon – seemingly reluctant to be wherever he is at any given moment – typically he'll be a Virgo. He's generally a large creature, either exceedingly tall and willowy or undeniably solid and hunky. In either case, he is sallow-skinned, a zodiacal symptom (like his bilious nature) of his sign's anatomical association with the liver and gallbladder. And, as purported, such peevishness is apparent in his demeanor: Virgo man has a crusty countenance (though decidedly upper), which mirrors the earth's own mutable mantle, the kiln containing the planet's molten core, the proverbial furnace of his patron Hephaestus, if not the fiery depths into which Faustus may have been flung. And despite any attempts at a coolly disinterested veneer, it's clear that Virgo man contains such hidden fire – latent creativity, sexual combustion, or both. This lends him a complex disposition, an intensity and sense of inner turmoil to which a keen, admiring eye might chalk up his usual condescension, seeing through these defenses to his infamous fear of intimacy, thus wishing to quell it. He may act eternally dejected, as if he's frightened out of his wits by life, in this way subconsciously playing on the sentiments of those friends and lovers who are forever trying to reassure him that the world's not *all* bad. But nine times out of ten, trying to cheer up a Virgo would be like getting Hephaestus to tango. Knowledge of the world and its less-than-rosy workings practically paralyzes the Virgo emotionally. And the comparison doesn't end there.

Envisioning Virgo man brings to mind an iconic shot of Elvis Costello from his first album cover – a scowling misfit whose stance is one of legs splayed out from under him as if unable to support his weight (read: worldly burden). Still, even literally, it's an apt image: No matter how buff he gets – and he's often quite the little gym bunny – Virgo man's torso sits atop slender, even spindly legs, made all the more apparent by his constant shifting about.

BIBLE + LITERATURE

Virgo draws upon the archetype of Cain, the equivalent of the Greek Hephaestus, both being smiths and potters who work in volcanic forges. God marks Cain, as Zeus made Hephaestus lame. Scholars claim that Cainite smiths self-inflicted leg injuries as initiation rites. Cain's story is one of wavering conscience. The aptly named Job (Virgo rules work) is caught in a bargain between God and the devil. The tale of the alchemist Dr. Faustus follows suit. The morality play *Everyman* explores this theme of virtue versus vice. Harry Potter is a modern alchemist, a disenfranchised wiz-kid, bearing the mark of good or evil, Zeus' trademark lightning bolt.

6TH ASTROLOGICAL HOUSE

service
work/job
obligation
matter
self-help
diet
hygiene
medical check-ups
habits
employment
staff
lodgers
attendants
dependents
routine
schedules
clothing
health/illness
aunts and uncles
self-adaptation
unconscious mind
service to public
nursing/medicine
effectiveness
sleep patterns
conformity
skill
ability
usefulness
craftsmanship
details
humility
discipline/discipleship
cleanliness/neatness
armed forces
tools
weapons
daily duties
pets/small animals

Otherwise, his bone structure is remarkably sturdy, his muscles thick and gnarly rather than smooth and sinewy. He often has a square-shaped head with a heavily lined brow and high hairline. Like other earth-sign males, he, too, tends to go bald early in life, his hair gradually shifting from a rather thick and coarse consistency in his youth to a feathery fineness as he reaches middle age. His face is stern and wide, made all the more stony by close, deep-set eyes and a long, beaky or beefy nose. His sexy sneer and sunken cheeks suggest an antithetical-boy-next-door disposition. There is, in fact, always something of the night owl about him – pasty skin, dark circles around the eyes, deep-creased nasal folds, jowls, and a near uncontrollable stubble. He typically dresses the part as well, wearing a lot of dark clothing – indeed, black comprises the bulk of his wardrobe, from suits to jeans to boxer briefs. Regardless of his profession, one might suspect he works in fashion – an industry that does boast a large population of critical-eyed Virgins – as he dons a usual penguin uniform, as many in that biz do, of white shirt, black everything else, and year-round sunglasses designed to ward off catwalk glare. He spends money on hard-core names – like his Mercury-ruled cousin Gemini, he's *au courant*; however, where that flitty air sign is supertrendy, Virgo is one of *la mode*'s cognoscenti, often opting for big-ticket European and Asian labels that those in the heartland have scarcely heard of. He has a hulking upper body, often barrel-chested and big-ribbed, which nonetheless tapers to a narrow but soft midsection, which can become blubbery if left unchecked. He's often hairy – the strands are wiry rather than wispy in texture – and occasionally hirsute in the extreme. Though thin, his legs and ass are strong, and any attempts at buffing them up (to match the rest of his body) will yield a worked, 'ripped' look. Much to his delight, Virgo tends to be amply endowed, generally enjoying an above average length and a circumference that measures nearly as much. (His balls, though, are typically as uptight as his disposition.) His hands and feet, like his heavy, beautifully bowed head, would have been worthy of Rodin's attention. Long, muscular, meaningful fingers suggest artistic as well as sexual deftness. He exudes erudition, indeed expertise, on so many levels, it seems only natural to assume he'd be erotically adept as well. And he could be – with a little perseverance. For here we see the most blatant manifestation of the Virgo male's 'virginity': He has less actual training than he'd lead you to believe as he takes that same poseur approach to sex as he does in so many other areas of his life.

∫ex + ∫exuality

Virgo man is infamous for his Svengali streak: a tendency to become involved with women he can mold to his critical vision, all the while escaping scrutiny himself. Even in his teenage years, he may enter into relationships with girls who seem unfortunate, taking them on as projects upon which he can project his Virgoan stricture. It's all somewhat patronizing, as he blatantly instructs his charge in adopting such behavior, attitude, and appearance as will better her station in life and, thus, reflect all the more favorably upon him. Being born under the sign of the Virgin means his moral judgments are severe; he expects any female worthy of his interest to carry a spotless reputation, sexual or otherwise. At a young age, he's already quite the little male-chauvinist Pygmalion, putting his girlfriend on a pedestal from which she dares not topple. He seeks a paragon of virtue, any etymological connection to the Virgin not withstanding. And though he may have chosen an outright guttersnipe to sculpt into his Galatean vision, he expects obedience to his moral mandates, already espousing a Madonna-whore vision of femalekind. After all, with so much energy put into making a girl over in his image of moral and physical flawlessness, precious little is left for simply loving her, let alone lusting after her – his partner may feel at once inadequate and sex-starved, that is, until she jumps from her pedestal and into the open arms of another man who wants to sex her, not dress her, up. Mighty Aphrodite, after all, the very embodiment of female sexuality, ditches her hubby Hephaestus to have a fling with lusty Ares, choosing to be sexually objectified rather than morally *petrified*.

Repeating this Svengali pattern in relationship after relationship is just one form of torture Virgo inflicts upon himself. Eventually, he may find a payoff for this pathology in a woman seeking as desperately to be mentored by a man as he is to execute such edification. This afflicted habit is often one from which he never truly breaks free. Many women may, at some time, invite the patronage of a mate, especially a man so urbane and well-connected as the Virgo – who'll make her feel she'll literally 'have it made' in hooking up with him. After all, it is his proficiency, as much as his leering good looks, that attracts a woman in the first place. And knowledge is power: Like Hephaestus, who was forever crafting the other gods' special endowments, it is natural for Virgo to be in (6th House) *service* to his loved ones; but in so doing, he also runs the risk of being used as a stepping-stone by a smart cookie looking for shortcuts to her own success. In serving as a vehicle for a woman's ambitions, instead of serving as one for himself, his bulk of time and energy goes into

KEY WORDS

fastidiousness
vexation
ability
discrimination
alchemy
perfectionism
metamorphosis
resolution
parsimony
suitability
austerity
erudition
transmutation
disenfranchisement
dexterity
responsibility
articulation
dissection
neurosis
generalization
retrospection
assistance
reclusion
modesty
industry
criticism
analysis
abstinence
concern
eccentricity
self-examination
anabolism
expurgation
didacticism
prosperity
respectability
productivity
divination
dissonance
interdependence
judgment
curiosity
empathy

coaching her, leaving little room for romance. Now, his persistent sense that something is *missing* is founded. Sex itself is often seriously lacking in Virgo's love life. Though his partner mightn't complain whilst being dutifully served by him, she may later throw the dearth of nooky in his face, using it as a bargaining chip when she inevitably finds sex elsewhere and seeks an 'out' from the relationship. It's sad but true that few other men are cuckolded as frequently as the Virgo. And adding insult to injury, he often accepts all the blame for his partner's infidelity – that Hephaestean punching-bag aspect of his personality is hard to shake.

No less selfish, though decidedly less driven, is another sort of woman Virgo might attract when stuck in his vicious Svengali cycle: a wee wifey type who, with no monumental aspirations of her own, allows Virgo man to make all her decisions – everything from what she eats or wears to the amount of collagen she'll inject into her lips. It's eerie just how literally the molding-a-woman-out-of-clay scenario plays out in Virgo's romantic bonds: A partner may let herself be physically reconfigured by Virgo, whose projected need for perfection takes on so real a manifestation. Like Hephaestus, who, cuckolded by Aphrodite, makes his own little dolly, Pandora, in her basic likeness – fashioning and fastening onto her face and body his favorite features modeled on all the other Olympian goddesses to boot – so, too, will Virgo man impose opinions regarding her appearance onto his mate, such that he practically cuts and pastes together a new partner. (Pandora here translates to *all-given* as opposed to Pandora, the *all-giver*, a pseudonym for the earth goddess Demeter, whose virgin aspect is the symbol for the sign of Virgo.) In some cases, Virgo may be, consciously or not, trying to turn a woman into the spitting image of a lost love. But as myth would have it, creating a Pandora is often opening a can of worms. One must wonder at the motives of any woman who allows herself to be so literally put-upon by a man. It is rarely, if ever, a healthy dynamic. Playing Virgo man's human dolly, this 'little woman' may convince herself she's fulfilling his fantasy of the ultimate female, when in truth all she's doing is disabling the already teetering Virgo man all the more. By indulging his whims and demands, he becomes more and more, well, indulgent – not only increasingly magisterial, but also more compulsive in general, perhaps even reckless in his appetite for food, drink, and even sex: With a Pandora in the picture, Virgo's own vices come flying out of the box. His Madonna-whore complex may be exacerbated to such an extent that he demands a lover look as pure as Dante's Beatrice when out in public, but remain as malleable in the bedroom as a paid-up-front prostitute. Still, no matter how much he tries to derive pleasure from controlling his partner, nothing is ever enough.

True satisfaction eludes Virgo until he learns to turn his infamous wizardry onto himself, *internally*. Too often, however, Virgo takes what seems like the easy way out, tinkering with his own appearance rather than delving into the furnace of his complicated psyche. For it must be said that, of all the men in the zodiac, Virgo may be the most ardent plastic-surgery patient. More than any other sign, he has a deep-rooted fear of aging and mortality, which is the true cause of this, and all, his obsessions. Ironically, it is often through his compulsions that Virgo finally arrives at the major turning point in his life whereby he forgoes such superficial ways. Like Hephaestus, flung by Zeus from Mt. Olympus, every Virgo man must hit his own rock bottom, wallowing in disgust and dissatisfaction with his circumstances, being forced, like the smithy god, into stillness and introspection, from whence his creative genius stems – Hephaestus' lameness giving rise to his very godhead. Eventually, he must stop feeling 'cut off at the knees' and become a conduit for serviceable productivity.

As anybody who knows him can attest, Virgo has terrible trouble in keeping scheduled appearances – often late, a no-show, hiding out, screening or not returning calls. Still, such behavior is nothing when compared to the disappearing act he'll perform once he experiences his inevitable bottoming out. But loved ones shouldn't fear: Virgo man usually resurfaces better than ever. Meanwhile, it would seem as if he dropped off the face of the earth, going into a hole like some Eleusinian initiate, secretly facing issues surrounding his own mortality. Still, he may spend as much time in 'solitary' as he did in Svengali mode. For many a Virgo man will, at such a time, take refuge in a monastery of his own making, cloistering himself in a lifestyle that runs completely contrary to his previous participation in the world of external trappings. He may even take a vow of chastity in the hope that abstinence will purify his tainted soul. Finding solace in this hermetic state makes sense: The term *herm-et* is derived from his patron god of alchemists, Hermes (Mercury), whose staff, the caduceus, possesses the power to turn base metals into gold. Similarly, Virgo man must *get the lead out* and wave a healthful wand over himself – ridding his psyche of base thoughts and habits, finding a wholesome vocation that will make him feel useful while inspiring devotion to his own callings as opposed to criticizing the endeavours of others. In short, he must discover his talents, where he shines and thus feels golden. In undergoing this transition in life, which usually hits around middle age (Virgo is associated with the ages 35–42 and exhibits the midlife crisis qualities of those years, in fact, all his life), he typically makes drastic, sweeping changes. Still, in assuming too mad-as-a-monk role, Virgo self-imposes severe rules, regulations, and indeed punishments, depriving himself of even the slightest indulgence, only further

BB King
Jose Feliciano
Branford Marsalis
Loudon Wainwright III
Jimmy Connors
Andy Roddick
Ted Williams
Lance Armstrong
Lyndon Johnson
Joe Kennedy
George Wallace
Bob Kerry
Charles Boyer
Maurice Chevalier
Seiji Ozawa
Hank Williams
Otis Redding
Leonard Cohen
Itzhak Perlman
Cardinal Cushing
O. Henry
Man Ray
Richard Wright
Johann V. Goethe
Jean Renoir
D. H. Lawrence
Upton Sinclair
Jean Luis Borges
James Wong Howe
Guillaume Apollinaire
William Saroyan
Wm Carlos Williams
Christopher Isherwood
Robert Indiana
Roald Dahl
Martin Amis
Leo Tolstoy
Stephen King
H. G. Wells
Theodore Dreiser
Ken Kesey
Elia Kazan
Friedrich Hegel
Prince Albert
John Locke
Milton Hershey
Chulalonghorn
Antonin Dvorak
Dan Loper
Yasser Arafat

BODY RULERSHIP

Virgo rules the general abdominal region, the intestines, gallbladder, spleen. Mercury, Virgo's ruling planet, governs the brain, sensory organs, reflexes, and the thyroid. The planet also controls physical changes, growth, and intellectual development.

fueling his phobias – disease, death, degradation. Short of bringing the hair shirt back into fashion, such pompous piety can be, however, just another pose, one more unfruitful incarnation to thwart his full self-realization. Even here, he avoids humility, his sole saving grace. Only by removing that chip from his shoulder, acknowledging his imperfections, and loving himself in spite of them, can he begin to love others, purely and unconditionally.

It is in embracing his astrological assignation as a mensch that Virgo may finally learn that he appeals to quality partners. Part and parcel of this often earth-shattering realization is seeing his innate feelings of disenfranchisement as an asset. That is, a built-in ability to keep a healthy distance in relationships. Vis-à-vis Virgo's association with the 6th House of *help* and *healing,* he adopts the mind-set of someone in service – doctors, social workers, charity volunteers – for whom emotional attachment is counterproductive, yielding only suffering. This is the attitude with which he was born; it just takes him half a lifetime to (re)discover how to properly employ it. Only then will Virgo man catch the eye of a self-sufficient woman who sees in him the opportunity for a healthy I'm-okay-you're-okay relationship wherein she might share the luxury of his loving detachment. It's little wonder that Hephaestus, despite all his marital problems with the high-maintenance Aphrodite, shared a temple with Athena – the embodiment of female independence. Indeed, the combination of Virgo man and Aries woman (whose archetype is Athena) is a classic one: Hephaestus and Athena were both patron gods of craftsmen and were worshiped together. This model relationship is mutually ennobling at its core. Similarly, when Virgo gets tired of being exploited by those flighty Aphrodites, he may be lucky enough to settle into an association with a strong woman who has her own agenda and individual spheres of influence that she, like he, wishes to inhabit solo. Such a strong, chill bond is the only one that's truly sound for the Virgo male psyche.

Even when all systems are go, Virgo's skepticism may hold him back from taking the sexual plunge. He tends to be fearful of proving lousy, or (almost worse) just so-so in the sack. Expertise is the very least Virgo expects of himself; but rather than practice his way to perfection, he often adopts an adept's air, skirting the whole issue, while continuing to live life *like* a virgin. This is why he generally prefers lovers with far less experience than himself (if that's possible), so that, in comparison, he will seem masterful, in every sense of the word: as sovereign, adept, and instructor. He believes love and affection should be unspoken – eschewing talky, cloying relationships. His mind must remain uncluttered and clear to focus on his personal projects – whether making that pottery, volunteering for the Peace Corps, or getting his Ph.D. He prefers a environment, whether alone or with a partner, that is quiet, meditative, and as

Zen-like as possible. And it must be the same with sex: Virgo wants to take it slow and appreciates a woman who'll likewise settle into a leisurely pace. Not to say he won't welcome proactivity in a partner, just so long as he is assured of having no demands made on him. He hopes a lover will take responsibility for her own pleasure in the bedroom, which is why, more often than not, he welcomes the woman-on-top position. He gets off on being viewed as an instrument for his mate's enjoyment, happy to provide the necessary tool(s) to that end, and grateful for not having to be the traditional male aggressor. Not that his sex drive isn't strong; it's just that it doesn't always manifest in a typical male way. He may be considered 'lame' by women looking to play the sexual submissive since his dormant volcanic libido requires proper stoking to get fired up. However, at the appointed time, Virgo will, in Hephaestean manner, hammer away, driving his lover's orgasm home. He has tremendous staying power and the earth may, indeed, move for his partner while she's being so diligently poked. Because of his association with the 6th House of *work* and *habits,* Virgo takes a dutiful approach to sex, choosing, and sticking to, a routine that works for him. Not one to soak the sheets – no fuss, no muss – the Virgo clean freak is squeamish about any 'funkiness' in the bedroom. Still, given his penchant for regularity, sex can take on a ritual significance, thereby becoming a means of reinforcing and solidifying his bond with a woman. And besides, putting himself on autopilot keeps Virgo from getting too 'in his head,' second-guessing his performance, subjecting himself to self-critical analysis. Better that he stick to his usual game plan, honing his technique more with every try.

Few men are better with their hands than Virgo man. The same might be said for his mouth, would he apply his workman's ethic to oral duties as well. But alas, he's not always so willing to oblige, preferring to use his increasingly calloused fingers with such alacrity as to slowly make a partner howl with pleasure. Likewise, he doesn't make oral demands, though he's willing to let his lover indulge any such fixations she may have. Virgo experiences orgasm as a full-body sensation, feeling an extended buildup that, unlike with many men, will see him shaking in precursory waves before he actually even erupts – and with the proper breathing exercises, he'll find this orgasmic period can be drawn out even longer. Whether or not he puts a label on it, sex for the Virgo has a tantric quality, being very much about prolonging pleasure and trying to achieve a sustainable ecstatic state. In fact, sex becomes a vehicle through which Virgo learns more about himself. As with any of his habitual practices, he generally goes deeper into the experience each subsequent time, thus emphasizing the importance of a steady partner as well as a steadfast routine. Though sex for Virgo is generally separated from its procreative purpose (of all

STR8 TURN-ONS

older/experienced females
Asian women
small breasts
skinny legs
waifs, wastrels
submission
girl-on-top
white shoes, stockings
handcuffs, harnesses
streetwalkers
(passive) discipline
(passive) s + m
nurses, secretaries
technicians
playing doctor
fingering
voyeurism/other couples
heavy porn
lite pain
humiliation/being cuckolded
(passive) teasing/torture
alcohol, downers
piercing, branding
gags, hoods, masks

the men in the zodiac, he may be one of the least interested in fatherhood), it is nonetheless not to be undertaken lightly. He rarely has sex for sex's sake, and when single, he doesn't sleep around – paying for sex is particularly out of the question for so sanitary a skinflint as he. In bachelorhood, his preferred outlet for sexual frustration is a female friend or acquaintance for whom he has no real affection but who will, most likely, fellate him for free whenever it strikes his fancy – no reciprocation required. Even when in a relationship, Virgo is often 'jumped' by his lover. As, like his neighbor Leo, he can go for long stretches without sex and may need to be forcibly reminded of his partner's needs. In the meantime he doesn't like to talk about his exploits and rarely reveals even the slightest humdrum detail, even to his closest friends. To the zodiac's Virgin, sex cannot help but be a rather sordid affair. As it is, he barely likes doing it with the lights on, preferring to see himself engaged in this most basic of human functions through a gauzed-and-Vaselined lens.

Yet, despite his sanitized vision of sex, Virgo has a wildly active fantasy life, as if the bawdier impulses he cleanses himself of come back to haunt his imagination. His more kinky longings are generally so deeply buried in his psyche that he may barely be aware of the range of proclivities he might actually possesss. In fact, because his more deviant desires don't easily surface, at certain points in Virgo's life they may come forth with signature volcanic vengeance. One classic Virgoan fascination is 'watching.' Specifically, this entails observing an attractive heterosexual couple have sex. Being astrologically predisposed to curiosity about the male-and-female dynamic – the mutable sign of Virgo synthesizes Mother fixation and Father fixation into a generic parental fixation – Virgo men find no greater turn-on than seeing these naturally opposite human forces in action. On a more banal level, he also tends to project a parental dynamic onto his platonic relationships, particularly those with the numerous couples who often adopt him as their friend. Mutable signs are all androgynous to some degree, or, as is often the case with Virgo, rather decidedly asexual – his traditional patron planet is named for the bisexual god, Mercury (Hermes), the original hermaphrodite. Archetypically, whether by virtue of Hermes or Hephaestus, Virgos don't feel as manly as all that – and so, even when decidedly heterosexual, he appreciates the power of machismo in a man, just as he thrills to the most feminine of female companions. The delight that he feels at witnessing the combination of the two wins him the title of the zodiac's preeminent armchair voyeur. Other sexual reveries generally involve nubile-looking women and, of course, virgins, whom, both in real life and in his imagination, he revels in deflowering. Sophisticated visions of corruption creep into the Virgoan mind, fantasies that focus on the degradation of innocent or 'proper' females – musings that incorporate a degree of social decorum – all very D. H. Lawrence (a Virgo, of course), if not ever so slightly *Story of O*. On the flip side, he may envision himself as the debased object, putting himself at the mercy of a dominant, vampish woman with whom he can play out any number of lurking submissive tendencies. Humiliation fantasies abound in Virgo's psyche, regardless of which side of a spanking he lands on. There is, too, an element of degradation in his voyeurism, especially if he wishes to watch his woman get it on with another man – being cuckolded is a signature Virgoan desire he mightn't even admit to himself. The zodiac's Hephaestus cannot but wonder what his mate might look and act like if being rodgered by a decidedly more aggressive man – it's an image that at once excites and torments him.

In astrological terms, Virgo is one of the more gay signs. Even the straight Virgo is bound to have homoerotic run-ins in his youth and is often suspected of being gay due to a natural, somewhat feminine soft-spokenness. As it is, straight Virgo gets a visceral satisfaction from a close relationship with a best male friend, typically a lifelong pal, with whom he'll play a wifey role, continually advising or lecturing him in dos and don'ts or along self-help lines. Virgo can't help but fall into preachy, caretaking behaviors – and with that as a basis for his heterosexual bonds, he naturally appears 'different' from other guys. He finds a closeness with other men more akin to the way women generally bond with each other. That, among other attributes, may make him 'appear' gay even when he's straight. Still, Virgos, by their very nature, if not actual behavior, invite suspicion (urban legend of Richard Gere and that gerbil comes to mind). This is due, in part, to his defensive demeanor, which others interpret as shiftiness – that mutable earthiness makes him hard to pin down. Indeed, nobody is more a chameleon than Virgo. And no Virgo is more a chameleon than gay Virgo man, who, being sexually self-aware from an early age, may view relationships with men, and typically older ones, as a way to mend his disenfranchised feelings and elevate his station in life. In deference to his alchemist archetype, he can be a real gold digger, exhibiting a particular aptitude for foraging his way into a rich boyfriend's deepest pockets. As well, Virgo guys, regardless of sexuality, have been known to fabricate whole pasts to support whichever character they're currently playing. Typically, gay Virgo will want to appear the young, cultured protégé to an older, richer man in whose image he's petitioning to be molded. Rarely does the young gay Virgo choose to bestow his affections on a lover of his own age, or one with neither social standing nor a beefy bank account, just as, in his more mature years, he may take up with a markedly younger lover whom he can similarly sponsor.

GAY TURN-ONS

submission
older men, executives
business suits, dress socks
Mediterraneans, Latins
straight men
role-play, faux identities
twinks, rentboys, 'chicken'
teacher-student role play
mutual oral, j/o
debauchery, degradation
(passive/active) analingus
foreskin
(passive) penetration
toys, plugs, gadgets
straight-sex voyeurism
private parties, sex clubs
theaters, backrooms
massages
saunas, bathhouses
uncle fantasies
servants
(passive) lite s + m
teasing, torture
enemas

Once in a relationship, in startling manifestation of his mutability, he may completely conform to his lover's vision of a perfect partner – think of a compliant Eliza Doolittle, only out of drag. Virgo purposefully becomes wrapped up in his lover's life – often working for his boyfriend, purchasing property 'together' or the like – legally and financially, as well as emotionally. If anybody's going to have an airtight palimony agreement, you better believe it's the gay Virgo. So total an entanglement as Virgo happily enters into becomes that much more of an obstacle to him when he seeks to fulfill his true purpose of becoming a 'self-made man.' Wholly blatant Batman analogy: He may find it difficult to break out of his Dick Grayson role and spread his fledgling wings while under the auspices of his Bruce Wayne-like benefactor. Despite the inevitable amassing of a spiffy wardrobe, Virgo's breakups, needless to say, can be the messiest on the astrological block.

Gay Virgo is quite the little conformist when it comes to sexual behavior as well. Neither vehemently dominant nor submissive a character, he wants what every freewheeling Virgo man wants, gay or straight: lots of blow jobs, with little effort or involvement. Still, the magnetic mentors to whom he's generally attracted may make more demands on him than he'd readily volunteer to perform. So it becomes a trade-off, at least in Virgo's early years, to weigh how much he gets from the relationship against what he's willing to give – compromise, negotiation – everything in his life having some price tag attached to it, if not a Dolce, Comme, Prada, or Yohji label. It's no secret, after all, that Virgo craves the finer things in life. To him, partnerships mean a trade-off of personal freedom anyway. He might allow himself to be eased into what are, at first, vividly compromising positions to keep his lover satisfied, thus insuring whatever cushy niche he's carving out for himself as ward, if not lord, of the manor. Think of it as *bottoming* out so as not to hit rock bottom. Indeed, sliding down the batpole, he realizes, has some valuable perks; and though he may be a *real* virgin on this exact sexual score, he soon learns to derive pleasure from being a versatile lover, one who'll switch more willingly from the giving to the receiving end over time. Still, even if his boyfriend possesses a tireless libido, emphasis for the Virgo will rarely be on sex. Indeed, he's far more interested in the pristine public image he and his lover present – he and his Bruce Wayne may also make it a point to keep their secret identities a secret. Not to suggest he necessarily masks his sexuality; he simply doesn't flaunt it (unlike Gemini, the zodiac's original Robin, who'd just as soon flit around in green tights and a Speedo). Virgo merely believes that sexuality should never define a person; fittingly, his own don't-ask-don't-tell policy is usually firmly in effect, and in his signature social-climbing, such subjects are seldom broached. His interest is in hobnobbing at posh parties, exhibiting an impressive knowledge of all things aesthetic, never feeling the slightest need to make anything near what might be considered a political statement.

Relationships of this sort provide the Virgo with a sense of parenting that he lacked as a child – not having been born sucking on that silver spoon, he finds a daddy willing to share his own. Such a bond feeds his ego, allowing him to play out a trophy-boy fantasy, all the while reinforcing his effete nature. Still, it's not all peaches and cream, as Virgo inevitably seeks to satisfy his lust with more exciting men, most, if not all, swarthy, earthy Mediterranean types – the consummate pool boy he'd love to finagle onto the payroll. Fleeting sexual interludes may be all his lifestyle allows, fearful as he is of losing his mainstay big-bucks bond. To be fair, the intellectual connection he doubtlessly makes with his mentor-mate – the basis of any gay Virgo relationship – is strong and sustaining. Since this love bond is really friendship first, Virgo doesn't get too hung up on issues of sex and/or fidelity. Just as he can dally with the pool boy guilt-free, he is naturally forgiving of his lover's forays, so long as they remain strictly physical. However, he has no desire to share tales of his experiences, mindful as always of keeping subversive worlds from colliding. Ask him no questions, and he'll tell you no lies.

Working toward a synthesis of sexual satisfaction and cerebral stimulation with one partner is a desired Virgoan goal; still, it's often one that will elude him. While he's happy to have an open relationship, unfortunately not everyone is capable of similarly compartmentalizing. Sometimes, Bruce finds a younger or more malleable Dick to show the ropes, and Virgo finds himself on the metaphorical train for Reno. But, again, such unexpected snafus are often blessings in disguise. In hindsight Virgo can look back on his former bonds as part of his sentimental education, as stepping-stones to self-sufficiency and the establishment of a lordly manor of his own making. Typically, around middle age, he will seek to pass the baton of his amassed knowledge, sharing his life with someone who reminds him very much of himself: a sorcerer's apprentice of sorts, who will regard him with as much love and affection as he does awe and respect.

Couplings

Virgo Man ∫ Aries Woman

They're a mystery to each other. Best-case scenario: This match means positive psychological change. When challenged, it disallows personal growth. With her, he's free to explore kinkier proclivities.

Virgo Man ∫ Taurus Woman

She has what it takes – beauty, virtue. After those dangerous types, he seems a safe choice. Their bond is about personal growth, newfound optimism. Sex involves experiment – swapping might be an option.

Virgo Man ∫ Gemini Woman

A challenging psychosexual dynamic. He's a Svengali to the plucky, 'youthful' Gemini; but surprise: She's more self-sufficient than he imagined. In bed, Virgo gets a reeducation – less repression, more expression.

Virgo Man ∫ Cancer Woman

He's in rescuer mode, sweeping Cancer off her sore feet. But her sexual history might be epic, causing him concern. With candor, such troubles are surmountable. In bed with no-holds-barred Cancer, Virgo really lets go.

Virgo Man ∫ Leo Woman

When Leo lands in Virgo's life, there's a shift: She's someone he won't seek to change. Heady on adoration, she relaxes into the role of queen consort to this gentleman. In bed, Virgo is eager to take Leo's orders.

Virgo Man ∫ Virgo Woman

Two exacting earth signs bound by matching modi operandi. They're an insular pair, cloistered as well as self-concerned – neuroses are amplified. Often labeled holier-than-thou, they may be puritanical in bed.

Virgo Man ∫ Libra Woman

Generally a sweet, good-natured couple. They often find each other when free of burdens. With Libra, life is productive. What they may lack in heat, this pair more than makes up for in tenderness.

Virgo Man ∫ Scorpio Woman

They appeal to each other's high standards, considering themselves of exceptional moral character. She helps turn lofty ideas into solid action. Friends feel their piety is just so much bluster. Sexually, they 'click.'

Virgo Man ♫ Sagittarius Woman
He sees potential – a beauty with brains – and sets out to sculpt Sag in his grand vision. He's the 'rock,' a stepping-stone for her own ambitions. In bed, she expects him to burn with desire: Does he?

Virgo Man ♫ Capricorn Woman
He's hot in cool Cap's presence. She's her own muse – a self-preservational package deal. Together, they pursue educational and cultural interests. In bed, this pair forms one fetishistic force – their routine is raunchy.

Virgo Man ♫ Aquarius Woman
They're compelled to caretake – he invests endless emotional energy. Privately, he's keeping a checklist: She owes him big. Aquarius is less selfish. Sexually, it's master–servant, with roles in constant rotation.

Virgo Man ♫ Pisces Woman
They fall head over heels, oblivious to any obstacles. But personality flaws manifest madly; it's often a murky, illusory existence. Sexually, he puts her on a pedestal – the fall from which is steep.

Virgo Man ♫ Aries Man
This might begin as a no-strings-attached sex thing. Virgo's aroused by Aries's authoritarian demeanor. But a bond between them yields soulful self-understanding. Sex remains free, 'open' to some extent.

Virgo Man ♫ Taurus Man
Erudition is the attraction. Communication is extraordinary. Each gives the other endless attention, without resentment. In the extreme, giving so much means enough is never enough. In bed, they're gracious, good-natured.

Virgo Man ♫ Gemini Man
They're buzzed in each other's company – in a literal sense, partying is a preferred pastime. Both are prone to rage, so tempers will flare; sometimes, fights feel dangerous. Frequent time-outs are taken. In bed, they're boisterous.

Virgo Man ♫ Cancer Man
Workaholics who tend to social climb. In tandem, sharp wit and sarcasm surface – it's a contest of who can be more clever. Professionally, this partnership is pure gold. In bed, they handle each other with care.

Gay

Virgo Man ∫ Leo Man
Virgo seems harmless and charming – captivating, but no threat to the Lion's alpha status. The Virgin is happy to be Leo's coveted companion. They transcend differences over time. Still, their sex life needs spicing.

Virgo Man ∫ Virgo Man
A detail-obsessed duo, waging a war of words from day one. Persnickety in the extreme, two Virgos nitpick each other down to a nub. Only the most mellow Virgins make it work. Sex often involves coaxing.

Virgo Man ∫ Libra Man
As they boost each other's bon vivantism, escapades easily turn excessive. Outsiders may say they're bitchy, exclusive. They make memorable moments. Sex is less about decadence, more about devotion.

Virgo Man ∫ Scorpio Man
Scorpio isn't looking to shock; here he seeks to service. It's all about digging deep and allowing for transformation. Sexually, too, this pair seeks something beyond standard – they unearth equally experimental natures.

Virgo Man ∫ Sagittarius Man
Virgo's neat; Sag is untidy. At first, they're anxious in each other's company. But a love of the finer things unites them. They'll make ideal travel companions. In bed, some disorder is desirable – never a dull moment.

Virgo Man ∫ Capricorn Man
Together, they master vital life lessons. Typically retiring Virgo does the pursuing. Cap finds himself uncannily attached. Just-sex is where it started, and each subsequent interlude feels fresh, like the first.

Virgo Man ∫ Aquarius Man
A liberating relationship, signaling a life change for Virgo and a sexual awakening for Aquarius. But freedom comes at a price: Anxieties augment and Virgo, especially, feels unsettled. In bed, these boys believe in bad behavior.

Virgo Man ∫ Pisces Man
They want to change the world. And it's worth trying. Still, one or both may go to extremes in pursuing a utopian vision. Regardless, they escape into ideology. Sexually, they're fickle fellows so variety is key.

Virgo Woman

the vessel

And God created woman. Virgo is the definitive earth mother, which, by this very nature, makes her a bundle of contradictions: She is at once an unassuming character and a powerfully feminine force to be reckoned with. Virgo woman is giving and nurturing, but equally reliant on others. Physically, even when she is small of stature, there is something of the brick house about her, with dramatic curves and generous cushions in all the right places. She exudes an air of accessibility, indeed a fragility, that inspires a man's lustful and protective urges in equal measure. Virgo projects a good-girl image, no matter how hard she may seek to shatter it – even engaging her in conversation feels like seduction, while bedding her can't help but smack of sweet corruption. Meanwhile, she is eager to give herself to a man, especially in servile capacities. Pleasing a lover tops Virgo's erotic agenda, and more than any other woman, she treats a guy like a sexual lord and master. In return, however, she demands a man possess studly power of the first order, such that many find themselves diminished in the mating process, unable to fulfill her lofty sexual expectations. The zodiac's antiwaif, she is eternally round and juicy, possessing sex appeal long after other women's charms have faded. Though notoriously deferential with men, with women she expects to be placed on a pedestal and worshiped with a combination of desire, indulgence, and a dash of envy.

Vi

PRINCIPLE

Principle of Reconciliation. Virgo makes *amends* in the world, *healing* and otherwise *contributing* to mankind. Virgo woman must take control of shaping her own character and thwart her penchant for being molded by others' actions or demands. Only then can she claim her birthright of being a guardian angel to humanity and fully embrace her sign's motto, 'I serve.'

Sign + Mind

There is plenty of controversy over the designation of Virgo's planetary rulership – many modern astrologers dispute Mercury's traditional rule, assigning the sign's government to the undiscovered planet Vulcan, or the fragmentary remains of what is purported to have once been a mighty celestial body, Chiron, or to Earth itself. If an argument were ever to be made for Earth's dominion over the sign, Virgo woman would serve as prime supporting evidence: She embodies the slow, cyclical change of the seasons themselves. She is often a warm and sunny personality, brimming with delight and enthusiasm; while at other times, she is a cold, stoical soul capable of putting even her closest friendships on ice. That her planetary government remains a riddle offers the most insight into the Virgin woman's personality. Her lack of definitive celestial origins gives her an aura of obscurity, a muddiness as befits her mutable-earth status. And as anyone intimately associated with a female of this sign would readily agree, what drives or inspires the Virgo woman, personally or professionally, is anyone's guess. She seems to lack ambition, even in the attainment of her particular goals, exhibiting no obvious drive or agenda. One might wonder whether she is conscious of her own motivations. In this way, Virgo appears to be an open book, a blank page – someone, often quite literally, up for grabs. When it comes to sexual relationships, especially, Virgo is rather like an empty vessel waiting to be filled, a quality that may make her seem vapid, if not outright venal, particularly to other women.

It is a mark of her being born into the 6th Astrological House of *service* that Virgo seems so willing to provide, essentially, whatever function one wishes of her. Nobody is more a piece of clay than she. As the personification of her mutable-earth status, she is highly adaptable, indeed malleable, to most any situation. Virgo represents the zodiacal Principles of Compromise and Conductivity, and as such, the Virgin female is willing to yield her own desires to the needs of others to achieve a sense of synthesis, a functional flow aimed at satisfying common goals as well as individual ones. In short, Virgo wants what you want. She's on this earth to help others attain their desired ends, and in so doing, she carves out her own expert niche along such glorified-helper lines. All one need do is glance at a list of famous Virgo women, which includes the likes of Mother Teresa, Margaret Sanger, Maria Montessori, Peggy Guggenheim, Kate Millet, Fay Weldon, and Sister Kenny, to see this signature quality embodied – so many females born under the sign are distinguished as teachers, health workers, patronesses, and other such exalted functionaries who *do* service for others and, thus, the world at large. Virgo woman, you might say, *is* the world. The grain-toting female that emblematizes this sign is the Greek earth/harvest goddess Demeter (in her virgin-daughter aspect, Kore). And like Mother Earth herself, the Virgo daughter of Demeter is in the business of nurturing life as a whole and yet, on some unseen level, she demands the kind of awe and respect that is naturally to be afforded her. The paradox of the Virgo female is the same as that of the planet: She can giveth, but she can just as easily taketh away. And, like the margarine-commercial lady said, 'It's not nice to fool Mother Nature.' Just as you can't pollute the planet without consequence, neither can you take advantage of the Virgo's servile nature and treat her like trash.

As the two preceding signs of Cancer and Leo, respectively, represent the Mother (source) and Father (dominion) view of the natural environment, Virgo becomes a synthesis of these parental principles. Virgo man *displays* the Virgoan precepts of compromise and resolution, seeking to blend the 'male' need to dominate the planet with the 'female' concern for its preservation. Virgo woman, in subtle contrast, like the planet itself, *embodies* this duality, at once an entity that could be exploited and/or protected. Her Virgin sign itself tells the tale: Here she is, Demeter-Kore, the symbol of unsullied femaledom, and yet she holds firmly in her hand the phallic shaft or sheaf of grain, filled with (male) seed, which, whether for good or ill, will change the landscape of her body, just as planting turns the natural wilderness into cultivated farmland, both manifestations of Virgo's mutable-earth energy. Whereas it is Virgo male's birthright to be a vehicle *for* change, Virgo woman's vocation is to be a vessel *of* change. She is a poster child for the aphorism 'change begins with me,' illustrating to all of us that as we treat ourselves so, too, do we treat the world. As such, Virgo woman is notoriously moderate in her habits, consciously taking a 'temple' attitude toward her body.

In addition to Demeter, Pandora is the archetype essential to understanding the character of Virgo woman. Although Demeter is also called Pandora ('all-giver'), the more famous mythological character of that name is the silly bimbo with the box who unleashed all evil into the world. This Pandora (here, 'all-given') was made of clay or marble by the tinker god Hephaestus, who, being cuckolded by his wife, Aphrodite, decided to forge his own little blowup version of her to play with, fashioning his favorite features of all the goddesses onto her malleable made-to-order body. Subsequently, she was entrusted by Zeus with a jar, really – not actually a box – which she was told never to open. Curiosity getting the better of her, she opened the vessel and out poured evil, pestilence, and disease into the world.

PLANETARY SYMBOL

The sign of Mercury. Virgo's traditional ruling planet portrays the hymen-crossed body, like that of the Venus symbol, with the additionally activated mind marked by the glyph's antennae. Whereas the planet points to cerebral and social behavior in the mental air sign of Gemini, also under its rule, for the substantial earth sign of Virgo, it illustrates a need for mind-body connection, as well as moral purity.

SIGN QUADRANT

The zodiacal quadrants correspond to the metaphysical planes of existence – physical, emotional, mental, and spiritual. The Second Quadrant is that of emotional environment, wherein a person's feelings about the world are of prime concern. Virgo is compelled to behave according to her conscience; moral virtue is her modus operandi.

SIGN GLYPH

The glyph of Virgo is the *M* for Mother Earth. It stands for Demeter, goddess of the harvest, who in her virgin aspect Kore is the Virgo. The *M* glyph's crossed arm suggests modesty and introspection. Virgo must ask herself, like the harvest goddess, how she will reap and sow in the world.

ELEMENT + QUALITY

The earth element connotes materiality and substance; the mutable quality, a call for versatility and change. Together the mutable-earth combination particular to Virgo is best illustrated as pliable clay that can be transformed in a fiery furnace – just as the magma bubbles at the earth's 'core,' a word stemming from the associative goddess Kore, the virgin of the sign.

So, we see, just as woman is a vessel for life, she can also be one of destruction – depending on what's gotten into her: if she feels loved and respected, Virgo has a mind to be likewise benevolent, giving, and famously mothering, like Demeter delighting in the company of her 'daughter' Kore, for whom all the world is bright and shining. However, if Virgo feels shafted, taken for granted, or otherwise put at a loss, like Demeter bereft at the rape of her 'daughter' by Hades, the world will become a desolate place, not just for her, but for everyone around her. Just as Kore is really the virgin aspect of Demeter herself, so, too, does Virgo woman seek to protect her inner child. Her happiness depends on whether her natural innocence is being guarded, or exploited, by men – or rather in what manner she is letting herself be treated by the masculine sex.

This my-mother-myself dynamic is endemic to the Virgo female experience. She's the zodiac's premier mama's girl, often the only daughter in the family with whom the mother seeks to bond, often in a cringey best-friends fashion. Virgo's mother tends to be neurotic and overbearing, in the extreme hormonally imbalanced or in a sexless phase with her spouse, with whom she lives more like brother and sister than husband and wife, during Virgo's formative years. Mother may also seem overly critical, perhaps even 'jokingly' picking on Virgo's more passive father. As well, she will tend to attack the (6th House) *habits* of the young Virgo herself, particularly regarding *hygiene* or *diet*. It's little wonder that many a Virgo girl develops eating disorders or weight problems, her self-image overly determined by the seesaw aspect of her mother's alternate tendency to offer and withhold approval. On some level, Virgo's mother tries to keep her daughter from growing up (and thus herself from growing old), which often results in an arrested development within Virgo's *unconscious mind,* an area that also fittingly falls under 6th House rule. There are visible symptoms of this phenomenon: First, the bachelorette pad of Virgo female will most often look like some glorified child's dwelling – nobody collects more juvenile trappings like stuffed animals, costume jewelry, trinkets, posters, photo albums, and the like. She is a walking-talking Wendy complex. In reflection of her mother's neuroses, Virgo seems likewise reluctant to mature, forever playing the part of dutiful daughter to an often increasingly destructive, doting mother. Virgo, in turn, adopts a den-mother demeanor with males, putting her in danger of being forever cast in that sexless Wendy role of cautioner and caretaker. She generally eschews the company of other females, instead tagging along with her male playmates; and even when she reaches college age, she'll continue to hang about the guys' dorm, gravitating, the way boys do, toward some charismatic alpha stud to whom she'll hope to romantically insinuate herself under the guise of being buddy-buddy – more often than not, it's an unsuccessful endeavor.

In childhood, Virgo is often close in age and sentiment to one or more brothers who, regardless of their birth order, she both looks up to and looks after. Often, given the self-conscious dynamic of her family relationships – for instance, she may already endure having to be 'dress-alikes' with her mom – Virgo and her sibling(s) are meant to be junior carbon copies of their parents. And so, she may confuse her sibling bond with that of the supposedly sexual love-connection of her parents; such that, as she matures through adolescence, she can't help but relate to the boys she fancies as a sisterly familiar. Unfortunately, her own actual sibling relationships may become blurred, in extreme cases, even, bordering on incest. Any bleak scenarios aside, Virgo can't seem to separate a sense of sisterly affection from that of sexual interest. Putting out such an innocent, filial vibe, however, suggests to would-be mates that she just plain old won't put out. While Virgo guy may cling to what vestiges of virginity he might possess, Virgo girl can't seem to give it away. Most men have no inkling that she is actually the Zodiac's most eager beaver. She thus embodies the flip side of virginity: its inherent frustration. She must wait, playing her childish games, until such time as a tall, dark stranger reaches out and grabs, plummeting her into delightful depths of exploring aching, untapped desires. Unaware that true love or lust is best when it finds her, Virgo meanwhile looks for it in all the wrong places. Another seeming contradiction of Virgo, vis-à-vis its Virgin symbol, is the sign's association with midlife, ages 35–42, when a woman is, at once, nearing her prime and the end of her fertile years. This is also mirrored by Virgo's zodiacal placement during late-summer harvest, when the ancients offered sacrifices to Demeter in hopes of her yielding enough sustenance for the ensuing winter. The Virgoan experience is akin to this time of life when a woman might make a last-ditch effort at motherhood or otherwise resign herself to eternal old-maidenhood. In a sense, Virgo projects this spinster vibe all her life, as if perpetually passed over and left to languish on the vine. It is baffling when you consider the list of famous Virgo beauties – Sophia Loren, Lauren Bacall, Ingrid Bergman, Greta Garbo, Margaret Trudeau, Peggy Lipton – that so many of them chose much older men, like old maids latching onto a last chance at love. Of course, some curmudgeonly female Virgos have found power in forgoing relationships with men all together, dedicating themselves, instead, to stricter definitions of their sign's principle of *service,* becoming the nuns and nurses of the world. In any case, Virgo gives off the air of a do-gooder, a sisterly if not outright saintly creature whom one feels compelled to do right by and treat with kid gloves. She is not one, it seems, to

POLARITY

Females in feminine (earth, water) signs are aligned with the gender polarity of their sign and thus embody the quality-element combination of the sign. The mutable-earth Virgo woman is a gorgeous lump of clay, typically molded into an hourglass-shaped vessel. She wants to be useful, productive, and sustain a happy life for herself and others.

SIGN NUMBER

The number six is related to sex, and more than just etymologically. The hexagram is a tantric symbol of erotic union: The two intertwining triangles signify the male and female engaged in sacred intercourse. It is the seal of Solomon whose book is the only potentially erotic bit of the Bible. Let's face it, the Virgo can't get around the holiness of horniness.

35–42

SIGN AGE
ASSOCIATION

Old maidenhood. At the metaphoric crossroads associated with this age, she's forever faced with a dilemma: whether to give up her (virgin) independence for the loaded and unreliable prospect of partnership. She wonders if time and energy couldn't be put to better 6th House use.

PSYCHOLOGY

Virgo may suffer from emotional blocks and arrested development. She can be highly neurotic, particularly about familial ties, to which she often clings. Easier said than done for her to be of service, as she is often overly dependent on siblings and plagued by resentments over loved ones' successes. She can be a fair-weather friend, appropriating the mannerisms of people whom she must then, as a result, discard.

be tampered with lightly. Virgo's brand of sibling affection works both ways, as men tend to love her, first and foremost, as a sister, succumbing to the mass hallucination that nobody is ever good enough for her, not even themselves. Still, it is indeed confounding that so voluptuous a creature, so desperate to express her sexuality, is so often left without a date on a Saturday night.

Body + Soul

Virgo woman is, in a word, *built.* Typically both big-boned and curvy in the extreme, her status as the mutable-earth sign of the zodiac translates into an undulating physicality of majestic proportions. She's as inviting to man-kind as a lush landscape of rolling hills, possessing a soft, fertile, peasanty body that would seem to demand rigorous attention. With the exception of occasional extraordinary bursts of rippling laughter, she is reserved, participating sparingly in conversation, though all the while wearing a somewhat vacant smile that she'll shine around a crowded room – it's her Virgoan veneer, a disclaiming grin that suggests she's void of strong opinions or judgments, a cheerful defense mechanism against being called upon for witty comment or conversation. When it comes to discourse, she generally sticks to accounts of her own dealings, often giving others blow-by-blow details of her life, picking up the thread of her last conversation – as with a daily soap opera, time spent out of Virgo's loop doesn't prevent one from tuning right back in. Of all the characters in the zodiac, she can be most like a broken record, with a running diatribe that is telegraphed, or at least telephoned, to everyone on her speed dial.

Still, if you see a quietly beautiful and beaming woman safely ensconced within the confines of a chummy group, scanning the room in one direction while sneaking furtive glances in another, she is most likely a Virgo. Generally shy, she often takes great pains to downplay a zaftig physique by wearing subdued clothing, if not something frumpish that recalls a nurse's, hygienist's, lunchroom lady's, or prison matron's uniform – anything decidedly unsexy (except perhaps to white-stocking fetishists). Feeling somewhat awkward, Virgo woman doesn't wish to attract attention to herself – as if she's overcoming something gawky in her nature, usually a throwback to having been one of the first girls to hit puberty and, therefore, to tower over most of the male population. The self-assured Virgo will embrace her gangly presence, embellishing it with a boisterous brand of humor that may later find her labeled larger-than-life. As an adult, too, Virgo may be quite tall, stooping somewhat to give her already rounded shoulders an even more delicate appearance. In fact, despite Virgo's trademark oomphy presence, there is something fragile about her upper body, as if her spine is just barely up to the challenge of supporting her ample breasts, which, even if not a large cup-size, will be dense, full, or heavy. Rarely is she the vigorously athletic type, sticking to more leisurely sports where the pace and competitive spirit are at a minimum. She is deliberate in her actions, not only moving slowly but cautiously, as if warding off a self-perceived clumsiness, which, ironically, lends her a graceful air that is still more earthy than ethereal. Indeed, if Virgo projects any message about herself, it is that she is a woman of substance. She wears an emotional sensitivity that suggests to a man that she isn't cavalier or easygoing – let alone plain old easy. However, he would only be half right.

The truth is, these earth girls *are* easy. And Virgo tries her damnest to signal sexual interest in a man, even letting herself be 'caught' with her eyes alighting upon his crotch. She hangs on a guy's every word, leaning into conversation, all ears and heaving cleavage, listening as if in a state of suspended fascination. She thinks she's sending out a clear message of sexual availability – instead, she merely makes a man feel at ease, winning her the dubious honor of being 'easy to talk to.' In most cases, he'll walk away feeling puffed up and prepared to crack tougher-nut female characters. Those scores of trollish men who think they can bag beautiful women have probably been indulged by fawning Virgo females. It takes a self-assured gentleman to recognize her subtle signals and sweet, albeit awkward way of flirting, finding pleasure in her old-fashioned demeanor and demure beauty: Virgo has a beneficent face, one reminiscent of an antique cameo: Big, round, soft puppy-dog eyes are fixed above prominent cheekbones that tend to be obscured by a cherubic face. Her skin is smooth as porcelain, though typically darker, more olive or oily than that of other members of her family. Virgo's nose is her most meaningful facial feature, being either suggestively plump, long and beaky, or both, often reaching low to just above her upper lip, which tends to look unpronounced in contrast to a full and pillowy lower one. On the whole, her face is youthful, sometimes distinguished by a well-placed beauty mark, a light sprinkling of freckles on her considerable schnoz, and fine fuzz crowning a high hairline. Her mop is thick, wavy or curly, and often grays prematurely. A monumental head on a fragile neck and shoulders gives her a Renaissance air as does her notoriously weak chin. In keeping with such a vintage ideal of beauty, Virgo is notably one of the roundest, most Rubenesque females on the astrological block, typically tending toward bottom-heaviness (like all earth signs), sometimes in the extreme, or so it would appear as her waist is often miraculously tiny in comparison. Like her facial features, which tend to float, there is something

ARCHETYPE + MYTH

Virgo draws on the archetype of Demeter, the harvest goddess who loses her 'daughter' Kore, really herself in maiden form. Virgo is likewise concerned with her own passing youth and mortality. Virgo corresponds with harvesttime, when bounty gives way to barrenness. Bereft that Kore must live half the year in Hades's house, Demeter, called Pandora ('all-giver'), punishes the earth with winter. Virgo can be just as generous or withholding depending on her whim. Myth's other Pandora (here: 'all-given') is molded out of clay, entrusted with a vase, and warned not to open it. Can of worms. Virgo, seen in this light, can be notoriously reliant on others, with often disastrous results.

BIBLE + LITERATURE

Virgo draws on the character of Mary Magdalene. According to the gnostic Gospel of Mary, she was loved better than the apostles by Jesus, echoing Virgo's typical role as an indispensable disciple to those she worships. Scholars say a vase of holy oil was her totem, just as Grecian Pandora had a jar or box. Mary was a sacred harlot who thus embodied both sides of the moral equation, just as Pandora's jar contained both virtue and vice. Mary lives on in such unexpected literary figures as Peter Pan's Wendy: Like the Magdalene, she is the consummate den mother, most beloved by Peter Pan but resented by his boy band. Everybody's little sister, Virgo can be likened to Sally Brown of *Peanuts* fame. She is embodied in Eliza Doolittle, the cockney Galatea.

mishmash about the Virgoan female's physique – a nod to her Pandora archetype, it's as if her body parts were borrowed from a number of different sources. Her ass is always ample to some degree, as are her obviously childbearing hips; and yet, her thighs seem always to turn slender, perhaps once past slight 'saddlebags,' running down to remarkably small feet. Her hands are often similarly diminutive in comparison to her long, supple, but not sinewy arms.

Virgo is one of those rare creatures who looks better naked than clothed. Though she's generously endowed with an hourglass shape, firm skin assures that all her parts stay pretty much where they should be – rarely does Virgo have a problem with loose blubber or cellulite. If her waist appeared remarkable when dressed, it would seem a feat of engineering viewed in the nude, just one of her many attributes that scream femininity. Virgo's body has a shifting, amorphous quality about it – what with those mixy-matchy parts of hers – seeming to change shape right before one's eyes. Like seeing a mirage, it seems impossible for a woman to be so curvaceous in reality. Her genital area also seems somewhat larger-than-life, distinguished as it is by a thick, wide shock of pubic hair that is considerably dark and lustrous with some of the longest short-hairs of anyone. The flesh of her yoni, by contrast, is ruby red and juicy, the lips being particularly pronounced. Her nipples are generally large, darkly colored, and insistent, changing shape and tension often during sex. Her body is sensually responsive in the extreme, seeming almost to have a mind of its own.

The feminine principle flows forcefully through the Virgo's being, and she needs no man to make her feel like a natural woman. Even her style of dress is aimed at portraying this overriding quality: Donning nonsynthetic, comfortable clothes, earthy shoes, and oil fragrances, the Virgo doesn't like to appear put-on. Still, she isn't stingy with herself – in her signature subtle style, the pricier touches she affords herself can easily go unnoticed. Under those crunchy Birkenstocks, there's a luxe pedicure; her 'natural' hair color will be maintained at the most expensive, exclusive salon, and her makeup-free face is actually slathered in a combination of top-quality creams. Body art is also often concealed beneath Virgo's bulky garments – a man may be shocked to find elaborate tattoos or piercings on one who seems so untainted. Still, Virgo's grooming efforts are focused on preserving the luster of youth, rather than presenting any sort of glamorous image. Occasionally, she'll 'miss' in her attempts at accessorizing, choosing garish tchotch-ke–like jewelry or juvenile trappings like macramé bracelets, beads, or a Mickey Mouse watch, touches that she is misguidedly convinced are cool. Even when gussied up, there is never anything too precious or pristine in her appearance. She seems attainable, if not a bit of a tagalong. Virgo hopes that, in looking down-to-earth, she will attract the kind of rugged, outdoorsy (but still boyish) characters that typically entice her. However, she magnetizes another type of male, as well – one who, when she least expects it, may swoop in and sweep her off her feet.

Sex + Sexuality

It is a testament to Virgo woman's angelic spirit that a guy won't readily 'jump her bones,' despite her often blatant invitations to do so. The zodiac's Virgin simply can't help but inspire respect for her 'person,' if even to the detriment of her conscious determination to incite lust. Virgo is no mere woman, but rather womanhood incarnate. She is iconic – ironic to someone so unsuspecting as she – Mother Earth made manifest, in all her gorgeous fleshy glory. Virgo woman instills both wonder and fear in the hearts of men. She is, simultaneously, sacred territory and a remarkably sexy bombshell, embodying many a man's conflicting view of femalekind as Madonna and whore, all pieced together into one jiggling, juicy package. Somehow, wanting to lay her, rather than marry, protect, and preserve her, is akin to littering at the Grand Canyon. And despite her den-mothering, she can never really be just one of the boys – one look at her says she couldn't roll with the punches of a casual fuck between friends. By definition, she cannot be that superficial in her dealings – Virgo's mutable-earth status points to profound intensity, like that of the churning, molten planetary core, a term derived from her namesake goddess, Kore. And it is on so fathomless a level that Virgo experiences her romantic and indeed sexual feelings, her disarmingly vacuous demeanor notwithstanding. Not only does this often spinsterish-looking sister have the proverbial fire down below, but she also experiences both her cached emotions and the pleasurable act of sex itself far more viscerally than most. For her, the earth indeed moves. Still, the fact remains that this earthy goddess can't just 'give away the farm' without forming nearly unbreakable emotional attachments.

Talk about loaded: Virgo is not only a whole lotta woman physically, she also places tremendous expectations on what another female might simply consider a crush. To most men, she is thus doubly intimidating – especially to the carefree 'boys' she seeks to bed, to whom the prospect of a relationship with her is akin to staring into a gaping abyss. First, some of those guys she goes for doubt their ability to sexually satisfy such a zaftig creature. Secondly, because relations seem to be so sacred to her, 'entering' a Virgo is like barging

6TH ASTROLOGICAL
HOUSE

service
work/job
obligation
matter
self-help
diet
hygiene
medical check-ups
habits
employment
staff
lodgers
attendants
dependents
routine
schedules
clothing
health/illness
aunts and uncles
self-adaptation
unconscious mind
service to public
nursing/medicine
effectiveness
sleep patterns
conformity
skill
ability
usefulness
craftsmanship
details
humility
discipline/discipleship
cleanliness/neatness
armed forces
tools
weapons
daily duties
pets/small animals

into a temple where most men feel unworthy to tread. Of course, being so diffident, she'd never suspect herself of making others feel insignificant – she'd just read it as rejection and internalize her pain, adding to those churning, burning, yearning feelings deep inside. It mightn't be until years later that Virgo finally appreciates the value of this natural weeding-out process: with lesser men – boys, really – kept at bay, it will be only the most self-assured 'grown-up' male who won't be intimidated by this unspeakable force, instead, desiring her for it. Despite Virgo's designation as the zodiac's empty vessel, she is nonetheless fairly incapable of being objectified by men – she is clearly so much more than a mere trinket. Still, it is particularly difficult for most men to resolve Virgo's double-barreled aura of saintly sister and sexy mama. Indeed, men tend to impose a sexual double standard on all women; but Virgo, by flagrantly embodying such seemingly dissonant feminine (Madonna-whore) themes, forces every man she meets to reconcile these labels. The sign of Virgo represents such universal principles as compromise and cohesion, a shift from discordant to the resolute, from dissonance to resonance. In none other than this personage do such conflicting characteristics alchemically combine to strike one resounding chord.

As befits her mutable-earth status and the 6th House quality of *conformism,* Virgo woman is designed to blend, indeed contour, herself to any given situation. When it comes to relationships, she naturally seeks to fill existing holes in a man's life, making herself useful as a tool for healing any ailing areas, whether he be professionally lagging or in need of rehabilitated personal habits. She is, in effect, attracted to men on the basis of their potential – to whom they might become, rather than to whom they already are. As that empty vessel, she enters into bonds with open arms, seeking to unburden a man from obstacles preventing him from self-fulfillment. The zodiac's efficiency expert, she helps shape a man's modus operandi, often forgoing much in the way of focus on herself. She's his premier consultant, pointing out blocks and implementing systems for positive change. The girl can't help it: She is driven to nurture a man in his ambitions, and to help heal any ills he experiences, personally or professionally. Notoriously attracted to erudite if not esoteric types – intellectuals, inventors, poets, writers – she is determined that a man focus solely on his creativity, happy to become his right-hand gal, giving him the increased manpower he needs to achieve his goals. But look out: The 6th House rule of *dependency* works both ways, and while a man may view his Virgoan helpmate as someone willingly under his command, she can also become a crutch on which to lean, unwillingly enabling any detrimental habits he might have.

More than anything else, Virgo needs to be needed – while she'd do better simply wanting to be wanted. As a result, relationships with her can take on the quality of an addiction. A man who would otherwise have developed a sexual interest in Virgo woman might fixate instead on her usefulness in the more workaday sectors of his life – those outside the bedroom – turning the eager beaver into a merely busy one: She'll perform all but that one very wifely 'duty.' Likewise, her romantic bonds may operate as business partnerships whereby administrative considerations take precedence over any exchange of passion. Such blurred relationship lines are part and parcel of the female Virgoan experience.

Like Charlie Brown's cartoon sister Sally, Virgo often invents situations that aren't strictly true: She may describe a 'relationship' with some Linus of her liking to friends in romantic terms when, if pressed, she'd have to admit that she and her clueless crush haven't even so much as kissed. In true Virgoan conformist fashion, she may, in the extreme, even mold herself in such a hapless man's image, literally taking on his traits, his tastes, his habits and affectations, so as to practically become his female doppelgänger. Somewhere, subconsciously, she might assume that if she, in effect, becomes an appendage of her love object, he won't think to dump her – doing so, she imagines, would be tantamount to chopping off his right arm. Meanwhile, by filling in all the glaring holes in his life, she mightn't even care that her own is going remarkably unstuffed. Life, for the mutable Virgo, is a collage wherein she borrows pieces of what experience she requires from various sources, all too often gleaning much of the symbiosis a love relationship might afford from other bonds – friends, particularly gay-male ones, bosses, or colleagues – leaving just the actual sex part lacking, something quite easily remedied via a one-night stand or an interlude with an electrical device, such behaviors that won't conflict, in time or energy, with the full-out dedication she already invests elsewhere. She is like a willing Eliza Doolittle of *My Fair Lady* fame (a character based on Pygmalion's Galatea, which is already a retelling of Hephaestus' sculpting of Pandora), whose name signifies Virgo's recalcitrance against doing for herself in favor of being molded in the image of some faultfinding Henry Higgins, who may come to depend upon, rather than love, her. It is all too easy for Virgo to stay in this, her signature rut. Despite her outsized desire to do so, it seems that no other woman has a harder time giving herself *fully* to another individual – the reason for this, quite simply, is that she often doesn't feel in full possession of herself, having done little in the way of owning up to her own needs.

Nobody, not even the protean Gemini, is more of a changeling than Virgo woman. She is like an empty vessel, a symbol of both Pandora and Mary Magdalene, waiting to be filled, seemingly devoid of personal boundaries, and

BODY RULERSHIP

Virgo rules the abdominal region, the intestines, and gallbladder. Mercury rules the brain, sensory organs, reflexes, and the thyroid. The planet also governs physical changes, growth, and intellectual development. Mental conditions can find physical manifestation in the body, as a result of stress or psychosomatic projection.

thus a bit dangerous, particularly to other women. Blatantly becoming the people she idolizes, her mimicry borders on body-snatching. In the broadest sense, being such a mosaic is a positive thing – Virgo doesn't miss a trick – taking in what she perceives in others as their beneficial qualities and incorporating them into herself. Much of who she is has been appropriated from outside sources, and sometimes inappropriately: Just as she might conform to a man's behavior, transforming herself into so exact a counterpart, so, too, will she assume the qualities of other women, whom she might only seek to emulate. Programmed to receive, this empty vessel can actually become a vacuum, sucking up to people in every sense of the word. With so few girl friendships, the wake of her existence is strewn with females whose identities she has assumed and then, as a result, discarded. Everyone, male or female, whom the Virgo encounters becomes another small portion of herself. In theory, this is true for all human beings; but for the living sculptural collage that is this mutable-earth female, the dynamic is most conspicuous. Like Mother Earth, Virgo woman will swallow you – little wonder that the digestive organs are associated with the sign.

Whereas heterosexual Virgo generally spits out the women she encounters, she gets her juices working on the men in her life, turning, churning them into individuals who can fully contribute to, indeed nourish, the world at large. She may view a man as her very sustenance, surviving off that which he might yield creatively or financially. Indeed, as the patroness of the zodiac, Virgo is uniquely gifted to aid other individuals – friends, lovers, or blurry combinations of both – in achieving, often artistic, aims such that both might enjoy monetary reward. This earth mama may nurse her man to financial health, but she will simultaneously milk him for her fair share of the bounty. Having fed off the fruits of a man whom she has metabolized into someone more functional and fertile, she has also developed the power to turn him, and his reputation, to shit (to follow the analogy). As unassuming, angelic, as this cherub-faced woman might appear, she will think nothing of accessing her Mercury-ruled communication skills, putting the kibosh – a 6th House *hex* – on whoever has stomped on her toes.

The irony Virgo must ultimately face is that the man for her is one who doesn't need her to blend or fold so fully into his life. Symbiosis might be allowed to occur on a strictly sexual, or indeed spiritual, basis, or perhaps both. Virgo is most attracted to a man who is rough around the edges – tough guys, rockers, bikers, tortured artists, or other such unwashed heroes waiting to happen, most of whom will fall into many of the aforementioned afflicted-relationship patterns with our codependent Wendy den mother. However, there is that rare breed of male, one whose career or creative life needs no tweaking, who still exhibits the in-the-rough male qualities that make the zodiac's Virgin lose it to love at first sight – often men somewhat older than the dorm-room denizens she typically adopts. A self-realized man, with no nooks and crannies for the Virgo to fill, is her most suitable, albeit most challenging, mate. Whether mature in actual years or in emotional attitude, this type poses the perfect detour to all Virgo's codependent behavior, flagging her to yield that symbiotic energy of hers into more strictly loving and sexual veins. It may take years for her to make such a love connection – many a Virgin doesn't settle into a healthy relationship until she is in her Virgoan ruled 35–42 years. Such a confidently masculine man is undaunted by the world of femininity that the Virgoan physically represents. He wants in – rather than perceiving her as a void that will swallow (read: emasculate) him, he sees her as his perfect match, the yin to his yang, the forcefully female equivalent to his masculine desire. Virgo woman, it must be said, so often wastes her time and attention on boys when what she really wants and needs is a man. And one day, when she's just finished tidying up some anemic Peter Pan's apartment – bam! – she might crash straight into the kind of man she's been trying to foster in relationship never-never land.

Such a man, who has no need for Virgo's Ms. Fixit routine, forces her to reallocate that energy – into a shared emotional, indeed spiritual connectedness and, of course, into sex. For her, the sacred-harlot Madonna-whore of the zodiac, sex is sanctified. What she teaches, by example, is that this should be true for all of us. But first, she must learn that lesson herself. Indeed, such a pure loving union with a man, free from all the administrative duties she usually feels compelled to perform, provides quite an education. Herein, Virgo realizes that, as the Madonna-whore of the zodiac, she is naturally tantric in the bedroom. The planet Mercury represents the principle of intelligence in the universe; and here, in the material (earth) sign of Virgo, its rule translates into a physical intelligence; that is, the body's awareness of how to perform its designated functions – digestion, ingestion, gestation, all being human capabilities that occur on the 6th House *unconscious* level. Such that, when it comes to the physical act of sex, Virgo's body *knows* what to do – one might even say it has a mind of its own, on occasion even surprising Virgo herself. Her body, the ultimate vessel, becomes a means of transcendence and, indeed, transformation. Sex induces in Virgo a near alchemical effect, making her feel more wholly confident, thus allowing her to get to the very Kore of her being – letting that inner juvenile she might so vehemently overprotect grow up and experience intense carnal pleasure. Sex puts Virgo in touch with parts of herself she wouldn't otherwise know existed, helping her to experience what a woman is most essentially designed for on the physical, sexual plane: mating.

Joey Heatherton
Claudette Colbert
Fay Wray
Mitzi Gaynor
Margo St. James
Cass Elliot
Shirley Booth
Martha Rae
Anne Meara
Julie Kavner
Jane Curtin
Lily Tomlin
Eileen Brennan
Kitty Carlisle
Amy Irving
Kristy McNichol
Dinah Washington
Valerie Simpson
Patsy Cline
Jessye Norman
Maria Muldaur
Alice Coltrane
Mary Shelley
Agatha Christie
A. S. Byatt
Cathy Guisewite
Agnes DeMille
Sylvia Fine
Mother Theresa
Sister Kenny
Grandma Moses
Margaret Sanger
Marguerite Higgins
Jane Addams
Althea Gibson
Maria Montessori
Christa McAuliffe
Faye Weldon
Ann Richards
Geraldine Ferraro
Peggy Guggenheim
Elizabeth I
Angela Cartwright
Marge Champion
Swoozie Kurtz
Linda Gray
Dr. Joyce Brothers
Joan Lunden
Tai Babilonia
Zona Gale

Still, any revelation that sex might offer will not occur overnight. Change for this earth girl happens slowly, and only with each successive romp in the sack will her sexuality *and* her sense of self progressively deepen. But letting sex take its natural course requires dedicated practice – which is why those Band-Aid one-night stands she experiences hardly scratch the surface of her longing. To boot, the quick-fix masturbatory stimulation she appeased herself with is paltry compared to the profound vaginal eruptions she will increasingly enjoy. Over time, and usually with a steady mate, Virgo comes to embody her mutable-earthiness, conforming comfortably to as hefty a package of manhood as a guy might have to offer. She mightn't realize it in her youth, but size, and length specifically, indeed matters to the Virgo, as does the frequency of lovemaking. She is a sturdy 'sex machine' and requires a similarly strapping man. One must think of her as the most powerful of sexual engines, all revved up and waiting to be taken for a long, fast ride by a seasoned driver – one who will undoubtedly enjoy the erotic trip of his life.

For the faint of heart, or simply the blatantly out of shape, sex with the Virgo woman can be a tough task indeed. Though she is rarely, by any stretch of the imagination, a gym bunny, odds are ten to one that most guys will tire before she does. To experience the full pleasure of sex with the Virgo female, a man must possess a heroic degree of staying power. Being result-oriented will get him nowhere. With her, it's all about enjoying the process, building excitement, giving and taking in equal measure – the sign of Virgo, after all, represents mutuality. Still, the sexual experience must be powered by love. Virgo can only reciprocate in her signature extraordinary way if that physical intelligence tells her a partner is deeply into her, literally and figuratively. Her perfect mate is someone who, unlike those guys who bolted when faced with her obvious emotional depth, welcomes so unfathomable a female as she. Likewise, Virgo has little tolerance for the Quickdraw McGraws of the world.

If all systems are finally go, that reciprocal energy can be mind-blowing: Virgo matches a man's every stroke with an ever so slightly anticipatory thrust of her own, upping the stakes by finely calibrated degrees, heightening the experience without wrecking the flow. Rushing is absolutely out of the question. Getting out of his head, giving over to Virgo's inherent physical intelligence and, thus, his own, a man will indeed feel the earth move, patiently giving over to pleasure. The more instinctually he works her, the more she'll become putty in his hands. Intuitively, she senses the subtlest of needs to ease or speed up, as if her yoni itself discerns the way to make his lingam grow without blowing its stack. At first, it might seem that Virgo is someone who just lies there. But any such impression is often more a reflection of a man's shortcomings than any on her part. As befits her Kore archetype, motion begins subtly for the Virgo, on the inside, where her body involuntarily teases, squeezes, and eventually vacuums a man into her without a kernel of knowledge of what's occurring passing consciously through her brain, her body delivering the information to her head, not the other way around. If a man doesn't tune in to these natural workings and instead seeks to assert his own rhythmic directives, they will never get in sync. In fact, there should be no conscious effort on the part of the guy. Given time – the term *quickie* isn't in her vocabulary – the zodiac's Virgin will gradually dispel any accusations that she's sluggish in the sack. Not generally multiorgasmic, Virgo will experience her one climax as seismic, originating from so subterranean a spot in herself as to throw her entire being into uncontrollable spasms. Linda Blair in need of an exorcism, thrashing about her bed, had nothing on the Virgo woman. Not into sexual abstractions or games of any sort, Virgo simply likes having some meat in her potato. Fantasy or role-play seems beside the point: She needn't pretend to enjoy what seems, to her, the most natural of experiences; she views what many females label taboo as a casual walk in the park. Fittingly, the Virgo seeks to serve, more than just simply please, and her penchant for submission is a surprising thrill to any lover. A willingness to be blatantly passive may easily extend to her offering up her Virgo-ruled rectum – she derives nearly as much pleasure from this orifice as she does from the other. If she's to join in any games at all, they might be along one bondage theme or another, as being held captive, and subsequently released, mirrors the evolution of her psychological process in life. She enjoys a touch of the dark side, often art-directing her own bedroom into some semblance of a dungeon, replete with candles that she might employ, expertly dripping wax on her partner in all the right places.

There is something fetishistic about this forcefully feminine woman who turns her intent to please a man into a ritualistic experience that might include a few pieces of paraphernalia – sexual toys replacing the juvenile doodads she's so fond of. Leather, typically part and parcel of attracting those motorcycle men for whom she will always have a weakness, is a particular Virgo fetish. If biker magazines are any indication, their readers seem to enjoy a zaftig female – a category in which the Virgo woman readily includes herself. It's a trademark turn-on for her to get down and dirty with a rugged bear of a man, thrilling with schoolgirl excitement at a rough rider with a Harley (especially if he bought it with the interest off his stock investments), making her all the more eager to ride his very own hog whenever and wherever she can. Virgo is a notoriously 'cheap date,' most content to hang at home and smoke a big fatty as a prelude to an evening in bed – Virgo, the zodiac's own little hell's

STR8 TURN-ONS

high-power creatives
rockers, painters
(passive) b + d
facial hair
hygiene
circumcision
business suits, bosses
(active) oral
bikers, skinheads
(passive) anal
doggy style
ribbed condoms
tantric techniques
toys, vibrators
candle wax
tattoos, piercings
maid/secretary role-play
degradation, humiliation
doctor/nurse fantasies
(passive) lite s + m
navels
corsets, garters
crotchless underwear
high leather boots
dungeons, goths

angel, revels in stoned sex. Mother, jugs, and speed: Virgo has all these essential elements that appeal to that most blatant brand of hetero male, having nary a desire to flirt with the sexual affections of any man who even slightly whiffs of ambiguity. Virgo is one of the least gay of female signs; although, despite her signature distaste for sushi, even the most heterosexual Virgin will indulge if and when it complies with the whim of the man she loves. Since lesbian fantasies abound among the straight men she takes up with, Virgo will submit to a man's desire in her eagerness to please, undoubtedly finding herself faced, at some point, with having to at least fake same-sex interest in a threesome scenario.

In gay relationships, Virgo woman tends to drop much of her servile tendencies and take on more of a prima-donna attitude. Gay or straight, she rarely feels a need to impress other women in the same way she does with men. With females, she won't pursue, playing a toned-down, traditional femme role during courtship. She is pointedly vague and vacuous in her sentiments, forcing a woman to make ever more bold advances or simply give up out of fear or confusion. Virgo is attracted to strong women, those who unapologetically take charge. To follow the *Peanuts* analogy further, she is like Marcy paired with Peppermint Patty, the demure other half to an often blatantly butch partner who may or may not have an affinity for sensible shoes and short haircuts. With such a woman, Virgo plays Alice B. Toklas to a Gertrude Stein, undertaking the role of a manicured majordomo and executive secretary, tending to her lover like a traditional heterosexual wife. She derives power in being the silent partner, ruling the roost while reveling in the femininity that so appeals to a lover. She may be the consummate homemaker, prettifying the environment she and her mate share, indulging in beauty treatments, potions, and perfumes. She will be literally quiet in the relationship, perhaps sensing that her natural shyness, even her vacancy, is perceived as part of a deep feminine mystique. The Virgoan secretary of the zodiac is literally a consummate keeper of secrets, inspiring trust in her lover, forever bolstering their bond. She is a fathomless source of consolation and consultation, a container and tender of rejuvenating home fires, forever urging her typically more worldly partner forward in pursuits that will bring mutual success. Her infectious laugh and infamously broad humor, especially, make a lover forget all the strife of life.

The larger-than-life Virgo can be an over-the-top lipstick-brand lesbian. She fetishizes, as she does all her passions, the signature trappings of being a woman – the clothes, the makeup, the sexy lingerie – confident that her most extravagant dalliances will only be met with appreciation and awe. She knows she's a catch. And she likes to be paraded around, a prized reflection of the power her lover must possess over her – when, more often than not, it's she who has her lover, if ever so gently, under her professionally varnished thumb. When it comes to sex, the gay Virgo finds herself getting served – passivity only drives her lover to please her all the more. As for her own modus operandi, Virgo enjoys being seduced by a woman, playing that Virgin role to the hilt, empowering her partner to introduce new sexual acts, positions, and techniques over time. She portrays a pretense of purity, as if her prudish boundaries were forcibly being pushed forward toward new delights. For Virgo's lover, the role of instigator becomes a sexual raison d'être: Excitement is derived from continually deflowering the zodiac's Virgin in some way or another. In this sense, the whole of the gay Virgo's sex life is one continual role-playing game. Similar to her straight counterpart, she may take her sexual ingenue act so far as to regularly partake in bondage scenarios – of course, cast as the captive damsel in distress.

As servile as the straight woman of the sign may be, the gay Virgo is far less accommodating, perhaps even unwilling to perform oral sex. Penetration is important to Virgo, however, and her lover may want to strap one on to satisfy the Virgo's deep need for physical symbiosis. Unlike some gay-female signs, Virgo is unlikely ever to consort with a man for the sole purpose of utilizing his tool. The Virgo lesbian is usually exclusively female in the company she keeps, though generally gravitating toward a circle of primarily straight female friends. Her sexuality doesn't define her, and like all aspects of her personal life, it is a private, even secretive affair – far too sacred a sector to discuss casually. She might even come across as puritanical: Many a Virgo is incorrectly labeled a 'lesbian by default,' as if she were so inclined out of an inherent fear of, or traumatic rejection by, men. In truth, gay Virgo, like her straight counterpart, often defers to men, crediting them as the natural mover-shakers, and thus infinitely more worthy of her respect than most females. She views her own gayness as a kind of über-femininity – she thus needs the kind of love and attention that only one of her own gender can convey. Since Virgo regards herself as the ultimate woman, fellow females will always seem somewhat inferior – this becomes the crux of her lesbian sexual identification: As one so extremely feminine – the zenith of a lover's desire – she hopes to inspire awe and envy in equal measure. Gay Virgo female is as haughty as she is humble, open to whatever sexual shenanigans her lover, whose responsibility it is to assert ever new and enticing erotic scenarios, might expose her to.

GAY TURN-ONS

older women
submission
kinky lingerie
butches, drag kings
erotica
dildos, vibrators
(passive) worship
intellectuals
mentors, professors
bathing, grooming
ingénue role-play
jewelry, piercings, body art
(passive) anal penetration
(passive) s + m
chastity belts
voyeurism
slaving
collars
enemas
fingernails
big breasts
latex, rubber
blindfolds
depravation, humiliation

Couplings

Straight

Virgo Woman / Aries Man
She seems pure as the driven snow; he embodies the ambition she finds so attractive. He'll accept her patronage: She may manage his career, if not his life. Often, needs are in conflict. Still, sex is a revelation.

Virgo Woman / Taurus Man
Marriage material: He's easily swayed by the adoration she showers. She accepts his tender tutelage. There are obstacles, but they're often overcome. Either way, it's a smoldering sex thing from the start.

Virgo Woman / Gemini Man
First impressions are deceiving: He seems perfect; she calls to mind mighty maternal figures from his past. But they're two fickle souls troubling to find a through-line; still, enjoying plot twists along the way. Exotic sex is their asset.

Virgo Woman / Cancer Man
They become fast friends. Together, they manage stresses. Life has a flow. She's happy to stay at home; Cancer softens into professional success. Craving each other completely, too much sex is never enough.

Virgo Woman / Leo Man
Leo's floored by Virgo's exceptional femininity. She recognizes a talent worth championing: He might become her mission. They'll enjoy an even-keel existence. In bed, she's the seductive schoolmarm; he's her dominant pupil.

Virgo Woman / Virgo Man
Two exacting earth signs bound by matching modi operandi. They're an insular pair, cloistered as well as self-concerned – neuroses are amplified. Often labeled holier-than-thou, they may be puritanical in bed.

Virgo Woman / Libra Man
Fast friends, but they struggle to reach relationship status. Both can be spoiled. What starts out as liberal may turn into taking liberties. With effort, they fix it. Sexually, she wants to be swept away; he won't work that hard.

Virgo Woman / Scorpio Man
She's an open book; he's in search of someone to write on. But does he have the whole story? She's a complex character. Finding middle ground may be difficult. Sexually, he's in control. She's grateful to be guided.

Virgo Woman / Sagittarius Man
They meet early in life, often staying together through thick and thin. She's overshadowed or 'sacrificed' to his success. Despite resentments, Virgo's satisfied being of service. Sexually, they've no need for enhancements.

Virgo Woman / Capricorn Man
They have a plan: to work as a team, to prosper, to live in relative luxury. They play house, taking traditional roles. Sex is rarely a focus. Surprisingly, in some cases, the marriage is comfortably 'open.'

Virgo Woman / Aquarius Man
They're born again – a spiritual overtone exists from the start. Still, there's a forbidden element here: She may be much younger or from a distinctly different background. In bed, they're like-minded. And full of surprises.

Virgo Woman / Pisces Man
Virgo is body-snatched by persuasive Pisces guy. Separating themselves from everyone, this pair is precariously complacent – laziness is often their undoing. In bed, she'll begin to expect the unexpected.

Virgo Woman / Aries Woman
They're a joy to behold: Aries finds her ravishing, reverential consort. Artistic leanings are lovingly pursued, creative passions sparked. Often, they're joined at the hip. In bed, it's Aries who's pussy-whipped.

Virgo Woman / Taurus Woman
Two cultivated sexual personae culminate into one powerful, potent whole. In the extreme, erotic appetites are unappeasable. More often, they're slaves to the ecstasy they experience together. Still, each is renewed via their association.

Virgo Woman / Gemini Woman
Both are prone to moods and whimsy. This combo is challenged from the start. Gemini must learn to compromise, almost constantly. Virgo morphs into a more mature self. Sexually, too, the energy is tempestuous.

Virgo Woman / Cancer Woman
Cancer seems lost at sea. But Virgo doesn't give in to the Moon woman's mood swings and changes of heart. Earthy-crunchy sensibilities are exacerbated. The scent of patchouli may well waft from the bedsheets.

Gay

Virgo Woman ∫ Leo Woman
A stimulating association. Life is lively. Often, a shared spiritual practice develops. Virgo finds power in passivity – especially in bed where she's the object of Leo's lust. Jealousy is a possible pitfall.

Virgo Woman ∫ Virgo Woman
The double-Virgo lesbian liaison is likened to a perpetual appointment at the psychoanalyst. Too much talk is a trap. To function requires physical interaction. Still, these sensual souls find blissful peace in bed.

Virgo Woman ∫ Libra Woman
Libra loves to be in love; Virgo is constantly forming crushes. In a partnership, each seeks perfection. Nothing ever seems enough. In bed, Libra is ladylike and Virgo longs for more demonstration, more desire.

Virgo Woman ∫ Scorpio Woman
With bewitching Scorpio, Virgo must learn to brandish her own power. Otherwise, Scorp's strength will destabilize. Both risk losing their footing. In bed, Virgo accepts the mentoring she has missed.

Virgo Woman ∫ Sagittarius Woman
They approach life, and love, so differently – a bond between them is bound to be stressful. Inconsistency and unreliability are persistent pitfalls. Compromises must be made. Sex, too, exposes conflict.

Virgo Woman ∫ Capricorn Woman
What begins with a bang may go out with a whimper. One or the other exists unceremoniously. To work, each woman must commit to compassion. In bed, domination incites desire. But most often, sex seems static.

Virgo Woman ∫ Aquarius Woman
Meeting halfway, they merge – differences disappear, similarities surface. They're a dazzling duo – creative in the extreme. Days spent together seem like a dream. Sex, too, is a point where fantasy and reality meet.

Virgo Woman ∫ Pisces Woman
Upon meeting, their immediate sensation: staggering. Still, Virgo struggles to tolerate an unpredictable Pisces. Their most memorable moments are spent in bed: Pisces responds extravagantly; Virgo is verbal.

Libra Man

the character

Libra is the zodiac's Renaissance man. For him life is art, and he approaches existence as would a painter faced with a blank canvas, feeling empowered to create a world based solely on his idealized visions while striving to encapture sweeping abstract realities that he perceives as having remained heretofore out of humanity's reach. He is naturally attuned to the ordered, nonchaotic energies of the universe and is thus both highly principled and philosophical. Libra is a perfectionist, if not a platonist, forever focusing on conditions that might bring betterment, both for himself and for others; and yet wearing rose-colored glasses can also set him up for great disappointment. He is liberal in his beliefs, a pioneer on the intellectual plane, which often puts him at odds with the more stodgy aspects of society. Despite his freethinking, Libra is typically traditional in his need for a steady relationship, which nonetheless doesn't preclude extracurricular dalliances, in thought or deed. He is attracted to an independent female, an intellectual equal, with whom he can live in mutual harmony, while still maintaining separate spheres of influence. Love, for him, is a meeting of the minds, and a woman must share his appreciation for highbrow ideals, aesthetics, and a sensual if not etheric approach to sex. Same-gender relationships take on a brotherly quality, often prohibiting him from accessing deep, romantic feelings. He keeps things light with a lover, his bonds smacking of glorified friendships, far more homoerotic in nature than blatantly hot and heavy.

Vïï

The Apollonian Principle. Libra seeks to live a life of order and reason. He is concerned with building a harmonious civilization based on beautiful ideologies and replete with a pleasing aesthetic. He sculpts out his own character, which he presents to the world as poised, disciplined, and equitable. His mottoes are 'I balance' and 'we are,' the latter expressing his penchant for perfect union.

Sign + Mind

Libra, like the earth sign Taurus, is ruled by Venus. Here, in this air sign, however, the planet's signature aesthetic energy manifests on the astral, mental, and social level rather than upon the physical, material one. Whereas Taurus is a fixed, feminine sign, therefore acting like a magnet for what are arguably *subjective* Venusian qualities of beauty, pleasure, unity, and even love, on the sensible plane, Libra is a cardinal (active, initiatory) *objective* masculine sign, who thus projects himself, on the intellectual plane, as a purveyor of Venusian principles in the abstract – love, grace, beauty, art, balance, and harmony as thought-forms and shiny ideals. Taurus is the zodiac's Adonis, Venus-Aphrodite's love object, while Libra man is rather a masculinized version of the goddess under whose namesake planet he was born, the proverbial Venus *as a boy.* Superficially, he recalls Cupid, not only in his signature cherubic appearance but in the combined energy of Venus and Mars, the imp's mythical parents, love and war respectively, being incorporated into the male sign of Libra, who, kicking off the second half of the zodiac, personifies a big switcheroo from the basic astrological layout initiated in the first half. There, Aries is a masculine sign fittingly ruled by warrior Mars (the objective Male Principle), followed by the feminine Taurus, aptly governed by Venus (the subjective Female Principle). On the flip side, in the second half of the zodiac, and thus the Third Quadrant of Mind, Libra represents the objective-male Venus just as its following sign, Scorpio, portrays the subjective-female Mars, being traditionally ruled by that planet. It's rather simple math. Libra is the higher 'octave' of Aries, its so-called opposite sign, while not really being its opposite at all. On the contrary, both are cardinal signs with the similar mottos, the Arien 'I am' and Libran 'We are' ('I balance' also being the sign's creed); both Aries and Libra are trailblazers in spirit (fire) and ideas (air), respectively.

Cupid comparisons aside, the overriding mythical archetype from which Libra draws his exceptional character is Apollo. He is, first and foremost, the god of light, the most vivid portrayal of Libra's exclusive cardinal-air combination, the very depiction of etheric power. Metaphorically, too, light, as in the term *enlightenment,* is a symbol of reason. Apollo is the god of reason, as well as order. His own Venus-as-a-boy status is well documented by scholars: A rather late addition to the Greek pantheon, Apollo usurped much of what were previously Aphrodite's special provinces, including the service of the Muses – music, art, history, dance, astronomy, etc. – as well as previously female-deity domains such as healing and prophecy. As a personification of classic, indeed platonic Hellenic civilization, the god symbolizes the imposition of patriarchal society on a previously matriarchal one. As such, Aphrodite was demoted to goddess of love and beauty once Apollo hit the scene. Apollo, as light, must be seen in contrast to Helios, the Sun god, just as Libra has a far different vision of the world than does the Leo man, who is ruled by the Sun and its more ancient archetype. The Sun and Leo typify the divine rule of kings, apparent in the Leo male personality. Libra, however, is associated with democracy, just one of many astral-Venusian high ideals, which sees power being spread out evenly upon the citizenry, albeit in the original Athenian version, a strictly male populace. This is certainly the most striking interpretation of the Libran motto 'we are,' and the sign's concept of *balance,* in that power is shared evenly, via vote, amongst the people. Indeed, as history will have it, time and time again, *reason* is the universal power of the human mind that causes the overthrow of monarchical rule. Just as Libra is associated with dusk, graced as it is with cool, even light and the appearance of shining Venus, in contrast to the blaring high noon of august Leo, so does the sole divine power of Leo become diffused via Libra among the many. Fittingly, the ancient Hebrew equivalent of Apollo is Lucifer, meaning 'light-bringer,' who attempted to snatch the Sun god's power to distribute to mankind. Of course he was later demonized, in biblical tradition, as Satan, a character who not only represents Libra's dark side, just as Apollo had his own shadow self, Python, the god of the pit, often referred to as the inclusive Apollopython; but, as we'll see, it is the male sign of Scorpio who tends to embody much of this underworld character since, as astrologer Dane Rudhyar once noted, signs respond to the excesses of previous signs. And indeed, Scorpio in many ways personifies a backlash to Libra's notoriously idealized visions of life.

Most individuals, however, are charmed by the principled, artistic Libran view of existence, even though he typically comes on strong, like his patron Apollo, unapologetically presiding over circumstance with an inherent superior demeanor that is rarely ever despotic enough to justify any outright attacks against him, even from the Leo and Scorpio men of the world. No matter how much of an imposer, if not a suspected imposter, he may appear, Libra is nonetheless a die-hard diplomatic envoy of democracy; still, even such civilized states require such a *president* as he. The sign of the Scales indeed represents the Apollonian Principle in the universe – that which is defined as 'well-balanced, poised, ordered, or disciplined' – and its native sons embody such attributes. As the natural ruler of the 7th Astrological House, home to such concepts as *harmony, equality, cooperation,* and *agreement,* for the sign of Libra, order is, well, the first order of the day. Over and over again, in myriad

PLANETARY SYMBOL

The glyph of Venus – circle of spirit above material cross – represents the divine mind. Called the mirror of Aphrodite, it symbolizes Libra man's preoccupation with the world of appearances as well as his obsession with self-image – the one he seeks to alter by emphasizing positive qualities and repressing any negative ones.

SIGN QUADRANT

The zodiacal quadrants correspond to metaphysical planes of being – physical, emotional, mental, and spiritual. The Third Quadrant is that of mental perception, particularly regarding the concept of existence. For Libra man, the visible world is paramount. He is the embodiment of the highly conscious mind and has little concern for what bubbles beneath the surface, whether in the subconscious or laboratory test tubes. For him life is all goodness and light (which can cast a dark shadow).

The Libran emblem is the planet Venus, the morning and evening star. It is also read as the Scales themselves. The only inanimate symbol of the zodiac, Libra can likewise give the impression of being unreal or just too plain good or talented to be true, depending on whom you ask. Whereas Libra woman weighs others with the Scales of her judgment, Libra man seeks to find balance within himself.

ELEMENT + QUALITY

The air element connotes mental and social experience. The cardinal quality signifies a call to action and initiative. Together, the cardinal-air combination particular to Libra is best illustrated as light. Indeed, the beaming character of Libra male is determined to shine as best he might, forever crafting his most dazzling qualities into a brilliant character. Some consider him a beacon of idealism, others a superficial lightweight.

metaphysical contexts, the number seven is employed as the numerical equivalent of order in the universe: seven heavens, seven vices, seven virtues, seven chakras, even seven notes to a scale (or the Scales), divined from the music of the celestial spheres. Seven is Apollo's sacred number and he drove a chariot of seven swans. Light itself is made up of the seven colors of the spectrum. Little wonder that Libra man is the personification of en-light-ened qualities, particularly that well-worn mental faculty of reason. He simply cannot abide the darker, more chaotic (read: subconscious) side of life. Not to mention his flying off the handle should a pipe spring a leak or someone throws a monkey wrench into his schedule. His focus is on such über-conscious notions as can be divined or imposed upon the world for the purpose of advancing ideas. To his mind, anything else is just self-absorbed wallowing.

So, the world of light – visible existence as well as enlightened ideology – is Libra's domain. Herein, he finds more than enough to occupy his time and energy, with little need for delving into the realm of the subconscious. He has a snap-out-of-it approach to other people's problems. Just as he tends to ignore his own darker feelings. However, being so oriented toward the lighter side of life, he may cast that much more of a shadow, repressing negative feelings that will, at some time, beg to be reckoned with. Meanwhile, Libra revels in the light-of-day world, arguably that of appearances, never feeling compelled to limit himself to any one area of interest, particularly in the realms of the liberal or fine arts. As the personification of the Venusian–Apollonian principle, he is bound to immerse himself in the objective creation of beautiful things just as he vividly illustrates the exploration of exquisite ideas. As well, given the inheritance of his patron god's myriad artistic domains, he tends to be talented in a great many areas – the word *talent* stems from the Latin *talentum,* fittingly meaning 'balance' – without necessarily specializing in any particular one. This laying claim to numerous disciplines often raises more than a few eyebrows, winning him the reputation for being a dabbler or a light-weight (pun intended). The medium through which he channels his talent is almost beside the point. To his mind, all is poetry – whether in writing, music, painting, dance, decorating, or design. Lyricism is a Libran keynote, and through it he forever seeks to uplift the spirit. He can't help but radiate those planetary principles that he personifies – he brims with notions that add more beauty, harmony, balance, equality, and indeed love to human existence. (When John Lennon sang 'all you need is love,' he mightn't have realized how Libran he was being.) Love, in its most basic form of appreciation, is what Libra beams outward in every which way, *appreciating* each situation in a threefold manner: First, he assesses that which he encounters; second, he accentuates the positive, focusing on and drawing out what is inherently good in any circumstance; and in so doing, he, third, improves situations, leaving them far better than he found them. He mainly turns this ameliorative energy onto himself, sussing out what he may best offer the world, and intensifying such qualities – the 7th House rules, amongst other things, one's *strongest personality traits.*

As the seventh astrological sign, Libra ushers in the Third Quadrant of the zodiac, that which is concerned with the metaphysical level of the mind, and thus the perception of existence. The Libra male is sexually aligned with the masculine-element polarity of his sign – air, fire, are masculine, while water, earth, are feminine – and thus embodies the cardinal-air evolutionary thoughts he espouses. In a sense, Libra man is himself an idea: The Scales is the only inanimate symbol in the zodiac, all others being either human or animal. He is so much his ideals, those principles that define his character, that his strongest personality traits are typically all he'll show to the world. Unlike Aries with its 'I am' motto signaling pure, physical being and the ego, Libra is focused on the cultivation of a character, both in the sense of a principled quality as well as in the development of an often eccentric persona, these two dynamics typically fused into one great, big personality. Some, like those Scorpios with their X-ray eyes, may feel that the Libra is put-on, phony, plastic, hiding behind his devised self to disallow others to glimpse the real him. To the zodiac's artist, however, there is no crime in self-creation. Indeed, Libra begs the question: are we not all, in one way or another, beings of our own divining? Though in truth, many Libran men adopt fairly over-the-top *alter* egos, lending new meaning to the sign's secondary motto, 'We are.' A list of famous Scales guys, which includes Sting, Flea, Usher, Eminem, Jelly Roll Morton, Meat Loaf, John 'Cougar' Mellencamp, Snoop Dogg, Buster Keaton, Groucho Marx, LeCorbusier, ee cummings, even John Lennon in declaring himself 'The Walrus,' reveals that the creation of an alias is a particularly Libran preoccupation. This fascination with characterization has also led many Librans to becoming playwrights, poets, and novelists – Arthur Miller, Oscar Wilde, Eugene O'Neill, Harold Pinter, Louis Aragon, T. S. Eliot, F. Scott Fitzgerald, William Faulkner, Gore Vidal, Truman Capote, Shel Silverstein were all born under the sign. Yet, despite a shiny outward disposition, most Libras hide a fiercely dark side, one that may eventually threaten to undo them. Viewing himself so subjectively, Libra systematically invents an image based on what he sees as his finest characteristics and polishes it to a shine. Venus' mirror-like glyph symbolizes the Libran's ability to look at himself, from this subjective perspective, as one would at a work of art, making any necessary changes to his person as he sees fit, accentuating the positive while obscuring any anti-Apollonian imbalances. He

POLARITY

Males in masculine (air, fire) signs are aligned with the gender polarity of their sign and thus embody the quality-element combination. Libra man is a beam of light, a projection of ideas, a walking-talking thought form.

7

SIGN NUMBER

The number of cosmic order: The musical *scales* comprise seven notes; the week is modeled on seven days of creation. There are seven virtues, deadly sins, pillars of wisdom, sacraments, and heavens. The Seven Sisters, or Pleiades, daughters of Aphrodite–Venus, are goddesses of justice. Light is made up of seven colors.

42–49

SIGN AGE ASSOCIATION

The age of achievement. This is a time of life when a man is polished in his accomplishments. In Libra's case, he is so all his life, and to a brilliant sheen. Focus for the Scales is on being a Renaissance man, an across-the-board great talent, from artist to thinker to connoisseur of all things aesthetic.

thus masks the pain of feeling deficient – for as much as the 7th House is that of striking personality traits, it also highlights *that which one lacks*. This selective perception of self is a source of much psychological suppression, and one that is deeply rooted in Libra's childhood rearing.

The Libra male child is typically born to bickering parents, or at least reared at a time in their lives when they are at odds. Because the cardinal-air child is precocious, often labeled a 'mini-adult' – an early nod to his sign's association with the human ages 42–49 – he sees his parents, and everyone else, as his equals. Whereas many children cower when faced with parental conflict, the Libra boy wants to mediate, indeed ameliorate, the situation. He may sit his parents down, one on either side, and seek reconciliation. His attempts to harmonize usually work, at least on the surface, and from an early age, he begins to believe that all difficulties can easily be smoothed over. His family life may look rosy on the surface, but tensions are lurking disastrously underneath. Tension, endemic to walking any tightrope, emotional or otherwise, is what actually necessitates the Libra boy's acquisition of balance. Just as his female counterpart is typically a child of divorce, giving rise to her ability to easily cut people from her life to retain an equilibrium, the Libra male, whose parents usually stay together, rather learns to justify, rationalize, and strike balances within given circumstances and even within his own psyche. Focused on keeping the peace, he presents himself to his parents as a goody-goody who won't add to their strife, but will instead be a source of pride and appreciation, itself a two-way street. Putting on a mantle of the perfect child, he hopes, will make his parents happy and, thus, keep them together. In trying to appear the ideal child, he may become a fusspot if not an outright worrier. Afraid of underlying tensions, he will stick close to home and become especially tied to his mother's apron strings, often panicked at leaving the nest as a kid for fear of not being on hand to mediate difficulties should they arise. He puts so much effort into 'tap dancing,' even at a tender kindergarten age, he may become aware of his own pretenses. He might be that child who'll haunt his parents with the perpetual question 'Do you *really* love me?' as a combined result of their distracted natures and his own inkling that he isn't quite showing them, or anybody for that matter, his true self. In a modern retelling of medieval tales of the *oaf,* literally defined as a child-substitute or imposter placed in the stead of a real child abducted by elves, fairies, or witches, the boy-robot David, in Steven Spielberg's film *A.I.,* standing for one very Libran concept of artificial intelligence, is an epitomic male Scales-child model. Coming along in his parents' life at a time when their marriage is hanging by a thread, David – ironically meaning 'beloved' – is programmed to be the perfect child and, as such, love his folks unconditionally. However, in so doing, he only ever seems to see parental love, devoid of selfishness, eluding him. Libra boy, like David, is wired to believe that he can make everything 'right' for his loved ones. And, because the Scales guy's own parents do typically stick it out, at least for appearance's sake, he is conditioned to believe that this is a possible dynamic – Venus signifying eternal unity – for which to strive. Well into adulthood, he is notoriously unable to let go of situations, people, and obstacles in his life. With rose-colored glasses firmly in place, he feels there's nothing in life that can't be 'worked out.' All one needs, he's convinced, is love.

By virtue of his planetary rule, Libra is attracted to feminine beauty from a young age, generally preferring the friendship of girls while avoiding the more rough-and-tumble world of male-bonding rituals, which strike his Apollonian sensibilities as disorderly and crude. With puberty, however, everything switches: Female friends give in to their burgeoning hormones and focus on the more physically overt males in their midst, often leaving the notoriously androgynous Libra suddenly out in the cold. Shunned, even ridiculed by other males who may label his artistic tendencies as mere artifice, part and parcel of his not being a real-functioning boy, effete if not effeminate, as well as, now, being all but ignored by the girls who once fueled his existence, the Libra finds himself at odds. As the masculine reinterpretation of his über-feminine planetary namesake Venus, the artsy Apollonian male feels caught in the balance in a world divided strictly along gender lines. He will try to find his niche, searching himself for those infamous strong personality traits, anything outstanding that might win him recognition and, thus, a place in the social pantheon. For although he may be concentrated on cultivating so distinct an individual character, he fears and hopes to avoid being relegated to the nether regions of peer oblivion. Talents become his focus, and he means to make a mark with any accomplishments he might display.

Likewise, he'll make up with stylistic flair what he lacks in manly appearance. If mankind still lived in the jungle, Leo, with his survival-of-the-fittest attitude, might indeed reign supreme; but in modern society, a world built upon high ideals and Apollonian rules of democratic civilization, a strikingly less 'natural' man, such as Libra, is able to thrive. Living by his characteristically Wildean wits, he is the preeminent intellectual and sophisticate of the zodiac. With these distinctions, he hopes to trump any inborn he-men at the game of life – and the game of love. Meanwhile, he may experience a sense of self-loathing (which he, of course, represses) if not feeling naturally equipped with enviably masculine endowments such as major muscles or rugged athleticism. Still, Libra masks his deep-seated disappointment behind an insouciant, devil-

PSYCHOLOGY

Libra can be rigid and emotionally inflexible. Life needs to fit into boxes, which it rarely does in actuality. He is overly idealistic and refuses to look at the 'darker' unconscious aspects of himself. Bon vivantism can border on the pathological, and he tends to overindulge in drugs and alchohol. Likewise, he may fall prey to sexual addiction. He can suffer repression on this score as well as with any number of emotional traumas, which may ultimately lead to depression.

may-care demeanor. He strikes attitudes as his best defense against feeling down-and-out. Reinvention, indeed re-creation of self, is his best weapon for survival in the dog-eat-dog world of male dominance and sexual conquest. Similarly, recreation, in that other sense of the word, becomes his main objective in life: Adopting a bon-vivant persona, the Libran sybarite seeks out those Venusian pleasures the world has to offer, dabbling in all things arty if not affected, employing his trademark *bons mots* in the courting of the *beau monde*.

Body + Soul

Libra man may be the most vivid character on the astrological block. From his naturally animated features to his exaggerated expressions and whimsical style of dress, the Scales guy certainly stands out in a crowd. Eternally youthful and more cute than classically handsome, he can appear almost cartoonish, if not decidedly comical in his appearance. Priding himself on the development of a personalized style, this baby-faced dandy likes to bounce around town, popping seamlessly in and out of diverse social settings, easily adapting, and cleverly wardrobed, to fit any given situation. Somewhat taller and leaner than other men in his family, he still manages to look positively cherubic. His face is round, rubbery, and wholly revealed by an extremely high hairline; his locks are curly or wispy, though fine; his slanting, deep-set eyes are encased by fleshy lids; his cheeks may be dimpled; his straight though slightly flattened and pliable nose seems almost cartilage-free. And then there's his mouth: a rather tiny horizontal slit that curls down at the edges into a slight frown, topped by a furled, aptly coined Cupid's bow of an upper lip, lending him an expression like that of a baby poised on the brink of a cry. Despite an almost Muppet-like appearance, there is something melancholic in his countenance, like a sad clown designed to make others laugh. Indeed, the possession of exceptional wit is a Libran birthright, and he is famous for pleasantly, placidly listening to others' discourse only to interject well-placed one-liners. He is a master of wordplay, innuendo, irony, and double entendre, though it may take others a moment to fully grasp the jist of his economic commentary – a raucous explosion of laughter ensues as the full import of what he's saying finally takes hold. Despite any feigned jadedness, Libra man loves to socialize; though, in truth, it is more apt to say he hates to be alone. Few people get chummier faster than Libra, as he tends to embrace strangers as if they were long-lost kin – his instinct is to be inclusive in all situations. Being so gregarious a creature, Libra is often misconstrued as a superficial partygoer by the more serious-minded individuals in the zodiac. But loneliness and depression are not unknown to the Scales guy. He simply considers it rude to brood in public, well-accustomed as he is to switching off the darker stirrings of his soul.

Often nearly pretty in appearance, Libra has a rounded musculature that only contributes to his Kewpie-doll countenance. His shoulders, especially, can be curved and narrow. He may be somewhat barrel-chested, his torso truncated and soft in proportion to trademark long, lean limbs. Libra is generally short-waisted with slender hips, a narrow pelvis, and a shortened lower back – this 'hinge' region is ruled by his sign, being the balancing point between the upper and lower bodies – which seems to correlate to many a Libra man suffering from sciatica, lumbago, and kidney complaints. He's less hairy than other men in his family, and what body fuzz he does have will be downy soft and lightly hued. He's rather flexible, often excelling at such graceful sports as gymnastics, diving, or even wrestling – he's as hard to pin down physically as he is psychologically. His private parts are rather textbook in nature; he's amply endowed though rarely overly so, boasting bits and pieces as user-friendly in appearance as he looks to be – all pink and prettily constructed, never distinctly dark or deviously shaped in any way.

Looking so much the cute and cuddly teddy bear of a man, Libra often has a hard time being taken seriously. Even when he's bone thin, there is always something of the little dough boy about Libra that may prohibit him, with few exceptions, from appearing purely lanky. His signature lack of beard – it can take him two days to grow a five-o'clock shadow – further enforces this air of artificiality. Not surprisingly, he may seem particularly suspect to other men, even when women find his conversation endlessly entertaining. Often, other guys are too quick to consider him no 'real man,' a label that may be symptomatic of his notorious interest in aesthetics, or of his predestined inability to divorce himself from the über-femininity of his ruling planet, Venus. Still, because Libra is a masculine polarity sign, he projects plenty of male agression, albeit on the cerebral and verbal level, that many men find confrontational, especially when coming from so floppy a Muppet. It doesn't help that Libra is so terribly driven in creative endeavors, those that strict machos might tag 'froufrou' in nature. On top of everything else, the Libran is no sheep, and die-hard conservative conformists tend to resent his naturally liberal outlook on life. If there's one thing Libra believes – and will have you know – it is that he's special, a total original. Having lovingly embraced and fostered his standout personality traits, Libra cloaks himself in these distinctions. That blanket-toting *Peanuts* character, Linus, comes to mind, a quintessentially Libran-male archetype – idealistic, intellectual, and rational,

BIBLE + LITERATURE

Libra draws on the character of Lucifer, meaning 'bearer of the light-stick,' the Prince of the Power of the Air, befitting the sign's cardinal-air status. He is the morning and evening star (planet Venus) who sought to over-throw the Sun as center of the universe. He rivaled God, Elias (Greek Helios). Lucifer sought to bring power to mankind and build an enlightened civilization. In Lucifer we see Libra as a *liberal* underdog seeking an exalted position. Literary prototypes include Charles Dickens's Pip in *Great Expectations*. Pip, meaning 'seed,' points to the Libran desire to impregnate the world with high ideals. The upstart Luke Skywalker with his light saber is Luciferian to the core.

7TH ASTROLOGICAL HOUSE

other
the non-self
union
one-on-one partnerships
business partnerships
love bonds
marriage/divorce
contracts
social engagements
agreements
compromise
lawsuits
civility
diplomacy
public response
what one lacks
grandparents
agents
identification with others
oneness with others
equality
harmony
the opposite sex
conflicts with spouse
attraction
balance
cooperation
other people
divorce
rupture
adversaries/detractors
close contact
who one attracts
open enemies
reciprocity
karma
compensation
public relations
fairness
impartiality
unification
strongest personality traits

but also ultrasensitive and insecure — who, like Apollo, is distinguished as a great orator, shedding light on situations by extracting their true meaning. Linus, a name derived from the Greek *linos,* meaning 'flaxseed,' was indeed a son of Apollo whom the god accidentally killed in sport, something of which Charles Schulz may have been aware. In classic literature, the male Libran character comes down to us as Pip, also meaning seed, in Charles Dickens's *Great Expectations.* Indeed, just as the sign of Aries represents physical seeds, the origin of life befitting its sparky cardinal-fire status, the sign of Libra is about the sowing of ideological seeds, creating new life and order on the intellectual plane in keeping with its cardinal-air assignation. Apollo's domain of prophecy is one and the same with having great expectations; Linus, too, had lofty prospects, lest we forget his waiting on that proverbial Great Pumpkin.

Libra man is a pip all right: Even if he works in a huge corporate hive, he will exhibit a decided flair in both manner and fashion sense: Libra pushes the envelope, often along whimsical, retro lines. But for all his panache, he may seem too forced a poseur. Indeed, there is startling archetypal truth to these sons of Apollo being imposing, and, like him, taking on what were previously female attributes under girly goddess rulership. In short, he isn't the butchest dresser on the block. In Wildean manner, he can be flamboyant to a fault, mixing and matching colors or patterns wildly, blending high and low fashion into an exciting mélange, clothing becoming a visible means of bucking societal conformity. To him, one is whom one imagines oneself to be — appearing false or phony couldn't be further from his mind. In fact, of all the astrological signs, Libra may have the most difficulty telling even the tiniest fib; when endeavoring to do so, he noticeably cannot make eye contact. But his inherent frankness may be taken as too in-your-face an attitude to quietly tolerate.

As the zodiac's consummate *artiste,* Libra is his own greatest, living masterpiece: He doesn't so much throw clothes on as he does art-direct himself and indeed his entire life. His hairstyle is often as edgy as his fashion sense — wedgy mushroom cuts, Prince Valiant bobs, or carefully coiffed rocker shags are some favorite looks. Since his hair is often wavy or curly, he may choose to leave it loose, embracing a hippy-chic aesthetic. In fairness to his detractors, there is something decidedly foppish about the Libra male. There is simply no avoiding that he has orchestrated his appearance. As that list of famous men of the sign denotes, Libra is a man of his own divining — a walking, talking thought-form. His imagination is famously hyperactive, and typically before he can talk, he's already performing the myriad characters brewing in his head; needless to say, this gives his parents pause. At so young an age, he seems already to be *acting,* not simply being himself. What his parents don't realize is that these mass characterizations *are* himself – remember that 'We are' motto? – each and every 'side' of his personality being cataloged into the formation of his singular psyche. Just as Libra is the Renaissance man, dabbling in a multitude of arts-and-leisure interests, he is, within himself, a multiple personality. His mind is a corrugated wall of characters from which he pulls his various faces. But what sounds like psychosis is a natural psychological process for the Libra. No one part of him is phony in the least. It's just that artifice – the word stems from *art* – is indigenous to the one male born under this inanimate star sign. But is art artifice? Or does it imitate life? Or vice versa? Libra man is a living, breathing exploration of these essential questions. He represents life lived as a sort of performance art, begging the question, can not the same be true for any one of us? Admittedly, organizing and coordinating the chorus of selves that makes up his naturally faceted personality does require a great deal of orchestration – in the strictest symphonic sense of the word.

Sex + Sexuality

From the time he's a small child, Libra feels other. His parents, recognizing their son's outsized imagination, personality, and antics, may label the boy 'special'; but more often than not, he is simply considered 'different' or 'weird.' When Libra hits adolescence and sexuality enters the picture, he feels unable to compete, especially physically, with the muscle-heads who are attracting girls' attentions. Having enjoyed lavish female companionship in his youth, he may suddenly find himself downgraded to the position of 'friend.' And if at such a disadvantage, Libra has difficulty scoring recognition as a sexual entity. Fittingly, he may feel himself to be an all-too-balanced combination of traditionally male and female traits, having to constantly defend himself against the barbs aimed at his seemingly dubious sexuality. Even the straightest Libra on the planet will have his sexuality called into question by the more simple-minded cookie-cutter population of the world. During adolescence, he may even wonder about himself, attributing his feelings of being 'different' to an alternative sexual orientation, which, even when Libra is gay, may not be the case: He simply suffers from an ongoing identity crisis, a tendency that unfortunately contributes to making him an obvious target for gay-male advances. In his quest for self-realization, many a Libra boy will sexually experiment with other males, often on the instigation of an older boy who senses Libra's innately searching nature. Libra is looking for that elusive love,

KEY WORDS

proportion
harmony
measure
charm
serendipity
idealism
composure
elegance
levity
pleasure
talent
character
decision
liberalism
justice
imagination
aptitude
order
appearances
democracy
prescience
progression
expectation
consciousness
civilization
diplomacy
negotiation
stimulation
agility
innovation
impudence
sensuality
suppleness
personality
imagination
peace
class
inference
wit
dalliance
talent

after all, in one form or another. For some, this is a departure point for committing to a gay lifestyle. While often even the straightest Libra will be a most gay-friendly individual, recognizing what may only be a purely theoretical bisexuality within himself. In fact, Libras of both sexes support the argument that all people are inherently bisexual. At the very least, he might be among those fellows who take a good long look at other guys in the locker room, predisposed to being as aesthetically intrigued by a godlike male form as he is by that of a lovely female – all things being equal.

And so, straight Libra man is rarely a homophobe. For everyone who says a Libra like Eminem is thus prejudiced, there is someone else who'll maintain that such anger is self-directed. In truth, sometimes the 'character' Libra adopts is a bad-boy persona geared toward completely warding off that sensitive Venusian energy that sends most Libran Linuses lunging for their metaphoric security blankets, if only to turn around and sport it, as that Peanut often does, in some dramatic fashionable flourish. However it manifests, the Libra's so-called artificial costume is in fact wrought from the very fabric of any sense of inferiority he feels, such bells and whistles meant to distract others, and indeed himself, from any real pain he might be feeling beneath his arty artifice. In general, he is far too intellectually enlightened to judge others based on race, creed, color, or sexual orientation. In fact, Libra believes it is his freethinking mind that offers him the best chance of impressing others, especially the women who appeal to his discriminating taste. Not typically comfortable competing in the more rustic arenas of male prowess – he takes to the tennis court or ski slope far more readily than the football field or baseball diamond – he commits to nurturing his urbane qualities in hopes of scoring points with such ladies who look to swim in so culturally sophisticated a pool. Easier said than done: Sadly, Libra is often rather unlucky in love. One so witty and charming surely makes an entertaining date; but the Libran bon vivant is not readily considered 'marriage material.' He is poised, polished, princely even – as if fresh from some finishing school of his own imagining. But why, women may wonder, does he make such a fuss about himself? The simple answer isn't because he can, but rather because he often must as such behavior is a by-product of the means for emotional survival he employed as a child. Betterment thus becomes the most striking through-line in any Libra man's life. He teaches us, by example, that we needn't necessarily accept the 'station' into which we're born; but that we may draft our own design for living, one that suits the person we see ourself to be in our greatest self-expectations. The flip side, however, is that Libra is hard-pressed ever to feel satisfied with himself, or with his accomplishments. It is his particular challenge: to learn to appreciate his current status, at any given time, if he wishes to see the value of his life continue to appreciate. Libra is living proof of the old adage that you must love what you have in order to get what you want. This is the precise karmic paradox upon which the Libran condition is predicated.

Unfortunately, Libra's notoriously freelance, artsy approach to life doesn't much impress the legions of women looking for security in a mate – one more strike against Libra in his search for lasting love. He'll always have girlfriends, but when it comes to marriage or any permanent form of a relationship, he finds that women have a hard time committing: He's at once 'too much' (ideas, read: hot air) and 'not enough' (substance, read: money on the table). It will require a woman with some foresight and a boatload of confidence to join with the Libra dandy. The faith such a steady mate might invest in him, something he's unaccustomed to – his own parents having pooh-poohed his loftier ambitions, attempting to steer him toward more bankable pursuits – would ironically work like a charm in helping Libra to profit from one of his many creative concepts. And he returns the favor: For better or worse, Libra sees those he loves in their best possible light – an idealized perception that others feel hard-pressed to live up to. He has the same lofty hopes for others as he does for himself, often making loved ones feel 'less' when they invariably fall short. While being seen through the rosy Libran lens may be inspiring, it can also be a window onto one's deficiencies.

In a sense, Libra picks up being Pygmalion where his predecessor Virgo left off: Virgo, wanting to make a woman into his ideal, chips away, sculpting her in Svengali fashion, while Libra beholds a woman as the finished artistic product, like Galatea on her pedestal, admiring her until his loaded appreciation causes her to come to life (and return his feelings). Such is the power of love, according to Libra. And in keeping with this Galatean analogy, Libra is drawn to statuesque, if not monumental women of classical beauty, those who are, in his estimation, perfect works of art. This poses yet another stumbling block to his securing a love connection, as the zodiac's Pip can't always easily win the affections of the world's aloof Estellas (meaning 'starlike'). Of course it's merely a matter of perception: Recognizing only the good, if not the perfect, Libra will plop the woman he fancies on that pedestal, regardless of whether it is universally agreed that Gwyneth Paltrow could play her in the movie version of his life, or even if she's wont to perch there in the first place. Dickens's story of the questionably beloved Pip is a remodeling of many an Apollonian romance myth, the most famous of which is the god's pursuit of the nymph Daphne (meaning 'honor'), who would sooner see herself turned into a tree than to have to hook up with a veritable god who,

Bam Margera
Luke Perry
Mark Hamill
Richard Barone
Roger Moore
George C. Scott
Jason Alexander
Mickey Rooney
Mario Puzo
Johnny Carson
Ed Sullivan
Lenny Bruce
Bishop Desmond Tutu
Gandhi
Jimmy Carter
Lech Walesa
Vladimir Putin
Stanley Kramer
George Gershwin
Dizzy Gillespie
John Coltrane
Chubby Checker
Art Blakey
Glenn Gould
Luciano Pavarotti
Ray Charles
ee cummings
T. S. Eliot
Michelangelo Antonioni
Pedro Almodovar
Shel Silverstein
Truman Capote
Oscar Wilde
Gore Vidal
F. Scott Fitzgerald
William Faulkner
Harold Pinter
Arthur Miller
Eugene O'Neill
Arthur Rimbaud
Auguste Lumiere
Le Corbusier
Alberto Giacometti
Caravaggio
Robert Rauschenberg
Mark Rothko
Shaun Cassidy
Peter Finch
Rex Reed
Jeff Goldblum

BODY RULERSHIP

Libra rules the lower back, lumbar region, kidneys and the appendix; common physical ailments include kidney complaints and lumbago. The kidneys perform a balancing act of their own, weighing and eliminating unwanted matter.

by all accounts, should be something of a heartthrob. But even in Daphne turning into that laurel tree we see the particular power of Apollo's love: It is ennobling, an expression of his attraction to high ideals as personified by a certain brand of female, one synonymous with honor. Likewise, Libra's love and appreciation are capable of having a profound transformative effect on a would-be partner. Looking into his admiring gaze, a woman will see herself as a simulacrum of the superior expectations he heaps on her, thus inspired to systematically begin seeing herself in the same light. The love of a Libra is indeed empowering. He doesn't seek to foster dependency – on the contrary, he wants those he loves to feel both free and accomplished, such that they may need no more from him, or anybody else, than reciprocated, requited love.

Of course, the glut of goodness and light with which Libra barricades himself only casts a more ominous shadow in his life, and in his psyche. He takes everything in, rationalizes it, then compensates for any disadvantage with an oft outsized optimism, if not extreme glee. But this is Pagliacci folks – the zodiac's little drama department: Libra man is both the theatrical Muses's masks, together – tragedy and comedy. Indeed, for all the Pollyannaism this guy exudes, he represses at least that much disappointment: Half-empty, half-full – therein lies the Libran quandry. The Scales tip back and forth, constantly, all day long, as any Libran's loved one will tell you.

As the cardinal-air guy, Libra is mentally active, forever drawing plans and philosophies, and inventing scenarios. (All Libra men are dramatists.) He looks for psychological action along experiential rather than purely physical lines. His character forever in full swing, he is continually out to achieve some objective; this is not the sit-quietly-by-yourself sign. Libra embodies his motto 'We are,' and a relationship with him can feel like a duet or dance-athon that has gone on too long. Every conversation is loaded. Every decision must be made by committee, relationships being a democracy à deux. (Why does Daphne run from Apollo after all? Like Libra man, he may simply be too much work.) A lot is going on in the mind of this man, and he's beaming with agendas. Added to which, Libra is notoriously anxious, and impatient to accomplish. Good intentions. Great Expectations. Every day he prepares a sweeping fan of activities that he invariably fails to achieve, thwarted by scrupulous self-demand. But for him, disappointment is de rigueur – it is his state of mind, roughly half the time. As friends and foes of the Libra know, this guy goes to extremes, exuding talent and torment in equal measure. Life with Libra has its tensions, but remember, he seems to thrive on it: As the Scales, life is a teeter-totter, or rather a tightrope. Propelling himself through the world in pursuit of his increasingly lofty aspirations, Libra slowly acquires finesse. With Apollonian grace and serenity, he eventually gets into a groove.

Meanwhile, he may struggle with his idealism in a relationship, such that his partner might easily tumble from the pedestal on which he has placed her. Unfortunately, as hard as he is on himself, he needn't be more than a fraction as tough on his mate to cause some major emotional damage. As appreciative, indeed flattering, as he might be, he can be at least that cruel and cutting. Apollo's arrows delivered the most painful wounds imaginable. What Libra wrestles with most in life are his conflicting needs for freedom and commitment – *marriage* and *divorce* are both 7th House attributes – and he often pro-jects blame for this quandry onto a loved one when he's feeling stifled by too-close-for-comfort circumstance. He wants his cake and to eat it, too, seeking stability and serendipity in equal measure.

Nor does Libra check his idealism at the bedroom door. Sex for him must be, in a word, beautiful. The mood, indeed the lighting, must be just so, preferably a cool blue haze akin to his sign-ruled twilight, as his vision of lovemaking is rather lyrical – no fumbling or false starts, but rather a slow, erotic journey with lots of crescendo and a sweeping, successful finish that should never leave him or his partner wanting. Placing such a tall order on himself in the sack, Libra may be too 'in his head' about performance. As a result, he indulges in lavish foreplay, determined to gratify a woman early on if only as a preventive measure, daunted by the prospect of not delivering a big bang during intercourse. In contrast to his opposite sign of Aries – aptly named the Ram – Libra uses his brain over whatever brawn he might possess. This boy Venus is far more erotic than he is explicitly carnal, his bedroom operations being tastefully artistic as opposed to blatantly pornographic. Fittingly, he is a 'light,' surfacey lover – orderly, yet improvisational. Kissing a woman's mouth, neck, ears, wherever, Libra expertly employs breath – sharp inhalations or hot blows – to awaken hidden erogenous zones. He is a master of the soft touch, barely tracing his fingers over a woman's body, allowing her anticipation to play a part in arousal. He is the most sexually intuitive of men, seeming to function on the astral plane, moving his hands over a woman as if casting a psychic spell of excitement, seeking to stimulate her aura as much as her actual body parts. He wants a lover to writhe in great expectation before he so much as licks a nipple. It never takes long for the Libra to bring his lover, thus warmed up, to orgasm. A particular specialty of this cunning linguist is the art of the oral: His style is slow and steady, deep stimulation mixed with unexpectedly quick and breezy touches, leaving plenty of space between

STR8 TURN-ONS

intelligence
tall women
classic beauty, models
(active) worship
long, straight hair
alabaster skin
kissing, licking
cleavage
cunnilingus
vanilla
voyeurism
female masturbation
(passive) lite bondage
girl on top
side entry
licking, blowing, biting
(active) nipple play
m-m-f threesomes
couples
private clubs
erotica
(passive) nipple play
sensual touching

applications of his creative tongue-lashings. Still, despite what may seem like a brilliantly manufactured form of lovemaking, sex with Libra doesn't preclude pure passion. The orderly manner in which he expresses himself sexually stems from a 'place' of true feeling and inspiration. As in any successful artistic performance, Libra is blessed with the ability to channel his ardor into a skillfully honed technique.

If a woman is looking for a real good rodgering, however, Libra is typically not the man for the job. Even when generously endowed – visions of Tommy Lee leap to mind – he's bound to equally share in the experience of lovemaking rather than taking the lead and giving a woman the proverbial lay of her life. Like his closest astrological neighbor, Virgo woman, Libra is engineered for a tantric style of lovemaking. Committing to his slow, if-we-build-it-you-will-come modus, he and his partner may attain ecstatic levels of pleasure. By taking a more yogic approach to sex – visions of Sting leap to mind – the erotic act with Libra can indeed be a transcendent experience. The Scales guy is typically wise to strike sexual goal-orientedness from his thinking. For, if the Libra is going to suffer from any snafus in the bedroom, premature ejaculation would probably top the list. Luckily, what the zodiac's perfectionist may lack in staying power he makes up for in prevention if not repeat sexual performances.

As one might expect from a man born under the antiseptic Apollonian principle, Libra cannot abide much of a mess in the boudoir. He can barely tolerate rolling into a wet spot on the sheets, not wanting such a vivid reminder of what most other signs might simply consider evidence of a rousing good time. There are distinct advantages to the Libra's being in-his-head in bed; his mind surfaces as more of a sexual organ than any other he possesses: Our little god of prophecy seems to nearly divine desire in a woman, touching her as would a painter knowing where to next stroke, playing a woman improvisationally, like a piano. Artful and attentive, Libra, unlike many men, considers the pleasure of his partner in tandem with his own and is actually so sympathetic to her (or him) that he makes sure she climaxes first, or solely. It's the same in all aspects of his life – if he shares a sandwich, he's sure to offer up the larger half, simply because it would displease him so much to be the cause of any one-sidedness. 'I balance' typically entails taking the short end of the stick. With the brain being by far the Scales' most powerful tool, sexually or otherwise, he may, in extreme cases, become so immersed in the erotic that it replaces any real, physical contact, intrigued as he is by no-fuss, no-muss hands-off experiences. Classy strippers, phone sex, autoeroticism, as well as elaborate mind games of domination and submission and voyeuristic fantasies are Libran domain. Projecting his erotic expectations into the atmosphere, he may imagine sexual tension where it doesn't exist. Even his platonic relationships can be charged and ambiguous – a big 'what if' always hangs in the air. Group sex, too, befits his 'we' attitude. Still, if ever involved in such a scenario, Libra will typically take the role of fly-on-the-wall. He's a sexual dabbler who believes that one should try everything at least twice. He rarely becomes psychologically or emotionally invested and is uncommonly able to exit most sexual scenarios unscathed. Even in his intimate one-on-one lovemaking, Libra adopts an impersonal perspective: He's particularly aroused by being used as an inanimate object, a sexual tool for a woman's pleasure. Indeed, nothing gives Libra a larger hard-on than a woman who can't get enough of him, hungrily using his phallus every which way for her own masturbatory pleasure.

In his blasé, cool blue vision of erotic activity, Libra doesn't believe in making a big deal out of sex. He has an aversion to rules, and he scoffs at sexual labels. As one of the truly bisexual signs of the zodiac, he is especially paradoxical in his sexual attractions. In reflection of his placement on the astrological wheel, Libra feels very much in the middle. Placed in the role of mediator between his parents at such an early age, he learns to see both sides of the argument in the ongoing battle between the sexes. And, more often than not, it's in the middle that he'd like to stay. In brass tacks, Libra is prone to liking threesomes, of either the female-male-female or the male-female-male variety. Having a bisexual female partner is an especially thrilling possibility to the Libra, as the possibilities seem endless. With two women, he may prefer to be all but ignored, left to kick back and observe the action – unless, of course, he's being used as that dildo. He also enjoys being in bed with a straight couple, though typically under the guise of sharing 'with a buddy,' any same-sex contact seeming accidental. (Whoops!) As if Libra's paradoxical nature wasn't confusing enough, he's at once attracted to the straightest of men and the most ambiguous of women.

But Libra's free-love attitude doesn't prevent him from having those *lifelong bonds* attributed to his 7th Astrological House. Sex, it seems, is often beside the point: As liberated and sexually ambidextrous as Libra might be, his primary goal will always be unity with one individual. He's far more interested in sharing a committed emotional life with a partner in the light of day than he is with what actually happens in bed in the dark of night. For all his self-objectifying, what he truly longs for is love. Even when sexually ambidextrous, Libra must bond with one person, monogamously, at least in theory, and typically with a woman. Whereas the Scales guy is more likely than most to experience a homosexual encounter, he is one, ironically, of the least likely to self-identify as gay. In a nod to his 7th House of *opposites*, Libra finds it

GAY TURN-ONS

younger males
straight, married men
models, pretty boys
long hair
Scandinavians
mutual j/o
body contact
gymnasts, swimmers
surfers, skaters
marble skin
bisexuality
threesomes
artists, landscapers
(active) nipple play
low hangers
voyeurism
(passive) analingus
(passive) lite b + d
treasure trails
spas, saunas, steam rooms
edging
soccer kit, players
(active) oral

difficult to merge emotionally with someone of the same sex. He worships male beauty, so physical attractions to men come easily. But at the end of the day, two males in one household, not to mention two stiff piggies wrapped in one blanket, tends to strike the Libra as redundant, tipping the Scales' precarious sensibilities too far in one direction.

Just when life with straight Libra seemed liberal enough, the gay man of the sign takes his open sexual policy in relationships that much further. Of all gay men, Libra is perhaps the least naturally inclined toward steady relationships. His attraction to straight-acting, -appearing, and indeed -identified men finds him hooking up with the most barely bisexual characters – 'closet' cases – with whom he shares a homoerotic, rather than strictly homosexual, approach to same-sex contact. Fittingly, so many Libras' first gay experiences are with older, supposedly straight and invariably married men. With his pretty-boy looks and AC/DC demeanor, Libra has a way of making almost any guy consider a walk on the wild side. Perhaps it is his light attitude toward homosexual contact that makes sex feel like no bigger a deal than a handshake or, more accurately, a wrestling match. Libra can be quite the little male Lolita, precociously prevoking whatever submerged gay fantasy another man might possess. Since the Scales himself isn't looking to be somebody's househusband, the no-strings-attached sexual agenda he projects suits those bi-curious males just fine, insuring a discreet atmosphere in which to explore cached desires.

Libra's soft, childlike looks – something he retains well into middle age – tend to attract a more dominantly inclined man. And though Libra is always open to exploring his receptive side, he will, as the zodiac's compensator, eventually seek balance by taking an aggressive position in bed. Still, Libra likes his men to be men, and so he usually learns to accept a sex life spent on the bottom. Not to say he'll ever just lie there: A need for order and control prohibits Libra from ever being the consummate submissive. Instead, he might be described as an aggressive bottom. Like his straight counterpart, gay Libra likes to keep sex light and lively: So some of the manly tops he attracts push his envelope a little further than he typically likes. He is orally adept, though perhaps not especially talented in the deep-throating department. Sixty-nine is standard sexual fare for the Scales guy, again, all things being equal.

Particularly drawn to suit-and-tie conservatives, Libra plays his freelance virtuoso act to the hilt in same-sex relationships, deriving pleasure from being wilder, if not crazier, than his lover's usual circle of friends. In cases where he has dragged his partner out of the closet, Libra thrills in shaking up the stodgier dinner parties and business gatherings to which his mate might invite him, gauging other people's reactions to his infamously candid comments and liberal political views. Artists, he believes, were put on the earth to provoke, and Libra feels duty-bound to capsize conformist codes of behavior. Never off-color, however, he typically ends up as the life of the party – and his attendance only augments his lover's popularity. Indeed, gay Libra is a beautiful reflection on his partner, a power that he and his mate might use to other advantages as well. Forever on the lookout for new and exciting experiences, Libra may, from time to time, hope to lure a third party into the bedroom, willing to give his lover an eyeful of his interaction with such a lucky 'stranger.' It's a scenario his partner would be wise to welcome as, with or without him, Libra will always look to spice up his sex life with an occasional infusion of variety.

Couplings

Straight

Libra Man ∫ Aries Woman
Allies from the outset, they share a need for sexual freedom and intellectual expression. As a couple, believing themselves an exclusive elite, they have cachet and others buy into the perception. In bed, she's the aggressor.

Libra Man ∫ Taurus Woman
They take time to warm up, but then it's hot. Each invests much energy in the other's emotional health. In artistic pursuits, this partnership is peerless. Sexually, imaginations are stimulated: Role-playing is one ritual.

Libra Man ∫ Gemini Woman
Where she goes, he'll follow: Libra is positively passive when compared with the enterprising Gemini. They have something to prove – success is the consequence. Sex is comfortably secondary in their nonstop lifestyle.

Libra Man ∫ Cancer Woman
Openness is this pair's ongoing theme: Sexuality is a liberal subject for Libra, giving Cancer license to color outside the lines. Their erotic repertoire will always be original – bisexual scenarios are stimulating.

Libra Man ∫ Leo Woman
Flattery gets them everywhere: Validation is the basis of their jovial bond. He learns to compromise; her energy is infectious. In bed, Leo wears the pants, but Libra's content to play passive.

Libra Man ∫ Virgo Woman
Fast friends, but they struggle to reach relationship status. Both can be spoiled. What starts out as liberal may turn into taking liberties. With effort, they fix it. Sexually, she wants to be swept away; he won't work that hard.

Libra Man ∫ Libra Woman
They're more aligned than most same-sign couples – a shared aesthetic is the centerpiece of their cliquey companionship. Scales of both sexes push the envelope of experience. Sexually, they're edgy, experimental.

Libra Man ∫ Scorpio Woman
She seems a self-sufficient sort; his aristocratic bearing is intriguing. Both are drawn to a grand lifestyle. They're happiest in the company of friends. Sex easily swings from precious to perverse.

Libra Man / Sagittarius Woman

His intellectual assets combined with her commercial capabilities create a powerful, profound partnership. He's her muse. This pair proves it's possible to have it all. Sexually, they may be into other couples.

Libra Man / Capricorn Woman

A contradiction – a harrowing emotional seesaw, a transcendent experience. A need for social status masks insecurities; success seems a way to overcome the past. In bed, there's baggage. But with time, the load is lightened.

Libra Man / Aquarius Woman

Defined by inventiveness and upheaval. Some say they're strange. Abstract thinkers, they share a mental affinity – each impacts the other's state of mind. Enthusiasm turns to zealotry. In bed, there are no hang-ups.

Libra Man / Pisces Woman

A wispy, waifish pair, predisposed to emotional sensitivity. They may drift into adverse behaviors, prone to hypochondria and procrastination. A profound connection produces works of art. Sex is a way to escape.

Gay

Libra Man / Aries Man

Aries and Libra make an impressive package – and they know it: Vanity is their defining feature. Life together is structured, but the Scales struggles to stay on the straight and narrow. Aries likes a little leather on his Libra.

Libra Man / Taurus Man

Taurus is Libra's homoerotic ideal. Beyond the physical, they share an appreciation of the finer things. Socializing is an art form. Food and drink are copiously consumed. They'll dote on each other. Sex is an intense exploration.

Libra Man / Gemini Man

They should agree to disagree. But a strong attraction exists: it's like going to bed with a best friend. Lively arguments lead to heated reconciliation sex. For both, fooling around should be fun, frisky.

Libra Man / Cancer Man

Cancer is Milquetoast to left-of-center Libra. But the Scales guy is famous for making exceptions, especially if sex is in the offing. Cancer acclimates to a spot of scandal in his otherwise spotless existence.

Libra Man / Leo Man

Ideological differences are a hindrance here. Leo's dogmatic; Libra's liberal. Still, a little lively debate stimulates. Sexually, it's simpler: Libra takes the lead, persistently inciting Leo's deeper desires.

Libra Man / Virgo Man

As they boost each other's bon vivantism, escapades easily turn excessive. Outsiders may say they're bitchy, exclusive. They make memorable moments. Sex is less about decadence, more about devotion.

Libra Man / Libra Man

Détente is the overriding dynamic in a double-Scales association: Hoping to avoid conflict, they choose quick reconciliation. Detachment is deemed easier than seriously dealing. Sexual communication, too, may be a struggle.

Libra Man / Scorpio Man

Scorpio is suspicious – Libra seems too good to be true. Here, the Scales guy endures Scorp's sadistic streak, but not for long. Sex is a struggle for power; Libra usually loses. He might seek a less intimidating lover.

Libra Man / Sagittarius Man

Together, they strike creative gold, having explored the limits of expression, often with dazzling results. In bed, Libra is a minion under a powerful Sagittarian spell. A need for adventure may mean messing with group scenes.

Libra Man / Capricorn Man

The Scales is like a gust of fresh air in Cap's life. Socially, they're absolutely matched. They may even dress alike. Sexually, there's intrigue: Libra is especially fascinated by Cap's fit, firm physique.

Libra Man / Aquarius Man

Libra's in the market for a soul mate when he meets the Waterbearer, bombarding him with a detailed life history. An abiding friendship ensues, one that may not withstand the complexities of deeper commitment.

Libra Man / Pisces Man

As a couple, they're complex: Pisces is unpredictable, Libra is easily thrown off-balance. To boot, both boast a love of the high life – who's holding down the home front? At the first sign of trouble, they take to the sheets.

Libra Woman

the charm

Libra woman is the zodiac's activist: The most principled person on the astrological wheel, she can't separate herself from her lofty convictions. To her, the world requires a redesign, as it lacks the very ideals that she most urgently seeks to project. If she perceives a wrong, she must strive to right it; the realm of human justice is her special domain. She possesses a powerful mind, a finely tuned faculty that is eclipsed only by her special brand of ethereal beauty. Of all women, Libra is most comely and fair – rarely one ever to be labeled sultry or, even, overtly sexy – but on this score, and many others, Libra's looks can be deceiving. Prized for her demure charms, she may risk being objectified as ornamentation, classy arm candy used by men for their own validation or as a means of impressing others. Meanwhile, her own agenda in love is to fall in with a true friend and equal, a liberal freethinker who shares her infamous love of the arts and all things aesthetic, as well as her often radical political views and egalitarian visions. She is unconventional in relationships, amenable to casual sex with a like mind, and leery, in fact, of legal, long-term bonds. When she does commit to a man, she demands total fidelity: Hell hath no fury like the lady Libra scorned. Notoriously attracted to other females, regardless of her sexual identification, she is principally drawn to extreme women – exaggeratedly beautiful supermodel glamazons or megaphone-toting, ax-grinding radicals; or, if she has her druthers, a righteous combination of both.

VII

With the 7th zodiacal principle, the dissonance of Virgo gives way to the consonance of Libra and its Apollonian precepts of order, reason, and beauty. Design replaces mere function, and societal rules are imposed on free-form nature. Libra woman stands for equality within the male-Apollonian vision of civilization, standing firm in her ideals, representing feminine authority in the world. Her mottoes 'I balance' and 'we are' expresses her need to stand up and be counted.

Sign + Mind

The planet Venus rules Libra, just as it does Taurus — only here, in the zodiac's seventh sign, this celestial sphere is focused on the mental and social (air-sign) plane as opposed to the material (earth-sign) strata of existence. Such that, just as the Taurus female strives for a substantially ideal existence, highlighted by her love of beautiful things and a concentration on her own appearance, the Libran woman is most concerned with exquisite ideas — high concepts and philosophical ideals — that she can project into the ethos. Just as Apollo, the god of light and order, is the prime archetype of the Libran male, the astral Venus–Aphrodite herself is the heavenly patroness rightly assigned to Libra woman. The goddess of beauty, grace, and charm whose namesake planet represents the universal principles of union, balance, and harmony, Venus–Aphrodite doesn't manifest her power literally in the personage of the Libra as she does in the Taurus, who embodies these precepts on a personal, tangible level. Here, in the sign of the Scales, beauty, grace, and charm are elevated to the status of abstract principles. As such, Libra woman sees the world as a system of inherently divine order, a unified environment ruled by the cosmic law of cause and effect, wherein justice will, and indeed must, be done. In Libyan mythology it is the goddess Libera (Greek: Astroarche; Roman: Astraea), the Lady of the Scales, who enacts the equalizing effects of karma in the universe. And, anybody intimately acquainted with a Libra woman would readily agree that, when she walks into a room, one can't help but think: Here comes the judge. Indeed, one would be hardpressed to pinpoint a more unequivocal individual, one who is ironically narrow-minded in even her most liberal ideologies, dogmatic in the expression of her loftiest principles. In her defense, Libra's intentions are typically for the democratic good, at least as she perceives it. Strictly speaking, no matter how tough a form or manner her proclamations take, this sharp-witted daughter of Venus acts out of love, albeit not as personal expression but rather as a universal prescript.

In symbolic terms, it is the Libra woman's birthright to better the world, just as it is the Libra man's preoccupation to better himself. *Appreciating* every situation she's faced with, and then taking the proper course of action — or making swift and, arguably, appropriate judgments or actions in response — is the way she leads her life. For better or worse, she always drops the other shoe as a way to bring her existence into balance. Amelioration is her modus operandi. The aptly named Amelie in the French film of the same name is a consummate Libran character: Out of love, *amour*, she makes it her life's mission to right every perceivable wrong that plagues those suffering in her midst, just as she is determined to punish anyone causing such pains. This is the Libra in a nutshell – a walking-talking dispenser of karmic retaliation, whether in the form of reward (grace) or vengeance (fury). The Graces are emanations of the goddess Venus–Aphrodite, their dreadful alter egos being the Furies – both are also considered variations of the Fates. In psychological terms, the Graces and the Furies respectively correspond to *charisma* (mother charm) and *miasma* (mother curse). And it is this double-edged power of the scale-toting Fates goddess that the Libra woman has archetypally inherited. She is the zodiac's lofty high priestess, a personage mythically endowed as a sorceress as in the classic figures of Circe (a personification of the karmic circle, the syllable *ka* aptly being the seventh, magic, sound in ancient Egyptian) and her niece Medea, who is the graceful aspect of the furious Medusa. As myth has it, Medea was a good witch who, when done an injustice, went bad, killing her children in a vivid act of miasma.

The sign of Libra is associated with the ages 42–49, the famed female prime of life, when a woman's focus shifts from childbearing to child rearing – bringing up, teaching and preparing offspring for adulthood. Indeed, such an epoch is distinguished by the imparting of knowledge, the instilling of ideals, and the designing of future fates of those under one's protection. The literary character who has most poignantly immortalized this period of 'prime' is Miss Jean Brodie – the name Jean means gracious and merciful, and Brodie is derived from *broderie* (embroidery), as the charismatic character is, like all Fate goddesses, a weaver of destinies. Throughout her life, Libra woman draws on this prime archetype, forever taking on the role of the freethinking, if not freewheeling, instructor who enlightens and empowers others, indeed casting her charges into such roles as she sees fit. Like Jean Brodie, the eternal lady of the Scales passes sweeping judgments, sentencing others to a life lived stamped with her permanent, albeit subjective, labels and instructions. Like a mother observing, and then weighing, the strengths and weaknesses of her growing children, Libra assigns everyone she meets a purpose, particularly those individuals who might be of service to her. Still, she sees others in their best light – so much so that one is often hard-pressed to live up to her expectations. She may sometimes miss the mark, prejudging rashly, over- or underestimating one's talents or, one of her most notable flaws, failing to sniff out self-serving hidden agendas. So preoccupied is Libra with grand conceits, putting her beautiful all-seeing notions and ideals 'out there,' that she can be oblivious to the intricacies of life looming just under her nose.

For this, the sole cardinal-air (active-mental) sign in astrology, knowledge is

PLANETARY SYMBOL

The glyph of Venus – circle of spirit above cross of matter – represents the divine mind. Called the mirror of Aphrodite, it reflects Libra's image of righteousness, lending new meaning to the phrase 'fairest of them all.' Viewed also as a wand, it portrays Libra's ability to cast her designs onto the world, urging others to examine their own principles.

SIGN QUADRANT

The zodiacal quadrants correspond to metaphysical planes of being – physical, emotional, mental, and spiritual. The Third Quadrant is that of mental perception, particularly as it relates to existence. For Libra woman, importance lies on the abstract level of conscious thought and the projection of principled thought-forms onto society. Venus' subjective beautifying power is mentally objectified into such lovely concepts as justice, art, and social order.

SIGN GLYPH

The Libran emblem suggests balance between day and night, summer and winter – the autumnal equinox ushers in the sign of Libra. Libra is the only sign with an inanimate symbol. The Scales represent equality in the sexes. Astraea, the Lady of the Scales, was goddess of justice and karmic law. Libra women inspire similar respect as 'symbols' of good. She is emblematic, especially to men, who view her as a pendant alternately meaning counterpart and ornamental trinket.

ELEMENT + QUALITY

The air element connotes mental and social experience. The cardinal quality signifies a call to action and initiative. Together the cardinal-air combination particular to Libra is best illustrated as light in all its symbolic forms: the visible world, reality, 'goodness,' order, truth, and illumination.

not only power, but also a force that can, and must, be pointedly directed. As the first sign of the second half of the astrological wheel, kicking off the zodiac's Third Quadrant – that of the metaphysical level of the mind and perception – Libra represents a flip-side reinterpretation of existence as originally put forth by the zodiac's first sign of Aries, Libra's lower 'octave' and so-called 'opposite.' The masculine sign of Aries, ruled by macho Mars, is followed by the feminine sign of Taurus, ruled by dainty Venus; masculine Libra is also governed by Venus, just as the following (feminine) sign of Scorpio is coruled by Mars. Long story short: Libra is the zodiac's Sadie Hawkins whereby Venus, purported to be the passive feminine principle, now becomes the active force of this masculine sign. And just as active-masculine energy can be characterized by the raw, overt physicality associated with the spear-toting sign of Aries, the active-female energy in Libra is the unseen, spirited power of the mind, personified by that sorceress-priestess wielding her wand. In Taurus, love, grace, beauty, and charm are physical, sensual possessions, passive attributes designed to attract a partner. For Libra female, those nouns become verbs: to love in the sense of appreciating and ameliorating; to grace in the sense of beautifying and honoring, as well as offering grace in the form of forgiveness and mercy, essential components to the overall ideal of justice that the lady of the Scales so vehemently represents. And charm, like grace, can denote a magic all its own, as both may be synonymous with a sort of invocation.

Just as Libran writer-philosopher Florence Scovel Shinn titled her famous treatise on the magic of positive thinking *Your Word Is Your Wand,* such a mantra seems to be encoded in the psyche of every female born under this sign. Like an ancient sibyl or sorceress, Libra is seemingly enabled, in keeping with the cardinal-air combination of her sign, to take action on the astral plane. Whereas the self-inventive men of the sign use this ability, intrinsically, to make themselves over into a 'character' thought-form of their own imagining, the Scales woman is rather blessed with the talent to cast her thoughts, like spells, into the ether with the pointed intention of seeing her designs materialize. In simple terms, Libra possesses such outsized conviction in her infamous ideals that she *realizes* them into being. In fact, it is a force of which she must take conscious rein, for even her slightest whims have a way of taking root, such is the power of even a suggestion of her will. Indeed, as the astrological purveyor of karmic activity, she proves the old adage 'be careful what you wish for.' The zodiac's little magistrate, she rarely wastes time or brainpower on interests or causes that may never yield her desired effects. She designs her life and is never one to sit idly by and passively go with the flow. And yet, her precise plans are often kept under wraps. Libra seems to always luck into situations – from the outside, she leads a charmed life – but the hard and fast truth is that she's a careful conjurer, a woman who takes great pains to weave her way into opportunities she has had the prescience to approach. She knows – and let this be a lesson to all of us – that in order to get what you want in life, you must behave as if you already have it. In so doing, she finds that life conspires with her; whatever road to success Libra chooses will invariably rise to meet her. Such is the energy of Venus, working actively on the astral plane: Libra strives to form a perfect union between herself and her desired circumstance, no matter how lofty, by psyching herself into being equal to it. It takes tremendous mental effort, but by sending the right messages, she convinces first herself, then others, that she is, indeed, a prime individual, one wrought from the finest human fiber. Consequently, she continuously improves the unfolding fabric of her life. Libra chooses to be choice, thereby priming herself for the best that life has to offer.

A list of famous Libra women – including the likes of Greer Garson, Helen Hayes, Gwyneth Paltrow, Emily Post, Julie Andrews, Angela Lansbury, Eleanor Roosevelt, Susan Sarandon, Olivia Newton-John, Deborah Kerr, Catherine Deneuve, Barbara Walters, and Linda McCartney – reveals that women born under the sign of the Scales are often, to some degree, beyond reproach: peerless, if not spotless, goody-goodies. (At the very least, one cannot help but think of them that way.) In actuality, Libra woman unequivocally abhors these labels – although she'd have to admit having a heavy hand in creating such an image. Whether she takes a high-minded political stance, puts on lofty airs, or otherwise plays the part of society's high priestess, Libra lives her life on a soapbox, pedestal, or pulpit of her own design. While she perceives all other women as wallowing, in one way or another, in the mire of their womanhood, she simply breezes in and takes what she assumes to be her rightful place in the world: as a man's equal.

Though Libra has no designs on dominating a mate, never wanting more or less than a fifty-fifty union, she can't help but come across as seeming 'above' most men. She is committed to living an ideal existence, a relative state of perfection that she perceives as an absolute – a dynamic symptomatic of her sign, distinguished, as it is, by the projection of Venus' subjective energy objectively out onto the world. After all, Libra is the sign of art, an ideal state itself, which, though forever bound to the realm of subjectivity (opinion), is arguably meant to achieve the absolute (truth). To Libra, it is essential that her life imitate art, and/or vice versa, ad infinitum. Undoubtedly, Libras of both sexes are true artistes, but whereas the male of the sign is his own most vivid masterpiece, the female Scales makes glorious compositions of her experience.

POLARITY

Females in masculine signs (fire, air) are not aligned with the gender polarity of the sign and thus enact instead of embody the quality-element combination of the sign. Libra woman seeks to cast light (cardinal-air) in her establishment of myriad thought-forms and high ideals. As the zodiac's illuminating counselor, Libra champions the causes of her intimates, with whom she seeks to share a higher 'courtly' love.

7

SIGN NUMBER

The number of divine order in the universe: Light is made of seven hues; diatonic scales in music are made of seven notes; as model for the week, the world was created in seven days. There are seven virtues, seven deadly sins, seven pillars of wisdom, seven sacraments, seven heavens. The Seven Sisters, also known as the Pleiades in Greek mythology, were daughters of Aphrodite–Venus, goddesses of justice and fate.

42–49

SIGN AGE ASSOCIATION

The age group associated with Libra: the *prime* of life for women; focus is often on mothering and educating children. A pinnacle time – the peak of sexual power, as well as personal ideology. One has spellbinding sway over others; and mental power culminates.

PSYCHOLOGY

The Libra woman often suffers from a superiority complex; she can be self-righteous, contrary, and argumentative. Fear of intimacy keeps her from committing and sees her bolting from relationships, seemingly without remorse. She is apt to be selfish and erratic, and she tends toward promiscuity as a way to prove herself passionate. Due to a highly competitive nature, she has difficulty befriending other women.

The rest of us are merely part and parcel of crafting her perfect world – it's her world, after all, and she'll let you know whether or not you're welcome to it. She is, in a word, superior. And to Libra's mind, that's not a bad thing, so long as she remains optimistic about finding a mate of equally premium quality. For her, men generally fall into two, or hopefully three, categories: those who are attracted to her exhalted stature, albeit all too often for their own selfish gain; those who might get a thrill from toppling Libra from her pedestal, convinced that 'playing on the ground' is what she really needs; and the odd fellow who, being similarly self-esteemed, makes in her a perfect match.

Rewinding back to Libra's childhood, we see the seeds of her self-righteousness already taking root. In general, a girl born under the sign of the Scales has either an idyllic childhood characterized by the presence of lovingly detached parents, both of whom dote on her every whim, or, and this is far more typical, she is the product of divorce. In the first scenario, Libra bears witness to a model marriage, one that allows her parents separate but equal power in the relationship as well as influence over their child's upbringing – Libra girl is almost always the offspring of two strong-willed individualists. Her parents are generally extroverted, liberal, career-minded types who treat the Libra child as their equal. In such a case, Libra is indulged, considered the perfect child, not having to put on a show like the Libra male to win such an honorable label, and continually given the impression that she can do no wrong. Instilled with so much confidence, the lucky little Libra born under Venus, called the lesser benefic, thus expects her charmed life to continue indefinitely. In the second scenario, in which Libra's parents are contentious, the domestic dynamic is markedly different. However, her resulting determination for perfection still surfaces – and one might say, with a vengeance. Here, her paradigm of coupling is based upon cutting one's losses – *marriage* and *divorce* are both attributes of Libra's 7th Astrological House. Unlike the Libra male, whose infamously incompatible parents typically stay together despite their differences, creating in him the tendency to rationalize, if not compartmentalize, experience, the second-scenario Scales girl is, ironically, sent the same message as the formerly mentioned perfect Libra princess: that she needn't 'make do' or settle for the status quo. Situations and people, even loved ones, are dispensable, she gleans, if they don't serve her ideal purposes. It is no great surprise then that, from the get-go, one feels scrutinized by the Libra woman – as if she is scanning your psyche with a brilliant searchlight, weighing your strengths and weaknesses, judging whether or not you're worth knowing or nurturing as a friend.

Body + Soul

It can take anywhere from an evening's conversation to a month's worth of vague interaction before Libra lets a person 'in,' while always reserving her right to opt out. Still, despite her signature and very conscious attempt to appear removed, there is something luminously attractive about her. As her sign's scales glyph suggests – the symbol alternately reads as the setting Sun or (twinkle, twinkle) the first evening star, Venus – Libra woman has a stellar quality that draws more men to hit on her, faster, than any other female on the astrological block. But clearly, her astral projections proceed her: Rarely is she ever approached in a brusque or brutish manner, as even a total stranger will feel inspired to clear his throat, slick his hair, and be on his best behavior before uttering, or stuttering, his first introductory word. From the start, a man can't tell whether he's coming or going with her – Libra's mien is as much warm and welcoming as it is standoffish. Like that sign-symbol suggests, she seems to hover on some distant horizon: not the blazing-noon August Sun of the Leo woman with her blatant intentions, but rather the still, soft light of dusk October, a balanced, chilly heat. To be sure, it's a mixed message she's sending; being enigmatic, she finds, buys the discerning Libra time to decide whether to assign a person some placement in her life or to reject him or her altogether. The decision is always hers – which may explain why one feels an unconscious need to impress her with a sense of worthiness. Indeed, it is remarkable how the most esteemed individuals find themselves bowing and scraping in the presence of the zodiac's seemingly impartial judge. Meanwhile, it's the reserve of her judgment that sends the rest of us jumping through hoops.

Like her planet, Venus, which only appears to be a star – reflecting the Sun's radiance back to we mortals here on Earth – Libra doesn't necessarily manufacture the beneficence she seems to be beaming. Even when in the foulest humor, she cannot help but exude a sense of goodness and light. This is a blessing for Libra, and also a curse: Just as Libran actresses often have to fight against being typecast in upright, if not uptight, roles, the typical Libra woman sends forth an exemplary aura, one that attracts others to her, men in particular, as naughty children to Mary Poppins. And though she is constantly fielding men's advances, they are rarely of a strictly sexual nature. Rather, Libra registers as the ideal girl to whom one must pop the question, though not necessarily to the exclusion of popping anything else – she isn't entirely immaculate or innocent-seeming. Unlike Virgo, who preceeds her on the zodiacal wheel, Libra isn't so weighty and loaded a female character as to

ARCHETYPE + MYTH

Libra personifies the high priestess, seer-sorceress, counselor-goddess arche-type – psychological emana-tions of her patroness Aphrodite-Venus – as Fates, Muses, Graces, Gorgons, Furies, symbols of feminine power. The Furies were karmic redeemers for crimes against women – those breaking the *ius naturale,* or maternal law. They tor-mented Orestes for slaying his mother Clytemnestra, though Apollo (Libra man's archetype) acquitted him based on the imposition of patriarchal rule. The sorcer-ess Medea/Medusa (who kills her sons in a vengeful reversal of Apollo's creed), like her 'aunt' Circe (circular wheel of karmic fate), are manifestations of Astarte, the morning star or Astral Venus, also called Astraea, Libra's Lady of the Scales – sovereign goddess of law.

BIBLE + LITERATURE

Libra draws on the archetype of the Great Whore of Baby-lon, a demonization of the goddess Astarte or Ishtar, meaning 'light of the world.' She was lawgiver and judge. Euripides' *Medea* immortal-ized the sorceress as a right-eous feminist who seeks revenge for being wronged. Muriel Spark's *The Prime of Miss Jean Brodie* portrays a masked goddess of fate — referring to *broderie* or embroidery — a weaver of others' destinies. Dickens's Estella is the stellar figure of Pip's *Great Expectations*. Ten-nessee Williams's Heavenly in *Sweet Bird of Youth* is the object of Chance's affection, hoping she'll be his lucky star, or charm.

represent a vortex of moral responsibility to men. Instead, she can give off quite the opposite vibration: Many a man presumes life with the cardinal-air lady Libra would be an absolute breeze — that he's found an ethereal female who is unfettered by the burdens of this world, one with whom he imagines his own spirits and loftiest aspirations will soar. Such is the auspicious air that Libra portrays. Naturally elegant and composed, she fits the bill of even the most sexist view of femininity despite being a feminist of the first order. She is too poised and classy, in fact, to come right out and tell one of the myriad men who fall in love with her daily to get lost. Libra always rises above, dismissing even the most cringing or difficult situations with a kind word, smile, or apology of her own.

Given the way she lights up a room, it's little wonder a man might expect Libra to illuminate his life. Over time, the Libra becomes very conscious of turning on, and (not always) being able to turn off, her shining allure. Strangely enough, feature for feature, Libra women aren't the most classically beautiful females on the astrological block; often, they look rather elfin, if not blatantly boyish, far more *jolie-laide* than a first impression might portray. But such a description comes as no insult to Libra, who is actually grateful for any slight absurdity in her appearance, hoping it might eclipse the perfection others are forever projecting onto her. The ability to undermine her beauty becomes important to the lady Scales, who develops a knack for passing people unnoticed. But going out with bed-head, draped only in a drab gray sweatshirt and distressed jeans, isn't enough — she has to *consciously* decide not to appear attractive, performing a bit of a spell by keeping her beaming energy under wraps. By the same token, no matter how offbeat-looking Libra woman is, all she need do is decide to appear beautiful, and everyone within view will find it difficult to keep their eyes off her. She possesses glamour in the most abstract sense of the word; not merely the physical charms that her Taurean sister often so desperately cultivates, but an automatic mental capacity for switching on, or off, so charismatic, indeed enchanting, an air that it often overrides the actual appearance. As glamour is etymologically akin to *grammar,* we herein again see the Libra's word-wand connection. It seems she is aware of the power she holds over us: A sure way to spot a Libra is by her smirky look of suppressed laughter, as if all existence were one great cosmic joke that she alone has been let in on. Think about it: Kate Winslet, Suzanne Somers, Heather Locklear, Gwen Stefani, Olivia Newton-John, the aptly named Jenna Elfman, Gwyneth, too, all seem similarly tickled when appearing in public. Really zeroing in on the Libra, one begins to notice the little twists and imperfections in her face — a crowded mouth, lank hair, big, pointy ears, blotchy skin, a turtlelike, thrusting throat – features without which she might just look too ethereal or other-worldly. Lest we forget she is born into a masculine sign, this fact rings true in Libra's trademark square, broad shoulders, her rough, veiny hands, slim hips, or other more overtly hormonal attributes such as a bit of an Adam's apple, a faint 'treasure trail' leading down from the navel, or a strained, croaky voice that often cracks like an adolescent boy's. Still, such traits only ever make her appear companionable – lending a masculine edge to her delicate femininity that augments a palsy accessibility and prevents her high-priestess persona from becoming prohibitively off-putting. In fact, for all her powerfully enchanting qualities, nothing seems to prevent Libra from being considered a lucky charm, ever so dazzling while dangling from a man's arm.

In a way, Libra's physical appearance belies her need to be respected for her intellectual capabilities. First of all, she is often blond, though a dirty version. Even when of a dark-skinned ethnic extraction, in comparison to other females in her family she will be the *fairest* of them all – if only such a label were more readily applied to her judicious mind, the Libra mightn't work so hard at concealing that signature grin. Her skin appears poreless, though sometimes dry and flaky, her cheeks flushing apple-red with every registered emotion. Her eyes, regardless of racial heritage, are pale: a gray-blue instead of bright, hazel-green or gold-flecked brown. Libra's face is serene but for that eternal grimace; her eyes, too, seem to be laughing. She boasts strong cheekbones in a rounded, rather meaty doll-face that rarely looks taut or gaunt. Her mouth is a perfectly drawn bow-shape, just ample enough to escape a thin-lipped look. Though often slightly taller than average, she's rarely towering – there are, as a result, few Libra supermodels – and despite her goodly height, she tends to be if only a tad waifish. A slip of a woman, she generally fits into so-called 'perfect' sizes: a 6 dress, 34-B bra, and 7½ shoe. Libra breezes in and out of shops, seemingly able to wear pretty much anything. Most Libras are notorious thrift-shoppers, drawn to vintage styles that project a classic workforce attitude – the 7th House is that of *grandparents,* and Libra especially emulates her grandmother(s), and all the more so if that esteemed elder was a career woman. Tweeds, tailored suits, and other such throwbacks define her trademark style. Generally long-legged and lanky, Libra has no problem donning a bikini: With hipbones protruding dramatically frontward, the waistband of her bottoms stretching over them, passersby are invited to sneak peaks, say, if she's sunning herself at the beach – something she should never do without maximum SPF. Her tummy is typically muscular, her Libra-ruled lumbar area being strongly supported, in contrast to that of her weak-hinged male counterpart. Indeed, like a poster child for Pilates, her every move seems to derive from this sturdy 'center'; likewise, she

7TH ASTROLOGICAL
HOUSE

other
the non-self
union
cooperation
one-on-one partnerships
business partnerships
love bonds
marriage/divorce
contracts
social engagements
agreements
compromise
lawsuits
civility
diplomacy
public response
what we lack
distance from self
grandparents
agents
identification with others
oneness with others
equality
harmony
the opposite sex
conflicts with spouse
attraction
balance
cooperation
other people
divorce
rupture
adversaries/detractors
close contact
who one attracts
open enemies
reciprocity
karma
compensation
public relations
fairness
impartiality
unification
strongest personality traits

makes a model student of dance, diving, skating, or other athletics that require great physical control and an outsized sense of balance. The Libra lady endeavoring in any sport is like poetry in motion; even if she undertakes a grueling physical challenge, she can't help but make it look easy to perform, as she does every task in her life – with exceptional grace.

Sex + Sexuality

Whereas other women might give their eyeteeth to be prized by the male population, the Scales woman feels a need to fight against such adulation. Unlike her so-called opposite sign of Aries – a woman who typically eschews overt feminine trappings so she might be treated the same as a man – Libra enjoys femmey Venusian-ruled accoutrements, but she sees no reason why that should stereotype her into some second-sex position in society. She embraces her gender-based differences, but doesn't feel they should preclude her from being considered absolutely equal. It burns her that, because she is prettier or more delicately wrought than a man, she is hard-pressed to find recognition for her mind and, in particular, her all-important principles.

Being born under the only inanimate sign of the zodiac is a phenomenon that cannot be overstated if one is to understand Libra woman's personality – or if she is to fully come to grips with herself. For men of the sign, being the inanimate Scales gives rise to the need for a strong concept of self – he feels innately unreal or unnatural, his 'issues' surrounding superficiality, artificiality, and plasticity in his notoriously indecisive character. For the Libra female, however, for whom certitude is rarely, if ever, a problem, the inanimate quality of her sign doesn't point to any sense of unreality in her notion of self, but rather an unerring desire to emblazon the world with her high-concept principles. You might say that Libra man is an idea while Libra woman stands for ideals. She is emblematic, a living symbol for what is good and right, a poster child for absolute moral guidelines – laws – that must be established to ensure social order and equality. She is the most noble-minded of all females in the zodiac, and yet her pleasing, comely appearance often belies the seriousness of her activism. Like her Libra brother, she can be viewed superficially, although for her it is in a most flattering (albeit, to her mind, fatuous) light.

One negative consequence of Libra's ethereal countenance may be that she is misunderstood as pretty but perfunctory – a knee-jerk reaction that suggests she lacks the passion, if not the courage, of her convictions. Especially in a society ruled by good old boys, Libra struggles against being considered nothing more than ideological window dressing. Like Catherine Deneuve or Bridget Bardot, for instance, both of whom lent their likenesses to be cast in a bust of Marianne, the female embodiment of the French republic and its idealistic credo – *Liberté! Égalité! Fraternité* – Libra woman often becomes the face of beautiful principles, eclipsing whatever personal axes she might have to grind. Gwyneth Paltrow, the American neo-Deneuve, is a symbolic persona whose very presence in the public consciousness has meant the return of intelligent entertainment in Hollywood cinema – she classes up the industry; but that is a role that has been assigned to her rather than one she may herself have taken on. Global notoriety aside, all Libra women fight this sort of glorious objectification in their personal life. Upon meeting the Libra, most men will project an exalted symbolic meaning onto her. Unlike other women who may have to combat sexual objectification, Libra struggles against being cast in stone as a sort of domestic Marianne, plopped onto a pedestal not of her own design. To most guys, she seems the perfect trophy, and to very few will she ever appear to be anything else. Her physicality, she feels, betrays her: Looking too much the 'little woman' and, even more infuriatingly, 'the good wife,' she invites advances by an endless stream of men who see her as a prime candidate for 7th House *marriage* and a conceived fairy-tale existence. But faster than you can say 'two-car garage,' Libra learns to stop such a man in his tracks. Like Jean Brodie thwarting what she deems the 'petrification' via the status quo, Libra woman rears her Medusan head, turning a man's symbolic designs on her to stone. Still, such love lessons don't necessarily come easy, and Libra's love life may be one of trial and error.

Libra can sometimes become preoccupied with having the upper hand with men, going overboard in taking a stand against being trifled with as a trinket. For this daughter of the astral Venus, a cardinal-air sign with its emphasis on the power of principles, uppercase Love is not just another four-letter word to be bandied about. There should be inherent rules of conduct that this woman, the zodiac's judge, expects to be followed to a tee. Only around a Libra diva like Eleanor of Aquitaine could there have sprung up the medieval tradition of 'courtly love,' a movement that, as the expression suggests, embraced nobility and certain order in the manner by which the paragon of all passions should be made manifest – ironically, somewhat dispassionately. Eleanor, historians have noted, was highly conscious of the ideals she sought to foster. All Libra women share her exacting romantic vision to some degree, courtly love being predicated, as it was, on the notion that the fairer sex held the power to bequeath or withhold loving or indeed sexual favor. By adhering to a chivalric code (gleaned from legends like Arthur and his knights, so

BODY RULERSHIP

Libra rules the lower back, lumbar region, kidneys – the organs that weigh and eliminate what is unwanted – and the appendix. Common physical ailments include kidney complaints and lumbago. Venus rules feminine attributes in the body, estrogen, and the centripetal flow of blood back to the heart.

popular at this period) men might woo their ladies fair. This is an Apollonian view of love, to be sure, one that sees human passions being elevated above the lusts of the body and civilized into set modes of behavior. No wonder the movement saw such a flourish in Libra-ruled art – poetry, prose, and music written and performed by the errant troubadours and trouvères (many of whom, we now know, were women), along with painting and scads of expert embroidery and tapestry work that would have rivaled that of any fate-goddess weaver. 'Courting' thus became a twelfth-century craze, fictional chivalry made factual human behavior, remnants of which have survived and are strongly ingrained in modern Western culture. In ushering in a custom that placed the power to bestow love in the hands of women, a rich court indeed grew around Eleanor at Poitiers, attracting noblemen from far and wide who were attracted to this dynamic of having to deserve women as opposed to purchasing them, in some form or another, or simply dragging them off in some dark-ages version of caveman style. To win a noble lady, in courtly love tradition, was a reflection of a man's own worth and principled countenance.

Indeed, as a young woman, Libra attracts more than her share of social climbers and would-be mover-shakers bent on raising their own stock via an association with her – ambitious fellows banking on Libra to be their Lady Luck. Needless to say, Libra learns to be a cautious dater, reviewing the men she meets like a lawyer deciding whether or not to take a client's case. Sometimes, against her better judgment, she falls for that tradition-minded man, willing to play the part of perfect hostess provided she feels the relationship will allow her the freedom to pursue her own passions – and not all of them the high-minded sort. In truth, Libra is an aggressively sexual being – don't let that cool Venusian remove fool you – a woman who hungers for sex as much as, if not more than, she does for truth, beauty, and goodness. Since this innate lustiness may, in rare instances, escape even her own notice, it's unsurprising that a man's pursuit of her hand in marriage mightn't be predicated on physical attraction but rather on a need for moral edification. This dynamic may be in no small way the fault of the Libra herself, who, in her zeal for elevated experience, overlooks the significance of her sexuality, suppressing her animal nature in favor of loftier concerns.

The famed character in Philip Barry's *The Philadelphia Story*, Tracy Samantha Lord, springs to mind (her middle name, from the Hebrew Samuel, the preeminent ruling judge in the Old Testament, means 'listener,' while her surname signifies her sense of divinity). A veritable goddess draped in white column dresses, she is harshly judgmental, indeed unforgiving of human frailty; she thus attracts a fiancé who loves not necessarily her, but the nobility she represents – in this case, nobility meaning both her principles and her aristocratic lifestyle. Eventually, she experiences a fall from this state of grace, via some comical run-ins with alcohol and lust, and in forgiving her own imperfection learns to forgive the shortcomings of others, particularly her once drinky ex whom she cast out for being flawed. Likewise, Libra's biggest stumbling block to romantic bliss is often not so much the symbolic perfection that men heap upon her but her own willingness to buy into it – a vanity based not upon physical beauty but supposed moral perfection.

Often, Libra finds herself locked into a committed relationship before she realizes the passions she's pressure-cooking. When these are of a strictly sexual nature, she might feel like Deneuve in *Belle de Jour* (a day-time equivalent of a lady of the night), playing the part of a dutifully pristine wife or girlfriend while, at least metaphorically speaking, her captive libido finally gets loose and sends her on a sexual spree of near-prostitutional proportions. Even more debilitating to her than carnal starvation, however, is the deprivation of intellectual power, though, typically, both aspects go hand in hand. Especially if Libra has tied the knot with some status-seeking suit under the guise of being the perfect bride, she will eventually have to break the news that he's gotten way more than he bargained for. Like Samantha Stephens of *Bewitched,* the American sitcom version of Deneuve's dirty-secretive Belle, she will need to let her mere mortal lover know that she possesses extraordinary powers. As for the zodiac's beautiful sorceress, nothing can substitute for the freedom to exercise her mind – the seat of her particular brand of creativity – which is linked with the more southerly located source of her sexual desire. Mental stimulation is the aphrodisiac of the Libran astral Venus. And any relationship that requires the suppression of her intellect will also anesthetize her erotic urges. In the world of creative ideas, the cardinal-air Libra, with her pointed intellect, rules; even Darrin Stephens soon catches on that Samantha is more brilliant than he is at coming up with snappy commercial slogans; and indeed, when she is 'allowed' to work her magic on the astral intellectual plane, as witch or behind-the-scenes advertising whiz, she's a much happier camper on the home front, if not specifically between the sheets. Likewise, the telegenic Libra, who, incidentally, tends to speak in clever sound bites, is seen by many men to be the proverbial woman behind the man, empowering him to go forth and conquer in the professional world (if not secretly doing his homework for him beforehand).

As the primary archetype living and breathing in every Libra woman, Medea (media?), that sorceress-princess extraordinaire, was sought out by the famously questing Jason to help him achieve his heroic aims. This is exactly what Libra represents to men; and even if she has thus far managed to sidestep all the slick opportunists seeking some pretty paragon of virtue to parade

Neve Campbell
Janeane Garafolo
Suzzy Roche
Sharon Osbourne
Rachael Leigh Cook
Fran Drescher
Lynn Anderson
Romy Schneider
Helen Hayes
Lillian Gish
Eleanora Duse
Sarah Bernhardt
Heather Watts
Emily Post
Marcia Kilgore
Donna Karan
Madelyn Kahn
Barbara Walters
Margaret Thatcher
Eleanor Roosevelt
Doris Lessing
Florence Scovell Shinn
Carrie Fisher
Penny Marshall
Wendy Wasserstein
Annie Liebovitz
Martina Navratilova
Martina Hingis
Jane Smiley
Janet Gaynor
Mary McFadden
Ethel Rosenberg
Frances Willard
Edith Abbot
Lilly Langtry
Katherine Mansfield
Anne Rice
Edith Galt Wilson
Margot Kidder
Melina Mercouri
Lotte Lenya
Eleanor of Aquitaine
Juliet Prowse
Linda Hamilton
Moon Zappa
Jenny Lind
Sarah Ferguson
Linda Darnell
Rona Barrett
Annette Funicello

through life for their own self-aggrandizement, Libra woman is still astro-logically designed to take up a loved one's case, to champion his causes in such a way as will benefit them mutually. First, like Medea, Libra is the original creative director, PR or talent agent, uniquely qualified to cast her partner, like a seed, into the ether of public awareness – she is the zodiac's premier broad-caster and she will do everything possible to speed the plow of her main man's pursuits. For her, intellectual and artistic interests go hand in hand with romantic investment. Second, she usually performs the exact same professional function as her lover, and helping him achieve is part and parcel of her own job or position – unsurprisingly, she is usually involved in media to some extent.

Prizing artistic truth above all other virtues, Libra is drawn to those Jasonian 'indies' who have already demonstrated autonomy by striking out on their own. Such a man appeals to her own love of *liberté* – women solely seeking *sécurité* have, according to Libra, fallen victim to the status quo. Even when going for the guy in the suit, Libra will harbor the hope that her man is operating from a 'place' of creative integrity – after all, it's the artist, not the adman, in Darrin that Samantha cherishes. She has no deliberate designs on working together with her lover, since such an arrangement smacks of co-dependency; instead, she seeks interdependence, such that her efforts might contribute to his goals while also fueling her own. It's a man's self-sufficiency that attracts her in the first place – as a child she learned that togetherness is only airtight when founded on that 'perfect' balance of autonomy and co-operation. So long as it is her decision to be a helpmate, she will do her equal part, and all is right with the world. Unless, of course, she finds herself being used. Then watch out. As a reminder, the Medea myth doesn't end well: Discovering that Jason has another princess on the side, Medea destroys all they created together (their children) in a gruesome but accurate symbolic repre-sentation of Libra's total retaliatory wrath. For one so loyal, boorish treatment comes as a particular shock. And as recompense for compounding injury with insult, she will seek vengeance in multifold fashion. In this way, she truly personifies the principle of instant karmic payback.

Even when all remains rosy in her relationship, Libra will only surrender to commitment in small increments, over time. Especially when she comes from a broken home, her signature detachment is designed to ward off the hurt she felt and witnessed as a child. Actually, it's this very distance that, on the negative side, causes her to be objectified by men; on a positive note, it helps her to function objectively in those notorious love-work relationships. Not investing too deeply, too quickly, also enables her to remain friends with her exes, a slew of whom often make up her close circle of cronies – such a casual attitude would be impossible for most of us to muster. But with her continual crushes Libra can't afford to fall in love easily. A real lookist, the Scales lady is the male-modelizer of the zodiac, her Venus-ruled masculine sign being most concerned with manly beauty. And the prettier the boy the better: She is drawn to often younger, smooth, and arguably androgynous guys, never one to be turned on by the rugged, hairy he-men of the pack. Sadie Hawkins that she is, Libra doesn't hesitate to make the first move on a man, sex being a rather casual affair. Even when directly hit upon by this stellar female, men will consider her aggression a flattering anomaly, convinced she is the demure princess she appears – that is until such time as she's chewing the buttons off his jeans. Only then will it dawn on a guy that this good-looking girl, one he'd willingly bring home to mother, is able to do some bringing it on home all on her own.

In bed with Libra woman, there are no set gender roles or pat responsibilities to perform. Her all-important insistence on equality comes startlingly into play when she and some young Apollo are stripped naked, one gorgeous androgen to another with only their sexual apparatus to define them. Just as we affectionately call Scorpio man the male lesbian of the zodiac, the argument can be made that Libra woman is the female gay-man, the über-male-mindedness of her sign freeing her from viewing sex as a loaded emotional experience. She allows herself to approach sex from a surfacey standpoint of two buddies just needing to have it off. As it is, Libra relates far more readily to the directive quality of the male mind than she does to the traditionally subjective feminine view; and so, with her mate, she's just as naturally aggressive as he is. Assuming responsibility for her own pleasure, she takes the pressure off a guy as well – still she won't objectify a mate to the point of using him as a dildo the way ultra-aggressive Aries might. There is instead a pervasive sense of mutual masturbation when in the sack with the self-sufficient Scales woman.

Libra is somewhat of an efficiency expert in the bedroom, far more proficient at getting the job done than she is passionately abandoned in the process. If orgasm is her aim, she'll have no bones about achieving one quickly, then opting to go on with her day. She isn't generally a sexual marathoner, not one of the girls who revels in being 'bored' for hours, pun intended. In keeping with being born into the sign of 'light,' she prefers prolonged bouts of foreplay, with intercourse brought into the mix at the right time, to all out fuck fests – this is another manifestation of her general disdain for purposefully macho men who, she'd be loathe to discover, feel they've something to prove. Sixty-nine is by far her favorite sex act: She seems to derive as much pleasure from blowing a guy as she herself gets from being munched – while it's the combination of simultaneous acts being performed, the inherent yin-yang, that truly drives her

STR8 TURN-ONS

younger men
artists, sensitives
smooth, sculptural bodies
veiny forearms
morning sex
sixty-nine
(active) grooming, shaving
hairy, muscular legs
Europeans
cross-dressing
nipple, navel piercings
romance novels
long, straight hair
bisexuality
quickies
foursomes
inverted positions
voyeurism
licking, nibbling, sucking
m-m-f fantasies
jetsetters, sugar daddies
(passive) intense nipple play

forward. The very thought of it alone is enough to get her juices stirring. Type-A Libra is always conscious of what she's doing in bed, and the mental picture of herself and a lover is highly erotic to her. Fittingly, she relishes watching herself with her man, whether in a well-placed mirror or via playback of a homemade video. She may pour it on if the cameras are rolling, if only to ensure not being disappointed when she later views her private porn.

Libra is confident in her sexual performance, aware that she possesses expert talents. Oral sex is her special province, and being on the giving end is, well, a heady power-trip for her. She thrills at having her man, literally, by the balls. In fact, it is a particularly Libra-female fantasy to render a pretty boy helpless, toying with his orgasm, bringing him to the brink, only to beg off and leave him whining for a finish. At this type of teasing foreplay, and screwing too, she is intuitive, economic in her movements, imaginatively mixing speeds, pressures, and positions. She'll keep her eyes open – the lights are on – fueling excitement through the looks and sounds she elicits from her lover. The best part: All this comes naturally to Libra woman; there's rarely anything planned or tricky in her erotic repertoire. She loathes dirty chatter, as well as feigned moans and groans – she is a silent sexual persona, of the school that talk is, indeed, cheap. Still, afterward, lazing about in bed, she's not above critiquing or praising the highlights of their performance. For Libra loves to linger in the glowing aftermath, and despite her pristine appearance, she's not put off by a messy sexual atmosphere. Men are not as 'foreign' to her as they are to many women, and so she feels as little revulsion for the male sex as she does reverence. Admittedly, the guys she chooses are often as smooth and pretty as she is, making her ability to feel such empathy not so much of a stretch. In a committed relationship, she may commandeer her mate's grooming regime, picking, plucking, and polishing him up, making him appear ever more her very own PYT. For Libra, familiarity apparently breeds the need to engage in grooming rituals as, consciously or not, she is determined that she and her lovely lad will turn as many heads as any handsome couple could.

Libra is a fairly vanilla character, not the type to be attracted by kinky scenes of any kind. Though, like her Libra brother, she possesses a potent bisexual streak, ménage à trois holds little interest. If she were to opt for a threesome, she'd ironically prefer adding a guy into the mix, instead of a girl – and only out of curiosity in seeing her mate explore any hidden gay fantasies he might harbor. As with Gemini and Pisces women – the zodiac's preeminent fag hags – gay men hold a fascination for Libra; but unlike those other signs, she doesn't look to them for love. Rather, she feels herself to be like one of them. Libra is gender-bending personified: With a man, she's decidedly ungirly, far more like one of his guy friends who just happens to look like a beautiful woman – again a fairly butch gay man trapped in a demure debutante's body. On the other hand, when exploring sexual interest in another woman, Libra adopts an ultrafemme character. Typically, she is attracted to even more extreme towering infernos of femininity than herself, women with vivid, over-the-top qualities and similarly fierce type-A objectives. For all the worship Libra receives in life, dating from the time she uttered her first edict, it's nothing compared to the total salaam she'll conduct in her bond with such a babe. Regardless of sexual identity, Libra woman has a generally lofty view of lesbianism – the romantic love of two women is far more scared than any attachment to a mere mortal man. This certainly explains why she tends to avoid including girl-on-girl activity in her straight bonds. Women are never to be objectified – men, yes; women, no.

The stakes get higher with the so-called lesbian Libra – and we preface it as such because even the most gay-identified Scales gal will keep the door to heterosexuality slightly ajar just in case she gets the urge to revisit the penile system. Sexuality for Libra is one big gray area (her brain) wherein anything is possible and labels don't readily apply. The woman she falls for is generally an iconic embodiment of Libra's highest or most radical ideals. With such a lover, Libra may assume an almost initiate role, holding her mate up as a kind of high priestess. The tables now turned, Libra plays a blatantly obsequious Pygmalion role to a Galatean figure of galactic proportions. Libra's choice of a female love interest might very well shock friends and family – her partners are often radicals who seem so extraterrestrial in contrast to said petrifying status quo.

Glamour and militantism appear to combine in the gay Libra, who seems to have invented the concept of 'lipstick' lesbian. Beauty (her ruler Venus's domain) coupled with the objective masculine energy of her sign makes for an in-your-face sexual agenda that demands the planting of political flags – so long as they also look pretty. The gay Libra woman espouses the notion that women are indeed the fairer sex, and her own sexuality is based on the exploration of female beauty. For all Libra women, looks are indeed of primary concern, but appearances become an almost bizarre keynote in the gay Scales's relationships: Her partner of choice is often very much an outrageous version of herself in appearance – taller, notably voluptuous, more vividly dressed in cutting-edge designs or the rarest vintage fashions, pierced, tattooed, dramatically made-up, and flamboyant in her body language, yet typically of the same complexion, coloring, or ethnic background as the Libra. They are at once look-alikes, yet with the Scales gal ever remaining the more demure rendition of the two. Highly social, the Libra likes to make the scene, mingling

GAY TURN-ONS

tall, powerful women
Africans, Scandinavians
models, athletes
femme on femme
girl bars
rocker chicks
mutual masturbation
humping, scissoring
erotic massage
(passive) b + d
mutual grooming
lawyers, politicians
lights on
chic style
boycut briefs
high-water booties
mutual exhibitionism
mindgames
friendship-blendships
double-dildos
(active) worship
f-f-m threesomes
male humiliation
teasing, edging

with a decidedly chic crowd. She relishes making an entrance with her lover, turning up her inherent glamour to its highest setting, eliciting stares and whispers from what she perceives to be jealous and worshipful onlookers. Such parading about elicits a sexual thrill for the Scales gal; and still, though she is quite the little exhibitionist, she is never overtly so. She thrives on suggestion and seduction – titillation – not on obvious display.

Libra is a homoerotic creature, and it is always the idea of sapphic love that she finds most enticing. She has an urbane view of her gay sexuality – as if it's something that defines her as a sophisticate – the actual act is almost incidental, as if she and her girlfriends just happen to fall into bed with one another, by chance. Meanwhile, Libra gets a lot of chances, appealing as the consummate femme, to the greater part of the gay-girl world. Just as her own sexuality is typically not concretely set in stone, she is likewise attracted to women who are similarly iffy, more bi than gay per se, such intrinsic duality providing an added tingle to Libra's sex life. She won't be pigeonholed, finding a strictly gay-girl existence to be as narrow as living exclusively within the straight system. She and a lover will rarely suffer from heterophobia; in fact, they are not above entertaining the occasional power-play bewitchment of an unwitting man of model mien – not only for the use of his most cherished equipment, but for the pure shared kick of seduction.

Not having any specific role she feels compelled to fulfill – neither a submissive with the hots for dominant dykes, nor the short-haired sister swinging some strap-on – Libra takes pleasure from making love to a strong, feminine woman *as* a strong, feminine woman in no way eager to see either of them emulate the behavior of a man in bed. Her usual repertoire includes endless deep kissing, licking, nibbling, fingering, blowing, and otherwise creating a pastiche of tactile sensations designed to arouse her lover everywhere at once. Her nightstand always contains a few requisite goodies – vibrators and two-headed dildos especially, as she particularly enjoys 'riding double' toward a perfectly timed mutual orgasm. To the Libra's mind, after all, what's good for the goose is, well, good for the goose. Despite any hero worship of a lover, equal partnership is crucial to the Libra, who rarely ventures out into the gay social scene on solo missions. Stimulation is what her bonds are all about; fittingly, there is little focus directed toward the nurturing and nesting that defines most lesbian couplings. For her, life should be a shared spree steeped in cultural events, swap meets, book and music discussions, and other entertaining or intellectual pursuits. Libra and her mate must be friends first, lovers second; and typically, if and when romance fizzles, she will remain lifelong pals with what could easily be just one in a string of former lover-gals.

Couplings

Libra Woman / Aries Man
She's searching for an unfussy affair; he appears the perfect unbeholden partner. From the start, it's a power struggle – both are opinionated, if not combative. In bed, they make the peace – sex is quiet, but kinky.

Libra Woman / Taurus Man
She storms into his life, introducing new sensual experiences. They luxuriate in all manner of excess. This bond may never push on past superficial – they're in different 'places' – but the erotic connection is serious.

Libra Woman / Gemini Man
There's a natural flow – an easy rhythm into which they fall, often forever. If one attempts to take the upper hand, their groove turns into a grind. Creative freedom is crucial. Sexual drama is alien to such cool characters – it's all about ease.

Libra Woman / Cancer Man
He's that rare 'regular' guy; she seems, at first, too perfunctory a personage. Relating requires tolerance. At best, they're harmonious and hilarious. Sex eases tensions: Cancer's passive so Libra has the power.

Libra Woman / Leo Man
They connect as intellectual equals, each inspiring the other to think more progressively. A fast-paced, industrious duo. In the bedroom, they're bonded: Sex is fun-loving, relaxed – no head trips, no taboos.

Libra Woman / Virgo Man
Generally a sweet, good-natured couple. They often find each other when free of burdens. With Libra, life is productive. What they may lack in heat, this pair more than makes up for in tenderness.

Libra Woman / Libra Man
They're more aligned than most same-sign couples – a shared aesthetic is the centerpiece of their cliquey companionship. Scales of both sexes push the envelope of experience. Sexually, they're edgy, experimental.

Libra Woman / Scorpio Man
They disarm each other, an unusual experience since neither is accustomed to surrender. Over time, these zodiacal 'neighbors' notice how much they have in common. Sex with laid-back Libra means Scorpio's 'layers' peel away.

Libra Woman / Sagittarius Man
She's in unknown territory; he's relaxed in the company of such a cool character. In bed, Libra loosens up, accessing her naughtiest needs. Sag is spellbound: He's scored a sophisticated woman willing to satisfy his every wish.

Libra Woman / Capricorn Man
Forming a culture club of two, these characters draw up their own design for living, often passionately participating in the worlds of fashion, art, or media. Their sex life, though secondary, is equally progressive.

Libra Woman / Aquarius Man
Unusual and spontaneous, marked by constant change and intense affection, this pairing is rare. They're private, possessive. Lovemaking is elaborate, energetic, and all-consuming; even as a fling, sex is unforgettable.

Libra Woman / Pisces Man
Pisces is the maestro orchestrating Libra's life, perhaps with a heavy hand. She can't resist his inspiration. She's his muse. Best-case scenario: Their collaborations become classics. Sex is an ecstatic exploration of the senses.

Gay

Libra Woman / Aries Woman
In the glint of each other's eye, there's a challenge: Who's the more evolved sexual animal? Antagonistic from the start, they process tension as pent-up erotic aggression. Sex is each woman's wildest.

Libra Woman / Taurus Woman
This starts as a crush. Taurus explores femininity; Libra experiments with androgyny, allowing latent longings to surface. In bed, Libra takes charge, lavishing her lover with all manner of sexual attention.

Libra Woman / Gemini Woman
An aesthetically inclined couple with a common vision: to be expressive in all aspects of life. Et voilà: They easily engage in a liberating, invigorating liaison. A no-fuss affair in which both partners thrive — sexually and otherwise.

Libra Woman / Cancer Woman
Cancer seems the ultimate catch, but she, too, falls, infatuated with vivacious Libra. This relationship is romantic — gifts are constantly bestowed. At home, they're surrounded by beauty. In bed, atmosphere is utmost.

Libra Woman / Leo Woman

Libra plays hard to get, often abstaining until Leo absolutely insists. Socially, they're a superficial pair. With the focus on personal pursuits, they mightn't develop much depth. Sexually, stimulation comes from confrontation.

Libra Woman / Virgo Woman

Libra loves to be in love; Virgo is constantly forming crushes. In a partnership, each seeks perfection. Nothing ever seems enough. In bed, Libra is ladylike and Virgo longs for more demonstration, more desire.

Libra Woman / Libra Woman

This coupling is complicated, to say the least. Their ensuing efforts to surpass each other are arousing. Sex is urgent: The lovely Libras engage in an erotic battle that would frighten the faint of heart.

Libra Woman / Scorpio Woman

They're at cross-purposes: One only tolerates the other, secretly feeling superior. Jealousy is the culprit, causing them to misbehave. Disloyalty is their default action. In bed, the Scales is uncharacteristically worshipful.

Libra Woman / Sagittarius Woman

They are each other's ideal, but in different ways. Libra challenges her lover to utilize untapped talents. In turn, the Scales gal is lifted beyond self-made sexual limitations. Often it's a forever affair.

Libra Woman / Capricorn Woman

Neither lady suffers fools gladly. They're unabashedly elitist. Bolstering each other professionally is a focus. Libra extols her lover's accomplishments, ad nauseam. In bed, Cap finds new self-assurance.

Libra Woman / Aquarius Woman

An overwhelming attraction. They buzz with physical and intellectual energy. Libra indulges artsy-craftsy interests while Aquarius accelerates entrepreneurial success. The comforts of home carry more allure than any social circle.

Libra Woman / Pisces Woman

Libra hopes to make languid Pisces over in her image. What she doesn't realize: The Fish has her own plans, and machinations are taking place on the spiritual level. Still, the compulsion to repackage rarely abates.

Scorpio Man

the stranger

Scorpio man is a severe individual, strict in his behavior and belief systems. He is narrowly focused, always putting his own needs ahead of any responsibility to others. A solitary figure, if not a subversive one, he stays far from what he considers the maddening crowd. For this serious man, life is a loaded experience, not to be frittered away in superficialities – every day must be seized and squeezed to extract as much benefit as might be afforded him. He is a naturally probing character, drawn to investigating life's mysteries, propelled to scratch beneath the surface of every situation. No wonder others find him intimidating: He is bound to provoke and often unnerve anyone with whom he comes into contact. He can't look at bowl-of-cherries circumstance without immediately contemplating every possible pitfall. Pessimism, indeed nihilism, is his default perception, preventing him from being duped by phony appearances, while allowing him to root out hidden obstacles in his path. He takes this same approach to love, aware, first and foremost, of its inherent suffering. Reluctant to invest his feelings, he waits and studies prospective partners until he's convinced a woman possesses inner beauty to equal the bright, sunny look and personality for which he, ironically, falls. Lavishing attention on his lover, he seeks to be everything to her, thus perpetuating an insular existence. When it comes to men, he's attracted to someone with wealth and power to match his own, herein willing to be all-consumed by a psychologically and sexually intense bond.

Vĩĩĩ

PRINCIPLE

The Chthonian Principle. That of unseen nature and the inner workings of the planet, cosmos, and the human subconscious. Directly opposite to Libra's Apollonian exploration of appearances, Scorpio isn't concerned with forms but with the veiled *content* of nature – no matter his profession, he's a scientist or detective at heart. His sign's motto 'I desire' points to his signature secret and deep motivations.

ſign + Mind

Scorpio is the only sign in the zodiac to be coruled by two planets, Mars and Pluto, the influence of which manifest in equal shares, packing a constant one-two punch in his approach to life. Mars is the solitary ruler of the zodiac's first sign of Aries, followed by Venus-governed Taurus. Here, in the second half of the zodiacal wheel, we see the flip side of this pattern: Libra, a masculine sign like Aries, is ruled by delicate Venus, followed by Scorpio, a feminine sign, propelled, in part, by macho Mars. So, just as in Libra where Venus's feminine (subjective) view is cast outward into the visible objective (masculine) world of appearances – giving rise to conceptual thought, such as the branding of 'art' and other ideals and aesthetics – in the sign of Scorpio the opposite is true: Mars's masculine (objective) view is plunged inward into the unseen subjective (feminine) realm of mystery, engendering investigative thought, 'science,' and other such deductive systems for uncovering nature's secrets. Just as Libra, regardless of profession, approaches existence as the zodiac's artist, Scorpio meets it as astrology's scientist, philosopher, or detective. He finds it impossible to simply accept life, especially its arbitrarily assigned 'pleasure,' without at least trying to uncover some inherent meaning. Little wonder that the sign presides over the 8th Astrological House, which is concerned with, among other things, *regeneration, sleep* (regeneration of the body), *sex* (regeneration of the species), and *death* (a possible regeneration of the soul) – some of life's greatest mysteries. Most notably, it is also the house of one's *indwelling of spiritual being,* and indeed it is at this level of self that the Scorpio 'lives,' as he is concerned with the uncovering of his own secrets and hidden desires, not content to distract himself with what he considers a fatuous participation in external frivolity. He'd just as soon be alone, although he never quite manages to escape feelings of loneliness.

Like every fixed sign – the second in a trio that make up each of the zodiac's four quadrants – Scorpio can be seen as responding to the excesses of the rather opposite sign that precedes it, Libra, in a sort of point-counterpoint relationship. Whereas Libra male is the personification of the formal Apollonian Principle in the zodiac, Scorpio represents what is best deemed the Chthonian Principle – *Chthonia* and *Chthonios* being suffixes meaning 'subterranean,' which were attached to the names of goddesses or gods, respectively, to indicate their underworld aspect. In her book *Sexual Personae,* Camille Paglia recognizes that the Chthonian is, indeed, the opposite of the Apollonian, using the term to substitute for the Dionysian Principle, itself long held to be the antithesis of the Apollonian. In astrological terms, she's only half-right: Logic does indeed dictate that the Chthonian 'subterranean' Principle would be the opposite of the Apollonian precept; however the Chthonian and the Dionysian cannot be used interchangeably as they represent two distinct cosmic energies, the latter corresponding, as we'll see, most specifically, to the male sign of Sagittarius. In fact (and Scorpio man loves this brand of discovery) our interpretation of the zodiac reveals that, contrary to age-old scholarly belief, the Dionysian Principle isn't the opposite of the Apollonian at all, but rather a synthesis of Apollonian and Chthonian energies, just as Sagittarius is an amalgam, as all mutable signs are, of the two signs that precede it on the wheel, thus wrapping up a particular astrological quadrant – in this case, the 'light' and 'dark' signs of Libra and Scorpio.

Scorpio's Chthonian nature not only dictates his scientific approach to life's mysteries – his inherent need for proof – but it also points to his signature self-indulgence: That which is going on inside of Scorpio is truly all that matters to him. His own subjective nature becomes the prime objective, the only fact of life truly worth noting. In the fixed-water sign of Scorpio, assertive Mars energy is rigidly rooted in all realms that the feminine element of water would suggest – emotion, the subconscious, intuition, mystery. Fiery Mars, locked in on the subterranean level, makes for a masked aggressive personality – and a potentially explosive one. It also points directly to the sign's secondary ruler, Pluto. Named for the Roman god of the underworld (Greek: Hades), the planet controls unseen Chthonian forces on both the macrocosmic and microcosmic levels. Pluto is associated with the regenerative forces in the universe, such as cell growth or root functions in the natural world. The Scorpion 8th House also governs *growth via elimination,* which is akin to a plant losing its foliage so as to revert energy to its roots, from whence new growth might stem – Scorpio is, of course, an autumnal sign corresponding to such occurrences. The planet Pluto functions very much like the planet Mars, but on an underground level; in any case, their combination into a corulership is clearly an organic link. One sees this same connection in mythology, as Hades-Pluto, dressed in black armor and helmet of invisibility, is an underground version of Aries–Mars, the war god, war and death being thus connected. But in this link paradox abounds, revealing the kinds of mysteries Scorpio men find so fascinating. Mars, though mythically symbolic of war, is the primary life force in the zodiacal system, as if to say that life is a war of survival. Likewise, Pluto, the mythological personification of death, is astrologically associated with regeneration of life. Scorpio man seems to embrace this paradoxical understanding, as his way in life is to embody gloom as a means of

PLANETARY SYMBOL

Pluto is associated with subterranean forces, both literal and metaphoric. The planet's energy is concentrated on digging out secret and hidden qualities. The Scorpio male is unafraid of dark forces lurking in his subconscious and investigative of others, pushing people to reveal what they mightn't even care to admit to themselves.

SIGN QUADRANT

The zodiacal quadrants correspond to metaphysical planes of being – physical, emotional, mental, and spiritual. The Third Quadrant is that of mental perception, and in particular the concept of existence. For Scorpio, the unconscious mind is of prime interest; he feels that truths lie in the hidden realm of the unfathomable psyche. To reach reality, Scorpio asserts, one must dig. A life well lived involves solving one piece of the ever-unfolding cryptogram that is our world.

The *M* of the sign of Scorpio, as with Virgo, signifies Mother Earth. The upward arrow, recalling the scorpion's or devil's tail, portrays the sign's concern with uncovering what lies beneath. Scorpio has a number of associative symbols – the serpent depicts the sign's exploration of the underground; the dragon, a concern for riches; the phoenix, an ability to rise from life's ashes; and the scorpion signaling a tendency to paralyze others via his control.

ELEMENT + QUALITY

The water element connotes emotion and intuition. The fixed quality denotes intense concentration and magnetism. The fixed-water compound particular to Scorpio is likened to ice or other such crystals as salt or precious and semiprecious stones. Scorpio wants to crystallize aspects of experience that remain mysterious or concealed into a solid understanding.

transcendence. Finding positive thinking to be Pollyannaish drivel, he tramples rose-colored optimism underfoot and approaches existence from the departure point of pessimism and nihilism, on the premise that, from there, life can only get better.

The difference between Scorpio and Libra is like night and day – the often dilettantish Libran male, in particular, is always 'looking on the bright side' to the exclusion, in Scorpio's view, of life's harsher realities and hidden land mines. He sees such 'characters' as whistling in the graveyard via their superficial interests and social distractions instead of focusing on facing one's demons, of fear, failure, and self-loathing in particular. Such remaining in light, Scorpio feels, is being blinded by optimism and only casts a wretched shadow. Just as the Libran god-of-light archetype, Apollo, has his own shadow self, Python, the god of the pit, often uttered in the same breath, Apollopython, so, too, is the Scorpion male a pure embodiment of that darker archetype. It's the same in biblical terms, Lucifer 'the light-bringer,' when cast into the Chthonian pit, becomes Satan. The serpent, the snake, the dragon, the spider, the phoenix, the sphinx, and of course the scorpion are all dark, if not outright creepy, symbols associated with Scorpio, distinguished as it is in the zodiac for having a range of totems. Fittingly, Scorpio focuses on the dark, unseen realities of life, often wallowing in outright negativity in hopes of attracting a reverse shadow – light – into his life. His sign's motto is 'I desire,' pointing not to mere want or will but deeper, often darker hidden yearnings that are daunting, if not most dreadful, to embrace. In the Scorpion view, a life of quiet desperation is the direct result of not owning up to one's true desires or facing repressed psychological issues. The problem is, it's painful for most people to connect with, let alone admit, what they truly hunger for in life. And yet, it is through such an absolute commitment to deep desire, shutting the doors to all the so-called easier ways in life, that one may find exaltation – glory and distinction – at least, that's the way Scorpio sees it. Still, there's a price to pay: This dedicated life requires blocking out all distractions, which is exactly what Scorpio accomplishes with his seemingly antisocial behavior. Still, in so doing, he runs the risk of becoming a vacuous black hole – a fate that he can never fully escape.

In what might come as news to even the supersleuth Scorpio, his main concern in life is not to create bad karma, or for that matter, any karma at all. Immediately preceding Scorpio man on the astrological wheel is Libra woman, that lady of the Scales who is the embodiment of karmic law. Scorpio's placement after her suggests that he would seek to transcend this law of karma. And so he does: First, in his avoidance of undue personal interaction, he limits his capacity to cause and effect the flow of others' lives, as well as their ability to influence his own. Next, by fixating on his own truest yearnings, always seeking to focus energy inward in hopes of excavating personal truths, Scorpio avoids the trap of creating increased suffering – regret, resentment, repression – as the result of having expectations from, or smilingly tap-dancing for, others. Sure, he may meet with disappointment, fear, and anguish – demons that surround his desires like a dragon guarding its treasure – but by facing such feelings, he might slay them. In so doing, he hopes to feel redeemed; and as the poets and philosophers have long had it, it is via redemption that one escapes the eternal, or infernal (depending how you look at it), karmic wheel.

Like Orpheus, the quintessential Scorpion male figure, whose descent into and deliverance from Hades's underworld realm is the symbol of redemption, Scorpio espouses a 'to hell and back' model of existence. Orphic rites, a precursor of the Christian sacraments, prescribed set ascetic rules and acts to be followed to escape the cycle of life and death. Orpheus's rescue of Eurydice (the goddess of the karmic wheel) is an enactment of this escape in allegorical form. And as anyone intimately acquainted with him would readily admit, nobody is more ritualistically set in his ways than the Scorpio man. The whole of his existence, he feels, is a solitary journey into the depths of his own psyche, just as it is an exploration, often in ritualistic terms, of life's greatest mysteries. This explains why so many Scorpios become adherents of organized religion or exacting philosophical systems – they believe that by dedicating themselves to one strict, formal paradigm, they have a shot at being led out of the depths of damnation they feel, unfortunately, born into. In short, they hope their adopted dogma will eat their negative karma.

The sign of Scorpio corresponds to the age group 49–56, a time when one might feel the first chill of the autumn of life settling in. For men, especially, this becomes a time of solitary reflection when one is no longer distracted by the raising of a family or the building of a career. It is also often a time when many men divorce, start second marriages, or pursue dreams and desires long discarded. It can be a painful period, fraught with a sense of disillusionment; one seeks true meaning and, thus, redemption for wasted time or energy. In a sense, Scorpio man is this fiftysomething fellow all his life. Like Orpheus, whose mystic religion introduced the notion of 'original sin' to those cursory Apollonian Greeks, Scorpio feels himself born into a damnable state of affairs, often hell-bound to a childhood upbringing where he was emotionally outcast, if not treated like an all-out pariah. Mother love, especially, is seriously lacking for the Scorpio, who is typically born at a strained time in his parents' marriage or when the family is coping with

POLARITY

Males in female (earth, water) signs are not aligned with the gender polarity of the sign and thus enact instead of embody the quality-element combination of the sign. Scorpio man, therefore, isn't crystallized to perfection like Scorpio woman, a beautiful diamond in the rough and/or the salt of the earth. Instead, Scorpio man is a miner for such qualities in others, just as he seeks to unearth anything beautiful or valuable as might be concealed from the eyes of the world.

8

SIGN NUMBER

The number of mystery. The black eight ball in billiards is a signal of death, ending the game (of life). The lucky-eight-ball toy is a revealer of secret answers. The number is the symbol of infinity – in other words, not death but regeneration, akin to the message the totem phoenix delivers. It depicts not simply a cycle of life, but a spiral forever turning on itself. Cabalistic teachings associate the number eight with material wealth.

49–56

SIGN AGE
ASSOCIATION

Age of introspection. A time when external attributes and manly prowess are in decline. Inner resources are uncovered as a source of happiness. Scorpio embodies the quality of this age all his life, focused on internal longings and solo pursuits that see him in careers where he's left to his own devices. Many men get divorced during this time, corresponding to planet Pluto's energy of growth via elimination.

PSYCHOLOGY

Scorpio suffers from suspicions. He is intrusive and confrontational and can be bullying in youth. Teasing can become outright abuse. He has a notoriously pessimistic view of society, which can lead to nihilism. He may suffer from obsessive-compulsive behavior. Particularly focused on money, he can have a maniacally stingy streak. When he feels slightly crossed by others, they will be frozen right out of his life.

hardship or, in the extreme case, even death. As a toddler, he may be made to feel like a nuisance, rather than embraced as a bundle of joy. And so, he feels tainted; at the same time he may take on the character others have projected onto him, becoming a 'living terror' to his family as well as a tormentor to other children, more psychologically bullying than physically so. It will be a long, hard road from rejection to redemption, and often bumpiest for those who come into contact with Scorpio, particularly in his childhood and as a young adult. The good news, though, is that he only becomes nicer as he gets older, growing through the elimination of the pain he acquired early on.

The phrase 'children can be so cruel' was probably first coined after a Scorpio boy, whose notoriously devilish manner twists the might-is-right framework of boyhood so nobly embodied, for example, by the Leo boy-king into a sort of *Lord of the Flies* survival-of-the-fittest mentality wherein the weak are to be rooted out and exterminated. Unsurprisingly, he doesn't make friends easily, incurring the wrath of kinder kids who might, if called for, still kick his ass to the curb. Of course, his harassment of others is just mislaid retaliation for the treatment he receives at home, specifically by older siblings, who tend to treat him as a nonperson, his hands-off parents offering little or no moral support. He may form minipacks with other bullies, hanging on the fringe of child society, picking on any so-called weaklings who cross his path. Eventually outgrowing such behavior, and having formed few to no close bonds, Scorpio will retreat into an ever more satellite existence. Meanwhile, his manly planetary Mars thrusts him into an early puberty: Suddenly he's the kid, sitting in the back of class, scribbling battle scenes and growing a beard, much to the distaste of his still childlike peers who cannot help but label him 'strange.' He's eleven, he plays with G.I. Joes, but he's practically covered in pubic hair – it's not a pretty sight. At least not to those his age.

But older girls see what his classmates do not. Even the odd female teacher will eyeball him with carnal intent. Tabloid-magazine scenarios aside, Scorpio's mature looks tend to invite seduction at a tender age, with some advances stemming from older boys or men. Whatever the case, early sexual behavior seems to be de rigueur for the Scorpio male, at once awakening hidden desires while perpetuating a sense of shame, if not sin. Self-loathing only gives Scorpio more of a sting; and though he may at this point in his teenage years form a few friendships, he'll still come across as some modern-day Eddie Haskell, bullying the 'little beavers' of the world, in every sense of the word. Indeed, of the male signs, Scorpio is most likely to exhibit a sadistic streak, and though he's typically far more confrontational toward other guys, he can also be brutal to girls whom he doesn't necessarily find attractive, sexually teasing with a sting of negative attention, while projecting a 'knowing' sexual aura toward those he does.

Body + Soul

Though Scorpio is closemouthed about his libidinous exploits, of which there may be surprisingly few, he is an erotically charged individual – his very presence buzzes with sexuality – the result, perhaps, of having been so objectified, indeed sexualized, at so infamously young an age. Having already felt emotionally mistreated or outcast as a child, he is somewhat desensitized to the painful aspects of human interaction by the time he hits adulthood. Just as Pluto is the solar system's outermost planet, men under its rule are similarly peripheral. The 'loner' routine, Scorpio learns, really works for him, especially attracting women who suspect him of being 'hurt' or 'deep,' both typically correct assumptions. Not shy in the least, however, he's actually a powerfully present person when pinned down, face-to-face, nonetheless retaining as much distance as politeness will allow. He makes quick, pointed connections, careful to shake the necessary hand, making social appearances only when pressed or required to do so, slithering in and out of gatherings, for the most part, undetected. Though this behavior stems from feeling socially forsaken, Scorpio's signature stealthy comportment only serves to make him appear ever more mysterious and captivating a male figure. In a nod to his serpentine archetype, he has a sinuous physique, his torso thin but wide, like a cobra, his oblique and lateral muscles tapering to a typically narrow waist. He often boasts the lowest percentage of body fat of any man in the zodiac, except perhaps for Aries, with whom he shares his muscular Mars rule. Viewed from the side, Scorpio's posture makes a gentle S-curve, his long neck stretching slightly forward above square but sloping shoulders whose blades jut out dramatically; his spine is strong but supple, each of its tiny muscles rippling noticeably beneath his shirt, suggesting that, when it comes to sex, he'll really put his back into it. Scorpio's torso can be rather elongated, his lower stomach stretching endlessly toward an outward-projecting pelvis that, being bendy kneed and centering his weight on the balls of his feet, thus completes his S-shape. He has a springy bearing, like a snake, coiled but ready to strike. On average taller than most men, he is nonetheless not lumbering, ever light and slinky in his movements. If anyone can sneak up from behind to scare or tickle you, it's Scorpio, who, in a nod to Hades's shroud of invisibility, can seem to appear out of thin air. Most Scorpio men are swarthy, matching that signature

ARCHETYPE + MYTH

Scorpio draws on the archetype of the underworld god, Pluto or Hades. Not simply the lord of death, he is also the god of riches, pointing to the 'underground' realm that contains gems, just as the human unconscious contains priceless truths. Hades' myth centers on his abduction of Kore-Persephone. Scorpio man likewise gets to the core of experience with others. Hades wears a helmet of invisibility. Like him, Scorpio man is a stealthy character who finds mainstream social activity supercilious; he, too, falls hard in love and seeks to whisk a woman off her feet to live some private underground existence.

BIBLE + LITERATURE
Scorpio man draws on the archetye of Satan, the shadow side of Lucifer. A serpent-phallic god who impregnated Mother Earth in whose womb he resides, he mirrors the underground Scorpio persona. The serpent's seduction of Eve reflects Hades' rape of Persephone. The tale *Beauty and the Beast* recalls these myths. The little Scorpion devil is characterized by such antagonists as Jack in *Lord of the Flies* and Draco Malfoy (malevolent dragon) in the Harry Potter series. Scorpio at his most subversive is likened to the Grinch, a hairy lizard with a nihilistic view, lusting after other people's money.

The sigil of Mars, Scorpio's coplanetary ruler.

dark and brooding demeanor. Some, however, are so pale and bloodless, often with icy white hair, as to appear downright vampiric, a startling look that is that much more dramatic than that of his more dusky fellows. Whatever the case may be, there's a definite sheen to his skin, a waxen glow that reflects white under light. Photographs of Scorpio often develop with flash marks obscuring his face – he is unable to be captured, in any sense of the word. All such spookiness aside, Scorpio is often the unfortunate recipient of combination skin, such that his signature shine can be chalked up to a moist complexion that is often also, alternately, dry, flaky, and well, chalky. Since his coruler Mars is associated with outward, excretory functions in the body, Scorpio can also be profusely sweaty, if not hairy and greasy, the planet's protruding glyph speaking to certain other outwardly mobile attributes of his anatomy.

The sign of Scorpio rules the reproductive glands in both sexes, and this zone, both his own and that of others, becomes a burning area of interest. He can be sexually obsessive, raising his fascination from a purely physical level to a rather fetishistic one. But there's more: Scorpio's rulership of the sex organs seems to determine that this serpentine fellow – there's no sensitive way to say this – looks as much like a penis as any man has a right to. His whole person, frankly, appears phallic. It doesn't help that he tends to go bald early, often preferring to keep his hair severely short in any case. His locks are generally G.I. Joe-like – coarse, wiry, or otherwise reminiscent of pubic hair – usually reaching down into an uncommonly low hairline or Eddie Munster peak, lending him an even more 'hooded' appearance. The odd Scorpio has uncharacteristically ultrathin, even wispy hair. Like a snake, his features are all flattened together high in front of his face, his bulging, signature wide-set eyes, perpetually half-shut, recalling his 8th House's association with *sleep,* and often topped with a serious unibrow that requires plucking into submission. Scorpio's mouth, a grinchy tight, lizard-lipped slit, gives no less remarkably penile an impression than do his head and neck, which form one continuous weenielike flow as if he were forever trying to touch his chin to his Adam's apple. If only the prick-ly comparisons would end there.

Given the tormentor he can be in his youth, adult Scorpio still gets a secret thrill from winding other people up. Because of his probing astrological nature, he loves to deliver zingers to male friends or colleagues, reserving a similar, though stealthier, sting for women. He particularly delights in riding the more airheaded females in his midst, casually insulting what he considers bimbo-esque coworkers or acquaintances, albeit in so masked a manner as to be undetectable. He delights in seeing his slings and arrows soar clear over the heads of unsuspecting victims. Playing mind games is one of his favorite pastimes. Never quite outgrowing his Eddie Haskell tendencies, he charms the clueless, mainstream, cookie-cutter Cleavers of the world, forever in search of friends and lovers who'll let none of his put-downs, often disguised as humor, get past them. Individuals who pass Scorpio's combined test of intelligence and tolerance are allowed entry into his close association, never again forced to suffer his provocative barbs. When it comes to women, especially, he'll fall for someone who can thus disarm him, an honest beauty who refuses to dignify anything beastly in his nature. Such a display of salt-of-the-earth character is what melts Scorpio's cold, cold heart and is far more a factor in affecting his loving interest than is any excess of female pulchritude. Salt, as that expression suggests, is symbolic for the crystallization of internal human values upon which the fixed-water (representative of minerals, gems as well as literal ice) sign of Scorpio places so high a price. Indeed, despite the popular astrological opinion that the Snake is some sort of lecher or sex fiend, he is, in fact, one of the most, if not *the* most, discerning of males in the zodiac. As such, in his covert quest to find that perfect beauty on whom to unleash the beast, he remains the consummate undercoverman.

A list of famous Scorpio men, including the likes of painters Pablo Picasso and Francis Bacon, photographers Helmut Newton and Robert Mapplethorpe, scientists Jonas Salk and Carl Sagan, writers Albert Camus and Dostoyevsky, behind-the-scenes political string-pullers such as Robert Kennedy, Spiro Agnew, and Nehru, and explorers of the subconscious such as Hermann Rorschach or Lee Strasberg, reveals that this is a cast of covert characters fascinated with the Chthonian aspect of life: physicists, spy novelists, war correspondents, and other such subterraneans, subversives if not outright revolutionaries. These are not your happy-go-lucky types, but rather cryptic cats with hidden agendas and the requisite attire to match. Fittingly, many a Scorpio man dresses like a spy, in trench coat, turtleneck, and dark glasses, his 'double O's and 7' often bulging noticeably from sleek, pinched trousers, his infamously mighty high-water booty filling out any fabric in back. And Scorpio doesn't rule the sex organs for nothing: This boy tends to be healthier than most in this area; his serpent is generally thick, mighty long, and heavily veined, as are all his extremities, particularly his pythonesque forearms. And his signature smooth-talking snakiness, along with a whispering hiss of a voice, match his usual reptilian good looks, all of which seem designed for one singular purpose – seduction.

In every circumstance he approaches, sexual or otherwise, Scorpio can't help but come across as invasive, if not confrontational, like a hard-nosed

8TH ASTROLOGICAL HOUSE

sex
death
joint ownership
endings, resolutions
physiological regeneration
reconstruction/reformation
dysfunction
financial assistance
morale boosting
spiritual support
legacies/trust/wills
taxes
inheritance
insurance
secrets
curses
possession
sexual behavior/attitude
sexual climax
sixth sense
psychological rebirth
the occult
sleep
in-depth research
investigation
examination
mysteries
hidden assets
other people's money
spiritual change
spiritual indwelling
shared material resources
joint funds
money from marriage
conflict over wealth
wealth for glorification
material dependence
corporate money
control/manipulation
coercion

reporter or detective launching a probe. His every remark seems ever so slightly cutting, as if designed to dig ever further into the mind of whomever he's addressing, gauging their reactions, as he does, in a search for chinks in one's armor. Fittingly, he is not above making scatological comments or using bawdy gross-out 'humor' to provoke or embarrass. He's continually excavating for truth, the real story behind the endless sea of quietly desperate smiles. His constant searching of people's psyches is no blind ambition; rather it is meant to serve a definite purpose: To borrow from a luminously shadowy Scorpion songwriter, he's a perpetual 'miner for a heart of gold.'

Sex + Sexuality

Just as the Scorpio is continually performing a profound exploration of self, embracing instead of ignoring his deepest fears and desires, so, too, does he snap a searchlight on his metaphoric Hades helmet and delve into the hearts, minds, and indeed the souls of others in a subconscious attempt to inspire a rooting-out process. Scorpio cannot trust anyone he suspects of hiding from his or her own self. As a result, he tends not to trust many people. Indeed, his signature sting, he realizes, can only hurt those who have dark secrets they wish to protect. Liars, cheaters, cowards, closet cases, or any such individuals tap-dancing as fast as they can to avoid certain truths in themselves . . . beware! In adolescence, when other boys were desperately seeking to sully their innocence any which way, the Scorpio was already trying to heal the 'damage' he had sustained both on the home front and/or from his premature sexual experiences. Compared to others, he lives inside out, not so much seeking to make his mark, but to erase the marks he feels have unfortunately been impressed upon him. In regard to creativity, Scorpio will approach art, as he does life, antithetically to the Libra, who generally seeks to impose order if not an aesthetic veneer upon the world, beautifying the surface of experience. The Serpent, in contrast, likes to wriggle around in the dirt, burrowing beneath the surface, and when it comes to art, specifically, uncovering, often dissecting nature, or allowing its mysteries to work their magic.

The ironically named character Ricky Fitts in the film *American Beauty* seems the consummate Scorpion character. He is a social outcast, disdainful of superficial societal shenanigans, having to cope with a dearth of domestic love, channeling his attention into the probing art of film documentation that borders on voyeuristic invasion of privacy. Of all he's witnessed on film, what strikes him as most beautiful is a lengthy scene of a plastic bag being blown around by the wind – nature itself captured as art. This is the Scorpion view in a nutshell: Life and art should be about nature revealing its beauty secrets, as well as its uglier aspects, not the imposition of human ideas onto nature. And the same goes in love; one mustn't seek it based on a predetermined agenda of perfection, but rather allow it to be revealed by silently waiting and watching. This, after all, is the exact dynamic of the Hades myth: Alone in his under-world realm, this gloomy god had his eye out for the perfect mate; then, with one fell swoop, he plucked the springy Kore–Persephone from her hilltop, plopping her on the throne he had prepared. The fairy tale of Beauty and the Beast picks up from there, the willingly captive Belle's love bringing redemp-tion to the hairy beast who thus, via her affection, turns into a handsome prince. Scorpio man's love life, for better or worse, follows these precise thematic lines.

Damned to shame and isolation, most Scorpio males 'act out' in youth in destructive ways – going through some form of compulsion or addiction early on, whether it be drugs, sex, food, rage, or marathon games of Dungeons & Dragons. Still, his regenerative Plutonian energy is already sending him, while still at a tender age, on that road to redemption. Barely emerging from his teens or twenties, he may feel he has already experienced the depths of human despair. So, like any individual 'in recovery,' Scorpio vehemently focuses on his own self-preservation, often becoming so completely self-absorbed as to perpetuate his accustomed alienation from others. Fine by him. Being 'a bad seed,' he finds, has its perks, as it piques the curiosity of women who expect nothing more from him than sex, providing him with no-strings release while he continues to search for his own innocent and unsuspecting Kore, whose name suggests inner substance worth its salt. Indulging in this sort of near-anonymous sexual interaction wrongly wins him the reputation for being some sort of predator or unfeeling fiend – in fact, nothing could be further from the truth. It's simply this: Until Scorpio meets 'the one,' he feels he can't afford to be distracted by imperfect relationships for fear of missing the real thing when it reveals itself. A man as naturally libidinous as this Mars-ruled chap is compelled to engage in purely sexual experiences – in and out – before going back to lying in wait for love to rear its lovely head. So totally hands-off is he with these temporary sexual partners that he mightn't do more than unzip and be serviced, say, orally, otherwise remaining utterly composed if not completely dressed. This do-for-me 'position' is very Scorpion indeed, part and parcel of the infamous distance he insists on having from others. It's his particular dual dynamic: to be totally dominant over those whom he cares little about, while longing to lavish attention on a one

BODY RULERSHIP

Scorpio rules the reproduc-tive system, genitals, blad-der, urethra, anus. There is a tendency to genital afflic-tions, venereal disease, rec-tal polyps, as well as sinus and adenoid trouble. Pluto rules regenerative cell growth and the gonads.

true love. Still, on either side of the spectrum, Scorpio will always end up asserting his signature control.

His attraction to that salt-of-the-earth female he seeks to capture is a double-edged sword – a taste of the Serpent's forked tongue. On the one hand, he prizes such an untainted soul, whose pure expression of femininity is just as nature, not society, intended. As a rule, he loves bouncy, voluptuous, or even suggestively bottom-heavy, pastoral creatures with a blissful ignorance of urbane affectation or jadedness. On the other hand, as sexist as it sounds (macho Mars is his coruler, remember), he feels that such a guileless rustic of a girl will be vulnerable to his often compulsively controlling nature. As his so-called opposite axis sign of Taurus, with its motto 'I have,' is one of material possession, watery Scorpio, whose alternative motto is 'We have,' is one of emotional, if not spiritual, possession. After all, he is the Serpent, a son of Hades; and his devilish nature is nothing to be sneezed at. The mythic lord of the underworld didn't politely escort Kore–Persephone to his subterranean realm. He pounced and pulled her down, body and soul, in one deliberate move. Subconsciously, Scorpio feels he must trick that 'innocent' woman into wanting him, a symptom of his being treated as a pariah in his past. He does this by behaving opposite from the way he usually does – he treats her like absolute gold, sympathetic and administering to her every need. Sometimes he becomes so much the 'Mr. Sensitive' man, it's sickening; there is a breed of Scorpio guys – though all of them are guilty of this behavior at some point – who become so absorbed, indeed attuned, to a woman, you'd think this former macho man had turned into a girl himself. He is an example of how ease with the Chthonian feminine nature can go too far: Before you can say 'menses,' this man is sautéing tofu, arranging crystals, and crocheting tampon totes, all for the benefit of his woman's comfort and well-being. Just as the Libra gal is astrology's gay man trapped in a woman's body, Scorpio man is the zodiac's male lesbian. However, in laying himself at his 'lady's' feet, seeking to fulfill her every whim and be 'everything' to her, we glimpse Scorpio's ever-present ulterior motive: He doesn't want the woman in his life to need anyone else but him. Hades, whose Roman name, Pluto, means 'riches,' if we remember, tried to compensate for Kore–Persephone's abduction by showering her with jewels and other underworldly goods. Indeed, she becomes like an embedded gem herself, cold and isolated in his subterranean experience. He is often referred to as the narcotized god, as he, like the animal scorpion, induces a sort of suspended animation as befits the sign's 8th House association with *sleep* as well as *death*.

To be fair, Scorpio himself desires such a state of total absorption in a relationship that he doesn't even entertain the possibility that his partner wouldn't be likewise inclined. Fixed-water connotes a concentration of emotion, and Scorpio, in expressing his feelings, tends to freeze his lover in her tracks, making her a permanent fixture in his life, if not paralyzing her into a rather limiting role as his everything. Scorpio expects his mate to be his link to the outside world and, often, to take up all the slack – better known as the house, the kids, all administrative duties – in what will undoubtedly become an increasingly rooted relationship, so that he might go even deeper into his own, trademark solo-career pursuits. What, she might wonder, happened to the man who prepared homemade aromatherapy treatments for her cramps? Lest we forget, that same Scorpion songwriter also wrote the lyrics 'a man needs a maid,' which, on some level, can't help but become the Serpent guy's natural anthem. As the sting of the scorpion paralyzes its prey, the male of this sign can unnerve his cherished victim of love. In the extreme, Scorpio, like his fellow fixed-sign Leo man, may be a controlling Archie Bunker-type – his name seems a nod to the sheltered life he leads – expecting his Edith to anticipate his every desire, but to otherwise 'stifle' herself. And yet, since he only reveals his true self to her, Edith sees in Archie what nobody else can. Likewise, Scorpio man only lets the one person he truly loves glimpse his own deep vulnerability. This scary monster that the rest of us see actually *needs* to cuddle; starved for affection, he requires a dash of mother love mixed into the adoration his lover offers. Conversely, in the bosom of a true-love relationship, he begins to express love as well, a painful process for him as he was discouraged from doing so in his youth. In the Scorpio's defense, he knows life with him isn't easy, and he almost has to fight the urge to apologize to his partner upon waking each day in advance of the difficulty she may have to face. Sometimes, this hardship takes an extreme form as, like Persephone, Scorpio's partner is often removed from the usual surroundings of her upbringing and relocated to parts unknown. Being naturally disposed to gloom, he can only do so much to brighten her existence; and in any case, she generally won't see much of him. A die-hard workaholic, Scorpio starts his day early and ends it late, rarely taking time for the ritual of regular meals. But a bond with Scorpio is mainly an unspoken one, based on trust, typically devoid of constant discussion or overanalysis.

Sex plays an enormous part in reinforcing a relationship with Scorpio – something that also goes without saying. Indeed, what often transpires in bed with Scorpio is too lewd to discuss in the light of day. He may prefer to make a distinction between the bouncy, sunny figure he wakes up next to and the licentious lady (generally, of his own creation) he cavorted with the night

Umberto Agnelli
Neil Young
Gavin Rossdale
Larry Mullen Jr.
Lyle Lovett
Adam Ant
Ike Turner
Dick Cavett
Dick Smothers
Larry King
Martin Scorsese
Danny DeVito
Ed Asner
Dylan Thomas
Albert Camus
Don DeLillo
Ivan Turgenev
Tiberius
Hermann Rorschach
Francis Bacon
Robert Mapplethorpe
Pablo Picasso
Auguste Rodin
Roy Lichtenstein
Stanford White
Paul Valery
Fyodor Dostoyevsky
John Keats
Sam Shepherd
Claude Lelouch
Louis Malle
Lee Strasberg
Alain Delon
Peter Martins
Aaron Copland
Robert F. Kennedy
François Mitterrand
Jonas Salk
St. Augustine
Edward Morehouse
Diego Maradona
Martin Newland
Prince Charles
Leon Trotsky
Ezra Pound
Art Garfunkel
Ted Turner
Kurt Vonnegut
Alistair Cooke
Voltaire

before. In one respect, sex with a Scorpio man who's in love can be a sappy affair, the absolute flip side of his former draconian dalliances with what basically amounted to faceless orifices. With the woman he loves, he dives in headfirst, reveling in every inch of her body, squeamish about nothing and eager to leave no possible approach to pleasure unexplored. The challenge for this man, though, is to reconcile his more obsessive, often fetishistic sexual desires with a need to maintain a pristine vision of respect for his partner. No easy task, for instance, if you get off on your girl wearing a leash and barking like a dog. Luckily, for most Scorpios' sakes such requisite turn-ons aren't so extreme. Still, a gulf typically needs to be bridged between his fantasies and his fear of expressing them to the one person he most loves. He only feels more beastly; but, not one to repress his desires, he'll deal with them one way or another. As it is, he will have introduced his partner to his 'lighter' prurient pleasures such as anal sex, the focus usually being, but not limited to, her posterior alone. As well, a bit of bondage generally makes its way into the Scorpio's bedroom, first perhaps as an off-the-cuff suggestion (pun intended); soon, however, like so many other turn-ons he stealthily introduces, it becomes a rotating staple in their repertoire. Both in and out of the bedroom, a relationship with the Scorpio feels something like being body-snatched. Just as, over time, he may systematically isolate his partner from as much outside social interaction as possible – unconsciously, he fills her dance card with his own needs – so, too, does he (re)program her sexually, slowly acclimatizing her to sharing his desires. His hope is that she'll come to crave them of her own free will, and whether she does or doesn't is eternally debatable. With Hades, after all, Kore, the goddess of spring, becomes crystallized into the goddess Persephone, queen of the underworld, a female carbon copy of her controlling hubby. (At least she gets six months off for good behavior, which is more than can be said for the bride of Scorpio.)

Echoing the eccentric orbit of his planetary ruler Pluto, Scorpio man takes a woman on an unconventional journey into the depths of sexual desire – drawing out her profound, hidden yearnings – as a means of reaching the heights of ecstasy and, indeed, self-discovery. His partner should set aside a good amount of time, as sex with the Scorpio is rarely rushed or simply a matter of physically getting off. On the contrary, he seems to have mastered the lessons his early, far more experienced, lovers taught. Scorpio takes total control of the proceedings, fucking with his partner's mind from the outset; building her expectation, he sets a mood of anticipation that sends her wriggling in excitement and frustration. He loves for his mate to lie perfectly still while he ever so slowly caresses and kisses her, not allowing her to take his own pressing matters into her hands. He may even remain dressed, purposefully putting his partner at a disadvantage, using his notoriously large, long fingers to probe and pinch, tracing his suggestive digits along the length of her body. To the Scorpio's mind, restraints or blindfolds may only help to keep the focus on pure sensation, as well as intensifying the atmosphere of his wielding all the power. Egging his partner on, the Serpent hopes to force a declaration of her urgent desire. The buildup of sexual ardor to an ever-increasing crescendo is more important to Scorpio than the advent of release. Even once he has freed the beast, he may make his woman beg for it, rubbing it around her face, breasts, or pussy, teasing and 'torturing' her with the tip.

By approaching sex from this angle Scorpio is exonerating himself from the responsibility of being so naturally overpowering in bed. As mentioned, he is generally well-endowed and possesses a good deal of staying power; if anything, it takes him *too* long to reach a climax. Also, as befits his nature, he likes to go deep, often only being able to get off when he's sure to have hit bottom. He puts his whole self into the act, seeming to crawl all over a woman. Though he's rarely rough in bed – he moves as smoothly as his serpentine association would suggest – there is a strongly psychological edge to the Serpent guy's sexual relationships. A most poignant symptom of his fixed-water status, representing not just focused feelings but also stuck or blocked ones, is Scorpio's infamous development of fixations. In fact, all emotion, including love, cannot help but smack of obsession for this fellow. And he expects his mate to match that intensity. In the process, or rather as the process, he employs a bit of mind control, even if it only amounts to a Disney version of *The Story of O.* Sometimes, given his more lascivious fixations, Scorpio realizes that his partner will never 'go there,' nor would he expect or even want her to. A bit of bondage, role-playing, or a few toys is one thing, but his lurid needs don't always end there, and he's right to keep them out of the usual bedroom mix. These fascinations may manifest in a secret porn stash or through cyber sex in which he can explore hands-off games of master-and-servant. However, if Scorpio is drawn to more elaborate 'scenes,' ones that might even require a leather wardrobe or whips and chains, he's perhaps better off remaining a bachelor. And he knows it: Never one to lead a double life, the Serpent guy is nearly incapable of hiding something so heady as an S&M lifestyle from someone he loves. In such cases, he might consciously take a pass on the shiny happy women he feels a love connection with and find himself a female denizen of the night who shares his fetishistic fascinations. In such extreme circumstances, Scorpio's need for control only increases, and he definitely plays the lead in this theater of psychological sex games – one that might include enslaving willing females in

STR8 TURN-ONS

blonds
salt-of-the earth types
big breasts
ample asses
innocence
body odor
body hair
body fluid
(dominant) s + m
(dominant) b + d
teasing, tickling, torture
probing, fingering
mutual analingus
(active) anal penetration
maids, secretaries
mind games
leashes, collars
latex, leather
water sports
dungeons, vaults, cages
ob/gyn equipment
pimping role play
kink

a dungeon of his own design or at after-hours clubs that provide such chambers of sexual commerce. Acts of degradation and humiliation directed toward self-declared submissives are radical examples of his need for psychological worship and utter obedience to his powerful will.

Scorpio man's sexuality is black-and-white, decidedly straight or gay, with no room for gray guesswork in between. He doesn't believe in bisexuality, for men, that is – another symptom of that sexism that he projects, regardless of his particular sexual preference. Being born into so powerfully feminine a sign, straight Scorpio puts women on a pedestal (if not binding and gagging them there), despite his domination fantasies or, indeed, as a twisted result of them. He can, thus, easily entertain attraction shared between two women, gay or straight; however, he can't quite make the leap when applied to his own sex. By the same token, gay Scorpio commits to his sexual identity completely, and often at an early age – he invites the same sexual seduction in adolescence as does his heterosexual counterpart – in signature Scorpion manner, accepting his homosexual feelings as fact, not so much coming out of the proverbial closet as never stepping into it in the first place. To him, sexually ambiguous males are actually no such thing: They are simply fence-sitting cowards whom he'd like to see knocked off. In keeping with the Chthonian ideal that people are defined by their subterranean forces, not capable of mentally choosing whom they want to be, but rather bound to commit to who they already are, Scorpio chalks homosexuality up to simple biology. That his sign is steeped so deep in nature, and thus the feminine-subjective experience, mostly manifests as a need to surround himself with fierce female friends, rarely one to even pal around with another gay-male friend or, worse, a group of such buddies – he'd sooner have the odd straight male friend; indeed, he often does.

Gay Scorpio is that much more a loner than his straight brother: He seems to haunt the world rather than actively participate in it. Like heterosexual men of the sign, he likes to work alone, so much so that he's not likely to be contented with a remote corner office; he needs utter solitude and is often drawn to professions that require it. Whether a scientist, cartoonist, designer, architect, or superhero of some sort, Scorpio's private work space is of prime importance as this lair serves as a place of solace and regeneration, as well as creative output. He must be alone to function, a fact that is often lost on acquaintances who engage him in small talk. Scorpio seems to look through people, as if (he oft wishes) they weren't there; apparently, he doesn't have even one moment to spare for anyone other than himself. And this is one of the secrets to his success: As ambitious as he is, even when young and 'climbing,' he never seeks to impress or eagerly make his mark. On the contrary, he often shuns such publicity or hobnobbing as might speed the plow of his success. Rather, he's confident that he will succeed and sees no use in feeling rushed or riled. So remember, if a Scorpio seems to be giving you the brush, it's nothing personal – and for the gay Scorpio, this is especially true.

The gay Serpent guy doesn't casually date. Like any self-respecting Scorpio, he's holding out for the real thing, with little interest in interim interaction. In his youth, Scorpio seeks the company of a sophisticated man with whom he fuses on every level. While other males his age are barhopping and boy-hopping, the Scorpio might be found at his mentor's home, receiving instruction in the finer things. Typically, with sexual overtones, the Scorpio plays a 'boy' role to such a 'daddy' – in the extreme, he's trained as a slave to a fiercely dominant master. To one degree or another, this dynamic is intrinsic, a materialization of the submissive position Scorpio may have been seduced into during adolescence. In most cases, he'll soon slip out from under the wing of this friend and/or sexual guru and commit to the serious, solo pursuit of his ambitions. Single, Scorpio may procure a small coterie of fuck buddies who share his nonemotional, no-strings attitude to sex. Though a deeply emotional person, Scorpio can't invest even a drop of feeling in the mechanical processes of purely sexual experience. In such instances, he ritualistically takes the top position, enjoying an oral servicing before bending his buddy over. Detachedness is key and emphasis is placed on his physical power – many a Scorpion sports the requisite cock ring to, shall we say, reinforce this impression. But his association with such individuals will rarely, if ever, see the light of day. To those with whom he interacts from nine to five, Scorpio's personal life remains one huge question mark.

Though he's secure in his own sexuality, many a gay Scorpio will stay completely silent on the subject if only to perpetuate an aura of mystery. Inquiring minds may find themselves frozen out of society with him should they ever have the gall to broach the subject. Others may write him off as an asexual anomaly. Then, suddenly, one might learn that the cryptic Scorpio, who for years has never so much as hinted at where his proclivities lie, is shacking up with a rich and famous man – often someone connected to his own career field. The big question answered, one may still be left wondering how such an insular guy ever ended up meeting so major a mover-shaker. In typical Scorpion logic, the question is the answer: In biding his time, unbeholden to any other distracting entanglements, Scorpio has left himself available to pounce on the 'perfect' opportunity when it eventually presents itself. Unseen, he's been laying the psychic groundwork for the inevitability of such an occurrence. Still, it can be explained away in far more nutsy-boltsy terms: Via

GAY TURN-ONS

master/slaves
(active/passive) s + m
(active/passive b + d
(active) anal penetration
pornography
water sports
infantilism
tea rooms, glory holes
sweat, body odor
rubber, latex, leather
skinheads
(mutual) swallowing
felching
cockrings, pumps
anonymity
dungeons, clamps, slings
fisting
kink, raunch, scat
sex clubs, private parties
jocks, briefs, socks
masks, gags
blindfolds, hoods
(active) ball, nipple torture
branding, piercing
poppers, stimulants

his aloofness, gay Scorpio creates a mystique of (self-) importance; through focus on his career, he begins to receive the sort of creamy social invitations he finally deigns to accept. All he needs is the introduction to a mogul who sexually appeals, and before you can say his-and-his hand towels, these two are setting up house.

Like attracting like, Scorpio is most at ease with someone rich and powerful – his patron's name Pluto means 'riches,' remember, giving rise to the term *plutocracy,* rule by the wealthy – indeed, to Scorpio, money is power. To boot, the 8th House is that of both *sex* and in particular *other people's money,* those two attributes being inextricably linked in the Serpent's lustful mind. Face-to-face with some magnate, Mr. Aloof suddenly comes to life, fixing such a man in his suggestive icy-hot gaze. What he hopes to see in the eyes of this heavyweight is the same brand of self-assuredness luridly staring back. Unlike his straight counterpart, gay Scorpio is no fan of vulnerability – what he looks for in a man's eyes is confidence, conviction, and courage, if not just a pinch of czarish cruelty.

Sex, cash, and mutual career interests are the perfect ingredients for the kind of relationship Scorpio can get with. This sounds more shallow than it actually is: Because he is so obsessed about career, leaving little time for a serious bond, it just makes sense to share his life with someone he might also merge with professionally, in some capacity. The truth is, he, like his straight counterpart, wants to share everything with his partner – Scorpio can be the most exclusionary gay man on the astrological block when it comes to his romantic commitments. Sexually, then, he and his lover will try to fulfill any and all of each other's needs – and though Scorpio is the consummate top in casual carnal circumstances, love relationships often bring out his submissive side, without completely eclipsing his more dominant needs. What the bedroom menu consists of, from night to night, is anybody's guess – nothing, from the sordid to the sublime, is beyond possibility. His Chthonian nature doesn't preclude Scorpio from certain scatological experimentation to be sure but he only does unto his significant other what he would have done unto him. Group sex is generally out of the question, and even the odd third would need to be nothing more than a glorified rent boy who could be used by Scorpio and his mate, like two vampires tearing into their prey from either end. After all, when it comes to love and sex, the Scorpio believes one should share and share alike.

Couplings

Scorpio Man / Aries Woman
They might not embody each other's ideal, but their similarly defiant natures intrigue. A subversive pair with a complicated sexual dynamic – both hot *and* heavy in the extreme. Erotic addictions are explored in tandem.

Scorpio Man / Taurus Woman
Illicitness is inherent; they turn on to the taboo of togetherness. In the long run, their love may be a barren landscape in which little grows. But an extraordinary sexual connection keeps them from taking a hike.

Scorpio Man / Gemini Woman
He's bewitched – she's the one who'll alter his perception from dark to light. As time passes, she hopes he'll remain so reliant. Their commitment appears unbreakable. In bed, lavish fantasies are revealed.

Scorpio Man / Cancer Woman
Her effect on him seems instantaneous – she's that princess he'll perch on a throne. Cancer is unafraid of his spooky disposition. This is rarely a casual coupling. Sex is vigorous and athletic; still sensitive and intimate.

Scorpio Man / Leo Woman
A stressy couple, exceptionally intent upon success. She's out to prove her worth, no matter the cost; he'll cash in on her credibility. Tempers often flare. His fantasies can be hard-core, but she may well entertain them.

Scorpio Man / Virgo Woman
She's an open book; he's in search of someone to write on. But does he have the whole story? She's a complex character. Finding middle ground may be difficult. Sexually, he's in control. She's grateful to be guided.

Scorpio Man / Libra Woman
They disarm each other, an unusual experience since neither is accustomed to surrender. Over time, these zodiacal 'neighbors' notice how much they have in common. Sex with laid-back Libra means Scorpio's 'layers' peel away.

Scorpio Man / Scorpio Woman
A match marked by material, psychological, and sexual obsession. Strong self-regard coupled with righteousness might make them somewhat insufferable. In bed, already intense emotions reach an orgiastic apex.

Scorpio Man / Sagittarius Woman

Her worldly radiance is kept under wraps – she's a valuable commodity who should only shine in his sphere. He's such a persuasive partner – a departure. Sag feigns being forced into acts she's only too eager to try.

Scorpio Man / Capricorn Woman

He vows to make her life better, ease her stresses, and see her succeed. She's his steadfast confidante. Sex is most satisfying on the heels of an intense argument or inspired conversation. A mysterious mix.

Scorpio Man / Aquarius Woman

Any antisocial tendencies are expanded. Feeling superior, they team up in a you-and-me-against-the-world bond, but later they might turn against each other. Sex is primal, but inclusive: This pair enjoys other partners.

Scorpio Man / Pisces Woman

They'll experience sweeping highs and lows – everything is an issue. Living with him often means being displaced. He lands more lucrative positions with her on hand. Sex feels like sparring; the rumble is raucous.

Gay

Scorpio Man / Aries Man

Their connection is elemental: Sexy, aggressive planet Mars rules both signs. Aries and Scorpio share a profound physical compatibility. Scorpio is often the instigator. Emotionally, their dynamic is complex – anger is ever present.

Scorpio Man / Taurus Man

Evasive, indirect characters whose sexual relationship often remains secretive. Contempt and power struggles are built into the bond. A classic male skirmish, like Archie and Reggie. Scorpio's sadism may be their undoing.

Scorpio Man / Gemini Man

Scorpio is subversive; Gemini is the happy, shiny creature who exists on the inside track of life. Often, this is simply a sex thing – the Twins entertains prostitution fantasies and stern Scorpio longs to enslave.

Scorpio Man / Cancer Man

They're masked and cool in public, but not so behind closed doors. Their object: to live and love ecstatically, in sustained rapture. A completely compatible couple who merge mentally as much as they do sexually.

Scorpio Man / Leo Man

This pair is polarized: Leo seems too sunny to Scorpio, who lingers even longer in emotional darkness, as if to annoy the Lion. In bed, they do battle. Leo is enlivened by the scrappy Scorpion force.

Scorpio Man / Virgo Man

Scorpio isn't looking to shock; here he seeks to service. It's all about digging deep and allowing for transformation. Sexually, too, this pair seeks something beyond standard – they unearth equally experimental natures.

Scorpio Man / Libra Man

Scorpio is suspicious – Libra seems too good to be true. Here, the Scales guy endures Scorp's sadistic streak, but not for long. Sex is a struggle for power; Libra usually loses. He might seek a less intimidating lover.

Scorpio Man / Scorpio Man

If they can create an atmosphere of trust – good luck – old issues are resolved and life seems rosy. Otherwise, secretive natures have the opposite effect: The path is treacherous. In bed, old dogs learn new tricks.

Scorpio Man / Sagittarius Man

Sag is seduced and shocked by shadowy Scorpio. Physical compatibility is assured; emotional understanding takes time. Sexual expectations are great. In this case, the agile Archer has a hard time keeping up.

Scorpio Man / Capricorn Man

Scorpio is inspired by Cap's ease and acumen. As a couple, confrontation is their way of dealing with disagreements – soon, such struggle wears thin. Still, their sex life thrives: Even if they part, they may end up back in bed.

Scorpio Man / Aquarius Man

If seeking a support system, they might find it in each other. But turning joint plans into actuality proves arduous – they need a third-party perspective. Though they often drift in and out of love, sex might keep them together.

Scorpio Man / Pisces Man

A peaceful and productive pairing, especially if Pisces is the older of the two. Over time, they cultivate an avant-garde aesthetic that appeals to outsiders. Sex might be rough – Scorpio plays at being 'trade.'

Scorpio Woman

the specimen

Nobody has a higher opinion of herself than the Scorpio woman. Hers is an indomitable spirit that cannot be penetrated by even the most vehement detractors. Too self-possessed to struggle, Scorpio achieves her ambitions by amassing supporters who pave the way, if not roll out the red carpet, for her. She oozes feminine allure and foreboding egotism in equal measure, bidding would-be mates to 'come hither,' but to do so at their own peril. The zodiac's indisputable femme fatale, she appears unmoved by a man's advances, using such insouciance to bait him into working ever increasingly for her attention. Scorpio invented hard-to-get, an expertise for insinuating herself into the psyche of those whom she desires, without so much as lifting a pinkie. She's all mystery, wearing a perpetual poker face – cajoling, challenging, and holding all the cards. Naturally assuming a superiority with whomever she comes into contact, Scorpio cannot help but see a man in terms of what he might do for her. With that in mind, she sizes up each candidate for her affection, weighing his inherent potential, as partner, coprogenitor, and professional success. Scorpio wants the full package, and she's wary of men and their ambitions, which she mostly considers half-baked. In a relationship, she'll seek to coax out a man's best qualities while killing off his bad ones. With women, whom she generally admires more than men, her bonds are at once more spiritually and sexually based. Sapphic by nature, Scorpio is highly romantic in her gay relationships, which always seem to smack of schoolgirl crushes.

VIII

PRINCIPLE

The Chthonian Principle. That of unseen nature and the inner workings of the planet, cosmos, and the human subconscious. The term is derived from Chthonia 'underground,' yet another name for Persephone. It relates to the machinations of the internal feminine experience – the earth being personified as female. Regenerative forces of the planet and the reproductive process of women are both called into question during the 'cold storage' associated with the onset of autumn and menopause respectively. Her sign's motto 'I desire' signals this femme fatale's infamously hidden agendas.

Sign + Mind

What lies beneath: Scorpio woman, coruled by Mars and Pluto, is like fire and ice, the burning aggression and sexual urgency associated with the former planet encased in the frosty, elliptical energy of the latter. Physically, tiny Pluto rules the unseen, regenerative forces in the body, at the cellular level, just as, psychologically, it rules the reformational workings of the subconscious. From our earthly perspective, this small, most remote planet in the solar system soars to great heights at certain times, then seems to dip far below median range in the sky at others – representing the heights and depths of the human experience. Similarly, one of Scorpio's coterie of mysterious sign-symbols, the phoenix, is mythically purported to dive from a great altitude, crashing and burning, only to rise again anew from the ruin of its ashes. Not surprisingly, Pluto, named for the Roman god of the underworld (Greek: Hades), is associated with the astrological precept of transformation via elimination. Originally an ancient female deity, Pluto was at one time synonymous with Persephone, who later devolved into the male god's wife. Pluto–Persephone is likewise etched into the mythos as being plunged into the depths of the underworld, heralding autumn, only to return to the sunny surface world at spring. This is Scorpio woman to a tee: As anyone intimately associated with the female Phoenix of the zodiac will readily concur, there is no keeping her down. Indeed, it seems the harder she falls, the bigger she becomes once brushing herself off. There appears to be no end to the Scorpio's ability to reinvent herself. A survivor of the first order, she endures life's natural disasters, both big and small, parlaying the most paralyzing setbacks into subsequent successes in a perfect expression of her transformational planetary principle of growing by letting go.

In Libra, the previous sign on the astrological wheel, the über-feminine planet Venus rules a distinctly masculine air sign of ideas – the result is a pretty Apollonian vision of the surface world with its requisite focus on man-made order, art, and ideals. In Scorpio, a masculine Mars rulership is submerged into the depths of this richly feminine sign, giving rise to a Chthonian view of existence. The term, meaning 'subterranean,' denotes the underside of life in every aspect, from the wormy womb-tomb of Nature herself to the dark recesses of the human subconscious to the bubbling chemistry or buzzy physics of life at the microcosmic level. Chthonia is yet another title given to the Black Demeter or Pluto–Persephone as she is called in her death-goddess aspect. Here in the zodiacal Third Quadrant of Mind, the focus of its native signs – Libra, Scorpio, and Sagittarius – is primarily on the perception of existence. Scorpio delves into these subjective, aforementioned Chthonian realities, specifically those of the subconscious, with the objective purpose of isolating and cataloging if not rooting out what she discovers there. While Libra woman, the *fairest* of them all, holds a mirror up to the world, bidding others to consciously reflect upon high ideals and principles, Scorpio woman is, like Alice through the looking glass, bound to investigate the wonderland of her own psyche. As any actor worth his salt will tell you, this is what the dramatic craft is all about – having so firm a grasp on one's own inner life as to draw upon it at will. No wonder so many top actresses are Scorpios – they possess the required depth.

Nobody has a better handle on her own feelings than the Scorpio woman. As the zodiac's only fixed-water sign, the element symbolizing emotion, she seeks to control sensation so as to never have it control her. Indeed, this fixed-water status can often make her seem frozen. Pluto's remote energy keeps Mars's impulsive expression in check, allowing Scorpio a comfortable distance from feelings – meaning, she rarely acts rashly upon them. To her mind, carrying on in any manner, whether with angry outbursts, crying jags, sentimentalism, or even excess enthusiasm or elation, is all a blatant waste of energy that could, and should, be put to other uses. The ability to contain and control what the rest of us experience as spontaneous sensation makes her a most coolheaded character – she is uncannily composed under pressure, or in times of crisis. Never flustered by unexpected circumstances, not easily swayed by flattery nor even hurt by outright insults, the Scorpio woman doesn't feel victimized, daunted, or even challenged despite others' intentions to thus affect her. By the same token, the fixed-water crystallization of Scorpio's emotional life dictates that she experience her own feelings as facts. Other people have humble opinions, but Scorpio has all the answers. In relationships, especially, it is typically her way or the highway. Scorpio's beliefs are nonnegotiable – her likes and dislikes are definitive, her inscrutable hunches self-evident, the whole of her mental framework a consolidation of subjective views into a hard-and-fast system of personal truths as airtight in formulation as Einstein's theory of relativity, and just as easy to disprove.

Perception beyond the five senses is one of the attributes of the 8th Astrological House. Indeed, Scorpio is all sixth sense. While Libra woman projects her thought forms onto the astral plane by waving her wand of idealization, Scorpio operates in the reverse, psychically drawing experience to her like a crystal ball attuned to what life might have in store. With such an advantage, she picks and chooses opportunities, enviably avoiding most

PLANETARY SYMBOL

Pluto's power is one of transformation, growth through elimination, regeneration, and renewal. From an earthly perspective, the planet rises to great heights and dives to profound depths, echoing the phoenix's rise and fall and the seasonal descent and return of Persephone. It is through self-imposed exile, eliminating the distractions of 'surface' experience, that Scorpio gains 'insights,' which, in turn, fuel her loftiest ambitions while nonetheless providing grounding.

SIGN QUADRANT

The zodical quadrants correspond to metaphysical planes of being – physical, emotional, mental, and spiritual. The Third Quadrant is that of mental perception, in particular the concept of existence. Scorpio is about the dark recesses of the subconscious and the objective exploration of this subjective realm. Like dormant Persephone, entranced on the throne of the underworld – itself an image of the subliminal – Scorpio woman is focused on self-examination and the elimination of deep-seated blocks that might interfere with psychological growth.

SIGN GLYPH

Of all Scorpio's associated symbols – dragon, serpent, spider, scorpion, phoenix – it is probably the latter mythical bird that is most appropriate to the character of the Scorpio female, as both birds only ever rise stronger than ever after even the most startling crashing and burning. The second dictionary meaning of phoenix is 'one of peerless beauty or excellence.'

ELEMENT + QUALITY

The water element connotes emotion and intuition. The fixed quality denotes intense concentration and magnetism. The fixed-water compound particular to Scorpio is likened to ice or other such crystals as salt or precious and semiprecious stones. Scorpio woman is just such a gem, perfected by the internal machinations of her pressurized psyche. As perfect a ten as she may be, she sees herself as salt of the earth, a precious, (self-) preservational commodity.

obstacles. Like all fixed signs, especially those whose sex is aligned with the gender polarity of their sign (as are the females of the feminine sign of Taurus and Scorpio), the Spider woman operates as a magnet. In fact, what Scorpio woman teaches the rest of us, by example, is that less is more – that those who fight for, finagle, hunt down, or meticulously plan their ambitions are often too narrowly focused, blind to the big picture, and unable to recognize what life might naturally afford them. A spider, after all, doesn't need to stalk its prey. Similarly, lest we forget the scorpion is an arachnid, Scorpio woman isn't compelled to make life happen or to build a future: As the personification of the unseen intelligence of nature, one that 'knows' the appropriate seasonal time for every purpose, Scorpio waits her turn (turn, turn), trusting in the cyclical character of existence, jumping on the carousel of time when the right opening comes around. Patience, for the zodiac's Spider, is the ultimate virtue. Meanwhile, she spends her time weaving as perfect a web for trapping the bounty she feels entitled to amass. To Scorpio, preparing for her good is paramount, and it mainly entails removing any and all impediments to its accession.

Another crucial quality of the 8th House, and one that particularly pertains to Scorpio woman's psychology, is *self-sacrifice;* this all-important element of elimination that gives rise to her personal growth is truly the crux of her being. It's a dynamic with roots in her earliest childhood. Scorpio is typically born at a time when her family's life is disordered, though often a happy chaos, characterized by geographic change or the jumble of many children. Her parents tend to be remote, both individually and as a couple, allowing for a loose, undisciplined atmosphere. Her father may be an especially absent entity. Rather than adding to the confusion, or becoming lost in the shuffle, Scorpio girl becomes instead the voice of authority, regardless of her birth order, taking on a parental role and generally sorting out the domestic muddle by pointedly telling everybody else what to do, and when to do it. Her blatant bossiness is welcomed by both parents, while her siblings see her as an anchor, granting her superior status in return for the constant support and definition she brings to their world. Working in tandem with her somewhat more lenient mother, they form one complete maternal presence – Scorpios tend to have a close, respectful relationship with their mothers. Scorpio's rootedness is considered invaluable to everyone concerned, winning her the role of family 'treasure.' In taking on such a vital position, however, Scorpio generally sacrifices a carefree childhood, digging down and tapping into her latent maturity well before it might otherwise have emerged. She strives for stillness, weaving that spiderweb around her own emotional issues, to chew on later, so that she might also create a more stable environment in which she and her siblings can meet their myriad challenges – school, family obligations, the formation of friendships, and ultimately, the negotiation of sexual issues – from a perspective of calm. The family with a Scorpio female in its midst is marked by a solidarity amongst siblings, who rally around one another in an all-for-one spirit of survival, with yours truly leading the group cheer, emboldening them with her inherent sense of superiority. By her digging in and choreographing their so-called turmoil, the chaotic pressure of family life is systematically honed into a charismatic power. To the (Chthonian) Scorpion mind, life is supposed to be random and unruly – it only becomes utter pandemonium through our panicky reactions to it. If one gives in to the chaos, it will, in turn, give way to *natural* order. The trick, she learns, is to clear a path for providence by obliterating any obstacles in its path.

It's little wonder, then, that Scorpio woman is the zodiac's personification of the Destroyer goddess: Her sign is steeped in associations with underworld/afterlife figures such as Persephone just as the Scorpio 8th Astrological House governs the concept of *death,* as well as *regeneration.* As the symbols of Virgo and Scorpio, respectively, suggest, these two signs are related, most poignantly, through their sharing of the Demeter archetype, the capital Ms being interpreted as variations on Mother Earth. In mythology, this earth goddess's 'virgin' aspect, Kore, is abducted by Hades–Pluto at the autumnal equinox, which marks the end of Virgo; later, she transforms into Persephone, the death crone – Mother Earth in a deep freeze – who haunts the autumnal sign of Scorpio. Persephone, by all accounts, isn't the happiest camper – at least, not at first. Like Scorpio woman, her happy-go-lucky childhood aspect has been entirely sacrificed, albeit in order that she might wield a power so great as to scare the bejesus out of anyone, god or man alike. She *is* death, giving a person either the thumbs-up or -down on where they might spend eternity. She is the last word, the bottom line. This is the same role Scorpio woman plays in life – the one who ultimately calls the shots in all her relationships. Like Persephone sitting motionless on her cold, jeweled throne, deadpan Scorpio releases her opinions like edicts, deciding the fate of everyone she encounters, always in terms of what they might offer her. Others barely exist for the Scorpio, except in so far as they relate to her. Family exists. Friends exist. Enemies don't – she doesn't have any, as she immediately eliminates such negative distractions from her life. All people are pawns – she just prizes some pawns more than others, purposefully pushing them forward in this game called life.

Like Scarlett O'Hara in *Gone With the Wind* (presumably referring to ashes, if not Ashley), Scorpio woman takes matters into her own hands. Penned by Margaret Mitchell and played on film by Vivien Leigh, both Scorpios, Scarlett

POLARITY

Females in feminine (earth, water) signs are aligned with the gender polarity of their sign and thus embody the quality-element combination of the sign. The fixed-water status of Scorpio means she is often as icy as can be. She has firmly fixed beliefs. Moreover, she is perfectly crystallized in her understanding of self, completely convinced of her motivations and unwavering in her emotional attachments.

8

SIGN NUMBER

The number of regeneration. Tradition equates eight with transcendence to a higher plane of consciousness. It signals eternity, the spiral shape folding unto itself. It is also associated with moneymaking and worldly possessions.

49–56

SIGN AGE
ASSOCIATION

The menopausal period. The cessation of maidenhood, akin to virgin Kore having turned into her crone aspect, Persephone. The hormonal change occurring at this time puts a woman in touch with the unseen chemical workings of her body, something of which the Scorpio is forever aware. Just as a tree drops its leaves and the energy of growth shifts to the internal root level, so, too, does this age signify the shedding of the last bloom of physical fertility in favor of the psychic fecundity of womanly wisdom.

PSYCHOLOGY

Scorpio is imperious. Her brand of superiority complex rivals Leo man's. Like frozen Persephone, she can be rigid, icy, and expectant of others to do her bidding. Her sting manifests when faced with strangers, of whom she's almost pathologcially leery.

is the Persephone archetype incarnate. Plunged into ruin, her beloved Tara (named for the Gaelic Demeter) pillaged – her mother, like her own youthful aspect, destroyed – Scarlett must rise, phoenixlike, from the cinders, not just for her own survival but for that of her entire brood. She thus embraces her troubles, unearths a root-vegetable snack, puts on some drapes, says, 'fiddle-dee-dee . . . I'll think about it tomorrow,' and starts manipulating the hell out of people to get back on top. Mitchell even gives us Hades–Pluto in the form of the black-clad Rhett Butler. Pluto means 'riches,' and it is mainly Rhett's greenbacks that Scarlett is after. Embodying her 8th House attributes of both *sex* and *other people's money*, Scorpio woman isn't necessarily above trading one for the other. She doesn't subscribe to any pristine, puritanical vision of her sexuality, seeing no good reason not to use it to her best advantage. Nothing the Scorpio does, in fact, could diminish the high esteem she has for herself. And, as we've seen, life's struggles and pressures only make her harder-edged and more valuable to others. Whether you take Persephone paralyzed in her crystal palace, bejeweled by Pluto as recompense for her imprisonment, or Scarlett O'Hara, vowing to 'never go hungry again,' soaring from the ashes of calamity to new wealth as a kept woman, this fixed-water lady's determination, in expression of her sign's motto 'I desire,' only becomes that much more crystallized amid chaos. Like a diamond, the vernacular ice – the hardest, purest, most perfect crystal – her worth and beauty, particularly the 'inner' kind, only increase the longer she remains rooted in the pressure cooker of Chthonian nature.

Scorpio woman periodically embarks on deep psychological descents, generally not more than twice or three times in her life, while an individual bout might last up to a year or more. These are not the baby blues, folks; but something darker, more profoundly, if not turbulently, indigo. The Chthonian realm is that of the internal mysterious feminine, and as the purest personification of this archetypal energy, Scorpio has subliminal tempests raging inside her, regardless of the cool lid she might be keeping on them. At these crucial times in her life, and they do surface as cruxes, she feels fairly forced into self-reflection. As it is, nobody else possesses the power of concentration that she does, evident if one is ever to glimpse the Scorpio at work, particularly, on a creative project. She often appears to be in a trance. This same ability to shut out externals and delve deep into her own subconscious becomes a bit of a curse in that she can't suddenly, on command, put a cap on that fathomless connection she feels. Thus when others might be able to repress underlying excitation in their psyches, or not be able to make contact with its workings even if they tried, the Scorpio has no choice but to be swallowed up into the pit, like Persephone, and face every last secret, skeleton, demon, and craving that, for most people, would be quietly lurking in the subconscious, but, for her, are building bonfires and waging holocausts there. Again, her motto, 'I desire,' points to no mere whim, but suggests a distillation of wants and needs into a diamond-hard determination. When she does ultimately resurface, she does so with an air of dead calm, as if, like her totem phoenix, she is wholly renewed with nary a trace of the torments that had threatened to overcome her.

Body + Soul

Scorpio woman wears an expectant expression, as if perpetually watching and waiting for something to occur, or someone to arrive. In conversation, she anticipates one's every word, often hurrying conversation along with quick nods or hissed yeses, visibly annoyed by even slight digressions. She often seems to only half listen, as if engaged by other thoughts or biding her time until she might interject her own strong opinions. This preoccupation stems from the strength of Scorpio's perceptive antennae, feeling the atmosphere surrounding what's being said, compelled to read between the lines. Never much satisfied with face-value discourse, she scans for signs of subtext, disingenuousness, or deceit, noting the ease or lack thereof in a person's voice or mannerisms. Befitting her fixed-water status, Scorpio woman is like a crystal radio, zeroing in on unspoken signals. This may account for her blank, often trancelike stare; she seems to listen more than look for clues about a person, opening up all available frequencies to her notoriously fine-tuned intuition. She often appears to be looking through a person, keeping silent tabs on other interactions, stealthily minding every minor coming and going. As you enter a crowded room, her eyes will meet you at the threshold. If, in that instant, she finds you interesting, sexually or otherwise, she won't let you out of her sight. With a prying look – as if to ask, 'Do I know you?' – she bears down on an individual, her squinted eyes and Sphinx's smile silently signaling her piqued curiosity. She is the zodiac's original spiderwoman, remember – and this seductive creature bids those she considers 'fly' to enter into her parlor, the world itself being Scorpio's living room.

Few woman are more comfortably ensconced in their surroundings, whatever they might be, than Scorpio woman; and unlike her male counterpart, who is eternally slithering about, she really digs into her environment. Not one to party-hop or even make more than a single plan in any given day, she'll leave the cozy confines of her domestic digs only if she knows that once she

ARCHETYPE + MYTH

Scorpio draws on the archetype of the destroyer goddess. Persephone personifies the earth at the dying time of year, just as the sign corresponds to the onset of the autumn of one's life. Death in the Scorpion view is a door to transformation. The Eleusinian mysteries associated with the goddess underscore illumination stemming from darkness. Persephone is about renewal – she turned mortals into gods, a pattern repeated by the Scorpio woman in love relationships where she is oft in the business of killing off her mate's impairments such that he/she might emerge as a more divine entity. She is also associated with the Sphinx, who holds life's riddles and kills men if they don't answer them correctly.

BIBLE + LITERATURE

Scorpio is the she-devil.
Ancients personified death
as female, the bosom of
Mother Earth to whom we
all return. The femme fatale
character lives in such figures as Delilah, 'the weak-
ener,' whose name also
means 'opening,' both as
yoni and grave. Sex and
death, both attributes of
Scorpio's 8th House, are
metaphorically interchange-
able. The femme fatale character in literature uses sex as
a device for her own gain.
Scarlett O'Hara is most infamous, her name recalling
the deep red associated with
the sign; her union with
Rhett Butler, a devilish Plu-
tonic character clad in black,
coincides with the desola-
tion of the earth (Tara).
*Alice's Adventures in Wonder-
land* also depicts the Scorpio
female who is undaunted in
delving into her own psyche.

The sigil of Mars, Scorpio's
coplanetary ruler.

reaches her destination, typically by the quickest means available – cabbing it even a couple of blocks isn't out of the question – she can comfortably park her queenly butt and be waited upon. As fate would have it, Scorpio woman is naturally still: Like a fine portrait whose eyes seem to follow one around the room, she emits a glacial (fixed-water) composure – she can be downright frosty when she wants to be. Her general countenance is that of one held in suspended animation, if not eternal suspense. She wants answers, and she induces a person, particularly a potential lover, to reveal himself – even the most closemouthed man will find himself spilling his guts to Scorpio. She *is* that Sphinx, putting a guy, especially, in the hot seat, demanding he do some fast talking, while she remains as silent as the grave, as cryptic as befits the zodiac's Persephone, forever entranced and enthroned. When she does deign to speak, she is succinct to say the least, as if keeping much of what she is, nonetheless obviously, thinking to herself. But she can say more with fewer words than any other being on the planet, often making a person feel he or she has received a subliminal transmission rather than taken part in polite conversation. This same capacity is used to its best advantage by the Scorpio woman who works with words, as a writer, poet, or songstress. Still, even the Scorpion CEO might employ dripping metaphor in the description of events surrounding a recent board meeting. This Chthonian in-dweller, in even her most banal expression, fairly proves that poetry is indeed the language of the soul, or at least that's how it surfaces in the translation to us, mere surface inhabitants in comparison.

Scorpio can appear particularly cold and calculating to other women, who might sense that she's concealing a secret sting operation behind her dis-armingly arctic exterior. With the combined rule by fiery Mars and subzero Pluto, Scorpio masks whatever hots she has behind a totally chilly demeanor. Ignorant of this, men find themselves babbling all the more, while she simply cracks her Mona Lisa half-smile, a countenance art historians have long attributed to the subject's being pregnant – expecting. Meanwhile, that iconic artist's model was probably a Scorpio, a most anticipatory female forever fixed in a metaphorical state of hatching some plan or another. On the subject of actual pregnancy, as well, Scorpio tends to be the broodyest baby on the astrological block. Indeed, despite her pat depiction as a sex-crazed harpy, Scorpio is rarely on a search for sex for sex's sake. Instead, she stakes out a permanent mate with whom to propagate. In the meantime, she doesn't like to be single, and in lieu of dating, she'll generally enter into one heavy relationship after another. Even when convinced a man isn't 'the one,' she'd still rather take him on, as a hobby if not a hubby, occupying her mind with making him over in her image – chewing him up only to spit him out again, to her mind, better than she found him. In this and most of her relationship scenarios, Scorpio is convinced she's doing a man a favor by being with him, whether for a fortnight or forever. As vampiristic as it may sound, any man she takes up with is in some way hers, everlastingly. Given the indelible mark she makes on the men she's been with, they'd all be first to agree.

The Scorpio brand of beauty is best described as Gothic. She is as beatific as that Mona Lisa, looking very much the 'eternal beloved,' in keeping with her archetypal assignation as the zodiac's interminable Persephone. There is even something ghostly in Scorpio's appearance: Often either raven-haired or icy blond, she seems drained of color or dusted with frost, her skin often white, like alabaster – even those of darker extraction will be not so much fairer than other members of their family, but rather more wan. Her enigmatic eyes, revealing nothing, are often so wide set that fixing her in a gaze seems impossible. Her hairline is low and often marked by a widow's peak, frequently fringed with the finest peach fuzz, as may be her neck, giving her a hooded or cowled appearance. Her hair itself, though often straight, is nonetheless springy and difficult to manage, lending Scorpio a cowlicked look unless she takes great pains to tame it. Her nose is typically long, straight, and sharp, contributing to her suspicious countenance, as does her notoriously sly smile – a perfect half-moon caricature of a mouth. Her neck, not overlong, seems stiff; she may appear to turn her whole body round to face in any given direction, a symptom, perhaps, of her fixed, ground-in stance. Her movements are quite staccato, in any case, and she is typically not one of the zodiac's best dancers. Her shoulders are strong without being square, her pale, luminous arms, throat, and bosom typically revealed in décolleté styles no matter the season. Often richly robed in clean-lined clothing – her penchant is for minimalist or mint vintage designs – she tends to show a lot of skin, not out of any exhibitionist need, but rather because, feeling so inherently private, she is oblivious to being on display.

The mark of a great screen actor, it has been said, is an ability to feel completely private with a camera shoved in one's face, in a studio packed with technicians. A list of famous Scorpio women – including the likes of Julia Roberts, Louise Brooks, Dorothy Dandridge, Maggie Gyllenhaal, Parker Posey, Winona Ryder, Vivien Leigh, Hedy Lamarr, Veronica Lake, Jodie Foster, Sally Field, Grace Kelly, Goldie Hawn, and Demi Moore – reveals the most success-ful, prolific, and highest-paid female stars in filmmaking history have been and still are Sphinx ladies. It would seem that not only the Serpent's extraordinary beauty but also her innate ability to be so intimate, indeed visceral, on camera makes a captivating impression on-screen. Simply put, Scorpio woman smolders. She seeps sex appeal, making her the perfect screen siren, if not

8TH ASTROLOGICAL HOUSE

sex
death
joint ownership
endings, resolutions
physiological regeneration
reconstruction/reformation
dysfunction
financial assistance
morale boosting
spiritual support
legacies/trust/wills
taxes
inheritance
insurance
secrets
curses
possession
sexual behavior/attitude
sexual climax
sixth sense
psychological rebirth
the occult
sleep
in-depth research
investigation
examination
mysteries
hidden assets
other people's money
spiritual change
spiritual indwelling
shared material resources
joint funds
money from marriage
conflict over wealth
wealth for glorification
material dependence
corporate money
control/manipulation
coercion

box-office treasure. It doesn't hurt that she tends to have a primo bod, too. Lean and sinewy, but at the same time round and meaty, Scorpio woman obviously benefits from Mars' masculine, athletic influence on her otherwise feminine-water-ruled physique – even when petite, she looks like a long, cool drink of water. In appreciation of the serpentine influence on her sign, Scorpio's firm though weighty breasts feature vividly indignant 'snake eyes,' an effect, perhaps, of combining Mars' outward protruding energy and Pluto's nippy effects. Likewise, she's typically tiny waisted and slim-hipped without ever looking bony or boyish. Like Aries woman, with whom she shares Mars rulership, as well as a tendency toward being long-legged and short-waisted, Scorpio woman can slip on a pair of men's jeans, no problem; and on her they won't boyishly hang, but will cling in all the girliest places. Like her breasts, the very feminine swell of her stomach, and even her pubic mound, is often perceptible through her clothes – which makes sense since she often wears slinky fabrics. But Scorpio's nature is to let it all hang out, as she is notoriously not hung up on cosmetic perfection. She mightn't even be terribly meticulous in her beauty regime, slapping on some makeup without washing her face, going without deodorant, shaving, plucking, and waxing sporadically. Completely comfortable in her body, as a new lover will soon learn, she'll lounge about naked with nary a thought to so much as crossing her legs, always advertising, if unwittingly, her Scorpio-ruled 'ruby fruit' that works like a guidance system for this sex-driven female – just as Persephone's own pomegranate decided the direction of her fate.

ʃex + ʃexuality

If any woman knows what she's made of sexually, it's Scorpio. The female body and sexuality is the human representation of the Chthonian Principle, its mysterious inner workings an intricate, hidden laboratory from where life springs, a woman's libido as well as her hormonally dictated moods and Moon phases circumventing rational thought. Sex is irrational, its natural workings not easily fitting into a pretty picture of idealized thought and higher love. And as with all life's mysteries, Scorpio has a far better grip on it than the rest of us. Scorpio is the sign of sex, Mars and Pluto's active-regenerative combo platter of energies determining the impetus to love, which, for the zodiac's subterranean dame is not a lofty, cerebral, 'courtly' urge but rather a blatantly chemical one. She doesn't need any man to make her feel like a natural woman, she was born that way. Scorpio exudes sexuality, as if cheering each attractive pheromone on as it makes that journey out into the ether to be sensed by any man. Typically, she has her pick: Scorpio's symbol can be read as an arrow sending out yonic signals, just as Virgo's glyph implies protectiveness of purity – screw that, says Scorpio, and in the most literal sense. Scorpio's attitude toward sexuality reflects her sign's association with the ages 49–56, which correspond to the time of menopause. Symbolically, menopause represents another facet of mysterious female sexuality: It is impossible to control the cessation of the reproductive, regenerative force in a woman. This age association certainly fits the bill of Scorpio's Plutonian rule, mirroring that planet's correlation to growth via elimination and the diverting of life energy at the root level. Menopause remains a giant mystery to doctors and scientists; while the ancients, like certain New Age sects, saw menopause as the onset of the crone age, when a woman's power to foster physical growth in the womb shifted to develop her own mental and spiritual prowess into the proverbial wisewoman. Needless to say, when of menopausal age, a woman is particularly ruled by her Chthonian hormones – metaphorically, Scorpio is menopausal all her life, preternaturally mature at so early an age, her psychology ruled by a resigned and fatalistic nature, not to mention being notoriously given to mood swings, running alternately hot and cold in her interaction with others. In a strictly carnal sense, to boot, she's rather blasé towards bonking, as if the advent of sex itself were old hat. She makes little fuss over the loss of her virginity, not easily impressed – often quite the opposite – by what men might have to offer in the way of physical endowments or performance between the sheets. It can be off-putting enough that Scorpio seems typically unmoved and trancelike, in any case, during sex; others, still, will find sex with her to be outright demoralizing, as if she were suppressing a yawn the whole time.

Chemistry being a two-way street, Scorpio, too, follows her nose, which may explain why there isn't any one 'type' of man she fancies. She trusts her sixth sense far more than her eyes, and though she appreciates a hot stud when she sees one, she is definitely not a lookist. As an inhabitant of the mental Third Quadrant of the zodiac, Scorpio seeks a meeting of the minds; still, not so much an intellectual connection as a psychic one. She needs to get a vibe – it's one and the same with chemistry, the heights-and-depths dynamic of Pluto demanding both a psychic *and* yonic attraction. She doesn't generally give a fig about shared interests and ideals. Rather, she craves an unspoken bond based on a mutual need to utterly merge, to become as much one entity as two people possibly can. Scorpio doesn't merely pair up, she psychically possesses, approaching her partner the same way she does herself – with a searchlight and a pickax – plunging into the depths of a lover's personality to

BODY RULERSHIP

Scorpio rules the reproductive system, genitals, bladder, urethra, anus. There is a tendency to genital afflictions, venereal disease, rectal polyps, as well as sinus and adenoid trouble. Pluto rules regenerative cell growth as well as the revitilization of the mental faculties.

help him unearth and fully realize any hidden talents to treasure, while seeking to root out and destroy problems or negative habits. In keeping with Scorpio's signature femme-fatale nature, whole parts of the man she takes up with must simply die. Some men won't allow her such powers of execution; others eagerly welcome it, happy to find so managerial and mentoring a mate. In every culture, death goddesses possessed a cauldron of regeneration – one more interpretation of Scorpio's fixed-water status – in which male gods or heroes were restored to life anew. Guys that fall for the Spider lady, too, soon find themselves in a similar stew, as she hopes to stir a man into full possession of himself, helping him to grow by killing off what might be holding him back. New Agey as it sounds, the Scorpio ice queen is like a crystal, utilized to transform atmospheric energy, neutralizing negativity and allowing for more beneficial vibrations.

Of course, Scorpio comes to relationships with nothing to lose and certainly nothing to prove. Having been conditioned since childhood to think of herself as a perfect gem, she has a healthy self-esteem – and don't think she doesn't let a man know it. One of her fatal flaws, however, is not being able to admit when she's wrong – a bitter pill for Ms. Flawless to swallow – and she sometimes loses friendships, or even love relationships, due to her absolute distaste for humble pie. Rather, she is programmed to repeat the role she played growing up, and as a result, Scorpio settles into serious relationships early in life, anxious to start mining the psyche of some male. She's that wifey girlfriend who gets her hooks into a guy as early as eighth grade, rattling off directive dos and don'ts – coming face-to-face with this Persephone, even a young male gets the sense he's meeting his maker. She is sexually wise beyond her years, the signals she even unwittingly sends out piquing the curiosity of older men, as well as boys her own age. She may even be the one to make the more major moves on her boyfriend, and as she always has a steady one, she could have already deflowered a string of lads before hitting her twenties. Still, every boy she romantically befriends is better for having known her – those with Madonna-whore complexes will have overcome them for life. So self-respecting, she likewise demands to be treated like gold; yet, as an unabashedly carnal person as well, she smashes any archaic double standards about women that a young man might harbor.

All the guys Scorpio goes for will tend to have at least one thing in common: They're typically all mama's boys. Though she can put up with more macho than most women, a man must also possess this particular brand of emotional deference for females to fully strike her fancy. So accustomed to sharing the motherly role with her own mom, she quickly bonds to a guy via dangling apron strings in front of him, muscling past the mother to whom he was previously attached. It's just the first in a string of his relationships that she puts, somewhat, on ice. Beyond that requirement, what she looks for is 'potential,' preferring a guy who is slightly underconfident and undeveloped in his understanding of how to consummate his life's ambitions to one who believes to have life all sewn up. A man with a clearly defined mission presents a problem for Scorpio, making it difficult for her to stir ingredients for his success into the 'pot'; but a guy with lofty notions who simply lacks the know-how to achieve them is just the right candidate to pop into her cauldron. Once Spider woman gets finished with him, he'll be a real catch; but woe to any lover who gets too big for his britches – sometimes she fuels a man's confidence so much that he develops a superior attitude, even hinting than he can 'do better' by falling in with another female. Look out: Given such a sorry state of affairs, Scorpio will either release so burning a sting as to reduce her mate to castrated rubble or she'll launch a cold-shoulder campaign the likes of which would simply freeze a guy's balls off. With that healthy dose of macho Mars submerged behind her icy countenance, when push comes to shove, she packs more (metaphoric) muscle than most males.

As she's the zodiac's Sphinx, the burden is always on the man in her life to think fast, do her bidding, and come up with whatever goods she demands. He, however, can ask zilch of her – she owes nothing to anybody and offers no explanations for her actions. Perfect in every way, Scorpio woman is completely beyond reproach. Her opinions of others are endlessly forthcoming, but even in deep distress, she keeps her lip buttoned, as asking others for help is tantamount to admitting weakness – something she simply cannot do. She's fine. It's everybody else who needs sorting out. When it comes to her own career, she focuses solely on internal affairs. Though notoriously creative, she cannot be bothered with public opinion, leaving any promotion of her talents to the spin doctors of the world. And like the Sphinx, she truly does think in metaphors – just as her acting talent is characterized by a strong but subtle 'inner life,' so, too, is there poetic mystery in any of her artistic endeavors. This may explain why this sign also boasts some of the best female songwriters – Joni Mitchell, Bonnie Raitt, Maggie Roche, Rickie Lee Jones – as well as other artists, thinkers, and scientists who probe the interior, unseen world of the mind and body: poet Sylvia Plath, scientist Madame Curie, painter Georgia O'Keeffe, comediennes Roseanne and Whoopi Goldberg, sex reporter Shere Hite. This is not a sign of superficial pop stars: Scorpio woman's notoriety stems from her exploration of the depths of the human experience. She is an unapologetic woman, committed to her own callings – other people be

Louise Brooks
Marie Dressler
Tina Brown
Hillary Rodham Clinton
Anna Wintour
Pauline Trigere
Patti Page
Jane Pauley
Maria Shriver
Roseanne
Whoopi Goldberg
Calista Flockhart
Sally Kirkland
Loretta Swit
Kate Capshaw
Tatum O'Neal
Joni Mitchell
Ricki Lee Jones
Bjork
Eve
Bonnie Raitt
Grace Slick
Maggie Roche
kd Lang
Ruby Dee
Sylvia Plath
Fran Liebowitz
Pascale Smets
Edith Head
Ruth Gordon
Mabel Normand
Fanny Brice
Imogene Coco
Barbara Hutton
Georgia O'Keeffe
Marie Antoinette
Shere Hite
Ethel Waters
Margaret Mitchell
Joan Sutherland
Florence Chadwick
Nadia Comaneci
Indira Gandhi
Petula Clark
Joan Sutherland
Marie Curie
Mamie Eisenhower
Brenda Vacarro
Helen Reddy
Marla Maples

damned. She is unimpressed with celebrity, her own or anybody else's. This total immersion in herself and in her private pursuits, whatever they may be, is what beckons others to her.

It's the same with love and sexual relationships. One must seek out the Sphinx with its possession of universal secrets and the power they hold. The Sphinx certainly isn't coming after you. So, too, does a man happen upon Scorpio woman: on her own terms and on her home turf. A partner must be prepared to lose himself – body and soul – in a pact with this she-devil, allowing her full possession. She will do her damnedest to help him fulfill his every wish, but in return, all he has, henceforth, is hers. She simply won't be used as a stepping-stone – any man who tries will find he's the one being trampled underfoot. Investing in a man is a full-time job for which she feels entitled to be paid. In fact, many Scorpio women sacrifice their career, at least for a designated time, upon tying the knot. Little wonder so many Sphinxes with strong artistic callings choose to remain single – in any case, femmes fatales don't generally hold down day jobs. So pity the poor fool who tries to throw the 'self-sacrificing' Scorpio over. If anyone will fight tooth and nail to take an ungrateful, unfaithful spouse to the cleaner's, you can bet it's our deadly little Persephone with her secret weapon of warring Mars energy – with her luck, she'll end up in a better, new relationship with her (ex's?) lawyer.

Of course, under the best circumstances, this inherent aggression and power also has its perks: Sex is one activity that taps into Scorpio's hidden fire. Despite her blasé femme-fatale facade, she burns for sexual contact, her urgency made all the more ironic by her unruffled, unapologetic tone. If any woman were to force a guy to go down on her in that cab she's hopped to avoid walking those few blocks, it's our, shall we say, in-your-face Scorp. To be sure, she is most uninhibited when it comes to making love. Perhaps only the Aries, who is exclusively ruled by Mars, is likewise so forthcoming in the sack. Unlike the aptly named Ram, however, Scorpio isn't so exclusively focused on the physical aspect of sex; rather, she is as inclined to fuck with a guy's brain as she is with the more evidently available organ. Notoriously experimental, especially in the early stages of a relationship, she really knows how to wow a guy – fastening him via fascination, that psychic hold she seeks to secure. She's a real tease, that girl who'll play footsie with a guy's crotch under the table, groping or even briefly going down on him, offering blatant titillation to stay erotically connected with her man at all times. She is in no way precious about sex. Indeed she may be Machiavellian in its usage, employing it as a means to an end. Since she emotionally invests so much, so quickly, in her man of choice – he mightn't even realize it given her signature chill – Scorpio may use sex as a safeguard to seal the deal. She pours it on in bed, pulling out all stops to ensure she'll rank among, if not be, his best. Embodying the fixed-water (focused-feeling) combination of her sign, she seeks to be a man's obsession, a crystallization of his desire – it's the primary manner in which the Scorpion paralyzes her prey. Bidding him to be still and just kick back, she goes to town pleasing him with a battery of acts most wouldn't dream of performing. She can be a veritable succubus, even having at her man while he's asleep. To this Chthonian character, practically nothing is a gross-out as her hands and mouth may make their way to places where the sun *don't* shine. She enjoys getting to the root of a man's matter, well acquainted with hidden areas that serve as male G-spots. Completely unsqueamish, Scorpio is apt to actually enjoy 'swallowing' or, say, indulging in a man's feet or armpits – even water sports may be in-bounds for Scorpio woman. In general, she's more turned on by the European model of penis than the standard American sort, preferring people in their natural state. She likes a little messiness in a man – fussy types who wax, shave, or overly preen themselves won't last long in her favor – just as she likes to sweat up and otherwise soak the sheets, totally aroused by healthy body odor, especially a man's musky scent. In rare instances, she will forgo showering postsex, perhaps even swapping undies with her lover to keep the excitement going throughout the day.

Scorpio's oral skills would put many a porn star to shame. Naturally equipped with a deep throat, she greedily gobbles up her lover, able to accommodate even a jumbo-sized schlong. Though it may take her some time to achieve her own climax, Scorpio's eventual explosion could be so extreme as to practically knock her unconscious. Not especially bendy, sex is rarely acrobatic – rather, she is her version of groovy, easily getting into a steady staccato rhythm. Scorpio is the sign of sex, after all, with the Serpent as one of its symbols – in tantric thought, a female serpent, Kundalini, is said to be coiled around the lowest chakra, that of the pelvis. More tantric even than Virgo woman, Scorpio naturally knows how to wake the snake inside, her breathing during sex working in perfect synchronicity with the muscles of her vagina – this accounts for any delay in orgasm, as she lets it come rather than forcing it to happen. She becomes one with the sex act, which seems to put her into a trancelike state. Not heady in the least, the bedroom is one place where she doesn't play any mind games, barely uttering a word to her lover, though she may make a great deal of primal, guttural sounds. Losing herself so completely in a sexual frenzy, Scorpio doesn't always know her own strength; her lover needs to be a sturdy fellow with a great deal of staying power, as she requires a long, hard ride. Quicky Dickies need not apply; she seeks a real slow Joe with

STR8 TURN-ONS

swarthy looks
body hair
(active) ass play
(passive) anal penetration
m-f-f threesomes
voyeurism
watersports
underarms, body odor
humiliation/cuckolding
(active) oral
(mutual) masturbation
mirrors
toys, gadgets
lesbian and bi porn
(active) b + d
(active) lite s + m
strangers
clothed sex
erotica
lite pain
biting, fighting
foreskin
swapping underwear

no place to go. And she requires a daily dose of it, too. Indeed, Scorpio always looks as if she's just had a good romp – her hair disheveled, her lips somewhat swollen or chaffed, her gait a bit stiff (from soreness, one imagines), her appetite forever hardy. In fact, few women benefit as readily from the actual physiological shift that sexual release elicits – Scorpio is famous for wearing a look of just-fucked freshness.

Of all the women in the zodiac, Scorpio may be the most open to anal sex. She likes the inherent naughtiness of such an act, always wanting to be that much more 'advanced' than her female friends, shocking the more prudish ladies in her set with matter-of-fact recountings of whatever new trick she has tried in bed. Variety spices things up, and she feels as much at ease shopping for dildos as she does lacy doilies. If any woman has a toy or two stashed in her undies drawer, it's the Scorpio, forever seeking to reach new heights by the down-and-dirtiest means imaginable. Like her male counterpart, the female Scorpio has a wee sadistic streak. She finds great pleasure in rendering a man helpless, tying him up and torturing him with, at the very least, a little tickling. Disciplinarian fantasies perfectly fit her psychological bill – she may be an outright dominatrix, turned on by enslaving a submissive man, seeing him grovel for her sexual attention, saddle-soaping her leather unmentionables in the meantime. Of course, her need for control rarely manifests in such an extreme or fetishistic manner – typically, she just bosses her mate around, telling him where to touch, lick, nibble, or penetrate and at what appointed time. Scorpio is never the docile damsel who'll make a man feel like big daddy even by feigning innocence or ignorance. However, as authoritative as she notoriously is, she is hardly the jealous type. In fact, Scorpios are surprisingly open and forgiving of lovers who go astray – sex is sex, not something to be morally hung up about. (She isn't as revealing about her own sideline activities, however.) On occasion, she may be amenable to letting another woman join in, the hapless third being used rather like a toy for their amusement. In such scenarios, Scorpio's latent sadism seeps out as she may subconsciously punish the other woman for simply being there.

Pretty women pretty much turn every Scorpio female on, the latent masculine Mars energy within especially inspiring clitty hard-ons for dewy-faced natural beauties. Gay or straight, all Spider women have a bit of the sapphic about them. She is sometimes angered by the palpable effect women have on her since, when faced with the hottest stud imaginable, she hardly bats an eye. And she doesn't like being taken unawares. To mask any flustered feelings, Scorpio overcompensates, acting all the more superior, immediately taking the power position. When she does actually identify as a lesbian, Scorpio is notoriously mysterious about it; like her astrological neighbor Libra, she is not a big believer in hard-and-fast labels. Drawn to wholesome girls-next-door, she adopts a worldly-wise demeanor, trying to appeal as both mentor and mother hen. The girliest girls have the greatest appeal – round little-dumpling ingenues, fresh as daisies and just as sweet to pluck. Adopting an adept's attitude, Scorpio looks to educate such a lovely Rita, literally leading out what sexy instincts might be lurking beneath the surface of so spotless a psyche.

Playing the sophisticated lady, Scorpio seduces that wide-eyed beauty in such a subtle manner that it all seems innocent enough at first. It may begin with an invitation to the gym or for a beauty treatment or simply a girly 'sleep-over' with the swapping of stories and pedicures accompanied by cocktails or champagne. But soon, the conversation swings toward sex, with the Scorpio grilling her 'friend' on every particular of her erotic history, alighting on the subject of lesbian contact. Given the Scorpio's instinctual power, she's pretty confident in her gaydar. She enjoys uncovering a closeted woman's secret tales of sapphic love, hoping to be the next page in that chapter herself. Though as a teen the gay Scorpio will be out clubbing every night, as an adult she steers clear of queer bars, finding such an environment too obviously based on sex. On some level, she needs to be entering virgin territory, sensing a woman thrills to the experience as only a relative neophyte can. Appealing to her need for control, she slowly takes a woman on an erotic journey, in full charge of the proceedings, as always. As the zodiac's daughter of Pluto, she shows a lover the ecstatic heights that might be achieved via the depths of – sometimes degrading and debauched – sexual delights. Unlike her gay-male counterpart, Scorpio lesbian lands herself in relationship after relationship, never alone for long, often overlapping her liaisons. Sexually aware at a young age, she will have had many schoolgirl experiences, whether initiated by older superiors on a sports team or within fuzzy best-friend bonds. If anyone were to be head cheerleader, dating the football captain, only to be secretly rubbing pom-poms with her squad mates on the side, it's the Scorpio, whose youthful lesbian history reads like erotica, or all-out porn, albeit geared to a male audience. Indeed, she'll be the first on the block to have engaged in group fun, with members of both sexes, if not having hosted such a soiree while her parents were out of town. Sex is power to the gay Scorpio girl, who taunts the more prudish femmes in her midst – a dynamic that continues throughout her adult life, as she scratches, if not sniffs, at the surface of another woman's puritanical standards, seeking to corrupt her with prurient deeds. Often working in industries flooded with females, typically at the top of the heap where her bossiness is best put to use, Scorpio has a pool of pretties to pick from, pets

GAY TURN-ONS

younger females
submissives, femmes
straight women
hour-glass physiques
seduction
mind games
(active/passive) anal sex
aphrodisiacs
body fluid
tattoos, piercings
body hair
mastering
(active) heavy b + d
(active) s + m
(mutual) nipple play
teasing, torture
costumes, uniforms
genital piercings
madaming, swapping
fingering
leather, dungeons
ejaculation
cross-dressing

whom she'll both prep for promotions and wield her power over. Minus the butch wardrobe, she plays Peppermint Patty to a submissive Marcy, decidedly wearing the pantsuit in the relationship.

Whether or not she mixes business with pleasure, allowing a work relationship to veer into a sexual one, Scorpio is imperious with the lassies she latches onto, slowly but surely putting a woman through her sexual paces. Scorpio uses the element of surprise in the bedroom, introducing new techniques and toys that will continually push her lover to the edge – faster than you can say nipple clamps, what may have started with sweet talk could end up far more slap than tickle. All Scorpios, male and female, gay and straight, welcome a little pain mixed into their pleasure, but the lesbian Spider lady is perhaps the most imposing on this score. Introducing her lover to new levels of excitement, she wants to assure her dominance, inculcating a lover in her specific brand of sex. She may be far more compulsive about sex than her hetero counterpart, but only because the straight Scorpio tends to substitute procreation for purely sexual experience. Still, gay Scorpio, though the dominant female, may also yield to her maternal instincts – she is typically the one in her long-term bonds who will choose to give birth. In fact, gay Scorpio hopes to wear as many hats as possible in her relationship, as breadwinner, household boss, mother, mentor, and sexual master. Her partner will have to be content with, indeed relish, worshipfully following in her wake, tying up all the loose ends, attending to life's little details – Scorpio's hacking into life with bold strokes necessitates the love of so amenable a maid.

Couplings

Scorpio Woman / Aries Man

She seems unattainable; he struggles to win her affection. Blasé in the beginning, she eventually assents to his ardor. Often, they have it all: looks, glamour, wealth. Their sex life is enviably active.

Scorpio Woman / Taurus Man

He's the submissive sort she hopes to reshape. Any alliance between these astro-opposites is nothing short of obsessive. Sexual addiction — to each other — is to be expected: Passion borders on savagery.

Scorpio Woman / Gemini Man

Living proof that chemical attraction exists: There's a tug too powerful to resist — pheromones are flying. Other aspects are less harmonious — ideologically, there's opposition. In the long run, their lust won't wane.

Scorpio Woman / Cancer Man

Cancer requires mothering; Scorpio's a cunning caretaker. Together, they cultivate a snug coexistence. Prosperity and progeny are anticipated. In bed, it's all-out eroticism. But mum's the word.

Scorpio Woman / Leo Man

Life is a banquet — a feast at which they devour separate areas of experience. Together, they're 'takers.' This couple craves notoriety. Offspring are inevitable. Sexual hunger for each other seems insatiable.

Scorpio Woman / Virgo Man

They appeal to each other's high standards, considering themselves of exceptional moral character. She helps turn lofty ideas into solid action. Friends feel their piety is just so much bluster. Sexually, they 'click.'

Scorpio Woman / Libra Man

She seems a self-sufficient sort; his aristocratic bearing is intriguing. Both are drawn to a grand lifestyle. They're happiest in the company of friends. Sex easily swings from precious to perverse.

Scorpio Woman / Scorpio Man

A match marked by material, psychological, and sexual obsession. Strong self-regard coupled with righteousness might make them somewhat insufferable. In bed, already intense emotions reach an orgiastic apex.

Scorpio Woman / Sagittarius Man

His good luck creates their fortune. Her hold on him is firm. What each craves individually is willed through the relationship, especially in bed: For the sake of staying together, nothing is refused.

Scorpio Woman / Capricorn Man

Slowly, she insinuates her way into his life – once she's gained entry, they're inseparable. She takes over, which suits his armchair approach to living: He's the prima donna. In bed, too, he's happy to hang back.

Scorpio Woman / Aquarius Man

Hard work, but often worth it. Restrictions are stripped away and there's nothing to keep them from individual success. An abiding sexual attraction sustains them through inevitable rough patches.

Scorpio Woman / Pisces Man

It seems something's being kept hidden. At best, they're a confident, conscientious couple with big dreams they intend to realize. In bed, decorum is their default demeanor. Sex is subdued, but never standard.

Gay

Scorpio Woman / Aries Woman

Scorpio holds herself up as a prize – the role Aries ordinarily assumes. Tables turned, the Ram is floored with feelings for the sultry Scorpion sexpot. This all-consuming tie might not last, but it's lusty.

Scorpio Woman / Taurus Woman

Taurus sends a shock wave through Scorpio, who, in turn, takes the role of guru to the suggestible Bull. A sexual relationship may develop ever so slowly. Months could pass before so much as a kiss is risked.

Scorpio Woman / Gemini Woman

Two become one: From the start, they're happiest alone. Scorpio transforms jumpy Gemini into a serene sort. The pressure to be everything to each other may overwhelm. Sexually, outsiders are off-limits.

Scorpio Woman / Cancer Woman

Hooking up means hitting partnership payload. Both carry baggage, but togetherness treats old wounds. Conflict may surround domestic duties. Sex seems always to involve the element of surprise.

Scorpio Woman ∫ Leo Woman
A shift: Leo's agenda is unalterable, so Scorpio's forced to face herself. Often, she'll simply lose interest. Sex is their way to recover from distress. In the light of day, it's far more difficult to doctor.

Scorpio Woman ∫ Virgo Woman
With bewitching Scorpio, Virgo must learn to brandish her own power. Otherwise, Scorp's strength will destabilize. Both risk losing their footing. In bed, Virgo accepts the mentoring she has missed.

Scorpio Woman ∫ Libra Woman
They're at cross-purposes: One only tolerates the other, secretly feeling superior. Jealousy is the culprit, causing them to misbehave. Disloyalty is their default action. In bed, the Scales is uncharacteristically worshipful.

Scorpio Woman ∫ Scorpio Woman
Scorpio is always the most captivating woman in the room – so who wins the distinction here? Like two powerful magnets, they repel. For a forever bond, they'll seek a less fierce female. But 'just sex' suits them.

Scorpio Woman ∫ Sagittarius Woman
They're a cloistered couple who'll often relocate to a remote locale. Together, it's a life of learning – self concerns are the focus. Both are erotically accessed, especially together. They bond best in bed.

Scorpio Woman ∫ Capricorn Woman
A mutual interest in women's issues or human rights will often draw them together. As a couple, they clash constantly. But fascination, even obsession, finds them forever connected. In bed, they keep it simple.

Scorpio Woman ∫ Aquarius Woman
An unusual sexual liaison that soon turns serious. Assuming a maternal role, Scorpio nurtures the Aquarian's ambitions. With the Waterbearer, Scorpio finally gets some respect. In bed, one or the other feels eclipsed.

Scorpio Woman ∫ Pisces Woman
It's kismet when these sensorial water signs connect. Destiny, it seems, has brought them together for a specific purpose: to heal, themselves and others. They're sexually in tune from the start.

Sagittarius Man

the maverick

Sagittarius man is the zodiac's libertarian. A freewheeling extremist, nobody lives larger than he does. Forever shaking up existing codes and mores, he colors outside the lines in life, succeeding in his endeavors by taking great risks. Being so naturally expansive a character, Sag embodies a sense of abandon, emancipating situations from the restraints of small-mindedness, resetting standards and ushering in new orders. By rights, he can be excessive in attitude and behavior, a living testament to the adage 'Think big and be big.' Indeed, Sag is a born citizen of the world – his oyster – and he approaches any and all experience with an easy exuberance if not an outright sense of exaltation. His lifestyle may appear reckless, but what others label 'out of control' is often, to him, a natural state wherein he feels securely composed. Rather, it is static circumstance that sends him off the rails. In love, he is wildly romantic and effusive: His emotions manifest in a heightened manner, and his displays of affection are often over-the-top. He is physically drawn to perfect tens and, unlike most men, never shrinks from making a play for such glamazons. Sag exudes an untamed energy, a renegade charm, which, along with his signature strapping physique, makes him a highly sought after heartthrob. He wants a playmate in a female partner, one who'll share his optimistic vision of life as a great adventure. With men, he's a big player, only settling down with a lover who possesses extraordinary looks, personality, and an extremely open mind.

ix

PRINCIPLE

The Dionysian Principle of expansion, ecstasy, exaltation, and optimism. All mutable signs negotiate the opposite energies of the two signs that precede them on the wheel. Libra's Apollonian Principle of orderly civilization is followed by Scorpio's Chthonian Principle of messy nature. The Dionysian precept paints civilization with a wildly natural brush. This is romanticism in a nutshell, allowing an unfettered stream of consciousness to take form. Sag's motto is 'I see' or 'I understand' a nod to his psychedelic vision of life. Another is 'we think' signalling his forays into the collective conscious.

Sign + Mind

Sagittarius is ruled by the planet Jupiter, named for the Roman king of the gods (Greek: Zeus), representing the Principle of Expansion in the zodiac. The Sagittarian male experience is hinged on an inherent need for growth, optimism, in the most literal sense – excess as might give rise to ecstasy and, thus, discernment in knowing when enough is enough. As the third sign in the astrological Third Quadrant of the Mind, therefore a mutable one, Sagittarius synthesizes the energy of the two opposing signs that precede it on the astrological wheel into a single cohesive understanding of existence: Libra, with its Apollonian vision of the world as a 'conscious' civilized place of light (reason, order, beauty, social harmony), is followed by nihilistic Scorpio, with its Chthonian (subterranean) view of existence as a dark, mysterious environment, emphasizing the unseen workings of nature and the unconscious. Mutable Sagittarius asserts that these perspectives are not mutually exclusive, that the world is neither all goodness and light nor is it all shadow and pessimism, but characterized as extending beyond such duality. Together, human civilization and nature form the Chimera, a shape-shifting mythical creature symbolic of the cyclical nature of existence that incorporates opposites into an endless wheel of alternating experience. Fittingly, in modern terms, *chimera* is defined as 'reverie' or 'daydream,' just as it scientifically describes an organism of both sexes. All such meanings, as we'll see, are embodied in the Sagittarian male.

Sag guy personifies the expansive Dionysian Principle, which is a chimeric amalgam of Apollonian and Chthonian forces. Think of a tree meant to symbolize, like classical architectural columns, Apollonian order and consonance; then consider the roots of said tree as representative of the unseen, Chthonian, subterranean jumble in which Nature is, nonetheless, doing her stuff. The Dionysian is then an amalgam of these dynamics, a vine – Dionysus is god of the vine – mirroring the rootsy hodgepodge, but now above ground in the seen world, digging its tendrils into those trees and columns for support. And this is an apt metaphor for the way Sagittarius male lives his life: He takes what is heretofore hidden, repressed, wild, or taboo in society and exposes it, building upon it a new model of civilization that reflects the savage interior of the natural world. The philosopher Nietzsche associates Romanticism with the Dionysian experience as it was a movement that evoked the subconscious wilderness just as it praised such forms in nature; still, because it sought to establish itself in the formal world – via art, philosophy, music, and architecture

– Romanticism wrapped itself around domains that were already clearly established as Apollonian. This is the eternal function of Sagittarian energy: To manifest as a new grapevine of communication by winding its wild, fresh, natural expression around existing mainstays of society. In a nutshell, Sagittarius man is a maverick, the consummate freethinker, who shakes up and reshapes the pillars of civilization from the inside, as opposed to some subversive outsider seeking to topple them at their roots.

Just as the wild Dionysus is earmarked to inherit Zeus' throne, Sagittarian male is in no way seditious toward mainstream society; rather, he feels himself heir to it. Sag is astrologically entitled to worldly influence. Once he has it in his grips, he hopes to freely expand the *collective mind,* something that falls under the Sagittarian rule of the 9th Astrological House, by bringing nature back into the mix. This is the very spirit that gave rise to Romanticism, Transcendentalism, and for that matter the Beat movement and rock 'n' roll, genres that tap and then channel the seemingly random energies of nature and the subconscious into a single stream-of-conscious, though still formal, expression. Mythology mirrors this pattern: Dionysus, in effect the reincarnated Zeus 'born' from his father's thigh, is an anomaly, a half-mortal male nature god who nonetheless wins a coveted seat on the Olympian dais. Indeed, as the thirteenth, he is the last god to enter the pantheon, where there is only room for twelve, thus signaling a new beginning. (Some variations of the story have it that Hestia gave up her throne to him.) The orgiastic, rustic god of wine and so-called disorder, he is, indeed, Nature *as* male – a new twist certainly – signifying, among other things, a patriarchal usurpation over even this most divinely feminine of realms. As it is, Zeus has already taken on the function of mother. As the living-breathing personification of the Dionysian spirit, Sagittarius male personifies the heretofore free-form Chthonian feminine made manifest in the directive Apollonian male – the wild-beast-cum-human-archer embodied as the Centaur. Like a leafy vine, he runs rampant upon the ramparts of civilized restraint at once signaling its ruin and veneration, all the while marrying what is man-made to the natural landscape – art, science, ideology, indeed all that is deemed societal progress back to Nature himself.

Just as there was an inherent method to Dionysus' madness, Sagittarius is likewise not a sign of disorder, but rather of new order. When abstract expressionism, jazz, or the equally improvisational musings of the Beat writers and poets first came onto the scene, they seemed erratic, frenzied, crazed. Yet, once taken hold, these movements revealed themselves as valid forms meant to express life's underlying realities. Sagittarius male personifies this seemingly wild, random energy that only the luxury of time tells us isn't as aimless as it

PLANETARY SYMBOL

The first letter of the name Zeus, like the glyph of Sagittarius itself, it depicts human evolution via the mind (the crescent) as an extention of the cross (a symbol of the material plane). This mirrors the 9th House rule of lessons learned through the physical experience of living. Sagittarian man embodies the Jupiterian sense of adventure.

SIGN QUADRANT

The zodiacal quadrants correspond to metaphysical planes of existence – physical, emotional, mental, and spiritual. The Third Quadrant is that of mental perception, in particular of the concept of existence. For Sagittarius, importance is placed on the superconscious mind and the imagination. He seeks to expand beyond dualism. Neither the cockeyed optimist nor the dour pessimist, Sag rises above the fray and joyfully participates in the sorrows of life.

The arrow of inspiration fired from the material cross. This is the sigil of the centaurs, who were wizards or shamans, also called magnetes or 'great ones.' Sacred brothers of Zeus-Jupiter, they were magical shape-shifters – the half-horse/half-man figure being a preferred form. After all, if a guy could choose what to be below the waist, horselike isn't so bad an option.

ELEMENT + QUALITY

The fire element symbolizes life energy, spirit, or the divine force; the mutable quality, versatility and change. The mutable-fire combination particular to Sagittarius is best described as lightning, the power of supreme gods like Zeus-Jupiter; this force represents both sagacity and aggrandizement, ecstatic states of consciousness as might appeal to the shamanistic Sag.

seems from the outset. As the only mutable-fire sign in the zodiac, Sag blazes his way through life, untamed by existing rules or limits. It is his birthright to 'break on through to the other side' of imposed restrictions, the confines of an overly conditioned mind included. In astrology, fire symbolizes the life spirit, while mutability signals versatility and adaptability. Sag is the Dionysian vine, adapting its life force to that which it climbs and covers. Likewise, Sag exhibits the qualities of lightning, a variable atmospheric substance of fire that fittingly wraps itself, vinelike, around trees and columns in a flash that is the very symbol of omnipotence, being Zeus' special weapon – the spectacle of which caused the death of Dionysus' mother and necessitated his being the 'twice born' god, ultimately delivered from the thigh-womb of his father. Sag man embodies such ravished exaltation, that chimeric flight of fancy, relating to the world as an all-powerful being for whom there are no impediments to attaining his wildest dreams. The 9th Astrological House, ruled by the sign of Sagittarius, is, among a slew of attributes, one of *aspirations*, the *higher* or *superconscious mind*, as well as that of tapped *inspiration, dreams, visions*, and *the need to experience life beyond commonplace limits*. It is a house of exaltation, a state of which Sag is in continual throes. He is 'out there,' both in thought and in action, participating in life on a grand scale, whether in business, travel, sports, or in his higher-minded philosophical or signature religious, indeed shamanistic, pursuits.

Perhaps the most poignant expression of the Centaur's mutable-fire mix, one that combines all the isolated musings on his psyche, is the interpretation of him as a shape-shifter. As anyone intimately acquainted with a Sag man will readily admit, this guy is a self-styled Zelig, continually lost in one of his many glamorous identities. As the famed Sag impostor Esternado Waldo Demaro did in real life, the Archer man can, in a flash, reimagine himself, making enormous changes to his lifestyle, embarking on incredible journeys, real or imagined, stunning supposed intimates, who are often left in the unsettling dust. One never knows when, or from where, the Sag man might reappear, or as whom. He is that freely expressive. The 9th House also contains the *collective conscious*, plus all brands of *big business* and *global commerce* – and it is on this sweeping level that Sag men live. Little wonder his sign is associated with the age group 56–63, those good-old-boy years when a man is at the peak of his power and influence, having nothing to either prove or lose – Sag embodies such aplomb all throughout his life. He can only relate to the world as an omnipotent spirit might – on a grand scale – struggling with his intimate associations like a farsighted tailor, unable to focus on the fabric (of life) at hand. The Sagittarius Archer symbol represents this man's proclivity for projecting himself 'out there' in the distance, both temporally and spatially. He lives life armed with a meta-phoric bow and arrow, which necessitates that he hold on tightly (to his far-reaching dreams and visions) and also let go lightly (of close familiar relation-ships, often needing to be sacrificed to achieve such aims). Connections are made on the broadest of levels, whether it's his knack for lucking into powerful global networks or his talent for tapping into the collective conscious in his creative pursuits. Either way, he is endowed with a sense of omniscience. Aptly, his sign's two mottoes are 'I understand' and the collective 'We think.'

Meanwhile, of all males, Sag is the most readily accepted by other guys. He is assumed to be a real man's man – the perennial first boy picked for basketball. He easily infiltrates the inner sweat-lodge circles of all-male societies and it is through such masculine association that he feels comforted, validated, and, most importantly, glorified. A signature Sagittarian dynamic sees him being recognized, for whatever his particular talent, by an elite group of males. In general, it is the top dogs in Sag's chosen field or creative arena who acknowledge his transcendent genius. Indeed, the term *genius* is never applied lightly here. Originally, the word was employed to mean 'a spirit of paternal ancestry,' a genie or jinn, thus a shape-shifting fire spirit of patriarchal inheritance. Indeed, the Archer's entrées in life seem always to stem from the top – Sag shoots by any and all interim steps on the way to success.

In the twisty-turny life of the Sag male, like Zeus unto Dionysus, Sag man's dad is a warm and fuzzy, nurturing, near maternal figure, while his mother is an expectant, authoritative, 'fatherly' disciplinarian. First and foremost, Sag is his father's son, a miniature version of his sire, whom he showers with an abundance of affection. Sag is rather more measured with his mother, whom he feels compelled to please. Dad is an old softie – all fun and games – who is nonetheless a busy, often absent character caught up in a whirlwind of travel and heavy scheduling generally associated with a creative, glamorous, or even frivolous career. In downtimes, however, Sag goes where his father goes and does what his father does and, as he matures, finds himself happily folded as an honorary member into whatever network of male comrades his father fosters. He happily plays the sports his dad plays, absorbs the hobbies his father espouses, and will often wish to emulate his dad by embarking on the same or a similar career, or one that the father had wished but failed to pursue. Most significantly, Sag's dad instills in his son the importance of following one's dreams. Meanwhile, mom has a strict vision of her son's agenda that typically entails serious academic or business endeavors. Whether through insinuation or by coming right out and saying so, she uses her husband's shortcomings as a guidebook for what not to do

POLARITY

Males in masculine (air, fire) signs are aligned with the gender polarity of their sign and thus embody the quality-element combination of the sign. Thus, he is like the personification of the male fire spirit – the jinn, genie, or genius, meaning inherited 'paternal spirit.' This fits the archetypal pattern of Zeus' giving birth to Dionysus, who thus inherits supreme masculine power.

SIGN NUMBER

The magic number. The term stems from the magi, like the 'seers' who predicted Christ's birth, which naturally had a gestation of nine months. It is also related to the realm of imagination. Nine always reduces to itself: Whatever number it is multiplied by (say 2), that number (18) always adds back to nine.

56–63
SIGN AGE
ASSOCIATION

The age of the magnate, a word derived from *magnete*, 'great one,' a synonym for centaur. The Sag male finds acceptance into the big-boy networks of the world all his life. Personifying the qualities of that age, he exudes a sense of relaxed entitlement and acquisition, perceiving the world as master of all he surveys.

PSYCHOLOGY

The Sagittarius can be reckless, feeling overly optimistic and expansive due to Jupiter's energy. He has difficulty with commitment and fidelity as his lust for experience calls the shots. He may be wildly experimental with drugs and sexual activity, perhaps inviting danger. He has difficulty recognizing the limits of mortality, considering himself more than mere flesh and blood.

in life. As a result of wanting to align with his father *and* please his mother, the Centaur strives to do it all . . . and give it all his all. Not a dabbler like the Renaissance Libra with his hands in many pots, Sag aims to outshine others in all his undertakings – he will be president of the student body, captain of his sports team, play lead roles in dramatic productions, and provided he has the brains, become valedictorian of his graduating class.

Mentally, the Sagittarius learns to wrap what he perceives as the needs of both his parents into a single modus of experience, a skill he will eventually hone without having to hit so many bases. As he reaches maturity, one particular way he might kill two parental birds with one stone is to surpass the success of his father (in that same field or a similarly 'fun' career) to such an extent that his mother can not find fault. Sag naturally begins to divine a tertiary path upon which he can tread, an all-encompassing chimeric vision of his future whereby he may continually have his cake and eat it, too: He does both what comes naturally to him, satisfying his (Chthonian) desires, and makes so huge a mark on the world as to fulfill any civilized (Apollonian) agenda. The Centaur character of his sign, in fact, is the perfect symbol of Sag's combined 'wild nature' with 'human ingenuity.' (As legend has it, this magical being is a shape-shifter, the horse-man guise simply being its favorite form to take.) On a mundane level, Sag is assumed to have it all, as well – brawn and brains – still, it's that knack he has for coming up with tertiary resolutions that wins him points with other people. Particularly in his professional life, Sag gains a reputation as an 'answer man' or wizard of sorts, one who invents solutions that require no compromise by either side. It is his special talent to contrive expanded visions with an (third) eye on fully incorporating divergent needs. Thus, the zodiac's shape-shifter becomes all things to all people, further fostering – in himself as well as others – a sense of his being omniscient. Seeing beyond black-and-white dualities, surpassing any gray areas of concession, Sag experiences life in living color. His being a native of the 9th House of *dreams* and *visions* is no small distinction – Sag's whole life is like a wild reverie, reality unfolding before him as if he were imagining it into being.

Body + Soul

As anyone who knows a Sag man intimately will tell you, the word *can't* simply isn't in his vocabulary. Perpetually losing himself in the phantasm of life, Sag may be the most adventurous soul on the astrological wheel. He is a risk-taker, a predisposition that results in either great personal payoffs or the advent of true peril. Of all the 9th House attributes, it is that of *growing through experience* that manifests most poignantly in the male Archer – he is bound to fling himself way into the world, gaining the insight that thrills and exaltation provide. Mostly, his adventures are real, and Sag learns about the reaches of his own human capacity through skydiving, mountain climbing, or any number of extreme sports and activities. Other Sagges, embark upon journeys in consciousness, such that this whiz kid, with his third-eye troubleshooting abilities, graduates to the position of full-fledged shaman seeking to sustain his enlightening glimpses into a lifelong vision quest. Just as Sag's archetypal Zeus is endowed with the power of lightning and passes that baton onto his reincarnated self-son, Dionysus, so, too, do we see that Sagittarius' personal power stems from a lighten-ing of his own condition, a freedom to embark upon life as a fantastical journey.

In literature, the Sagittarian soul is personified by such supernaturalist Dionysian characters as Heathcliff, Tom Jones, or Huckleberry Finn, whose Sagittarian author's pen name, Mark Twain (the point between), perfectly illustrates his sign's tertiary, third-eye perspective. And it is in the expression of their wild side, their sense of adventure or indulgence, that these characters, paradoxically, end up socially redeemed. This quality is evident in such imaginative, real-life Sagges as William Blake, Jonathan Swift, C. S. Lewis, Walt Disney, and Stephen Spielberg, as well as those who turned to drugs for their ecstatic shamanistic visions – Jim Morrison, Jimi Hendrix, Keith Richards, Richard Pryor, Billy Idol, Greg Allman, Dennis Wilson – all men who, arguably, tuned in by turning on. One way or another, Sagittarius male requires release. Fortunately, most seek it in the chemical flood of extreme exertion or thrilling adventure rather than in substances. Dreams provide that same alchemical shift – to the Sag, remember, life *is* a dream. Being on a natural high, even that which endorphins offer, contributes, indeed corresponds, to Sag male's expansiveness and signature sense of immortality. It is often remarked how scarce Sagittarius men make themselves – while we're scratching our heads on the subject, Sag is out there getting lost in his audacious reveries. Similarly, when he does make the requisite social appearance, he wears a wild, faraway expression. As a result, he is often accused of being either shy or snooty; but he's neither of those two qualities exactly, just some inexplicable combination of both. He hopes to remain unfettered, even in the press of a crowd, typically avoiding eye contact, mumbling some disclaimer, or otherwise displaying a total lack of enthusiasm if approached by a small-talking stranger. He is, in a word, apprehensive; rarely one to mix and mingle, Sag finds himself a roomy corner in which to comfortably flop, otherwise keeping his back to

ARCHETYPE + MYTH

Sagittarius draws on the archetype of the supreme godlike Jupiter-Zeus and his favorite son, Dionysus. Zeus gave birth to Dionysus, having sewn him into his Sag-ruled thigh after rescuing him from his dying mother's womb. The meaning of this male birth? Dionysus, like Sag male, is cherished by the patriarchy. He is the only Olympian male nature god, mirroring Sag's own wild nature. His disciple Teiresias was a shape-shifter who took both male and female form. (Enter Sag's sexual experi-mentation.) He was blinded by Hera for siding with Zeus in a debate over who, male or female, has more pleas-ure in sex: He said women. In recompense, he was given the gift of second sight. His sageness stems from having looked at life from both sides.

BIBLE + LITERATURE

Christ is modeled on Dionysus. Christian Communion is a tame echoing of the wine god's orgiastic rites that saw worshipers feast on the torn body of the god, in human proxy. Both were born of mortal virgins and attracted a cult of disenfranchised followers. Agony and ecstasy figure into Romanticism and Beat literature, which fuses the beatific and the beaten down into one tertiary Sagittarian view. Mark Twain, a Sag whose nom de plume illustrates that very 'point between,' gave us Huckleberry Finn, a wild rustic like the wine god. Tom Jones embodies Dionysian excess. Brontë's Heathcliff is a male personification of nature, the *Wuthering Heights* symbolizing superconscious ecstasy achieved via expansion of mind and spirit.

the wall so as to remain as far from the fray as possible and yet able to take what's happening in all at once. To be sure, he exudes a whiff of superiority, whether intended or not; he is often literally head and shoulders above the rest. Even when Sag isn't tall, he'll manifest a certain largesse in any number of areas, such as a massive head, bulging arms and legs, a commanding barrel chest, or other outsized portions of his anatomy.

Regardless of size, Sagittarius' body language is best described as sprawling: He's forever standing spread-eagle or lurching back and forth like a tennis player awaiting a serve, stretching his arms up, arching his back, sitting with his legs splayed, lounging as if, like Dionysus, eternally couched upon a commodious dais. This broad self-expression, a nod to the expansive energy of his planet Jupiter, carries a presumptuous edge, as if anyone and everyone assembled before him is present for the sole purpose of providing amusement. Like all fire signs, Sag is indeed a man's man (only with a twist, as we'll see), and he typically attracts a circle of other males to him, forever engaging in what appears to be locker-room banter, constantly delivering asides that result in large bursts of hearty laughter that dissolve around him while he is left wearing his signature self-satisfied smile. He is forever sizing up every female within view, often on the basis of her looks and sex appeal, unapologetically dismissive of those that don't fit his strict, albeit closeted, chauvinistic criteria. Women, no matter how confident, may find themselves reduced to shy schoolgirls in his presence. Sagittarius, it must be said, seems entitled, a quality that even his famous brand of self-deprecating humor cannot belie.

A list of famous Sagittarius males, which includes the likes of Billy Connolly, Ben Stiller, Jon Stewart, Harpo Marx, Rodney Dangerfield, Garry Shandling, James Thurber, Flip Wilson, Redd Foxx, Buck Henry, Dick Van Dyke, Tim Conway, Noël Coward, Richard Pryor, Woody Allen, and Mr. Twain reveals that this is a sign of comics, humorists, and satirists. Still, even a nebbishy self-put-down artist like Woody Allen exudes a definite swagger, having the *cojónes* to continually cast himself as a romantic lead linked with beautiful and, often suspiciously younger, women. All Sagittarius males embody a similar braggadocio, believing themselves worthy of the most glamorous, loving, attractive . . . the list of superlatives goes on infinitely . . . woman in the world. As a native of the 9th House of *aspirations,* Sagittarius doesn't simply strive for sublimity, he expects it. Indeed, magnificence is assumed in every aspect of his life. And though he tends to be ruggedly handsome, even the more looks-challenged Sagges can be notorious modelizers, inspiring wonderment and an is-she-really-going-out-with-him? line of inquiry. Meanwhile, in keeping with his outré planetary ruler, when Sag is attractive, he will be extremely so; and he knows it, putting this heady self-awareness to prolific use.

More than any other man, Sagittarius is a woman's rough-and-tumble, take-charge sexual fantasy come to life. He possesses an overt masculinity, a predatory power and natural abandon that make him the consummate stud, whether or not he actually boasts such sizable equipment as befits his horsey symbol. That, it seems, is rather a hit-or-miss scenario, in one extreme or another. Meanwhile, everything else about his big persona speaks to a rousing sexual ride. Ye-ha: Genital apparatus aside, Sag tends to be a big ol' boy – lanky if not a bit gawky, large boned and limbed. His shoulders are often enviably broad, if not perfectly square, his arms roped with thick muscle, his manly hands usually rough and calloused, regardless of his profession, only adding to his hale, lusty appeal. Topping his typically massive noggin is a dense shock of thick hair, sometimes coarse or unruly, like a dog's, often making a flip or feathering action originating from a natural middle part. Separating his eyebrows is a wide, flat space – his 'third-eye' spot made all the more marked by the contrast of small or doleful, puppy-dog eyes, slanted, like beefy almonds. His forehead may appear bony or protruding, the shape of his face narrowing at the temples, then sinking deeply at the cheekbones, only to fill out again at his jaw and meaty chin. His nose is often flat but flared about the nostrils, his lips are full and sensuous, naturally curled upward at the corners creating a joker's smile, itself generally more gummy than toothy, and marked by small, square, considerably spaced-out choppers. He wears a slack-mouth expression, lending him a loose, peaceful, if not panting appearance. Sag has a particular penchant for whimsical shows of facial hair – soul patches, goatees, muttonchops – not to mention a preference for the odd piercing on his face, tongue, nipple, navel, or even elsewhere. He has a similarly fanciful style of dress, often overdoing it in the color department or being too on-the-nose when it comes to sporting trends. No matter how gaudy or glitzy his garb, he will typically tug at his clothes as if terribly uncomfortable, visible evidence of this man's basic burning need to be au naturel.

Sag has a sturdy, somewhat stiff torso – he's forever pulling muscles and otherwise injuring himself, as evidenced by such fashion accessories as splints, crutches, and slings – which may explain why he always seems to be limbering up, even in the most formal of settings. He is a natural hardbody, with bulbous or knotted muscles, rounded and well-defined pecs, and a stomach that easily shapes into a neat little six-pack. Yet, despite his overall mighty musculature, it is his Sag-ruled steel thighs that stand out, extending to fierce indented flanks and a rock-solid rear, all visibly ripped beneath his trousers, becoming the seat

9TH ASTROLOGICAL
HOUSE

aspirations
higher mind
systemized thought
higher education
superconsciousness
world view
law
religion
ethics
principles
philosophy
psychology
intense consideration
long journeys
foreign transactions
foreigners
big business
trade/import/export
church as spiritual sanctuary
clergy
in-laws
grandchildren
inspiration
meaning
public opinion
court decisions
universal energy
lessons learned
second marriages
manifest social concepts
careers in publishing
academia
developing wisdom
intellectual synthesis
passage of principles
cultural pursuits
growth of consciousness
out-of-body experience
shamanism

of much of the desire he incites in a woman. Indeed, the most cerebrally transcendent female, thinking herself immune to mere appearances, may find her loins surging with just one glance at the Centaur's hindquarters. Though this stallion hasn't cornered the market on magnitude in the penis department, Sag's overall athleticism suggests a tireless roll in the hay. Any such supposition would be absolutely right: With unparalleled stamina and staying power, this bucking bronco can kick it all night long, hardly ever needing to slow down or beg off; considering his peerless, perpetual thrust-ability, one might actually be thankful if he's not hung like a horse. Of course, there are plenty of downsides to being labeled (wo)mankind's mindless lay; but, for the whole of his youth, and much into adulthood, Sag man doesn't see any. Instead, his prime preoccupation is finding a female who will approach sex the same way he does: as an electrifying journey on which no possible path to pleasure should go unexplored.

Sex + Sexuality

Sagittarius has incredible luck with the ladies. From the moment he possesses a libido, Sag finds he has ample opportunity to act upon it. As an adolescent his signature athleticism makes him a hero and a heartthrob to hormonally raging girls to whom he appeals on that very visceral level. Typically, all through his teens and twenties, Sag will sow more than his fair share of wild oats. Sex is yet another activity that offers him those signature sought-after thrills. In fact, he can become addictive in his behavior, particularly in his desire to experience the ecstasy of climax. If Sag isn't having sex, he's thinking of having it, or, as is frequently the case, enjoying sex all by himself. Of all the males in the zodiac, nobody is more the notorious masturbator than the Sagittarian – and not just as a quick means to an end, but often as an elaborate processional of pleasure. Even when involved in a heated sexual relationship, or serial-dating as he is wont to do, Sag will still enjoy his onanistic practice. To the mind of this Dionysian son of Jupiter, quantity can be as significant as quality when it comes to the erotic experience: Any sex is good sex, and he wants to experience it with women, and sometimes men, too, of every size, shape, descent, and disposition. Fortunately for Sag, his own brand of looks and blatant virility meet with widespread appreciation. More than most, he personifies the type of man about whom women fantasize – a charismatic yet carefree character, naturally athletic but a bit messy and rough around the edges. In the savage world of sexual conquests, Sagittarius man is considered big game. And though he often fulfills a woman's wildest imaginings, many females might choose to relegate such a man to the realm of fantasy or a one-off sexcapade, opting for a more docile, down-to-earth male as a long-term partner.

Despite his desire for a variety of sexual partners, Sag is looking for a monogamous, permanent relationship once all such oats are sown. He seeks a major merger with a woman who must be willing to utterly join with him. Granted, he typically shops for his ideal mate amongst a population of women with model-worthy looks – Why not? he figures – and yet, it is a sense of humor, an insouciant, jovial nature that he'll prize more than beauty. Still, Sagittarius is turned on by glamour, proud to be carting around an awe-inspiring beauty that other men are sure to ogle. The Archer, rarely at a loss for dates, starts shooting 'higher and higher' in his attempts to score a relationship, thriving on the challenge and thrill that such romantically lofty pursuits provide. Often, it is flamboyance or even fame that Sag finds most attractive in a mate; again, not because he is a status seeker per se but rather because such an association suggests excitement. Notoriety, particularly of the global variety, is an attribute of his ruling big-daddy planet, Jupiter, just another expression of Sag's expansive nature – more is more, bigger is better. By the same token, Sag doesn't deal in trifling, casual relationships: He either sleeps with someone and moves right along, sending the occasional maintenance postcard should he later decide to dock again at that port, or he seeks to fold a woman completely into his life, like some large conglomerate swallowing up a smaller, vital enterprise.

To be with the Sagittarian long-term, a woman must realize that resistance to being absorbed into his imaginative vision of life is futile. This rare, willing woman he stumbles upon might already embrace her own soaring view of existence; though typically Sag is drawn to someone for whom he can unlock the doors of perception, exposing a more insular partner to his particular brand of wide-eyed optimism. The irony, however, is that Sag's mate must be so confident as to never feel threatened by his need to perform such a spiritual makeover. He will rarely try to change her external qualities or superficial aspects – nonetheless, one might notice a rather marked alteration in the Archer's mate's appearance as he begins to rub off on her – for, like Dionysus, 'the Liberator,' Sag wants to free a woman's subliminal self of all psychological and emotional limitations. After all, someone as expansive as him requires an equally buoyant, bouncy, if not outright elastic partner. In his zeal to lift his mate's spirits, though usually unbeknownst to our ebullient Sag, he ends up, over time, turning his woman into a female version of himself. Woody Allen's mates – Louise Lasser, Diane Keaton, Mia Farrow – all accessed their inner nebbish through intimate association with him. Other examples abound: Sinatra's true love was his free-and-easy alter ego, Ava Gardner. Top male pop icon Joe DiMaggio was eternally bound to top female pop icon Marilyn Monroe. Kenneth Branagh was paralleled by Emma Thompson. Ben Stiller found his comedic counterpart in Christine Taylor; Benjamin Bratt his female doppelgänger in Talia Soto. Even Jennifer Aniston loosened up her hairdo while augmenting her box-office appeal upon attaching herself to bohemian ex-hubby Brad Pitt's Sag-ruled hip. What Sag wants is to rescue a woman from the mire of mediocrity, especially that which results from either fear or societal convention. He hopes to expand her outward horizons while widening her internal scope – self-revelation is the be-all-end-all of experience from the Sagittarian male vantage point. Ironically, he imagines the simplest way for his loved one to achieve such a state is to model herself on him, the self-proclaimed poster child for a limitless spirit.

Sagittarius James Thurber's masterwork *My World and Welcome to It* perfectly sums up the Archer's attitude toward love relationships, let alone life in general. A significant other enters into his experience – never vice versa – yet his perception of existence is so expansive and imaginative that a partner need never feel constrained or restricted playing by Sag's free-form rules. Whereas Scorpio man, the native of the 8th House of *sleep,* seeks to nearly narcotize a mate, Sagittarius, in light of the 9th House of *dreams* and *visions,* wants to be on the same 'trip' with a woman, to meld with her as completely as possible, particularly on the superconscious level. His sign's association with the *collective mind* is, ironically, nowhere more vividly illustrated than in his most intimate relationships. As one of the zodiac's four mutable signs, Sag's particular brand of synthesizing life's inherent opposing forces is fusion. To him, one and one makes one. Yet, at the same time, Sag and his true love together create something greater than the sum of their two individual parts.

For Sag guy, a love relationship takes on a life of its own: It is the embodiment of his trademark tertiary perspective. And he almost can't help but look at himself and a lover from this outside, third-party viewpoint, a tendency that manifests most as overromanticizing. (Little wonder the Romantic poets are described as tapping into the Dionysian.) The Sagittarian man embodies a heightened sense of reality, wherein experience itself, and not least of which his relationships, becomes an inspired magical child to be both nurtured and celebrated. No man is more the type to commemorate his love bonds with over-the-top overtures such as showering his lady with gifts, whisking her off on a surprise excursion, or other such trademark displays as scattering the boudoir with rose petals to memorialize some special occasion –

every day – or to solemnize the sexual experience. One potentially detri-mental dynamic of being the zodiac's son of expansive Jupiter is an inability to perceive experience from any other perspective than the Archer's signature wide-angle remove. Like some Mr. Big Businessman swinging a major merger, Sag *acquires* a mate, a move he subconsciously sees as contributing to his 'company's' growth. As well, his outsized fire-sign ego is convinced that any woman would benefit greatly from an association with him. Focus is thus aimed at the burgeoning strength of their consolidation, rather than their intimate, individual needs as experienced privately from inside the bond. To be fair, Sag is similarly unconcerned with what he considers the minutiae of his own life – he rarely stops to analyze, let alone heal, any psychological or emotional rifts he might harbor. He naturally harnesses his tremendous energy for use in targeting loftier aspirations. He expects his mate to do likewise: Never wallow; keep riding the chimera of life. For all the stops, starts, and stabs that his opposite-axis sign of Gemini makes at tapping the power of positive thinking, Sagittarius man, on the contrary, often can't seem to turn it off. For that reason, many would-be partners feel he doesn't 'deal' with his internal issues enough to sustain a healthy relationship. What these doubters misunder-stand is that Sag copes with even his intrinsic struggles by letting them run as rampant as wildfire until such time as they simply burn themselves out.

Unleashing energy is a prime Sagittarian leitmotif. And along with extreme sports and adventurous journeying, sex is one area where the Centaur really lets himself go – no male is more abandoned in his approach than the Sag, who is enviably free of inhibitions and insecurities. (Even those Archers with physical, *ahem,* shortcomings will possess that much more irresistible aplomb as compensation.) Sag male embodies the notion that, in letting go sexually, one inevitably rides out any foibles or failings. Sag is free from both the self-satisfying urges of his fire-sign brother Aries, as well as any compulsion to please his partner, which plagues many men. Because Sag is beyond even so blatant a duality as the vividly described 'beast with two backs' – inherently unconcerned with either his own pleasure per se, or that of his partner – he may more fully meld with the *experience* of the sexual act than anyone, male or female. Sex, by nature, is ecstatic; yet, especially for men, sustaining this rap-turous state presents quite a challenge. But not for our ever-loving Sagittarius: Blessed with the ability to 'become one' with the carnal act, despite even the pressing tension of ensuing orgasm, he can relax all the more into the peaking pleasure and plateau for quite a while without popping his cork. Meanwhile, his lover reaps the obvious benefits. It is often said that sex with a Sagittarian man is, in a word, superlative. Sometimes (though not always) without even

John Mayle
Randy Newman
Garry Shandling
Richard Pryor
Sammy Davis Jr.
Dick Van Dyke
Flip Wilson
Red Foxx
Buck Henry
Ossie Davis
Spike Jonze
Tim Conway
Don King
Tom Waits
Billy Idol
Harry Chapin
Mario Cantone
Asa Somers
Denny Doherty
David Merrick
Noël Coward
Billy the Kid
Winston Churchill
Jacques Chirac
Andrew Carnegie
Toulouse-Lautrec
Paul Klee
Ludwig van Beethoven
James Thurber
Adam Clayton Powell
William Safire
Jonathan Swift
C. S. Lewis
Rainer Maria Rilke
Thomas Beckett
V. S. Pritchett
William Blake
Eugene Ionesco
Jean Genet
James Agee
Gustav Eiffel
Mark Twain
André Gide
Bruce Lee
Friedrich Engels
David Carradine
Robert Hand
Gustave Flaubert
Keith Richards
Donny Osmond

knowing it, Sag's signature surrender to the sexual experience allows a woman, nature's little receptor, to take the baton (forgiving the pun) and run with it.

Just as Sag wants to free the woman he loves from the status quo, so, too, does he seek to liberate her from any sexual inhibitions: Nothing arouses Sag man more than a woman giving herself over to sex. From his trademark tertiary, third-party perspective, he sees the two of them, his lover and himself, as a whole – a chimeric being composed of male and female parts, the he-man sexual-libertine-cum-liberator who provides the proverbial key to opening a woman to the full extent of erotic experience. Sagittarius is the one male who identifies with the inherently sublime pleasure principle within a woman, something he feels uniquely qualified to access and drive to new, unlimited heights. If anything, the Sag male seems to surrender his own pleasure for the sake of increasing that of his partner. Here, the characteristically Sagittarian myth of Tiresias comes into play: This devotee of Dionysus, a human chimeric priest/priestess of the archetypal new god, is famed for his revelations on rational sexuality. In an argument between Zeus–Jupiter and Hera–Juno, on the subject of who gets the most pleasure out of sex, man or woman – both deities claim the opposite sex gets off better than the other – Tiresias is employed to settle the difference, having lived, for a spell, as both man and woman. Legend has it that Tiresias, erring on the side of Zeus, claimed that women derive the most enjoyment from the erotic experience – curiously, nine times more pleasure to be exact – a conclusion for which Hera blinded him. As compensation, Zeus bade Athena give Tiresias the gift of second sight, that signature sage Sagittarian vision. Indeed, in terms of sex, Sag personifies Tiresias's perspective, combining objective masculine thought with an unparalleled empathy for feminine feeling. The sign of Sagittarius portrays this paradoxical battle of the sexes from a third-party perspective, which, like the second-sighted, second-sexed Tiresias, looks at life from both sides at once.

In brass tacks, if anybody is going to have a mirror on his ceiling, it is the Archer, who, as the sign's symbol would have it, is naturally removed from any effects of the swift shaft he may be shooting. This is the rub in making love to a Sag; as present and penetrating as his pounding may be, there is a sense that he's somewhere else, as if undergoing an out-of-body experience. Sag guy, like Dionysus, might *represent* the principles of disorder, frenzy, or orgiastic ecstasy, but, like that splendid male god, he will often himself be as blasé as can be. Even when in the extreme throes of sexual rapture, his partner might sense that Sag is somehow in the role of observer, sometimes wearing an almost voyeur-istic smile, no matter how active a part he is obviously taking in the procuring of her pleasure. Mirror or no, he sees himself from a sort of aerial view, working, in his mind's eye at becoming a screenworthy sex symbol if not providing one long, continuous money-shot. As a nod to his Dionysian association with the vine, his conduct is spontaneous and 'twisted'; he is notorious for coming at a woman every which way, often to climactic results. So, too, does Sagittarius seem to embody that which women find most lacking in other men: a need to cling and entwine himself, which he does with passion and persistence. In any case, he is random in his sexual manner – everything goes everywhere, with no predicting where his fingers, tongue, or penis might next alight. Typically, he's a legs and ass man, a woman's tits sometimes generating little more excitement than his own. Whether for the sheer love of this area or because it represents just that much more a sense of taboo, Sag, like his neighbor Scorpio, tends to push the envelope on anal sex more than most guys. (For many women, anal sex represents a major milestone, a possibility that incites his expansive nature all the more.) He relishes seeing his lover reach beyond set sexual limits, in hopes that she'll eventually beg him to do something she had originally considered outrageous. If Sag is to be continually fulfilled by a woman, she must, in effect, become more hedonistic, if not outright raunchier in her approach to sex, and indeed, to life. Every day, Sagittarius man proves his theory that transcendence is achieved through a certain sense of abandon. Little wonder he can be so addicted to sex, an activity in which there is always a new act to encounter and an ever-increasing opportunity to let down one's guard.

Sag likes sex to be long on time, cool on tone, but always with a twist: He is, quite simply, kinky by nature. Just as he likes to wrap his physical body around a woman, giving her the sense that he is as omnipresent as Zeus himself, so, too, does he seek to infiltrate every corner of a woman's psycho-sexual being. He is an explorer of fantasies, driven to uncovering desires that may lie dormant in the recesses of his lover's mind. He may employ erotic 'play,' lightly entertaining his partner in pointed directions en route to piquing curiosity and inevitably making carnal inroads. Being the zodiac's chimera often means he is mixy-matchy in both temperament and sexual behavior – a quality that may manifest as a simple swapping of undies with his lover (leopard-print bikinis are his favorite) or progress more elaborately to role reversal, swinging, or full-on group sex. If any guy will welcome his wife or lover strapping on a dildo and giving him what for, it will be the Sag man, who enjoys that act's topsy-turvy essence. His famous third-party perspective means he's very much into threesomes – whereas many signs might welcome an occasional third wheel rolling into the bed he or she shares with a partner, Sag man tends to be that wheel himself, tired of just eating his own tail (believe us,

STR8 TURN-ONS

tall females
blonds, Scandinavians
flight attendants
(passive) erotic massage
married women
anonymity
verbal action
role-reversal
pantyhose, nylons
pansexuality
onanism
m-m-f threesomes
spit-roasting, tag-teaming
foursomes, swapping
bisexuality, homoeroticism
orgies, hedonism
exhibitionism
(passive) worship
outdoor sex, public sex
leopard skin
wild-woman fantasies
hunting/capture games
gigolo role-play
(passive) ass play
drugs, asphyxiation

he would if he could) – happily careening into the lives of couples looking to round out their sex life. Sagittarius loves to step in, sizable reputation and infamous staying power in tow, to please a woman with a proper pummeling. In this scenario, it is not only the notion of a sex-starved woman begging for release that arouses him, but the sense of humiliation being directed at the comparatively 'lesser,' lacking husband or boyfriend also strikes an erotically sadistic chord. In certain cases, if everyone involved is so inclined, Sag might even take things an infamous step further, 'topping' the other guy and thus simultaneously satisfying and shaming this fellow in the face of his woman. Such is the Sagittarian seat of power: to prove how much more superhuman he is than the next guy and be gone. For better or worse, in a purely sexual context, Sag is rarely inspired to revisit the same experience – for him, once is usually enough. Sag fancies himself the quintessential gigolo: Indeed, in hiring a paid consort, one might hope he turns out to be a Sagittarian, built to deliver that much more bang for the buck. As a sexual persona, the Archer is at once breathtakingly masculine and radically open-minded, allowing for endless possibilities in the pursuit of pure pleasure.

As a rule, Sag male is not so much bisexual as he is pansexual. Regardless of whether he self-identifies as straight or gay, the Archer is most at ease in the intimate company of other men. By nature, he embodies a sense of the homoerotic: Totally steeped in über-masculine experience, the straightest of Centaurs is so confident in his masculinity as to never feel threatened by, or phobic about, the gay world. In a signature twist, Sag guy is rather more like most women in regard to same-sex relationships; platonic or not, bonds with other men are naturally strong and intimate. In either case, Sag guy is not one to subscribe to the same-sex double standard many men espouse: that sex between women is a natural erotic behavior that shouldn't necessarily be defined as lesbian, while even a subtext of attraction between men signifies weakness, provoking revulsion. Sag man, no matter which way he swings, tends to apply the former vision of girl-on-girl sexuality to the world of men as well. Intimate relations with another guy, whether of a sexual nature or not, are seen as an expression of male empowerment, just as, say, the lesbian movement is viewed as reinforcing feminism as a whole.

From adolescence, Sagittarius inhabits a testosterone-themed world, being the consummate rough-and-tumble boy thrusting himself headlong into masculine experience. As a boy, he forms infamous crushes on older males, gratefully playing batboy or other such subtly insinuating roles where his hero worship can be put to constructive use. The Archer boy aims to please those giants in his midst and will be witness to, or an initiate in, any such passing homosexual fancies that invariably arise among the hormonally charged older adolescents he idolizes. Such erotic play is part and parcel of many a secret society of this age when such acts are shrugged off as an antidote to blue balls, an interim release on the way to consistently scoring with females. 'Sharing' with the somewhat older males he admires sets Sag up for feeling psychologically superior to boys his own age. Later, as a straight man, this experience breeds in Sag a sense of absolute ease amongst male peers, as if he alone has passed through some clandestine rite of passage. He may maintain an anything-goes attitude toward sex all his life, one that includes bisexual activity as 'no big deal' – this explains why so many Sag guys enter long-term relationships with bisexual women, since, as a couple, they can swing any which way.

As a gay man, Sag's masculine-chic boyhood lends him an elevated status amongst peers, typically becoming the fabled straight-looking/straight-acting stud that many a hopeful homo is seeking to hook up with. Gay Sag is almost pathologically male. Like the other fire signs, Aries and Leo, he may be the consummate 'top,' and yet, unlike those other characters, he is drawn to ethereal pretty boys, if not outright femmey men, for mates. Ironically, of all the gay men in the zodiac, Sag may be hands down the most misogynistic, as if taking his sign's astrological alignment with patriarchal experience all too literally. In his particular gay world, women are anathema: He finds all the femininity he may need in the gorgeous Tiresias he seeks to sexually befriend. Like his straight counterpart, the gay Centaur pushes a lover to the limits, and his attraction to docile, demure, if not obviously straitlaced lads is where this grand fantasy begins. His combined romantic and sexual needs are complex: Like a wild stallion for whom the presence of geldings is a calming influence, a pretty, submissive fellow tends to soothe his soul, while other aggressive types like himself pose a challenge, firing him up, a dynamic best reserved for Sag's sporting or other physical endeavors. Indeed, gay Sag will typically enjoy a large group of like-minded, mostly straight butch friends, but these rugged lads are rarely the type with whom he seeks to mate. Besides being a calming influence, the coy, somewhat sissified partner he opts for should be submissive enough to make the Sag feel overpowering within their sexual exchange. It's a fine line: Sag needs a lover who will take whatever he dishes out, though not so bottomless a bottom that there'd be no stimulating struggle to cope with the demands Sag might make.

Just as women praise the prowess of the straight Centaur, gay men will swear that their best-ever sex was with a Sag. Still, in signature fashion, trysts rarely proceed beyond one-night stands, mainly because it is so difficult for the Archer to pinpoint that perfect partner who will be eternally hard-pressed to

GAY TURN-ONS

bodybuilders, athletes
top on top
straight-male seduction
strong thighs, musclebutts
groups, orgies
bisexuality
deliverymen
frat boys, preppies
military, uniforms
cops, firemen
(active) humiliation
jockstraps, sports kit
equestrian gear
foreigners
foreskin
buttplugs
(active) anal penetration
(passive) analingus
rough trade
wild, kink
hallucinogens, ecstasy
variety, multiple partners
toys, dildos, gadgets
rentboys, twinks

enjoy the surpassing erotic experience that Sag is known to deliver. Perfect sex, to the Sagittarian mind, should always involve his being considered 'too much,' a blatant manifestation of his quantitative Jupiterian rule. Taking a lover to the limit might include exposing him to the more 'out there' world of gay life, bringing him on excursions through the feral landscape of group parties and after-hours clubs, perhaps inviting another dominant character to fully explore, if not exploit, his lover's ever-expanding submissive side. Still, even amid what might be considered a spiraling chaos of sexual depravity, the nobly savage Centaur never seems to lose his footing – something that can not always be said about his partner, whom Sag will inevitably be there to 'catch.' This is part of the thrill for Sag: to bring his lover to the edge, even push him over it, and then fulfill his ultimate Dionysian role, not only as orgy master but as savior as well. Relationships, and indeed sex itself, with the Sagittarian male are, in effect, one big, long trust exercise. He is a trip – and he knows it: One night spent with this extraordinary being proves him capable of offering the kind of wild, fiery, abandoned ride to which no other man can hold a candle.

Couplings

Sagittarius Man ∫ Aries Woman

Bucking authority, they live way outside the rules. He's unhurried and askew; she's unbeholden and autonomous. This is a supercouple that easily finds professional success. Sexually, they're exceptionally open-minded.

Sagittarius Man ∫ Taurus Woman

Fixation at first sight. Sag's colossal self-confidence transforms this twosome. In her, he's found a 'savior.' Financially, they don't see eye to eye. She's one lover who'll satisfy his outsized libido.

Sagittarius Man ∫ Gemini Woman

She's addicted to bold, beguiling Sag man. They're in absolute accord – their bodies, too, snap into place like puzzle pieces. Sex, like all aspects of their shared life, is wild with rounds of overt experimentation.

Sagittarius Man ∫ Cancer Woman

He's undaunted by her turbulent temperament. Exhausted from taking life so seriously, she finds relief in his lively approach. A notoriously wild couple, they might live hard and fast. In bed, immense appetites are indulged.

Sagittarius Man ∫ Leo Woman

Their courtship is formal, enveloped in etiquette, played by the rules. She's a nurturing presence; he's that stud she's been searching for. 'Waiting' is a way to build excitement – their first encounter is explosive.

Sagittarius Man ∫ Virgo Woman

They meet early in life, often staying together through thick and thin. She's overshadowed or 'sacrificed' to his success. Despite resentments, Virgo's satisfied being of service. Sexually, they've no need for enhancements.

Sagittarius Man ∫ Libra Woman

She's in unknown territory; he's relaxed in the company of such a cool character. In bed, Libra loosens up, accessing her naughtiest needs. Sag is spellbound: He's scored a sophisticated woman willing to satisfy his every wish.

Sagittarius Man ∫ Scorpio Woman

His good luck creates their fortune. Her hold on him is firm. What each craves individually is willed through the relationship, especially in bed: For the sake of staying together, nothing is refused.

Sagittarius Man / Sagittarius Woman

Like a god and goddess on Mount Olympus, two Sagges make a mythic match. Together, they feel entitled to the material wealth that seems to seek them out. Sexually, this is the stuff of which legends are made.

Sagittarius Man / Capricorn Woman

A glamorous pair with an iconic allure that both impresses and intimidates anyone outside their social set. Still, the focus is inward and their home is a cozy cocoon. In bed, though, it's down and very dirty.

Sagittarius Man / Aquarius Woman

They may seem ill-suited, but it's an illusion: With her, he's found a lifeline. Paired with Sag, the Waterbearer sets herself up for a brighter future. In bed, they break from old behavior – together, it's earthy-crunchy.

Sagittarius Man / Pisces Woman

From the start, they enjoy an unspoken understanding: Both know it's time to stop running from love. Bohemianism is their mode – she's a gypsy at heart; Sag trades his bowler for a beret. Sex is messy, unfussy, fabulous.

Gay

Sagittarius Man / Aries Man

These fire signs share a slew of qualities – palpable masculinity, love of adventure, a bawdy sense of humor. Still, there's discord: Aries is a neat freak; not so Sagittarius. In bed, both men will try anything twice.

Sagittarius Man / Taurus Man

A force of nature. Together, they seem capable of ruling the world. Still, there's trouble – Sag takes the upper hand, Taurus tags along too willingly. A purely sexual scenario is perhaps preferable.

Sagittarius Man / Gemini Man

Volatility is their shibboleth. Gemini's temperamental nature knows no bounds; the Archer is a fiercely fickle fellow. One or the other may be unwilling to commit. Still, for a few nights, this pairing is unparalleled.

Sagittarius Man / Cancer Man

Cancer is a tough nut to crack – especially guarded with straight-shooting Sag. Soon, it's clear their quality-of-life concerns correspond. The Archer's extensive sexual past shouldn't prohibit partnership: Cancer's hiding quite a history himself.

Sagittarius Man / Leo Man

Together, two high-rolling he-men live even larger – Sag is especially audacious. Fortune seems to surround them. Sexually, too, they've hit the jackpot: It's all a game; extreme behavior gets much play.

Sagittarius Man / Virgo Man

Virgo's neat; Sag is untidy. At first, they're anxious in each other's company. But a love of the finer things unites them. They'll make ideal travel companions. In bed, some disorder is desirable – never a dull moment.

Sagittarius Man / Libra Man

Together, they strike creative gold, having explored the limits of expression, often with dazzling results. In bed, Libra is a minion under a powerful Sagittarian spell. A need for adventure may mean messing with group scenes.

Sagittarius Man / Scorpio Man

Sag is seduced and shocked by shadowy Scorpio. Physical compatibility is assured; emotional understanding takes time. Sexual expectations are great. In this case, the agile Archer has a hard time keeping up.

Sagittaris Man / Sagittarius Man

Together, two Archers polarize into distinctly different aspects of their archetypal natures: the Student and the Teacher – especially in bed. They're a can-do couple, personifying the power of positive thinking.

Sagittarius Man / Capricorn Man

Sag is a macho choice of mate. Still, they share a satirical sense of humor and an affinity for flashiness. In their downtime, it's all about long, leisurely sex sessions. Inviting a third, perhaps a stranger, is status quo.

Sagittarius Man / Aquarius Man

An extraordinarily passionate pair. Sadly, each may surrender to his own instability. Grandiosity is a pitfall – self-mythologizing means they live in a land of make-believe. Sexual antics often border on out-there.

Sagittarius Man / Pisces Man

The Archer admires and often emulates the poised Piscean. It's a surprise to see Sag put through his (psychological and sexual) paces. In bed, it's all about role-play: Sag is subject to the imperious Fish.

Sagittarius Woman

the maven

In life's rich pageant, Sagittarius woman is the contestant most likely to walk away with the crown. A radiant, regal figure, she presides over experience, exuding an air of deservedness directed toward all that she desires. To her, the world is an abundant place where she can reach out and grab all she envisions. Struggle is anathema to Sag: She keeps her eye on one particular prize at a time and, sensing the right opportunity, lets her Archeress arrows fly with swift precision, hitting her far-reaching marks while remaining removed from the fray of embattling human interaction. She appears the perfect leader, one who has it all – brains, body, beauty, and the ability to amass as much devotion from others as she does coins for her coffers. Wealth, it would seem, is her personal birthright. A vividly glamorous character, Sag does not merely slip into situations; rather, she explodes onto the scene. Meanwhile, despite such signature resplendence she tends to be skittish, often harboring emotional anxieties and low self-esteem. Still, more-more-more is Sag woman's motto, both in her professional and private lives. Not one to live on love alone, she makes a successful match with a man who will share the auspice of 'power couple,' drawn to dashing father figures who indulge her trademark fairy-tale expectations. Conversely, in a same-sex bond, she seeks a serious-minded mentor who might expose her to a world of knowledge and vast cultural influences.

PRINCIPLE

The Principle of Expansion: exaltation, optimism, and quantitative experience. In the Sag view, *more* is more, both materially and culturally. Exposure is what it's all about for mutable Sag. She imposes her feminine nature onto the world, objectively expressing a divalike supremacy that nonetheless stems from her subjective desires along the two-way theme of awe and adoration. Her sign's secondary motto 'we think' carries this collective understanding while expressing a fittingly royal air.

Sign + Mind

Sag woman lives a life of exaltation. For her, being born to the sign ruled by mighty Jupiter – the planet representing the astrological Principle of Expansion – optimism, growth, and wealth – means she can't help but view existence as a state in which the stakes are perpetually high. Even the most quotidian aspects of her life appear heightened. Sag woman is like a thoroughbred, a nod to her horsey sign, built to outstrip all others and, in a shot, take her rightful place in the winner's circle, basking in glory and adoration. As a female born under the solar system's largest planet, whose namesake, Jupiter (Greek: Zeus), is the omnipotent king-god, Sag woman thus draws her archetypal energy from his female equivalent the supreme queen-goddess Juno (Greek: Hera), who, as myth would have it, was the one deity capable of reducing her almighty hubby to a comically henpecked character. Likewise Sag woman is the quintessential haughty matriarch: A vehemently proud, even supercilious, personage who holds herself up as a paragon of perfect womanhood. Though such pomposity is often overcompensation for a lack of confidence in her natural femininity, the fact remains that she exhibits an elevated sense of self that demands she be treated like gold by her man. She believes wholeheartedly in the sanctity of relationships, particularly marriage, and is not one to be ever so slightly slighted on that score. Juno's patronage of women and marriage rings startlingly true in the ideology of the Sagittarian woman – the goddess's provinces being as much recurrent themes in the work of Archeresses Jane Austen, Joan Didion, George Eliot, and Louisa May Alcott as they are in the actual lives of every living, breathing Centaur female on the planet. Personal independence and permanent bonds are not mutually exclusive or in any way in conflict in the Sagittarian viewpoint. Au contraire: To her, the most sanctified of marriages offer a means for expansion, both in terms of material and spiritual wealth.

Just as the mythical bickering of Jupiter–Zeus and Juno–Hera represents the clash of combining a patriarchal deity system with a matriarchal one, the two sex signs of Sagittarius represent these highest orders of gender-power in the universe. For Sagittarius male, the zodiac's little Dionysus, patriarchal power is his inalienable inheritance as if handed to him on a silver platter by Zeus. For the Sag woman, however, astrology's own high and mighty Hera, a sense of omnipotence is not something she needs to be granted – it is her birthright – however, she often ends up in struggles with a mate whose male ego won't easily allow for the outsized status Sag typically maintains. For the Archeress requires a partner who is at least as powerful as she – in modern terms: Wealthy, professionally successful, socially elevated, if not celebrated, and of sound mind, body, and moral conviction – so as not to breed slings and arrows of jealousy or resentment aimed back onto her, in the bond. Besides, anyone less ambitious and successful than herself is a huge turnoff, as only a mogul, indie or otherwise, can get and keep her juices flowing.

Sag author Dawn Powell once wrote, 'Luxury is living within your means.' Though this missive might sound noble on the surface, the oft-missed point to this statement is that luxury, to the Sagittarian mind, can and *should* be had at any income level – it is the Archeress's one essential. Among other things, the 9th Astrological House rules *life experienced beyond the everyday,* which is fitting, given planet Jupiter's association with the energy of expansion. Taken together, these influences instill a yen for exhilaration, glamour, and glory in the Sagittarian female. Unlike her male counterpart, for whom the sign's energy works internally, forever driving him to mind-blowing rushes of experience, Sag woman needs external augmentation, which manifests in a number of ways, not least of which is a desire to be seen as important if not magnificent. Just as the shamanistic Tiresias is a perfect symbol of the Sagittarian male sex – this mythological 'seer' was blinded by Hera for deciding against her in a dispute with Zeus – Hera's own blinding force represents the brand of power Sagittarius woman herself seeks to wield. The infamous ride of Lady Godiva (literally 'goddess-diva') is a medieval reenactment of the ancient ritual display of the supreme female deity at her peak of power, the time in her virgin-mother-crone cycle when she is at her most majestic – and her blinding of the Peeping Tom is a brash echoing of the Tiresias–Hera myth. Dazzling radiance is a prime symptom of goddess power at its most supreme – Hera–Juno's symbol is an emphatic asterisk on a stick, pointing to this signature radiance – a beacon of a lavish female condition, that is the Sagittarius woman. The naked Godiva astride her steed is not only an emblem of female resplendence, but, when you think of it, the mounted lady, in all her glory, is also the perfect picture of the female Centaur.

Sagittarius is the only mutable-fire sign in the zodiac; and though one might assign any number of interpretations and embodiments to such a designation, it is the image of lightning – that changeable fire in the sky – that best expresses the sign's most poignant meaning. Sagittarius, as the name implies, is associated with flashes of *sagacity, inspiration, dreams,* and *visions,* additional attributes of the 9th House. Like Lady Godiva, Sag woman hopes to demonstrate her thoughts and feelings in such a dazzling (lightninglike) manner as will leave an indelible mark on people's minds – expanding others's noggins with her own notions means an ever-growing global influence. Another 9th House

PLANETARY SYMBOL

Like the Sag symbol, this glyph illustrates superconsciousness (the half-circle) stemming from worldly experience (the cross of matter). Jupiter is called the lucky planet: and Sag woman tends to encounter serendipity and fortune in all her life's travels. Like her archer's arrow, her radiance precedes her.

The astrological sigil of Juno illustrates Sagittarius's especially emphatic nature.

SIGN QUADRANT

The zodiacal quadrants correspond to metaphysical planes of existence – physical, emotional, mental, and spiritual. The Third Quadrant is that of mental perception. For Sagittarius, importance lies in the ability to project an image of whom she imagines herself to be. She lives a life of optimism, as magnanimous as she is materially acquisitive, in contrast to the inwardly (mind-) expansive male of the sign.

concept, the *world view*, is something she actively seeks to infiltrate and influence with ideals that are characteristically geared toward empowerment, especially that of women, if only because society has for so long dictated that her sex must take a backseat in the world's socio-evolutionary journey.

Sagittarius is the third and final sign of the zodiac's Third Quadrant, which is primarily associated with mental capacity. Indeed, as the mutable sign meant to fuse the ideological influences of the two preceding ones – Libra and Scorpio respectively represent objective (conscious) and subjective (subconscious) thought – the placement of wise Sagittarius (superconscious) on the wheel tells us that evolution toward spirituality, represented by the ensuing Fourth Quadrant, lies in adopting a third-eye perspective that combines these conscious and subconscious modes. In the cosmic design, Sagittarius is focused on communication with *universal forces,* and the development of a *higher mind* that would connect us all on a psychological and philosophical level, thus overriding the limitations of our more mundane waking thoughts. This is all a heady way of saying that the Archeress woman naturally 'rises above' and directs her mind beyond any limiting external conditions or emotional wounds, regardless of how traumatic they might be. If anything, the opposite is true: The more Sag has to overcome in life, the further she pushes herself away from any such damaging influences, and toward whatever she envisions as a consummate, exalted life experience. Most often, her superconscious mind leads the way to personal milieus and professions where she might tap into a global network of thinkers, if not amass her own worshippers, in the world of academics, publishing, commerce, big business, science, law, or religion, all such pursuits falling under the influence of her sign's 9th House.

Regardless of her chosen arena, Sag feels the deep need to make an impact. She embodies the adage 'knowledge is power' – from early on, she is the model student, dedicated to making top grades, which will later serve as a ticket out of her childhood surroundings. In sharp contrast to her opposite-axis sign of Gemini, whose domain is the familiar and the familial, Sag is a born citizen of the world, and the whole of her upbringing feels like being waylaid in customs. Her parents tend to fall into a certain mold: Her mother is a domineering character, vain and pampered, her father the premier 'Mr. Nice Guy,' who nonetheless has difficulty meeting his wife's constant, tremendous demands. Though outwardly overbearing, Mother is often a weak character, a bonbon eater who resents having to pitch in and pull her own weight. Father is devil-may-care toward responsibilities. Nothing is ever enough for Sag's mom, a materialist of the first order, and the blame for her frustration falls heavily on Dad's shoulders. He is typically an adventurer of sorts, often an overgrown kid who prefers to spend what cash he earns on extreme sports or cultural interests, hobbying, far-flung travel, or other such big-ticket outings. Not surprisingly, Sag is often the product of a broken home. Even when her parents remain married, her mother may break out in search of the elusive *all* she's missed, filling her wallet and/or footing the bill for extravagances herself with earnings from a solo career, typically started later in life and all but exclusively for monetary gain. Or, she may simply hope to have a luxe lifestyle 'rub off' on her via hobnobbing with people who inhabit the right side of the tracks. Sag's dad only goes further afield in his trademark excursioning, emotionally retreating from his wife and sadly often sacrificing close ties with his children, especially the Archeress, who is hardest hit by this dynamic in her formative years. Sag feels torn in two directions. Like her mom, with whom she'll ultimately share a common bond of rancor if and when times are tight, Sag wants more from life than what might be considered 'enough' by comfortable standards; still, longing for fatherly love, she glorifies her dad as even more an exciting adventurer than he actually is. By the same token she buys into her mother's labeling him an underachiever, just as she might see his side of the story – that her mother is an inveterate money-grubber. As a means of coping, the Archer girl focuses her attention beyond this overwhelming domestic duality, forward toward the future. She takes aim at specific targets for her lifelong ambitions, often alighting on a career direction and beginning to pursue it as early as teenage, so long as it fulfills two requirements: one, that it all but guarantees big financial reward, as will impress her mother, and two, that it offers the kind of cultural or daring enterprise as would excite her father's imagination. And it will be these same two prerequisites that form the basic criterion for what she insists upon a mate wanting out of life.

Needless to say, Sag does much in the way of self-parenting. If her upbringing teaches her anything, it is an ability to see both sides of any sweeping argument, a quality that saves her from any feelings of resentment. Indeed, Sag is remarkably forgiving, or rather she doesn't quite recognize when she's being done harm, a by-product of not admitting she may have been, emotionally, left holding the bag as a child – which she generally is. (You can often criticize a Sag, and somehow, with a 'thank you,' she'll manage to twist your words, in her own mind, into a compliment, glowing all the more at the notion you've been giving thought to her.) She will not see the bad, and would that we all could think this way, she can never quite imagine herself as having done any wrong. This, too, is a result of her childhood upbringing: She copes with emotional unrest by being the consummate overachiever, and she'll rarely ever see herself as anything else, oblivious therefore to any shortcomings. She

SIGN GLYPH

The Sag Archer is armed with an ability to project desires and effect change far into the distance. Human will stems from mastery of the physical plane. Earthly goals are organic offshoots of her perception of existence as an expansive, abundant experience. She hungers for temporal goodies and worldly knowledge. Her sign's main motto is 'I understand,' pointing to her need to approach the world with maven expertise.

ELEMENT + QUALITY

The fire element symbolizes life energy, spirit, or the divine force; the mutable quality, a call for versatility and change. Together the mutable-fire combination particular to Sagittarius is best described as a certain radiance or glory. It is that sort of glamour that the Sagittarian displays, something that silently says she's a force to be reckoned with.

POLARITY

Females in masculine signs (fire, air) are not aligned with the gender polarity of the sign and thus enact instead of embody the quality-element combination of the sign. Sag projects her (mutable-fire) radiance outward, parading herself in the expectation that others will want to bask in her glorious presence. She breathes that fiery spirit of optimism into others, instilling confidence and causing them to blossom into more vibrant versions of themselves.

may be such a type-A personality, in fact, that teachers may worry about her working too hard and heading for a fall. Sag is notoriously mature, responsible, and all-business from early youth, quite in keeping with her sign's association with the 'established' age group 56–63. Though she's often nerdy, if not gawky or clumsy as a girl, many a keen-eyed adult can spot her as a potentially spectacular beauty. This is just one example, in a lifelong series of instances, of how Sag experiences a need for having to catch up with herself. As a teenager, when most girls' eyes are on frivolous trappings and appearances, Sag is preoccupied with SAT scores, internships, and securing early acceptance to the top school of her choice.

Certainly, of all the women in the zodiac, Sagittarius is the most future-oriented. Finding it difficult to live in the moment, she is in fact prone to anxiety disorders. For her, the grass seems always to be greener up ahead, and she may experience continual dissatisfaction with her present circumstances, no matter how stellar. Sag is infamously plagued by thoughts of roads not taken. Still, like an arrow-shot, she is often rocketed to top spots in life, granted leadership positions, which, though she targeted them, may make her feel undeserving or out of her depth. This only contributes more to feelings of panic or fraudulence, a sense of having skipped certain steps and struggles that most anyone else would have had to endure. It's a classic Sag woman dynamic, one that makes her highly self-conscious. Whereas Sag guy can't help but embody a third-party perspective toward life, being neither objective nor subjective in view but rather tertiary, like the double-sexed Tiresias looking at life from both sides at once, Sag woman takes that dynamic a wee bit further. Our Godiva feels that it is she who is continually *being* watched from that third-eye perspective, as if a camera were always rolling, putting her on display. Experience is always heightened and strangely celebratory for the Sagittarian, like some queen under constant public scrutiny. Along those same metaphorical lines, in her career Sag typically rises to figurehead positions, invariably called upon to lead others as an 'expert,' though she often feels not quite up to snuff. Still, as one might imagine, she puts on a great show – though always somewhat faking it, which only fuels her feelings of being, well, a fake. Eventually, however, she will catch up with herself, learning by doing the lofty work she lands. Life for Queen Sag is one long on-the-job training, and she meets her every challenge with a reflex smile and a brilliant gift for delegating. Indeed, and heed, empowering others is her signature key to success – as what she might lack in know-how, she never fails to make up for in trust and confidence in those who support her, do her bidding, and – they better – make her look good.

Body + Soul

Sagittarius woman loves, indeed lives, to be seen. She makes a bold statement, grandly entering a room, not so much hoping as assuring that all eyes will be on her. She is born understanding the power of first impressions, and she is always determined to make a glorious one. Slowly, often exaggeratively, sauntering into a social setting, Sag's arrival is announced by her voice, a laughing, built-in fanfare as would herald Hera's entrance into the hall of Olympus. And like that high and mighty queen of the gods, Sag will not be overlooked, underestimated, or in anyway outshone. For her, life is as much pomp as it is circumstance, and she lives every day as if in celebration – similarly, she herself expects to be celebrated. So long as she meets with attention and appreciation, Sag is a beaming, upbeat figure, one who positively glows, as if literally lit from within – the whites of her narrow eyes flash, her skin gleams, health and vitality shining as if from every pore of her statuesque being. Larger-than-life, Sag is the tawny Texan of the zodiac, no shrinking creature of subtlety, but one eternally committed to giving life all she's got. As a quick perusal of a list of notable Sag ladies reveals, the sign boasts a bevy of emblazoned women – to Austen, Didion, Alcott, Powell, and Eliot are added Willa Cather, Emily Dickinson, Rita Mae Brown, and Margaret Mead – those who managed to shine through man-made social barriers and often literally get their stories heard. Global fame, against all odds, seems to be an inalienable Sag-female birthright. Personifying Hera's haughty aplomb, Sagittarius embodies the greatness of woman, proving the so-called second sex possesses as much, if not more, superhuman prowess as the most high and mighty man. Fittingly, the Centaur girl can not help but appear a potent, often towering figure – literally, Junoesque – just as she is the very apt picture of coltish, if not downright horsey, beauty, such as the looks of the likes of Sagittarians Kim Basinger, Daryl Hannah, Jane Fonda, Jamie Lee Curtis, Susan Dey, Tina Turner, Maria Callas, Cicely Tyson, Dionne Warwick, Mariel Hemingway, Liv Ullman, Lee Remick, and Felicity Huffman vividly illustrate. Indeed, no sign boasts a more remarkable roster of gorgeous glamazons, a line-up of living, breathing depictions of über-feminity, veritable goddesses as would seem beyond the grasp of mere mortal men. And that's just the way she likes it: Especially in her search for a mate, Sag isn't interested in attracting anyone less than a similarly exalted icon of masculinity, one whom she considers head and shoulders above the rest. Like a would-be queen adorned in all her resplendent glory, she parades herself before admiring eyes, taking

9

SIGN NUMBER

Magic number of initiation or blessing, a word with dual meaning, French (*blesser* = to wound). Scholars suggest the word *nine* is derived from the Hebrew root meaning 'to gaze upon.' The blinding illumination of Hera or Godiva is inherent in the number. There are nine planets in the solar system, nine months of pregnancy, nine choruses of the angels according to Jewish mysticism.

56–63

SIGN AGE ASSOCIATION

The age of mavenhood. This time of life suggests a certain glorified station whereby a woman can play the expert role of madam hostess or ambassador to the hilt. It is an honorary age, when one feels deserving of creamy figurehead status, the sort of position of power, regard, and influence to which the Sag feels entitled all her days.

Like a thoroughbred, Sag woman can be high-strung and skittish. She is prone to panic attacks. Projecting herself so far ahead in life may lead to feeling unworthy or fraudulent. To overcompensate, she puts on imperial airs to convince herself she's deserving of success. She has a pathological need to be liked. She is people-pleasing and oft falls into two-facedness. She can be overly materialistic and succumb to a 'let 'em eat cake' attitude.

great pains with her appearance – no creature of subtlety is she – so as to project so divalike an image as would weed out any man who lacks the confidence and charisma necessary to make a compatible partnership.

Sag naturally possesses the necessary ingredients with which to properly pull off such a dazzling demonstration. Typically wholesome, with a corn-fed beauty, she is as healthy in her body as she is in her mindful ambition. Born with an athletic build, solidly boned and sinewy, she is as much a potential tomboy as her fellow fire-sign sisters – Aries and Leo – yet, unlike them, she neither, respectively, embraces her boyishness nor blends it into a tough-girl brand of womanhood. Instead, Sag seeks to subdue her more strapping qualities, going the extra mile to feminize herself in so absolute a manner as only the farsighted Archeress can do. Typically, she grows her hair into cascading tresses, often lightening her locks while plucking, tweezing, or bleaching any errant fuzz on her body or face. With her protrusive forehead (made all the more pronounced by a concave 'third-eye' space), dramatic cheekbones, a small nose with dramatically flared nostrils, deeply creased nasal folds, thin lips, and a strong, often jutting jaw, there is something extreme about her features. Her chiseled countenance might even lend a masculine or handsome air, which she takes great pains to compensate for, thinning her brow and plumping her lips cosmetically and otherwise feminizing her appearance. With large, squared shoulders and powerfully muscular arms, she knows to wear draped, rather than fitted styles of clothing that hang from her frame, further contributing to her goddesslike look – long column dresses are a favorite Sag fashion choice. Such styles also offset a short waist while enhancing her greatest feature: those endlessly long legs, which she shows off to maximum effect. Exposing a fair amount of skin works well for the Sag, whose natural brand of beauty is at once fresh and wildly forboding. As a nod to the sign's horsey symbol, her body is streamlined, her typically small breasts a mere afterthought, barely masking her pronounced pectorals, her sleek torso tapering down to slim, shimmering Sag-ruled flanks and a rather flat behind. Her pelvis may be wide, which makes her pussy appear small and shy in comparison, in any case a typically unhairy affair, if only due to regular waxings. Her appearance is all-important to the Sag, who knows that her body is the best advertisement for a superior mate. The long-range-minded Archeress leaves no stone unturned in making herself over in the likeness of some pampered queen who, at a glance, seems strictly fit for a king.

Having such foresight, in addition to being born under planet Jupiter's limitless power, allows Sag to see beyond obstacles and successfully target her aims, sexual or otherwise. The rub, however, is that she sometimes goes too far in putting herself 'out there' and is not always 'up' to the emotional challenge of fulfilling the role of the iconic maven that she projects. The result: a disconnect of sorts, whereby, though styling herself as some towering luminary, she simultaneously retreats into a little-girl personality, an attempt at psychological self-protection against the lofty expectations (of herself) she instills in others. Such a dichotomy in character is often interpreted, by men, as an unassuming allure along the girl-can't-help-it line; while other women might mistake her often genuine giggly guilelessness as just another arrow in her quiver of self-motivated manipulations. When it comes to pure appearances, Sag may, too, be guilty of overshooting her mark, styling herself as a big-time gal seeking to leave any humble or underdog origins in the dust – though she never quite escapes her horsey sign's more hayseed roots. Simply put, Sag can be all too obvious, *prinking* herself – that is, dressing for show – in such a manner as will telegraph her desired goals. If she's determined to become chairwoman of the board, for instance, she'll don the most conservative garb and get the most teased-and-sprayed hairdo on the planet. If she wants to be seen as fashionable, she'll sport an on-the-nose replica of what *Vogue* has laid out on its latest pages. In youth, because she inherently seeks praise, Sag might be the consummate junior-beauty-pageant contestant who begs her parents, rather than being pushed by them, to compete. She yearns to dazzle, notoriously drawn to sparkling sequins, exaggerated styles, and ultrabright colors. This is not the sign representative of the 'best' in life, but the 'most.' If it's new and expensive, Sag will take two. She seems not to have an understated bone in her body, let alone a sedate item of clothing in her closet. She is an overt, decided diva, though an often gawdy goddess, if deified she must be.

Sag female is often catapulted into top professional positions, seeming to pole-vault over any and all competition, because, or so say her detractors, she looks the part. What most people fail to recognize is that she has actually put herself there: That giggly little-girl act of hers isn't really an act at all but rather a reaction to her realization that she's the most power-hungry (read: ruthless) broad on the astrological block. Partly because she doesn't want to be seen as a bitch, and partly because she feels bad that she often is one, she pours on the sugar all the more. With a man, especially, she strikes a harmless, even passive pose, subconsciously seeking to counteract her imperialist purposes. She tilts her head when she talks, oohing and aahing in agreement while she listens, her infamously whinnying voice warbling and catching with apparent enthusiasm and excitement. She makes a point of touching a guy when chatting with him, perhaps running her hand reassuringly, or outright flirtatiously, up and down his arm, literally stroking a person while she metaphorically does likewise. In

ARCHETYPE + MYTH

That Sag woman is Junoesque is no big surprise: She draws on the heavenly queen archetype of Juno (Greek: Hera). She is a glamorous deity, the prima diva who is especially demanding of her mate, Jupiter–Zeus. Like Hera, the goddess of wives and matrilineal tradition, Sag demands respect and dignity for her womanhood. Hera is no warrior or huntress – her power is her blinding glory. She causes Tiresias to lose his sight when this priest of Dionysus sides against her in an argument. Similarly, Sag doesn't like to be challenged or told she's wrong. Hera–Juno especially despises Zeus's heir Dionysus just as Sag herself is protective of the supreme power she invariably wields in male-dominated society.

BIBLE + LITERATURE

Sagittarius draws upon the Book of Ruth, whose name means 'friend-partner.' The text outlines ancient marriage laws and customs, like those concerning Hera–Juno, goddess of women. The ride of Lady Godiva – a female centaurean image – sees her blinding Peeping Tom, the poet-seer from the 'Ballad of Thomas the Rhymer.' This is a retelling of Hera's blinding of Teiresias, with Tom being given the same shamanistic vision as recompense. Charlotte Brontë's Jane Eyre (Eire, Hiera or Hera), a woman struggling against societal prejudice, ends up with a blinded man. The overtheme of Sag Jane Austen's oeuvre is courtship and marriage. Virginia Woolf's Jinny (Juno) from *The Waves* is a haughty diva like her namesake.

this way, she suggests total availability, an utter presence in the moment, which of course, she hardly ever is. She is spinning further and further into the future, gauging how her current actions and behavior might impact her ambitions, knowing that listening attentively (or seeming to) while looking attractive is how to win friends and influence people. She is obvious, too, in her body language, which often amounts to a fair amount of squirming, crossing and uncrossing her legs, and otherwise projecting an excitable, eager persona. As a nod to her optimistic Jupiter rule, she is the most convincing yes-woman in this business we call life. Never, never, will she shoot an idea down. She always makes others feel that they can do anything they set out to achieve, precisely the kind of appreciative person one wants as a friend, society fund-raiser, chief financial officer, or steady sex partner. One look in the Sagittarian's eyes and all is right with the world – everything seems possible – and that smiling, beguiling radiance blinds a man, not only to any fears he may have, but to any flaws she might possess.

Sex + Sexuality

Whether in business or in the bedroom, Sag's modus operandi is to make others feel empowered, often through simple flattery, which, experience tells her, turns people to putty in her hands. She is easy on the ego, as she affixes those around her with superlatives, everyone she comes in contact being deemed the most . . . (fill in the blank). One of her sign's mottoes is 'We think' – the other is 'I understand' – a nod to the *global communication* associated with the 9th House, sure, but something that also translates quite vividly into quintessential Sag female behavior, especially when she's with a man whom she's earmarked as a potential mate: She not only tends to agree with everything the guy says, making him feel like a veritable genius in the process, but she also makes it clear she shares his prodigious thoughts, on anything from politics to the philosophy of existence, to such a degree that the two of them are cerebrally if not spiritually connected. Miss Heightened Experience can't simply acknowledge that she and a first date might, say, have a lot in common – to her, such shared sentiments are tantamount to their being pre-destined soul mates. As it is, in Sag's celebratory company, one feels compelled to toast at steady intervals, in large part because she may perpetually be proposing one, with glass raised and eyes glazed over in a loaded appreciation of even having just met. Of course, she attracts her fair share of bons vivants, if not outright loafers, who don't see much beyond her appearance as an enthusiastic party girl. It doesn't help such slouchers that, in her admiring eyes, they've become exalted epicureans. At least momentarily. For once Sag is convinced that a guy has obvious problems, she will label him a 'loser,' completely steering clear of his company in the future – ironically, in light of her notably generous nature, Sag may be the least likely female to give a guy slack in the face of his faults or foibles. It's one area where she simply cannot be forgiving.

Sag's life is lived in an eternal winner's circle, and though she initially assumes the best in everybody, she has no sympathy when it's proven otherwise. Though native to the zodiacal sign of benevolence, which rings true in most cases, the Archeress's abundance consciousness might nonetheless precludes her from altruistic understanding of those less fortunate than herself. This insensitivity shows up in some small ways: For one, she is notoriously dismissive of those in service positions – waiters, janitors, hotel maids, shop clerks, for instance – whom she regards as beneath her, unable to get that regal Sag brain around the fact that these are just jobs, not evidence of innate inequality. More obviously, she may shy away from involvement in charitable causes, except maybe to write the occasional check. Otherwise, she can be guilty of a rather let-them-eat-cake take on abjection. It is as if she is too programmed toward optimism to be consistently aware of pain and suffering – it simply doesn't fit her exalted vision of existence. Likewise, when it comes to choosing a mate, her ruling Jupiter comes startlingly into play. Called the higher benefic, the planet brings luck on *both* the astral and the material planes – unlike Venus, the 'lower benefic,' which, for instance, charms the Libra woman's life on the ideological/astral plane alone. And whereas the Scales lady can easily settle in with a starving artist so long as she and her mate lead a principled, creative existence, the Sag is not so willing to sacrifice bucks for a beautiful mind. Why should she have to 'settle,' she wonders, when she might be able to have it all? And to have it all, she believes, requires giving her all.

Sag can be so unsubtle in her approach to a man she fancies that, at times, she might just as well wear a sandwich board announcing her loving (and sexual) interest. The mighty mutable-fire (changeable life-energy) of her sign means that Sag gal puts her whole spirited self into action with an eye on making herself so radiant a presence that a man will be blinded to anyone else. Of course, the Sagittarian rearing determines that she adopt such an ultimately imposing MO. Having missed much in the way of mother-daughter bonding, Sag can't help but overcompensate where issues of femininity are concerned. Less, she fails to realize, can actually be more. Just as she notoriously overextends herself in professional scenarios, relying too heavily on underlings, often leaving a mess in her wake, so, too, does she take an inflated view of romantic feelings

9TH ASTROLOGICAL HOUSE

aspirations
higher mind
systemized thought
higher education
superconsciousness
world view
law
religion
ethics
principles
philosophy
psychology
intense consideration
long journeys
foreign transactions
foreigners
big business
trade/import/export
church as spiritual sanctuary
clergy
in-laws
grandchildren
inspiration
meaning
public opinion
court decisions
universal energy
lessons learned
second marriages
manifest social concepts
careers in publishing
academia
developing wisdom
intellectual synthesis
passage of principles
cultural pursuits
growth of consciousness
out-of-body experience
shamanism

KEYWORDS

fortune
glory
magnitude
expertise
celebrity
entitlement
vicissitude
ecstasy
growth
hyperbole
agitation
luxury
procurement
beneficence
ambiguity
vanity
enterprise
adventure
extroversion
accomplishment
exuberance
pomp
exploration
liberation
challenge
fidelity
versatility
expectation
ambition
ostentation
rivalry
self-promotion
exposition
extravagance
deservedness
generosity
agility
sentience
perception

or relationships. Lest we forget the event-conscious Sag needs to celebrate, even trumpet, the most minute milestone in the progression of a love bond, putting the onus on her lover to commemorate each and every tiny anniversary they might have shared – 'A toast, my darling, to the first time we saw each other pee!' Would that all of us had such gusto for life – Sag woman teaches the world, by example, how to truly commemorate our existence.

That camera-rolling third-eye perspective of hers often amounts to an overintellectualizing of emotions, a need to telegraph feelings instead of simply, privately, expressing them. For the Sag, precious little of her life is left unspoken, her inherent sense of feeling under some lens developing into a near compulsion to be *seen*. She may, for instance, relay to friends the details of what was meant to be a romantic interlude à deux. Such behavior would be annoying if it didn't come from so guileless a place – indeed, one can hardly help getting caught up in Sag's honest exuberance. Eventually, however, she will need to 'get real' and connect any highfalutin ideas about herself with what she truly feels inside. This is the crux of her sign's mutable nature – she is meant to justify the world of appearances (Libra's Apollonian view) with her visceral experience (Scorpio's strictly subterranean perspective). The good news is, most Sagittarians do eventually 'mind the gap,' filling in any emotional holes that a far-reaching idealism initially creates. Still, before she successfully achieves her emotional catch-up in life, Sag will trip, stumble, and fall through a fairly set pattern of experience, specifically in her love-sex relationships.

Having been so beyond her peers in youth, typically seeking a ticket out of her childhood experience by the time she hits college age, Sag is fairly itching to find a guy whose lifestyle matches that which she wishes hers had been like, already eager to project herself into such a milieu and begin one more leg of her far-flung journey. She can't help it: As shallow as it may sound, she latches onto guys who, to some degree, have had far more privileged upbringings than her own. That Archeress within convinces her that a certain guy, just like a particular career, is the one bull's-eye to go for; and so she leaves no stone unturned in achieving such a love connection. Still, her jumbo sense of self cannot abide so one-sided a dynamic whereby she is the pursuer. In typical Sag fashion she is both objective and subjective in her approach to a guy: She bags her big-game boyfriend on the premise that she is just as much a prize as (she thinks) he is, if not more so. For, like her male counterpart, she looks for vulnerability in a mate that might allow her to infiltrate and, in a sense, take the upper hand. So often does a young Sag woman bond with a moneyed or otherwise entitled character who nonetheless feels disenfranchised by his upbringing that the dynamic of 'remedy' in the relationship will be a two-way street, she healing him of any emotional lack he might have experienced, she gaining the sense of advantage she feels is due her. Naturally splendid-looking, Sagittarius woman definitely appeals to a guy's vanity, ready to take on the role of trophy wife or girlfriend and run with it. In keeping with Sag's 'the future is now' philosophy, she tends to marry young, eager to assume a position of young society maven such that even her lofty career goals might be approached from a 'place' of ease rather than hungry desperation. If the zodiac's personification of Hera is nothing else, she is the consummate wife-queen who marries well, happily accepting all that such a distinction might afford her if only to use it as a stepping-stone to begin wielding her own mighty powers.

With such an aforementioned mate, Sag finds all the indulgence she may have missed growing up. For a while, she will let herself be spoiled by what additional luxury her love match may offer. Of course, if she and her partner are true equals, their power-coupledom will stand the test of time. However, as is unfortunately more often the case, that element of compromise Sag accepted by taking on a weak but wealthy character might come back to bite her in the Chanel-clad ass. Eventually, the problems or shortcomings she may have overlooked in favor of putting her career on a fast track will begin to wear on her true self: the once independent student of life who, in *expecting* more from existence, fully embodied the open and versatile spirit that *is* the mutable-fire sign of Sagittarius at its core. Fittingly, what Sag woman must (re)connect with in life is what was aptly referred to in antiquity as her inner *juno,* a woman's personal spirit-god whose male equivalent, *genius,* is still used to mean 'one inspired.' It may take a lifetime of soul-searching for Sag woman to recognize herself as reality's answer to television's Jeannie (again, Juno), a female who chooses to costume herself as a belly-button-baring bimbo though possessing enough personal power to blow any guy out of the water.

This is the Sagittarian female paradox in a nutshell: Despite her inherent might, cerebral or otherwise, she still wants most, in her heart of hearts, to be seen as a physically desirable, beguiling, and indeed passive female. ('Yes, master' might easily be added to the list of Sag woman's mottoes.) Still, like the small-screen Jeannie, one thing the Archeress cannot abide is being ignored, if even ever so slightly. A lack of attention makes the Sag highly suspicious, her overactive imagination left to assume that the overage of attentiveness she fails to elicit must then be being directed toward another woman. Sagittarius is famous for such projections. Often it is a symptom of her own dissatisfaction, as envy, a notoriously Hera–Junoesque trait, can be a distraction from her own all-too-familiar sense of lack. In fact, as brutal as she

BODY RULERSHIP

The sign of Sagittarius rules the thighs, hips, buttocks, sciatic nerves; Jupiter governs the liver (coping with Sag's rich lifestyle) and the pituitary gland, thus growth. Common ills may include sciatica and rheumatism. The sign's rule of the limbs ensures that the Sag filly has some of the best gams going.

is in her assessment of other women with whom she feels a certain rivalry, she is typically that much more unhappy in her personal life, albeit reluctant to admit it. In brass tacks, those would-be power marriages that the Sag woman often makes, prematurely, tend to be mere learning curves on her way to full understanding of what she wants from love. Many a Sagittarius, as a result, will marry at least twice in her lifetime.

If anybody is bound to outgrow an early relationship, it is the Sag woman, especially if she sacrificed lust for an assured income or inheritance. Particularly as she approaches her sexual prime, Sag will insist on finding a mate who might access her feminine genius on more primal levels. Because so much of what young Sag initially looks for in a mate is representative of the lifestyle she seeks to lead, she and a first love or husband might become overly preoccupied with professional issues such that their life together smacks of corporate collaboration rather than conjugal interchange. Typically, a drastic lack of sexual connection is what leads Sag to pursue new romantic opportunities. To be fair, she is often less than libidinous in her early bonds; but, of all the things the Archeress ignores in favor of casting her eyes on the future, her own sexuality is most vengeful in the manner in which it eventually catches up to her. Being half of a working partnership begins to pale in light of her wanting nothing less than worship. As it is the Sag nature to long for something 'better,' a complacent mate might one day be shocked to discover that his lady-wife has just run off with someone more solvent, more successful, more handsome, more talented. More, more, more. The trick about 'jeannies,' after all, is that they mustn't be neglected if they're to work their mutable-fire magic in a man's life – inspiring the belief that nothing is impossible to achieve. In fact, the only way to steal a fabled genie away is to appreciate her more than her existing master. And that's typically how it works if Sag is to leave a relationship – she rarely does so to be on her own, rather she will move man to man in the direction of the most mutual appreciation and benefit.

Predisposed to wanting the most out of life, Sag woman, often while still young herself, might easily make a love connection with an older man. Never the blushing bride, Sag was born to be the *madame,* the most glaring evidence of her sign's association with that mature 56–63 age group. Most of the men who are able to fulfill her requirement as 'accomplished' are older, distinguished gents. Even in an early bond with a partner her same age, the couple acts older – while their peers might be out seeing bands and grabbing bites at a street vendor, Sag and her mate are boning up on opera and building a wine cellar. Such shows of splendor are like an aphrodisiac for the Sag, but all too often materialism becomes the main focus, while sex and love slowly slip away. Indeed, a disproportionate focus on 'goods' may make Sag woman one of the more spiritually challenged characters on the zodiacal wheel. And yet when it comes to her soul's enrichment, she eventually plays catch-up on that score as well. Undaunted, the Archeress will continue to shoot for the moon, rarely blaming luxury for her bond's undoing, determined as she is to have it all. With an older man or a foreign fellow or both – like Leo she has a lust for aliens, but whereas the Leo hunts for passionate Latin or Mediterranean hunks, Sag has a yen for Northerners, whose inherent stoicism she finds intriguing – the lady Centaur hopes to feel that much more desired for being younger and, comparatively, exotic. One way in which the Archeress's infamous far-flung sensibility manifests is in her often relocating to distant lands, typically via some extravagant cortege, like a bejeweled queen being shipped off to wed her king.

Having finally landed a lauded Mr. Big, one who showers her with heartfelt attention and gifts, our divine Miss Godiva is eager to show her gratitude. In light of her sign's knack for display, she is a generous and highly enthusiastic lover. Typically, Sag uses her parents' discontented marriage as a strict guide on what *not* to do. But lacking some essential grounding in this area, Sag's relationships always smack of fantasy – her love life needing to be glittering and glamorous, the home she shares with her mate sometimes ludicrously well-appointed, both her body and her man's exercised and sun-kissed to perfection. Regardless of her actual looks, Sag will tend to imagine herself as a long, lean, leggy 'babe' – this state of mind is a clear example of the sign's focus on mind over matter. Still, if Sag is even reasonably attractive, her home might be strewn with mirrors and photographs of herself, often in highly stylized portraiture poses. The message here: that her lover so adores her that he must be reminded of his gorgeous Godiva at every turn.

Subtlety is certainly not a strength for this child bride of Jupiter whose often outlandish energy makes for fierce, often very public displays of affection. As it is, most of Sag woman's love connections are made in the workplace; where others might feel it's taboo, the wild Centaur woman sees no need to stick to strict decorum should the right suit-and-tie stroll by. Rarely, though, will she mingle with an underling, while priming the rumor mill with fodder of her playing footsie with a superior sexy exec imparts a secret thrill. Once in a relationship, she can't help but flaunt her feelings, stroking and hanging all over her man in mixed company, inspiring such silent wishes as 'Get a room.' Sagittarius woman needs visible shows of devotion from a lover, those she can wrap around her like a pashmina shawl as proof that he is likewise rapt. Fittingly, she loves to sleep with her man all entangled and

Dorothy Lamour
Lillian Russell
Christina Onassis
Anna Nicole Smith
Mia Tyler
Sheila E.
Joan Armatrading
Béatrice Dahl
Sinead O'Connor
Dionne Warwick
Rita Moreno
Nelly Furtado
June Pointer
Britney Spears
Christina Aguilera
Monica Seles
Billie Jean King
Chris Evert
Florence Griffith Joyner
Lesley Stahl
Susan Seidelman
Caroline Kennedy
George Eliot
Edith Cavell
Louisa May Alcott
Jane Austen
Madeleine L'Engle
Frances Hodgson Burnett
Joan Didion
Helen Frankenthaler
Christina Rossetti
Willa Cather
Margaret Mead
Emily Dickinson
Mother Mary K. Drexel
Violette Verdy
Ada Byron
Mary Todd Lincoln
Mary Queen of Scots
Carol Alt
Margaret Mead
Terri Garr
Ellen Burstyn
Katarina Witt
Deanna Durbin
Amy Grant
Carrie Nation
Jaye P. Morgan
Christina Ferrari
Helen Eisenbach

entwined; showering with him is another way to perform for that ever-rolling camera. Toting this tendency to demonstrate into the bedroom, one has never heard such moaning, squealing, if not outright whinnying at the top of her lungs. From that third-party lens, she has a fantastic vision in her head of what ultimate lovemaking should look like. Building sex up to such cinematic proportions may cause her lover to feel incapable of providing fulfillment. Indeed, it takes a man with a mighty ego, not to mention impressive staying power, to live up to Sag's loaded sexual longing; and not to feel deflated despite her enthusiastic eggings on.

No bones about it: The Centauress is a size queen. Particularly when it comes to girth, Sag's lover had better be as thick as his bankroll if he plans to hang around. Result-oriented, Sag is a stickler for having an orgasm during each and every sexual interlude, and if her guy is reasonably well hung, she is happy to take the reins from there. Indeed, she is self-serving in the sack, a big believer that one should take responsibility for one's own pleasure. Certainly, nothing turns Sag on more than herself: As if ubiquitous photos of her weren't enough, there are generally plenty of mirrors around in which the Archeress can see herself reflected pre-, during, and postcoitus. Just as real horses are vain (equine creatures are forever checking themselves out in mirrors when trotting along an indoor ring), so, too, does the Centaur lady love to see herself in the throes of passion, especially when her man is groveling at her feet. Not that Sag likes a passive man per se, but she needs to feel elevated by the sexual experience, never put-upon or made submissive herself. Her favorite position is on top (preferably watching herself), riding her guy to orgasm. She enjoys being orally stimulated, although it's not a fixation, and she doesn't much relish reciprocation. Just as in business, she's the consummate delegator in the bedroom, constantly giving her man gentle hints if not outright directives on how to drive her pleasure home that much harder. Action, for the most part, is centered below the belt, as her breasts generally offer little in the way of erogenous excitement.

Control is important to Sag during sex, and with her typically athletic body, particularly her strong thighs and legs, she can sustain vigorous positions longer than most women. Whatever she may lack in limberness, she more than makes up for in sheer stamina. Enthusiasm, however, only seems to take Sag so far. Men might remark on how different she is in bed compared with how one would have imagined her based on the big buildup of courtship, or for that matter, foreplay, wherein she writhes, moans, and groans. She will experiment, and in areas many women wouldn't think of visiting, but when it comes to specifics, Sag is basically a 'good girl' who merely fancies herself someone with exotic tastes. The kinkiest she gets is in exploration of her exhibitionist tendencies. Indeed, most every Sag enjoys masturbating for her boyfriend far more than she likes to do so alone. Just as Sag male elevates his own onanism to new heights, so, too, does his female counterpart make art out of popping her own cork, reveling in her ability to blind her lover with graphically elaborate displays of self-appreciation, as being 'naughty' becomes something of a fetish for someone so naturally nice and wholesome as Sag. Besides, such 'shows,' she feels, are her duty to perform if she wishes to be considered 'spectacular.' As for her foibles, Sag definitely doesn't believe in false advertising. She has endowed herself with greatness, projecting such majesty onto her bond with an imperial mate, and she isn't about to let the relationship down with anything less than a bang-up job in the bedroom. So, once 'show-time' arrives, our overly zealous Archeress must live up to the image of herself projected in preproduction. Enter: Mmore reasons for repressed anxiety and her overachiever's sneaking suspicion of questionable self-worth. Deep down, Sagittarius has an inherently low-key attitude toward sex, but she feels compelled to add a bit of pomp to each carnal circumstance. Alas, it all looks so much better in her head then when in the midst of a sweaty mess, let alone when having to strip the sheets – reason enough to hire a maid. For the most part, Sag is really in love with the seduction and romance. While even her most intimate acts smack of that ever-present exhibitionism, one specific sexual arena in which the Sag woman might overindulge.

There can be something very *9½ Weeks* about the Sag brand of outré eroticism, albeit a somewhat sanitized version. What appeals is the temptation of bringing her sexual life with a man into public view. As it is, she and her mate are forever surreptitiously groping and snogging, even in the finest of restaurants and at the most prestigious of events. Life, for Sag, should be all build-up, a prolonged state of over-the-top foreplay. And, of course, our Lady Godiva even enjoys a healthy dose of shock value. The thing is: The more she projects a sexy-vixen persona, even to total strangers, the more she comes to see herself as such, a nod to that ongoing autoerotic mind-trip she's forever on. She must see herself as wildly sexy, and heaven help any mate who gives an indication to the contrary. A boyfriend's or husband's slightest peripheral vision, for instance, is enough to send her into a jealous rage; even suspecting that another woman has caught her guy's eye, Sag is capable of erupting into days of outburst and recrimination. Envy is Sag female's most fatal flaw. Though quite hypocritically, if she finds herself in a tepid relationship, she will flirt wildly and openly with other men, often the husbands or boyfriends of the myriad 'couple friends' who make up the bulk of Sag's social circle.

STR8 TURN-ONS
executives, athletes
luxury gifts
wining and dining
spontaneity
northerners, Nordic types
flattery, fawning
married men
thick penises
deep penetration
tennis players
rock hard thighs, asses
exhibitionism
girl on top from behind
standing positions
stockings, garters
photos, videos, mirrors
little-girl role-play
father, boss fantasies
(passive) analingus
sixty-nine
call-girl role play
standing sex
staying power

GAY TURN-ONS

older females
mentors, intellectuals
athletes, glamazons
look-alikes
money, travel
femme on femme
vanilla
outdoor sex
erotic massage
(mutual) worship
deep-kissing
cuddling, spooning
exhibitionism
stripping, erotic dancing
baths, grooming
spas, steam rooms
(passive) penetration
vaginal orgasm, g-spot
(passive) ass play
rubbing, humping, tribadism
vibrators, dildos
(passive) lite b + d
threesomes, couples
bisexuality
male voyeurs

After all, people, to her mind, come in pairs. And as a married woman, especially, she has little contact with single females. Among other attributes, Hera is the goddess of marriage, and Sag shares her sign-sister Jane Austen's obsession with that sacred bond. Couple scenes, though generally not swapping per se, are often among the fantasies that Sag woman entertains. However, these imaginings usually begin and end, as they should, with the 'other man' feeling desperate to have her − as always, she must be the most sought-after woman in the story.

The sign of Sagittarius is not known for having a vast number of strictly lesbian natives. In any case, regardless of how she sexually identifies, the Archeress is naturally and powerfully attracted to other strong women. Like fellow fire sign Leo, she typically surrounds herself with a bevy of females in the workplace, 'delegates' who will do her bidding. Still, as a boss, she is often a serenely benign leader who never plays mind games or subtlety abuses her 'bitches' the way the Leo can. Likewise, when it comes to a same-sex relationship, she isn't looking to overpower a woman like her catty fire-sign cousin. As in her relationships with men, she is drawn to successful, self-realized leaders who personify a more elevated social, educational, financial, or indeed intellectual status than her own. She falls in love with ladies who are all she would like to be, lust and envy entwined into a searing crush that has far more than faint narcissistic overtones. In imperialist Sag spirit, she consumes those traits and tastes she most covets in other women, openly folding them into her own ever-expanding personality, albeit in an artless way, much in the manner of a young schoolgirl forming crushes and modelling herself on popular queen-bees. Straight or gay, she makes a terrific girlfriend, caring and generous to a fault, physically demonstrative and at ease holding a lover's hand or arm just strolling down the street. Even a card-carrying heterosexual Sag looks on lesbianism as absolutely natural and normal. As is her nature, straight Sag may enjoy several friendships that ride the fine line between close and downright intimate. Sexual bonding between her and a buddy may be another symptom of her repressed need for closeness and gender indentification stemming perhaps, in no small part, back to her self-absorbed mum. In any case, Sag is erotically charged around other ladies, an over-the-top girlie girl in her indulgences, which lie, of course, along luxurious lines. She frequents spas and resorts, get massages or goes on grooming and shopping sprees, gaining a sense of empowerment as one of two gal pals out on a lark. She needs the validation regardless of her sexual orientation − of men's affections, she is generally secure, but she worries about breeding resentment and jealousy in other women (you see, there's always a hint of vanity in even her most modest of emotions), and she is eager to prove herself capable of female-to-female affinity. If a sudden kiss after an intimate conversation or an excess of wine has happened between Sag and a close girlfriend once, it's happened a thousand times.

When the Archeress does indeed outright identify as gay, her appreciation for extraordinary women becomes that much more apparent just as, starting in her youth, she latches onto teachers, bosses, and other such mentors who inspire her on that signature Sagittarian superconscious level. With such figures she may form intense sexual and psychological bonds oftentimes lasting no longer than a few months. This is the rub: The strong, independent types to whom she is most attracted typically prefer to remain that way. Meanwhile, Sag herself is a worshipful lover, ritually proferring up as much pleasure to her partner as possible, with equal zeal and reverence. In obedience to her lover's whims, she may be more experimental in the sack than her straight counterpart. Remember, there's always a hint of narcissism afoot: As part and parcel of being drawn to Pulitzer Prize winners, CEOs, and top-paid professional model-athletes, Sag sees herself as a (usually younger) version of a lover on whom she seeks to imprint, if not find the proper tutelage for, her lofty goals, which will be, remarkably, along the same or similar lines as her lover's. The expansive Archeress typically wants into whatever world of sophistication a lover inhabits, as much if not more than wanting into her pants. The most exciting thing for Sag is to have both – a lover she truly desires, and one who also promises that all-important element of entrée.

Couplings

Sagittarius Woman / Aries Man

She's a clear conveyor of sexual messages; he readily acts upon them. Aries and Sag share a body consciousness – fitness is often a fetish. Sex is straightforward, spontaneous; no head trips, but never ho-hum.

Sagittarius Woman / Taurus Man

Sharing much in common – especially a need for attention – they clash when it comes to the essentials: She's happiest out in the world; he prefers the pleasures of home. Still, sexually, it's sumptuous.

Sagittarius Woman / Gemini Man

She lives large; he invites such expansiveness, living vicariously. She believes his strengths offset her weaknesses. Sex is touchy-feely, with lots of flirtatious foreplay. She encourages his lewder tricks and touches.

Sagittarius Woman / Cancer Man

She's unpredictable, something he's unequipped to handle. Sexually, she falls into a category: fantasy fling. They share a soulful ideology. She uses sex to fasten his affections. In bed, he'll feel like James Bond.

Sagittarius Woman / Leo Man

Vigor and drive are what they share in common. Two colossal egos, in tandem, produce one of astrology's quintessential power couples. In bed, he's robust and ever-ready; Sag matches such heartiness.

Sagittarius Woman / Virgo Man

He sees potential – a beauty with brains – and sets out to sculpt Sag in his grand vision. He's the 'rock,' a stepping-stone for her own ambitions. In bed, she expects him to burn with desire: Does he?

Sagittarius Woman / Libra Man

His intellectual assets combined with her commercial capabilities create a powerful, profound partnership. He's her muse. This pair proves it's possible to have it all. Sexually, they may be into other couples.

Sagittarius Woman / Scorpio Man

Her worldly radiance is kept under wraps – she's a valuable commodity who should only shine in his sphere. He's such a persuasive partner – a departure. Sag feigns being forced into acts she's only too eager to try.

Sagittarius Woman ♀ Sagittarius Man

Like a god and goddess on Mt. Olympus, two Sagges make a mythic match. Together, they feel entitled to the material wealth that seems to seek them. Sexually, this is the stuff of which legends are made.

Sagittarius Woman ♀ Capricorn Man

Slick Sag and classy Cap man are drawn to the best circles in society, smoothly and successfully threading their way through the social fabric of their choosing. In bed, they're brassy and no holds barred.

Sagittarius Woman ♀ Aquarius Man

They meet, and lives are turned upside-down. At first, they're formal; then suddenly, it may be love and marriage. Aquarius learns to lavish attention in bed – the estimable Archeress won't accept anything less.

Sagittarius Woman ♀ Pisces Man

Each requires some solitude to survive this busy bond. Liberation might be their modus operandi; everything else is secondary. Pisces reassures Sag of her sex appeal. She finds new ways to get him going.

Sagittarius Woman ♀ Aries Woman

Competitiveness creates a healthy sexual tension. Aries is the more overt character; Sag keeps her emotions uncharacteristically cached. Superficiality is a pitfall. Still, it's a homey, cozy twosome.

Sagittarius Woman ♀ Taurus Woman

They're a testimonial to the good life. Though Taurus is easily sated by simple luxuries, Sag can't help but yearn for more, more, more. Even if they end up just friends, an erotic connection endures.

Sagittarius Woman ♀ Gemini Woman

A winning twosome. Gemini rides strapping Sag's coattails. Their partnership means more professional power. But business and pleasure blend beautifully. In bed, it's a question of who's the boss.

Sagittarius Woman ♀ Cancer Woman

They embody different aspects of womanhood – here, opposites attract as much as they annoy. Physical contrasts are exploited for erotic potential. Still, on an emotional level, this couple struggles.

Gay

419

Sagittarius Woman / Leo Woman

A classic combination: Friendship is foremost, but sexually they don't suffer. Arguments erupt over extravagant spending. Life is glamorous. Lovemaking smacks of luxe: Pampering each other is a passion.

Sagittarius Woman / Virgo Woman

They approach life, and love, so differently – a bond between them is bound to be stressful. Inconsistency and unreliability are persistant pitfalls. Compromises must be made. Sex, too, exposes conflict.

Sagittarius Woman / Libra Woman

They are each other's ideal, but in different ways. Libra challenges her lover to utilize untapped talents. In turn, the Scales gal is lifted beyond self-made sexual limitations. Often it's a forever affair.

Sagittarius Woman / Scorpio Woman

They're a cloistered couple who'll often relocate to a remote locale. Together, it's a life of learning – self-concerns are the focus. Both are erotically accessed, especially together. They bond best in bed.

Sagittarius Woman / Sagittarius Woman

Sag is more spontaneous and social in the presence of a sign-sister. But a long-term bond proves difficult to sustain: With so little downtime, nobody's dealing with the details. Sex is vigorous and revitalizing.

Sagittarius Woman / Capricorn Woman

They consider each other stepping-stones. Sag's audacity and Cap's common sense combine; their influence and affluence augment. In bed, it's a randy rumble to determine who's in charge. Both are exhibitionists.

Sagittarius Woman / Aquarius Woman

Anything's possible. The Archer takes aim at the Waterbearer's grand plan, and bull's-eye: Their partnership pays off. They're a sexy twosome, public about their lust. They exude an ecstatic energy.

Sagittarius Woman / Pisces Woman

Sag seems so aggressive to the pacifistic Piscean. Later, the Archer admires and even fears her partner's profound intuitive powers. Together, they have a greater purpose. In bed, both are passive-aggressive.

Capricorn Man

the stickler

Capricorn man is the zodiac's consummate sophisticate. An anachronism of the first order, he is a living, breathing anomaly who, while existing in a thoroughly modern world, nonetheless eschews all things new or culturally mainstream. Like some deposed royal, he is at once grand and stately in his demeanor as well as perpetually jaded, wistful, and dejected in his outlook. Nothing much impresses or excites the Cap – his personal protocol is to remain unruffled and aloof in every circumstance – embodying an ultimate sense of relaxation that remains his eternal raison d'être. An ironic amalgam of highbrow and lowbrow sensibilities, Cap is both a self-taught epicurean and a bit of a prankish wag, an unadulterated sybarite who puts the pursuit of pleasure and laughs first in life, while still being a dyed-in-the-wool mensch who isn't afraid of hard work. For the Capricorn man, life truly is a banquet, and he's the first in line at the buffet table, never feeling a need to struggle or strive, which, to his mind, only leads to strife. When it comes to love, he's drawn to a woman with old-guard values, if not solid old-money investments, one with whom he can share a traditional lifestyle, he as the front man, and she happily supporting and providing him with a stable, functional home life. As archaic as it sounds – Cap is somewhat of a relic when it comes to relationships – his perfect mate is a lady-wife type who'll share his conventional family views while not questioning his autonomy. In gay bonds, the Goat is drawn to guileless, pastoral characters, wholesome farmboys and innocent cowpokes, whom he relishes introducing to his dandy, disenchanted ways.

X

The Principle of Conservation. For Cap man, experience can be rather qualitative – he finds the gluttonous, gaudy parvenus of the world odious, to say the least. He is leader of the astrological old guard, determined to sustain what is sanctioned. To inspire true culture in this petri dish called life, Cap seeks to block certain influences so that civilization's soul might flourish; he considers a dose of self-denial nourishment for his own spirit.

Sign + Mind

Saturn is the sole ruler of the sign of Capricorn, and in astrological terms, it represents, among others, the Principle of Restriction and Containment. Capricorn is thus in sharp contrast to its preceding sign of Sagittarius, ruled by Jupiter, which signals expansion and growth. In mythology, Saturn (Greek: Cronus) is the father of Jupiter (Zeus) and is overthrown by him. The elder Titan deity's reign, the mythical Golden Age, ends when the Olympian Zeus casts his padre down. These two gods perfectly represent the difference between the Sag and the Cap man – the former, the scion archetype, the arriviste Zeus, is on his way *up,* and the latter, the fallen archetype, the superannuated, ousted incumbent 'Grandpa' Cronus is on his way *out.* Cap man, whose sign is fittingly associated with the retiring age group 63–70, personifies this lame-duck energy, for better and for worse, throughout his life. On the positive side he is Saturnian, living the good life, having done his time in the rat race, endowed with a sense of peaceful happiness and prosperity. On the other hand, he is saturnine: wistful, melancholy, or often gloomy in the extreme, overly cautious if not plain old sluggish. It must be noted that Cap's animal totem is not pure goat but a Sea-goat, pointing to the contradiction of a capriciously determined spirit that is nonetheless dragged down by fishy feelings or emotional floundering. The eternal retiree, Cap man is forever open to spontaneous plans or sudden whims. His focus is less on ambitions than any other male sign in the zodiac, whether in terms of his career or even in his personal life.

As the 10th Astrological House associated with his sign is one of social and financial *status,* the age-old misconception has been that our fishtailing mountain Goat is a real climber. This is rarely true. Like his archetype Cronus–Saturn, Cap man looks upon status as something he was born with – indeed, he sees it as every person's inherent birthright – but he's over that hill, metaphorically speaking. What the Cap guy embodies is the other shoe dropping on power and status: He is the personification of graceful decline, the notorious dissident or backslider of the zodiac (befitting the Sea-goat's slippery, sluggish tail) who takes his own greatness or achievements with a huge grain of salt. Even the most famous Cap men seem to constantly fall into some form of declivity, if not woeful degradation, after scaling the heights of whatever mountain they sought to ascend. Falling from grace, the Cap man proves by example, is part and parcel of attaining such heights as others might only dream of – knowing that elusive glory is glimpsed but never truly grasped. Of course, the more notable Caps of the world slip back into their proverbial armchair perspectives of existence (or hush-hush decadent behaviors) so quietly and demurely that the rest of the planet hardly notices their periodic retreats into 'downtime,' whether it be the joy and protection of family life, the haze of hedonism, or a wallowing in melancholia, all distinctly Cap male possibilities. Indeed, no matter how famous he might be, Cap guy, whatever his profession, takes some fairly heavy hiatuses between his more heady achievements. Like the female Scorpion, who falls only to rise again phoenixlike from the ashes, our masculine Goat wins a similar title of the perpetual comeback kid. Of course this propensity only perpetuates his infamous picky-choosy persona, one who holds out for quality over quantity of experience, in professional endeavors, social minglings, or in his pursuit of romantic relationships.

Another solid misconception about the sign of Capricorn is that Saturn's rule makes Goat people of both sexes closed and restrictive as compared with their expansive and accepting Jupiter-ruled Sagittarian predecessors. Though this assumption may be true on the surface, it must be remembered that the wheel of the zodiac is ever-evolving as it spirals ad infinitum through the signs, such that, Capricorn embraces the expansive Sag energy, containing it as to keep it pure, like a mountain lake or reservoir. Saturn isn't arbitrarily limiting in response to Jupiter simply to put a damper on existence; instead, Saturn insures the recognition of knowing when enough is enough. Indeed, Saturn's sovereignty over the sign signals preservation rather than prohibition. The word *Capricorn* means 'goat horn,' the mythical cornucopia, which was the she-goat Amaltheia's ambrosia-spouting horn that fed Zeus in his infancy while he was being hidden away from the infanticidal Cronus. This horn of plenty perfectly symbolizes the Capricorn experience as the containment and preservation of abundance, not the outright restriction of it. Without such a holder as the horn represents, bounty becomes excess, glut, waste, and thus pollution. So how does all this out-there symbolism relate to the Capricorn person in real life? One may wonder. The answer is – in many ways.

Caps of both sexes are most concerned with self-preservation, especially on the spiritual level, the 'ambrosia' they seek to keep pure representing their own immortality – even mere mortals were granted everlasting life with just one swallow of the food of the gods. Capricorn is the first sign of the final Fourth Quadrant of the zodiac, which is metaphysically concerned with the spiritual level of existence. As are all first signs kicking off a quadrant, Capricorn's quality is cardinal, distinguished by an initiatory, essential energy. It is the only cardinal-earth sign in the zodiac, and can thus be described as portraying the key, essential (cardinal) substance of matter (earth), akin to Saturnian *structure,* which preserves the purity of the universe's inherent

PLANETARY SYMBOL

Nearly the inverse of the Jupiter glyph, the sigil of Saturn portrays material, earthly concerns (the cross of matter) weighing on the evolving spirit (the divine curve or semicircle). Restriction is the order of the day, and struggle works as a pressurized means or path to perfection. Structure is paramount, along with patience and discipline.

SIGN QUADRANT

The zodical quadrants correspond to metaphysical planes of existence – physical, emotional, mental, and spiritual. The Fourth Quadrant concerns the soul and one's relationship with the divine or eternal. Religion may or may not have anything to do with it, but Capricorn man approaches life from a perspective of atonement (at-one-ment), cautious not to add to the glut of the world – his motto 'I use' carries the subtext 'what I already have.'

SIGN GLYPH

The Sea-goat is a symbol of the ancient culture gods that brought age-old knowledge to mankind, enriching their lives. The fishy bit signifies primordial instincts and understanding of natural law, while the Goat suggests methodical application of such knowledge.

abundance. The implications of Capricorn's cardinal-earth status are manifold: For one, the sign rules the skin and bones of the body, the essential structure, minus the meat and fat of the physical self. Like the cornucopia holding the pure nectar of the gods, Cap views his body as a container if not a temple. Caps of both sexes, particularly females, seem to embody this understanding in their infamous love of meditative exercise and moderation in food and drink – a theme in Cap man's life as well, but one that sees him going to extremes. 'I use' is the Capricorn mantra, which, in the best light, refers to the ability to utilize the self as an implement for spiritual growth. For this reason, many Caps find yogic, or other such 'soulful' disciplines, to their liking. On the other hand, this motto might have a more colloquial implication if applied to the reliance upon 'substances' often endemic to the Capricorn man. The quintessential image of cardinal-earth is a mountain, a symbol of importance, preservation, and eternity. Fitting, too, that Cronus–Saturn is also referred to as Father Time as his namesake planet signifies discipline, patience, and other such principles as perseverance and preservation, which indeed do require time. Of course, the concepts of eternity and immortality suggest having time forever on one's side – a sense the Cap man experiences acutely.

Indeed, life for Cap guy would appear to be one long stint at the country club where he enjoys a distinct, though somewhat faded, VIP standing. But he is no entitled glory seeker or bristly member-of-the-club. Au contraire: Cap man is rarely rude or snooty, and his truest buddies in life are often those in so-called subservient positions who make his life that much more a picnic on a daily basis – waiters, bartenders, doormen, caddies, mechanics, heads of state. For, being a stickler for fairness, Cap will attempt to be as gracious to his boss as he is to his bookie. In truth, as an employee, Cap embodies his sign's in honorarium status, inspiring a certain awe, fear, and respect in a professional setting, often even from those who are his supposed superiors. He simply defies pecking orders or chains of command. Cap might be a purposeful underachiever, taking on jobs that he could do in his sleep, those that afford him time and all-important ease. For the Goat man is far more concerned with being rich in spirit than he is with financially rolling in it. That said, he is notoriously bad with money: He has a devil-may-care attitude toward such banalities as bills piling up or rent being due. If he wants to fly down to Rio, he does; if he wants to buy a Jaguar, he will. Of course, he will have found the most inexpensive flight and lodgings at some ancient hotel in a delicious state of decay, and the wheels he purchases might be twenty years old and questionably sound. It doesn't matter. Like some geezer, he feels 'they don't make 'em like they used to.' That motto of his, 'I use,' could easily carry the subtext 'it down to the bone,' that essential part of the body being under Capricorn rule. If and when his tastes and whims do exceed his credit limit, he'll simply apply for another credit card. Life is too short to worry or deprive oneself of pleasure — besides, there's always personal bankruptcy to wipe the slate clean.

Life is, metaphorically speaking, mountainous for the Capricorn man. Like the capricious but gloomy goat-god Pan, best known for frolicking through his native Arcadia (a hilly region of Greece, literally 'place of arcs'), Cap man's life is a bumpy terrain, defined by continual ups and downs. Just as Pan — the name means 'all,' pointing to the abundance of life, for better or worse — is a whimsical character, half the time suffering from depression and his namesake panic attacks, Capricorn man finds existence a fifty-fifty affair. He is a brooding bon vivant, believing in his brand of dandyism if only by default: Since life can be looked at as a half-full or half-empty experience, he does typically choose to err on the sunny side, if only *just*. Human imperfection, to his mind, is something to embrace, not ignore, and certainly not root out. In fact, it's often something to celebrate. The Capricorn man shows us that, by falling, the individual becomes enriched, just as societies begin to thrive culturally when in a state of decline. The word *culture* itself means a richening of social experience just as it denotes a fermentation, moldering, or decay, like cultured growth in a petri dish. Life for the Cap is that petri dish: He is, like Cronus, a fallen refugee from a distant golden age, a sort of male Auntie Mame, having learned his life lessons at the proverbial school of hard knocks. He is the ultimate survivor who remains, throughout his life, a transcendentally insouciant character despite, or indeed due to, any past struggles.

Sadly, Capricorn boy doesn't experience much of a childhood. His father is often a distant if not a debilitated figure, leaving the Goat to shoulder far more manly burdens around the house than his male peers. In some instances, he plays surrogate husband to his mother, siding with her emotionally, much the way the mythical Cronus conspired with his mother, Gaia (Earth), in the overthrow of his 'out there' father, Uranus (Universe). Even when Cap's father is in the picture, he is rather remote, and the Goat boy learns, if only from his father's failing to show for Little League games and the like, that supposed moments of glory can't help but feel hollow. He gleans early on what it takes many of us a lifetime to appreciate: that all worldly eminence is ephemeral, subject to Father Time. Indeed, the Capricorn of both sexes is an exceedingly worldly-wise if not a jaded child for whom life is never black-and-white, good-or-bad, but one huge gray area that rarely provides him with a reason to jump for unadulterated joy. In extreme cases, the intense Cap child sees through the veil of 'rosy appearances' all too clearly and finds himself stuck in

ELEMENT + QUALITY

The earth element connotes materiality and substance. The cardinal quality signifies a call to action and initiative. Together the cardinal-earth combination particular to Capricorn is best described as a mountain, a symbol of preservation, a running theme for the restrictive, sometimes elitist Capricorn.

POLARITY

Males in female (earth, water) signs are not aligned with the gender polarity of the sign and thus enact instead of embody the quality-element combination of the sign. Whereas Cap woman is likened to a mountain of self-preservation, Cap man seeks to safeguard culture by instituting restrictions and upholding traditions. This, he feels, enriches the soul of humanity.

the harsh realization of samsara – that life circumstance is all but illusion, and suffering, the nature of samsara, is simply par for the course. Carrying more burden – literally, with an outsized number of chores, and figuratively, in the emotional weightiness that is an inherent aspect of Saturn's heavy influence on this sign – the Cap becomes the child on whom most 'baggage' is heaped. To wax biblical, he is the proverbial scapegoat, a sort of savior, especially for his siblings, who are thus more able to live, think, and dream freely. He is mature beyond his years and urbane in character, transcending such small-town attitudes to which he is typically born – rural life leaves little impression on the preternaturally polished, sentient Cap boy. Capricorn J. D. Salinger's Holden Caulfield in *The Catcher in the Rye* is the model, perhaps even autobiographical, portrayal of the Goat boy: Wise and even gray-haired beyond his years, he is pathologically aware of samsara, sickened by modernity, finding its phoniness fatuous, taking on the burden of all societal 'sin' just as he becomes a sacrificial victim of everyone else's personal vices. He is, in effect, left holdin' the bag, just as he wants to catch, indeed save, other innocents as they, too, fall. Incidentally, *caul* is defined as a protrusion or a cap, a field of which would recall that same hilly Arcadia where our sometime gloomy Pan loves or fears to tread – a metaphoric place where the guileless might easily fall and a savior scapegoat could do some catching of these unwitting souls.

Like Holden, along with many of Salinger's other male characters, members of his fictitious Glass family in particular, Capricorn man lives somewhat like a refugee from, and indeed *of,* the past. (It's so fitting that, residing in a mountain region of New Hampshire, the reclusive Salinger has found an Arcadia of his own, a safe haven removed not only from many modern conveniences but from an arguably fatuous phoniness of the world.) *Sanctuary,* meaning both a retreat as well as a shrine, carries just the sort of double meaning that every Goat guy metaphorically seeks in life. The mountain is, again, the perfect symbol of Cap's cardinal-earth status while often quite literally being just the kind of landscape where he'll look to find refuge from the grand illusions of the world. This meeting place between heaven and earth has, cultures over, been considered a most holy environment, the ultimate sanctum – from Mt. Olympus to Mt. Sinai and beyond. The pinnacle of material experience befitting the *status* associated with the sign's 10th House, it figuratively portrays a physical means to a spiritual end. As such, the Capricorn employs the corporeal experience of life, and any materialism as might come his way, as a vehicle of elevating his élan. Easier said than done: For Capricorn isn't automatically some Moses whose hair goes white in a flash meeting with God. Still he might be on his way to such communion, being, figuratively speaking, like Holden, prematurely gray, as much a symbol of Cap's sophistication as it is would-be spiritual enlightenment. The mountain road is a tough one, an uphill battle at least half the time, but one worth tackling – transcending the material *via* the material. However, the zodiac's stickler (read: dissident or backslider) takes his sweet time on his particularly bumpy journey called life, alternately reaching great heights and experiencing personal falls, often seeking safe haven from his roller-coaster existence, arms metaphorically outstretched in aiding others to do likewise.

Body + Soul

Capricorn man is by far the most affected male character on the astrological wheel; and though such a statement may sound like a slight, it isn't. For the Goat guy puts on such delightful airs, beginning at so young an age, that by the time he hits his twenties, his many infamous poses will have become so utterly woven into his psyche that what would be perceived as pretension in anybody else surfaces in him as an organic second nature. As perhaps a manifestation of the age group 63–70 associated with his sign, Cap's old-fashioned eccentricity is often uncannily represented in his signature style of dress: classic, leisurely looks akin to what his grandfather would have sported some fifty years ago. Indeed, given his sign's rulership of the 10th Astrological House of *tradition,* if anyone is going to show up anywhere wearing plaid trousers, a cardigan, and even the odd neck scarf, it is our vintage Capricorn man. Even in youth, his attire suggests a just-slipped-into-retirement feeling, as he clothes himself in the distinct identity of one who has earned the right to just kick back and relax. He oozes indifference as if from every pore of his strong yet willowy physique, itself perpetually prone, if not supine, as he drapes himself across furniture or leans his body along an entire length of wall. Both in his physical demeanor and his discourse, Cap communicates that he lives, almost ridiculously at times, in the moment; and in every sense of the word one witnesses his inherent propensity to *dwell* – particularly, on the past.

The world, as Capricorn sees it, is in decay, evidenced not only by his style of dress and manner but in his love for gilded relics of forgone eras, whether they be vintage cars, ancient cities, venerable social venues, or old-world manners and charm in other people. Upon entering any social setting, he is easily spotted as the longest, coolest drink of debonair water you ever did see. Even when he's not terrifically tall, he will appear so, having the perfect proportions for being the notorious clotheshorse that he is. Dressed to the nines

10

SIGN NUMBER

The zenith number. Ten is the culmination of all that comes before it, the start of a new set of order. Most number schemes are built on systems of tens, hundreds, thousands, etc. This represents man's relationship to natural perfection as humans have ten fingers for counting. There are ten commandments or Saturn-ruled prohibitions.

63–70

Age of retirement. This is a period marked by pulling back, an antidote to living large in earlier years. It is a time of getting back to those Capricorn-ruled bare bones. All his life, Cap man embodies this spirit of denouement, attending to his goals with unparalleled relaxedness – this is one of his most charming qualities.

but oh-so coolly and casually, in trademark gray, slate, charcoal, and silver, Cap will nonetheless sport some form of flourish – a modish mop-top haircut, pastel tie, notable absence of socks, elegant antique watch, his signature signet pinkie ring or, a real dead giveaway, that neck scarf. With martini, manhattan, or old-fashioned firmly in hand, this larger-than-life fellow is hard to miss at a party, speaking, as he does, in a smarmy stage whisper of a voice, often with perfect Shakespearean pronunciation, which might seem to be some sort of put-on. But no: Here is no victim of pretense, sycophant, or kiss-assy corporate yes-man. Cap man simply does not seek to impress, particularly in his professional dealings. He lives life as if it were all one long, languid cruise to his namesake isle of Capri. Never is his demeanor even slightly anxious or harried, and whether his bankroll is big or small, he's cavalier about spending, feeling, by virtue of his Saturnian astrological placement, that he has nothing to lose.

Suffice it to say, Capricorn male is more than happy to social-direct, typically holding court on some cliquey scale even in the midst of a massive gathering. Slipping his lissome self into a loungey corner, he stretches out, luxuriating in his infamously sardonic sermons and bottom-line litanies on everything cultural under the sun – provided it happened twenty years ago. It's a pretty safe bet that Cap won't be discussing current events, the gist of his tales typically centering on some Auntie Mame–ian event that occurred many years ago, the moral of his stories always along some wistful theme with a conversational coda akin to 'those were the days.' He will have you know he's 'seen it all,' and what he doesn't know – new stuff – he'll fake, quickly gearing discourse toward more familiar, *old* territory. Heaven forbid the dialogue should lag; to the zodiac's stickler, that would amount to a loss of cultural obligation and politesse. Cap is on hand to make the rest of us feel gorgeously woven into a single social fabric – which is why the blatant parvenus of the planet really get his back up. By example, Cap man teaches that people shouldn't have to work so hard climbing, changing things, or otherwise proving themselves in life. Rather, he personifies a feeling of falling comfortably in and accepting the way things are, even in a downturn. Though somewhat of a fringe dweller, particularly when left to his own devices, Cap is also a vividly gregarious being when in the company of others. Of course, he has favorite haunts – well-worn watering holes and warhorse restaurants – where he'll invite a rotating roster of friends and acquaintances, preferring to be on home turf, catered to by familiar faces, who'll make just enough, though never too much, of a fuss over him.

A perfect match to those antiquated settings he enjoys, the Goat guy embodies a classic appeal, his looks recalling matinee idols of yore. The Cap actor, for instance, is 'distinguished' for being a dashing, swellelegant gent, though one with an offbeat, often screwball sensibility that, if not evident in his public persona, manifests in his less-than-pristine private life – Cary Grant, Danny Kaye, Anthony Hopkins, Mel Gibson, Ted Danson, Denzel Washington, Jude Law, Jared Leto, Jim Carrey, Andy Kaufman, Elvis Presley, Ricky Martin, David Bowie, Rod Stewart, are just some of the typically cleft-chinned, psychologically complex characters of the sign. Known for exhibiting flair and sophistication, Capricorn seems a throwback; even his lithe physique suggests he's never been anywhere near a modern exercise machine. Naturally fit, Cap's body is kept trim via casual sports and time-tested means such as running, swimming, or afternoons on the treadmill or tennis court. Typically taller and leaner than most men, his stature may be somewhat stooped, his spine curving near his square but fine shoulders, as if in a perpetual shrug of resignation. Indeed, Cap man does let out a goodly number of audible sighs in the course of conversation, like someone who's resignedly given up on the hurry-scurry world, choosing to let the chips fall where they may. Ironically, though he's an acquiescent character, Cap is also quite an imposing one, his nonchalance lending him a heady confidence and strong, comfortable presence. As a physical reflection of such a sanguine spirit, this sardonic sophisticate has a weighty, immovable stature framed by large, sturdy bones – the skeleton is ruled by his sign – not to mention fairly hefty boners as well. In fact, all of Capricorn's extremities, including his hands and feet, are of the long, thick, and heavily veined variety.

Cap man is a beguiling combination of boyish beauty and an almost careworn, craggy crustiness. Though his skin may be as soft and moist as a baby's, his forehead may become deeply lined early in life, his mug creased with deep nasal folds. His face is often beauty-marked by moles and subject to a sharp, dense hairy stubble. His wide-set and generally dark, oblong eyes are fringed with lustrous, long lashes; his nose is somewhat flattened; his wide, meaty mouth is rose-dipped and dewy like an infant's, his teeth weak and milky – Caps often *have* caps; and as if branded by the cloven hoof of some mythological goat deity, Cap man usually bears that infamous cleft in his chin – one title of the goat-god Pan/Baal is 'god of the cleft.' Like Pan, too, the Goat guy may have a hairy body, which, despite its heavy structure, still tends toward being bone thin. In comparison to his elongated torso, Cap's legs can look short, giving him a low center of gravity and a swivel-hipped gait made all the more remarkable by an arched lower back and buttocks. Though his legs are slender and also covered with dense, coarse hair, his ankles may appear thick and sturdy, belying that they, like all his Cap-ruled joints, are prone to injury. Overall, his body is spry, sinewy, and seductive, though saved from

PSYCHOLOGY

Melancholia plagues Capricorn. He can be as dark as a black cloud. He seems to be almost in love with suffering, disinclined to make positive changes when opportunity knocks. He can be an elitist – closed to new people and ideas. He tends to dwell on the past and is almost pathologically behind the times. He is an infamous know-it-all and is fearful of competition.

appearing too adolescent by a stiffness in his movements. His chest can be somewhat concave, with negligible nipples; and his stomach, though not always solid, is often flat, fleeced with a shock of hair that extends down to his pubis. His package tends to be loose and floppy, boasting a rather fleshy phallus as well as low-hanging *cojones,* a signal of an inherent sense of calm in males throughout the animal kingdom as well as another visible symptom of his association with the sagging group 63–70. Likewise, Cap guys go gray earlier than most men in the zodiac – snowy temples lend him that signature air of sophistication, often while still in his twenties. It is as a worldly and erudite figure, after all, that Cap hopes to appeal to those to whom he finds himself romantically and sexually attracted.

Sex + Sexuality

In his youth, Cap man is notoriously attracted to older girls and women who, even when having numerous years on him, are continually surprised and challenged by his ripe adult nature. Being tall and somewhat careworn while still in his teens, the Goat can, and often does, dupe a woman into believing he's *d'un certain âge*. Ironically, though he seeks a certain form of caretaking from a woman, the typical Capricorn man requires no guidance or nurturing: He is comfortable and collected, confident in his ability to achieve lifelong ambitions on his own. Though he may be loath to admit it, what he wants is someone to pick up, rather than look, after him. Cap is rarely attracted to domineering women, drawn instead to seemingly shy and retiring types, if not outright wallflowers or would-be spinsters who'd otherwise wither on the vine, in whom he feels he'll find protection, undivided devotion, or outright servility. Sometimes he goes for arguably 'used goods' – broken-in girls with a track record seem more real to him than self-professed debutantes whose perky, bright-and-shiny demeanor he finds suspect. In fact, Cap man is either attracted to absolute innocents, which can be a sketchy scenario in extreme cases, or women who make no bones about having been around the block.

Though generally popular in grade school, it is a typical Capricorn scenario that he'll see his social status slip early on in life, such that by the time he hits high school, he's already something of a has-been. Like our hapless Holden, the teenaged Capricorn is often labeled odd by peers who fail to understand his complexity and innate sense of dejection – to boot, he is so blasé toward current trends that he seems out of step with his peers and invites ridicule on that score just as he does for reaching puberty early, standing out like a sore, hairy thumb. Not caring much what other boys think, it nonetheless cuts him to the quick to be made fun of by girls, especially popular ones who set the tone for everyone else. The 10th House also determines *how the world sees and evaluates you,* so judgments are felt that much more acutely by the Cap. In truth, such negative attention is actually a misguidance of the sexual feelings he stirs in the opposite sex; and though girls might play hormonal catch-up and soon throw themselves at him, the de rigueur Capricorn damage will already be done. But all is meant to be: Henceforth, the Goat, even when fawned over with heaps of flattery, will take such sycophancy in stride, having developed a strong allergy to any 'in crowd,' saved from ever being swayed by his own vanity or pride. Meanwhile he goes where the love is – often to girls with a Janis Ian sound track running in their head who relate to his nonconformist, misfit appeal and seek to share in his dissident view of existence. And so, faster than you can say 'You and me against the world,' Cap becomes romantically linked with nebbishy nymphs just as he himself is developing into something of a suave sophisticate. It is definitely to Cap's credit that he's not much of a lookist, leaving importance placed on outward appearances to his externally minded predecessor, Sagittarius; instead he focuses on what beauty a person harbors on the inside, though often to a fault: It might be argued that, being such a downcast sort, Cap tends to 'shoot low,' a result of feeling so deeply rejected by the more physically gorgeous girls he truly fancies, like Pan failing to score with all the nymphs he chases. Then again, when speaking of Capricorn man, there is an upside and a downside to every issue.

The main point, when it comes to sex and relationships, or really any life goal, is that the Goat guy simply cannot cope with competition. This makes him a unique character, as whatever successes he does achieve are accomplished in so signature a manner that he stands in a category all of his own – otherwise, he's rarely in the running. Herein we see the quintessentially Capricorn-male modus for operating in the world: He starts out on top, typically entering an arena of human awareness, whether on an intimate or global level, at the top of the heap. Think of Salinger's Glass children, at the height of fame in tenderest youth, with nowhere to go but down, life being one long anticlimactic denouement. This is the Cap male experience. If he lands a new job, he'll be ushered in as some sort of wunderkind whose elevated position is precarious to say the least. In popular culture, the Capricorn doesn't merely tap into a partic- ular slice of the zeitgeist, he personifies the pinnacle of that genre, 'capping' it off: There was rock 'n' roll, then there was Elvis. There was boxing, then Joe Frazier and Muhammad Ali. There was the Hollywood leading man, then Cary Grant. The great American novelist, then J. D. Salinger. The list goes on and on.

BIBLE + LITERATURE

Capricorn is associated with the 'scape-goat' and the Day of Atonement or Yom Kip- pur. Azazel was the same as Baal-Gad, the goat lord and the Greek Pan. Atonement is a Capricorn theme, and he seeks to limit, restrict, and indeed repent. The most vivid Capricornian character is Moses, a mountain climber, who returns with a list of ten restrictions and a new snowy-colored hairdo. Holden Caulfield, despite his young age, already has gray hairs; he, too, feels the world is in need of repentance for its 'phony' excess. As *Catcher in the Rye,* he hopes to save others from a fall. An inability to do so is the downfall of Salinger's Savior- culprit Seymour Glass. Capricorns play the role of scapegoat in their families, taking on undue emotional pressures.

Indeed, the zenith brand of Capricorn greatness is near impossible to sustain. However, the Sea-goat knows when it's time to slide back into obscurity, self-imposed or not, and (as time is always on his side) regroup before navigating his next big ascent. This same peaks-and-valleys pattern, the archetypal legacy of the fallen god Cronus–Saturn, is applied to Capricorn's personal relationships as well. In new romantic bonds, Cap is seen as the ultimate catch, particularly to friends and family of his new mate. People flock and defer to him. He is the front man, showing his partner the town, painting it red. He is everybody's favorite and can do no wrong. But soon he falls from grace – typically, because he simply rears his very human-emotional head and those who saw him as the most happy fella suddenly have a hard time accepting him as a melancholy baby. This is another reason why he often goes for shrinking violets, guttersnipes, or mail-order brides as romantic partners: so that he can experience any such personal falls as (he knows) he's often wont to and not have to face derisive tsk-tsking by people who (he thinks *they* think) are 'better' than him. Ironically, though he's famously jaded by limelight seekers, Capricorn himself likes to feel like a star, at least in whatever ragtag circle he might amass. He's like some deposed czar, still doing his golden-age royalty routine for courtiers-cum-barkeeps. He's the cat's meow, the tarnished star on an aluminum Christmas tree, the masculine equivalent of Mame or Nora Desmond, the very Saturnesque pièce de résistance, in other words, 'the very limit.' His challenge is to shoot as high as he might in love, not settling for second-best scenarios, and yet to still secure the same kind of laissez-faire lifestyle with a righteous babe with brains, bod, and spirit (read: expectations) as he would be guaranteed to share with some compliant child-bride maharincess from Franistan.

The character that Goat Cary Grant fittingly played in the film version of Philip Barry's *The Philadelphia Story* serendipitously illustrates the Capricorn male's vision of relationships. The 'fallen' man, in this case a former boozer, C. K. Dexter Haven, is all the better, not worse, for wear. His name ('seek right haven,' *dexter* being the opposite of *sinister*) says it all: He's on the lookout for a haven, a source, as the name suggests, of both safety and sanctity, Cap's modus in a nutshell. Even his Sea-goat totem, itself half-land animal and half-fish, says he'd be snuggest nestled into some harbor. But safety can be a trap, breeding complacency in the Cap, who unfortunately looks at relationships as a source of convenience first, and love second. In fact, of any man in the zodiac, Cap is the most likely to disbelieve in love altogether, often, in his jaded sophistication, throwing that baby out with the bathwater of what he considers to be phony social contrivances. Typically it's a subconscious excuse. Our melancholic Pan wants, in adulthood, to avoid the feelings of heartbreak he experienced in his youth. As well, the zodiac's old man doesn't want to work so hard or make compromises to his set ways. Like C. K. Dexter Haven, having made a go at love with the woman he truly adores, the monumentally virtuous Tracy Lord, he can only experience a signature fall – a woman's best, principled qualities bring out his most decadent behavior, almost as if in defiance. It's a Capricorn guy-thing: to push the envelope on sophistication all the more when faced with condescending paragons of uprightness. There's something about moral rectitude he's simply tempted to shove up society's rectum. And so C. K. and Tracy's marriage goes on the rocks – the couple's sailboat, the *True Love,* goes into dry dock – and they divorce. Of course, once C. K. eases up on his decadent confections and Ms. Lord comes down off her high horse, they reunite. This is the exact dynamic that Cap man must often navigate if he himself is to get a sense of his capacity for true love. Still, it can't be overstated enough how often the Capricorn guy will miss that boat altogether. If he only realized when considering taking the plunge, into marriage especially, that he would save himself so much more emotional anguish facing up to his love of bright and challenging women with an agenda and expectations (yes, even of him) than he would in looking for safe, easy, convenient 'arrangements.' They are usually anything but. Still, it's as if this melancholy baby would rather feel sorry for himself and live a life of emotional unrest and mediocrity, rather than budge one iota or make the slightest concession to be with the kind of woman that really gets his heart thumping. Unfortunately, most often that sensation only reminds him that he has something fragile, which might too easily break.

There is a good deal of the Capricorn male population, as well, who subscribe to the antiquated belief that women are on the planet to procreate and otherwise do a man's bidding. It's where the *tradition* of Saturn's rule over the 10th House can negatively manifest; generally what goes along with this sort of Cap-male personality is a strict adherence to an organized religion. When it comes to spiritual beliefs, Cap can be ultrarigid and steeped in dogma, if not clouded in incense (Mel Gibson, gesundheit). Let's just say he might take the biblical Moses-going-to-the-mountain aspect of his sign a little too literally. For this kind of Cap, love may have even less to do with marriage than it usually does for this emotionally enervated fellow. A devout stance takes the place of a decadent one, and he may hide his underlying call to degradation in a God-fearing lifestyle of which marriage might just be part and parcel. Indeed, it may be due to repressed prurient desires that he makes such a point of living a catholic, that is, a 'widely accepted,' existence regardless of his religion or even if he subscribes to one at all. Whatever his routine, for the

KEY WORDS

dissidence
recession
fortification
assertion
calculation
establishment
decadence
stricture
refinement
fantasy
wisdom
profundity
duration
repression
exclusivity
inaccessibility
maturation
imprudence
determination
resignation
sophistication
fatalism
development
command
sophistication
learning
ostentation
obsession
stature
economy
status
perfection
tradition
repartee
élan
atonement

metaphorically mountain-roaming Goat, relationships are no mere walk in the park, nor are they for his mate.

Even the signature martini-swilling Capricorn city slicker, free-falling his way through life, will thus look upon relationships as safe places to land. And as the preeminent serial-marrying man of the zodiac, he may do so time and time again. However, when he finds a compliant spouse who'll conform to the structure of a bond he tailor-makes to suit his needs, he will be loath to leave it. And because he can be almost pathologically pragmatic in his search for a safe-bet bond, Cap may think nothing of marrying for money. A boy's gotta eat after all, and heaven knows, if properly financed, he'd happily trade in his thrift-store threads for brand-spanking-new ones, provided of course, they came from an old-world establishment, say, like one somewhere on Savile Row. An autodidact of the first order, Cap typically spends his entire youth cultivating his mind with intellectual, religious, or philosophical study, just as he hones his knowledge of social grace. In this respect, he fancies himself a catch, worthy of imparting his priceless knowledge to a partner, sometimes in return for pocket money. In this way, a shy, dowdy, and devotional heiress could easily become Capricorn male's most compatible mate. He sees a certain practicality in marrying well; should some form of affection or his cagey sort of love be a by-product, then all the better. Meanwhile, his signature dashing good looks and impeccable charm guarantee him a secure spot in his partner's heart, despite his eternal detachment, which is typically impossible to broach. Such ready-made relationships appeal to Cap for the same reason he makes those sudden, gigantic career moves or creative successes: It is his nature, like that of his archetype Cronus, to start at the top and then slowly find his comfort level in situations. And so, when he spots that safe haven of a woman, he really pours on the charm and puts all his energy into sweeping her off her feet, such that, before she realizes it, she's managing a household and affairs for two while he slips ever further into the retirement that is the whole of his life. He finds, too, that the more emotional weight and pain a woman already carries, the more likely she will be to put up with his.

That our snappily attired Scapegoat is metaphysically burdened does not prevent him from dumping it all onto his partnership. In part, that is its purpose: Entering into a marriage with Cap man is akin to having an elderly grandfather come to stay, for good – and not just in terms of the wardrobe he's toting. In his bonds, Cap hopes to reap the benefit of being attended to while being afforded the freedom and respect due to a worldly wise elder. (This dynamic gives rise to a rather negative interpretation of his sign's motto, 'I use.') The sign of Capricorn is associated with the principle of elevated status, which, as we see, he perceives as his birthright. Like attracting like, the Goat is naturally drawn toward the rich and powerful, both in his professional dealings and in his search for a mate. Despite having, perhaps, grown up on the 'wrong' side of the tracks, Cap is *dexter*ous at fitting into lofty, socially Arcadian milieus. The mainline magnates and mavens of the world take an immediate shine to this old boy, as he is a walking, talking historical society, and more importantly, find him a perfect match for their more old-maidish daughters. Love aside, the Goat is equally unmoved by sexual stirrings, which are rarely a determinant factor in his choice of a partner, ironic since few men experience the lofty level of libidinous urges to which he is party. Erotic desires may be somewhat of an annoyance to him, an indecorous distraction he subconsciously seeks to subdue, if not submerge in more socially civilized pleasures like champagne, caviar, or collecting silk cravats.

Even when courting, a woman may have difficulty sussing out whether the Cap man is sexually interested or not. Many, many dates might transpire before he even so much as makes a move. Still, *satyriasis,* defined as an uncontrollable sexual desire in men, isn't named after his goatish archetype for nothing. But the more he feels it, the more he seeks to restrict its libidinous hold on him, the psychological pressure, let alone the physical strain, continually building and building to bursting. Everything, it would seem, turns him on, and his more lascivious sensations, those that call into question his sexual identity, torment him no end. Especially in his youth, with Saturn's influence weighing so heavily, every sexual stirring feels loaded. He is, like Hamlet (synonymous with *harbor* or *haven*), an eternally tragic figure – the word *tragedy* itself comes from the Greek word *tragoidia* meaning 'goat song.' And let's face it, there's no easy way of telling these skull-gazing Hamlets of the world to simply lighten up.

As time goes on, the irony becomes more acute as the Cap increasingly withholds from having sex just as his more prurient tendencies begin to surface – the repression of that mighty, healthy libido is what ultimately begins to twist it in more perverted directions. When young, his outsized stirrings and lurid fantasies further preclude him from seeking a relationship with a fresh-faced virgin his own age; rather he welcomes an experienced, if not a well-worn, woman whom he feels wouldn't be shocked by his ruder erotic ruminations. When finally settling into a marriage, say, with a safe and notoriously straitlaced mate, he will need to make other arrangements for his more ribald longings. Just as the 10th House rules *interests outside the home,* which manifests in Cap man's deferring the day-to-day details of existence to his mate-cum-maid, so, too, might he find release for his more shocking sexual

Harry Shearer
Steve Allen
Charles Nelson Reilly
Ray Bolger
Quentin Crisp
Stephen Hawking
Sir Isaac Newton
Louis Pasteur
Ben Franklin
Martin Luther King Jr.
Anwar Sadat
Isaac Asimov
Henry Miller
J. D. Salinger
J. R. R. Tolkien
A. A. Milne
Jack London
Robert Bly
Carl Sandberg
Kahlil Gibran
Alvin Alley
Rod Stewart
Robert Palmer
Maurice Gibb
Robin Gibb
Cab Calloway
Jimmy Buffett
Muhammad Ali
Joe Frazier
Rod Serling
Matt Lauer
Albert Gore Sr.
Woodrow Wilson
Howard Hughes
Aristotle Onassis
Cardinal O'Connor
Conrad Hilton
Phil Spector
Mao Tse-tung
J. Edgar Hoover
Jim Bakker
Dennis Hastert
Konstantin Stanislavsky
William Howell Masters
William James
Anthony Hopkins
Richard Nixon
Henri Matisse
Carlos Castaneda
Alan King
Oliver Hardy

Capricorn rules the bones and skeleton as a whole as well as the knees and skin. Knee trouble is typical as are skin disorders due to excess worry or the suppression of emotions. Ruling Saturn is also associated with the gall-bladder and spleen.

urges from a third party, almost out of courtesy, far from home base if only so as not to trouble his partner. Of course the perfect solution would be to form a lasting partnership with a woman who is as equally suited to mothering the plentiful offspring Big Daddy Cap is wont to bear as she is open and eager to engage in all the dirty behaviors the Goat wouldn't typically dream of introducing to his mate. This is the zodiac's tragedian's fatal relationship flaw: In hiding large chunks of himself from a significant other, he often finds himself stuck for life with a safety type to whom he can only return after enacting such desires elsewhere. What Mr. Hamlet or Mr. Haven needs to realize is that the safe-harbor scenario is really a two-way street: The paragon of virtue that is Capricorn's lady-wife and mother to his children can, and indeed should be, someone who has just as many sleazy inclinations as himself so that together they might explore their nastiest notions, keeping each other's decadent secrets securely sequestered in the bosom of their bond. In his quest to negotiate a serviceable but dispassionate relationship, Cap man only increases the manufacture of repressed sexual baggage; but in admitting his baser, bawdier inclinations and indulging them with a like-minded mate, true affection may be allowed to bubble up from the beautiful quagmire of their mutual lust.

Sophistication, in its purest sense, means a lack of simplicity. So to call the complicated Cap the zodiac's premier sophisticate hits more than one nail on the head. His fantasies, and his actual sexual behavior, are typically no straightforward affair, but rather layered with deviations, fetishes, and more than his fair share of hang-ups. His brand of sex is salacious and often more depraved than most people might even begin to imagine. At the core of his desire is his interest in contrast, which typically manifests as him taking on the role of aristocratic master, whether subtly or in full costume and makeup, while his woman plays the perfect wench or scullery maid. Perhaps his proclivity for debasement and degradation might manifest in a simple desire for naughty no-no sex such as anal penetration, his personal favorite, or even an oral variation on said theme. Like his so-called opposite, Cancer man, Cap also has a fetish for women dressed as nubiles, in the whole pigtails and shorty-pajamas regalia. One is struck, again, by the relationships in Salinger's stories of grown men and young girls, as in 'For Esmé – with Love and Squalor,' which just about sums up the jumbled sentiment Cap feels at these more prurient leanings, which, in the case of Seymour Glass, might've been the very cause for his suicide. One has to wonder, in 'A Perfect Day for Bananafish,' what plantain-shaped *poisson* Seymour was pointing out to the little girl he was cavorting with in the ocean. Such penal violations aside, Cap might go in for a bit of role-play whereby his partner must do all that he says; he might even get off on paying for the right to have his sexual mandates carried out. As it is, Cap's most quotidian of lovemaking practices follow a 'do me' theme whereby his woman must take on much of the responsibility for driving even the most obvious actions, climbing on for a ride while he kicks back in signature leisure mode. In many of the scenarios that further float Cap's boat, the woman should do stuff *to* him, as he experiences an extra wave of excitement when certain acts pose a challenge, taking some practice, if not some stomaching, to get the job done right. Patience, however, is the Saturn-ruled Goat's most striking virtue; and to the delight or chagrin of his partner, he is never in a rush. Often that which turns him on most in bed are things he may have shared, in his youth, with the more seasoned older women he tends to attract at a tender age. Past experiences, traumatic or erotic, make a heavy impact on the Cap, and he will want to repeat the pleasurable behaviors of a bygone era, sometimes ritualistically – it is acts of this ilk that he most fears broaching with his more prudish mates. But even he'd have to admit that what gets his sexual Goat most is the idea of corrupting a puritanical priestess, just as C. K. Dexter Haven wants to topple his lady love, the fictitious Tracy Lord, from her patrician pedestal and tap her smuttier self.

In a nod to Saturn's 10th House rule of *restraint*, Cap is notoriously titillated by prim, repressed-looking women with priggish trappings. Nurses, secretaries, librarians, teachers, clerks, and tellers top the list of those whom the Sea-goat would most like to drag down into the depths of blissful degradation. His masturbatory images, in fact, often focus on such female goody-goodies gone bad. The person who said, 'Men don't make passes at girls who wear glasses,' had no insight into the Cap's sexual psychology. Perhaps it's a matter of sensing, or imagining, frustration and subjugation in such characters akin to his own. Though aroused by the idea of a woman becoming ensnared in her own desires, his actual activities usually stop short of any form of S&M – a bit of bondage perhaps, but he's really not one for whips and chains. He has a *Lady Chatterley's Lover* erotic vision, intrigued by the idea of social restraint being ripped apart at the corsets by raw, rustic desire. (Of course, he'd just as soon sit cross-legged in a comfortable armchair and watch some brutish gardener have at it with a supposedly prim, chaste lady or some other such dignified-meets-dirty scenario.) It is terribly sophisticated, after all, for a man to allow his female partner to cavort with other men; of course that's just a fancy way of saying that Cap gets off on watching a woman being screwed by another guy – it tops his fantasy list far more than the prospect of witnessing her mix it up with another sexy minx. Unlike the Virgo man, it isn't a matter of getting off on being cuckolded; rather it is the female's degradation that imparts a thrill, and so, in

STR8 TURN-ONS

older women
submissives
dark skin, dark hair
Asians, Latinas
female repression fantasies
small breasts
big bottoms
(active) b + d
swapping
mastering
schoolgirls, spanking
primitive, native women
corsets/binding clothes
(active) humiliation
voyeurism
pimping, being cuckolded
(active) anal penetration
(passive) analingus
voyeurism
female masturbation
librarians, nurses
buns, chignons
masks, hoods
transsexuals

his fantasy, the more bestial and rough a character having at his woman, the better. Of course, the whole concept of playing with other couples is one of those infamous urges he usually hides from his mate. What the French call *l'échangisme* could become a habit for our randy Cap; the whiff of secret society that surrounds such a world is right up his seedy, sordid alley.

Sexual feelings for other men are something most Cap males experience. Loaded and weighty as these sensations are for the Goat, it is difficult to determine what might be a passing fancy and what constitutes latent interest. As an adolescent he, like many, will participate in ye olde circle jerks; but he will red-light any such activity lest it develop into more involved conduct. The irony here is, he makes such a big deal of these feelings and behaviors, dwelling on them endlessly while denying himself further involvement, which he labels 'wrong,' that the issue never quite gets resolved, and he carries on in life with a huge question mark in the back of his mind – straight Capricorns force themselves to outgrow such behavior and gay Goats may remain fairly repressed. Either way, Cap man is sensible on the subject, being the sensitive sod he is, and remains sympathetic to gay individuals, many of whom make up the bulk of his closest friendships. Meanwhile, our fishy Sea-goat has a sexually 'ishy' air about him. That inherent satyriasis causes Cap to eroticize experiences and sexualize most people, further predisposing him to attracting those of his own gender. Whereas his expansive astrological neighbor, Sag guy, is forthright about his feelings, willing to try anything at least once (including sex with another guy), Cap is so essentially emotionally restrained, a stickler for what is 'right' and 'traditional,' that even having homosexual urges can set off bouts of intense psychological pandemonium. But like a shabby-chic cardigan, Cap wears his inherent confusion as part of a sophisticated character, one that signals to others that he is unshockable and, indeed, that there's most likely nothing sexual he hasn't tried (if only in his fertile fantasies). Needless to say, Cap's sexual character keeps people guessing. Often he literally is as the bisexual Goat, playing it straight with a wife and family while keeping a boy or two on the side.

Still, even when admittedly queer as a three-dollar bill, Cap guy is loath to be categorized by others, eschewing sexual labels even while lifting up his dress to give it to a bent-over buddy. You heard us. Though he may have a string of boyfriends all through his life, and one or more everlasting relationships at that, Cap is rarely one to settle into an all-exclusive domestic role with a mate. The gay Goat is a bundle of contradictions, the zodiac's notorious top man in drag. Though he might work in an erudite or artsy field, typically surrounded by other well-dressed guppies with an eye on going places, it is generally not in this pool where our fishtailing Goat gets his jollies. Indeed, Cap is attracted to completely guileless country boys, rugged rednecks and straight-acting bubbas with down-home charm and manners (and often a girl waiting back at the ranch), whom he hopes to flip over faster than you can say 'cornhole.' Something about a wholesome, straitlaced character gripping his ankles tops the Caps must-see list, particularly when he can be the first to lay claim to virgin territory. One is reminded of Capricorn E. M. Forster's *Maurice*, a suave, urbane city slicker with same-sex longings who, like many Goats in real life, undergoes a form of psychotherapy to rid himself of such impure thoughts only to eventually find the bliss of erotic self-realization in the arms of the rustic gamekeeper, Scudder. Indeed, nothing unfetters the brow of the gay Cap guy more than a jaunty romp in the hay with an uncomplicated rustic – indeed, if pressed to pick his favorite Village People persona, Cap would undoubtedly choose the cowboy. Cap can be quite fetishistic about all that surrounds such a character, feeling a surge of excitement even by such paraphernalia as boots, chaps, and ten-gallon hats. From an astrological perspective, there seems to be something safe about bonding with a sexy ranch hand who embodies a groundedness that puts the Goat on solid sexual footing. Being lofty enough in his own right, he feels he can truly land when making whippeeee with such a man.

With these lovable lugs he so admires, gay Cap plays an Auntie Mame role to the hilt, opening his lover's eyes to all the delights the metropolitan world has to offer, though he remains just as willing to be whisked back to the farm to fraternize with his partner's family. Like the mythic Sea-goat-culture deities who brought civilization to the pastoral innocents of rocky Arcadia, Cap enjoys being an anomaly, happy to feed the chickens, milk the cow, or, mechanics forever being his strong suit, recustomize a tractor engine albeit dressed in a Gucci thong. Let's just say Cap can put the *boy* in *flamboyant*. He is gloriously inappropriate and people love him for it, especially his lover, who benefits from all the nasty pleasures Cap is prone to impart. He is, hands down, the zodiac's ass man, and much of his bedtime shenanigans center around that certain spot. He is deliberate, often ridiculously drawn out, in his concentration there, hoping to extract as much pleasurable response as he can by stimulating it any which way. Penetration is never hurried or, seemingly, about him – rather it is meant to transform his manly mate into a pleading pussy boy of the first order, something others might never assume. Cap knows that, to look at them, most people would suspect that his typically hapless hunk of a mate was the pitcher and he the catcher, and it thrills him no end knowing it's the opposite that is usually true. Like his straight counterpart, the gay Goat

GAY TURN-ONS

younger men, twinks
chicken
skinny physiques
topping
(active) analignus, ass play
cowboys, farmers, laborers
leather, chaps, boots, denim
Latin, Mediterranean men
waiters, busboys
role-reversal, virgin bottoms
backrooms, sex clubs
secrecy, anonymity
(active) body worship
kink, raunch
heavy (active) b + d
cross-dressing
(active) humiliation
straight men, bisexuals
cock rings, piercings, pumps
body fluids, watersports
pornography
(active) lite torture
waifs, wastrels, prostitutes

takes a leisurely approach to lovemaking, as considerate in playing with his lover as he is arranging flowers or installing a new carburetor. When it comes time to return the favor, his lover, too, must be prepared to pace himself, generally a challenge when it comes to oral sex given Cap's notoriously hefty size and gradual buildup to orgasm. Patience will be particularly important in a lover's expectations of pure shows of affection, as it can take a lifetime to hear the Cap say those three little words, if he ever utters them at all.

Couplings

Capricorn Man / Aries Woman

If looking for complication, she'll connect with complex Cap man. A messy match – dramatic, chaotic, unclear. Extreme fantasies are comfortably expressed: gender-bending, swapping, or S&M may be status quo.

Capricorn Man / Taurus Woman

He often keeps his women undercover – not so now: She's a classy piece of arm candy. She exists to create a stable environment in which he might thrive. Life together is haute everything: Only the best will do.

Capricorn Man / Gemini Woman

From the start, they seem set on different speeds – he's slow; she's swift. At best, they help each other adjust to a more moderate pace. Sexually, she feels snubbed; but he's dreaming up ways to draw out her desire.

Capricorn Man / Cancer Woman

A first, mind-blowing sexual encounter paves the way for a commiserative bond – whether as carnal cohorts or something more committed. Erotic activity borders on extreme – strange, rough sex is standard.

Capricorn Man / Leo Woman

Two precocious characters whose individual independence dwindles once they're a duo. He is especially possessive. In bed, it's 'dirty,' perhaps more daring than either would venture with another. *Worship* is the key word.

Capricorn Man / Virgo Woman

They have a plan: to work as a team, to prosper, to live in relative luxury. They play house, taking traditional roles. Sex is rarely a focus. Surprisingly, in some cases, the marriage is comfortably 'open.'

Capricorn Man / Libra Woman

Forming a culture club of two, these characters draw up their own design for living, often passionately participating in the worlds of fashion, art, or media. Their sex life, though secondary, is equally progressive.

Capricorn Man / Scorpio Woman

Slowly, she insinuates her way into his life – once having gained entry, they're inseparable. She takes over, which suits his armchair approach to living: He's the prima donna. In bed, too, he's happy to hang back.

Capricorn Man / Sagittarius Woman

Slick Sag and classy Cap man are drawn to the best circles in society, smoothly and successfully threading their way through the social fabric of their choosing. In bed, they're brassy and no-holds-barred.

Capricorn Man / Capricorn Woman

Two old souls. They're a handsome couple with refined tastes, sharing a somewhat superior self-perception. Her set-in-stone values may cause him some consternation. Sex is slow and steady; they're respectful, even courteous.

Capricorn Man / Aquarius Woman

They may be explosive in each others company, thus overly conscious of not instigating a scene. Still, there's plenty of hilarity here. In bed, emotional intensity is put to its best use: Sex is ardent and unruly.

Capricorn Man / Pisces Woman

It begins as best friendship – they inspire each other's wildest dreams. Pisces must keep her misty eyes wide-open; he relies on her to be their collective conscience. Cap's mission: to gratify the ravenous Piscean lover.

Gay

Capricorn Man / Aries Man

Aries is the arm candy who worships a worldly, well-bred Goat guy. After fascination fades, the focus turns to friendship. From overtly sexual beginnings, this pair may slowly become abstemious.

Capricorn Man / Taurus Man

A fondness for each other might go unspoken; sexual involvement, too, might stay under wraps. Friendship is guaranteed – Taurus–Cap combos are great roomies. In bed, the Goat's well-honed handiwork unearths the Bull's desire.

Capricorn Man / Gemini Man

Financial gain may inspire this twosome's togetherness. Little wonder tensions arise if resources dwindle. Taunting each other is a way to play – they call it quipping. Sex is 'dirty,' the kinkier the better.

Capricorn Man / Cancer Man

These astro-opposites face many challenges. There's trouble lurking behind the straight surfaces they present. In the end, Cap is labeled the villain. But from the first, sex is so fine as to become a fetish.

Capricorn Man ∫ Leo Man

Leo feels out of the loop: He's a neophyte compared to the cultured Goat guy. But the Lion learns to accept the guidance of such a socially adept sophisticate. In bed, Cap hopes to expose his 'hick' to a soupçon of sin.

Capricorn Man ∫ Virgo Man

Together, they master vital life lessons. Typically retiring Virgo does the pursuing. Cap finds himself uncannily attached. Just-sex is where it started, and each subsequent interlude feels fresh, like the first.

Capricorn Man ∫ Libra Man

The Scales is like a gust of fresh air in Cap's life. Socially, they're absolutely matched. They may even dress alike. Sexually, there's intrigue: Libra is especially fascinated by Cap's fit, firm physique.

Capricorn Man ∫ Scorpio Man

Scorpio is inspired by Cap's ease and acumen. As a couple, confrontation is their way of dealing with disagreements – soon, such struggle wears thin. Still, their sex life thrives: Even if they part, they may end up back in bed.

Capricorn Man ∫ Sagittarius Man

Sag is a macho choice of mate. Still, they share a satirical sense of humor and an affinity for flashiness. In their downtime, it's all about long, leisurely sex sessions. Inviting a third, perhaps a stranger, is status quo.

Capricorn Man ∫ Capricorn Man

One of the least common same-sign couplings. When two guarded Goats get together, it's a standoff that's sometimes insurmountable. Both are prone to posturing – reality is lacking. Each may search for outside sex.

Capricorn Man ∫ Aquarius Man

Cap is afraid of being waylaid by the strange-seeming Waterbearer. But in a bond, Aquarius champions Capricorn's cause. Their sex life is eccentric, at times conservative, otherwise notable for its perverse nature.

Capricorn Man ∫ Pisces Man

With fishy Pisces, Cap's serpentine side surfaces. But rather than expanding, the Goat meanders more, perhaps losing his way. Still, they have clever ways to capitalize on their strengths. It's an effort to keep sex lite.

Capricorn Woman

the sleeper

Capricorn woman is a class act. The most self-composed, least showy lady in the zodiac, she is an understatedly elegant character, largely unimpressed by 'externals' such as fame, high finances, or family pedigree. Self-respect is of prime importance – largely unswayed by others' opinions of her, she focuses on cultivating a quality of life distinguished by moral courage and a quest for spiritual knowledge. On this score, reputation is paramount to her, determined as she is to be valued as a person of substance. Life, the way she sees it, is a long, hard road that requires pacing and careful negotiation. No frivolous risk-taker, Capricorn lives in infamy for being purposeful, even premeditated. Circumspection, however, is the particular key to her success – she never ventures what she's unsure to gain. Instead, she deliberately takes signature baby steps toward success, avoiding shortcuts that might bring about a meteoric rise in either her professional or personal pursuits. Cap believes nothing worth achieving comes easily; that is, not without the proverbial other shoe eventually dropping. She takes a similar attitude to love and sex, rarely if ever rushing into relationships, but rather letting bonds blossom over time. She is drawn to a man with creative intelligence and a strong inner life, appealing to a guy's need for a meaningful long-haul relationship. Cap is the consummate *significant* other – one look in her eyes and it's clear she won't be trifled with. Her same-sex relationships tend to be less loaded: Notoriously attracted to younger women, she easily maintains a casual but erotically charged bond.

X

PRINCIPLE

The Principle of Containment. Structure is a means of conservation just as a reservoir of water, with restricted entry, keeps the resource pure, guarding against waste. Capricorn shifts the focus in life from quantity (a Sagittarian concern) to quality. The horn of plenty is a container of bounty, just as Capricorn woman's reserve and conservatism ensure she will, in time, meet with her own bountiful lot in life.

ʃign + Mind

Capricorn is ruled by the planet Saturn, which represents, among other attributes, the astrological Principle of Containment, and the concepts of reserve, resource, and recuperation, ideals that have particular meaning when discussing the female of the sign. *Capricorn* literally means 'goat horn,' the mythical horn of plenty, that of the she-goat Amaltheia (the goddess Rhea in her totem-animal form), who nourished baby Zeus, her son, after rescuing him from the clutches of her husband, Cronus (Roman: Saturn). Cronus, having devoured all his children to ward off a prophecy that he would be overthrown by his offspring, was duped into swallowing a stone wrapped in swaddling clothes that the goddess disguised as her child. As scholars have noted, Rhea, the anagrammatical crone-aspect of the queen-goddess Hera, was originally called Rhea–Cronus, herself possessing such powers as are now attributed to her consort, who survives to this day as Old Father Time. Rhea, as her myth suggests, is a preserver goddess, and Capricorn woman comes to personify this archetype in all her stodgy, methodical glory. Like Rhea anticipating Zeus' maturity, the Goat girl bides her time, waiting for the right moment to launch her secret grand plans. Rhea's smuggling away of Zeus on the surface signifies Capricorn woman's need to safeguard and, moreover, sustain the creative life she's been given. She perceives what certain Native American tribes refer to as the 'long-body' of her life: living not just in the now, but for the future and all time. Ironically, however, because she considers the whole of her life in every little thing she does, pacing herself appropriately, Capricorn woman probably lives more consciously in the present than any other individual in the zodiac.

Saturn's energy manifests as a correction, like that which occurs after a wild rise in the stock market: and indeed Cap woman embodies this sense of recovery and repooling of resources. In her, we find one who is unwilling to squander time and energy. She is not restrictive in personality for restriction's sake, but rather, as the horn of plenty incarnate, she contains such bounties as she perceives to be her birthright – intelligence, health, and an overall ability to contribute to the betterment of the world – wanting to preserve these personal resources. Like Rhea, Cap woman often has the last laugh, in the same sense that the tortoise has it all over the hare. While many people press to achieve the external trappings of success, ill prepared for the lumps existence inevitably doles out, Cap generally has the wherewithal to meet challenges face-on, tackling them before continuing forward, and thus is the life contestant left standing when so many others have faltered. Time is on this

Saturn-ruled lady's side; and hindsight being twenty-twenty, she is the proverbial sleeper, one who eventually rises to importance after a long period of obscurity. By example, she teaches us the ultimate virtue of her 10th House attribute of *patience*, that rushing through life only makes one old before one's time. A want for more, more, more, she instinctively understands, only creates more want. Whereas in needing less, less quickly, the Capricorn preserves the reservoir of 'plenty' she feels she already contains. She saves her energy, and it shows: She looks well-preserved far into her golden years. Indeed, she seems to get younger as she grows older, as if she were living backward.

Capricorn is the only cardinal-earth sign of the zodiac, the cardinal quality signifying initiative, and what is essential, and the earth element representing substance. The ultimate symbol of the cardinal-earth combination is a mountain, the rocky firmament, the very emblem of eternity and prudential preservation, the natural container of river valleys and especially lakes, where water is protected and pure. Aptly, Capricorn's symbol is not simply the mountain-climbing goat, but a Sea-goat, the sign's glyph traditionally being read two ways – as the horned animal with a fish tail, or a mountain with a lake. Since Capricorn is a feminine (negative-polarity) sign, the female native *embodies* the quality-element combination of her sign: Cap woman is therefore like a mountain, a looming, solitary figure who cannot help but appear iconic to those she encounters. Ancient cultures associated mountains with the 'great mother' goddesses, from whom all the gods are born, and the significance of the goat as Rhea's totem, for instance, is as an 'all-giving' animal providing nurturing meat and milk and protective clothing. The original aegis was a goatskin, from which the modern definition of preservation stems. Indeed, the whole of Aegean civilization was based on the goat, the form of which ancient culture gods took. Capricorn woman personifies this fundamental energy, a living, breathing representation of the Great, or Grand, Mother goddess. Fittingly, the sign of Capricorn is associated with the age group 63–70, which manifests in the Goat lady in myriad ways.

Like Cap man, but in less obvious, superficial ways, Cap woman is something of a throwback to the past, old-fashioned in her values, hobbies, and interests and, like a little old lady, meticulous and exacting in her daily habits. A self-styled loner, she easily becomes cranky in a crowd of more than a few others. Even when in a relationship, she carves out a solitary lifestyle, sequestering herself from her mate for most of any given day. The age group associated with her sign is also evidenced in her signature pared-down mode of existence. A neatnik minimalist of the first order, Capricorn eschews the accumulation of 'stuff.' She may even embody that elderly spirit of taking up

PLANETARY SYMBOL

Nearly the inverse of the Jupiter glyph, the sigil of Saturn portrays material, earthly concerns weighing on the evolving spirit. Restriction is the order of the day and struggle is a pressurized means or path to perfection. Structure is paramount along with patience and discipline.

SIGN QUADRANT

The zodiacal quadrants correspond to metaphysical planes of existence – physical, emotional, mental, and spiritual. The Fourth Quadrant concerns one's relationship with the eternal. Capricorn woman is focused on achieving a spiritually meaningful existence via her actions in life. She wants to do the best she can with what she has – her motto is 'I use' – treating her physical body as a container of soulful energy.

one's begging bowl and renouncing much in the way of material goods. Indeed, spiritual communion is often as much a part of her life as it is for the aged, whose thoughts become naturally more focused on the ever-after. Death, too, could easily become Capricorn female's constant preoccupation, but being acutely aware of her mortality is what helps her to appreciate being alive. As the zodiac's soaring alp, we see in her personage all that the mountain has come to represent down through the millennia – for it is atop these mounds of cardinal-earth where one is meant to commune with God. It is indeed, as in the case of Mt. Olympus, Mt. Sinai, and any number of other hilltop dwellings where the immortal deities reside. It is where Moses received his rather Saturnesque tablets of restrictive shalt-nots and from whence Jesus delivered his sermons. Such spiritual understanding – the concept of life as a 'gift' isn't lost on Capricorn woman – is only had at the acme where our earthly abode meets the sky. And our Capricorn mountain mama is thus in a perpetual summit meeting with such lofty powers-that-be. This lends new meaning to Capricorn's rule over the 10th Astrological House of, among other attributes, *people in high places.*

The 10th House, as Capricorn's motto 'I use' would suggest, is one concerned with *status, achievement,* and *a need to establish oneself through honorable means – rising to the occasion, usefulness, responsibility, hard work,* and *self-discipline.* Not one ever to rely on luck, the way her predecessor Sag female does, Cap woman is instead steeped in active faith, something that manifests in her life in a number of ways. First, she typically adheres to a belief in a benevolent spiritual power that sustains her through life's ups and downs, keeping her more levelheaded than most individuals when encountering either extreme hardship or boon. As well, she physically acts, as much as any layperson might, like one leading a religious life, ridding herself of excess, particularly a glut of ego, and naturally seeking to conserve the soulful aspect of herself. In short she *uses* her life to gain spiritual strength, a living testament to the adage that 'what doesn't kill you only makes you stronger,' and she thus eschews shortcuts and easy ways, happily working her fingers to the Capricorn-ruled bones to get what she wants out of life – not just the resulting fruits of such labors, but the spiritual awareness and conditioning that come with the process. In so doing, the Sea-goat gal builds a metaphorical muscle for survival that most people simply never develop. Water is symbolic in astrology for feelings, intuition, and the loving contents of the soul; and the watery aspect of the sign's totem represents a reservoir of ever-purifying emotional well-being as well as 'age-old' spiritual wisdom that is conserved by taking a slower pace toward achieving life goals, nonetheless providing more lasting sustenance for survival. The zodiac's little

Sherpa, Capricorn often has more than her fair share of emotional baggage, if not outright pain and hurt, which she totes around. But unlike Cap man, who views such aspects of his life as a literal drag, Cap lady finds a way to use her suffering as a springboard for any number of positive employments, from creative inspiration to spiritual enlightenment. Nothing is lost on the pragmatic Capricorn – she has a knack for turning what others might see as drudgery into a dedicated practice. Truth be told, she's not always a bundle of sunshine; many people find their Capricornian friends, colleagues, or spouses rather dour. In a sense, the whole of her life is one long, dark night of the soul. But it makes her deep. And it nurtures in her a spirit of compassion.

As the first sign of the final Fourth Quadrant of the zodiac, that which is associated with the metaphysical level of the soul, the cardinal-earthy Cap can be something of a crusader who often eventually puts the whole of her being into spiritual pursuits. She is naturally ascetic, the poster child for Saturn's principles of correction and atonement (at-one-ment), both in the sense of striving for a strong mind-body-spirit connection as well as endeavoring to form a perfect union with the essential energies of the universe. At the very least she is a gnostic gnome – a decidedly grounded earth dweller with an innate knowledge of spiritual workings. Joan of Arc or Thérèse de Lisieux couldn't be born under any other sign but Capricorn. In the former character we see embodied active, physical cardinality on the spiritual level, and in the latter, called 'the little flower,' we see a startling example of redemption via growing younger along the specific 'be ye like little children' theme in an intentional recuperation of purity and innocence in both thought and deed. One look at Cap woman is all it takes to sense her saintliness; she doesn't sin often or easily. She appears to be as solid as the rock of ages, which, for better or for worse, gives the impression that Cap is a safety zone, the proverbial life preserver, a role that she might have found herself cast into early in life.

The Capricorn girl is typically born into a strict household and at a time when her parents are experiencing growing pains in their marriage. Generally an older child in birth order, the Cap girl is heaped with responsibilities, which tend to rob her of a relaxed childhood. The Goat girl, often saddled with a sort of scullery work, may be kept down by self-absorbed parents who also count on her to offer emotional rearing to other, usually younger children. In the extreme, her mother is incapable of bonding with the Capricorn or even showing her the slightest affection; Cap's father is often an emotionally detached, though verbally opinionated, character with whom achieving closeness is difficult. Still, Cap will relate more readily to her father, often sharing at least an intellectual connectedness. If ignored, Capricorn girl

ELEMENT + QUALITY

The earth element connotes materiality and substance. The cardinal quality signifies a call to action and initiative. Together the cardinal-earth combination particular to Capricorn is best described as a mountain, a symbol of preservation. Cap woman strives for self-sustainment and the edification of her spirit as a valuable natural resource.

POLARITY

Females in feminine (earth, water) signs are aligned with the gender polarity of their sign and thus embody the quality-element combination of the sign. The cardinal-earth status of Capricorn determines that she be like a mountain herself, a tower of self-preservation and a rather insurmountable character. People are drawn to her, like Moses to the mount, as a dispenser of revelatory rules to live by.

may find self-destructive ways to scream for attention – eating disorders and other such manifestations of acute perfectionism might come into play. There is a certain chaos in Capricorn's household of origin, and she finds it difficult to secure a sense of privacy, just as she seems to be lost, if not forgotten, in the shuffle of quotidian confusion. The Goat girl is extremely sensitive, and the emotional scars she forms make her seem a hardened, guarded, and somewhat defensive individual. It is the undoing of this dynamic that can be seen as her signature 'growing down' as she grows up. The further she climbs in her personal or professional ambitions, the more she'll need to jettison the baggage that threatens to weigh her down. The good news is, she generally does. In fact, Capricorn female's life is primarily about lightening her load. She is rarely the materialist most astrologers make her out to be. Still, even the more monkish Sea-goats have a weakness for shopping at designer boutiques – quality is her credo – though material wealth is rarely an end in itself. Rather, financial abundance is a means by which Ms. 'I use' might more readily achieve the peaceful, carefree lifestyle she lacked as a kid. She may drop five hundred bucks on shoes, but they'll be one of the few precious pairs she owns – Cap is notoriously careful with all her belongings.

Growing up, Cap is typically the quintessential bookish type, often made to feel that she shouldn't or, worse, couldn't ever rely upon her looks. It's the ugly-duckling story come to life: She is the proverbial late bloomer, often not getting her first period or filling out a bra until well into her teens. And then *boom* – seemingly overnight, Cap blossoms into womanhood, ill-equipped to handle what she perceives as negative attention for her more eye-catching physical attributes, which she summarily begins to play down. Above all, Cap girl wants to be respected for her mind, having adopted a studious persona, primarily as a means for winning some notice and securing her emotional survival. The worlds of ideas, philosophy, and indeed all the liberal- and fine-arts disciplines are endlessly fascinating to her. She slips easily into a bohemian crowd, sipping espresso, visiting museums, early on seeking out the more progressive, intellectual advanced-placement, and later, graduate-level courses. But having been raised in a sexually repressive home – dating may have been a distinct no-no – she is often disarmingly unaware of the natural appeal she possesses, somewhat at a loss to fully express her erotic urges as they arise.

Body + Soul

PSYCHOLOGY

Spontaneity is an issue for the Capricorn, who some-times misses opportunities due to overcaution. She might stifle her creativity by being too pragmatic, just as she might repress her sexu-ality. An often pathological need for control and struc-ture might see her falling into obsessive-compulsive behavior or eating disorders.

Capricorn woman seems the most untouchable of any female in the zodiac, little about her suggesting interest in inviting the attention or affections of the opposite sex. Saturn's conservative rule over the Goat girl determines that she focus on herself, in the cultivation of private inner resources, rather than in any outward concern for, or solicitation of, others. Anything but showy, Cap is an earthy and elegant creature whose prime occupation is her own contentment, intrinsically achieved through the ever-increasing proliferation of self-esteem. Not wishing to be approached by anyone on what she might deem a superficial level – sexual advances are generally lumped into this category – she may downplay her sometimes extraordinary good looks, wearing understated, even decidedly unsexy clothing in dark, shadowy hues – black being not only her favorite color but the one associated with her sign – intent upon remaining as inconspicuous as possible. With her hair generally pulled back and her infamously large, dark, almond-shaped eyes often hidden behind studious spectacles – her ovoid peepers are prone to myopia – there is something emphatically Marian the Librarian about our Cap lady. As in depictions in film and literature, such a Goody Two-shoes–looking character as the real-life Cap seems to be just waiting, if not fairly itching, to lose the specs, loosen the bun, and let her hair down. She chooses to realize her full sexual potential slowly, blossoming in her own good time rather than seeking to make some sort of splash and, perhaps, end up attracting flash-in-the-pan experiences. She doesn't relish the idea of being hit on, and so she stays away from the social fray, sometimes going so far in her attempt to appear off-limits as to defeminize her appearance. A list of famous Capricorn women – including the likes of Diane Keaton, Maureen Dowd, Patti Smith, Sissy Spacek, Marlene Dietrich, Annie Lennox, Diane Sawyer, Joan of Arc, and the aptly named Marianne Faithfull – reveals a bevy of austere beauties who choose to butch it up a bit in tailored trousers, suits, and even the odd tie. Goody-goody Goat girl Mary Tyler Moore went so far as to battle network TV execs in the 1960s for the right to wear her trademark Capri(corn) pants on *The Dick Van Dyke Show.*

On a deeper level, Cap woman is a serious sort, no mere dolly who would tolerate being toyed with. As insurance against any such attempts, she cultivates a no-nonsense, sometimes severe and intimidating character that will keep feeble flirts and flatterers at bay. Indeed, Cap seems to have invented stand-offishness – it is her default demeanor to keep people from ever getting too close, physically, emotionally, or otherwise. Cap man might fancy himself a VIP

The archetype associated with Capricorn is the 'Grand Mother' or mother of the gods. The classical term *aegean* means 'of the goat,' a nod to the Titan queen of the gods, Rhea, in her animal-totem form. Called Rhea–Cronus, it is from her we get the word *crone*. She is a preservation goddess, a symbol of divine sustenance who seeks to have her wisdom carried on for generations. In her goat form, Amaltheia ('god-nurse'), she fed Zeus from her *capri cornes*, the horns of plenty. She separated the land from the waters and was the Mother Mountain from whose milky snowcaps came the flowing rivers. *Rhea* means 'to stream or flow.'

member of some club of his own conception, but Capricorn woman is an exclusive league of her own, and she's typically not accepting any new applicants. Only the closest of family and friends, a teensy coterie of loved ones, ever experience her highly selective offerings of affection. At her utmost, she is the epitome of self-containment, a living embodiment of her preserver goddess(es) archetype. First and foremost she is concerned with her own survival, especially financially and spiritually.

In a room filled with people, Cap camps out on the periphery, digging into a comfortable corner, a vantage point from which to people-watch, sometimes for hours, where she can carefully avoid the actual press of a crowd. When verged upon by someone, even in the most harmless, casual manner, her immediate reflex is to recoil, often literally pulling in her noble chin and leaning backward as if approaching luge position. Setting her face into a blank expression, she'll offer only quick, monosyllabic responses to whatever is being said, refusing to make eye contact in hopes of nipping any unnecessary interaction firmly in the bud. The Goat is especially suspicious of compliments (though often secretly thrilled by them), wary that such comments are a precursor to a full-fledged come-on. Faced with small talk of any sort, she turns on her heel, making a hasty retreat with an economic, though ever polite, excuse. She is, by all accounts, a tough nut to crack – and she appears the part: Typically tall and aristocratic-looking, as upright in posture as she is in moral conviction, the Goat can't help but emit a haughty air. Holding her head high upon her long, slender neck, she literally looks down her prominent nose; her exotic eyes are ever watchful and defensively darting, her perfectly bowed brows arched suspiciously and crinkling under a vast dome-shaped forehead, distinguished by a high hairline that predisposes her to those stern, signature swept-back hairstyles. Though she possesses strong cheekbones, they tend to go rather unnoticed as her cheeks themselves are robust, rather than sunken, her jaw and bold chin proportionately strong. Though pointedly upturned at the tip, her nose is generally meaty, never needlelike; and she boasts a substantial soup-strainer space between it and her lips, which are full and sensuously drawn, but often absentmindedly pursed or puckered into some sort of pout or another, generally one signaling disdain. Perhaps as a nod to Capricorn's association with enduring hardship, the Goat girl often manifests physical evidence of her sign's metaphoric recuperation as actual scars, typically on her face. It's a visible reminder of having been dealt a bit of a brunt in life, emotional or otherwise.

There is one sure way to penetrate Cap's defenses: Launch into a conversational topic that instantly reveals intelligence and, most of all, insight. She is entertained by her own astute running commentary and is willing to bat around other's perceptions as well. One may thereby see a sudden shift in her countenance as caution turns to capricious concentration; screwing up her brow and narrowing her eyes, she'll nod and cluck her tongue in acknowledgment should something along the lines of social criticism enter into discourse. Cap is a keen observer, an eternally attentive student of life, and she cherishes that quality in others. In her youth, much to the eye-rolling derision of her peers, she was that girl who sat front and center of class, pencils sharpened, hanging on the teacher's every word. As Cap matures, a certain studiousness continues to define her. At some point, it may conflict with whatever inherent creative impulses she may possess; those that beg free-form expression. Seriousness, structure, and scholarliness are fused together into a solid mountain of determination that defines the Goat girl's essential struggle: how and when to let her signature reserve slip and make room for spontaneity and serendipity. Or, when it comes to a potential sexcapade, how to move from haughtiness to naughtiness – a transition that is particularly difficult for Capricorn to make.

Cap's trademark circumspection may be attributed in part to her sign's association with the age group 63–70, which also goes a long way in explaining her conservative, unadorned style and love for funerary black, granny glasses, cross pendants, and other such religious talismans. Likewise, snow-capped Cap tends to go gray early in life, which, combined with her alabaster skin, makes her appear older than her years in her early days. Cap women of darker extractions, too, will likewise be lighter and more porcelain-skinned than other females in their family. But as she matures, the reverse happens, such that the Cap begins to look younger and younger. As the years pass, Cap's appearance seems to alter little and, like a mountain, she appears the very symbol of self-preservation. When it comes to exercise, meditative disciplines such as stretching, yoga, Pilates, or dance – forms that call for the proverbial mind-body-spirit connection, appeal to her most; besides, given her delicate Capricorn-ruled joints, and those fragile knees especially, the zodiac's old lady doesn't fare too well with high-impact activities. Yoga especially suits astrology's sleeper, as one tends to master it only with time.

Capricorn appears anything but sporty in the traditional sense. An explicitly hourglass figure precludes any aerodynamism in movement, as does a dense, often weighty bone structure. Though delicately shouldered, with long, skinny arms, the Goat generally possesses hefty breasts, dual horns of plenty, and a typically tiny waist, which gives way to wide hips, creating anatomical hairpin turns – one might say she looks like a Modigliani. Long-waisted in the extreme, she is rarely leggy; and while she's happy to expose her dainty forearms, wrists, calves, and ankles, Cap tends to conceal her more solid

BIBLE + LITERATURE

Capricorn draws on the Israelite goddess Jael, a she-goat synonymous with the biblical Deborah 'queen bee' and the Grecian Rhea, who, in goat form, poured out nectar and ambrosia. Cap's 'Grand Mother' prototype is typified by Sarah, meaning 'queen or throne,' the matriarchal wise woman of Abraham's tribe. The crone figure entered into fairy tales as Mother Goose, in her Capricornian black cloak and hat, and as the ubiquitous fairy godmother. She is Spencer's Faerie Queene and Shakespeare's Titania (Rhea the Titan) from *A Midsummer's Night Dream,* who steals away a young prince, just as Rhea whisked off prince Zeus.

thighs and ample behind. Similarly, the cleft between her legs is demure and understated, veiled by a wispy patch of fine hair, the folds of her privates not the least bit protrusive, while her clitoris is pronounced and easily pinpointed. Despite any external attempts at androgyny, the ultrafemininity of Capricorn woman naked is indisputable. Indeed, it is monumental. Still, it typically takes some finagling to get this iconic figure of womanhood to let down her guard and simply hop into the sack.

Sex + Sexuality

Capricorn isn't the kind of woman to opt for a quick roll in the hay – she must share at least some measure of familiarity with a man. Even if she were to opt for a rare impromptu interlude with, say, some stranger on a train, she would have had to experience an immediate intellectual and, indeed, spiritual connection, such that the whole affair smacked of kismet and not just some sort of sordid exchange. The brain is the only organ about which Cap is a size queen, and it is typically those guys who wear-glasses at whom she'll make passes. Such signs of intelligent life, whether real or imagined, pique her curiosity; but should he turn out to be an actual Rhodes scholar, then so much the better. To be sure, there is a certain vanity in Cap's selection of a man, as she believes that she herself would appeal to a 'thinking man' far more than a guy with a football for a head. From youth, she has been rather gun-shy of macho guys, all too often having suffered their slings and arrows during her uglier-duckling days, having found solace in a brainy, artsy crowd among whose geekier members she may have inspired crushes. Like her, she hopes, the spotty, bespectacled boys often manage to mature into rather smart-looking artistic types. And so, it is for the brooding would-be Arthur Millers, J. D. Salingers, or Sam Shepards of the world that she generally carries a torch – long, lean, lanky lads with colossal cerebrums. Since youth, she is fascinated by guys with some apparent genius and the potential willingness to realize it. Even when choosing to marry, Cap rarely thinks in terms of whether a man will provide her with financial stability. This stalwart Saturn-ruled logician learns, early on, to furnish herself with any necessary material grounding – looking older than her years, the typical Cap will have started securing paid work for herself (often disguising her age) since before her teens, often socking money away for her highly anticipated foray into living independently, far away from home. She is a firm believer in the human right, indeed the human responsibility, to soar to whatever heights that can be achieved through dedication to one's artistic or scholarly callings. The 'necessities' of life (e.g., money) are thus to be used as a means of achieving such ends, not as an end in themselves.

Relationships, like everything the Capricorn undertakes, are shows of active faith. She goes on instinct, sussing out the kind of latent prodigiousness in a man that might, over time, give rise to an extraordinary life – that is, she sees beyond the mundane, into which category she even lumps such luxuries as might make other women drool. (Expensive cars, elegant restaurants, precious jewels, and all such stereotypical shows of wealth can seem wasteful extravagances to the ascetic Cap, who prefers to invest any extra cash in items that enrich her life in more meaningful ways.) Still, sometimes her nonpecuniary expectations of a man are too lofty; or she may confuse creativity with craziness, talent with mere talk. Often, her early partners, though notoriously few and far between, simply cannot live up to the hope she heaps upon them. Indeed, there is always an element of pressure to being Cap's mate as the mountain lady becomes the projected embodiment of a man's own potential, if not his elusive greatness – and the flip side: his inability to live up to such exalted aims. However, it must be said that the Cap woman is often guilty of more than a little projection, or even hypocrisy of her own – she is a tough-lover who urges a man to take on tremendous challenges, but she might not even admit to her own towering hopes and dreams. This dynamic goes a long way in explaining why the zodiac's sleeper can be such a late bloomer: Eventually she applies those same expectations to herself, usually once her partner no longer requires, or desires, her tutelage. It's a hard lesson for Cap to learn as she has been programmed since childhood to play caretaker, particularly to younger siblings. Of course there are those men who look for such mothering, and then those who see it as smothering – ironically, the former scenario ends badly while the latter might provide the Goat with just the right kick in the pants to keep the focus squarely on herself. After all, her best match is a man who is able to achieve all she foresees for him on his own terms, while she steadily unearths and nurtures herself.

Suffice to say, Capricorn doesn't readily appeal to the good-time Charlies of the world. She is a solemn lady who looks at life and relationships as requiring hard work, that is if they're to be ultimately beneficial. Relatively speaking, she is considered something of a moral giant, and as such, most mere mortals feel lacking, even diminished, in her intimate association. Life for this Saturn-ruled creature is one long state of recovery, as she is typically plagued by compulsions, more food than drink, or a certain addiction to spending, which she is forever atoning for with signature monkish intent. Still, when

KEY WORDS

endurance
capriciousness
eternity
posterity
restriction
reserve
religion
patience
promotion
resource
polish
qualification
concern
strength
aristocracy
elegance
haughtiness
mastery
authority
success
society
faith
practice
obstinacy
organization
method
distinction
certitude
thought
devotion
aspiration
assertion
temperance
domination
convention
work
reliance
prudence
care
discretion
encouragement
loyalty
acumen
constancy

such so-called demons arise, she is notorious for exorcising them forthwith, healing faster than most. The rub, however, is that she expects those in her life to do likewise. Indeed, it is fitting that the New Year falls during the Capricorn period as the female of the sign is continually locked into one Saturnian resolution or another. She exudes austerity even in her pared-down, modest appearance; so much so, at times, you might say Cap woman puts the *nun* in renunciation. One look at her and a man might feel daunted by this decided bastion of goodness – looking up to her is natural, but living up to her is often nothing short of a nightmare. She is the one and only cardinal-earth sign, exhibiting a look of Everest, she is the epitomal uphill battle, worth the climb but still posing a real challenge if not a barrier to people, would-be partners in particular. She is like that private club of one, automatically discouraging the rabble-male population from crossing her chilly threshold, while hopefully inviting someone equally self-important to ring her proverbial bell.

Once Capricorn sees a man she wants – an intellectual, spiritual, as well as physical revelation – she keeps her eyes on the prize, eventually securing subtle ways to make him do the pursuing. For no matter how sought after a man is whom she makes the target of her affections, Cap woman will always some-how turn the tables, making her own self seem the more enviable catch. She approaches sexual relationships as she does everything else: She's in it for the long haul, uncannily able to focus her attention on solid objectives, and not willing to entertain anything extraneous along the way. With her high standards in tow, she rarely stops for dillying dalliances with the men she meets en route to securing the successful match she pictures, often since childhood, in her mind's eye. It is little wonder, then, that when Cap makes her long-awaited love connection, she is eager to see it stick. For this reason, it is not unusual for Cap to marry her first boyfriend, often doing so at a relatively tender age, fueled by the feeling that she is more mature, thus ready, than most. As the embodiment of the 'preserver' goddess archetype, Capricorn isolates what she perceives as good in a man and meditates, indeed prays, upon it, putting her belief fully in him, building him up to heretofore unimaginable heights. The concept of prayer is itself a quintessentially Capricornian one, as it signifies forward cardinal movement, in the form of active faith, on the spiritual level – the only sort that might move mountains. Cap woman, putting such spiritual stock in the one she loves, becomes a man's rock, his anchor. But seeing only the good in a loved one, she may all too easily underestimate his negative qualities. She isn't so much forgiving as she is oblivious to human frailty – she is continually wiping out her own weaknesses – often having little patience for people who are troubled or otherwise treading a slippery slope.

Her holier-than-thou attitude may manifest literally in an espousal of a particular faith system, though she is generally saved from relying on organized religion by her infamous pragmatism that dictates she remain, feet firmly planted, on the material plane.

To be fair, Cap woman avoids what she deems negative influences because she perceives herself as being overly susceptible to them. She is predisposed to Saturnian sentiments – sudden, crushing feelings of gloom if not impending doom. (The word *tragedy* comes from the Greek *tragoidia*, meaning 'goat song.') And so she consciously strives, daily, to transcend the mire in which she might otherwise wallow. This rallying of spiritual forces within her often reads as arrogance, a sense that she is 'high' on herself. But in truth, she must keep herself above the status quo – that lofty metaphoric 'place' to which she was born – to stave off falling into the kind of depression she was prone to in childhood. So men who represent a run-of-the-mill lifestyle are simply not for her – such relationships she sees as flatliners, those that threaten to make her feel dead inside. In a partnership, she seeks the sublime and is thus drawn to vivid, extraordinary, often eccentric and erratic types with whom life, she imagines, will never be boring. Ironically, she is usually the one imposing relationship ground rules and regulations – the goddess Rhea, it must be remembered, brought 'commandments' to the people in the same way as Moses did, and Cap woman mirrors this need to impose restrictions, albeit on these highly intellectual, often extraordinarily talented types – entrepreneurs, scholars, philosophers, actors, playwrights, producers, and the like – to whom she is invariably drawn. Still, laying down the law is really a preventative measure employed by the cautious Cap to avert potential domestic conflict – any such disturbances smack of second-rate mediocrity, and she simply won't have it. After all, she is in search of an uncommon love experience. This also explains why the zodiac's most mindful, indeed traditional, character is famous for taking up with unconventional mates, those so seemingly unlike herself. However, such intense men who at first seemed so cool and unusual may soon become cruel and unusual, and Cap learns that living with a guy who goes too much against the societal grain is tantamount to gluttony for punishment, only repeating a childhood pattern she so desperately sought to escape.

Although there may be an element of opportunism in Cap's signature choice of a mate – she may exploit his talent, making *his* management *her* career; otherwise, she could copy his creative lifestyle, hoping to become well-known as 'the couple who . . .' – it is more accurate to say that she educates herself via her relationships. Still, she rarely does so with an older, wiser mentor. Instead, she subconsciously seeks out someone her same age or slightly

Joey Lauren Adams
Joan of Arc
Annie Lennox
Joan Baez
Odetta
Naomi Judd
Janis Joplin
Patti Smith
Marianne Faithfull
Donna Summer
Dido
Sade
Mary J. Blige
Françoise Hardy
Sophie Tucker
Ethel Merman
Marilyn Horne
Renata Tebaldi
Crystal Gale
Charo
Eartha Kitt
Gelsey Kirkland
Katie Couric
Diane Sawyer
Cokie Roberts
Maureen Dowd
Judith Krantz
Zora Neale Hurston
Simone de Beauvoir
Anne Brontë
Clara Barton
Betsy Ross
Lady Bird Johnson
Elizabeth Arden
Helena Rubenstein
Countess D'Agoult
Eva LaGalliene
Theresa Helburn
Diane Von Furstenberg
Carolina Herrera
Cindy Sherman
Berthe Morisot
Gina Garan
Dolly Parton
Shari Lewis
Pal Benetar
Thérèse de Liseux
Patricia Neal
Gypsy Rose Lee
Faye Dunaway

BODY RULERSHIP

The sign of Capricorn rules the bones and skeleton as a whole as well as the knees and skin. Knee trouble is typical as are skin disorders due to excess worry or the suppression of emotions. Saturn is also associated with the gallbladder and spleen.

younger. This is the trade-off: She performs a parental role, as she did in childhood, but at the same time learns how to play, something she never quite had the chance to do, given the restraints of her early years. For this reason, Cap's partner must, above all, be a playmate. Slowly, through recreation and disport, she begins to access her own creativity, which has for so long been stuck. The free-form part of herself, represented by the fishy tail of Cap's Sea-goat symbol, becomes her ultimate resource to draw upon. All her stifled untapped talent that threatened to pull her down into a depression, eventually becomes her most valuable asset, the sustenance she comes to live on, and that which keeps her young, seemingly for aeons. And so the story goes that Capricorn sometimes surpasses her playmate, having that much more determination and pent-up inventiveness screaming to be expressed. In this way, she eventually switches roles with her partner whereby he must learn to become that rock upon which she might rely. And the once discouraged, dour duckling does indeed develop into a wonderful, wise, and often wacky swan.

Meanwhile, the creative geniuses Cap generally goes for are drawn to her as well, since at first glance she will not seem to be a competitor, in any sense. To be sure, she is a supportive energy in a man's life, never one to suggest he keep his day job. On the contrary, Cap's notorious shows of faith are contagious, and her mate might soon find himself being paid for talents he once only expressed in obscurity. She is devotedly loyal and deeply loving, expecting perhaps too little in return. Indeed, she is one of the more emotionally low-maintenance females on the astrological wheel – strong and independent, she offers little in the way of head trips, rarely indulging in such girlish role-play as might require excess attention or the showering of gifts. She can, in fact, seem a rather businesslike mate, typically less frivolous even than most men. Capricorn woman isn't comfortable being coddled and cooed – it's not something she ever knew as a child, and any lingering lack of confidence in her femininity only further prohibits it. Having been discouraged from embracing her sexual self as an adolescent, Cap has no real handle on the concept of feminine wiles. Flirting, especially, is not her forte. She is too essentially honest to engage in such frothy, phony behavior, often not dating until her twenties, sometimes taking as long to lose her virginity. This could explain why so many Caps date younger men, and sometimes ones who are considerably so, especially later in life – she wants to get a taste of sexually peaking boys if only to see what she was missing. The unmarried Cap woman, and there are many of them, often take up exclusively with these callow fellows as they provide plea-sure but allow her to maintain psychological control as well as her solitary lifestyle. In general, she is less intimidated by younger men, giving rise to sexual 'teacher' fantasies, particular to the academic Cap. Besides, she just likes all that locked-in freshness the odd college freshman has to offer.

In sharp contrast to her astrological neighbor Sagittarius woman, the most obvious flirt on the astrological wheel, Cap is wary of overt public displays, even when in a relationship, choosing to keep her private life exactly that. She isn't looking for intrigue from a bond, but a solid working arrangement that can serve as a backdrop for all she seeks to accomplish as an individual. Her relationships are not typically of the sizzling sort, and sex is rarely the main motivation for forming a partnership in the first place. She is a fairly conservative sexual character when it comes to her erotic regimen, viewing the intimacy that sex provides as a source of safety and comfort far more than as an acrobatic workout or psychological journey. Still, sex for our Marian the Librarian is something of a big deal, as she probably came to it relatively late in life. Freeing her libido often requires as much coaxing as it took to tap her creative spirit – sex, the literal act of creation, and artistic expression are locked, if not blocked, into the same 'place' in the Cap's emotional cloakroom. Patience on the part of her lover will therefore be the ultimate virtue. Needless to say, her sex appeal is anything but superficial, and it takes a certain kind of man to withstand the necessarily slow freeing of Cap's carnal appetite – there is simply no rushing the Goat girl's lust. She is intent on setting the pace and must sense no hidden agenda in bed.

It might come as some surprise that Cap isn't specifically marriage-minded: The whole idea of being legally bound to another individual seems a rather specious notion to her, one that conflicts with her inherent philosophy: that we are all essentially alone – born alone, die alone – and should it come to any legal entanglements, she'd just as soon be left alone. The loss of control that marriage signals frightens her, particularly when she is involved with an erratic genius; she doesn't much fancy the notion of being left holding the bag. Sexually, too, she doesn't adhere to a belief in 'wifely duties,' rarely being one who'll switch on autopilot just because her mate expects it of her. There is no coercing or even cajoling Cap into doing anything, especially in the bedroom. All a guy has to do is apply even the slightest pressure – his hands on her head, for instance – and all sexual bets will instantly be off. For that reason, too, anal sex tends to be a definite no-no – the act smacks of feminine submission – whereas doing it doggie style might satisfy that same urge in her man while hitting all the right spots for Cap as well – not to mention allowing for free clitoral manipulation by either herself or her lover. She is not experimental by nature, preferring to stick to the same well-loved, reliable routine, even in the same order, so she knows what to look forward to next. Nowhere do we see Cap's need for control as fiercely as in the bedroom. To her credit, she doesn't require a lot of bells and

STR8 TURN-ONS

younger men
dark, curly, wavy hair
lanky physiques
collegiates, intellectuals
tweed, flannel suits
big noses, cleft chins
spectacles
men in uniform
laborers, contractors
strangers, travelers
executives
(passive) worship
masturbating during intercourse
stripping, teasing
exhibitionism
domination
teacher/student fantasies
hands and feet
high heels, hose, garters
lingerie
(active) seduction
delivery men
missionary
doggy style
(passive) oral
tantrism, spirituality
stoicism
hygiene, soapy smells

whistles to make sex special, rather she prefers to achieve a certain greatness by sticking to her usual path. Sex is not a jaded affair for the Goat girl, and as cliché as it sounds, for her each time feels like the first time. This is another reason why she likes bedding those considerably younger guys – she shares the sense of newness that is naturally felt by guys still sexually wet behind the ears. When with an older partner, an unjaded exuberance must still be a relationship keynote, particularly palpable between the sheets. Cap finds the very anticipation of sex as exciting, if not more so, than the nitty-grittiness of the act itself, and the man who needs ever increasing stimuli will not be long for her world. She will always be as wide-eyed as a schoolgirl, forming endless crushes on men, if not those barely out of boyhood, letting her mind wander through all the romantic, intriguing possibilities that could serendipitously occur.

The wildest thing about Capricorn woman is her love of fantasy, and especially the idea of covert sexual activity. She invents dream lovers in her waking hours, possibly fantasizing during a masturbatory moment over the landscaper, her mechanic, or the FedEx guy. As pornlike as it may sound, she enjoys interaction with men in the service industries whose job it is to be polite while doing her bidding. She might offer such a worker a cup of coffee or enter into a jovial chat that could be considered out of character by those who know her as a discerning, somewhat terse individual. But caught unawares, Cap would surprise her closest intimates. She also often has a 'real' dream lover as well; that is, a figure who regularly factors into her nightly revelries and with whom she shares in a recurring sexual theme, often climaxing in actuality, which can give the flesh-and-blood mate lying next to her something of a jolt. What she experiences in her subconscious affairs is lovemaking with an insatiable and indefatigable sort, mirroring what she truly desires in her waking life. She may be rigid, but Capricorn is anything but frigid. However, because sexual requirements don't top her list for a loving partnership, it can be hit-or-miss for her in the nooky department. Eventually, as with everything, Cap will realize the importance of sexual satisfaction in her life, and if her man isn't quite cutting the mustard, she may look elsewhere for that particular brand of satisfaction. Enter the tireless twentysomething guy, as well as her need to be free of a marriage contract. Cap woman may see no conflict between satisfying her sexual needs elsewhere while still devoting her emotional self fully to a primary relationship. When it comes to love, her heart is forever in the right place; but if other parts of her aren't being used to full capacity, Cap might fill that particular hole with another more willing and able to help. Her attitude is sophisticated: Sex is an isolated experience, something she simply wants done, and done right. It might matter little that she's in love with one man who falls short of pleasing her while she employs a lover who will take her to such sexual heights as can be had, most often, via the straightforward act of intercourse. Still, she's not a big believer in unbridled passion as it seems all too precarious a 'place' to go; she is, after all, most concerned with taking Saturn-ruled responsibility, if even for her own rapture. She may even try to restrain her partner's more ebullient expressions – indeed, if any woman were to emit the librarian's cautioning shhhhing during sex, it would be our *comme il faut* Cap. There is a very practical application, in fact, for Cap's reasoning that it is best to contain oneself, even during sex. She finds, in so doing, a further building up of her own excitement. Chances are, given her slow-climbing nature, that the Cap woman orgasms at a higher level than most, perpetually staving off the temptation to pop her cork until such time as it is impossible to stop. Talk about your transformative experiences. By surpressing her pleasure, Cap seeks to enhance the purity of the experience. For this ability, too, she thanks her lucky stars she's a woman, as, all too often, she witnesses a man's inability to pace himself and prolong the ecstasy of the sexual act. Hastiness is what she most dislikes in people, whether it's rushing into friendships or to conclusions, and she judges men most guilty of this.

Capricorn tends to have more respect for women than she does for men. In general, she may relate better to the opposite sex, but when she happens upon a woman who transcends hackneyed societal role-playing, whether as a heroine – musician, politician, author, artist – or someone in her own life, Cap is completely in awe. She is often pleasantly surprised to find that so many of these strong females she emulates, those who take their place in an otherwise exclusively male world, are themselves born under her sign. Ava Gardner, Marlene Dietrich, Berthe Morisot, Simone de Beauvoir, Janis Joplin, Zora Neale Hurston, Clara Barton, Eva Le Gallienne, Patti Smith, and Dian Fossey are all such Goats who strike that particular chord in Capricorn, and it is for such strong women that she invariably forms a crush. However, when it comes to actual lesbian experiences, she tends to be attracted to pretty young girls (just as she is to pretty young boys) whom she hopes might regard her in that same exalted fashion. Still, Cap lives in a fairly black-and-white world, and one finds few bisexuals among her order. She is inherently too decisive to fence-sit in any respect, and though straight Cap can have her female crushes, and the gay Goat might fancy the occasional man, Cap doesn't let herself frolic in the gray area – blurring is anathema to this border-conscious lady.

Though she rarely casts herself in the butch role, she will nonetheless be the one wearing the pants in a same-sex relationship. Living even more for herself than her straight counterpart, she embraces her solitude, keeping herself elevated and ever so out of reach from a lover. In gay bonds, she plays a

GAY TURN-ONS

younger women
tall, lean, curvy bodies
long dark hair
extended foreplay
vanilla
femme on femme
(passive) penetration
(passive) oral
(passive) worship
multiple vaginal orgasms
(active) breast play
sensual massage
thongs, demi-bras
boots, heels
mutual grooming
cross-dressing
feet, toes
straight women
casual, no-strings sex
(active) lite discipline
sober sex
afterplay, intimacy
erotica

parent/teacher role to the hilt, demanding attention and obedience in equal measure. At the same time, she encourages her lover to be her own woman, to strike out solo, except, that is, when it comes to extracurricular affairs. Cap woman, regardless of sexual preference, is hard-pressed to sit down and analyze the inner workings of a partnership – she shows love rather than professes it, and she requires a lover who is self-sufficient and confident enough to forgo such indulgences. In a brilliant stroke of narcissism, Cap woman is often attracted to younger, more exotic, or foreign, versions of herself. Even the straight Goat has her fantasies about these types of women who catch her eye: mirror images who might have enjoyed a more cultured upbringing than she. Call it jealousy, projection, transference, whatever; but this feeling of longing for a life Cap never led is often what draws her to the callow clones who she feels benefited in ways she never did. They both intimidate and turn her on, and by taking up with such a woman, Cap gains the sense of recapturing a part of herself, the careworn, humble Rhea embracing her youthful, more imperious Hera aspect as embodied in a lover. In short, there's no use telling the gay Cap to go fuck herself, she's way ahead of you there.

Despite the mixture of love and envy Cap feels for the sultry beauties with whom she invariably bonds, she will still need to be the one catered to in bed. She yearns to be pleased soothingly and deliberately, wanting a lover to take her time, particularly in her oral practices, as she lies back and luxuriates in sensation. She doesn't go in for any rough stuff or urgent expressions – all must be a continual, relaxed flow. Sexy lingerie gets her juices flowing, on herself as well as a lover, and she enjoys prolonged tactile stimulation, running her fingers lightly over a lover's body, lingering in all the right places, as her lover does likewise. Dildos are de rigueur, but generally employed by her mate slowly and at the appointed time, in combination with other means toward Cap's arousal. She is rarely inclined to return the favor, however, just as she isn't overly giving with oral sex, typically willing to comply when asked but otherwise not jumping at the chance. Simply put, she'd rather somebody else did it. Indeed, though Cap won't tolerate her girlfriend going behind her back for sex outside the relationship, she is happier than most to mix a third into the proceedings, particularly someone who can please her lover the way her lover pleases her. Watching, in any case, is a big turn-on for the Cap, but she particularly enjoys the sensation of holding, hugging, and kissing her partner while a third party is providing most of the entertainment. As a twosome, Cap and her lover are rather high on themselves, feeling they're the envy of the entire lesbian population. The Goat gloats over such primo-pussy status, whether it be real or imagined, and sometimes she can't help but literally rub other women's noses in it.

Couplings

Capricorn Woman / Aries Man

A rare pair. Her unrelenting faith plus his fighting spirit means life is lived like a crusade. Still, independence is their mutual mantra. Sexually, Cap is less hesitant with him. Indeed, she submits to his will.

Capricorn Woman / Taurus Man

Each finds a counterpart capable of true love. Still, though these earth signs are emotionally aligned – feathers rarely ruffle – she, thinking he'll stray, imposes restrictions. In bed, clearer communication is called for.

Capricorn Woman / Gemini Man

Cap is a conquest for Gemini. For the Goat, he's a guilty pleasure in her otherwise serious existence. Still, they share an interest in all things au courant – fashion, news, culture. In bed, she takes control – he's not complaining.

Capricorn Woman / Cancer Man

He's the Eagle Scout of her dreams; she's that perfect, postmodern beauty. These astro-opposites are often ideal counterparts, easily finding a comfortable, conducive middle way. Sex is a slow process of chipping away at constraints.

Capricorn Woman / Leo Man

Often a snobbish 'power' sign pair. They share traditional values, an old-fashioned work ethic. Still, as they're emotionally dissimilar, disappointment develops – she's capriciousness; he expects compliance. Sexually, it's cozy, but careful.

Capricorn Woman / Virgo Man

He's hot in cool Cap's presence. She's her own muse – a self-preservational package deal. Together, they pursue educational and cultural interests. In bed, this pair forms one fetishistic force – their routine is raunchy.

Capricorn Woman / Libra Man

A contradiction – a harrowing emotional seesaw, a transcendent experience. A need for social status masks insecurities; success seems a way to overcome the past. In bed, there's baggage. But with time, the load is lightened.

Capricorn Woman / Scorpio Man

He vows to make her life better, ease her stresses, and see her succeed. She's his steadfast confidante. Sex is most satisfying on the heels of an intense argument or inspired conversation. A mysterious mix.

Capricorn Woman / Sagittarius Man

A glamorous pair with an iconic allure that both impresses and intimidates anyone outside their social set. Still, the focus is inward and their home is a cozy cocoon. In bed, though, it's down and very dirty.

Capricorn Woman / Capricorn Man

Two old souls. They're a handsome couple with refined tastes, sharing a somewhat superior self-perception. Her set-in-stone values may cause him some consternation. Sex is slow and steady; they're respectful, even courteous.

Capricorn Woman / Aquarius Man

They fuse into a package deal of practicality and purpose. Still, Cap won't sacrifice her own objectives. They are notoriously accomplished. In bed, it's an ongoing master class – student and teacher roles are rotated.

Capricorn Woman / Pisces Man

At its core, a friendship founded on fondness and respect. Thick as thieves, they're protective of each other, fiercely loyal, and endlessly understanding: Capricorn, especially, serves as 'savior' to Pisces. Naturally, sex is tender.

Gay

Capricorn Woman / Aries Woman

Their learning curve is steep, but knowledge gained is power: Self-improvement takes precedence; individual pursuits are promoted. The infatuation lasts. Sex is rapturous – it's all about worship.

Capricorn Woman / Taurus Woman

Taurus pushes all Cap's buttons: How does one dare such outlandish relaxedness? To Taurus, Cap is a wise woman to be worshiped. Together, they live a principled, luxurious lifestyle. In bed, Cap takes command.

Capricorn Woman / Gemini Woman

It's a learning experience. With a glib 'Get over it,' Gemini stills the Goat's soulful, strained searching. But it's Gemini who's subdued in bed: Her lover demands the command position.

Capricorn Woman / Cancer Woman

They're searching for salvation – a soul mate. With Cancer, Cap learns to heed her sign's watery half: that tendency to emotionally fishtail. It's all about forgiveness. In bed, patience is required.

Capricorn Woman / Leo Woman

They're a formidable pair – stylish, ambitious, ostentatious. Making mischief is their social modus. Still, with mature Cap, Leo gleans life lessons. As for sex, it's purity in public and prurience in private.

Capricorn Woman / Virgo Woman

What begins with a bang may go out with a whimper. One or the other exists unceremoniously. To work, each woman must commit to compassion. In bed, domination incites desire. But most often, sex seems static.

Capricorn Woman / Libra Woman

Neither lady suffers fools gladly. They're unabashedly elitist. Bolstering each other professionally is a focus. Libra extols her lover's accomplishments, ad nauseam. In bed, Cap finds new self-assurance.

Capricorn Woman / Scorpio Woman

A mutual interest in women's issues or human rights will often draw them together. As a couple, they clash constantly. But fascination, even obsession, finds them forever connected. In bed, they keep it simple.

Capricorn Woman / Sagittarius Woman

They consider each other stepping-stones. Sag's audacity and Cap's common sense combine; their influence and affluence augment. In bed, it's a randy rumble to determine who's in charge. Both are exhibitionists.

Capricorn Woman / Capricorn Woman

Together, they climb the ladder toward professional success, though slowly. They're best friends on an unhurried, extraordinary journey. Developing a snug sexual link, too, takes time, but there's no need to rush it.

Capricorn Woman / Aquarius Woman

A battle of the wills wherein the Waterbearer tries to assume authority – and Cap's having none of it. Still, they're an enterprising pair, if verbosity doesn't obstruct action. In bed, the Goat gets the better end of the deal.

Capricorn Woman / Pisces Woman

There's a kink: Pisces harbors so much envy, which stands in the way of intimacy – sexual or emotional. With problems resolved, this couple can be one of the most creative. Cap feels whole; Pisces learns patience.

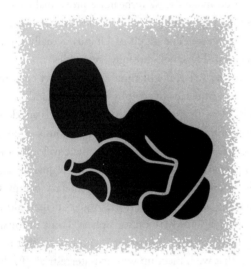

Aquarius Man

the visitor

Aquarius man is the most estranged character in the zodiac. He exudes an air of detachedness, an ironic symptom of his sign's infamous association with human liberty. On a one-to-one level, he feels set apart from others, while he is often predisposed to belonging to a larger, set social group, class, or even a philosophical ideology. For much of his youth, Aquarius is considered a bit of a freak, eccentric in his signature offbeat perceptions and predilections. Still, though he starts out feeling like an oddity, Aquarius develops into a social vanguard, capable of breaking existing molds and conjuring new ways of viewing the world. The roster of Aquarians is filled with revelatory thinkers and scientists who were ridiculed for their ideas before being recognized as veritable seers. Indeed, Aquarius has the power to glimpse truths that are yet to be proven – as if gazing into the future. Thus, he is the consummate man of conviction, no matter how outrageous his belief system, and his signature utopian notions are often catching. The most adept guru (or cult leader), Aquarian's demeanor says, 'I know something you don't know.' As such, potential mates fall under this demigod/demagogue's spell. To women, he seems sorted and self-sufficient in a sea of unstable men, only to exhibit his notoriously skewed if not sordid side in the sack. Typically cautious of other men, he tends to prefer no-strings sexual bonds, taking his sweet time (and sometimes never) settling into a steady relationship.

Xi

PRINCIPLE

Principle of Deviation. As the model of evolution of the species shows us, survival depends on mutations that meet with the requirements for adaptation. The Aquarian view is that universal or spiritual survival of mankind is based on sudden, new forays into the vanguard.

Sign + Mind

Aquarius's primary ruler, the planet Uranus – Saturn is the sign's subruler – represents the cosmic Principle of Deviation and Independence in the zodiac. As the male embodiment of this precept, the Waterbearer is somewhat of a pioneer, if not a human mutation who breaks with traditions and so-called normalcy. He is like that genetic quirk that occurs in a species that nonetheless ensures its evolution, a necessary departure to ward against extinction. The sign of Aquarius represents seeds of change that often make the Waterbearer a proverbial solitary voice in the wilderness trumpeting a new future, one that lies on the horizon that he is specially engineered to perceive. The glyph of Uranus, actually the *H* of the planet's discoverer, William Herschel, fittingly resembles a satellite designed to explore the far reaches of space, if not time, and to report back on what is 'out there.' Like that satellite, Aquarius telegraphs new understandings to humanity as a whole – this is his often lonely, solo mission. Aquarius is an ideological explorer, naturally forward-thinking and progressive, notoriously planted on the avant-garde of human experience, the guy who pushes the envelope more than anyone in almost every aspect of life. The concept of the Aquarian age (purported to begin in 2020) is all about change – Uranus's planetary energy is of sudden and sweeping, irrevocable alteration – and the Aquarian man alone represents the human character as catalyst for such drastic upheaval on a universal level. There are some (probably many of them Aquarians) who believe that it is during this time in our evolution that we'll meet up with extraterrestrials. In the meantime, Aquarius man does his best to fit that bill himself.

Aquarius guy appears so ridiculously detached and preoccupied because, on some level, he is forever lost in far-out revelations. This quirky fellow, who seems to be a visitor from the future, is already living realities that the rest of us won't get our brains around for ages. Even physically, planet Uranus signals 'freakish growth' in an organism that, as noted Aquarian Charles Darwin himself first theorized, provides a glimpse into the eventual norm of said species, evolution following where mutation leads. Aquarius is simply living those eventualities now. And though he may be labeled a freak, in hindsight (where Aquarians are always perceived in the best light) he will often be credited with contributing to the growth of humanity. His 11th Astrological House is that of *reformative activities, social consciousness*, and *spiritual unity*. Archetypally speaking, Aquarius is the zodiac's dispenser of immortality, an arbiter of social change and a progressive who gives us a taste of mankind's future. On a metaphoric and spiritual level, there is more to Aquarius than might readily meet the eye.

The story most widely associated with Aquarius male is that of John the Baptist — the waterbearer connection here being self-evident. He was a man raised free, in the wild, living the biblical version of a granola lifestyle, as we're told, existing on nothing but nuts and berries. No figure is more the single voice in the wilderness than he, the consummate 'mad man' in a constant state of revelation. Water, a symbol of divinity, is held by the bearer, immortality in a cup — the promise of everlasting life, which is mirrored perfectly in the secular ideal of evolution. Moreover, via the act of baptism, John initiated the concept of freedom from original sin, at least in the Judeo-Christian vein (he didn't originate it at all, as many so-called pagan religious rites involved the same dynamic). Still, the Baptist is a dispenser of grace, enabling those with whom he comes in contact to be free from the mark of damnation. In Aquarius, we see embodied the male archetype as not only a spiritual cleanser but one who sees no good reason for any such divide between mortal experience and eternal life. Via John the Baptist's out-there visions and anointment, he prepares the way for Christ, often symbolized as that water-inhabiting fish, just as the sign of the Waterbearer gives way to the Piscean Fish whose male archetype is the messiah.

In Arthurian legend, Merlin is the wild man of the woods, a druidic John the Baptist whose name means 'containment of the sea,' a fittingly cupping image — as the story goes, he had X-ray vision, lived backward, coming from the future, and was said to have forged a magic chalice synonymous with the Holy Grail. As such, Galahad is also an Aquarian archetype, untainted by original sin and thus able to seize the grail — *gala* meaning milk or in this case manna, or 'divine milk,' is contained in the name *Galatea,* referring to the eternal-life-giving goddess, and in the word *galaxy,* our own being the Milky Way. In Greek myth, the Waterbearer, Ganymede, the figure of the Aquarian constellation, embodies this same dispenser role, only with a decidedly gay twist. Fittingly, Uranus rules homosexuality: Father Zeus falls in love with Ganymede, a beautiful shepherd boy, and in eagle form sweeps him off his feet and up to Olympus where, before you can say 'sugar daddy,' Zeus grants him immortality and installs him as cupbearer to the gods, replacing his own daughter Hebe (actually his wife, Hera, in her maiden form). This switcheroo signals a change in Hellenic culture toward the elevation of male love-bonds if not Aquarian sexual liberation. Again, the 'water' is the ambrosia of immortality, manna, grace, the liquid essence of life everlasting. This infamous rape of Ganymede represents a mortal's transcendence to the experience of spiritual rapture, one that parallels the biblical and Arthurian tales. In the Aquarian Age, and especially to the Aquarian male mind, sexuality and

PLANETARY SYMBOL

Uranus is the masculine personification of the sky or universe. The planet signals sudden *change* or mutation on a massive scale and the ushering in of entirely new waves in thought, technology, discovery, or invention. Aquarius males, especially, are purveyors of the effects of this planet's extraordinary effects.

SIGN QUADRANT

The zodical quadrants correspond to metaphysical planes of existence — physical, emotional, mental, and spiritual or universal. The Fourth Quadrant concerns one's relationship with the whole or soul of mankind. Aquarius is looking to evolve the human spirit through revelatory means, if not revolutionary ideas, which he seeks to firmly establish as truths.

SIGN GLYPH

Herein we see the streaming waves, a symbol of heavenly manna, whether in the classic sense of liquid ambrosia, which would make a mortal immortal, or the baptismal waters, which likewise allow one to enter into life everlasting with God.

ELEMENT + QUALITY

The air element signifies mental and social experience; the fixed quality, intense concentration and magnetism. The fixed-air combination particular to Aquarius implies a certain corner of the sky, whether it be heaven, a distant star, or such visions as a rainbow. The combination also symbolizes truth, a fixed idea, which is ever so important to the Aquarian, whose motto is 'I know.'

spirituality can go hand in hand. Funny that many cult leaders have been Aquarians. Not ha-ha funny, necessarily, when you consider how many men, under the guise of religious leadership, use their 'godly' position to bed as many devotees as possible. Two forms of rapture rolled into one. Not that being an Aquarian male is the only prerequisite to zealotry; but it is a predisposition that cannot be discounted. In any case, the Aquarian male condition is one of being freeze-framed at the point of contact with the great beyond, the eternal, the infinite, the universal, and often the galactic, as evidenced by the many spacey notions of noted Aquarian men.

Mythically, too, Uranus is the universe, the preeminent male sky-god and father of the Titans, who begat Saturn–Cronos, who begat Jupiter–Zeus, the two respective rulers and archetypes associated with the precedent male signs of Capricorn and Sagittarius. Uranus was cut down by his son, Saturn, with his handy scythe simply because Uranus was too lofty a godhead for his own good. As we know, the Baptist similarly lost his head. So, too, does every Aquarian male become overly enraptured by his imaginings, often delusional about his own grandeur. Aquarius is the one fixed-air sign in the zodiac: Air symbolizes mental and social experience; and fixedness is just that, a steadfast resolve and focused concentration. Taken together, Aquarius has such set ideas about existence that he can't help but perceive even his most whimsical thoughts as uppercase Truths. Genius, as well as insanity, seems predicated upon such staunch conviction – John the Baptist was both prophet and madman. Furthermore, Aquarius feels a need to convert others to his thinking: The wavy, watery symbol of his sign recalls electrical signals, pointing to the Waterbearer's need to flow, indeed pour out his trademark avant-garde revelations onto others. He doesn't merely think, he ascertains, his sign's motto being 'I know.' Uranus, from whom we get the word urine – in ancient mythic terms this fluid was synonymous with blood and semen – fertilized the sea when castrated or beheaded by his son – likewise being beheaded, John the Baptist evolved more fertile ground for Christ's teachings to take root – thus, rain was associated by the ancients with the urinating of the sky god and the fecundation of the world. Ganymede, too, means 'celebration of virility.' While in modern imagery, we have the Dustin Hoffman character in the film *Rainman,* both a freak and a genius, an idiot savant, who is an Aquarian character to the core. Being an air sign, the fertility Aquarius espouses is ideological, growing the seeds of social and intellectual change, on an impersonal, sweeping, universal level. Despite his notoriously mad countenance, every Aquarian is no mere futures analyst but a 'knower' of truths that are yet to be revealed to the rest of us who don't, like him, benefit and suffer from the blessing and affliction of funneling such theories into facts.

Any such mathematical allusions to that *Rainman* character notwithstanding, having such fixed ideas thus sees the Aquarian as the most calculating man in the zodiac. For him, there is no such thing as an isolated action, his every move adding up to furthering his grand agenda. If any man has a master plan for existence, it's the Aquarian, forever conscious of steering his destiny, leaving nothing to fate, seeking control not only of external environmental forces but of those natural ones raging inside him. It has been said that he is an impersonal being, which couldn't be more true; but in elucidating his signature emotional detachment from others, many astrological scholars fail to note that he is, likewise, separated from his own feelings – more often than not, he regards his sentiments as distractions, if not obstacles, to achieving the lofty aims he has firmly fixed in his mind. He is the personification of mind over matter, fully convinced he has the power to change tried-and-true traditions that he perceives as outmoded or universally unfair. And, in a similar fashion, he will root out undesirable qualities in his own nature. Aquarius rules the 11th Astrological House, that of one's *hopes* and *wishes*, as well as *adoptive behavior*; and so, whereas the rest of the zodiacal population is, in their own way, coming to terms with who they are, in one of the myriad variations on the theme of 'know thyself,' this is not the case for the Aquarian, who instead seeks to embody the idea of whom he wishes to be – in the future – with no regard for where he may be 'coming from.' Even his most far-out aspirations are never considered pipe dreams, but rather attainable goals that he then programs himself to achieve, almost mathematically, with no room for dillydallying or dysfunction. Despite his sign's association with sexual liberation, most poignantly illustrated via the Broadway musical *Hair,* Aquarius man may even seek to override his own sexual nature if he finds it in conflict with his fixed idea of how he ultimately hopes to be (self-)perceived. His ruler, Uranus, the planet of innovation and mutation, sets Aquarius on a path of self-invention from day one. Thus, the Waterbearer becomes the brainchild of his own fertile imagination, something that can gain him as much a reputation for being contrived as it does for being creatively original.

Aptly, the sign of Aquarius is associated with the age group 70–77, a time when one's thoughts might naturally turn to mortality and, thus, what it might mean to meet with the proverbial great beyond. It may also be a time of entering a 'second childhood.' At this age, one becomes, once again, more reliant on others, pointing to the Aquarian ideal of a socialized all-for-one system of civilization. Daftness of old age is something the Aquarian male seems to possess all his life. An oddball, he is ironically often born to incredibly traditional parents. His siblings, on the other hand, all seem to fit the familial

POLARITY

Males in masculine (air, fire) signs are aligned with the gender polarity of their sign and thus embody the quality-element combination of the sign. Aquarius guy is a revelation unto himself, lost in his own convictions – that is, utterly convinced of certain truths. Like John the Baptist, he is often a lone voice calling out in the wilderness.

11

SIGN NUMBER

The number of revelation. A page is turned with this number: After the completion of ten, eleven signifies the first 'reveal' of a new order. Joseph, with his Technicolor dreamcoat, is the eleventh son of Jacob, one blessed with revelatory power.

70–77

SIGN AGE ASSOCIATION

A time of life when one prepares, on some level, for that ultimate connection with the great beyond. This can also be a time of second childhood, which certainly lends new meaning to the term born-again.

mold. But he sticks out like a sore thumb. As the zodiac's wizened old man, he is constantly trying to 'keep up,' generally having difficulty with what peers might consider the most facile school lessons. He is a loner, often playing imaginary games, losing himself in revelry often to his own embarrassment when he is caught out by schoolmates talking or singing to himself, scribbling wild stories or drawings in his lesson book, or simply seeming dazed and confused when called upon. Luckily for him, he has little ego and the derision of others will roll right off his back. He is calm and contemplative, often divinely unaware of his social-misfit moniker. He is, like that eternal seventy-seven-year-old, far more concerned with making his own peace with the world, easily shrugging off any attachment to even the rat race existence of a second-grader, untouchable in his sense of self-worth and self-sufficiency.

Typically, his father will be involved in intellectual pursuits and have little to do with the Aquarian on the home front. His mother will be somewhat put-upon by daily existence if not a bit depressed or phobic in her social interactions, often immersed in her profession as well, or the experience of domestic life, to the point of obsession if not reclusion. There may not be much warmth in his upbringing, which engenders his signature detachment all the more, something that will nonetheless become the Aquarian's saving grace. Though he's a sort of Forrest Gump or, rather, an Owen Meany, sometimes brutally ridiculed and tormented by others, it doesn't much matter to him. In fact, in being labeled the local weirdo, his mind travels all the further into inner space in search of those trademark undiscovered truths that will ultimately become his anchor in this world. Alternately, or often simultaneously, he will look further afield for a less personal sense of belonging, joining organizations or involving himself in activities or sports that take him beyond normal experience, cutting him off from contact with schoolmates or even siblings. Meanwhile, on the home front, he definitely gets the ugly-duckling treatment, especially by brothers who ride roughshod over him, attempting the human equivalent of pushing this odd bird out of the nest.

The Aquarian male is, in every sense of the word, exceptional. By the time he hits high school he generally slips slowly below the radar – what was once an experience of peer ridicule becomes one of blissful social oblivion. His attention will go elsewhere: Classmates mightn't realize he is embarking on a career as a boy-genius chess player, or that he takes an all but exclusively adult advanced drama class in a nearby city, nearly landing some meaty roles in film or theater, or that he has written several novels that he is secretly circulating to publishers and agents. The odd duck close to home, he is perceived as a would-be swan in those far-flung environments. But such a dynamic has its downsides: This vulnerable and gawky fledgling might invite the unwanted attention of lecherous chicken hawks, a sort of 1950s term for the more pedocentric population. Like his archetypal Ganymede, some overbearing male or female predator with an eagle eye for virginal male beauty might swoop in and offer our Aquarian the kind of personal attention and affection he has lacked thus far. And even the straightest of Waterbearers might go along for any free ride as might land him atop some sort of Olympus.

The most poignant image of Aquarius's designation as the fixed-air sign is in his wish to attain a sense of glorious heaven, that fixed corner of the sky where a certain immortality is assured. He *is* Ganymede in this way, and he will happily let himself be taken up by others whom he perceives to be more exalted than himself in whatever arena, professional or social, he's seeking to infiltrate. He can do this far more easily than the rest of us because he doesn't possess such personal attachments as most humans do. He is readily removed from terrestrial trappings, certainly, even familial ones. And he is especially detached from any strict sense of self. That is, being so fixed on whom he sees himself becoming in the future, he is willing to sacrifice all present notions of personality by which he defines himself – such scruples even, which the rest of us might see as constituting literal integrity. But as he seeks complete and utter communion with what he determines to be greater than himself, whether it be a social or political organizaiton or spiritual system of his own divining or even a rarefied world to which gaining access might require selling out to some degree, for real or metaphorically, he won't let fear of losing himself stand in the way. Actually, that is his ultimate goal. Ganymede is the cupbearer just as Galahad ascends to heaven once grasping the Grail. Likewise, Aquarius male is seeking, in everyday life, to take up the cup of his own ideological exaltation. Often this makes him susceptible to cults and other such ersatz 'religions' – then again, he might be uniquely capable of perceiving them as the mainstay belief systems of the future. In any case, Aquarius doesn't stand on ceremony of ego, in the strictest psychological sense, and is thus easily swept up into heady, heightened situations and lofty opportunities. By example, Aquarius man teaches the rest of us that personality is an illusion and that we are made up of the same atomic particles as everything that surrounds us – he already knows we are all but dust in the wind.

Body + Soul

Aquarius is nearly mechanical in his manner, his deliberate mind-set translating into a skittish, somewhat robotic body language, if not a defensively cold

PSYCHOLOGY

Aquarius is almost pathologically self-aware, as if his every thought holds some earth-shattering truth. He often feels misunderstood by the world, which can give rise to seriously antisocial behavior. He is skittish in intimate settings. Signature emotional detachment can turn to depersonalization. Naturally attuned to abstract ideology, Aquarius may ride a fine line between genius and delusional hysteria. He may be inclined to sexual deviations that others consider depraved.

The god Uranus, namesake of Aquarius's ruling planet, is the universe, the über sky god, just as Aquarius is a sort of over-the-top air sign. The classic Waterbearer is Ganymede, 'lover of virility,' from whose name the term catamite is derived – a boy kept for pederastic purposes. Zeus had the hots for Ganymede and swept down in eagle form to whisk the boy back to Olympus to become the cupbearer to the gods. If anybody is the proverbial pool boy, it's Aquarius man. For his trouble, Ganymede is made immortal. The symbolic upshot is that Aquarius men get caught up (and carried away) in their own glimpses of eternity.

physicality – let's just say Aquarius isn't much of a hugger, as even simple shows of affection conflict with his carefully plotted programming. Interestingly, it is the Greek word *kybernet,* meaning 'helmsman' or 'steersman,' that has given rise to the modern term *cybernetics,* defined as both 'the study of human control functions,' as well as 'the mechanical system designed to replace them.' For the future-minded Aquarian, under whose rule fall such technological sciences (as well as the literary genre science fiction), the analogy is not an extraneous one: Just as the science fiction of today becomes the science fact of tomorrow, the contrivances of Aquarius man, given time, become the reality of his actual being. In the adoptive spirit of his 11th Astrological House, he seeks to replicate that which he most admires in other people, assimilating their best qualities into his own machination for living. Sure, all human beings imprint upon one another; but the difference here is that the Aquarius has a unique ability to consciously choose what, and whose, influences will be encoded into his own behavior.

It must be remembered that Aquarius man, more than engaging in mere transformation, *is* mutation, the embodiment of Uranus's revolutionary and, indeed, evolutionary energy – deviation, in Darwinian terms, being key to survival. In a variation on the ho-hum theme of humanity, Aquarius is the quirk, the vanguard forever pushing the human envelope forward. Sometimes this metaphorical truth is blatantly obvious in the Aquarian's appearance, kitted out as he might be in the latest techno-fashions, just as he may have been the premier hippy on his block back in the 1960s – literally wearing his ruling planet's principles of differentiation and freedom, fairly screaming societal change. At other times, fearful of any derision at letting his so-called freak flag fly, Aquarius goes to the other extreme, scrambling for some semblance of normalcy, adopting a cookie-cutter catalog-clothing style, such stabs at conformity being his attempt to gain acceptance from society at large. Still, like a sly alien body-snatcher, he may *look* like the rest of us, but any comparison typically ends there.

All joking aside, there is something vaguely unnerving about the Aquarian's tendency to co-opt experience – as if he envisages others as potential hosts upon whom he can feed for inspiration, thus fueling his ambitious fires. Like his fellow fixed signs – Taurus, Leo, Scorpio – the Waterbearer has a come-hither attitude, making him more concerned with what he gets from, rather than what he gives to, others. Especially, emotionally: His native 11th House is also associated with *the love one receives on a mass scale* and though his inherent distance makes it difficult for him to invest in others, he is disproportionately expectant of acceptance, if not love. Since, as a rule, air signs concern themselves most with the intellectual, ideological, and social planes of experience, the fixed-air sign Waterbearer strives for social security just as he seeks ratification of his often revolutionary ideas. Part and parcel of being a born radical is trying to infiltrate mainstream thought, and this is the very process by which the vanguard becomes the old guard – in the arts, science, politics, and religious reform – from time immemorial. The list of famous Aquarian men is distinguished by thinkers, indeed seers, and often mystics who are light-years ahead of their time – Mozart, Rasputin, Galileo, Copernicus, Thomas Edison, Jules Verne, Bertolt Brecht, James Joyce, Franklin Delano Roosevelt, Thomas Merton, Abraham Lincoln, Charles Darwin – all of whom sought to find security for their visionary thoughts in the social mainstream. Of course, not all Aquarians are genius inventors or social reformers, but a heightened sense of conviction exists in all men of this sign, as if they are convinced of those certain truths about life that have yet to be proven or come to pass. This feature makes John the Baptist the ideal biblical archetype for the sign, himself a Waterbearer who foretells the coming of a new age.

The first thing one might notice about Aquarius is that Baptistlike intensity, fixed as he is on whatever cause he is currently championing, his own self-interest perceived as one and the same with a universal raison d'etre. He seeks to impress people while impressing upon them a vision of utopian life that he is forever in the process of achieving. Though he has a cool and composed look, particularly around the eyes, which can be pale and icy, Aquarius man reveals a real zealotry in conversation, a characteristic made all the more ironic in juxtaposition to his trademark restrained body language. So if you were to encounter a physically hemmed-in fellow – arms notoriously held in at his sides as if by an invisible straitjacket – wildly gesticulating via facial expressions, unsuccessfully attempting to modulate undue excitement in his speech, eyes self-consciously darting off to the side as if into some imaginary rolling camera, chances are he is an Aquarian man. He has a particular delivery to his speech, and often a shticky one, punctuating his statements with a cymbal-crash *ba-dum-bum* – *chh,* laughing at his own jokes, that imaginary camera always rolling. Still, as something of an empath, he'll either turn up or tone down his 'performance' to suit the mood of the company he's in. Experience is all input-and-output for the Aquarian man as his sign's double-wave symbol suggests – with every word or gesture uttered he immediately gauges others' reactions to them, like a computer calculating data. It appears a struggle for him to listen when others speak, as if he's fighting the urge to react verbally; one often has the feeling he's always aching to interrupt. Eye contact isn't easy for him either, and he often strains to sustain it – this can also be

BIBLE + LITERATURE

The Aquarian male in biblical archetype is John the Baptist, that waterbearing purveyor of Truth who lived his life 'out there' much the way Aquarius does. His medieval equivalent is Merlin, who forged the Holy Grail. Also called Ambrosius, pointing to the manna he offered, he was Christianized into St. Ambrose. Merlin prophesies the coming of Arthur, just as the Baptist is the vanguard of Jesus. This dynamic finds outlet in James Joyce's *Portrait of the Artist as a Young Man:* Cranly presages the Christ figure, Stephen Dedalus. In the film *The Matrix,* the character Morpheus rebirths the savior figure, Neo.

**11TH ASTROLOGICAL
HOUSE**

social awareness
group dynamics
potential for friendship
potential for happiness
friends and associates
unemotional bonds
life objectives
ideals to live by
love received
mass appeal
money made via career
self-employment
step-children/foster chil-
dren/adoptive children
situations out of control
humanitarian concerns
how we perceive others
clubs/cliques/associations
hopes and wishes
collective bonds
new order
extraterrestrial life
quirks/foibles
mutations
technology
the unexpected
working for common goals
spiritual oneness
mental link with God
impersonal truth
identification within a group
unorthodox activities
creativity within a group
universal regard
applause
liberation
mental acuity
social progress
collective consciousness

unnerving as he has a keen and steady gaze, his eyes narrowed and nearly wolfish. Latching on to people as he does, with his smarmy conversational routine, he might be mistaken for a letch, which he isn't (at least not necessarily so). Still, those shifty eyes can make him seem like a big baddie who is only after a girl's basket of goodies – any attempts to appear all clean-cut may only make more of an impression that he's really a wolf in sheep's clothing. Truth is, he's just trying to fit in.

It's hard to believe, given the Aquarian's tendency to be both handsome and hunky, that he was probably an awkward adolescent. For the most part, the Waterbearer is quite tall with a ruggedly angular physicality, although the suddenly mutative energy of Uranus often sees him getting fat or bloating for extended periods in his adulthood, just as he may experience abrupt hair loss – rarely does he bald gradually. Uranus rules both the gonads and the pineal gland, which, given its frontal position in the brain, has been thought to correspond to the mystic third eye and is thus associated with clairvoyance. This gland is also credited with promoting accelerated development. Freakish growth like giantism is also associated with Uranus, and traces of it may sneak into the Aquarian's anatomy, often to his delight – though, in some cases, much to his annoyance such grandiosity might be centered just south of a desired target and settle in his very own gonads. Perhaps that's why he often prefers standing to sitting. In any case, Aquarius makes up a major part of any big-and-tall shop's clientele, which he may start frequenting from an early age. As a rule, he experiences his adolescent growth spurt far earlier than his peers, which can be a source of pain and ridicule. Already he will have felt unusual given his unique personality; and so, he often finds himself labeled weird, in more ways than one. Added to which, he may've had difficulty in school, since his brand of intellect is most often misunderstood and so rarely nurtured by elementary-school curricula. Only further along in his education will he find an outlet and any acceptance for his advanced form of abstract and scientific thinking. Of course, this will only see his nerd status become more specifically defined as an 'egghead' persona – it doesn't help that he also looks the part. Having typically shot up so quickly in his youth, the Waterbearer's body will be weedy, lending his head a looming appearance in comparison; and as if that isn't bad enough, Aquarius tends to have a lightbulb-shaped noggin, covered with peach-fuzz, fine, or wispy hair marked by a high Mozartean hairline such that he looks somewhat like the sketches of aliens made by those claiming to have been kidnapped by UFOs. The ridge of his brow is often drastically pronounced, in Frankenstein fashion, his nose long, thin, and aquiline at just the very tip – as if a nod to the Greek waterbearer Ganymede's own kidnapping by Zeus in eagle form. And yet, despite all these seemingly gruesome descriptions, those that may make him an ugly duckling in his youth, Aquarius nonetheless gels, swanlike, into one of the more beautiful men in the zodiac. His secondary ruler, Saturn, may take his sweet ol' Father Time in the Aquarian's physical development; but then, suddenly, Uranus sees the Waterbearer form fully into exquisite manhood, Ganymede's archetypal beauty causing more than a fair share of suitors, male and female, to swoop in and try to pick Aquarius up. Among the lookers born under the sign, we see the crystal-eyed likes of Paul Newman, Rutger Hauer, Peter Gabriel, Elijah Wood, Christian Bale, John Travolta, and James Dean.

It is a great part of Aquarius's charm that he was, generally speaking, such an ugly duckling. For, no matter how devastatingly handsome he may become, it never quite goes to that ET–shaped head of his. Even women who are quick to label him that 'wolf' soon realize that this guy isn't nearly so wrapped up in his external appearance as he is rapt by his eternal internal revelations about life. That he may have exquisite looks is just icing on the cake. Beefcake that he is: As would befit his zodiacal designation, the Waterbearer is generally blessed with an attractive swimmer's build. Though Aquarius generally fills out his Speedo just fine, the bulk of his bulge is, again, often based in his often jumbo balls. However, Uranus is the planet of the unexpected, after all, which is what one might encounter when this seemingly unassuming chic geek whips out a freakishly monster member. Anyway, he typically boasts a tight, compact upper body – more toned than buff – sinewy arms, and a nearly curvaceous waist. Likewise, he may have swelled hips, an arched or sway back, and an exaggerated bubble butt, lending a rather 'girly' look to his rear view, especially if wearing tight trousers. It doesn't help that he walks with a wee bit of a wiggle. His legs are strong and stocky, his calf muscles especially bulbous, while his hands and feet, long and tapered, suggest sensitivity and creative expression. Still, his gait has a duck-footed goofiness, which in some cases turns his wiggle into a waddle. Fairer skinned than his relatives, Aquarius's hair, in contrast, is typically dark brown or even black, though it goes salt-and-peppery prematurely. His signature pale peepers sometimes raise the suspicion that he's the milkman's child as his siblings might be all brown-eyed, making him that much more an anomaly. He isn't especially hairy, generally only scarcely so, looking like some future dweller who has evolved out of such caveman characteristics, there being nothing in his personality to suggest he'd ever cart a woman off by the hair. Indeed, it is he who is generally up for grabs, seeking adoption by a devoted partner who will allow him the freedom of his unique visions while helping him to assimilate into conventional society.

KEY WORDS

universality
egotism
populism
humanity
veracity
uniqueness
innovation
rigidity
zealotry
eccentricity
genius
originality
idealism
perversity
charity
obstinacy
independence
permutation
revelation
populism
modernity
pedagogy
innovation
separation
irregularity
inclination
complexity
mystery
rebellion
curiosity
experimentation
affability
heroism
virility
dispassion
truth
modernity

Sex + Sexuality

In a world where men are programmed to assert some sort of personal agenda, sexual or otherwise, the Aquarius seems not to fall prey to the machinations of his own libido. In a nod to his Galahad archetype, he quite simply seems beyond sex, far more obviously focused on his lofty ideals, aspirations, and a signature need to feel above the fray of base human experience. From a perspective of outside objectivity, which is the perspective the zodiacal visitor has of even his own self, a person driven by sensation, emotion, or even hormones is unsightly. He takes absolute control of his desires and makes damn sure they never show. Aquarius prides himself on being an evolved man; however, what he often ends up doing is simply repressing his natural physical, sensual, and sexual urges until they reemerge, in some alternate albeit controlled form. But, like Galahad, Aquarius believes you can't grab that chalice of immortality and achieve some heavenly form of idealized existence if you allow yourself to be weighted down by desire or attachment of any kind. His apparent lack of sexual beastliness makes a potential partner feel that she's found someone special, a man who is head and shoulders above the rest. This of course is what Aquarius wants most: Just as he became accustomed to being labeled odd as a kid, he now hopes to cash in on his exceptional status in adulthood. What he wants, and what he promises a would-be mate, is not ordinary love. He is, therefore, rather a tough catch to land, generally giving off the impression he's unavailable if not completely out of one's league. As a rule, suitors of both sexes tend to throw themselves at the Aquarian man as it seems anything less than an overt play for his attentions mightn't register on what is perceived to be his above-it-all nature. The Aquarius, and not altogether unconsciously, makes people feel base for having sexual feelings for him. But this is a bit of a ploy: Astrology's Galahad typically isn't as pure and beyond sex as he would let others believe. Indeed, no male has a sleazier side, albeit a highly secretive one. On any given day, he might be patting some pretty woman on the back with an air of 'better luck next time' as he lets her down easy, making her feel she's fallen short, while on any given night he might more pointedly slap and tickle some plaything, perhaps even a paid one.

When it comes to living publically with a person, he insists on maintaining an exalted position. He expects worship, not as the attractive beefcake Taurean Adonis does, but in a far more lofty manner. The zodiac's Ganymede demands near immortalization; and a mate must put, and keep, Aquarius on so high a pedestal that he feels tribute is continually being paid him by sheer virtue of the bond's existence. He won't play on the ground as some mere mortal; rather he requires bucket loads of esteem. On one hand, he needs a blind devotee. But on the other, it must be someone he deems of similarly high quality – or else his or her opinion won't count for much in his mind. He expects to be worshiped by something of a goddess or god who likewise inspires a kind of awe in others. When in a bond with the Aquarian male, all other power couples will pale in comparison. For this reason alone, Aquarius is often labeled a parvenu, a seeming social climber who seeks to marry above his station. Though this may often be true, it is a symptom rather than the cause of his efforts. As Aquarius makes little distinction between his utopian social visions and what might strike him as a cushy societal heaven, capable of being the people's prophet, while still out for personal profit. He is often accused of being venal – like Ganymede, up for grabs to the most flush bidder. If and when he does marry some social high priestess or professional mover-shaker, he will typically see her fade into the background, trading her own status for the mantle of his chief disciple. Having a calculated system for success, Aquarius must convert a woman to his programming and reinforce his every whim with affirmative nods – he can't, of course, live a life of debate or even open discussion of his ideas, which, from the instant he thinks them, must be immediately set, as solid fact, in stone.

There is nobody whom the Aquarian male thinks is out of his league. His self-conviction, thus, becomes the secret to securing relationships with the most eligible bachelorettes on the planet, even when he himself is less than a looker. That's what comes from seeing yourself as a god. Astrology has often made the mistake of describing the Waterbearer as socially liberated, and sexually emancipated as well, living life as if it were staged in a 1960s commune. Certainly, if such a lifestyle were a particular Aquarian man's vision, then it would unfold in actuality. But the real point is that Aquarius feels free to envision the world according to whatever his individual utopian ideal might be, and everything and everybody must then conform to this perception – or he simply cuts them out of the picture. If anything, the Waterbearer is a rigid person when it comes to his individual modus operandi. His ideologies and belief systems might seem 'bizarre,' a result of Uranus's rule, but the way he regiments his life in keeping to such avant-garde life philosophies is pure Saturn, distinguished as it is by time efficiency and a taskmaster's discipline. Take communism – a political and social view that falls under Aquarian rule – it is free, liberal, and, well, communal on the outside, but on the inside is rife with rules and regulations based on espousing such selflessness. It's the same with Aquarius man: He rules his most free-form belief systems with a firm, mechanical hammer and sickle. Fittingly, he cannot help but impose his sometimes severe ethics onto loved ones as well.

Eddie Van Halen
Phil Collins
Peter Gabriel
John Lydon
Graham Nash
Jack Nicklaus
Wayne Gretzky
John McEnroe
Michael Jordan
Christian Dior
Balenciaga
Charles Lindbergh
Charles Darwin
Galileo
Copernicus
Sir Francis Bacon
Thomas Merton
George Balanchine
Mikhail Baryshnikov
Edouard Manet
Robert Motherwell
Jackson Pollock
James Joyce
Stendahl
W. S. Maugham
Paddy Chayevsky
Langston Hughes
Anton Chekov
Charles Dickens
Sinclair Lewis
Jules Verne
Lewis Carroll
Christopher Marlowe
William Burroughs
Wolfgang Amadeus Mozart
August Strindberg
Franz Schubert
Franklin D. Roosevelt
Abraham Lincoln
Hadrian
Frederick the Great
Douglas MacArthur
W. Randolph Hearst
Bill Mumy
Fernand Leger
Sonny Bono
Ramakrishna
Joe Pesci
Garth Brooks
Stephen Crane

BODY RULERSHIP

The sign of Aquarius rules
the legs, from knee to ankle,
and the circulatory system.
Uranus is associated with
sudden nervous disorders –
fits, spasms, breakdowns –
as well as abnormal growth
such as that of tumors.

Like any guru, he seduces a would-be adherent into believing that he knows what's best for her: By following his lead, she'll live life the right way. Meanwhile, Aquarius makes his lover feel special, 'chosen,' and wrought, like him, of exceptional stuff. He thus anoints his partner, metaphorically sprinkling her with his divine blessing, letting her sip from his cup. Thus, he often attracts women who are seriously lacking father love – those looking for someone 'great' to please and adore – just as he tends to turn a woman into his primary caretaker. Suddenly, the self-sufficient Waterbearer can't seem to tie his own laces. It happens time and time again: Aquarius makes a woman his host of sorts, relying on her for his daily sustenance while he focuses fully on all those lofty, universal concepts that grace or plague his mind. He insinuates himself into a woman's life on the premise he's some god of a man who will offer guidance and protection, then he slowly turns into that seventy-seven-year-old who needs to be checked so he doesn't leave the house wearing two different kinds of shoes. (Especially not so attractive a trait in a thirty-five-year-old.) Still, such inability to pay attention to the little things typically means that Aquarius is achieving certain greatness on a universal scale.

The 11th House is that of *the love one receives,* as compared with the 5th House of *the love one gives,* associated with Aquarius's so-called opposite sign of Leo. Both signs are preoccupied with authority, which, for the Aquarian, often translates into his desired sexual activities. The passionate Leo, who is very vanilla in his erotic tastes, would be shocked to know what the dispassionate Aquarian gets up to in the bedroom, provided, of course, this setting isn't too banal and cliché an environment for the Waterbearer to perform in. Needless to say, Aquarius is probably the least emotionally involved sexual persona. For starters, he isn't above screwing his way to the top, since such behavior can't touch him personally. Uranus's rule over the 11th House is associated with *freedom via repression,* which sees the Aquarian being able to move on a dime in life by perpetually squelching his feelings, something to which an ex-wife of a Waterbearer will undoubtedly attest: He tends not to exhibit the slightest remorse at ditching relationships that were decades in the making. We see this dynamic, too, in his sexual exploits, as he will travel to the farthest reaches of erotic activity while his actual role in such scenarios remains incredibly restrained. For instance, a signature Aquarian sexual proclivity leans toward disciplinary action such as spanking a partner, if not something more extreme. He is also infamously turned on by humiliating a mate. Indeed, the Waterbearer might own several sets of rubber sheets but never involve himself in anything more so-called perverted than unzipping his fly and relieving himself on a playmate in all too graphic an expression of Uranus's golden-showering rule.

To this self-appointed god, even his tinkle should be considered manna as if sprinkled from on high. He is no Milquetoast sexual character to be sure. Indeed, the more pure and knightly our Aquarian Galahad might seem in public, the more prurient and kinky he may be in private. But here's the rub: Aquarius generally perceives his relationships as being part and parcel of his public, not his private, life. His wife, therefore, will generally not be the one squealing and squeaking around on those rubber sheets or wrapped from head to toe in latex. Indeed, she might find herself increasingly sexually wanting as her relationship with Aquarius man progresses.

Though he does sexually deviate more than most, a direct result of his skewed planetary rule, the Aquarian's erotic scope tends to be incredibly focused and specific. As with his ideological views, this fixed-air sign burnishes his thoughts into preoccupations. As he is hands down the most monomaniacal individual on the astrological wheel, sex with Aquarius always smacks of a mind fuck. Internet chat rooms geared toward sexual interest were made for Aquarius as he can democratically indulge his desires with an increasing variety of people. Not just some male cyber slut, Aquarius will meet women for anonymous real-time sex as well, preferring one-shot deals rather than casual ongoing sessions. Given his trademark hands-off interaction, he worries little about bringing anything home to his usually doting spouse, who assumes that her genius husband is only increasingly beyond sex, her eternal Galahad valiantly guarding his purity with mounting vigor. Truth be told, the spark tends to go out of relationships for Aquarius man very easily, and such bonds must then be supplemented, and fairly regularly if not daily, by these aforementioned vague dalliances. But eventually he'll long for something even more. In all his sexual relationships, one thing remains certain: He likes to be considered out of reach, necessitating his lover to petition if not beg him to bestow his sexual favors.

The Waterbearer, with his über-idealized vision, is perhaps overly concerned with the form, or look, of love, rather than the actual content of his relationships. Like most people, he enjoys the beginnings of bonds best, the thrill of newness; but unlike others he tends to become so attached to the feeling of freshness that he seeks to keep such heightened sensations of exhaltation alive in varying ways. When it comes to marriage or a primary relationship, he tends to act like a neophyte on a job where, so long as he's still going through some kind of orientation, he won't have to really dig down and do the work of managing the business of love. The zodiac's Mork from Ork, everything seems new to Aquarius, and he engenders that much more affection from his mate, who, at least for a time, sees his boyish exuberance as charming and without guile. He keeps his bonds superficial, becoming so lodged in the courtship aspect of love

STR8 TURN-ONS

dominant females
blonds, redheads
Africans, Indians, Asians
waifs, tomboys
executive women
(passive) seduction
extended foreplay
lesbian porn
(passive) b + d
(active) s + m
(passive) oral
lesbianism
m-f-f threesomes
phone/cyber sex
(active) mind control
swapping, orgies
kink, fetish
(passive) water sports
(mutual) anal play
(passive) deprivation
sex clubs, groups
female masturbation
being cuckolded
humiliation
(passive) worship

that it might border on the ridiculous, commemorating every minute anniversary with gifts or a celebratory dinner or getaway. He is so over-the-top in his praise, flattery, and very formal public displays of affection for his femme that strangers might assume he and his mate were on their honeymoon, rather than just running day-to-day errands. Quotidian existence, you see, is too ho-hum for our parvenu dweller of Olympus, and he does whatever he can in his demeanor to heighten even the most common circumstance. More times than not, Aquarius's partner will be the type of woman who requires this brand of constant lip service, lacking, at least initially, the ability to cope with deeper feelings and life challenges. It's as if, when it comes to marriage in particular, Aquarius leaves the proverbial building just after the preacher or justice of the peace says 'for better or . . .' Enough said, he thinks.

Another symptom of his need for thrills is that signature poking (if not actually screwing) around for what can only be described as adoration of the masses. Aquarius's 11th House association of *global relationship* and *large-scale community* means that blanket, not individual, attention is really what this man really craves. Like a many-wived zealot cult leader, he never stops seeking new brides to add to his conceptual harem. Everywhere he goes regularly there will be installed some fawning female whose affections he has fostered. There will be his favorite female fellow exec at the office, his preferred lunchtime waitress, the woman (rarely is it another man) who cuts his hair or gives him massages, and so on. Hanging in the air around him, these gaga girls imagine, is the possibility that at any moment he might swoop down and carry them away. Unfortunately, those thoughts begin to cross his spouse's or longtime companion's mind with increasing frequency as well: In a new relationship, Aquarius will make it an absolute point to have sex with his partner nearly every day. He has an amazing ability to psych himself up whenever he needs to do so – those cameras are rolling, after all, and they expect the money shot. All he demands from his lover in return is that she express as much pleasure with his performance as he typically takes. He's the 'How'd you like that, baby?' guy, and a woman needs to put on her most enthusiastic expression in assuring the Aquarian that sex, like everything else with him, is absolute heaven. God forbid she should ever get bored. Planet Uranus signals sudden change, accident, and serendipity. And it will be along such themes that the Aquarian will make his case for having found somebody else, even after years of what appeared to be the happiest of marriages. It 'just happened,' he'll maintain. Predator lust swoops down and carries the Waterbearer off to new means for maintaining his immortality – in layman's terms, younger women. Or men, for that matter.

Nobody has a trickier time negotiating his own sexuality than Aquarius. It's as if, being a naturally far-out character, he can fairly well entertain any erotic activity. If it can be imagined, it must be true – this is the Aquarian rationale, but one that scares the bejesus out of him sometimes. Like Ganymede, homosexuality is often thrust upon him, in some form or another, in his youth. And with this universal son of Uranus being so naturally ubiquitous, his sexual desires are typically all over the map. This is precisely why Aquarius must find his Uranian freedom in repression; something, in the case of this sign, that is an absolutely good thing. So our tall and handsome Galahad with the perfect lady wife and 2.5 children might just as easily be taking boys out to the woodshed as bending those girls over his knee for a friendly walloping. It doesn't matter. For because he remains so completely on the surface of sexual activity, something that allows him to experiment unscathed in any number of scenarios beyond the aforementioned paddling or pee-pee episodes, such interludes never touch him deeply. Thus, he doesn't feel defined by them. Rarely has a self-professed heterosexual Aquarian not had sex with at least one man – rarely, too, does the essentially straight Waterbearer ever do so with such frequency as would ever interfere with the utopian lifestyle he most obviously seems to espouse. In fact, Aquarius may repress homosexual stirrings, a tendency that later gives rise to a variety of fetishes. Since sexuality is so stigmatized by society, Aquarius might simply 'remove' that part of himself from his programming.

As planet Uranus rules homosexuality, one might say it rules homophobia as well: the male Waterbearers are especially cagey when it comes to man-to-man contact. Such displays are measured, contained, even when he is unabashedly gay-identified. Despite his sexual preference, the Aquarian native of the 11th House of *acquaintances* is actually more comfortable having casual, impersonal sex with a number of people than he is having an intimate relationship with one. This is why, when Aquarius does commit to a specific someone, he tries to keep the focus on the appearance of the bond, rather than on its substance. The Rainman of the zodiac, thus, is more about sprinkling himself around than he is pouring himself into one certain, perhaps limiting scenario. For this fixed-air sign, the atmosphere of any relationship can seem, by nature, stale and stagnant. Like John the Baptist, he must spread the word, even if it is about himself, reaching as many devotees as possible. The gay Aquarian, more than most, will be a subscriber to casual, if not anonymous, sex. Since his adolescence, when he may have been made to 'succumb' to a compromising sexual scenario, Aquarius has seen himself develop from an awkward, vulnerable chicken into a sharp-taloned sexual predator in his own right. Whereas other signs tend to repeat the patterns imprinted upon them in

GAY TURN-ONS

older men, mentors
hairy pecs
major penis size, foreskin
bears, bikers, hippies
skaters, skinheads
jocks, socks, sportskit
bottoming
passive) rimming
(active) oral, swallowing
groups, anonymity
(passive) heavy b + d
(passive) lite s + m
raunch, kink, lite scat
tea rooms, glory holes, baths
truckers, bluecollar workers
(passive) fisting
enemas
watersports
plugs, clamps, pumps
pornography, poppers
restraints, cages, slings
(passive) teasing, torture
low hangers
(active) ball play
tvs, trannies

their youth, the Aquarian evolves through the experience and, in an effort to overcome any lingering sense of victimization, becomes a kind of obsessive or controlling sexual character. Nothing must ever impinge upon his personal freedom in the way that an unsolicited sexual episode in his youth may have. Aquarius's silent mantra becomes: *I know* that such a thing must never happen again. So, straightaway, even when a tender Ganymede himself with as pillowy soft an ass as Rauschenberg suggested in his modern-art piece *Canyon* – he depicted the character *as* a pillow suspended (fixed) in the air by a rope tied through its center, implying a pair of buttocks surveyed by a stuffed eagle, Zeus' totem, perched above – the Aquarian will turn the tables and use his cheeky appeal to his best advantage.

Who really is getting the better, forgiving the pun, *end* of the deal – Zeus or Ganymede? Playing on his youthful allure, the young Aquarian is immediately aware of his value to powerful older men who might help rocket him to success, aiding him to avoid a years-long struggle. Indeed, the young gay Aquarian is the consummate Waterbearer, if not the epitomal pool boy who somehow ends up inheriting an older lover/mentor's estate right out from under even the closest family members. Being anything but sexually prudish certainly furthers his cause. He has a homing device for power, honed so early on in life that he ends up insinuating himself into the life of often brilliantly intelligent or artistic individuals. Not so much interested in just finding someone rich and influential, he is looking to be the majordomo for a veritable god whose talents are the source of immortalization. Aquarius wants to be passed the cup of preeminence, something he will carry forth as an emblem of his own rightly inherited state of grace. He is a heaven dweller, and he must live an exceptional, exalted life. Most any Aquarian who is on the fence regarding his sexual preferences, as many are, will 'commit' himself to being the lover of some great and glorious divinity of a man.

Just as a goodly number of Aquarian 'straights' could easily swim in the gay pool, so, too, are gay-identified Waterbearers perpetually attracted to women. When it comes to labels, Aquarius shrugs: If you had to peg any tag on the Waterbearer of any persuasion, one would be calling him not bi- nor pan- but rather über-sexual. He is anything but mysogynistic in his makeup as some gay male signs can be. Indeed, he is neither too turned on nor turned off by the same or opposite sex. He communes with a person, even sexually, based on the quality of their ideas first (and their gender second).

Meanwhile, because men seem to him more restrained by social obliga-tion, the bulk of the Aquarius man's friendships will be with women, albeit extraordinary ones, to whom he's drawn based on a certain outré aspect of personality. Simply put, gay Aquarius is the one with fabulous female friends; climbing his way into the cozy laps of lovely ladies who lunch, those who'll act as patronesses in his lifelong quest to evolve from the boy toy of some genius into a similarly exalted character in his own right. Such scenarios of sudden death and inheritance not withstanding, those that might see him simply slipping into the vacated throne of his all-too-typically older lover, it is de rigueur for the gay Aquarian to make a clean break from the man from whom he received his training in immortality, and to start constructing a heaven of his own making. His breakups are notoriously messy, mainly because, like those of his straight counterpart, they often come out of nowhere, that sudden-change aspect of Uranus being a painful blow to his loved ones. What he may do, then, is find a houseboy of his own, a combination lover-servant just as he had been, who'll now play the part of his majordomo unerringly. Think Lone Ranger and Tonto – sometimes this has a literal manifestation as the Aquarian is notoriously attracted to small, ethnic, often Asian men. Just in case you can't quite stomach the image of our proverbial masked man doing it to his faithful companion amidst grunting shouts of 'kemo sabe,' it might help to realize that the bonds into which the older Aquarian enters are fairly platonic. Submission, it must be said, has always been something every Aquarian man mainly seeks to inspire psychologically far more than physically. This points to a lifelong Aquarian truth: Sex is (almost) always just a means to an end. That the Waterbearer can be the most 'far out' in his sexual activity rarely has anything to do with his own desire. Rather, it is a symptom of his signature detachment from it. What every Aquarian male, regardless of his sexuality, seeks is ultimate authority – control on such a grand scale that, like Big Brother, it can easily go undetected. He thus makes himself available to fill the void, fixing an 'air' of utter conviction about the relationship, hitting home the fact he and a lover are a perfect tongue-in-groove fit. Having no strict adherence to an ego-driven personality there is always a sense of his being happy to be what you want him to be, that proverbial missing link in one's life.

Couplings

Aquarius Man / Aries Woman

He has a sobering effect; her remote nature mirrors his own. Each inhabits a separate sphere – the overall effect is either meditative or mismatched. Sexually, they're unrestrained: Limits might be lacking.

Aquarius Man / Taurus Woman

Lurking tension requires exploration. She must clear her mind of prior expectations. For him, it's time to get real. Another caveat: they must be careful not to constantly contradict each other. Saving grace: Sex is stellar.

Aquarius Man / Gemini Woman

Instant attachment. Codependence could be a pitfall. Emotionally bound, sexually rapt. At best, they embody the power of positive thinking. Otherwise, unreality dissolves into disillusionment. Sexual appetites are unwieldy.

Aquarius Man / Cancer Woman

He dotes, taking responsibility for her feelings. In a constant process of catharsis, this couple is exhausted and exhilarated. Sexually, they're often at odds: She needs intimacy; he's happiest somewhat detached.

Aquarius Man / Leo Woman

An indelible impression is made. Their bond develops via emulation – she might mimic him. Furthering ambitions is a prime motivation. He's inventive and erotic; she needs straightforward sexual expression.

Aquarius Man / Virgo Woman

They're born again – a spiritual overtone exists from the start. Still, there's a forbidden element here: She may be much younger or from a distinctly different background. In bed, they're like-minded. And full of surprises.

Aquarius Man / Libra Woman

Unusual and spontaneous, marked by constant change and intense affection, this pairing is rare. They're private, possessive. Lovemaking is elaborate, energetic, and all-consuming; even as a fling, sex is unforgettable.

Aquarius Man / Scorpio Woman

Hard work, but often worth it. Restrictions are stripped away and there's nothing to keep them from individual success. An abiding sexual attraction sustains them through inevitable rough patches.

Aquarius Man / Sagittarius Woman

They meet, and lives are turned upside down. At first, they're formal; then suddenly, it may be love and marriage. Aquarius learns to lavish attention in bed – the estimable Archeress won't accept anything less.

Aquarius Man / Capricorn Woman

They fuse into a package deal of practicality and purpose. Still, Cap won't sacrifice her own objectives. They are notoriously accomplished. In bed, it's an ongoing master class – student and teacher roles are rotated.

Aquarius Man / Aquarius Woman

They feel superhuman, seeming to live in a perpetually exalted state. For him, perfection is the goal; for her, the focus is to improve the human condition. Little energy is left for sex, so they might make it more a priority.

Aquarius Man / Pisces Woman

Restoration and atonement are the keys to this committed bond. Compensation is due – emotionally and financially, life pays them back in full. Sexually, too, they're making up for any losses.

Aquarius Man / Aries Man

Aries might need more affection than Aquarius is inclined to offer. But when it works, individuality and independence await. Somehow, sex stays comfortably casual. Other couples often enter the mix.

Aquarius Man / Taurus Man

A bond that's bound to have ballast. Each feels he's found the perfect partner. Dynamic Aquarius introduces his Bull boy to new and exhilarating situations, sexual and otherwise. They raise each other's professional profile.

Aquarius Man / Gemini Man

Gemini's fantasy of being devoured by a big, bad man – Aquarius is the sometimes scary, 'supreme' sign of the zodiac. This is a dynamic and exhilarating ride for two intellectually inclined guys.

Aquarius Man / Cancer Man

Cancer directs Aquarius down a more traditional life path – to the Moon man success is measured by the money one makes. Resentments resound if creativity is sacrificed to status. Sexually, tables turn: Aquarius is the authority.

Gay

487

Aquarius Man ∫ Leo Man
They exist to support each other. Before long, Leo reevaluates his lifestyle, reconfiguring priorities. Aquarius creates their new order – his rules take precedence. Passionate love frees Leo of any self-doubt.

Aquarius Man ∫ Virgo Man
A liberating relationship, signaling a life change for Virgo and a sexual awakening for Aquarius. But freedom comes at a price: Anxieties augment and Virgo, especially, feels unsettled. In bed, these boys believe in bad behavior.

Aquarius Man ∫ Libra Man
Libra's in the market for a soul mate when he meets the Waterbearer, bombarding him with a detailed life history. An abiding friendship ensues, one that may not withstand the complexities of deeper commitment.

Aquarius Man ∫ Scorpio Man
If seeking a support system, they might find it in each other. But turning joint plans into actuality proves arduous – they need a third-party perspective. Though they often drift in and out of love, sex might keep them together.

Aquarius Man ∫ Sagittarius Man
An extraordinarily passionate pair. Sadly, each may surrender to his own instability. Grandiosity is a pitfall – self-mythologizing means they live in a land of make-believe. Sexual antics often border on out-there.

Aquarius Man ∫ Capricorn Man
Cap is afraid of being waylaid by the strange-seeming Waterbearer. But in a bond, Aquarius champions Capricorn's cause. Their sex life is eccentric, at times conservative, otherwise notable for its perverse nature.

Aquarius Man ∫ Aquarius Man
Notoriously detached from one another. Little wonder this uncommon, double–Waterbearer pair struggles to find common emotional ground. Sexually, even the slightest dalliance is cause for relationship rupture.

Aquarius Man ∫ Pisces Man
Self-satisfied souls: Finally, Aquarius and Pisces quit trying to change. Spiritual purity is often their mutual modus operandi. Together, they simply stop stressing. In bed, egos are abandoned.

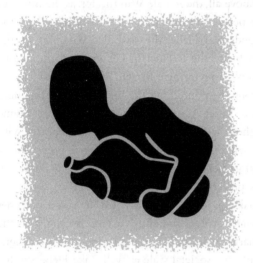

Aquarius Woman

the vision

Aquarius woman is an inspiration. Her natural disposition is to see the joy in every situation, and she's able to make even the dreariest of events seem like fun. To her the world is painfully beautiful, and she greets every day with an unscripted childlike awe, open to what cheery serendipity might cross her path as she whistles through her routine. She cares little for worldly trends or the trappings of supposed sophistication – that proverbial square peg who can't be fit to social convention. Aquarius can be an eccentric with a taste for the outlandish, and she is not in the least precious about herself or her appearance. She is the zodiac's finger painter, unafraid of rolling up her sleeves and getting messy in the expressing of her heart's content. Even when committed to a nine-to-five job – she is dutiful and regimented to the core – Aquarius tends to indulge in some arguably wacky after-hours hobby. In time, she may chuck the security of a steady paycheck and gamble on dreams that strike others as bonkers. Her choice in men is often similarly suspect: She is drawn to flagrant, overbearing, or megalomaniacal men whom she imagines lacking in love, but who otherwise offer her the liberal independence she requires, if only by virtue of being so wrapped up in themselves. She can be the quintessential woman who loves too much. Alternatively, one wonders if she loves enough, so dispassionate are her relationships. With other women, she adopts a pedagogical role, a sort of kind headmistress in bonds that invariably combine a shared personal life with professional aims.

Xĭ

PRINCIPLE

The Principle of Diversity. Aquarius celebrates uniqueness and eccentricity as a means of self-expression but also as a way to ensure the soulful health of humanity. Just as a gene pool mustn't become too restrictive lest it weaken, the Aquarian concept of spiritual diversity ensures the health of the collective consciousness, which must change and grow if it is to survive.

Sign + Mind

The sign of Aquarius is primarily ruled by the planet Uranus, that of 'sudden change,' which represents, among others, the Universal Principle of Diversity and Deviation, and such concepts as mutation, revolution, and indeed evolution. Saturn is the sign's secondary ruler, signaling a taskmaster's sense of structure and discipline, the ironic means by which Aquarius woman manifests and, indeed, dedicates herself to the cultivation of her sometimes deviant, if not outright freaky, persona. Above all, the female Waterbearer, as the moniker suggests, is in the business of renewal, and she's in it for life. In mythology, the original waterbearer to the gods was Hebe, the so-called daughter of the Olympic queen bee Hera — actually, she is Hera in her virgin form. Yearly, Hera took a dip in a sacred pool to revirginize herself, emerging as Hebe, or 'Youth.' As cupbearer to the gods, she poured out the immortal-life-sustaining ambrosia, the divine sustenance. Enter Aquarius woman: She does that same thing in life, forever feeding those with whom she comes into contact with life-affirming hope, instilling self-confidence in others' convictions. She is often considered the proverbial godsend, just the sort of person one phones in a pinch, that answer to one's prayers. This role in which she is cast seems encoded in her astrological makeup: Just as Uranus-ruled deviation becomes the very means by which a species evolves and, thus, survives, so, too, does the zodiac's beautiful mutant, Aquarius woman, become a saving grace to others, not just on a personal level, but on a societal scale as well. Like Hebe, she has already been 'made new' via the possession of an inherent, intellectually evolved outlook on life. Aquarius doesn't hold to the past, but rather looks toward the future, as dictated by her planetary rule. The 11th Astrological House associated with her sign is that of *future goals* as well as *reformative, communal activities* and the *identification of the self with mass objectives* — it is also, by rights, that of *spiritual unity*.

In considering the concept of spiritual unity, one thinks of commonality amongst peoples, which is of course one interpretation. But there's more: that of the individual communing with the eternal or, to coin another 11th House phrase, the *universal mind*. Indeed, Aquarius is naturally blessed with the understanding that any separation between the human condition and divine inspiration is an illusion — life, she inherently maintains, is a spiritual experience — but she isn't personally wrapped up in her insights. Whereas her male counterpart might be enraptured by a sense of revelatory understanding, Aquarius female has no ego attachment to such a perspective. She is ready to pour out her divine acumen democratically, to whomever she meets, because she believes that everybody deserves to experience heaven here on earth. This difference is also mirrored in each of these sex sign's Waterbearer archetypes: Ganymede was a mortal parvenu, handpicked by god (Zeus) to bear the albeit Greek Holy Grail; Hebe, who Ganymede replaces, is a 'born' immortal, nonetheless happy to perform a servile function. Moreover, being a goddess wedded to yet another mortal parvenu, Heracles (Hercules), whose name means 'glory of Hera,' Hera *as* Hebe, is thus a 'descending goddess,' that is, willing to come down to earth. In so doing, she elevates and immortalizes her spouse. This pattern is prominently echoed in the Aquarian female's relationships as well. To be sure, the Waterbearer is the living embodiment of such descending, or emanating, goddesses. Like Hebe, she isn't precious about her own 'divine' status; rather, she is happy to commune with the common man, if not romantically take up with the particularly male parvenu population of the planet. Likewise, she draws upon other 'emanation' deities such as Iris (the Rainbow), who is Hera's messenger, and Eos (the Dawn), whose main myth depicts her love for a mere mortal – both are personifications of natural manifestations that symbolically portray hope and renewal.

There is rarely anything lofty or stuck-up in Aquarius's nature. She is detached from the desire for status, preferring to be of the people, for the people, one who has seemingly let go of all worldly or material concerns. Fittingly, the sign is associated with the age group 70–77, a time of life when one is resigned to her own imminent eternal communion with the great beyond, having little to prove or be concerned with on the earthly plane. Her preceding sign, Capricorn, starts this ball rolling: Letting go of material concerns, she takes up an ascetic lifestyle, a way in which she distinguishes herself as better than others. To the Aquarius, however, whether one meditates and eats vegan, or chows fifteen bags of greasy chips while smoking and watching porn, is all the same to her. She's beyond making judgments, and best of all, she doesn't try herself with expectations of perfection. Aquarius takes herself as she is, and it follows she expects others to do likewise. This living embodiment of a renewal goddess is naturally forgiving and considers her fellow human beings deserving of absolution, mercy, grace, and ultimately salvation. More than any other astrological character, she wakes up thinking how she might help make others happy. As a nod to one of her patron goddesses, and to coin a classic Rolling Stones' lyric, 'she's like a rainbow': her raison d'être, indeed her very presence, seems designed to inspire and encourage. Open and forthright, her 'funny face' and whimsical style can't help but brighten a person's day. Proving herself a great listener, she'll pick up

PLANETARY SYMBOL

Uranus is namesake of the god of the universe. The planet signals change on a massive scale and the ushering in of entirely new waves in thought, technology, discovery, invention, and social experience. The Aquarian woman adapts easily to such changes and helps others adjust to evolutionary trends.

SIGN QUADRANT

The zodiacal quadrants correspond to metaphysical planes of existence – physical, emotional, mental, and spiritual or universal. The Fourth Quadrant concerns one's relationship with the whole or soul of humanity. Aquarius woman brings a sense of relief and reprise to the world, teaching others to detach from the weight of outmoded tradition and mores, to unlock their fears.

SIGN GLYPH

The waves: A symbol of the divine liquid manna, whether in the classic sense of ambrosia, the blood of the Holy Grail, promising everlasting life, or the baptismal waters without which one can't enter the kingdom of heaven. It also recalls radio or light waves, which signal new ideas of human invention.

ELEMENT + QUALITY

The air element signifies mental and social experience, the fixed quality, intense concentration and magnetism. The fixed-air combination particular to Aquarius implies a certain corner of the sky, whether it be heaven, a distant star, or such visions as a rainbow. The combination also symbolizes truth, a fixed idea, which is ever so important to the Aquarian, whose motto is 'I know.'

a conversation right where it left off, even if months or years have elapsed. One soon realizes that she's democratic to the core, doling out her sunny-funny disposition to anyone with whom she comes in contact. She may at first seem like the soul mate one has been waiting for, but in keeping with her archetypal patrons, those messenger goddesses who make it their business to appear, showering grace, to mere mortals, Aquarius woman is the spiritual mascot of the zodiac: that is, one who brings good fortune; and yet *mascot* also shares its etymological origin with the word *mask*. Her infamous love of costumes notwithstanding, Aquarius probably doesn't realize that it is her birthright to don the proverbial red rubber nose and floppy shoes. She is the zodiac's, and thus humanity's, comic relief. Aquarius lives all her life as if in the throes of second childhood (70–77 years old), literally taking every opportunity to dress up and play act. Even her everyday wardrobe suggests a bit of costuming. Metaphorically speaking, next to being a clown, cheerleader is Aquarius's favorite guise of all, both roles ensuring she'll bring joy and inspiration to others. Some say she does so to make up for her own sadness and disappointment, which isn't strictly true: Rather, Aquarius channels her personal grief and grievance *into* encouragement for others.

Aquarius's default disposition as the human equivalent of the smiley-face logo is perfectly in keeping with her status as the only female fixed-air sign of the zodiac: Air symbolizes the mental plane – thought – in astrology, just as it points to social experience. Thus, Aquarius deals in solid ideas, bent upon solidifying them into fact, i.e., uppercase Truth. A thinker like Ayn Rand could only be an Aquarius, her philosophy of objectivism based, as it is, on the concreteness (fixedness) of the abstract (air-ideas). To her, abstraction was real and the only evil was irrationality. Indeed, she is known for having reacted emotionally to broadest abstraction. The whole notion of an *ism* is itself an Aquarian one. Males of the sign are forever on the vanguard of new understanding, lost in their individual glimpses of fresh reality via revelation. She, in contrast, seeks to reveal Truth(s) to others. According to her, divine-truth experience exists in the here and now, as the ubiquitous though masked reality – and it is her specific role on the planet to tear away the veils of illusion that cover it. In mythology, Iris is Hera's messenger to mankind, forever bringing 'the good news,' the rainbow being a bridge between mortal and immortal existence. In the biblical vein, just as the male Aquarian is associated with John the Baptist, the female Aquarian is Salome. Her striptease 'dance of the seven veils' – one for each color of the rainbow – was a ritual performance depicting the goddess in her 'descending/revealing' form, drawing down to earth and unlocking the doors of the seven heavens via which her lover, typically a mortal priest-king who was sacrificed, could reach immortality and become a god. In this view, the Baptist is spiritually wedded to Salome (*shalom,* 'peace'), his beheading representing a ritual sacrifice aimed at his edification. Rainbows, in most ancient cultures, are ladders or bridges by which one travels to 'heaven' whether upon death or in revelatory trances.

Like a rainbow, Aquarius woman is an emanation of positive reinforcement. Inspiration, a word related to simple respiration, is the very air one breathes in her presence. It is no less than uplifting spirit that the Aquarius seeks to convey, hoping to see people's 11th House *hopes and wishes* come true by instilling absolute conviction. Needless to say, her company can be addictive. One feels incapable of doing wrong around her, a tendency that may backfire and breed complacency just as easily as it sparked motivation. And this seems to be somewhat the point of her Pollyannaism: Acting as a salve, if not offering salvation, comes to define the Aquarius. The list of famous Waterbearers is filled with women who set themselves up as beacons of empowerment to those who get the short end of the stick in society, particularly other women and minorities – Susan B. Anthony, Rosa Parks, Betty Freidan, Helen Gurley Brown, Toni Morrison, Oprah Winfrey, Alice Walker, and Ellen DeGeneres all urge others to embrace diversity in themselves and, in so doing, to achieve new levels of dignity and personal advancement. Aquarius represents, by example, the power of self-help. This may explain why so many great female writers are Aquarians as well – along with the aforementioned novelists, Edith Wharton, Virginia Woolf, Colette, Gertrude Stein, Ayn Rand, even Laura Ingalls Wilder and Judy Blume, are amongst the most influential, socially pointed minds ever to put pen to paper – the literary medium is, by design, meant to reach as wide an audience as possible. Indeed, nobody is more populist in her perspective than the female Aquarius – it is the overriding quality in her personality, the seeds for which are sewn in her early life.

Growing up, the Waterbearer's father is considered something of an oddball or anomaly. Typically, he will be a sensitive, creative type, if not a frustrated artist whose secret aspirations find little room to surface in the confines of the household. Her mother is most often a pragmatist, and she may even seek to override her husband's more free-form musings. While also still appreciating his quirky nature and inventive spirit, in some instances, she may overtly put her spouse down as a silly (even worthless) dreamer. Whatever the case, Aquarius girl identifies with her father, intellectually and spiritually, as do most females born into masculine (air, fire) signs. Her father might have a 'workshop' of sorts, what she considers a magic place and where, as a girl, she will feel most comfortable and inspired. As he often slips away to this, his

POLARITY

Females in masculine signs (fire, air) are not aligned with the gender polarity of the sign and thus enact instead of embody the quality-element combination of the sign. Unlike Aquarius man, who is caught up in his own universal truths and visions, Aquarius female is a revelation to others, a dispenser of joy, if not comic relief.

SIGN NUMBER

The number of revelation. A page is turned with this number: After the completion of ten, eleven signifies the first 'reveal' of a new order.

70–77

SIGN AGE ASSOCIATION

A time of life when worldly concerns and ambitions are left behind and one is focused on appreciating the lasting joys of life. This can also be a time of second childhood.

PSYCHOLOGY

The Aquarian female tends to shirk responsibility and to buck authority. She can be rather fanatical in her interests, susceptible to mind control and the cult phenomenon. If any sign is likely to wear a tinfoil hat and wait for the mother ship, it is Aquarius woman. She can suffer from escapist fantasies and exhibit deviant behavior.

sacred space, it is also one of the only environments in which she can bond with her dad, away from more utilitarian family influences. Aquarius girl may be written off as having inherited the oddest aspects of her father. But the Waterbearer is proud to be considered Daddy's girl. In the case of divorce, Aquarius will dream of leaving home and living the vagabond lifestyle, perhaps walking in her father's footsteps. The age-old childhood dynamic of wanting to run away and join the circus was undoubtedly ushered in by Aquarius girls the world over gleefully expressing such a desire. From early on, she feels like a freak, but unlike most people, she considers this a good thing. Aquarius is searching for identity, and she's conscious of doing so. At school, she might be a bit of an outcast, as conformity of any kind sets her teeth on edge. Typically she'll dive full force into artistic enclaves such as drama or music. She may consider becoming a majorette, if only to wear the goofy outfit. Otherwise, she steers clear of the social mainstream and sticks to the subversive, nerdish coffeehouse scene, one rife with other misfits in the wrong-style jeans who care little for the trappings peer pressure is pushing.

Though she's not the flashy kind of girl one would assume was 'fast,' looks can be deceiving as the Aquarius may be more sexually advanced than most. For her, however, this is a by-product of an emotional maturity developed early in life, one that equips her with a level head when it comes to negotiating boys and sex. She is her own person, generally slipping under the radar of her mother, to whom she seems too much of a goody-goody to ever get into any trouble. Poor deluded woman: The Waterbearer is naturally open to sexual experience, almost ridiculously grown-up when it comes to dating, playing at being wifey to a boyfriend as early as junior high. She is rather a mumsy character to begin with, and she will often dote on a guy from the first date. Inevitably she goes for fringe dwellers like her dad. She may lust after the eccentric brainiac with the pocket protector or the musical protégé who looks as if he's never been in sunlight or taken exercise. Ironically, however, she is most drawn to decidedly unacademic types – phantoms of her peer group who mightn't seem to frequent any other wing of the school than where the woodshop or autobody department is housed. She is turned on by such handy boys and grease monkeys, whom she senses have more going on than their oily hair and dirty fingernails would suggest. Indeed, her Aquarian viewpoint appreciates a guy who is already thinking outside the box, divining his own path apart from the well-worn conformity of the pop-media-influenced teenage mainstream. Such a guy, she feels, is on her adult wavelength and may want to commit to a serious, mature relationship despite the fact that his upper lip still exhibits its original peach fuzz. More times than not, that pretty but nerdy girl with the same boyfriend all four years in high school will be our cute little Aquarian oddball, forever immortalized in the collective memory of her high school classmates as walking through the halls with her partner, hands lodged in each other's back pockets, the sound of denim- or corduroy-encased thighs rubbing rhythmically together. *Shup-shup, shup-shup* . . .

Body + Soul

Aquarius woman is an unplugged personality. What you see is what you get: Even as she reaches adulthood and trades in her trademark T-shirts and jeans (still, heavy on the accessories), she seeks comfort in her clothing. She never puts on airs nor does she indulge in material acquisitions that might suggest status or wealth. Rarely will she dress in pricey designer duds, as labels mean nothing to this undisputed off-the-rack queen. As well, she prefers bold and colorful styles to subtle or staid fashion statements. Even when attending an elegant occasion, she can't help but add some quirky twist – sneakers, color-tinted glasses, a floppy hat – if not dress herself so outlandishly, from head to toe, that she leaves others visually reeling. When she dresses up, she does so with a vengeance. She has a love of ladylike silhouettes, but always far-out in some fashion. Think Laura Ashley on acid. We're talking bold prints, iridescent fabrics, neon. At times one might think her clothes should come with a packet of Tums instead of extra buttons. And if you think dressing down is any different, you have another thing coming. Truth be told, if anybody other than Mork from Ork or some rogue cast member of *Godspell* were to have a pair of rainbow suspenders stashed in his or her wardrobe, it's the cooky Aquarius gal. Indeed, famous Waterbearers who decline to be professionally styled will find themselves on a worst-dressed list faster than you can say gauchos-with-leg-warmers. Here, too, the sign's association with second childhood is unmistakable: To open the Waterbearer's closet, one might swear they'd stumbled upon the Miss Marple collection, or the entire wardrobe worn by the woman who played batty Aunt Clara on *Bewitched,* vintage mink stoles and all. If her style of dress doesn't provide enough of a clue, there are some dead giveaways for picking an Aquarius out of a crowd: With some notable exceptions, she tends to be small, if not somewhat childlike, in stature, with a juicy plumpness to her body and a pliable elasticity to her skin. Still, despite such youthful attributes, the sign's correspondence to the ages 70–77 is written all over her wizened face. Indeed, Aquarius is often distinguished by a rather old-looking head plopped on a sprightly physique. Astrology's answer to the

ARCHETYPE + MYTH

Aquarius woman draws on the classical archetype of the renewal or descending goddess, distinguished as 'coming down' from heaven to commune, help, or mate with mortals. The female cupbearer to the gods is Hebe, Hera in her renewed, revirginized form. It is as Hebe that Hera marries Heracles and thus bestows upon him the gift of immortality. Eos, the goddess of the dawn, inspires hope. Iris, goddess of the rainbow, skates down this colorful bridge between heaven and earth, delivering divine messages from Hera to mankind.

Aquarius draws on the biblical Salome, whose dance of the seven veils is a reenactment of the goddess's descent along the rainbow. The rainbow symbolizes a bridge to heaven, and each colored veil is a key to each of the seven levels. The rainbow also concealed the future, corresponding to Uranus' connection with evolution. In medieval literature, the Holy Grail associated with the Waterbearer was guarded by Queen Repanse de Joie (Dispenser of Joy). The character of the descending goddess is portrayed in Tennessee Williams's *A Streetcar Named Desire* by Stella, 'star,' who descends to reunite with her all-too-mortal husband upon his invocation: *Stel-laaaaah!*

renewed Hebe seems to bear the traces, metaphorically speaking, of the crone she once was.

So if you see what appears to be a perennial teenager from the back but who, upon turning face-front, exhibits a vacant, ancient look – all exaggerated cheekbones and sunken hollows – chances are this hoary-looking ingenue is an Aquarius. She is an offbeat beauty, possessing a strong, typically hooked nose and rubbery, comic expression, her mouth notoriously turned down into a grimace, if not an outright frown like that of a sad clown, made all the more marked by either a drastic underbite or an overly large chin, or both. Her face is long, but her cheeks appear puffed; her hair is shiny and bouncy, but often so springy that it takes much in the way of product to set it into place. As a result, she may opt for a short cut, which, given her hair's texture, tends to create a bit of a helmet head. Yet, despite the quirky looks of this sign, one that includes the likes of Jennifer Aniston, Mena Suvari, Christina Ricci, Heather Graham, Sheryl Crow, Jennifer Jason Leigh, Farrah Fawcett, Cybill Shepherd, Margaux Hemingway, Stockard Channing, Minnie Driver, Florence Henderson, Geena Davis, Vanessa Redgrave, Laura Dern, and both Stephanie and Caroline of Monaco, Aquarians are among the world's most vivid, never subtle, beauties. Her features are overstated, and as a nod to the spirit of those emanation goddesses she embodies, she literally beams with an almost cartoonish vitality. She can be goofy, with a loud, girlish laugh, her voice warbling but ringing clear as a bell. She tends to communicate outward, like an actress on a stage, even when having a close tête-à-tête, gesticulating when she speaks if those hands aren't shoved into pockets and making little mini-knee-bends for emphasis. Most strikingly, Aquarius is the original girl with the faraway eyes, as, in conversation, she seems to direct much of what she says to some spot over one's shoulder. She has googly peepers to begin with, which float around inside her head as if detached from their connective tissue; and it is an effort for her to make steady contact – easier to accomplish when she's listening than when she's doing the talking herself. Still, she is famously attentive, nodding reassuringly and hanging on every word, tilting her head inquiringly or craning her neck forward with a screwed-up, receptive expression. She adopts a casual posture, and there is rarely anything nervous or shifty in her body language. She is an open and forthright presence – her spirit is as voluptuous as her body tends to be.

Though her breasts are small-to-medium-sized, they are usually perfectly round, full, firm, and buoyant. Even when short-waisted, Aquarius possesses hairpin curves, her ample hips giving way to an even bigger bottom and thighs, lending her a sturdy, albeit ever so slightly pear-shaped look. In addition to favoring tight bodices and bodysuit tops, while opting for looser flowy skirts and roomy trousers on bottom, she often decorates her wrists and square, childlike hands with an abundance of bracelets and rings. The Waterbearer will tend to embellish and ornament herself with tattoos and piercings as well as slogan buttons, badges, and other decorative bells and whistles. Typically a decidedly youthful touch can be found here or there – a Mickey Mouse watch, glass Mardi Gras beads, or other such symbols of fun and frivolity. She consciously wishes to signal lightheartedness. And her career will even tend to allow for such overt freedom of self-expression as she generally gravitates toward professions in which she can be her own boss. When working for others, she is notoriously earnest and hardworking. Still, unconventional vocations appeal to her, especially those that include an element of amusement. For the Aquarian, clown college is a very viable form of higher education. You think we're kidding?

It seems simply in the stars that the rubbery-faced Aquarian feels an actual affinity for life under the big top. Her planet Uranus rules 'freakishness,' the mainstay of many a circus's main attractions, but there is a more primal connection still: As Joseph Campbell pointed out in *The Power of Myth,* clowns have a spiritual significance in most ancient religious rites. In donning such costumes, people ritually transformed themselves into sacred beings (usually creation gods), the purpose of the 'funny, grotesque form meant to keep people from getting stuck in the image' – that is, the costume would immediately keep worshipers from taking the appearance of the gods too seriously, as getting stuck in such appearance, again, in Campbell's words, 'short-circuits the contact with the deep mystery.' On some level, Aquarius understands that she is that emanation goddess revealing certain undeniable Truths to others – aptly her sign's motto is 'I know.' And back on planet Earth: By looking somewhat clownish Aquarius precludes others from building her up or putting her unduly on a pedestal, something that might easily happen to one so 'conscious' and 'evolved.' Put her in sleek Donna Karan pantsuits and she becomes Oprah – but remember 'O' before she hired a stylist? Eeesh – even Ms. Winfrey would be that much more venerated if she didn't crack silly jokes or feign that streety, Southern sass. Still, Oprah knows what she's doing, if subconsciously. For Aquarian ladies don't really want to be considered gurus – that's the sort of status her male counterpart seeks, and according to her, he can have at it. With humor, or visual signs of whimsy, she wants to make it clear that she, like the goddess Iris, is only the messenger. She shuns the responsibility of being the proverbial answer-lady even for practical reasons: She's protective of her free

11TH ASTROLOGICAL HOUSE

social awareness
group dynamics
potential for friendship
potential for happiness
friends and associates
unemotional bonds
life objectives
ideals to live by
love received
mass appeal
money made via career
self-employment
stepchildren
foster or adoptive children
situations out of control
humanitarian concerns
how we perceives others
clubs/cliques/associations
hopes and wishes
collective bonds
new order
extraterrestrial life
quirks/foibles
mutations
technology
the unexpected
working for common goals
spiritual oneness
mental link with God
impersonal truth
identification within a group
unorthodox activities
creativity within a group
universal regard
applause
liberation
mental acuity
social progress
collective consciousness

time and is all too easily bombarded by others seeking the kind of pacifying company she naturally provides. Sure, she's happy to be a bearer of divine inspiration and saving grace, but she doesn't want to be deified. So, by wearing red Converse sneakers and driving a vintage purple Volkswagen Beetle with flower-power appliqués, she keeps most would-be disciples at bay. The male of the sign is rapt by the self-importance of his own revelations, while the female Aquarius seeks to downplay her own significance in the equation of revealing epiphanies to others. She's determined not to lose her head over the missives she may be communicating. Thus laughing off even the most serious of situations is Aquarius's signature behavior. One can see it in her body language, a symphony of shrugs, thrown-up hands, and disclamatory muggings all designed to physically demonstrate that she doesn't fancy herself the final word on any subject. When push comes to shove, she doesn't want to be expected to invest much time or energy in anyone other than herself.

Sex + Sexuality

Emotionally, Aquarius woman tends to travel light. She abhors belabored friendships or overly dependent love bonds. From an early age, she prefers a steady someone with whom she can share life experience. Still, despite what might be considered evidence to the contrary, she isn't in the least sappy or clingy, being happy to be attached at the hip when together, but also pleased as punch to have solo time. The point is, it's all the same to her. She will generally have one close female friend as well, a lifelong chum; but, otherwise, everyone is simply a convivial acquaintance. She will belong to many 11th House *groups* and *organizations,* just the sort of dispassionate interaction she most welcomes. Socially however, Aquarius will never be part of some large pack – she can't abide complicated, interwoven dynamics. And she especially cannot stomach conflict. Unfortunately, in an ongoing attempt to never make waves, the Waterbearer may sublimate her needs. Especially in relationships with an overbearing partner (to which she's oft ironically drawn), or at times when a less imperious guy is in railroading mode, she'll sooner fold herself into the mandate of her man. Aquarius can go along for the ride so completely in relationships that other women, in particular, might label her a patsy.

But all is not what it seems: Consciously or not, Aquarius will play compliant as a sort of compounding bargaining chip: If and when she decides to call it quits, all the evidence of having tried to make the relationship work will be stacked in her favor. As the zodiac's cheerleader, she is always her partner's biggest fan – if things go south, then she is forever blameless. The 11th House is that of *impersonal relationships,* the impact of which her intimates will realize if she feels a bond is finished. That she doesn't fight won't mean it's all just water off a duck's back. She still keeps score. And one day, when she feels pushed too far, that last straw will break the camel's back and all her partner will see is the back of her head getting smaller and smaller as she makes a clean break. She'll never look back – Uranus isn't the planet of sudden change for nothing. And woe be to any man forced to hash out legalities with the blameless, put-upon Aquarius. For him, we have just two words: Mia Farrow. In a sense, one might look upon the utter complicity of the Aquarius personality as fairly insidious. In hindsight, a guy might prefer her to have piped up about her problems instead of smiling through a long list of resentments that she may later use as leverage for leaving, let alone taking him to the cleaner's. So absolutely final is the Aquarius's departure, it may feel as if the entire relationship was just a mirage, like that proverbial rainbow fast fading into the ether.

It's important to consider why it is Aquarius falls for some fairly megalomaniacal men in the first place. The simple answer is that, no matter what the particular dynamic of her parents' marriage, Aquarius feels cut off from her father, with whom she invariably connects on a soul-mate level. They really are cut from the same cloth, but he only becomes more and more unreachable a figure as time goes on. Thus, her model of the perfect man is someone naturally distant and independent, but also, ironically, on her same wavelength, a nod to both the wavy Aquarian symbol and the fixed-air status of her sign, which might be interpreted as a certain, solid frequency. Since childhood, she has been shopping for boyfriends in the 'irregulars' section, in search of an extraordinary mate. She seeks a rugged individualist – a revolutionary, an eclectic, a maverick if not a heretic – someone, like Ayn Rand's character Howard Roark (we won't even get into *The Fountainhead*'s significance to the Waterbearer), who has soaring aspirations *as* the common man, devoid of privilege or collectivist crutches, self-divining his own destiny. A man with singularity of mind, those all-important big fixed ideas, is whom our own rosy radical finds most riveting. However, what she might often end up attracting or, more accurately, *falling* for is a guy who is just deluded enough to fancy himself some great genius without having the right stuff to substantiate such a claim. Either way she'll label the lug 'misunderstood,' except of course by her – employing her astute Aquarian wavelength, not to mention her sign's 'I know' mantra. She feels all her potential would-be prodigy needs is encouragement, hope, and the courage of his convictions, exactly the kind of support our cheerleader is prepared to deliver. But, here's the rub: Because she

BODY RULERSHIP

The sign of Aquarius rules the legs, from knee to ankle, and the circulatory system. Uranus is associated with sudden nervous disorders – fits, spasms, breakdowns – as well as abnormal growth, such as that of tumors.

is so acquiescent a character, she actually brings out the raja in most guys who wouldn't otherwise be so domineering – it's a matter of self-fulfilling prophecy that she ends up with, or thus creates, somewhat of a monster. It's yet another symptom of her sign's association with freakiness and mutation – whereas Aquarian guy can be a real Frankenstein, Aquarius woman often ends up being the bride of the good doctor's creation. Like Hebe marrying Heracles, there is often a sense of her wedding a mate of lower status. The perfect Aquarius female archetype in literature is Stella (*star,* 'a fixed bit of firmament') in Tennessee Williams's *A Streetcar Named Desire.* The classic image of this character is of her making a descent, like the archetypal goddesses associated with the sign, to the bellowing demands of her husband, Stanley, an unruly 'beast' who is nonetheless able to see through life's illusions. And what Stella and indeed every Aquarius woman wants to feel is mighty real. As the zodiac's vision of loveliness, this far-out sign inherently feels all too etheric at times and, like her goddess archetypes, thus has an overriding urge to play 'on the ground.' Sex is one particular endeavor that gives the Aquarian the sense of having feet firmly planted on terra firma. And Williams makes it clear that this is what keeps Stella wedded to Stanley, their abandoned erotic experience being described as getting 'them colored lights going' – like a rainbow, Stella apparently comes in colors.

In this literary reference, we see most poignantly the Waterbearer's tendency to become involved with men who employ a sort of mind control over them, yet one more symptom of fixed-air (read: stuck thought). Aquarius virtually asks for it – she is ever in search of some guru of a man to whom she can conceptually attach to and model herself after. Indeed, behind most successful Aquarian woman there stands a man whom they, in some sense, mimic. When it works, it's the perfect meeting of the minds, indeed the quintessential spiritual marriage. But sometimes Aquarius finds she's in a cult of two from which it is difficult to extricate herself. It's no easy task to backtrack after being the consummate cheerleader to a man, his greatest fan, especially when she's ended up fueling the fanaticism surrounding his most prodigal, if not prodigious, notions. She may have a series of serious long-term relationships in which this dynamic continues to emerge, only to use her infamous 'get-out-of-relationship-hell-free card' as previously described. When you consider the effect her constant forgiveness, if not doormat status, has on the Stanley Kowalskis of the world (whom she can reduce to bellowing babies should she threaten to take a powder), we gain insight into why the Waterbearer quits her bonds so abruptly. She has to. Having been such a salve/slave to a man, she must tear herself away fast, like ripping off a Band-Aid.

Aquarian woman is grace personified. She is endlessly forgiving, mercifully understanding of a person's faults and foibles, able to see past such problems to the unadulterated good in others, particularly a partner. The problem is, most men waste her grace, taking her kind and adoring mien for granted, forcing her sooner or later to hop that first streetcar out of town. But just when one is ready to write off Aquarius woman as the emotional punching bag of the zodiac, there comes a realization: Despite being continually disappointed by the men in her life, she won't cease and desist from that signature modus of giving selflessly to relationships. Rarely jaded, the Waterbearer loses not one drop of hope in that seemingly bottomless loving cup she carries, willing to pour herself fully into the arms of yet another man. Of course, in time, she does develop an ability to discriminate, learning not to cast her pearls before swine. Et voila: Because she never compromises her utterly ungrudging, indeed altruistic, vision of love, she will ultimately happen upon a man who will appreciate all the joyful affection she is ready to gush, without taking her own (often tremendous) needs lightly. She is programmed to *give,* mainly in the form of lending her infamous compassion – this is what she is astrologically designed to do. And in finding a man on whom she can spew forth her feelings without having them trampled underfoot, Aquarius experiences rapture. Sometimes it so happens that a former flame will have learned his lesson about the Waterbearer's goodness, seeking suddenly to woo her back. ('Starting Over,' John Lennon's ode to rekindling his turbulent romance with Yoko Ono, springs to mind.) Uranus's energy is eccentric and unpredictable – stranger things have been known to happen than Aquarius giving love a second chance with someone whom she left in the dust or, alternatively, deserted her. If anybody could forgive the past, it's the zodiac's Stella, who, even when slapped in the face by love, can turn the other cheek.

When it comes to relationships, Aquarius asks for little. She is a low-maintenance mate whose idea of the perfect evening would sooner entail pizza and beer than caviar and champagne. And, despite the hippy association with her sign, a specious one in fact, she's rarely some granola-crunching health nut. In fact, she often doesn't take as much care of her physical well-being as she should, and she's similarly lackadaisical with her environment. Of all the woman in the zodiac, Aquarius is, shall we say, the most casual about her digs. She's overly relaxed when it comes to housecleaning and general upkeep, the hands-down Appalachian of the zodiac who, even if she were in a Beverly Hills mansion, would give the Clampetts' homespun lifestyle a run for its money. A lack of anal retentiveness comes to define her: She's never the lady of the house picking up after a man and his buddies, who will invariably come to invade

Vanna White
Lana Turner
Kim Novak
Stockard Channing
Carol Channing
Tina Louise
Sharon Tate
Laura Ingalls Wilder
Alice Walker
Edith Wharton
Virgina Woolf
Colette
Germaine Greer
Ayn Rand
Gertrude Stein
Mary Lou Retton
Rosa Parks
Susan B. Anthony
Caroline of Monaco
Stephanie of Monaco
Leontyne Price
Carole King
Lillian Armstrong
Etta James
Jacqueline Du Pre
Melissa Manchester
Yoko Ono
Natalie Cole
Jessica Savitch
Queen Beatrix
Oprah Winfrey
Diana Oughten
Angela Davis
Betty Friedan
Evangeline Adams
Stella Adler
Virginia Johnson
Alice Neel
Toni Morrison
Helen Gurley Brown
Chynna Phillips
Jane Seymour
Amy Tan
Jill Eikenberry
Linda Blair
Tallulah Bankhead
Christie Brinkley
Susan Sontag
Barbie Benton
Corazon Aquino

her home as it will always be that much more laid-back than any other, if not the proverbial poker party pad. Rather, she's right there with them, feet up on the furniture, making crumbs and not using coasters. It is a startling symptom of the Aquarian's lack of concern for materialism, but it often elicits the same response as that of Stella's sister Blanche visiting the Kowalskis for the first time. The Waterbearer's surroundings are typically a visual collage, rather than an orderly catalog, of the goings-on in her life. There will be effects from the endless string of her notorious hobbies, which often include crafty home arts. The curtains and bedspreads, like many of her clothes, may be direct from her sewing machine. There will be tons of requisite knickknacks and memorabilia, minimalism not being her default aesthetic disposition. She likes the lived-in look, and nowhere in her house will that be more in evidence than in the bedroom, where both in decor and in sexual philosophy, as a rule, the Waterbearer isn't above making a bit of a mess.

Formality is not an Aquarian watchword. She abhors anything stuffy or puritanical; in fact, many an Aquarius is a connoisseur of kitsch, Americana, if not the finer points of white-trash living. She's turned on by men who are rough around the edges, if not altogether red in the neck, at least in spirit. Sex should never be a laminated, sanitized affair, but rather a releasing of all inhibitions. Her attitude is laissez-faire – the Aquarian is never the demanding, domineering, emasculating type, au contraire – as she gives her man much in the way of space, not wanting, as many women do, to be involved in the lion's share of his experiences. The 11th Astrological House, after all, is one of *nonpersonal* and *nonemotional relationships.* (Let's just say, it takes a lot to make the Aquarius cry.) And that element of detachment from her mate ironically helps to ensure that their sex life remains alive and kicking. For the zodiac's renewal goddess, there should be a sense that sex forever 'feels like the first time.' For this Uranus-ruled sign, serendipity and surprise will always be important elements for keeping the erotic experience new and exciting. Not knowing everything about her partner's life, allowing for that whiff of mystery, keeps the Aquarian guessing – she comes to expect the unexpected. It's the same with sexual behavior itself. Spontaneity is arousing to the Waterbearer, whose fantasies often involve being 'taken' abruptly by a man. She doesn't relish or require long-drawn-out touchy-feely sessions and romantic gazings into one another's eyes. She'd sooner get off on being jumped by her mate from behind while she was absentmindedly washing the dishes. Real, sudden human urges are what she's all about; not playing footsie for hours at a restaurant as a precursor to foreplay – that's too drawn out and, frankly, frustrating. It is the bestial side of men that attracts her most. She turns to jelly for rugged, blue-collar types.

If any woman were to take an anonymous, impromptu plunge with the plumber, it would be our impulsive Aquarian, who, ironically, given her sunny, wholesome, somewhat nerdy disposition, might be the last female on the astrological wheel one would expect to do so.

Considering that Aquarian's ultimate 'type' is a sort of prodigy from the proverbial wrong side of the tracks, a biker-scientist, redneck-guru, mechanic-philosopher, janitorial genius, we see in this affinity for unusual hybrid species of guys not only evidence of her sign's association with mutative energy, but also its correlation to the experience of the 'divine' mind being made manifest in the common man. This is the kind of fellow who is both literally and figuratively going places; i.e., he is the man of the future, the self-possessed and empowered individual who, like the hero Hercules, lays waste to notions of social barriers based on some specious class system. In the Uranus-ruled future, that mythic Aquarian Age wrought with social consciousness, 'harmony and understanding,' where blanket 11th House *egalitarianism* is the order of the day, there would be no division between construction worker and wine connoisseur. Aquarius seeks to latch on to this man of the future, now. Besides, she simply goes bonkers for a brainiac with the body of a sexy beast.

It takes this certain breed of man to get those colored lights in the ceiling spinning. She likes big lugs, those who look as if they can manhandle her with just the right amount of roughness. Sex doesn't need to be meaningful – it is what it is – rather, it's about pure physical pleasure. Aquarius woman is not a sensualist, she's a sexualist, and she appreciates a man who won't, pardon the pun, beat around the bush. She wants all her buttons pressed, preferably all at once, with the least amount of ceremony possible. As a sexual persona, too, she is unplugged, any nods to her infamous appreciation for battery-operated devices notwithstanding. Indeed, more than any other female, the Aquarian will boast a so-called goody drawer filled with colorful plastic cylindrical objects, vividly flavored contraceptives, tickling devices, and the like. Sex is all fun and games for her, and toys tend to work their way into the proceedings between her and a lover. Still, unlike the male of the sign, she is surprisingly unkinky, given her sign's association with deviant energy. However, she has zero hang-ups nor any trace of religious or moral guilt surrounding sex. Her body isn't so much a temple as it is a fun house, and she is especially comfortable with artificial stimulation as either enhancement to sex with a partner or as a happy, solo substitute for human contact. She is a nitty-gritty character in the bedroom, and though she doesn't much go in for role-playing per se, the Waterbearer's overriding sexual character is along variations on the theme of righteous mama. Sometimes, she really embraces that biker-chick personality

STR8 TURN-ONS

younger men or big daddies
white trash, truckers, bikers
long hair, ponytails, hippies
zealots, libertarians
rough-housing, biting
wrestling
(active) worship
(passive) degradation
groveling, begging
body hair, treasure trails
armpits
goatees
casual, no-strings sex
cheating
m-f-f threesomes
tattoos, piercings, branding
extra large penises, foreskin
(active) oral, swallowing
(passive) anal sex
(passive) heavy b + d
enslavement fantasies
costumes, masks
hoods, blindfolds
posing, home porn
(active) ass play
role reversal
freaks, geeks, carnies
captive/slave fantasies

full stop, getting off on being a kind of 'hogs 'n' heifers' poster girl as might appeal to the gear-head guys she generally goes for. Her boudoir wardrobe is thus rarely top-of-the-line lingerie material – she's far more Frederick's of Hollywood than Agent Provocateur, or even Victoria's Secret for that matter. It's amazing how garish a girl can be with so little fabric per square inch of flesh, but she doesn't want to know from anything more glamorous than neon nylon. It's not that the Aquarius necessarily burns with desire to sexually please her man; but she does want to look the part of the sexy bitch that does. She and her mate may document their bedroom shenanigans, whether with still photos or videos in which Aquarius stars as the moxie vixen. It floats her boat to be dolled up in synthetic costuming as the zodiac's cosmic slut. It's part sex, part conceptual art. But when it comes down to actual activity, she's fairly straightforward in her desires – let's just say she likes to ride a mean fast hog, or be rigorously driven by one. Otherwise, she will do whatever pleases her man, but she may somewhat shut herself down in the process, performing oral sex but not especially delighting in it. Anal sex is usually off-limits for Aquarius woman, who prefers to keep what might be considered invasive activity to a bare minimum.

Astrology is forever labeling the Aquarian the orgy queen since the 11th House is associated with *groups,* but it's a specious conclusion. If the Waterbearer were allowed to attend such a gathering with the understanding she wouldn't have to do anything, or anybody, she'd probably show up out of her trademark dispassionate curiosity. But her interest in multiple partners tends to end there. And much to the chagrin of a male partner who'd like to see his righteous Aquarius mama get it off with another game girl, she is not generally bisexually inclined. Ironically, for this open-minded creature, when it comes to sex, there is little to no gray area.

As such, one would be hard-pressed to find a more empowered individual in the zodiac than the gay-identified Aquarian woman. She is such a beacon of confidence and self-esteem that, without inviting it, other gay women tend to rally around her and hold her up as a mentor, even during her tender years. The gay Waterbearer may come out early, finding peer groups and support systems where she can be with like minds. Not exactly comfortable cast in the role of chairperson of the sapphic-love committee, however, she is not inclined to politicize her lesbianism. As society as a whole evolves, whether or not a person is gay holds less and less importance; as a nod to the future-oriented planetary rule of Uranus, that which signals large-scale social change, Aquarius lives her life as if already in an advanced civilization, a world where sexual preference doesn't even warrant discussion. And so, with little effort or personal agenda, Aquarius possesses a sort of pied piper appeal to other gay people, lesbians in particular, who wish to emulate her liberated, carefree attitude. To the Aquarian, however, her own vision of life as a gay person matters on no other level than her own.

Gay Aquarius woman tends to be a good deal more romantic than her straight counterpart. As a rule, she is a dominant figure in relationships, often eschewing feminine trappings and fashions for a more androgynous, if not outright masculine, look to match her usual hoydenish mind-set. It's not that she's decidedly butch – indeed, the Aquarian doesn't subscribe to extreme posturings in personality, which she believes to be more a backlash symptom of sociosexual pressure – it's more a matter of expressing her natural condition: not so much a latent masculinity as much as a perpetual, childlike tomboyishness. But Aquarius rarely comes across as some sort of drag king; rather, she is a sporty, wholesome-looking individual with a glint of mischief in her eye, a decidedly indecorous demeanor that suggests she might at any moment impetuously run outside and build herself a tree house. This is the gay Waterbearer girl's particular brand of Aquarian eccentricity; and she seems the most liberated of all individuals born under this extraordinary sign. Her company is infectious: As with all fixed signs, an element of magnetism is associated with her personality, but the gay Aquarian woman is that much more compelling. She will have a close circle of intimates whose friendship she'll retain over a lifetime, her choice in cronies never being contingent on sexual orientation. Her best friend is often a man with whom she'll pal around in the most convivial manner – *good, clean fun* is Aquarius's social mantra.

Like some callow youth for whom love is a new occurrence, gay Aquarius woman is completely transfixed by the object of her pure, unadulterated affection. Oblivious to boundaries or, in this case, fences, she tends to be attracted to women with teeter-tottering sexual identities and vice versa. Like straight women of the sign, the gay Waterbearer also entices more than her fair share of opportunists who will take advantage of her wide-eyed, innocent outlook on love. As it happens, she is naturally gallant and protective of a lover, often indulging her with gifts and spoiling her with surprise evenings out and romantic trips. Less savory types might hang on for such perks, while brattily expecting more and more until nothing the Aquarian does ever seems to be enough. Unlike her straight counterpart, however, she doesn't go through a steady series of relationships (or serial-marry, for that matter). Instead, she'd sooner remain single than have her heart broken more than once, or maybe twice. When Aquarius commits to a steady relationship, she expects it to last for life; and so when it doesn't work out, it's typically not for lack of trying

GAY TURN-ONS

small, meek women
buxom bodies
submissives
mastering
servants, waitresses
secretaries
feminists, activists
panty hose, garters
str8 women, femmes
dominance
voyeurism
sitting on face
heavy mind control
(active) lite s + m
(active) shaving, grooming
(passive) oral
(active) penetration
drag
dildos, vibrators, sex toys
(active) discipline
(active) nipple play
(active) piercing, branding
exhibitionism, public sex
rentgirls, threesomes

on her part. She is often so devastated by breakups it takes ages for her to heal.

In a nod to her planet's association with the unexpected, love usually finds the gay Aquarian girl when she is least looking for it. Her ideal partner will be a rather retiring but often doting character who appreciates the Waterbearer, foremost, for her outsized intelligence and, next, for her signature absurdist sense of humor. Indeed, one reason people circle around the Aquarian is because she's so damn funny. She may also come across as quite intellectual, even though her appearance often suggests Dennis the Menace more than Gertrude Stein. A good match for the Waterbearer is a like-minded lady who is nonetheless demure and naturally deferential. In general, an element of accident instigates their meeting – anything from a harmless fender bender to a chance introduction via a mutual friend – and before she realizes what's happening, Aquarius is chattering away in her inimitable style while the lovesick lady hangs on her every word. A shared cerebral interest is what unites Aquarius with her lover, a mental fixation that they might discover is better tackled as a twosome.

Aquarius often finds herself in a relationship that entails showing her lover the lesbian ropes. The Waterbearer is a patient, albeit dominant, figure in the bedroom, playing a decidedly active role. She is the hands-down top girl in the sack, an aggressor who manages to focus on mutual satisfaction as opposed to strictly pleasing or being pleased. Passion takes precedence over sensual finesse, and Aquarius is ardent in her physical expression, coming on strong and remaining heatedly excited and urgent for the duration of any sex session. She is remarkably oral, but again, she rarely tucks in to eat her partner out unless she's being simultaneously reciprocated. Whatever toys they play with will be double-headed, a literal example of how Aquarius and her lover must remain forever attached at the hip – *ba-dum-bum-chhh* – achieving absolute symbiosis, coming to function as one entity, even in bed. If the Waterbearer achieves certain success or notoriety stemming from her unique brand of intellect, her partner may function as her agent, manager, or otherwise act as a liaison, running defense for Aquarius. In any case, once the Waterbearer finds a steady relationship of this sort, she will seek to sustain it for life. Her bond comes to define her, she and a partner achieving such symbiosis that they begin to function as a single entity, indivisible one from the other.

Couplings

Aquarius Woman ∫ Aries Man
She retains a strong selfhood; he's emotionally accessed via their association. Intellectual growth is the outcome. Sex is playful and plentiful. There's more pleasure than she'd imagined in the missionary position.

Aquarius Woman ∫ Taurus Man
She sets out to nest with someone 'normal.' Ironically, he's exploring the dark side of his psyche. Enormous, uprooting changes occur. Aquarius is accustomed to more passion; for him, she's the exotic exception.

Aquarius Woman ∫ Gemini Man
Their only concern: pleasing each other. He's her ideal fling; she relishes the role of minx and mentor. Free-spiritedness creates a combined social and political consciousness. Sex is robust and randy.

Aquarius Woman ∫ Cancer Man
She's his wake-up call. He's less an epiphany, more of a reality check – a sign it's time to get serious. They're an ideological society of two, living an inspired life. Sex is transformative – a step up for him, an enhancement for her.

Aquarius Woman ∫ Leo Man
Together, they're big and bold, gifted, but unpredictable. Leo adopts a contemplative countenance. Her unusual, extraordinary qualities emerge. Sex is passionate, energized by envy, as well as esteem.

Aquarius Woman ∫ Virgo Man
They're compelled to caretake – he invests endless emotional energy. Privately, he's keeping a checklist: She owes him big. Aquarius is less selfish. Sexually, it's master-servant, with roles in constant rotation.

Aquarius Woman ∫ Libra Man
Defined by inventiveness and upheaval. Some say they're strange. Abstract thinkers, they share a mental affinity – each impacts the other's state of mind. Enthusiasm turns to zealotry. In bed, there are no hang-ups.

Aquarius Woman ∫ Scorpio Man
Any antisocial tendencies are expanded. Feeling superior, they team up in a you-and-me-against-the-world bond, but later they might turn against each other. Sex is primal, but inclusive: This pair enjoys other partners.

Aquarius Woman ∫ Sagittarius Man

They may seem ill-suited, but it's an illusion: With her, he's found a lifeline. Paired with Sag, the Waterbearer sets herself up for a brighter future. In bed, they break from old behavior – together, it's earthy-crunchy.

Aquarius Woman ∫ Capricorn Man

They may be explosive in each other's company, overly conscious of not instigating a scene. Still, there's plenty of hilarity here. In bed, emotional intensity is put to its best use: Sex is ardent and unruly.

Aquarius Woman ∫ Aquarius Man

They feel superhuman, seeming to live in a perpetually exalted state. For him, perfection is the goal; for her, the focus is to improve the human condition. Little energy is left for sex, so they might make it more a priority.

Aquarius Woman ∫ Pisces Man

A fast and furious courtship for this couple. Beneath slick exteriors lie deeply soulful individuals seeking a source of inspiration. Their sex life reflects such profundity – in bed they move as if possessed, even hexed.

Gay

Aquarius Woman ∫ Aries Woman

At first, they hide their hookup from others. But taboo is what keeps them tempted. Even when committed, this coupling remains one of the most erotic and exotic lesbian combinations. Raunchiness is de rigueur.

Aquarius Woman ∫ Taurus Woman

In Taurus, Aquarius has an eager audience, someone who'll lovingly listen to her high-minded monologues and learn. Sex is best when conceptual – it's all about exaggerated role-play and complex mind games.

Aquarius Woman ∫ Gemini Woman

They'll say it was predestined. This connection is empathetic in the extreme. As a couple, they're insular; neither feels beholden to those on the outside, even friends. In bed, it's a question of who's the more generous lover.

Aquarius Woman ∫ Cancer Woman

Big issues abound when these supernatural sisters sign on. They're so in sync, it's scary. Still, they go through phases of fierce fighting. Chaos can be exhausting. Sex is like their social life – wild, fast, frenzied.

Aquarius Woman / Leo Woman

More reciprocity makes this relationship a success. So Aquarius should dodge some of Leo's demands. Best case: They're a droll duo – lively, larger-than-life. Sex is luscious when Leo lets herself be led.

Aquarius Woman / Virgo Woman

Meeting halfway, they merge – differences disappear, similarities surface. They're a dazzling duo – creative in the extreme. Days spent together seem like a dream. Sex, too, is a point where fantasy and reality meet.

Aquarius Woman / Libra Woman

An overwhelming attraction. They buzz with physical and intellectual energy. Libra indulges artsy-craftsy interests while Aquarius accelerates entrepreneurial success. The comforts of home carry more allure than any social circle.

Aquarius Woman / Scorpio Woman

An unusual sexual liaison that soon turns serious. Assuming a maternal role, Scorpio nurtures the Aquarian's ambitions. With the Waterbearer, Scorpio finally gets some respect. In bed, one or the other feels eclipsed.

Aquarius Woman / Sagittarius Woman

Anything's possible. The Archer takes aim at the Waterbearer's grand plan, and bull's-eye: Their partnership pays off. They're a sexy twosome, public about their lust. They exude an ecstatic energy.

Aquarius Woman / Capricorn Woman

A battle of the wills wherein the Waterbearer tries to assume authority – and Cap's having none of it. Still, they're an enterprising pair, if verbosity doesn't obstruct action. In bed, the Goat gets the better end of the deal.

Aquarius Woman / Aquarius Woman

A snowball effect: Togetherness may accelerate their separate descents: Loss of control, neurosis, even paranoia, are possible. Due to stresses, their sex life suffers. Still, there's hope: Focus on selves, not others.

Aquarius Woman / Pisces Woman

With passive, pretty Pisces, the Waterbearer butches it up a bit. Supportive, even doting, Aquarius may find the Fish strangely dispassionate. But in bed, this is one of the more erotic, ecstatic sexual couplings.

Pisces Man

the drifter

Pisces is the very definition of a self-made man. More than any guy in the zodiac, he is blessed with an ability to exist according to his own design, devoid of doubt and distraction. He doesn't stress or strive to achieve success; rather he patiently allows his plans to gestate while visualizing himself to be, in the present, what he is determined to become in the future. He never waits to 'arrive' at goals but rather behaves as one who has already attained them, his life being one long self-fulfilling prophecy. As a rule, he is drawn to artistic professions where his imagination can manifest. Infamously unbeholden to anybody but himself, he trails nary a trace of emotional or psychological baggage, often eschewing evidence of the past if it doesn't suit his typically mythic self-image. He sees no irony in adopting a personality, often a hoity-toity one, which arguably suits his spirit better than what he perceives to be the arbitrary self conditioned by birth or upbringing. Pisces boasts the dissolute soul of a poet, freely licensed to devise the landscape of his own experience. Despite any highbrow polish, which is in no small way aimed at providing entrée into more rarefied enclaves of society, he nonetheless has a taste for raw, unmade women – artless, unblushing types who provide a sense of *real* grounding, thus enabling him to creatively soar all the more. With other men, he is homoerotic to the core, forever flirting with the fine line between friendship and full-out sexual involvement.

XĬĬ

The Principle of Dissolution – a synonym for death, Pisces symbolizes a return to the primordial soup. A metaphoric fetus in the process of rebirth, Pisces is both a product of inherited traits and of evolution. Dissolution is also a dream state, Pisces representing imagination made manifest. Dissolution also symbolizes love, which embraces all diversity, deliquescing it into a wholism of humanity. His sign's motto 'I believe' is a mechanism for turning dreams into reality.

Sign + Mind

Although Jupiter is attributed as a secondary ruler of Pisces, providing those born under the sign a psychological backdrop of optimism and expansiveness, Pisces's primary ruler is Neptune, called the planet of imagery, which signifies, among other things, the universal Principle of Dissolution in the zodiac. Thus, those under its government view reality as rather, well, dissolved. Ancient and contemporary cultures and religions, the world over, speak of the visible world as, to use the Buddhist term, *samsara,* defined as the cycle of existence and the completely defiled state of mind, caused by *karma.* The dissolute Pisces, in seeing the world as a dissoluble patina, is thus able to live life beyond the veil of this cycle, which is what it means to reach *nirvana,* the liberation from the wheel of existence and, thus, the attainment of a purified state of mind. The master illusionist himself – Neptune is the planet of illusion – Pisces sees life as a sustainable miraculous condition which the previous sign of Aquarius man was only able to glimpse in revelations, the Aquarius woman, the zodiac's Salome, personifying the veil itself drawing back. Pisces, like the great and powerful Oz – the *zed* signaling an end to journeying whether along some brick road or round the astrological wheel – *is* that man behind the curtain, whether you pay attention to him or not. He is the original *dharma* bum, a drifter on the spiritual and the metaphorical plane, nonetheless equipped with a natural understanding of the absolute ironic truth of existence – that the world of appearances is but illusion, mere vapor as typified by this misty mutable-water sign, and thus able to be orchestrated as such. Neptune itself points to life lived on this metaphorical plane, and, thus, the natural-born poet Pisces is blessed (or cursed) with the gift of seeing life, indeed existing on, such a level akin to what Pisces painter Piet Mondrian pegged as 'abstract realism' – that of the essential, albeit unseen reality. Believing life to be fraught with illusion allows the Pisces to reach beyond its tricks and disguises, appearances being so ultimately deceiving. Pisces man teaches the rest of us, by example, that real life is what one *fancies* it to be. And in truth the Fish guy lives a life of 'fancy' in every conceivable meaning of that term.

First, Pisces man has a natural talent for creating whimsical, unreal worlds from the vast recesses of his imagination, typically possessing a romantic vision of existence via which he can elevate the most banal, or even degrading circumstances to a sublime level. His poetic soul is apparent in whatever he undertakes, though many a Pisces male does indeed pursue such creative vocations as painting, decorative arts, dance, and writing. In any case, to the

Piscean mind, all is poetry. Via Neptune, the sign is associated with the 12th Astrological House of *dreams* and *impressions,* which means he perceives reality most subjectively, driven by his internal senses and personal apprehensions rather than by solid external factors or sensible conditions, the harsher bulk of which he simply deigns not to recognize. Purposeful ignorance, one might say, is Piscean bliss and his private path to perfection, as the Fish chooses mainly to inhabit the dreamy waters of his own unconscious with a pointed disregard to outward influences, social mores, obstacles, or limits that might otherwise hinder his particular design for living. The personification of the old adage 'life is what you make it,' he exhibits a unique ability to eliminate anything from his path that might muddy his determination to fulfill his specific calling. Unlike most of us who find ourselves mired in emotional blocks, self-doubts, familial dysfunction, or discouragement, Pisces simply won't see such detriment as such; rather, he embodies the be-all self he *fancies* himself to be, not so much overcoming obstacles as obliterating, indeed dissolving, them with a direct disregard, living the dream of what his life should be, regardless of any given condition of birth or upbringing, particularly when they are decidedly dodgy.

It is fitting that the word *fancy* also means 'breeding,' as in the case of animals, i.e., developing points of excellence or beauty – the making, designing, growing, or adapting for exceptional quality or appeal to please the fancy – for the Piscean does exactly that: He propagates in himself that which he pinpoints to be his finest traits. As the last astrological sign, Pisces is associated with the age group 77–84 and the advent of not only death but, the zodiac being a wheel, reincarnation, leading to the premier sign of Aries and its representation of birth. The sign of Pisces is, in effect, the alpha and the omega – a phrase associated with Christ, the primary archetypal figure associated with Pisces – as depicted by the sign's opposite-facing-fish symbol. How does this relate to our Pisces guy? Well, from an early age, guys born into this sign live their life in a metaphoric womb-tomb state where they let dissolve the unwanted memories of the past as they reincarnate, indeed breed themselves, into somebody new. To Pisces, the world is a womb with a view to nurturing and developing his dreams and desires. Moreover, the male Fish perceives his environment as fluid, his life a system that provides both incoming nourishment (reinforcement for his self-development) and outgoing cleansing (psychological waste-removal), a washing away of distractions and other detritus that might hinder the full realization of his most fantastical ambitions – just as an actual womb system performs this same dual function by feeding the fetus while eliminating its waste. Bobbing away in life (as if it were one big isolation tank) gives rise to Pisces's infamously fantastical imaginings,

PLANETARY SYMBOL

Neptune is the planet of illusion and immateriality. It represents the need to experience life from a perspective devoid of practical or ideological structure. It puts Pisces man in touch with unseen planes of inspiration, just as it can leave him open to spiritual or mystical experiences. It is the three-pronged phallus of the triple god.

SIGN QUADRANT

The zodiacal quadrants correspond to metaphysical planes of existence – physical, emotional, mental, and spiritual or universal. The Fourth Quadrant concerns one's relationship with the divine or the eternal. Whereas Capricorn engages in traditional practices and Aquarius seeks to grasp new relevatory truths, Pisces combines these forces via the practical application of evolutionary ideals.

SIGN GLYPH

The opposite-facing Fish of Pisces are mythic totems of Eros and Aphrodite. They signify the alpha and the omega and the yin-yang (male-female) construct of the universe as the primal androgyne. The Fish is a womb symbol; the opposite-facing Fish here signify a dual system of incoming nourishment and outgoing elimination.

ELEMENT + QUALITY

The water element signifies emotion, particularly love, and intuition; the mutable quality, a call for versatility and change. Together, the mutable-water combination particular to Pisces is best described as the sea, itself a metaphor for the dream state, a primordial soup from which all life sprang. It also implies a fog, mist, or vapor synonymous with imagination, dreams, and so-called illusion.

whether artistic or purely delusional, just as he seeks to isolate and breed out wasteful attitudes or attributes, engendering only those traits that fit the self he specifically imagines himself to be. The power of Neptune signals refinement *via* its aforementioned principle of dissolution, such that Pisces man, as the possessor of this planetary power, emerges as a gleaming individual precisely because he is better able than most to let impediments to his successes simply melt away. Regardless of whether or not he was reared on the proverbial wrong side of the tracks, Pisces man tends to gestate decidedly genteel, well-bred characteristics, literally fancying himself some sort of aristocrat of exquisite pedigree, often much to the bewilderment of his parents. He is detached from family dynamics and is thus easily able to let go of his past, particularly if his kin conflict with his princely, peaceful self-image. For Pisces man, even what might be considered 'humble origins' can become grounds for cutting family out of his life, just as he performs a sort of psychic surgery on himself, determined to rid his mind of any squalid associations that might hinder his signature soaring plans.

Despite Pisces's notorious flights of fancy, he is the most resolute character on the zodiacal block. His whimsy and decisive determination aren't mutually exclusive, but rather one and the same: For the Fish, desire is purpose, and whereas many feel a conflict between their dreams and their reality, Pisces entertains no such chasms. To him, ambition and desire are impersonal – they are manifestations in the individual of some divine plan or other. Thus, in following his callings, no matter how lofty, Pisces on some level believes he is simply fulfilling his destiny. He sees ambition or desire, even of a sexual nature, as stemming from a divinely inspired source or force, upon which he'll happily hop and go along for the ride. Of course, as in Tennessee Williams' *A Streetcar Named Desire* where the choice stop is Elysian Fields – the mythic heaven where crème de la crème mortals are granted eternally blissful life – Pisces possesses a confidence that, in fully committing, if not sacrificing, himself to what he perceives to be his life purpose, that which is determined by his most pressing needs, he will also achieve certain immortality, a seat on the dais of heroic human achievement. And of course, living one's dream requires great fearlessness in the face of adversity, something that the Piscean possesses in abundance.

In coming to the last sign, the so-called end, of the zodiac, it makes sense that we encounter an individual with such resolution – a term that means determination, definition; thus an answer, or a solution. The word *solution* itself relates back to the dissolution energy of Neptune and comes from the Latin *solutionem* meaning a 'loosing or unfastening' – the word *solve* itself comes from the Greek *selvo,* meaning to 'release, atone, clear up, or wash away,' a fitting denotation for this be-all-end-all of water signs. And so, one might say, to the Piscean male mind the key to this wee riddle we call life is to let go of one's problems – a process of elimination, or casting of burdens – the literal solution being the liquidation of impediments, which, in their absence, reveals answers that have always been there, but blocked. To his mind, heaven is spread out here, on earth, if only we would see beyond the veil of life's illusions. Pisces male isn't trapped in the world of appearances; he lives life like a lucid dreamer, who brings about desired circumstances through concentration and total ignorance of distraction – no easy feat, something to which anyone who has ever awoken into a dream can attest. It is Pisces's birthright to be in touch with his one true calling. Everything else is dross – *refuse* being a principal attribute of the 12th Astrological House, fittingly referred to as the dustbin of the zodiac. Pisces has nary an emotional obligation, being unbeholden to anybody but himself. Those with whom he enters into a relationship must either fold themselves into his life, making his goals their own, or remain resolutely determined to pursue their own destined path, 'okay' with the inherent isolation that a relationship with Pisces man entails. Otherwise, bonds are an obstacle, and something that he will coldly cut loose in favor of drifting toward his divinely appointed destination. And somewhere subconsciously, he feels that if a relationship is able to survive given his total immersion in, well, himself, then that bond, too, qualifies as destined. For in a world where most people live quiet lives of desperation, Pisces man, by embracing his most exalted flights of fancy, can achieve a kind of profound connection with his life purpose – a direction others mightn't even allow themselves to dream of pursuing.

Still, it can take Pisces a lifetime to fulfill his destiny as he neither quests nor networks but slowly sails toward his goals – for that reason alone Pisces is a notoriously late bloomer. And if that wouldn't try the patience of a saint, his martyred life partner must also cope with his cavalier attitude toward money, taking on the role of bookkeeper, if not banker, until the Fish's infamous creativity begins to translate into hard cash. Even so, material matters will remain peripheral to the Pisces, for whom everything in life, people included, is easy come and easy go. But sacrifice is endemic to the sign of Pisces. Indeed, the Fish draws his persona from the archetype of the apotheosized deities, those who, typically through the sacrifice of death, turn from men into gods. Christ is the most obvious example of this sacrificial character. In the myth of Christ we see both his birth and his death as miraculous. Likewise, the sign of the Fish, an oft-used symbol for the Christ figure, is all about miraculous energy – the Greek word for fish is the same as that for messiah. As the third, mutable sign in the Fourth Quadrant of Soul, Pisces represents transformative change on the unseen,

POLARITY

Males in female (earth, water) signs are not aligned with the gender polarity of the sign and thus enact instead of embody the quality-element combination of the sign. Pisces man is not the soupy, dreamy mix that Pisces woman can be, but rather one drifting in a sea of reverie like a lucid dreamer, imagining his intentions into reality.

12

SIGN NUMBER

The number of divinity. Considered the higher vibration of the number three, which twelve reduces to, when its two digits are added together. There are twelve tribes of Israel, twelve stations of the cross, twelve zodiacal signs, twelve Olympian gods.

SIGN AGE
ASSOCIATION

The age of death: Pisces male lives as if drifting comfortably in some wondrous limbo where his pure intentions are free from distraction and all seems possible. With his froggy, fetal features, the world is like a nurturing womb, an isolation tank, giving rise to his infamous dreams and fancies.

PSYCHOLOGY

Pisces often exhibits some form of a messiah complex. He can be pathologically jealous of others' successes. He is hypersensitive and prone to drug and alcohol abuse. He may be oedipal. 'Attuned' to mystical occurrences, he may suffer from hallucinations, paranoia, or schizophrenia.

spiritual plane. Birth and death both fit these criteria, particularly when taken together as parts of the same cyclical wheel of life, forever repeating through a series of reincarnations or resurrections. As the only mutable-water sign in the zodiac, Pisces man's experience is like that of some divine being for whom the world is embryonic liquid, a nurturing and purifying, fluid experience that naturally forms him into a virtual deified man. Indeed, Pisces, and in particular the often messiah-complexed males of the sign, remind us that there need not be any division between the concept of god and man. It is an ideological energy that courses through Pisces's veins: the belief that he was put on this earth as the embodiment of a supreme being; albeit at such a great sacrifice, that is, having to put up with the disappointing shenanigans of the rest of the planet's unruly, unrefined inhabitants. As anyone intimately associated with a Pisces man would readily agree, he exudes a benign though subtly patronizing tolerance of others, even his closest loved ones, on whom he casts a patient but disgruntled gaze. In truth Pisces will always be let down by the all-too-human machinations of other people – while he has long ago cut loose and set adrift such effecting and finagling and struggling himself. Meanwhile, he manages to smile reassuringly, if not condescendingly, at the rest of us wallowing in such as mire.

Pisces's transcendence of the standard human cycles of existence finds its seeds in his earliest childhood. Fittingly, it all begins in the womb: Often, Pisces's mother has a difficult pregnancy; or she carries him during an incredibly stressful time. Problems may have occurred that lead to Pisces being born prematurely or with a vague defect – webbed toes or feet, a cleft palate, or birthmarks are not uncommon. The word *blessed* comes from the French *blessé,* meaning 'wounded,' which, given his biblical archetype, casts some foreshadowing on the phrase 'blessed is the fruit of thy womb, Jesus.' Pisces is so often the proverbial 'miracle baby,' whose birth, despite its complications, indeed due to them, is auspicious. Pisces's mother is a powerful force in the family, though perhaps not particularly nurturing. Instead, she forms a rather adult bond with the Pisces, who may be eerily mature for his years, one of comradeship that sometimes gets too close for comfort, giving rise to oedipal patterns in the Fish male. Pisces's dad tends to look on his son as strange, often concerned about the future of his sexuality as even the straightest Pisces boy will be somewhat foppish and effete. There is usually a tricky triangle of affection whereby Pisces's mother feels a strain in showing affection to both her husband and her son, who seem forever at odds. As the Pisces reaches teenage, he will have become a brooding dark-horse, one of the few aspects of personality he draws from his classic patron Neptune (Greek: Poseidon), whose namesake planet rules this squally boy. Poseidon is unique in mythology as a shadowy, stormy figure who rarely enters into myth. Like Apollo, he is a patriarchal god, depicted as greedy and jealous, who took over previously goddess-ruled provinces. His carrying of the trident, originally a symbol of the goddess in her triplicate form, as well as his marrying of Amphitrite (the triple Aphrodite of the Sea), is proof of this usurpation. This seeming digression is important: Aphrodite–Mari is equivalent to the Judeo-Christian Mary, whose name is synonymous with the sea *(mer),* the water womb from which Jesus emerges. As such, Jesus is then analogous to the Greek Eros who, unlike his Roman counterpart, Cupid, is at once the oldest of all gods and yet Aphrodite's eternal babe. Jesus, like Poseidon, is wedded to the triple goddess as well, having, as the God, fathered himself via his mother, taking Mary Magdalene as his consort – three Marys are present at crucial moments in his thirty-three-year life span, including, most notably, his crucifixion. Jesus is called the 'little fish' just as the constellation of Pisces is said to represent Aphrodite and Eros together, whose totems were fish, the particular animal form they were wont to change themselves into. Eros is love. Jesus is love. As father, son, and holy spirit, the male trinity, three points creating a circle, we thus have a wheel or cycle of life personified in one being.

This is the Pisces male in a nutshell: his own creation, self-begotten and self-contained, the 'holy spirit' bit signifying the mysterious, unseen aspect of his personality, which is the power of self-conception continually taking place in the protective womb that is the Pisces's world. The zodiac's own prince of peace is thus designed to carve out his destiny without unduly dealing with others' agendas. It is little wonder then that he recuses himself even from domestic dynamics as early as he can think to do so. The 12th House is one of *escape* and *asylum,* and Pisces may live out his adolescent years barricaded in his room, only interacting when arm-twisted into doing so. Even at school, he will find a rarefied enclave, generally surrounding an artistic interest, where he might find sanctuary. He will stay late, alone, after school to work on solo projects, typically art or music. He isn't awkward, shy, or trying to fit in like the Aquarian male, who precedes him on the wheel. Rather, he is heedless of others, living in 12th House *oblivion.* He attracts a great many girls, who find his searing sensitivity, as well as his utter insouciance, intriguing. If heckled by other males suspect of his masculinity, he goes all Christ-like and turns that proverbial other cheek. This untouchable nobility attracts a great majority of the school misfit population, who become disciples of sorts, elevating the Pisces to a champion among the meek and disenfranchised, a status that will define him well into adulthood.

ARCHETYPE + MYTH

Pisces man draws on the archetype of Eros (love), who is at once the son of Aphrodite and the oldest of gods. Pisces's fish are Eros and Aphrodite in their animal-totem form. Eros embodies the underlying energy of the universe, love, with which, Pisces believes, all is possible. Pisces's planetary namesake, Neptune (Greek: Poseidon), the god of the sea, personifies 'the middle way' in a world of opposites represented by his brothers, lofty Zeus and underworld Hades. Poseidon's trident is a triple phallus, key to coupling with his triple-goddess wife, Amphitrite, Aphrodite in her marine form. *Poseidon* means 'mate of the mother.'

BIBLE + LITERATURE

Pisces is associated with Christ, for whom the fish serves as a symbol. It is also the totem of the Greek Eros. Christ is love just as Eros is love; Christ is the son of Mary, who is equivalent to Aphrodite (Mari), mother of Eros. Both male figures are personifications of the supreme divine force in the cosmos. Christ figures abound in literature from Chaucer's Nicholas in 'The Miller's Tale' to Steinbeck's Jim Casey in the *Grapes of Wrath* to Stowe's Uncle Tom to Joyce's Stephen Dedalus to C. S. Lewis's Aslan in *The Chronicles of Narnia*. In the film *The Matrix,* he is the savior Neo. The Pisces man as Christ figure is defined by total immersion in his calling. The Greek word for 'fish' is synonymous with that for 'messiah'.

Body + Soul

Like all mutable signs, Pisces man lives in flux – for this and other reasons, he makes a fairly fair-weather friend. He prefers to remain a free agent, and even when married for fifty some odd years, he likes to mingle, solo, in any social setting, often springing on someone he may, silently, have been sussing out, determining whether a person would make interesting, or rather interested, conversation. Pisces man has a definite spiel, a verbal routine designed to impress, consisting of seemingly spontaneous insights and one-liners. He has a unique ability to key into a person, pinpointing and playing into one's state of mind. So if some man suddenly approaches you, say, at a party, keenly summing up the thoughts running through your mind at that exact moment you're thinking them with some witty aside or non sequitur aimed at striking up a conversation, ten to one he's a Pisces man. That 12th House trait of *clairvoyance* has a startling way of kicking right in. Otherwise, he exudes a quietly charismatic air, made all the less intrusive by a dulcet-toned voice. He loves latching onto strangers, simultaneously entertaining and impressing acquaintances with his witty repartee and worldly knowledge, regardless of their sex or his sexual identity. He can be a bit of a fancy-pants, if not an outright fop, all proper dress and pronunciation, qualities that suggest he might have enjoyed a luxury upbringing or, to some, that he's a big sissy, or both. Indeed, even the straightest Pisces are notoriously suspect in their sexual orientation, being so over-the-top and cultured a gallant – think television's fictitious Felix Unger or Frasier (both portrayed by Pisceans, Tony Randall and Kelsey Grammer, respectively), two of the queeniest heterosexual characters ever to grace the airwaves. Like these pompously prissy personalities, if not the men who played them, straight Pisces man in all his outsized flamboyance tends to, shall we say, put the *big* in *ambiguous*. Much to his chagrin, the male Fish must often break through such a barrier of suspicion surrounding his sexual preference.

Given the Pisces's inherent lack of machismo, women are not generally threatened, but rather intrigued by what they might mistake to be his ardent advances. He becomes so seemingly invested in a person, and so immediately, that one might expect a meaningful friendship, if not a romance, would naturally ensue. Physically, too, there is so much to recommend the Pisces. Despite a certain froginess to his appearance, particularly in his usually bulging eyes and wide, suggestively gaping mouth, Pisces man tends to be the best-looking, if not the prettiest, man in the zodiac. He has a distinctly feminine beauty, like so many male models of the day, his features being centered low and crowded together on his face, lending him an innocent, childlike mien. His forehead is high and unfettered, his eyes big and dramatic with a soft, unfocused gaze, framed by bushy, sweeping brows. Though his hair is typically dark, his skin is so extremely pale as to be translucent, his veins often visible beneath the surface; and his eyes are often of an indistinguishable color, a green or blue flecked with brown or so dark in hue as to appear charcoal gray. His peepers usually have a milky, opaque quality suggesting a shrouded, or clouded, impressionistic perspective. His pointy, though slightly hooked, nose is often dusted with tiny freckles, regardless of his race, his lips sensuously full and pillowy above a square but delicate chin. Indeed many male models are Pisceans. Otherwise he tends to be the proverbial boy-next-door Ken doll of the zodiac, like such pretty if not plasticine lads as Kyle MacLachlan, Rob Lowe, Chris Klein, David Duchovny, Kurt Russell, Freddie Prinze Jr., Barry Bostwick, and Pierce Brosnan. Being such a beauty boy is probably why Pisces has historically crossed cultural and racial lines more easily than other males. In popular culture, it has been Pisceans of African descent who have had the smoothest transition into what was once the white-dominated social main-stream. Sidney Poitier, Nat King Cole, Harry Belafonte, Al Jarreau, Quincy Jones, and Spike Lee are all men of color who were pioneers in infiltrating white-bread America. Besides their pretty looks and peace-loving personalities, Pisces of any extraction also get over on their mannerly, upper-crusty personas, most poignantly expressed via typically lock-jaw, socialite-sounding patterns of speech, such as a *yah* style of delivery that would have given Thurston Howell III a run for his money. Besides Randall and Grammer, Jim Backus, David Niven, Rex Harrison, George Plimpton, and John Updike are all Fish. Even when a troubled sort, as so many Pisceans can be – the 12th House is also one of *self-deception* and *self-undoing,* literal manifestations of dissolution – the Piscean male inspires a sort of sympathy on that score that other men wouldn't – think Kurt Cobain, Bix Beiderbecke, James Taylor, Pier Paolo Pasolini, Jack Kerouac, Dean Stockwell, and Robert Lowell. These characters all elicit compassion for their pain while troubled natives of other signs often seem just, well, like trouble. Being the most genteel man on the astrological wheel goes a long way to explain Pisces's prolific success, in particular in his sexual pursuits. With a decided lack of raw, male beastliness, he becomes the favorite boy-toy flavor of many men and women alike. Notoriously naturally smooth-bodied, he again wins points for a kind of mannequin masculinity, appealing to those who like their male lover to look as if he just stepped out of the pages of a magazine layout. And no man comes as close to fitting that bill as Pisces.

12TH ASTROLOGICAL
HOUSE

spirituality
extrasensory perception
profound imagery
non-material existence
evasion/aversion
psychological fitness
inner strength or weakness
surrender to a higher power
secret goings-on
secret societies
healing solitariness
places of reflection
confinement/seclusion
difficulties/dilemma
limbo and oblivion
unfinished business
obstacles
hidden problems
subliminal endings
health of a society
health of a marriage
bodies of water
unseen danger
grief brought on self
self-deception
behind-the-scenes activity
sympathy
understanding
mysterious stimulus
escape and asylum
unreality
public welfare
breaking barriers
monasticism
martyrdom
empathy
selflessness
aptitude for the arts

The Fish man typically boasts being what is referred to in the fashion industry as 'sample size,' a perfect 40-long most men will never in their life shimmy into. And the more flamboyant the garb the better, as Pisces man has a fanciful fashion sense, being drawn to romantic, indeed Byronesque clothing styles that visibly portray his signature poetic soul. However, in the world of traditionally minimalist men's clothing, Pisces can often look as if he's just raided the wardrobe department of some stock production of the *Pirates of Penzance.* He tends to wear his typically fine and wispy hair long, also in Byronesque fashion, or perhaps as a blatant advertisement of his Christ complex. Ironically, even in a physical sense, such a comparison is fairly fitting in that Jesus, infinitely depicted as a long-haired, blue-eyed beauty, was the Western world's original male model. And though Pisces has unfortunately inherited his powerful archetype's love of gauzy caftans and open-toe sandals, he also embodies the same peaceful demeanor, enviably lanky physique, and low percentage of body fat. His chiseled, angular facial features – high cheekbones and a delineated jawline – give way to a long and graceful neck marked by a pronounced Adam's apple and a deep dip at the clavicle. His shoulders are wide and bony, his arms thin but defined, as is his chest, which can have a sunken, concave quality that requires compensatory focus at the gym. He has a high, muscular rear, and long, thin, somewhat spindly legs. His Piscean-ruled feet, like his hands, are delicately attenuated and ever so slightly erotic. Still, despite all this seeming bodily perfection, there is often something amiss in the Piscean physique – a curvature of the spine, bowleggedness, flat-footedness, or other structural 'defects.' Though only ever moderately hairy, Pisces often has a definite dark and fleecy trail emanating from his navel straight on downward past his typically flat tummy. He has a loose and floppy basket, though he's pretty averagely endowed, his dick being perfectly proportion in length and thickness. Ironically, there is something decidedly nonsexual about the naked Pisces, as if his nudity is meant to inspire aesthetic appreciation rather than overt lust. Perhaps it's due to his overall anatomic definition, like that of a life-drawing model whose body composition makes one marvel at the magnificent human form.

ſex + ſexuality

As early as his teenage years, Pisces male will have set himself adrift from his family, often moving out of the house as quickly as he can, sometimes before legally of age, or otherwise living at home like some sort of shadowy boarder.

He will come and go as he pleases in that case, often disappearing for days on end. At college, his roommate will be pleasantly surprised to find that Pisces is a ghostlike presence, remaining decidedly detached from dorm-room life. Typically, he will latch on to a domineering female, often older than himself, whose company he'll keep to the exclusion of all others. Since taking up with girls, he will have been attracted to flamboyant, attention-getting females, gaudy, bawdy types with creative ambitions, if not for fame and fortune, very much like his own. His love life, too, will be Noël Coward–esque, as he adopts an adult character-personality who is perpetually bored even with his own sophistication – as if he knows and has seen everything. Nothing and nobody impresses Pisces, and he makes a point of undermining anything or anybody that appeals to the masses, whether out of jealousy or justifiable disdain. And his main criterion for a partner worthy of being called his own is a vocal and otherwise obvious corroboration of his views. He likes a bit of wear and tear on a woman as well, being turned off by the fresh ingenues that most men find so appealing. He looks for experience, seasoning in a woman. Even as a teen, he'll be attracted to older girls or those with reputations, warranted or not, for having been around the block once or twice or more. It's as if, being so subconsciously linked to the cyclical nature of life, he'd sooner make a Madonna out of a questionable whore than hook up with some snowy virgin who, by rights, might only become more blackened.

Though this won't sound particularly flattering on the surface to those romantically linked with Pisces man, the 12th House is oft referred to as the dustbin of the zodiac, associated with *the dregs,* sediment being an intrinsic result of Neptune's energy of dissolution, the remnants of experience as well as society. We have already seen this dynamic manifested in Pisces's appeal to the misfits and miscreants of his peer group, but the same pattern seems to apply to his love relationships as well. Even the kind of slaggish girl who might appear to be used goods is viewed by Pisces as a person who, via experience, has become a seasoned distillation of womankind, refined by circumstance, if not hardship, into her essential self, devoid of pretense, ego, or other such trappings of human falsification. In being undone, he believes, a woman's soul is laid bare. And it is the soul that this personification of the Christ archetype is seeking to wed, just as, using his Greek archetypology, Eros–Cupid is wedded to Psyche (Soul). And if you know anything about that myth, and the hell his mother Aphrodite–Venus put poor Psyche through, you might get an idea of the oedipal pressures that invariably plague the Piscean male. One never knows if Pisces's choice of a partner – which strikes most everyone acquainted with him as dubious – is the primary reason for his mother's disdain toward

BODY RULERSHIP

Pisces rules the feet, which comprise pressure points that connect to the entire body, just as the sign itself is considered the catchall of the zodiac. It also governs the lymphatic system. Neptune is associated with mental processes, brain and spinal fluid. There is a tendency to foot trouble, dementia, and brain disorders.

whatever girl(s) he tends to bring home, or if conflict on this score is simply written in the stars. Whatever the cause, Pisces's mother and mate typically don't see eye to eye; in time, however, they might begin to realize that they are eerily cut from the same cloth, if not born into the same generation.

Pisces is the sole mutable-water sign of the zodiac: Mutability represents change and adaptability, while the feminine element of water symbolizes feeling, intuition, and the primal origin of life (this is why baptism signifies rebirth). Of course, just as Eros is the primal god-force, Love, specifically of a sexual nature, is the essential impetus to life. Thus, throughout classical and medieval literature, water is used as a metaphor for love: One must be an open recipient to contain it, while it escapes those seeking to grab it for their own gain. Love, as they say, is not selfish. And that's the kind of love to which the Pisces male subscribes. He neither wants to own nor be owned by his partner. The zodiac's drifter, it seems, can never be tied down. Even in marriage, the Fish guy will pursue his individual ambitions even if they take him on solo excursions or retreats far from his lady-wife. Subconsciously or not, he seems to feel that an older woman might understand the concept of cling-free love, if only through hard-knocks experience. He cringes at the thought of some cleaving ingenue who will undoubtedly expect to be conventionally attached at the hip. Think of that Cupid–Psyche myth wherein the god of Love demands not to reveal himself, but simply to be loved without ever having it known who he is. This is unconditional love, devoid of any importance placed on appearances or ownership. He searches a woman's soul for this invisible quality – indeed, it would seem the contents of a woman's psyche are more readily visible to the Pisces's eye than are her style of dress or makeup. Perhaps as a result of the 12th House's association with *freedom from social barriers,* the Fish falls for women who exaggeratively color outside the lines – despite his own fussy appearance, his visibly incongruous mate may be the proverbial peroxide blonde, outfitted in the most outrageous manner.

Unlike his opposite sign of Virgo, Pisces is not a conscious Svengali trying to physically change the appearance of his mate. As befits our Fishy fellow, Pisces brings about a lover's change on an unseen, subconscious level, such that a woman might find herself transforming from the inside out. Pisces man is attracted to so-called guttersnipes, and in his loving them unconditionally, they tend to undergo an alteration all of their own volition. Mary Magdalene was literally loved into changing – Jesus didn't simply pick her out some new clothes. This is the effect Pisces man has on friends, as well as lovers. Since he has absolutely no expectations of others, those who want to win his affections end up jumping through hoops to please him – basically following in his footsteps, often vividly straining to win his favor. In this way, he turns those with whom he *enters* a love relationship into his disciples, worded as such since it doesn't seem as if Pisces ever *falls* in love per se. His form of loving is so removed and devoid of expectation as to border on apathy. Ironically, though he asks less of a partner than any other man in the zodiac, relationships are mainly all about him. It's little wonder behavioral psychologist B. F. Skinner was a Pisces as the Fish guy interacts with loved ones, albeit subconsciously, on a system of punishment and reward. Without ever saying a word, Pisces man will either tune in or tune out his partner based on her comportment. If he's pleased by his mate, she'll have his attention. If not, he leaves the proverbial building. And so a spouse or lover learns to conform to such manners so as to win the prize of even his vaguest recognition. Ever in his protective bubble, an in-box out-box system described by those opposite-facing fish, the Pisces decides what is jetsam and what is flotsam in his experience.

Even in love, the human filter system that is the Pisces man is in a sense designed to not create undo karma. Those opposite-facing fish are rather an illustration of the soulful mechanism of the elimination of karma — good in, bad out. This is, of course, in keeping with the sign's association with death: Conceptually speaking, the sign of Pisces is predicated on the employment of that 12th House ideal of *escape,* being able to jump off the karmic carousel (reincarnation) and apotheosize atman (individual soul) with Brahma (world soul). This is what the Pisces man is doing, here and now, daily — he simply doesn't become snared in entangling human drama, and only individuals who likewise create no undue karmic attachments are allowed to enter Pisces's custodial environment. Therefore he must, in turn, be loved purely and with no expectation. Most women who attempt to romance the Pisces end up singing 'I don't know how to love him.' He challenges potential partners to love in such a way as poets have described: by simultaneously setting him free, allowing him to escape into the solitude of his life's callings. This is the dynamic Pisces needs to keep love alive, and it is typically too unnerving for most women, or men for that matter, to abide. Even sex doesn't anchor the zodiac's drifter. If so, the Magdalenes of the world with whom he invariably hooks up would be able to rely on standard skills, not so hard-pressed to change attitude and behavior to cultivate a love bond with the unfathomable Fish guy.

Of all the gender signs in the zodiac, Pisces male is probably the least moved by sex. Not to say that his range of carnal experience doesn't outstrip the rest of the astrological population, because it generally does; it's just that sex doesn't much affect him one way or another. He could watch the most

Robert Altman
Sam Peckinpah
Luis Buñuel
Marcel Pagnol
Vincente Minnelli
Bernardo Bertolucci
Pier Paolo Pasolini
Spike Lee
Quincy Jones
Ralph Nader
Alan Greenspan
Rupert Murdoch
Bobby Fisher
Enrico Caruso
Lord Byron
W. H. Auden
Edward Albee
Robert Lowell
John Updike
Jeffrey Eugenides
Philip Roth
Victor Hugo
Ovid
Henrik Ibsen
John Steinbeck
Lytton Strachey
Wilhelm Grimm
Theodore Geisel
Tom Wolfe
John Irving
David Rabe
Kenneth Graham
Constantin Brancusi
Pierre Auguste Renoir
Ansel Adams
Piet Mondrian
Hubert de Givenchy
Andre Courreges
Albert Einstein
Rudolf Steiner
George Washington
Edward Kennedy
Peter Graves
Johnny Cash
Michelangelo
Rudolf Nureyev
Vaslav Nijinsky
Jack Kerouac
Maurice Ravel

hard-core porn with a roomful of grannies and not feel the slightest bit of embarrassment. Likewise, he can enter a decadent sexual landscape, even as a vague participant (which is the only kind he might ever be) and surface unscathed, without any residual battering to his peace of mind. As he's the personification of Eros, nothing shocks the Pisces, and by the same token, he finds nothing to be of overwhelming fascination. He remains outside sexual experience. Thus, it's often actually easier for him to put himself into environments where he can acknowledge and appreciate even blatant carnality without his own intimate involvement. Interestingly, in clinical psychological terms, the Eros refers to the instincts for self-preservation in people. Herein, we see the ultimate Piscean-male paradox as befits this character whose sign's Fish is a symbol of yin and yang: He is all and nothing, in everything he does. Christ-like to the core, he can go to hell and back again with his entire being unshaken and intact. No character will go further in his exploration of eroticism, a term primarily defined as the sexual quality of an experience, particularly those of an abnormal nature, rather than meat-and-potatoes sex, which to him is just ho-hum. Lest we forget, Neptune is the planet of imagery, and the Piscean sexual persona lives in this elusive realm. He thus appreciates quality erotica, and he's generally game to film and/or star in his own home movies, never one to consider such activities sleazy. Indeed, being the only mutable-water man, Pisces is metaphorically no stranger to primordial slime, which is why he could easily attend that sex venue, whether it be an orgy or the goings-on at some after-hours club, though, as easily as not. When he does, he will typically just pass through, perhaps stopping long enough to chat up some woman – having good conversation in a landscape of otherwise writhing, moaning bodies being the picture of Piscean insouciance – recruiting yet another disciple if not fishing in the murky mire for some would-be Magdalene to spiritually mold into his very own Madonna. In said instance, how could such a soul not get the sense she was being saved? Granted, the presence of the typically prissy Pisces in such a place might make anybody feel self-conscious; and despite this extreme example, the fact remains that the Fish guy tends to force others, particularly potential partners, to search their own soul and conscience and try to remove any impediments to their own peace of mind. Unlike the Pisces onlooker, it could be argued that most people who might be found groping in the dark of some sex joint are doing so as a result of some past trauma or compulsion, not truly, therefore, out of choice.

Not just notoriously prim and artsy, Pisces can also appear rather androgynous if not outright sexless – this is one instance where appearances are not necessarily deceiving. It makes sense, given his association with the sweet hereafter, that he is as genderless as one might imagine a pure spirit to be. Since adolescence, the Fish may have been startlingly aware that he doesn't fall prey to his libido the way others do. Sex doesn't strike him as a fresh or foreign concept, even in tenderest youth, and the natural transcendence with which he regards it at once makes him feel estranged from, and superior to, other males in particular. Instead of seeing himself as abnormal, he labels others as 'lesser' and holds himself up as that much more of a supreme being. That he's not sexually prolific doesn't bother Pisces guy in the least. The truth of the matter is, as the sexual urge is basically, biologically aimed at procreation and therefore linked to other creative energies, Pisces inherently channels such forces as might be aimed at his groin up toward his imaginative mind and crafty hands – not so much lacking libido as converting it into his signature artistic fuel. Sex is so not a big deal, a Pisces truism that may extend to his absolute understanding and forgiveness should a partner stray and hit the sack with someone else. The Fish is no hypocrite: He allows his partner the same kind of personal freedom he in turn demands from a mate, letting her experiment and make her own mistakes. The Pisces himself doesn't typically 'cheat' as a rule because it creates the kind of karmic baggage he simply cannot abide. That sense of freedom is enough; he needn't, and rarely does, exploit it, especially when in a committed relationship or marriage contract. For Pisces is among the most steadfast of men, apt to stay put in a bond with the same woman, the sanctity of which falls within the protective sphere with which he perpetually seeks to surround himself. Marriage, especially, is a womb wherein he can drift and dream and into which he can dissolve.

Another reason the Piscean might be so forgiving of even a spouse's extramarital dalliances is because he knows he doesn't always deliver in the rough-and-ready manner many a woman desires. His relationships are, first and foremost, spiritual marriages, and he won't necessarily begrudge his lady the luxury of that sort of meat-and-potatoes sexual experience he isn't wont to provide with any frequency. Then there's the age-old Piscean problem with just plain old getting it up. Sometimes, he needs a stronger erotic impetus than mere routine urges. As Pisces's long-term partners will readily agree, sex tends to happen more often than not when they're away from home: Having escaped the confines of routine reality, the Fish invariably finds his penis becomes that much perkier. Having to sneak or hide having sex – whether doing it in public, on a train or plane, or even slipping away if just to another room during a visit to friends – is not just a theoretical turn-on particular to Pisces man, it's often an essential practical part of sex play. In certain cases, the exotic is so alluring that he might only be able to have sex with strangers, even prostitutes, while his

STR8 TURN-ONS

aggressive, older women
zaftig builds
gothic beauty
corsets, garters, stockings
hardcore porn
prostitutes
role-reversal
submission, slaving
(active/passive) bondage
(active) humiliation
(active) oral
giving pearl necklaces
feet, shoes
voyeurism, straight couples
rubber, latex
(passive) watersports
being cuckolded/cuckolding
infantilism
lipstick, nail polish
tag-teaming
dungeons
alcohol, downers, narcotics
kink
strangers

marriage becomes a hands-off, strictly soulful bond. Drink and drugs, those proverbial Piscean fixes of forgetfulness, tend to provide enough of a crutch to keep the Fish's sex life, pardon the pun, limping along. Still, Pisces simply doesn't require the amount of sex that most men do. The 12th House rules both *convent* and *monastic life,* and Pisces and his partner, despite their often awkward attempts to keep up appearances to the contrary, might very well live a rather chaste domestic existence. Of course, as suspect as people generally are of the Piscean male's sexual identity, outsiders are always willing to jump to their own conclusions.

From early childhood the Pisces is often ridden for being a sissy. Though he meets such derision with a proud pacifism, typically turning the other cheek and never dignifying such ridicule, this sort of haranguing only further contributes to a sexlessness in the Piscean's nature, rather than forcing him to either repress or overcompensate for any preferences that he may or may not have. Instead, the Fish simply rises above the issue altogether and sweeps it into the 12th House dustbin. It's just that much more psychic surgery he'll perform on himself, dissolving the issue along with any other problematic concerns that cross his path. The last thing in life that the Pisces will tolerate is any sort of stigma being attached to him. Society still being the way it is vis-à-vis homosexuality, the Piscean would just as soon skirt the issue of any same-sex feelings he might have, often refusing to lend them any credence. So quickly will he nip such inklings in the bud that it will often be unclear, even to the Pisces himself, which way the wind might have ended up blowing for him. An astrological androgyne in any case, this man born into this über-feminine of zodiacal signs might be the most effeminate heterosexual you ever meet, even if he's never actually had a gay thought in his head. And even if the Pisces does declare himself gay, he might never do so formally. An undeniably homosexual sector of Piscean men, however, could never kid themselves, let alone anybody else, that they are anything but card-carrying queers. This nearly biologically female, lisping, limp-wristed sect of Piscean gay men, were they born into some expansive-thinking Native American tribe, would undoubtedly be prized and offered the shaman's special tepee. Indeed, sexuality aside, a large part of the transgendered community seem to be made up of Pisces men who rival the Taurus male population for the title: 'Most likely to undergo sexual reassignment surgery'. Aside from this distinct sector of undeniably gay Pisceans, who, incidentally, are often so caught up in their own intriguing natures that the issue of sex takes a decided backseat, while across the board, the sexuality of the Fish man, straight and gay, remains, well, fishy.

The gay Pisces, but for the aforementioned enclave, is generally a pretty hardy, masculine character, like his straight counterpart, all but fully focused on his career, also a decidedly creative one, making little of his sexual proclivities. For starters, he doesn't much mingle with other men, the bulk of his friendships being with single, somewhat fag-haggish women whom he tends to take under his wing and instruct on the more fascinating, if not the finer, things in life. Pisces, of any sexual persuasion, isn't ever caught up in materialism even when he embarks on moneymaking ventures. Rather, he seeks to buy freedom and the opportunity to color his world with the imaginative brush he brandishes. In his soul, he's a bohemian, and the gay Piscean in particular will inhabit a world of fringe or indeed forgotten artists, filmmakers, designers, and other innovators (typically like himself) who exhibit a certain evolutionary cultural vision. It's this which he hopes will rub off on his coterie of female friends, for whom he often plays surrogate husband, coming over to fix this or paint that, all the while exposing these bosomed buddies to the music, art, and other such influences that decorate his life. In such relationships we see that Jesus–Magdalene connection almost ridiculously crystal clear. Being that Virgo woman, specifically, falls under this female archetype, the world is populated with pairings of spinsterish Virgo girls and the gay Piscean guys who love them.

Queer Pisces is even that much more an unbeholden drifter than his straight counterpart. He generally gravitates toward artistic jobs that see him working whatever professional magic he possesses, going from place to place. A career as a photographer, stylist, writer, and the like suits him best, one where he never need be in the same spot for long. He is notorious for finding some terribly inexpensive flight to some far-flung exotic destination and, never carrying much literal or metaphoric baggage with him, becoming immediately immersed in said milieu, mixing and mingling with foreign strangers. He'll even live this sort of life back home, where he has an infamously low overhead – even a single room suits him fine, though he will whip it up into a decorator's paradise, living as if inside a dream landscape of his own elaborate design. As such, he's free to take up any long-weekend invitation or to house-sit for the league of well-heeled women and married couples who make up the bulk of his friends. A societal orphan, he often seeks, in a sense, to be adopted by his straight-couple cronies for whom he'll also pop over and cook a meal, decorate a room, or fix the plumbing in return for their affection. Pisces doesn't tend to have many gay male friends. Like his straight brother, he is rather unlibidinous and cynically prejudiced toward oversexed people. Meanwhile, he is incredibly secretive as to the types of activities he does get up to, when venturing forward to get his ya-yas out. He isn't much into bars as a means of meeting men, being happy to have a few cocktails but bored with

GAY TURN-ONS

straight, married men
masters, daddies, bears
body hair
Africans, Scandinavians
suits, dress socks
bikers, skinheads
(passive) lite s + m
(passive) heavy b + d
rubber, latex
(passive) anal penetration
(active) rimming, scat
substances, anesthetics
sailors
onanism
rough trade
(passive) torture
humiliation
backrooms, sex clubs
cross-dressing
pantyhose, nylons
branding, piercing
enemas
foreskin
(passive) discipline
hoods, blindfolds, gags

the ritual of cruising and chitchat: he'd prefer to get more directly to the point. As gay life provides more of the kind of dark, vague, dreamlike environments that Pisces man of any persuasion appreciates, the gay Fish finds no lack of venues to provide him anonymous, wraithlike erotic involvements. He never throws himself into the mosh pit of some orgiastic scene; rather, he floats around the periphery of such settings waiting to focus his typically orally fixated penchants on other such loners as strike his fancy. Even in such an environment, however, the Pisces is extremely picky, drawn to overtly masculine men whom he might even assume lead straight lifestyles back on the other side of the veil. This is, in fact, Pisces's biggest turn-on. Ironically, he is cynically prejudiced toward men who call themselves bisexual – his other notorious allergy is toward gay girls. However, if he comes across a fellow who is fiercely attached to labeling himself straight, except for what he might get up to with the Piscean guy alone, this is sexual nirvana for the Fish. A sign that boasts Michelangelo, Pier Paolo Pasolini, Jack Kerouac, and Lou Reed among its ranks, the Pisces man is homoerotic in the extreme. That fine line between straight and gay provides endless fascination for him stemming from his youth, wherein his first experience is often with a macho, closeted so-called heterosexual. As he matures, he gravitates toward such types, who tend to be of certain ethnic extractions, particularly Southern European or North African, where gay/straight boundaries are more readily blurred. Short of moving to a Greek fishing village, the infamously lithe and pretty Pisces does his best to land a type of man with whom much is left unspoken and the banal realities of their lives are checked at the bedroom door. This special someone, even though remaining a love for many years, might nonetheless just come and go, forming a bond with the Pisces that is thus comprised of a series of dreamy, vague interludes, which suits our fine Fish fellow just fine.

Couplings

Pisces Man / Aries Woman
With this ultrareceptive man, she softens, stimulating maternal instincts. He's expected to clean up his emotional act or take his exit. Sex is no simple affair: She wants it long and hard; he's comfortable cuddling.

Pisces Man / Taurus Woman
Allies: An emotional attachment develops instantly. He's ready to commit. If she accedes, life will be peaceful and productive. In bed, the focus is on entertainment – both require plenty of playful attention.

Pisces Man / Gemini Woman
Pisces appeals as a consort. He may hang on her every word. Together, worldly ambitions are given fullest focus; other aspects are often left in disrepair. Sexually, she gets a surprise: Mild Pisces makes many demands.

Pisces Man / Cancer Woman
They push each other's buttons, though with the best of intentions. An absorbing bond: He especially uncovers old burdens, healing in the process. Cancer opens up, too. Sex is an escape from stresses.

Pisces Man / Leo Woman
He's a mystery she's keen to uncover. Resolute, she pursues with a frightening intensity. Together, natural aptitudes turn a profit – everything is accomplished her way. Lovemaking moves at Leo's fast pace.

Pisces Man / Virgo Woman
Virgo is body-snatched by persuasive Pisces guy. Separating themselves from everyone, this pair is precariously complacent – laziness is often their undoing. In bed, she'll begin to expect the unexpected.

Pisces Man / Libra Woman
Pisces is the maestro orchestrating Libra's life, perhaps with a heavy hand. She can't resist his inspiration. She's his muse. Best-case scenario: Their collaborations become classics. Sex is an ecstatic exploration of the senses.

Pisces Man / Scorpio Woman
It seems something's being kept hidden. At best, they're a confident, conscientious couple with big dreams they intend to realize. In bed, decorum is their default demeanor. Sex is subdued, but never standard.

Pisces Man ∫ Sagittarius Woman

Each requires some solitude to survive this busy bond. Liberation might be their modus operandi; everything else is secondary. Pisces reassures Sag of her sex appeal. She finds new ways to get him going.

Pisces Man ∫ Capricorn Woman

At its core, a friendship founded on fondness and respect. Thick as thieves, they're protective of each other, fiercely loyal and endlessly understanding: Capricorn, especially, serves as 'savior' to Pisces. Naturally, sex is tender.

Pisces Man ∫ Aquarius Woman

A fast and furious courtship for this couple. Beneath slick exteriors lie deeply soulful individuals seeking a source of inspiration. Their sex life reflects such profundity – in bed they move as if possessed, even hexed.

Pisces Man ∫ Pisces Woman

A dizzying dynamic. Fate seems to have brought them together. Sometimes they stagger toward goals, but they usually arrive. Life is heightened – a too emotional approach is a possible pitfall. In bed, foreplay is foremost.

Gay

Pisces Man ∫ Aries Man

Often a purely physical pairing. Pisces man is unusually shallow in his perception of virile Aries as a mere sexual tool. Under such corrupting influence, the Ram's barbaric, conquering erotic spirit emerges.

Pisces Man ∫ Taurus Man

Pisces seems that 'missing link' in Taurus's life. It's a symbiotic bond. Being with the Bull is like a dream come true. Life is productive, professional goals are met – and more. In bed, selfish motives are put aside.

Pisces Man ∫ Gemini Man

Gemini is the 'little brother' to the Pisces mentor. The odd Fish guy will abuse such influence, reducing a green Gemini to mere minion. Sex is masterful, both an erotic work of art and a chance for Pisces to dominate.

Pisces Man ∫ Cancer Man

Together, they probe remote corners of experience – spiritual exploration is a possibility. Soul-searching enhances their chances of relationship success. They both crave romance and often find it with each other.

Pisces Man / Leo Man

A head-trippy gay-guy duo. Egos clash and verbal sparring is expected. Holding out emotionally becomes a game that no one wins. In bed, peace is restored – this is where these boys shine.

Pisces Man / Virgo Man

They want to change the world. And it's worth trying. Still, one or both may go to extremes in pursuing a utopian vision. Regardless, they escape into ideology. Sexually, they're fickle fellows, so variety is key.

Pisces Man / Libra Man

As a couple, they're complex: Pisces is unpredictable, Libra is easily thrown off-balance. To boot, both boast a love of the high life – who's holding down the home front? At the first sign of trouble, they take to the sheets.

Pisces Man / Scorpio Man

A peaceful and productive pairing, especially if Pisces is the older of the two. Over time, they cultivate an avant-garde aesthetic that appeals to outsiders. Sex might be rough – Scorpio plays at being 'trade.'

Pisces Man / Sagittarius Man

The Archer admires and often emulates the poised Piscean. It's a surprise to see Sag put through his (psychological and sexual) paces. In bed, it's all about role-play: Sag is subject to the imperious Fish.

Pisces Man / Capricorn Man

With fishy Pisces, Cap's serpentine side surfaces. But rather than expanding, the Goat meanders more, perhaps losing his way. Still, they have clever ways to capitalize on their strengths. It's an effort to keep sex lite.

Pisces Man / Aquarius Man

Self-satisfied souls: Finally, Aquarius and Pisces quit trying to change. Spiritual purity is often their mutual modus operandi. Together, they simply stop stressing. In bed, egos are abandoned.

Pisces Man / Pisces Man

'Let's get lost' might be their catchphrase. Left unchecked, this Pisces pair often escapes into subversive activity. Regardless, a so-called normal lifestyle often eludes them. Sexually, both expect to experiment.

Pisces Woman

the dream

Though she is the last lady in the zodiac, Pisces is astrology's undisputed prima donna. The proverbial Everywoman, she is the culmination, and an often chilling compilation, of all the other women who come before her on the wheel. A walking-talking paradox – all virtue and all vice wrapped up in one deceivingly demure package – she is at once victimized by and victorious over life. An empath of the first order, Pisces personalizes experience to such a degree that she is incapable of separating her emotions even from the most removed circumstance. She is drama personified, making a fuss over her every feeling and impression. Existence is a loaded affair for Pisces woman – overwhelming to her impressionable, high-strung nature. Then again, she will seem tough as nails, a true survivor who grows through even the most negative of experiences; and truth be told, Pisces has more than her fair share of hard knocks. Still, she is a cultivated creature, and regardless of the conditions of her upbringing, there will always be something decidedly high-hat to her countenance. She craves solitude, yet her escapist instincts ironically require others to do her bidding; thusly, she maintains a necessary connection to the world. Though, in her youth, she is attracted to sensitive, callow fellows who are even more fragile than she, Pisces will eventually settle down with an assiduous man who'll treat her like a princess, providing emotional sanctuary and proper pampering. With other women, she is at once acutely submissive and withholding of her affections, inspiring a partner to constantly please and appease her.

XII

The Principle of Dissolution, suggesting susceptibility and immateriality. Pisces woman lives in blissful oblivion, an unbeholden soul for whom life means sinking ever deeper into the unseen, eternal realities of existence. Her sign's motto, 'I believe,' would best be followed by the phrase 'only love transcends this mortal coil and keeps the wheel of life perpetually turning.'

Sign + Mind

From the perspective of astrological evolution, one could easily begin this book not with a chapter on Aries man but with one on Pisces woman. The sign represents the alpha and the omega, and whereas Aries guy embodies the energy of birth, his sign being associated with the age group 0–7, the Pisces woman embodies the zodiacal age group 77–84, which represents the advent of death. She is rather likened to the primordial soup from which life springs, whether individually in the womb or, on a universal scale, the teething slime from whence the first organisms slithered. Pisces is the only mutable-water sign in the zodiac, thus pointing to, amongst other interpretations, the concept of a quintessential sea-of-change. Fittingly, planet Neptune, named for the Roman god of the sea (Greek: Poseidon), primarily presides over Pisces, while planet Jupiter is considered the sign's secondary ruler. The trident glyph of Neptune is the illustration of a holy trinity of sorts, which, in the case of Pisces woman, reflects the manifestation of the triple goddess – ancient female deities traditionally took triple form. And whereas all the females signs that precede Pisces on the wheel generally draw on one or sometimes two specific aspects of any given goddess-archetype, Pisces metaphorically derives her persona from the triplicate form of the goddess – virgin, mother, and crone – all at once. Though watered down into the lovely Greek goddess of love who emerged from the sea foam on that infamous half shell, parentless or fathered by Uranus, whose semen fertilized the waters upon his castration, Aphrodite (Roman: Venus) was originally the Great Goddess or Sea Mother, recognized in triple manifest, who ruled birth, life, and death as well as the province of love. She is also called Mari, who took the form of a giant fish and is thus synonymous with the Christian Mary, meaning 'sea,' who appears in triplicate at, for instance, the death and burial of Christ. Borrowing from this weighty archetype, Pisces's status as the zodiac's Everywoman shouldn't be taken lightly. She is at once as beatific as the Madonna, worldly wise as the Magdalene, and mysterious as that other Mary who unpredictably pops in and out of biblical lore.

The actual manifestation of Pisces's archetypal legacy is practically palpable. First of all, as anyone familiar with the Fish lady will readily admit, she is no easy personality to pin down. She is at turns warm, aloof, accessible, untouchable, dignified, petty, righteous, and unscrupulous. She can be an emotional rock one second and seemingly ready to snap the next. She is the best of friends and a backstabbing bitch. And as her yin-yang, opposite-facing-fish glyph suggests, she is opposites fused into an irrepressible singularity –

curiously, just like life. Indeed, Pisces is a living testament to there being good and bad in everything, and everyone, such opposites being inextricably linked – life and everybody living it, she reminds us, expresses this same paradox. She may be thus equally lovable and despicable, just as any respectable diva should be. Like a mermaid or siren singing her mesmerizing song, which sees those drawn to it dashed upon the rocks or drowned, Pisces woman is the most enticing and enchanting of creatures; yes she can be incredibly difficult if not dangerous to navigate. Indeed, Neptune represents the Principle of Dissolution and the world of illusions, enchantment, imagery, and life lived on the metaphoric, imaginary plane. The 12th Astrological House (under Neptune's rule) is likewise that of, amongst other attributes, *sustained subjectivity,* which connotes a sort of dream state, ongoing trance, or delusion. Welcome to Pisces woman's world. Water represents emotions and impressions, as well as love and a feminine source of divinity, and our mutable Fish woman is a swirling mass of subjective notions and contemplative imaginings. On one level, she can be rather self-delusional, fancying truths about herself – some might call it lying – albeit so convincingly that she can't help but believe them herself. In fact, each time the Pisces recounts the same tale (and she does repeat herself), the plot invariably thickens, the tension builds, and her role in the drama becomes that much more exaggerated and exalted. As well, she approaches her relationship with the world from an inside-out perspective, by trusting in her own insights, rather than any hard-and-fast external facts to corroborate or disprove these views. She exercises this metaphoric muscle more than most people, which is why the sign often boasts psychics among its ranks – to the Piscean female mind, practice in extrasensory perception makes perfect. Those intimately associated with the Fish will forever applaud or pooh-pooh her ability to search and extract the contents of a person's psyche. Indeed, she does so soul-to-soul, keying into one's spiritual conscience, reading that person's 'energy,' infiltrating by tapping into and channeling others' still, small voices. Her ability to recognize and speak to one's emotional or moral condition may be uncanny. As an encounter with Pisces woman is often nothing short of cathartic.

There is, of course, a downside to being so, well, impressionable. For one, Pisces can be a real follower; especially in her youth, she is easily swayed by the opinions and demands of others. The zodiac's Everywoman is engineered to put on as many faces as people she meets, feeling a certain amount of expectation from each encounter. She wants to be loved universally. So should someone so much as look at her sideways, the sensitive Pisces can easily dissolve into tears. In an effort to feel sociable, she may not be a pillar of strength when

PLANETARY SYMBOL

Neptune is the planet of illusion and immateriality. It signals a need to experience life from a perspective devoid of practical or ideological structure. It makes Pisces woman a channel to unseen planes of inspiration, just as it can leave her mediumship open to spiritual or mystical experiences of the first order. It is the symbol of the triple goddess.

SIGN QUADRANT

The zodiacal quadrants correspond to metaphysical planes of existence – physical, emotional, mental, and spiritual or universal. The Fourth Quadrant is concerned with one's relationship with the eternal. Whereas Capricorn practices active faith and Aquarius strives for concrete truth, Pisces represents the energy of love, the power of creation and indeed procreation.

The opposite-facing Fish of Pisces are mythic totems of Eros and Aphrodite. They signify the alpha and the omega and the yin-yang (male-female) construct of the universe as the reunited primal androgyne. It is a symbol of the world as a womb, fish being embryonic emblems of a dual system of incoming nourishment and outgoing elimination.

ELEMENT + QUALITY

The water element connotes emotion and intuition; the mutable quality, a call for versatility and change. Together the mutable-water combination particular to Pisces is best described as the primordial soup from which all life sprang on a universal level, just as every human being was formed in the dreamy embryonic fluid of the womb. The combination is also characterized by fog, mist, and foam, like that from which Aphrodite was born.

faced with the opportunity to partake of substances, in particular alcohol or drugs, which contribute to her signature desire to live, to some degree, in oblivion. Neptune's dissolution is a concept akin to the sign's association with the advent of death, the proverbial return to the primordial soup from whence one came as befits the sign's mutable-water status. Pisces female often feels a deep need to dissolve: She avoids the spotlight in her pursuits, forever bent upon preserving total anonymity. As a naturally excitable type, she may learn early on that a quick snort or two will steady her nerves. Indeed, Pisces's association with the 12th House, that linked not only with *withdrawal from reality* but also *emotional blocks,* will see the Fish dropping herself into the drink more readily than most.

The irony here is that, physiologically, Pisces may be unable to tolerate even the slightest substance use. As the zodiac's daughter of befuddling Neptune, she is more susceptible than many to influences of this sort. Those who've pursued paths toward some brand of enlightenment often speak of the increasing danger of introducing artificial properties into their bodies as they achieve higher and higher levels of spiritual realization. Pisces woman is born with that sort of advanced spiritual openness, one that seems to leave her that much more vulnerable to deep intoxication, and even psychic, if not psychotic, episodes, as a result of such usage. Not that this will easily stop the Fish lady from trying to 'get lost.' However, the profound rock bottom Pisces inevitably hits will give rise to a wholehearted new lease on life – invariably, the recovered Pisces becomes a champion for spiritual wellness. Until then, however, she is generally in the business of medicating her soul, one way or another, attempting to evade the darker recesses of her subconscious mind that threaten to undo her.

As early as she can remember, Pisces woman is haunted by her past. Though she will undoubtedly love her mother, she views her as somewhat of an albatross – typically, her mother is a pragmatist who is plagued by pessimism, if not crippling doubts and fears; Pisces becomes her emotional anchor. Her father, by contrast, is a carefree individualist who feels unbeholden to family life. He is sensitive, possessing the soul of the poet, but marriage doesn't much agree with him. He may be a reckless or hapless character. Whereas her siblings might use any laissez-faire family dynamic to overindulge their own independence, if not express abandon or rebellion, Pisces plays the goody-goody, dutiful daughter to the hilt. She represses her need for autonomy, exchanging personal will for a certain martyrdom that comes from being 'old reliable.' Herein the seeds of resentment are sown. As a nod to her sign's association with sanctuary, Pisces leads a fairly sheltered existence by her own design. To peers, she is the proverbial priss or prude, one who prefers to stay attached to her mother's apron strings, eeking out whatever attention she might from her lovably untenable father, rather than focusing on the pursuit of a social life. What she perceives as the best quality in her father is his soulful sensitivity, indeed his vulnerability, and it is that very ingredient she looks for first in a boy. She mixes with other meek types like herself and is generally attracted to namby-pamby males whose eventual sexual identities may be dubious. Pisces is the most patently unrealistic of individuals when it comes to life and love, as is blatantly evident in the so-called romantic relationships of her youth. Still, being so sheltered, Pisces girl is rather squeamish about the opposite sex at this tender age, a sentiment that is only exacerbated by the early run-ins with at least some vague form of molestation she generally encounters.

Perhaps as a nod to Pisces's association with the 12th House concerns of *hidden dangers* and *secret enemies,* the curtained Fish girl seems so unwitting that she unfortunately finds herself falling prey, in some way, to lecherous types. Even the subtlest encounter may send Pisces reeling. Still, as is her nature, she will completely repress the incident, unconsciously rendering herself that much more skittish and susceptible to emotional fragility. Not only will this be the root cause of a need to anesthetize her secret suffering in some way and give rise to the subjective sustainment of a fabricated reality – the Fish's intricate woven net of casual lies designed to protect her from painful truths – it also determines her taste for males she feels might be harmless. All through her teenage years and into her twenties, she will take up with guys who are all but noticeably lacking in the requisite testosterone to fuel their pouncing on our supposedly prissy Pisces. On one hand, she wants it this way: She cannot abide the harsh hormonal reality of a male's pressing hard-on to have her – she prefers to live in a sanitized dream of what sex should be, just as she seeks to obliterate all other brutal realities in life, which she mostly avoids by sticking close to the safety and seclusion of her home, first that of her parents, and then her enchanted own. One is reminded of Sally Bowles in John Van Druten's play *I Am a Camera,* the story upon which the musical *Cabaret* is based, a character with a tad of an Electra complex like our Pisces who thus invents for herself an entire personalized reality via the enchantment of her own imagination, a role, incidentally, immortalized on-screen by the very Fishy Liza Minnelli. As in the case of Sally Bowles, we see tragedy and exaltation cohabitating in the character of the Pisces female, for whom life really should be a cabaret. Indeed, what the Pisces woman teaches us, by example, is that existence is exactly what one imagines it to be, something that lends more loaded meaning to her sign's motto, 'I believe.'

POLARITY

Females in feminine (earth, water) signs are aligned with the gender polarity of their sign and thus embody the quality-element combination of the sign. The mutable-water status of Pisces determines that she is like the ever-changing sea as well as the primordial soup or nurturing womb from whence all life springs. The sea represents an illusory dream-time, Pisces recognizing little difference between what is imaginary and what is true or possible.

12

SIGN NUMBER

The number of divinity. Considered the higher vibration of the number three, which twelve reduces to, when its two digits are added together. There are twelve tribes of Israel, twelve stations of the cross, twelve zodiacal signs, twelve Olympian gods.

77–84

The age of death. This period represents the sleep of death and dissolution. Pisces woman personifies a limbo or sort of dream state, the primordial spiritual soup between death and rebirth. She 'lives' in that mysterious realm, most often a psychic recipient of information and inspiration being communicated from the immaterial realm.

PSYCHOLOGY

Pisces is often overly passive and codependent. She may suffer from certain fears and anxieties, including agoraphobia, and be susceptible to drug and alcohol abuse. She can live in a world of fantasy and be pathologically dishonest. She sometimes lacks ambition despite her love for luxury. As a partner or parent she can be inappropriately overbearing and overprotective.

Unlike Pisces man, female Pisces isn't content to dream all on her own. Rather, she expects others to buy into the enchantment she creates for herself, such that all those who populate her life succumb to the mass hallucination that she is what she imagines herself to be. Furthermore, Pisces urges others to be all that they might wildly imagine *themselves* to be. In view of her motto, she believes in others' dreams, inspiring them as a muse, coming to reflect the utter conviction that one's fantasies are capable of coming true via the strength of belief alone. After all, despite what could be perceived as self-delusion, the Pisces woman literally thinks who the hell she is. Admittedly, being the zodiacal embodiment of the primordial soup, the Pisces is predestined to imagine any and all potentialities as might emerge from her fertile power of fancy. Thus, she is the most fabulous female on the astrological block, in every sense of the word, from the marvelous to the made-up. Being a child of Neptune, planet of the wondrous, even the miraculous, Pisces is a conduit for such energy as is represented by her ruling planet – little wonder that the Virgin Mary is her biblical archetype. The whole notion of the womb as a miraculous environment, the seat of quintessentially mutable waters, isn't lost on the symbology of the sign of Pisces. In Greek, the word for womb and fish is the same, *delphi;* and as the Fish, the mutable-water woman is herself likened to a womb just as, in perfect paradox, she represents a tomb, both environments denoting a 12th House sense of *isolation* and *oblivion,* an in-between dream state hovering amidst the ultimate opposites of life and death – the consumate interpretation of the sign's opposite-facing fish. In brass tacks, being the alpha and the omega translates into the Piscean female's fancying herself the 'be all, end all' of womankind. Despite her meek and meager emotional beginnings, the sometimes phenomenal myth Pisces creates about herself seeps into her very soul. Eventually, she owns the outsized persona of her own creating. Would that we were all such believers in ourselves, whether our legacy was based in fact or fiction – two more interpretations of the opposite-facing fish that fuse into one singular reality in the Piscean female mind. Fabulous is as fabulous does, and our Fishy female is the most over-the-top dame to spin round the astrological wheel. As a nod to her sign's association with death and dissolution, it's as if she approaches life with a built-in hindsight akin to the old lament 'If I had it to live all over again . . . ,' making such amends, automatically, as she goes. She has the confidence, even, of her most dubious convictions (or is it a total lack of self-esteem?) to feel she has nothing to lose by being as extraordinary a character as she can. Either way, her divadom is assured. As the personification of dissolution, Pisces inevitably surrenders to life, sacrificing her humility along with the strict responsibility she imposed on herself in youth. She is completely unbeholden to others, just as she is more reliant upon people than any other individual in the zodiac. This is, after all, the mark of a true diva. Like Tennessee Williams's Blanche DuBois from his play *A Streetcar Named Desire,* the most startlingly clear portrayal of the Piscean female archetype in modern literature, the Fish lady depends on the kindness of everybody, strangers included. The whole of her life is one huge trust exercise whereby she lets herself free-fall, fully believing there will always be outstretched arms to catch her.

Body + Soul

Pisces woman causes a commotion without even knowing it. Though she fancies herself fairly demure and ladylike, she has the distinct ability to send those around her into a bit of a tailspin. The polite princess on first impression, she will, for instance, drive a waiter nuts asking for a new glass or utensils should they be even slightly spotted, insisting on knowing every ingredient and mode of preparation of items on the menu – never seeming quite satisfied with the answers – and ordering her food and drinks with substitutions and special directives, sending her meal back if it isn't just so; and yet, at that point, should her dish still not be to her liking, she'll slip into martyr mode and – she'll have one know – suffer through it on the grounds of not wanting to be a bother. Too late. Perfection, according to her subjective specifications, is something of a preoccupation for Pisces, and she is constantly put off by the searing lack of it in her life. Sometimes there is just no pleasing her. Like Blanche, Pisces expects enchantment in every moment; but this can't help but elude her in the generally harsh light of reality. As the zodiac's Aphrodite, forever emerging fresh from her seashell, Pisces woman's constant reliance on others continually sees her courting disappointment if not personal disaster. But when it works, it does so like a charm: She is forever soliciting worshipers who find themselves hard-pressed to do right by her. She is clueless as to the turmoil little ol' Pisces is capable of causing, couched as she must generally be in the lap of luxury, though typically at someone else's expense. If any female stops short at a door, unapologetically waiting for it to be opened, it is the Fish. She truly is a muse, and as such she must have the homage due her; in return, she grants those in her life the endless gift of inspiration.

Pisces moves as if in a dream, her body language so slow and meditative that even when undertaking arduous physical tasks, one might suspect she is continually popping Valium. One sure way to spot a Pisces woman is in the

ARCHETYPE + MYTH

Pisces is associated with the triple goddess. She is the zodiac's everywoman, personifying feminity in all its aspects – virgin, mother, crone – at once. She is Aphrodite, the primal triple goddess, born from the foam of the sea, whose son Eros is also, ironically, the oldest of the gods, father of heaven and earth. This mirrors Mary as the mother of Christ, who is also the god of creation. Aphrodite's classical portrayal as the goddess of love lends insight into the Piscean character, who demands adoration more than any other woman. The nine Muses, the triple goddess in triplicate, depict Pisces's myriad talents. Water sprites, naiads, mermaids, and sirens portray how men often 'drown' for love of her.

BIBLE + LITERATURE

Pisces draws on the Mary archetype. Just as she is associated with the triple goddess, Pisces embodies all three Marys present in various Bible scenes. Mary is synonymous with Aphrodite–Mari and likewise personifies the sea. Her blue gown trimmed in white is akin to sea and foam. The Fish is both symbol of baby Jesus *and* of Mary's womb – the Greek word for 'womb' and 'fish' is the same as that for 'messiah'. In Arthurian lore, she is Morgain, Igraine, and Viviane. We see her in Lady Anne who forms a 'pietà' mourning Henry VI in Shakespeare's *Richard III*. She is Giraudoux's Ondine and Tennessee Williams's Blanche Dubois, whose own 'young boy' is killed – Blanche wears Mary's della Robbia blue gown. In the film *The Matrix*, the male savior, Neo, is linked with the female character Trinity.

way she eats: Cutting her food into manageable morsels, she chews each bite numerous times, placing her fork back on her plate and her hands daintily in her lap, making barely a dent in her meal by the time others have finished. She is entirely graceful in her carriage, sitting and standing erect as if toting the proverbial invisible book on her head. For all her seeming composure, however, Pisces is inherently nervous, her placid demeanor necessarily cultivated over the years in her attempt to 'keep it together.' Sometimes even the simplest things can set her teeth on edge – social gatherings, in particular, bare the essentially fragile Fish to an element for which she's simply not engineered. The thought of having to be 'on' makes the Pisces feel dangerously exposed, like Blanche held under an electric light. And she really isn't much interested in hearing tell of other people's lives, loved ones excepted. Though Pisces will have few female friends, she may flaunt a best gay-male pal. She will also be surrounded by people who, in one way or another, work for her, thus being paid to endure the peculiar Piscean prima donna. She prides herself on being a beneficent dictator, patting herself on the back for leaving a big tip or sending her housekeeper home with leftovers. What her regular waiter or cleaning lady mightn't realize is that they are just about all the extrafamilial human contact the Pisces has. It becomes very clear, in analyzing the Fish lady, that she not only relies on the kindness of strangers, but she often does so to the exclusion of others.

When called upon to be social, at a party say, the Pisces generally escapes into a corner, typically bending the ear of some unsuspecting character – she is naturally drawn to what she perceives as disenfranchised types. Though her patronizing attitude will be wholly unconscious, she latches onto whomever in the room she assumes might feel out of place (the way she does). So if you see a somewhat dramatic-looking creature with the elegantly eccentric gesticulations of an aging starlet chatting up the only Eskimo, old lady, burn victim, albino, or midget in the room, it's a pretty safe bet to assume she's a Pisces. The Fish lady doesn't so much have a conversation or recount stories as she does act them out. She literally channels experience as a means of communication, making hyperbolic sounds, taking large intakes of startled breath, or otherwise pantomiming that which she's discussing. She doesn't so much look a person in the eyes as she does sort of inward, lost in the private reliving of even the most ordinary occurrence. Pisces's eyes are at once bulging – though slitted as the result of heavy lids – misted, clouded, and often drifting in different directions. (When she drinks, the effect becomes that much more extreme.) Even when beautiful, there is something decidedly froggy or fetal about the Fish's appearance. When not particularly blessed with good looks, however, Pisces can end up looking somewhat like Edward G. Robinson in drag. Though again, this is typically not the case as suggested by a list of famous pointy-chinned Pisces princesses, including the sweet-faced, similar-looking likes of Elizabeth Taylor, Isabelle Huppert, Charlotte Church, Thora Birch, Cyd Charisse, Jennifer Jones, Claire Trevor, Jennifer Love Hewitt, Kristen Davis, Gloria Vanderbilt, Lee Radziwill, Paula Prentiss, Jennifer O'Neill, Vanessa Williams, Sharon Stone, Téa Leoni, Patsy Kensit, Niki Taylor, Ursula Andress, Kathy Ireland, Cindy Crawford – a lot of lovelies with more than their fair share of beauty marks. Still, many of them possess a frogginess in their gorgeous, bug-eyed looks, a trait strikingly evident in the more eccentric faces of Fishes such as Liza Minnelli (inherited from her Piscean father, Vincente), Drew Barrymore, Holly Hunter, Anna Magnani, Joanne Woodward, Jean Harlow, Sandy Duncan, Glenn Close, Nina Simone, Irene Cara, Ruth Bader Ginsburg, Sally Jessy Raphael, Rue McClanahan, and the ever-enjoyable drama queen Tammy Faye Bakker. Another giveaway is Pisces's tendency to speak out of the side of her mouth – as if everything she says is a confidential aside – just as she, figuratively, speaks out of both its sides. A nod to her opposite-facing-fish symbol, she is often guilty of playing all sides of an argument, feigning agreement with opposing factions among friends, family, or in professional experiences. She presents such a puritanical, if not pedantic, image that one would scarcely suspect her of gossiping or backbiting – but truth be told, she's an infamous tattletale, just as she's the stealthiest of snoops.

Pisces's typically straitlaced, bluenose appearance can be deceiving. She is, after all, one of the more sexually game girls in the zodiac. But that's not what people see first. She invariably presents a rather moral, virginal, if not downright uptight image, her mouth pursed, as it is, into a tense pucker, her generally pale, thin skin drawn tight in her face and throat, giving her the stringy, sinewy look of a ballet dancer whether or not she's ever stepped into a toe shoe in her life. She is fond of wavy hairstyles, regardless of whether she wears her locks short or long, and she will rarely leave the house without at least some hint of makeup, being drawn to green-blue eye shadows and pearlescent lip tones. Fairly hairless over all, Pisces often has a remarkable lack of eyelashes and eyebrows, necessitating the use of a liner to frame what are often unusually colored peepers – gold, bright green, cobalt blue. Indeed, only a Pisces like Elizabeth Taylor could be credited with unmistakably violet eyes. Of all the women in the zodiac, Pisces might be called the prettiest, that is, rarely a smoldering beauty, even when astonishingly gorgeous. What typically saves her boasting too perfect a doll face is a signature hooked nose, albeit button-sized – a crooked beak one might bait to catch a fish. Befitting her character, Pisces

12TH ASTROLOGICAL
HOUSE

spirituality
extrasensory perception
profound imagery
non-material existence
evasion/aversion
psychological fitness
inner strength or weakness
surrender to a higher power
secret goings-on
secret societies
healing solitariness
places of reflection
confinement/seclusion
difficulties/dilemma
limbo and oblivion
unfinished business
obstacles
hidden problems
subliminal endings
health of a society
health of a marriage
bodies of water
unseen danger
grief brought on self
self-deception
behind-the-scenes activity
sympathy
understanding
mysterious stimulus
escape and asylum
unreality
public welfare
breaking barriers
monasticism
martyrdom
empathy
selflessness
aptitude for the arts

KEYWORDS

love
symbiosis
grandeur
illusion
transcendence
clairvoyance
gentility
escape
reverie
compunction
reflection
beatitude
euphoria
delusion
vision
contemplation
devotion
decorum
intricacy
insouciance
prayer
divinity
timelessness
reliance
eroticism
incandescence
imperishability
affectation
enchantment
self-sacrifice
subtlety
immobility
inspiration
fascination
leisure
affluence
pulchritude
absolution
rumination
uncertainty
imagination

espouses a rather femmey fashion aesthetic – drawn to muted colors, meshy or webby knits, and tapered, princess-cut silhouettes. She can be New Age in style, too, wearing crystals, beads, and talismans for jewelry. She is generally understated in her appearance, forever determined to look like a lady. However, though she's loath to admit this to herself, the prim, indeed aristocratic persona that Pisces puts forth is just a delicate veneer begging to be shattered.

Unclad, she is something special to behold: Her skin soft and dewy, her figure curvaceous though compact. Even the most Rubenesque Fish, and there are some famous modern Burlesque queens who leap to mind, boast so integral a form that nothing extraneous will jiggle, just such bits that are meant to neatly bump and grind. There's rarely anything even slightly boyish in her physique, even when bone thin; and always, she exhibits an economy in her form, which prevents her from ever being overly bodacious in the bosom department – even when in the rare occasion she is amply hipped, she will still glide as if on a cloud. Her private parts are as demure as her character, her bush seemingly trimmed to a whisper whilst she's typically never required a single waxing in her life.

Sex + Sexuality

In the mythical character of Aphrodite, we see Pisces's complicated vision of sex. The great love goddess is wedded to the divine Everyman, Hephaestus, is ardently pursued by the brutally masculine Mars, but is most enamored of the delicate 'boy' Adonis. Blanche DuBois's first love, too, is a rather fragile youth – like Adonis, the tender fellow dies for the affection she heaps on him – and being rather stuck on these tender sorts, she is later run out of town for taking her teacher job too far with the juvenile male student-body. Blanche's Mars equivalent is Stanley – in the play, she even suspects he's an Aries, the male personification of the Mars–Ares archetype; and her Hephaestus, whom she aims to marry, is the safe, menschlike Mitch. Let's deconstruct: Most every Pisces woman will have a painful if not tragic memory of her first love for that 'sensitive' boy, a bond that was never meant to be. Blanche's family home, the aptly named Belle Reve, symbolizes her beautiful dreams, including the (Piscean) delusional hope of love shared with a harmless, hormoneless boy. And the fanciful Fish is forced to ditch her delusions when faced with a similarly harsh reality: The pretty boys she's attracted to in her youth are themselves often attracted to the macho men who make her bristle. Any lifelong lust for ambiguous jailbait notwithstanding, Pisces eventually realizes her own attraction to these sexy beasts, too, finding herself at delicious odds with the more blatantly red-blooded males of the world who give off a whiff of base animalism to her refined signature hooked nose. She inherently feels that such overtly masculine types are nearly another species, altogether separate from herself. The mythical Venus and Mars (Aphrodite and Ares) are as much archetypal lovers as they are irreconcilable rivals, love and war being at once the most extreme of concepts and yet, all being fair in both, metaphorically relatable and indeed combined into the love-warrior character of Venus' son, Cupid. Again, we come up against a Pisces female paradox – she is equally attracted to and repulsed by the he-men of the world, enticed and intoxicated by their nature, and yet unable to reconcile such stereotypically male characters with her 'beautiful dream' of life, which was never meant to include smelly sneakers or back hair.

No woman finds affront to her delicate sensibilities faster than Pisces female. Whether her natural disposition or such airs as she puts on – the real and the fabricated being one and the same for the Fish – Pisces comes across as the bluest of prudish princesses. (Blueness is a synonym for purity, the supposedly snow-white Blanche being costumed in della Robbia blue, the color drawn from the gown of the Madonna, whose blue dress, fringed in white, is the ancient costume of Aphrodite–Mari, representing the sea edged with foam.) In fact, Pisces is so purposefully proper that this overriding trait comes to define men's attraction to the zodiac's eternal belle, for better or for worse. First of all, this exaggeratedly *comme il faut,* if not holier-than-thou, diva continues to attract every worshipful homosexual male on the gaydar. And sometimes the attraction extends far beyond friendly. Many a Pisces woman won't have readily awakened from a liaison with one of her signature dreamboys: having so many sensitive, decidedly female qualities in common with a man that it overrides any potential sexuality questions. Like Gemini woman, the Fish might find herself in a series of marriages or serious relationships à la Blanche or Sally Bowles with closeted gay men, thinking nothing suspicious in their shared desire to regularly redecorate to the sooth-ing strains of Liza with a *Z.* To be fair, Pisces might purposely have opted for such a bond wherein she and an equally persnickety male can live a sexless, sequestered life – she won't be put upon to put out. For, in a sense, Pisces woman can be somewhat sexless, that is, when she's not completely nympho-maniacal, the most striking paradox of our pretty Fish. Meanwhile, she has her fetishes, which typically include those innocent young lads, as she can't easily abide what she considers the sexual tyranny of heterosexual relationships. This daughter of Neptune is more about the special effects in life than she is about any sort of solid plot. Just as she eschews the more banal

BODY RULERSHIP

Pisces rules the feet, which comprise pressure points that connect to the entire body, just as the sign itself is considered the catchall of the zodiac. It also governs the lymphatic system. Neptune is associated with mental processes, brain and spinal fluid. There is a tendency to foot trouble, dementia, and brain disorders.

realities of her conditioning and puts on extravagant airs, so, too, does she not only have, but heartily enjoy, her own illusions about sex via which she seeks to escape the grimmer dynamics of it. In brass tacks, she's easily grossed out by the actual carnal function and machinations of sex – the sweating, the odors, the emitting of fluids, totally clash with her dreamy visions. As a nod to the 12th House's association with *inhibitions* and *isolation,* she is the zodiac's very own Untouchable. Some Pisces women are so vehemently squeamish about sex that, when they become pregnant, friends and family who know them best are inclined to suspect some form of immaculate conception. Pisces female tends to associate sex, often inextricably linked to any inappropriate sexual contact she may have suffered through in her youth, with feeling dirty; and the Fish is in the business of washing away any such sins she detects in herself. We see this in the characterization of Blanche, who is forever taking her long, fragranced baths – absolution if not utter dissolution – like Aphrodite ritually renewing her virginity, a trick to which any card-carrying Pisces would appreciate knowing the secret. But it's only half the story: for Aphrodite was the original nympho who would have had cause to renew that virginity on a regular basis.

And besides attracting every gay man within earshot of her siren's call, the enchanting, sanctimonious Pisces attracts that many straight men, who view her as a top-drawer lady, a class act, a princess worthy of the royal treatment. The poor unsuspecting suckers – they don't stand a chance: Thinking the Fish lady a demure female character deserving of all the finer things in life, a regular joe might romantically approach Pisces from the perspective of her being 'too good for him,' but by whom he will 'do right.' Treating her like some insatiable muse, he may bankrupt his spirit, if not his bankroll, trying to elicit a passionate response to his tributes. What he typically gets in return is the luxury of calling her his own. A man who claims her is thus endowed with a status similar to one toting around some golden-age starlet, such is the statement she makes, by her very presence, to any and all persons with whom she comes into contact. One way or another, she'll have you know she's special. And in scoring her as arm candy, many a man counts himself the beneficiary of some cosmic miracle. Wondering why she is so willing to give herself to a man she mightn't even love is akin to pondering why it is the ancients wedded Aphrodite, the epitome of female beauty, to the only lame and ugly god, Hephaestus. The answer: He's safe, and so totally grateful to be linked with her that little demand will be placed on her. In most cases, Pisces negotiates herself into relationships that promise sanctuary, a kind of sponsorship by a mate who functions for them both. The Fish seeks to remain protected in a fishbowl of sorts, her partner sprinkling whatever she needs for sustenance while providing those attractive accoutrements – the house, fine furnishings, and holidays – that keep the muse from becoming bored. Sally *Bowles* serves as this type of muse. Sometimes there's simply no pleasing her, as the Pisces petitions for more and more comfort and stability, as opposed to outright luxury, while lifting nary a finger. And still, it is she who calls the shots. When and if, however, circumstances don't go exactly her way, Pisces is not one to abandon ship; rather she slips back into that martyred role she played so readily in her youth. Sighing her way through hard times, Pisces woman makes her partner feel that much more responsible for having disappointed her. Again, this buys her more personal freedom within the bond, as the least her partner can do is to leave the poor, put-upon Pisces in peace. The best that could happen, for all concerned, is for the mouse of a mensch to act like a man and stand up to the Pisces. Invariably, the Fish will find this macho display, from a partner she'd happily written off as meek, makes her surprisingly weak in the knees. Indeed, their relationship only survives in the wake of this man becoming less worshipful. By the same token, Pisces gradually allows herself to grasp the latent male animal lurking within this sort of mate as he progressively asserts himself by palatable degrees. Indeed, the whole of Pisces's metaphorical allergy to he-men is based on either an inbred or conditioned fear of susceptibility to their power over her. Again, this is often a result of an unfortunate liason in her youth. Sooner or later, however, every straight Pisces woman will, in one way or another, be forced to face the natural attraction that she, as the zodiac's über-female, feels for those more overstated males of the species.

Just as a gay man might find Pisces the perfect icon, and the regular joe will see her as a sort of step up, the self-possessed, ego-driven alpha male views Pisces as grade-A pussy that needs to be taken down a peg. Any Piscean partnership with a man less eminently masculine than she is feminine is bound to be precariously lopsided. Still there is such a mental, indeed psychic, gulf between her and a proverbial man's man that it is no easy task to fuse the two, except on the level of physical attraction. Part and parcel of Pisces's prim properness is her signature repression of sexual energy. Taking again Blanche DuBois as an example, she is as repulsed by Stanley's base behavior as she is betrayed by her innate attraction to him. Every Pisces female, no matter how many homo or henpecked husbands she hides behind, is fairly itching to play Lady Chatterley to some raw and hunky gameskeeper. In the case of the bath- and booze-happy Blanche, eventually raped by Stanley, she suffers a nervous breakdown so severe that it sends her, at play's end, bundled up in della Robbia

Mercedes McCambridge
Dana Delaney
Paula Prentiss
Patsy Kensit
Jeri Ryan
Jasmine Guy
Irene Papas
Nancy Wilson
Irene Cara
Keely Smith
Nina Simone
Queen Latifah
Lisa Sergio
Erika Badu
Alberta Hunter
Barbara Feldon
Larraine Newman
Moms Mabley
Dorothy Gish
Anne Lee
Mia Hamm
Jackie Joyner-Kersee
Ivana Trump
Ruth Bader Ginsburg
Alice Hamilton
Gloria Vanderbilt
Lee Radziwill
Pamela Mason
Patty Hearst
Chelsea Clinton
Chastity Bono
Patricia Nixon
Benedicte Newland
Edna St. Vincent Millay
Elizabeth Barrett Browning
Anaïs Nin
Diane Arbus
Janet Guthrie
Sylvia Beach
Harriet Tubman
Alice Hoffman
Adele Davis
Anne Wigmore
Sally Jesse Raphael
Lady Augusta Gregory
Rosa Bonheur
Tammy Faye Bakker
Jennifer O'Neill
Paula Zahn
Patricia Heaton
Claire Trevor

blue, to the funny farm – remember that profound Piscean rock bottom. And yet, according to Gore Vidal in his autobiographical *Palimpsest,* Tennessee Williams claimed that Blanche experiences a full recovery and reclaims her diva status by opening New Orleans's premier dress shop. Stanley's right 'rodgering' shatters Blanche's illusions, allowing her to surface a real, productive character. She, like all Pisces women, finds her true self-esteem, which had been repressed along with past pain and fear. Still, a good screw isn't the only key to Pisces female's well-being. The sexy-mama aspect of herself doesn't miraculously replace the virginal Madonna or the psychic wise woman – these two of her three faces keep her more latent libidinous tendencies in check, even when they surface with a startling vengeance. The message isn't that the Piscean Blanche truly needs a beastly Stanley in order to find happiness. Au contraire: Despite the perks of being poked by a straightforward male sexual figure, such a rough-and-ready guy is, ironically, not nearly man enough for her. A relationship with so singularly macho a character tends to be an explosive match, wherein the love bond does remarkably take on the dynamics of war. Nope, the zodiac's triple-goddess incarnate needs a far more well-rounded male than that.

Though the trident is a symbol of the triple goddess, it is clearly a phallic one. Wielded by male gods – the Hindu Shiva, Trefuilngid Tre-Eochair (the shamrock god) in Celtic Ireland, Poseidon and Hades in Greece, as well as the demonized Christian devil who begot the Antichrist upon the medieval Blanchefleur, the Lilymaid whose symbol is the fleur-de-lis, a symbol of the yoni, tridentlike in form – it represents the triple penis, the exact endowment required to mate with each aspect of the Pisces threefold goddess, all in one go. Likewise, to avoid disappointment, Pisces needs a partner who is a combination of all three aspects of manhood that have heretofore appealed to her various needs. As anybody who has ever had a relationship with a Pisces will concur, she can be the most demanding and least easily satisfied of women. Whether it is her archetypal nature that dictates this quality, or her nature that gives rise to comparisons with the threefold cognate goddess, is a conundrum akin to the familiar chicken-or-egg, alpha-or-omega, dilemma. Pisces's perfect mate, therefore, is one-third male love-object, one-third humble provider, and one-third masculine beast. A man must hold the three-pronged key to accessing her multifarious affections – he needs to be emotionally sensitive, materially servicing, and sexually virile. She neither requires a man of whom she can take control nor one who will be controlling; rather, the Pisces gives a man charge of the relationship, unwilling as she is to take on such a role herself. All responsibility is delegated to him – but it must be clear that it is hers to entrust in the first place. Even in this most perfect, and thus rare, relationship scenario, the Pisces will still seek to dissolve into the protection of the bond. With his triple-prong key, her man is the ultimate gatekeeper, entrusted with the duty of keeping the world at bay. Not to say that Pisces mightn't hold down a job or otherwise interact with people – though in many cases she won't – it's just that being a Pisces woman is alone a full-time occupation. She is thoroughly preoccupied with herself, not to mention how well or not she is being treated by others. Her partner comes under the most direct scrutiny, expected as he is to display the kind of respect due a virtuous Madonna, to express the sort of sexual desire any sacred harlot would require, and to afford her the brand of material comfort she deserves, laid out at her dainty Pisces-ruled feet. And yet, her mate might find, all this won't be quite enough.

The unsuspecting fellow who falls for the Fish always gets more than he bargained for, which generally becomes apparent in short order. For someone who seems so untouchable and hard to get, she expects the bond to become almost instantly serious. Indeed, Pisces typically moves from one major relationship to another in her search for Mr. Right, in the meantime craving the confines of even a troublesome bond on which she can depend. When she happens upon a man who fits her unconscious criteria as the perfect mate, she wastes no time securing the love connection, often not being above using sex as a means for cementing a man's interest. She needs so full of a man's attention as to border on obsession – this is evidenced by her nearly maniacal jealous streak, one fueled by her infamously wild imagination. Of course, in suspecting her mate is taking up with every floozy that crosses his path, there is an element of the pot calling the kettle black. Indeed, Pisces may stop at nothing if she spies a 'prime mate,' and his marital status is of little consequence. Dissolving as she does into every experience, the sexually seasoned Pisces who has had her illusions gloriously shattered more than a few times will be extracompliant when it comes to a man's demands in the bedroom, or any other room in the house for that matter. This is particularly true when it comes to negotiating herself into a new relationship. In fact, she may pull out the whore card when she feels she has to. Providing a guy with a profound sexual experience is the quickest way she knows of putting a man under her enchanting spell. Indeed, no woman can sweep a man off his feet, or often out of his marriage, faster than the Fish girl. She is one female other women are loath to find themselves faced off with in a love triangle – she is always victorious. Like Aphrodite at the Judgment of Paris, she knows what men want more than wisdom or worldly power: the best lay imaginable by the most feminine female they can find.

STR8 TURN-ONS

father figures or young boys
sensitive men
androgynous looks
smooth bodies
swimmers, models
delicate features
bone structure
artists, poets, creatives
married men, homewrecking
extended foreplay
tender sex, massage
lite submission, b + d
(passive) oral
slow, sleepy sex
erotica, softcore porn
(passive) analingus
(passive) tickling, teasing
(passive) anal penetration
long fingers, toes
flattery, (passive) seduction
nibbling, licking
pillow talk
gifts, surprises
bisexuality, lesbian erotica
prostitute role play
alcohol, narcotics

Nowhere is the Pisces's paradoxical nature more evident than in her sexual behavior. For such a subjectively fueled creature, sex, something meant to be so personal an experience, is probably the one thing in life toward which she is ultimately wholly objective. Rarely will her urges be so pressing as to rule her, something that even a prolific Pisces such as Anaïs Nin seems to escape in her multitude of experience. Indeed, Pisces enjoys eroticism, even in the form of a dime-store novel, generally endowed with a talent for exteriorizing sex herself, whether it be in her own writing or in her blatant exploration of the subject in what is otherwise meant to be polite conversation. That dynamic follows her into the bedroom. She is open to activities that might make other women's hair curl. She isn't so much passive, or even receptive, as she is susceptible to the desires of her partner. It's as if she needs nothing more or less than what's needed of her by her man. She is utterly available in the moment, willing to comply with a partner's penchant for sexually going 'around the world,' open to any and all oral or anal activities with equal nonchalance. Pisces is not a passionate lover, any pleasure seeming to take her unawares. On the other hand, she never quite loses her untainted and innocent vision of what sex should be, more likely than not fantasizing about some underage stud with peach fuzz on his lip when left alone to her own masturbatory devices. Between sexual bouts, she seems to regrow her own pure virgin vision, a bubble that is continually burst much to her astonished delight. She simply never expects to enjoy the depths of sexual delight or debauch as much as she does, and her partner must be prepared to encounter her unfathomable source of pleasurable participation. This is certainly where the he-man aspect of a mate must make itself known, for once Pisces gets started, she certainly won't expect to stop anytime soon.

Still, Pisces isn't particularly active in the sack. Remaining the passive recipient is in great part from whence her gratification stems. Her particular proclivities, aside from the norm, tend to include being plundered in one way or another. The proverbial victim of love, she might easily be persuaded to engage in a bit of bondage if, and only if, it is with a trusted partner. As it is, even when Pisces has celebrated a golden wedding anniversary, her mate will always remain somewhat a stranger to her, and she to him. She is never one to discuss her internal workings with a man – she'd sooner do so in group therapy or a twelve-step program. There must remain a line between the sexes whereby she is allowed to stew in the juices of her own imagination, whether pursuing a solo creative yearning or simply alternating her days between good books, good naps, and a few good nips in the evening. When it comes to spending time with her partner, she generally gives all her attention and energy to listening to his worldly workings, issues, and problems and offering him her sage consideration and counsel. It's the same with sex — it's all about him, as she is most likely to get off on a man indulging himself with, in, and all over her. She wants to be confronted with a guy's lust far more than she wants to share in some mutual expression session. Sex should take Pisces to the limit, whether it be via straight-up intercourse aimed at continually breaking her record for the most orgasms had in a single night, or by the playing out of a man's sexual fantasies, particularly those that involve imposing control over the ecstatically floundering Fish. Submissive fantasies abound as do any such activities where she is prone to elicit as much of a man's dominant nature as possible. And then theres that kindness-of-strangers dynamic that, in more cases than she'd care to admit, drives the Pisces in search of a steady stream of one-night stands or no-strings booty calls. The personals' sex ads and their online equivalents, where women are doubtless the minority placing notices. Well, the majority of said minority is comprised of this most wanton of signs.

While in a longterm relationship, the unerring desire to please her man — really an unconscious guise for satisfying herself — will come to a screeching halt at the mere mention of lesbian play for her partner's benefit. Pisces is loath to introduce another woman into the sexual mix as, being too jealous of and competitive with other females, she wouldn't generally be able to bear her man's attention directed at anybody else. After all, she works harder than most at indulging even her guy's most outrageous demands; she's not about to then see her allure, and his appreciation, diluted by a guest appearance by some auxiliary T&A. But it's definitely not the idea of girl-on-girl action that puts her off. Truth be told, most Pisces women have a sapphic side that points at a double standard where same-sex contact is concerned: Despite being a magnet for gay men, the Fish typically finds the notion of gay male sex rather repulsive, and she would be especially hard on a mate who is prone to switch-hitting. But when it comes to girl gayness, she is most forgiving — to say the least. To generalize wildly, it seems that a large proportion of Pisces women possess a latent lesbianism. Often, she is blatantly bisexual and makes no bones about it. Many a straight, even married, Pisces woman has gay fantasies, not to mention girl friendships that border on flirtation. Indeed, even when she doesn't have such feelings, Pisces will be surrounded by a bunch of lesbian cronies — she may be the 'honorary dyke' amongst them. As her personal demons are faced over time, Pisces loses herself less and less in substances and immerses herself more and more into a self-help milieu that inevitably leads to her helping others. This gives rise to her involvement in charitable causes and public-welfare concerns in general — a positive manifestation of Piscean dissolution wherein she gives

GAY TURN-ONS

dominant females, butches
straight women
sapphism, erotica
deep kissing, body contact
vanilla
(mutual) masturbation
(passive) oral
(passive) penetration
triadism, scissoring
spankings
hygiene
feathers, ticklers
sensual massage
performing striptease
(passive) penetration
vibrators, dildos
straight couples
threesomes
diva role-play
pansexuality
men on the side
intimacy, monogamy
anonymity, strangers

herself over to selfless deeds and profound service to others. Straight or gay, she increasingly associates with people who are on similar tracks, owning up to themselves and clearing away their subconscious cobwebs. As a result, she may encounter men and women with issues surrounding addiction. Forming friendships with these individuals is de rigueur for the Fish, and that many of these bonds are based on a code of anonymity is perfectly in keeping with her sign's association with secrecy and isolation. Bonds with other women are generally formed on the basis and theme of the female societal condition. When it comes to feelings and concerns about being a woman, including the topic of sexual relations between ladies, Pisces doesn't bat an eye.

In accordance with the eternal paradox that is Pisces woman, there is no glitch between the beliefs or behaviors of those who identify as gay or straight (most considering themselves to be bi). It would mean as little to any heterosexual Pisces woman to admit to gay tendencies as it would to a lesbian Fish to exit a long-term relationship and find herself falling into something serious with a man. Where sexual preference is concerned, she is, in a word, fishy. Her modus operandi changes little whether involved with a man or a woman: She wants to be coddled and catered to. Though she's drawn to strong women who possess qualities Pisces finds enviable, worship goes right out the window by the time she and a lover hit the sheets. There, it's the same old story: She wants to be done for, pretty much shying away from any substantial form of reciprocation. Despite how orgasmic activity might be for the Pisces in the privacy of her home, her lesbian relationships might appear rather sexless to the public eye. Indeed, with the bedroom out-of-sight-out-of-mind for the Fish, her gay bonds smack of a sort of nunnish, monastic life. Relationships are a kind of sisterhood, based on mutual betterment and shot through with shared spiritual aspirations. Still, Pisces will play the homebody, planning and cooking meals while her lover willingly takes on the breadwinner role. The Fish flourishes in situations where she can make her partner proud. Should her lover invite friends around, Pisces will always pride herself on furnishing the most elegant of gatherings, understated and unladen by ceremony, always marked by a quality of creating memories as befits this eternally creative creature in whose company one feels blessed with the ability to take part in some epic unfolding of life, the way it was meant to be lived. The world of the Pisces woman truly feels enchanted, as if existing outside of time, and those in her presence gain the sense of escaping the banalities of life that typically threaten to plague them.

Couplings

Pisces Woman / Aries Man

He's found that ultimately demure damsel – few are so willing to be swept off their feet. Subconsciously, she seeks to smother him. Still, they settle into an easy give-and-take. Sex is tender, with oedipal overtones.

Pisces Woman / Taurus Man

She's the über-feminine female of his fantasies. His instant devotion is all the proof she needs: He's 'the one.' Harmony is in the stars. Their sexual desire is pressing – each pleases and pampers the other.

Pisces Woman / Gemini Man

They share a classy, cosmopolitan sensibility, a worldliness that allows them to live large, beyond the status quo. A divide-and-conquer approach to career means they often make it big. In bed, she's a queen.

Pisces Woman / Cancer Man

Two sensitive souls with acutely creative spirits. With him, she delves into a vocation, inching closer to goals. He transcends lingering emotional limitations. Bed is their messy center of activity.

Pisces Woman / Leo Man

She's their spiritual barometer; he keeps the romance rolling. Emotionally, she underwrites his quest for professional power. Their bond affords a dose of detachment from others. In bed, Pisces is his estimable goddess.

Pisces Woman / Virgo Man

They fall head over heels, oblivious to any obstacles. But personality flaws manifest madly; it's often a murky, illusory existence. Sexually, he puts her on a pedestal – the fall from which is steep.

Pisces Woman / Libra Man

A wispy-waifish pair, predisposed to emotional sensitivity. They may drift into adverse behaviors, prone to hypochondria and procrastination. A profound connection produces works of art. Sex is a way to escape.

Pisces Woman / Scorpio Man

They'll experience sweeping highs and lows – everything is an issue. Living with him often means being displaced. He lands more lucrative positions with her on hand. Sex feels like sparring; the rumble is raucous.

Pisces Woman ♒ Sagittarius Man

From the start, they enjoy an unspoken understanding. Both know: It's time to stop running from love. Bohemianism is their mode – she's a gypsy at heart; Sag trades his bowler for a beret. Sex is messy, unfussy, fabulous.

Pisces Woman ♒ Capricorn Man

It begins as best friendship – they inspire each other's wildest dreams. Pisces must keep her misty eyes wide open; he relies on her to be their collective conscience. Cap's mission: to gratify the ravenous Piscean lover.

Pisces Woman ♒ Aquarius Man

Restoration and atonement are the keys to this committed bond. Compensation is due – emotionally and financially, life pays them back in full. Sexually, too, they're making up for any losses.

Pisces Woman ♒ Pisces Man

A dizzying dynamic. Fate seems to have brought them together. Sometimes they stagger toward goals, but they often arrive. Life is heightened – a too emotional approach is a possible pitfall. In bed, foreplay is foremost.

Gay

Pisces Woman ♒ Aries Woman

With utterly unlike agendas, Aries and Pisces feel free to protect and promote each other's pursuits. Together, life is richer. In bed, Pisces is the consummate femme fatale to the ardent, adoring Aries.

Pisces Woman ♒ Taurus Woman

Initially, they clash. But it's intriguing. They have career goals in common; each works to reinforce the other's reputation. Often, emotional balance is elusive. Sex is untamed – a workout, if you will.

Pisces Woman ♒ Gemini Woman

From inauspicious beginnings, Gemini and Pisces build a solid bond. First, they'll weed through a litany of harsh preconceived notions. Often a haphazard, compulsive relationship. Sex is too often an afterthought.

Pisces Woman ♒ Cancer Woman

They experience their first meeting as a 'religious' experience. Little wonder: Vivid déjà vu accompanies an intense, undeniable physical attraction. A long-term bond will be life-altering. Sex is heightened.

Pisces Woman / Leo Woman

Romantic and unrestrained, this relationship is at turns exhausting and enlivening. Pisces is attached; but the Lion needs her space. Professionally, they're perfectly suited. Sexually, Pisces has her lover by the short hairs.

Pisces Woman / Virgo Woman

Upon meeting, their immediate sensation: staggering. Still, Virgo struggles to tolerate an unpredictable Pisces. Their most memorable moments are spent in bed: Pisces responds extravagantly; Virgo is verbal.

Pisces Woman / Libra Woman

Libra hopes to make languid Pisces over in her image. What she doesn't realize: The Fish has her own plans, and machinations are taking place on the spiritual level. Still, the compulsion to repackage rarely abates.

Pisces Woman / Scorpio Woman

It's kismet when these sensorial water signs connect. Destiny, it seems, has brought them together for a specific purpose: to heal, themselves and others. They're sexually in tune from the start.

Pisces Woman / Sagittarius Woman

Sag seems so aggressive to the pacifistic Piscean. Later, the Archer admires and even fears her partner's profound intuitive powers. Together, they have a greater purpose. In bed, both are passive-aggressive.

Pisces Woman / Capricorn Woman

There's a kink: Pisces harbors so much envy, which stands in the way of intimacy – sexual or emotional. With problems resolved, this couple can be one of the most creative. Cap feels whole; Pisces learns patience.

Pisces Woman / Aquarius Woman

With passive, pretty Pisces, the Waterbearer butches it up a bit. Supportive, even doting, Aquarius may find the Fish strangely dispassionate. But in bed, this is one of the more erotic, ecstatic sexual couplings.

Pisces Woman / Pisces Woman

The fishy female needs constant verbal validation; so a relationship could be exhausting. To thrive, they must depend more on friends for fussing. In bed, too, they might say less, play more.